Books by John Updike

POEMS

The Carpentered Hen (1958) · *Telephone Poles* (1963) · *Midpoint* (1969) · *Tossing and Turning* (1977) · *Facing Nature* (1985) · *Collected Poems 1953–1993* (1993) · *Americana* (2001) · *Endpoint* (2009)

NOVELS

The Poorhouse Fair (1959) · *Rabbit, Run* (1960) · *The Centaur* (1963) · *Of the Farm* (1965) · *Couples* (1968) · *Rabbit Redux* (1971) · *A Month of Sundays* (1975) · *Marry Me* (1976) · *The Coup* (1978) · *Rabbit Is Rich* (1981) · *The Witches of Eastwick* (1984) · *Roger's Version* (1986) · *S.* (1988) · *Rabbit at Rest* (1990) · *Memories of the Ford Administration* (1992) · *Brazil* (1994) · *In the Beauty of the Lilies* (1996) · *Toward the End of Time* (1997) · *Gertrude and Claudius* (2000) · *Seek My Face* (2002) · *Villages* (2004) · *Terrorist* (2006) · *The Widows of Eastwick* (2008)

SHORT STORIES

The Same Door (1959) · *Pigeon Feathers* (1962) · *Olinger Stories* (a selection, 1964) · *The Music School* (1966) · *Bech: A Book* (1970) · *Museums and Women* (1972) · *Problems* (1979) · *Too Far to Go* (a selection, 1979) · *Bech Is Back* (1982) · *Trust Me* (1987) · *The Afterlife* (1994) · *Bech at Bay* (1998) · *Licks of Love* (2000) · *The Complete Henry Bech* (2001) · *The Early Stories: 1953–1975* (2003) · *My Father's Tears* (2009) · *The Maples Stories* (2009)

ESSAYS AND CRITICISM

Assorted Prose (1965) · *Picked-Up Pieces* (1975) · *Hugging the Shore* (1983) · *Just Looking* (1989) · *Odd Jobs* (1991) · *Golf Dreams* (1996) · *More Matter* (1999) · *Still Looking* (2005) · *Due Considerations* (2007) · *Hub Fans Bid Kid Adieu* (2010)

PLAY

Buchanan Dying (1974)

MEMOIRS

Self-Consciousness (1989)

CHILDREN'S BOOKS

The Magic Flute (1962) · *The Ring* (1964) · *A Child's Calendar* (1965) · *Bottom's Dream* (1969) · *A Helpful Alphabet of Friendly Objects* (1996)

HIGHER GOSSIP

John Updike

HIGHER GOSSIP

ESSAYS AND CRITICISM

Edited by
Christopher Carduff

Random House Trade Paperbacks • New York

Acknowledgments

Grateful acknowledgment is made to the following magazines and publishers, who first printed the pieces specified, sometimes under different titles and in slightly different form:

THE NEW YORKER: "A Desert Encounter," the opening section of "The Beloved" (as "Love: First Lessons"), the tribute to L. E. Sissman, "Visual Trophies," "The Valiant Swabian," "In Love with a Wanton" (as "An Ode to Golf"), and the fifteen reviews collected in "Book Chat"

THE NEW YORK REVIEW OF BOOKS: Seventeen of the reviews collected in "Gallery Tours"

AARP MAGAZINE: "The Writer in Winter"

THE AMERICAN SCHOLAR: "Nessus at Noon"

THE OBSERVER MAGAZINE (LONDON): "The Football Factory"

TRANSATLANTIC REVIEW: The second and third sections of "The Beloved"

GRANTA: "The Lens Factory"

ONTARIO REVIEW: "Cafeteria, Mass. General Hospital"

POETRY: "Not Cancelled Yet" and the comment on poetry in the marketplace (as part of an interview conducted by mail and posted at poetryfoundation.org)

PEN AMERICA MAGAZINE: "Humor in Fiction"

PROCEEDINGS OF THE AMERICAN ACADEMY AND INSTITUTE OF ARTS AND LETTERS: Tribute to Raymond Carver

LOS ANGELES MAGAZINE: "The Enduring Magritte"

LE TRANSRÉALISTE (PARIS): Tribute to Jean Ipoustéguy

NATIONAL GEOGRAPHIC: "Visions of Mars" and "Extreme Dinosaurs"

FORD TIMES: "Ipswich in the Seventies" (as "The Dilemma of Ipswich")

AUDIENCE: "Three Texts from Early Ipswich"

BOOKBUILDERS OF BOSTON NEWSLETTER: Tribute to Lovell Thompson

GOLF DIGEST: "Walking Insomnia" (as "Never to Sleep, Always to Dream")

THE NEW YORK TIMES BOOK REVIEW: "The End of Authorship" and "In Defense of the Amateur Reader"

TIMES LITERARY SUPPLEMENT (LONDON): "An American View of English Fiction" (as an untitled comment)

LE NOUVEL OBSERVATEUR (PARIS): Replies to questions occasioned by *Licks of Love*

PHYSICS TODAY: Note on "The Accelerating Expansion of the Universe"

THE ATLANTIC MONTHLY: Contribution to the symposium "The Future of the American Idea"

CHRISTIANITY AND LITERATURE: Remarks upon accepting the Lifetime Achievement Award from the Conference on Christianity and Literature

EUROGRAPHICA (HELSINKI): "The Football Factory" and "The Lens Factory," in *Love Factories: Three Short Stories*, and "Basium XVI," in *Recent Poems, 1986–1990*, both books in editions of 350 copies

HOUGHTON LIBRARY, HARVARD UNIVERSITY: "Basium XVI" (as "Kiss 16"), in *Poemata Humanistica Decem*, an anthology of Renaissance Latin poems with English translations by divers hands, edited by Rodney G. Dennis

ALFRED A. KNOPF: "*Head of a Girl*, at the Met," in *Facing Nature*; "A Poetics of Book Reviewing," from the foreword to *Picked-Up Pieces*; and the critical matter from *The Carpentered Hen*, *The Poorhouse Fair*, *Buchanan Dying*, and *The Early Stories*; also the foreword to *The Complete Lyrics of Cole Porter*, edited by Robert Kimball

LIMBERLOST PRESS (BOISE, IDAHO): "An Hour Without Color" and "Not Cancelled Yet," in *Not Cancelled Yet*, a chapbook of thirteen poems in an edition of 700 copies

LORD JOHN PRESS (NORTHFIELD, CALIF.): "The Beloved," as a small book in an edition of 400 copies, and "Humor in Fiction," as a small book in an edition of 126 copies

LITTLE, BROWN & CO.: "Søren Kierkegaard," in *Atlantic Brief Lives: A Biographical Companion to the Arts*, edited by Louis Kronenberger

QUILL AND BRUSH (ROCKVILLE, MD.): Contribution to *F. Scott Fitzgerald at 100*, edited by Jackson R. Bryer, a small book in an edition of 500 copies

STERLING PUBLISHERS (US) / DUNCAN BAIRD PUBLISHERS (UK): Foreword to *Coffee with Hemingway*, by Kirk Curnutt

THE ECCO PRESS (US) / CANONGATE (UK): Introduction to *The Haunted Major*, by Robert Marshall

PENGUIN GROUP LTD (UK): Afterword to *The Luzhin Defense*, by Vladimir Nabokov

HOUGHTON MIFFLIN HARCOURT: Introduction to *The Best American Short Stories of the Century*, edited by John Updike with Katrina Kenison, and "Playing with Better Players," in *The Ultimate Golf Book*, edited by Charles McGrath and David McCormick

HARRY N. ABRAMS: "Harvard Square in the Fifties," in *Harvard Square: An Illustrated History Since 1950*, by Mo Lotman

ALOE PRESS (NEW YORK): "Ipswich in the Seventies," as *A Good Place*, a booklet in an edition of 126 copies

THE SEVENTEENTH CENTURY DAY COMMITTEE OF THE TOWN OF

IPSWICH (MASS.): "Three Texts from Early Ipswich," as a keepsake printed on the occasion of the pageant's first performance

THE TRUSTEES OF RESERVATIONS (BEVERLY, MASS.): "Open Spaces," as the foreword to *Land of the Commonwealth*, by Richard Cheek with Libby Ola Hopkins

MASSACHUSETTS GOLFING ASSOCIATION (NORTON, MASS.): "Memoirs of a Massachusetts Golfer," in *A Commonwealth of Golfers, 1903–2003*, edited by Laurence Sheehan

THORNWILLOW PRESS (NEWBURGH, N.Y.): Four of the five essays in "The Game," as *In Love with a Wanton: Essays on Golf*, a small book in an edition of 250 copies

WATSON PUBLICATIONS (UNIVERSITY PARK, FLA.): "Being Senior," in the souvenir program of the 2001 U.S. Senior Open Championship

STEWART, TABORI & CHANG: Foreword to *Lost Balls*, by Charles Lindsay

SIMON & SCHUSTER: "Reply to Paul Boyer," in *Novel History*, edited by Mark C. Carnes

EVERYMAN'S LIBRARY: Introduction to *Rabbit Angstrom*

FAWCETT BOOKS: Foreword to *Too Far to Go*, and the "original ending" of *Self-Consciousness*, in *Literary Outtakes*, edited by Larry Dark

THE BENEDICTINE MISSIONARIES OF BLUE CLOUD ABBEY (MARVIN, S.D.): Note on "The Indian," a short story printed as an eight-page special issue of *The Blue Cloud Quarterly*

WILLIAM B. EWERT, PUBLISHER (CONCORD, N.H.): Note on *Bech: His Oeuvre*, a small book in an edition of 110 copies

HARPERCOLLINS PUBLISHERS: Statement on one's own style, in *The Sound on the Page*, by Ben Yagoda

OHIO UNIVERSITY PRESS: Letter included as an afterword to the introduction to *Updike in Cincinnati*, edited by James Schiff

WARNER BOOKS: "The Courage of Ballplayers," as an untitled contribution to *What Baseball Means to Me*, edited by Curt Smith and the National Baseball Hall of Fame and Museum

Grateful acknowledgment is made to the following sources of previously published material:

RANDOM HOUSE, INC.: From the Modern Library edition of Cervantes' *Don Quixote*, translated by Pierre Antoine Motteux, revised 1791 by John Ozell. Copyright 1930 by Random House, Inc.

PENGUIN BOOKS: From the Penguin Classics edition of Voltaire's *Candide*, translated by John Butt. Copyright © 1947 by John Butt.

THE LIBRARY OF AMERICA: From *Adventures of Huckleberry Finn* (the corrected text of the first edition, published by Charles L. Webster & Co., New

Contents

Book Chat

AMERICANA

Gallery Tours

OLD MASTERS

ROMANTICS AND REALISTS

VAN GOGH AND SEURAT

SECESSIONISTS AND SURREALISTS

Foreword

A REVIEW DONE WELL, John Updike tells us in his foreword to *Hugging the Shore* (1983), is "gossip of a higher sort"—the dirt dished out by a trusted and stylish confidant who got to the party early, who read the book in uncorrected galleys or saw the exhibition as the last wall label was going up. The words of this privileged insider, this ideal reviewer, come to us in the carefully weighted syllables of a well-schooled but largely self-educated connoisseur ("a wise and presentable man," Updike calls him, "in suit and tie") and we lean in close to hear them, not only because we feel more intelligent and worldly in his company but because *he's got the goods.* He knows the story; he quotes directly; he's qualified to judge and takes delight in judging. He brings us the juicy cultural news we crave: who's been good and who's been bad, who's just said or done something beautiful and who's fallen wide of the mark. And he does so with a taste for fine discriminations and (only sometimes, in a seemingly throwaway line, and all the more effectively for his usually being so humane) for the hot and salty drop of blood. His account of the proceedings approaches the definitive.

For many readers of a certain age, myself included, Updike was the ideal reviewer—indeed the preëminent literary journalist of our times. And the learned yet never pedantic, civilizing yet gossipy "I" of his criticism ("a figure," the author claimed, "no more or less fictional, somehow, than the heroes of *Rabbit, Run* and *The Coup* and *Self-Consciousness*") became a familiar and welcome voice in our heads. Over the course of five decades we came to know, trust, and appropriate his pronouncements and predilections. We flipped to the back of every new issue of *The New Yorker*, where his book reviews appeared almost monthly from the middle Sixties on, and were disappointed if we couldn't find him there; later, after 1990, we hopefully scanned *The New York Review of Books* in search of his art writings. Updike told us what to read, or skip, or fight the crowds to see; more frequently he provided us with such vivid and memorably phrased responses to whatever was under consideration that—by some mystery of vicarious experience, by a contact-high communication of imagery and sensibility—we felt we'd read the book or seen the show ourselves. His verdicts were the final word, and they live on in our memories: Though John Cheever's journals make "a spectacular splash of bile and melancholy," of "lusts and failures and self-humiliations and crushing sense of shame and despond," his confessions also "posthumously administer a Christian lesson in the deep gulf between outward appearance and Christian tradition" and, "in their unstructured emotion, reach higher and certainly descend lower than anything in the fiction." Though Tom Wolfe's *A Man in Full* occasionally "touches us with its grand ambition," it still "amounts to entertainment, not literature, not even literature in a modest aspirant form. Like a movie desperate to recoup its bankers' investment, the novel tries too hard to please us." Though the many nudes among Andrew Wyeth's "heavily hyped" Helga paintings, on pink-and-cream display in cold gray puritan Boston, "make the show sensational," they also "make it worthwhile. They significantly add to a venerable genre rather undernourished in America, where the menace and sadness of naked flesh have impressed artists as much as its grandeur and allure." This is gossip, yes, but gossip in service of higher, even lofty, things, witty but exalted talk that, by getting at what is alive (or not) in works of art, enhanced our aesthetic lives immeasurably. No living critic can approach its style, its special mixture of warmth, elegance, and impressionistic brilliance, and I doubt we'll hear the likes of it again.

Because Updike liked the way I'd put together posthumous editions of Daniel Fuchs and William Maxwell, and because we'd collaborated happily on his *Hub Fans Bid Kid Adieu* (2010), I was asked by his wife and literary executor, Martha Updike, to assemble this volume of his uncollected prose. The notion of such a volume—the capstone to the series of miscellanies that began with *Assorted Prose* (1965) and included, most recently, *More Matter* (1999) and *Due Considerations* (2007)—was on Updike's mind during the weeks before his death. In a letter to me dated December 16, 2008, he wrote, in the context of other unfinished business, that he would soon be making a final deposit to his papers at Harvard's Houghton Library, namely a carton of recent and fugitive magazine pieces. He hoped that this was only a temporary deposit: "I might yet make a book of them," he said, "if there is time and energy." He died, of inoperable lung cancer, on January 27, 2009.

When, nine months later, I began to pinch and knead this volume into existence, this carton provided me with starter dough. Its contents consisted of three shirt boxes, one containing all the book reviews that Updike had published in *The New Yorker* since he wrapped up *Due Considerations* in 2006; another containing twenty years' worth of uncollected art writings, most of it written for *The New York Review of Books;* and the last containing what Updike called his "oddments"—editorial commissions from every corner, and of every length and weight, including pieces on Harvard Square in the 1950s and Ipswich, Mass., in the 1970s, on the bones and horns of dinosaurs and the iron-red dust of Mars, on the courage of ballplayers and the effervescence of Cole Porter, on the best American short stories of the twentieth century and the disappearance of the professional writer in the digital age. (Some of these oddments had been copyedited for, but in the end omitted from, *More Matter* and *Due Considerations*.) The texts of these pieces were not, as I'd expected them to be, corrected tear sheets of the original printings; they were instead clean printouts from Updike's personal computer—double-spaced, in fourteen-point Georgia, easy on his aging eyes and mine. Each piece had been meticulously revised for eventual collection in book form, and some pieces were much expanded from their published versions, with new titles, sentences, paragraphs, parentheticals, and footnotes.* All are reproduced faithfully here, just as Updike left them.

This carton of pieces did not come with instructions for assembly: Updike left no outline, and no proposed title, for his hoped-for final book. He did leave, however, the example of his six previous collections, with their charmingly diffident two-word handles (*Picked-Up Pieces*, *Odd Jobs, More Matter,* etc.) and their characteristic organization (from fiction and humor and personal essays that aspire to the condition of fiction, to reviews of books and museum shows, to lighter, shorter, varied fare and, lastly, essays on the author's own work). These helped me strike a tone and build a tome. I brought to the task a few assets of my own: thirty-five years' close acquaintance with the writer's work, a compulsive habit of bibliographic stone-turning, and what Updike once termed "the collect-

---

*In the matter of footnotes in Updike's texts: only those marked by asterisks are his. The unkeyed bibliographic notes at the beginning of pieces, like the titles and descriptive headnotes in "Table Talk," are mine. (So are five other titles: "Plain and Simplified," "The Enduring Magritte," "Aftermaths," "Ipswich in the Seventies," and "Open Spaces." I should also say, in the spirit of full disclosure, that I have silently abridged or otherwise adapted a handful of the pieces I brought to the mix, including "A Poetics of Book Reviewing," the foreword to *Too Far to Go*, and the "apology" for *Buchanan Dying*. A bit of pruning and grafting was necessary to keep the collection a living thing. This is a book for the common reader, not an arrangement of bracket-strewn specimens in a museum case.)

ing instinct," which delights in sets of things. Fed by my editorial additions, the starter dough doubled and then almost overflowed the pan—but this wouldn't be an Updike collection if it didn't offer a sense of yeasty, ever-rising abundance, of all-this-and-then-some, of almost-too-muchness.

The first section of *Higher Gossip*, comprising memoir, humor, short stories, and poetry, is titled "Real Conversation" because I recall Updike saying in a radio interview that while criticism is written by a mind engaged with art, fiction is written by an artist engaged with reality. (The closest I could find to this thought among his written works was this, again from the foreword to *Hugging the Shore*: "An artist mediates between the world and minds; a critic merely between minds. An artist therefore must . . . maintain allegiance to the world and a fervent relation with it.") These pieces, it seems to me, bring us Updike the artist in fervent conversation with the real.

The opening pair of items, both first-person meditations on old age, are among the last he published: "The Writer in Winter," in *AARP Magazine* for November/December 2008, and "A Desert Encounter," in *The New Yorker* for October 20 of the same year. "Nessus at Noon," a comic playlet occasioned, like his early light verse, by a printed artifact, in this case a "customer note" from his neighborhood dry cleaner, is also of the latest vintage: it comes from *The American Scholar* for Winter 2009. The next three items are fugitive short stories—my pick from a field of, by my count, eight—arranged by the age of the protagonist, oldest to youngest. "The Football Factory" (1989), which antedates and perhaps inspired Rita Cohen's visit to the Swede's glove factory in Philip Roth's *American Pastoral* (1997), is the semi-journalistic byproduct of Updike's chance visit, in the spring of 1988, to the Wilson Sporting Goods factory, in Ada, Ohio. It was published in the magazine of the Sunday *Observer* (London) and revised for the privately printed 1993 collection *Love Factories: Three Stories* (Helsinki); this printing, however, marks its North American debut. "The Beloved" has had perhaps the most tortuous publication history of any Updike story. It was accepted by *The New Yorker* in 1971 and was already in proof when, as Updike relates in *More Matter*, "the magazine's head editor, William Shawn, expressed such qualms about the theatrical background I had concocted . . . that we agreed to kill the story, though I, along with the typesetter, had already been paid. I was troubled by this outcome, and offered to return the money, but Bill"—fiction editor William Maxwell—"extracted from the story's thirty or so pages six or seven that he thought would make a *New Yorker* 'casual.'" These pages were published, as "Love: First Lessons," in the issue of November 6, 1971; the remainder ran, as "The Beloved," in *Transatlantic Review* for Fall 1974. The reunited whole was at last printed, as a small book limited to four hundred copies, in 1982; this version, much revised from the then ten-year-old original, is the text made public here. The final story, "The Lens Factory," was published in *Granta* in 1989 and, like the football-factory outing, revised for *Love Factories*. It is a latter-day Olinger story, its controlling consciousness that of the onetime boy David Kern, the protagonist also of "Pigeon Feathers" (1961), "Lunch Hour" (1995), "The Road Home" (2005), and other short works of autobiographical fiction.

I've concluded "Real Conversations" with five poems, four of them previously uncollected, the other ("*Head of a Girl*, at the Met") printed in the long-unavailable *Facing Nature* (1985) but not in *Collected Poems* (1993). They are here to give those readers who know only Updike's prose a taste of his verse, and also to return the section—in a series of lyrics on erotic love, art, and death that approximates a spin of the Wheel of Life—from the youth of David Kern to the old age of the narrator of "The Writer in Winter." The dates of publication are as follows: "Basium XVI" (or "Kiss 16"), 1986; "*Head of a Girl*, at the Met," 1985; "Cafeteria, Mass. General Hospital," 2007; "An Hour Without Color," 2003; and "Not Cancelled Yet," 1994.

The second section, "Book Chat," collects literary tributes, speeches, introductions, and reviews. If the present volume were typical of Updike's other non-fiction collections (which, beginning with the second, appeared at regular eight-year intervals), the book reviews from *The New Yorker* would number in the sixties and make up half its contents. *Higher Gossip*, which is published hard on the heels of 2007's *Due Considerations*, collects only thirty months' worth of "new" reviews, from "Hugger-Mugger" (September 16, 2006) to the posthumous "Basically Decent" (March 9, 2009). Consequently these book reviews (counting also "Visual Trophies" and "The Valiant Swabian," reprinted in later sections) number a mere seventeen—exactly the number published in Updike's first such collection, the comparatively slim *Assorted Prose*. While I was pleased that they fell neatly into three focused groupings, I was surprised that they lacked Updike's customary catholicity: where's the evocation of a neglected novel from colonial São Paulo or the pocket history of court intrigue in the middle Yuan Dynasty? If Updike could have continued adding to it through 2015, "Book Chat" would surely have wound up less parochially American. Of the four introductions and afterwords that help round out the section, the Cole Porter piece is from 1983, and the

Nabokov a 1994 rewrite of a review first published in the Sixties and collected, as "Grandmaster Nabokov," in *Assorted Prose*. The others were published in 1999. I am especially happy that the lecture "Humor in Fiction" (1970), which Updike remembered as "one of my most ambitious flights of criticism, on a topic dear to me," is reprinted here, in full, in the version revised for a limited edition issued in the year 2000. A tantalizing excerpt was a highlight of his youthful *Picked-Up Pieces* (1975).

If the book reviews tilt heavily toward the American, the art reviews, as if to balance them, are preponderantly European. This is partly because most of Updike's writings on American art were previously collected in the richly illustrated pages of *Just Looking* (1989) and *Still Looking* (2005); it is also due to the Eurocentric nature of the retrospective shows hosted by New York and New England art museums during the three decades he was active as an art critic, from 1979 to 2008. A major retrospective in itself, the third section here, "Gallery Tours," brings together twenty of Updike's art essays, the largest sampling ever assembled. (Still more uncollected art pieces, all just as strong but crying out for full-color plates, have been reserved for a future, glossier collection.)

Updike's history as an art writer deserves rehearsal here. As a young man a cartoonist for the *Harvard Lampoon* and then a scholarship student at the Ruskin School of Drawing and Fine Art, Oxford, he had planned to become a writer and graphic artist both—a second James Thurber, perhaps, or a combination Robert Benchley–Gluyas Williams. Although in his middle twenties he turned away from drawing in favor of writing fiction, he always made verbal picture-making a central element of his storytelling. He treasured Joseph Conrad's definition of the artistic impulse as "a single-minded attempt to render the highest kind of justice to the visible world." He also adopted Conrad's apology to his readers as his own: "My task which I am trying to achieve is, by the power of the written word, to make you hear, to make you feel—it is, before all, to make you *see*."

In 1973, twelve years into his career as a book reviewer, Updike ventured his first critical piece on visual art: a roundup, published in *The New York Times Book Review*, of the first three volumes in Putnam's *World History of Erotic Art* series. He followed with considerations of other art books, including *Two Hundred Years of American Illustration* (Norman Rockwell, N. C. Wyeth) and Peter Gay's *Art and Act* (Manet, Gropius, Mondrian). Then, as Updike later remembered,

in January of 1979 an American edition of the French art magazine *Réalités* began to be published. . . . The French original and then the successful

British version had contained brief essays on art by non-specializing belletrists; I was invited by the editor, James Forsht, to contribute one such, and I did, on a favorite painting of mine by Richard Estes [*Telephone Booths*]. It appeared in the November/December issue.

Updike then offered Forsht a second essay, on an eighteenth-century Japanese woodblock print, and asked if he might also have his say on an Adam and Eve by Lucas Cranach.

Seeing that I was a game columnist, [Forsht] gave my contributions the general title "Impressions," and, to feed my inspiration, sent a batch of museum postcards [Homer, Sargent, Diebenkorn, Johns]. . . . Every month or two I would write about five hundred words based upon one of these, or upon two that compared amusingly. . . . Seven essays in all were published before the ambitiously elegant magazine, not surprisingly, cut its losses and folded.

Though its life was brief (1979–81), the American *Réalités*, to its lasting credit, launched Updike as an art critic. Soon he was writing further "Impressions" for *Art & Antiques*, *Travel + Leisure*, and the recently revived *Vanity Fair*. Beginning in 1983, Leon Wieseltier asked him to review museum shows for *The New Republic*, and then, in 1990, Robert Silvers made him a regular art critic at *The New York Review of Books*. Updike dedicated *Still Looking* to Silvers—"editor, enabler, connoisseur."

In his introduction to *Just Looking*, Updike writes movingly about museumgoing as a kind of churchgoing, and about how the habit of looking at visual art helped him to maintain a fervent relation with the world. Here he is in 1989, a man in his middle fifties, remembering himself as an untried writer in his twenties, when, to refresh his spirit after a day writing Talk pieces for *The New Yorker*, he would often visit the Museum of Modern Art:

Within the museum, Brancusi's statues were grouped in a corner room . . . and emanated an extraordinary peace and finality—the floating *Fish* of gray marble whose stratifications became events in an imagined water, the soaring *Bird in Space* that etherealized the viewer into an elongate reflection. . . . These pet shapes . . . had acquired, in the decades of the sculptor's obsessed reworking of them, a sacred aura, which I imbibed as in a chapel, in that softly lit corner space. . . .

I was looking for a religion, as a way of hanging on to my old one, in those years, and was attracted to those artists who seemed to me as singleminded and selfless as saints. . . . Picasso seemed a bit too noisy, too bustling and carnal, for my hagiography, but there was a painting by fellow Spaniard and Cubist Juan Gris which I often contemplated with reverence.

Breakfast, though a less sunny and matinal work than Bonnard's *The Breakfast Room*, tastes more like breakfast: a stark but heartening outlay of brown coffee and thick white china, with a packet of mail and a piece of newspaper at its edges. . . . On the table, the impudent yet somehow earnest use of commercial paper imitating wood-grain moved me . . . and the perfect balance and clarity of this crayonned collage . . . exuded the religious overtone I sought.

A religion reassembled from the fragments of our daily life, in an atmosphere of gaiety and diligence: that was what I found in the Museum of Modern Art. . . . Gaiety, diligence, and freedom, a freedom from old constraints of perspective, a freedom to embrace and memorialize the world anew, a fearless freedom drenched in light: this is what I took away each time, from my visits of just an hour or so, usually in the afternoons, my day's journalism done, before heading south to my wife and apartment and daughter on West Thirteenth Street. I took away, in sufficient-sized packets, courage to be an artist, an artist now, amid the gritty crushed grays of this desperately living city, a bringer of light and order and color, a singer of existence.

As Updike's life as a writer unfolded, he found artistic inspiration and aesthetic bliss not only in the chapel-like galleries of MoMA but in other, less likely, public places: Fenway Park, for instance, when Ted Williams played there; the workrooms and galleries of the Museum of Natural History; and Wheatland, the home of President James Buchanan, in Lancaster, Pennsylvania. The fourth group of pieces here, "Pet Topics," records moments of revelation experienced in the open air—on the marshes and beaches of Massachusetts' North Shore, and, especially, on golf courses just about everywhere. Golf was for Updike what chess was for Nabokov: a recreation but also a restorative; a discipline but also a drug; a muse and a mistress; a personal quest for simplicity, self-mastery, perfection, and grace. Updike wrote: "I thought I'd had my wistful final say on golf with the publication, in 1996, of *Golf Dreams* . . . but the mighty topic exerts such interest that neither editors nor writers are ever quite quits of it." Here, then, along with essays on science and New England places, are five final rounds with Updike, a name that now joins Robert Marshall, P. G. Wodehouse, and Herbert Warren Wind among the game's great poet-players.

Updike often felt impelled to apologize, to readers and reviewers alike, for including golf essays in his literary collections. He also made excuses for rounding out such volumes with "snippets" and "bon bons" and "feuilletons," and so-called narcissistic writings about his own works. Indeed, as a maker of novels and stories and poems he frequently seemed defensive about writing essays and criticism per se. "As eminent a critic as Malcolm Cowley once, after some kind words about a review of mine of James Joyce's letters, wondered if I ought to be doing this sort of thing at all," he wrote in the preface to *Odd Jobs*. "I wondered, too. . . . And a perspective looms from which all of it was, if not a mistake, an aberration."

But another perspective looms, one from which "all of it" is only as it could be, from which Updike the literary artist can only be seen whole in relation to Updike the critic. He was, after all, equally the child of his mother, the short-story writer Linda Grace Hoyer, and his father, the high-school teacher Wesley Updike. The urge for him to do, to make, to create, was complemented always by the impulse to teach, to share his discoveries, if not in the classroom then in print. The sun gives light from dawn to dusk, and the moon the sun's reflection throughout the night; together they make the day. Fiction and poetry, essays and criticism: these were the sun and moon of Updike's days, twin aspects of the light and order and color that he was born to bring, the counterpoint of existence that he was born to sing.

A collection like *Higher Gossip* is, by its very nature, a collaborative effort. In the foreword to each of this volume's predecessors Updike expressed gratitude to the editors who commissioned the pieces and who, in their various professional attentions, improved them. Had he lived to write a foreword to this seventh collection, he would have extended his warmest thanks to all, and perhaps especially to David Remnick, Henry Finder, and Ann Goldstein of *The New Yorker*, and Robert Silvers, Michael Shae, and the late Barbara Epstein of *The New York Review of Books*. For my part, I am grateful to Judith Jones of Knopf, and her assistant, Ken Schneider, for their enthusiasm for this project, and to Updike's longtime copyeditor, Terry Zaroff-Evans, for her close attention to the text's finer points. Rachel Jirka, formerly of the Boston Athenæum, helped me track down Updike's many fugitive pieces, and Sarah Almond secured permission to reproduce the art in "Gallery Tours." Leslie Morris, curator of modern books and manuscripts at Houghton Library, always made my visits to her basement office seem a welcome distraction from her work cataloging the Updike papers, and never flinched when asked to bring me yet again those three shirt boxes. My deepest thanks, however, go to Martha Updike, for her counsel, generosity, and trust. This book belongs to John Updike, but it is in your hands due to Martha's energy and love.

—Christopher Carduff
April 2011

Real Conversation

THE WRITER IN WINTER

YOUNG OR OLD, a writer sends a book into the world, not himself. There is no Senior Tour for authors, with the tees shortened by twenty yards and carts allowed. No mercy is extended by the reviewers; but, then, it is not extended to the rookie writer, either. He or she may feel, as the gray-haired scribes of the day continue to take up space and consume the oxygen in the increasingly small room of the print world, that the elderly have the edge, with their established names and already secured honors. How we did adore and envy them, the idols of our college years—Hemingway and Faulkner, Frost and Eliot, Mary McCarthy and Flannery O'Connor and Eudora Welty! We imagined them aswim in a heavenly refulgence, as joyful and immutable in their exalted condition as angels forever singing.

Now that I am their age—indeed, older than a number of them got to be—I can appreciate the advantages, for a writer, of youth and obscurity. You are not yet typecast. You can take a distant, cold view of the entire literary scene. You are full of your material—your family, your friends, your region of the country, your generation—when it is fresh and seems urgently worth communicating to readers. No amount of learned skills can substitute for the feeling of having a lot to say, of *bringing news*. Memories, impressions, and emotions from your first twenty years on earth are most writers' main material; little that comes afterward is quite so rich and resonant. By the age of forty, you have probably mined the purest veins of this precious lode; after that, continued creativity is a matter of sifting the leavings. You become playful and theoretical; you invent sequels, and attempt historical novels. The novels and stories thus generated may be more polished, more ingenious, even more humane than their predecessors; but none does quite the essential earthmoving work that Hawthorne, a writer who dwelt in the shadowland "where the Actual and the Imaginary may meet," specified when he praised the novels of

Anthony Trollope as being "as real as if some giant had hewn a great lump out of the earth and put it under a glass case."

This second quotation—one writer admiring a virtue he couldn't claim—meant a lot to me when I first met it, and I have cited it before. A few images, a few memorable acquaintances, a few cherished phrases circle around the aging writer's head like gnats as he strolls through the summertime woods at gloaming. He sits down before the word processor's humming, expectant screen, facing the strong possibility that he has already expressed what he is struggling to express again.

My word processor—a term that describes me as well—is the last of a series of instruments of self-expression that began with crayons and colored pencils held in my childish fist. My hands, somewhat grown, migrated to the keyboard of my mother's typewriter, a portable Remington, and then, schooled in touch-typing, to my own machine, a beige Smith Corona expressly bought by loving parents for me to take to college. I graduated to an office model, on the premises of *The New Yorker*, that rose up, with an exciting heave, from the surface of a metal desk. Back in New England as a free-lancer, I invested in an electric typewriter that snatched the letters from my fingertips with a sharp, premature *clack*; it held, as well as a black ribbon, a white one with which I could correct my many errors. Before long, this clever mechanism gave way to an even more highly evolved device, an early Wang word processor that did the typing itself, with a marvellous speed and infallibility. My next machine, an IBM, made the Wang seem slow and clunky and has been in turn superseded by a Dell that deals in dozens of type fonts and has a built-in spell checker. Through all this relentlessly advancing technology the same brain gropes through its diminishing neurons for images and narratives that will lift lumps out of the earth and put them under the glass case of published print.

With ominous frequency, I can't think of the right word. I know there *is* a word; I can visualize the exact shape it occupies in the jigsaw puzzle of the English language. But the word itself, with its precise edges and unique tint of meaning, hangs on the misty rim of consciousness. Eventually, with shamefaced recourse to my well-thumbed thesaurus or to a germane encyclopedia article, I may pin the word down, only to discover that it unfortunately rhymes with the adjoining word of the sentence. Meanwhile, I have lost the rhythm and syntax of the thought I was shaping up, and the paragraph has skidded off (like this one) in an unforeseen direction.

When, against my better judgment, I glance back at my prose from twenty or thirty years ago, the quality I admire and fear to have lost is its carefree bounce, its snap, its exuberant air of slight excess. The author, in his boyish innocence, is calling, like the sorcerer's apprentice, upon unseen powers—the prodigious potential of this flexible language's vast vocabulary. Prose should have a flow, the forward momentum of a certain energized weight; it should feel like a voice tumbling into your ear.

An aging writer wonders if he has lost the ability to visualize a completed work, in its complex spatial relations. He should have in hand a provocative beginning and an ending that will feel inevitable. Instead, he may arrive at his ending nonplussed, the arc of his intended tale lying behind him in fragments. The threads have failed to knit. The leap of faith with which every narrative begins has landed him not on a far safe shore but in the middle of the drink. The failure to make final sense is more noticeable in a writer like Agatha Christie, whose last mysteries don't quite solve all their puzzles, than in a broad-purposed visionary like Iris Murdoch, for whom puzzlement is part of the human condition. But in even the most sprawling narrative, things must add up.

The ability to fill in a design is almost athletic, requiring endurance and agility and drawing upon some of the same mental muscles that develop early in mathematicians and musicians. Though writing, being partly a function of experience, has few truly precocious practitioners, early success and burnout are a dismally familiar American pattern. The mental muscles slacken, that first freshness fades. In my own experience, diligent as I have been, the early works remain the ones I am best known by, and the ones to which my later works are unfavorably compared. Among the rivals besetting an aging writer is his younger, nimbler self, when he was the cocky new thing.

From the middle of my teens I submitted drawings, poems, and stories to *The New Yorker;* all came back with the same elegantly terse printed rejection slip. My first break came late in my college career, when a short story that I had based on my grandmother's slow dying of Parkinson's disease was returned with a note scrawled in pencil at the bottom of the rejection slip. It read, if my failing memory serves: "Look—we don't use stories of senility, but try us again."

Now "stories of senility" are about the only ones I have to tell. My only new experience is of aging, and not even the aged much want to read about it. We want to read, judging from the fiction that is printed, about life in full tide, in love or at war—bulletins from the active battlefields, the wretched childhoods, the poignant courtships, the fraught adulteries, the big deals, the scandals, the crises of sexually and professionally active adults. My first published novel was about old people; my hero was a ninety-year-old man. Having lived as a child with aging grandparents, I imagined old age with more vigor, color, and curiosity than I could bring to a description of it now.

I don't mean to complain. Old age treats free-lance writers pretty gently. There is no compulsory retirement at the office, and no athletic injuries signal that the game is over for good. Even with modern conditioning, a ballplayer can't stretch his career much past forty, and at the same age an actress must yield the romantic lead to a younger woman. A writer's fan base, unlike that of a rock star, is post-adolescent, and relatively tolerant of time's scars; it distressed me to read of some teen-ager who, subjected to the Rolling Stones' halftime entertainment at a recent Super Bowl, wondered why that skinny old man (Mick Jagger) kept taking his shirt off and jumping around. The literary critics who coped with Hemingway's later, bare-chested novel *Across the River and Into the Trees* asked much the same thing.

By and large, time moves with merciful slowness in the old-fashioned world of writing. The eighty-eight-year-old Doris Lessing won the Nobel Prize in Literature. Elmore Leonard and P. D. James continue, into their eighties, to produce best-selling thrillers. Although books circulate ever more swiftly through the bookstores and back to the publisher again, the rhythms of readers are leisurely. They spread recommendations by word of mouth and "get around" to titles and authors years after making a mental note of them. A movie has a few weeks to find its audience, and television shows flit by in an hour, but books physically endure, in public and private libraries, for generations. Buried reputations, like Melville's, resurface in academia; avant-garde worthies such as Cormac McCarthy attain, late in life, best-seller lists and *The Oprah Winfrey Show*.

A pervasive unpredictability lends hope to even the most superannuated competitor in the literary field. There is more than one measurement of success. A slender poetry volume selling fewer than a thousand copies and receiving a handful of admiring reviews can give its author a pride and sense of achievement denied more mercenary producers of the written word. As for bad reviews and poor sales, they can be dismissed on the irrefutable hypothesis that reviewers and book buyers are too obtuse to appreciate true excellence. Over time, many books quickly bloom and then vanish; a precious few unfold, petal by petal, and become classics.

An aging writer has the not insignificant satisfaction of a shelf of books behind him that, as they wait for their ideal readers to discover them, will outlast him for a while. The pleasures, for him, of bookmaking—the first flush of inspiration, the patient months of research and plotting, the laser-printed final draft, the back-and-forthing with Big Apple publishers, the sample pages, the jacket sketches, the proofs, and at last the boxes from the printers, with their sweet heft and smell of binding glue— remain, and retain creation's giddy bliss. Among those diminishing neurons there lurks the irrational hope that the last book might be the best.

A DESERT ENCOUNTER

IN OUR FIFTH WINTER in the Southwest, my wife discovered that her gardening skills could be turned to xerophilous plants. All afternoon, she had served as my assistant and directress in pruning some ocotillo, and was enough exhilarated by the results to turn my attention to our overgrown hedge of mixed olive and oleander. Ocotillo is a tall, wandlike candlewood with vicious thorns and a feathery orange flower at its tip; handling it, even with thick leather gloves, requires the concentration of a bomb squad.

The electric trimmer I had borrowed for the massy hedge was dull and noisy. Further, the electric socket on our porch was distant, a hundred-foot extension cord away. I had to keep crawling on my hands and knees through gaps in the hedge to take the trimmer, trailing the gnarling extension cord, to the other side. And then there was the spindly aluminum stepladder that I had to keep shifting and leaning against springy branches to gain access to the hedge's overgrown top. Our condo sits on a slant, in the foothills of a pink-and-tan mountain range, which made moving the ladder one-handed and then balancing my weight on its higher steps feel heroically precarious.

My sense of triumph when my wife and I agreed that the job had been completed was marred by a mysterious circumstance: my hat had disappeared. Repeatedly getting down on my hands and knees to search beneath the hedge and circling the stony area of caliche where I had labored, I failed to find it. At this latitude, the elderly need to shelter their heads against the intemperate desert sun, and I discovered within myself an agitating grief in regard to the disappearance of the hat, a simple, brimmed floppy affair bearing the logo of an organization of which, years ago, I had been pleased to be elected a member.

Even as the shadows were deepening in the saguaro-studded mountain clefts, and the sun was lowering over the blue range to the west, I, with the circular compulsions of an aging brain, kept wandering out of doors, convinced that one more search in and around the hedge and the ocotillo would produce my missing headgear.

A breadth of paving passes close by the hedge. There, on the slanting asphalt, part parking lot and part side road, a curious confluence arose: an ancient man, brightly dressed in white trousers and a striped, starched shirt, made his ragged way downhill with the help of a cane, while, nearby, a Roto-Rooter operative in a khaki uniform was packing up his truck at the end of his workday. Oleander roots work their way into the clay drainage pipes of our aging complex and obstruct flow.

The gentleman in white trousers greeted me as if we had often met before, though we had not. "What are you doing?" he asked, tilting his head to receive the answer.

I decided to be honest, however foolish it made me seem. "I'm looking for my hat."

The Roto-Rooter man overheard us. "Hat?" he echoed. "There's a hat over here."

By "over here" he meant the curb on the far side of the asphalt, where it had never occurred to me, in all my peering around and under the hedge, to cast a glance. The hat must have fallen from my head in the course of my awkward, preoccupying struggles, and the desert breeze that springs up in the late afternoon had moved it twenty feet away.

"My hat!" I exclaimed. "It is!" I hurried over and, as if to prove my ownership to my two new companions, put it on my head. "Thank you, thank you," I said to each.

The man in khaki smiled, his share of my pleasure appropriately moderate, as he coiled his rooter and distributed the last of his tools to their places in the back of his truck. The older man, however, bent and bowlegged as he was, made my happiness his own. Quizzically beaming, he came closer to me, the shadow of his cane elongating to the east, where the last golfers at the local country club, calling to one another like birds at dawn, were finishing their rounds before darkness fell. "What does it say on your hat?" he asked me.

In the world of retirement, customary reticence is discarded, as needless baggage from the forsaken world of midlife responsibilities. We say what we think and ask what we wish. I was taken aback only for those seconds I needed to remember that this man had been a party to my finding what I was about to assume had been lost forever, my precious hat. I took it off my head and read aloud to him, in case his eyesight was poor, the words stitched on its crown. "American Academy of Arts and Letters," I enunciated.

"And what is that?" he asked, his eyes as lively as those (as I imagine them) of Socrates driving a pupil, question by question, toward an inarguable conclusion.

I did balk, a bit. My privacy began to feel invaded, and I could hear from behind the hedge the brittle sounds of my wife preparing dinner. Yet the other witness's silent eavesdropping and the benign mood of a desert sunset enabled me to locate a certain humor in his effrontery; I took the plunge and held nothing back. "An honorary organization in New York City," I explained, "that includes writers, composers, painters, sculptors, and architects. Two hundred and fifty of them, no more and no less. Fewer than one for every million Americans—think of it! Some years ago, the Academy celebrated its hundredth anniversary, and as part of the celebration all the members were given, in a spirit of dignified fun, hats like this."

I felt the sun reddening the western side of my face. My interrogator was slightly downhill from me, wearing, I noticed now, a hat of his own—a daintily checkered wool cap, with a bill too small to keep out much sun. His hair crept out from under its protection in white curls whose length suggested that he had not yet surrendered a youthful self-image.

"Isn't that wonderful!" he exclaimed. "Did you hear that?" he asked the Roto-Rooter man, who softly slammed his truck's back door. "Did you ever hear of such a nice organization? Writers, composers, painters, and sculptors, the best in the country."

"Well," I said, my embarrassment growing. "They'd like to think that. Some people would disagree."

"Of course," he said. "There are always those. There's always that."

"I was elected to it years ago. It cheered me up at the time." I refrained, modestly, from also telling him that I had been chairman of the anniversary observances. It all seemed long ago, and, at this distance of two thousand miles, rather preposterous. I had wanted everybody to dress up in formal clothes, but, in the event, only I wore a tuxedo. Arthur Miller didn't even wear a necktie. Yet my new friend could not be detached from his glow of approbation; it was as if he had, from my meagre description, bored straight into the inner essence of the Academy, its stately and elitist hopes for itself at its founding, more than a century ago—hopes long since run afoul of modernism, East Coast parochialism, the decline of print, and diverse scorn for any notion of a canon or an elect.

"This is so exciting!" he affirmed. A fresh idea struck him. "You must do something for me. Please. Could I dare ask you?" His bright eyes grew brighter. He took a step closer, uphill, as if he were about to impart a whispered secret. "Could I ask you to sign a piece of paper?"

I would have begun to suspect a put-on, an impish tricksterism leading to some intricate fraud, except that irony doesn't carry across the Mississippi; Ivy League graduates have to fly it over the nation's great heartland direct to Hollywood. Itching to turn my back on this encounter, I reminded myself that here in the desert people have a stake in one another, especially people over a certain age. We have come out here to put our striving to rest, amid barren landscapes and big-box stores. "I'd be happy to," I told the other old man, "but I have no paper, and no pen. Do you?"

Together we looked around for a piece of paper lying on the asphalt or among the cacti, and saw none. "What do you need?" the younger man called over to us. "Paper?"

"And a pen," the merry old gentleman said. Both items were produced, and, when I scanned the environment for a desk or lectern to sign at, a clipboard appeared. Sighing with the unexpected exertion, I signed my name. Still, my fresh acquaintance wanted more. "And the name and address of the organization," he said. "Did you hear," he asked our provider, who was patiently waiting for the return of his pen and clipboard, "what a wonderful organization he belongs to? It does all this good."

"You know," I confided to him, willing to be frank now that I foresaw our encounter soon ending, "this is beginning to be humiliating."

"I know." He smiled. "But isn't it nice? Writers, composers, sculptors." They were for him, it seemed, a faraway frieze, on the eastern rim of possibility. They loomed, as our membership had been intended to loom, as immortal. "And its phone number."

This was too much. "I don't know it," I told him, truthfully.

I had signed the back of a Roto-Rooter invoice. My petitioner tucked it, twice folded, into the pocket of his striped shirt, and handed back to the third man his ballpoint pen. "Hasn't this been something?" he asked the repairman, who didn't deny it. I could hear my wife calling my name, beyond the shorn hedge and the pruned ocotillo. Trash collectors will not touch ocotillo — it is too invincibly thorny — and my trimmings lay in an uninviting heap on the dusty, stony caliche. Slipping backward out of the old man's magnetic field, I looked for the first time at his shoes; they were not the bloated patchwork running shoes with which the elderly in the Southwest anchor and ease their weary feet but real shoes, two-tone wingtips, like those of a dancer in a musical comedy. Along with the point of his cane, they held him there, on the slant surface, defying gravity. Dressed with a brave brightness, he had been headed for some festivity, and had confused the festivity with me. The encounter, when all was said and done, had been no stranger than those in *Krazy Kat*, which had given me my first idea of the American desert.

The dusk was threatening to enwrap us. The calls of the golfers to one another had been silenced. At our feet a sizable city had begun to display its shimmering grid. The Roto-Rooter operative moved, uncertainly, toward the driver's door of his truck. I felt that some concluding statement was expected from me. "I am delighted," I announced, "to have my hat back," and tipped it, floppy as it was, to the two of them, first one and then the other, overcoming my fear that they might suspect irony, where none was intended.

NESSUS AT NOON

SCENE: *A dry-cleaning establishment, between a pizza parlor and a nail
salon, in a small American strip mall. Cleaned clothing hangs in transparent bags from movable racks on tracks, right up to the ceiling, thick as bats
in a cave before sunset. The counter, on the other hand, is exiguous.*

CUSTOMER (*entering, brandishing garment*): I've inspected this garment
carefully and can find nothing the matter with it.

CLEANER: Really? Oh, dear. You honestly don't see it?

CUSTOMER (*rotating garment once more under his eyes*): No, frankly. To me
it seems perfectly fine.

CLEANER: Well, our customer notes *say* we did the best that could be
done.

CUSTOMER: But what was wrong with it in the first place? A spot of
gravy? Salad dressing? Sweat stains under the arms or around the
pockets? Be honest. Don't worry about my hurt feelings.

CLEANER (*gingerly inspecting, at a polite distance*): You know, sir, we really
can't be expected to remember every garment that passes through our
system. We meticulously clean hundreds of garments every day.

CUSTOMER: Yes, but you're implying here in this note that you somehow *failed*. Something successfully resisted your best effort. You did the best that could be done, and it still wasn't enough.

CLEANER (*up on his toes, almost smiling*): Where do we say that it wasn't enough?

CUSTOMER: You say "Sorry." How can I go anywhere wearing something that made my dry cleaner say "Sorry"? See, here it is, right after the checked box. "Sorry."

CLEANER: We don't say you shouldn't wear it. That's your choice. Among your family and close friends, it probably won't matter. They're used to you. Poor old Pops, his clothes a disgrace, his shirttails always hanging out. There's something in it for them, I'm sure, in forgiving you your little eccentricities. (*Sneeringly.*) Your foibles, your lovable weaknesses. (*Chuckles to self.*) Who was it who on his deathbed, asked by some officious person if he thought God would forgive him, responded, "Yes. Forgiveness is His *métier*"?

CUSTOMER: I have no idea. You wonder about these clever deathbed remarks, if they ever really got said, don't you?

CLEANER: Yes, one does wonder. It was allegedly Heinrich Heine, the German poet.

CUSTOMER (*persisting*): But, in this instance, what's to forgive? Tell me what didn't pass muster with this garment.

CLEANER: Sir, please. I can't say it's against our policy to tell, because such a request is so rare that we *have* no policy. If *you* see nothing wrong with the garment, then there is nothing wrong. Wear it with pride and confidence. Frankly, it's not the worst piece of goods we've ever had to handle. See no evil, hear no evil, smell no evil—isn't that the rubric?

CUSTOMER: *Speak* no evil. (*Holds garment up to face, and inhales.*) I don't smell anything funny about it.

CLEANER (*as if in happy conclusion*): There you are! Forget our fussy old customer notes! Sally forth, as the bridegroom said whose previous three wives had also been named Sarah. (*Attempts to turn to the next customer.*)

CUSTOMER (*obdurately standing and continuing to inspect garment*): Here's a thread that might start to unravel some day. Is that what you meant? Or, at the seam, you can see where the two fabrics might not have been from exactly the same dye lot . . .

CLEANER (*gazing, with a pointed serenity, over* CUSTOMER's *shoulder*): We did the best that could be done.

CUSTOMER (*desperately confiding*): This is destroying me, you know. How can I sally forth, as you say, dressed in your relative failure? It will eat me alive. Like the mythical shirt of whoever it was.

CLEANER: Nessus. He gave it to Hercules to wear. It took off pieces of the hero's skin and led him to build his own funeral pyre and immolate himself.

CUSTOMER: Is that what you hope to drive me to?

CLEANER (*at last relenting*): Oh, very well. Hold the garment up to yourself. Under your chin. That's it. Try to smile, and look in the mirror. Now do you see it?

CUSTOMER: See what? No.

CLEANER: That garment. Dear boy, it's simply not you.

THE FOOTBALL FACTORY

THE DIGNITARY was surprised that the factory was located in farm country—a gently rolling plain hazy with pollen and tractor exhaust, not so different from the guileless land where, a half-century ago, he had been born. Corn had been the crop there, while here interminable dull-green rows of potatoes dominated, with some fields given over to the slightly broader and brighter stripes of pick-them-yourself strawberries, tidily mounded between weed-suppressing strips of black plastic. The factory itself was low, its flat roof only one visual notch higher than its parking lot, and but for the violent, multi-colored glitter of the rows of parked cars would hardly have interrupted the landscape.

The company president and the floor manager, both wearing shirts and ties but coatless, greeted the dignitary's party at the entrance, a small door to one side of a long concrete loading platform. The chief of the delegation, the local mayor, introduced first the dignitary, then the reporter and the press photographer who would accompany their brief tour. The mayor, knowing the dignitary's tight schedule, emphasized the "brief." The company president, who wore conspicuous cufflinks in the form of gold footballs, was pink with pleasure, whereas the floor manager, who was to conduct the tour, appeared relatively sallow and tense; he gave them all their protective goggles and red plastic safety hats without any of the playfulness, the sheepish sense of childish fun, that such a procedure usually elicits. To be polite and to lubricate the encounter, the dignitary asked the president if there had been any significant recent changes in their manufacture of footballs.

The question seemed to be an awkward one. The president's china-blue eyes slid around his office, from desktop to filing cabinet to industrial-performance plaques to an oversized display football to a framed letter from a former regional sports hero to the face of his floor manager, finding the answer nowhere. "Well," he said, "there's always subtle changes—an eighth of an inch here, a degree or two of curvature there—but the last revolutionary step was the half-circle on the end, instead of the full circle. That was really the last major innovation. Before that, all I can think of is the clear plastic bladder, for the less quality models."

The dignitary became interested in spite of himself. "Who determines these changes? The league heads?"

"Supply and demand, like everything else," the president said, his pinkness intensifying but his appearance of pleasure ebbing. "Changes trickle down from the leagues, yes, but there's also a trickle-up effect, from the schools and colleges. You get younger pro players used to a certain style of pebbling on the leather, a certain specific amount the laces are spaced and raised up, they're going to be most comfortable with it all the way along, way into their careers. We don't make policy here, we just make footballs."

The president's palpable relief at having arrived at a joke of sorts, after so long a traversal of what seemed to be thin ice, communicated itself to the group and released them to their tour. The floor manager led the visitors down a long wooden hall, past a bulletin board and time clock and production charts and a pair of lavatory doors marked *Heifers* and *Steers*, and opened a steel portal into bedlam—a controlled, steady bedlam of clanging, huffing, rattling, stitching, stamping, and breathing. A giant presiding set of lungs seemed to be inhaling and exhaling through the mechanical din, as if about to pronounce an anguished word. To the almost blinding richness of activity and noise was added the intermittent flash of the photographer's camera as he recorded the dignitary intently observing different aspects of football manufacture.

The delegation was led around to the far side of the huge room, through lanes of machines and workers who seemed no more conscious of the visitors than the machines were, to a corrugated wall half hidden by mountains of hides. "We try to keep the inventory low," the floor manager explained, slapping a broad stack that came up to his chest. "Inventory ties up cash." In the din, his shouted words were precious, and had to be strained after. Often, he merely gestured.

First, the hides (imported from Argentina, Florida, and Texas) went to a young woman at a machine that stamped big pumpkin-seed shapes from them. It was wonderful, to see how quickly she placed the oval die, snatched back her hand, let the machine descend and lift with a hollow plucking sound, laid the punched piece of leather in a stack, and shifted the hide and die for another such quick subtraction. When all the pieces were stamped out, the waste remnant, minimal and tangled like a wet bikini, was tossed into a barrel. It somehow surprised the dignitary that the hides, whitish on their unpebbled side, still testified to the four-legged shape of the steer, and bore organic irregularities that were taken into account by the deft worker: she did not relegate all the leather pieces to the same stack but graded them into three or four stacks as she worked. She had the pensive pale profile of a maiden rendered in Art Nouveau stained glass, and ringleted blond hair caught up into a tight red polka-dot kerchief, and long arms whose motions unfailingly glided in silent obedience to the rhythm of the machine; she formed, in her young and pensive beauty, a human island in the midst of clatter. Even through the veils of mechanical fervor, the intensity in the dignitary's contemplation of her profile must have made itself felt, for she glanced aside, risking in that moment's inattention severance of her fingers.

The floor manager, his initial tension expansively relaxing as he settled into his field of expertise, was explaining the nuances of hide—the relative thicknesses and consistencies of the shoulders versus the flanks, and the problem of barbed-wire scratches and gorings acquired by the animal in its wandering, irresponsible, pre-football condition.

The group moved on, to terrible machines where whiningly revolving bands of steel shaved the ovoid leather pieces to a uniform thickness. The workers here were sitting down, and with a certain insouciance flipped the pieces in and out and onward. Travelling belts transported square gray buckets of leather from one process to the next. Four pieces made a football, and soon the pieces met their fated companions and travelled in quartets, in two-pointed four-ply sandwiches, of which two pieces were punctured with lace-holes and one with another hole to admit the bladder valve. At a kind of printing press fed with gold and black foil, one of the four pieces was branded with the company's name and logo. At rows of industrial sewing machines, pairs of sides were sewn together; huddled women peered into spots of light where their tenacious fingers guided the doubled leather along a single curved edge stitched by a chattering needle. Then the two halves, nested together, shaped like open pods, were sewn into a single unit, at machines even more powerful, by women and men even more highly trained, than at any previous stage. The floor manager shouted, "Takes four to six years' experience to be trusted with this procedure. Toughest part is the tips. See how they trim a little bit off? Otherwise there'd be too much to drive the needle through. You'd get a sort of lump at the end."

The dignitary stared at the brightly illuminated hands that with habituated sureness and strength perfectly pulled the doubled leather along its curve, around the acute corner, back up the other side, around the other corner, back to the patch for laces, cut the thread, and finally tossed the wadded, limp, hopeless-looking result into a waiting square gray bucket. The photographer's blue flash kept bursting in his face; he hoped his expression was suitably fascinated. He asked, "Don't they ever get bored? I mean, do you ever get employee burnout?"

A hint of tension returned to the manager's sallow visage. "Not at the prices we pay 'em," he said. "This is one of the top jobs. Like I say, four to six years' experience before they can handle it." Quite unexpectedly, he smiled. "Now I bet you're asking yourself the question everybody takes this tour asks themselves."

"What's that?"

"How do the footballs get turned right side out?"

Belatedly the dignitary realized that the hopeless-looking assemblages of leather were inside-out footballs. Amid the many impressive, implacable machines he had lost sight of basic objectives. He wondered if he were especially stupid or merely innocent regarding the rigorous, intricate, and yet basically blunt steps whereby things are made. His whole adult life had been spent in the realm of the immaterial—speaking, thinking, performing, conferring, making impressions on men's minds. His childhood acquaintance with matter and its earthly principles had been perfunctory and not pleasant enough to prolong. He had yearned for a life free of dirt and calluses, and his success was measured by how much time he now spent on airplanes. Only in airplanes, above the clouds, going somewhere at someone else's expense, did he feel fully himself—impervious, clean, transient, a lord of thin air.

"People always love the turners," the floor manager assured him, smiling as if an obscene treat were in store.

Before they could witness the turners at work, the delegation had to admire the computerized assembly lines, whereby a laborer at any machine could, with a touch, signal for more units to stitch or punch, and a gray container would be sent on its programmed way. The lanky lad manning the multi-colored computerized control panel slapped down a bucket of grayish ovoid liners, of what looked like felt or cardboard; the dignitary had somehow missed the part of the process where the leather was lined. And then another slapped-down bucket, of half-moon-shaped reinforcement patches for underneath the lace-holes, skimmed on its zigzag way. There was more to making a football than met the eye. The flashbulbs went off with less regularity now, and the dignitary felt his brain wearying. The mayor, too, who had been on this tour many times, and the press reporter, his ballpoint pen tucked back into his corduroy jacket, looked drowsy and overwhelmed, here at the acoustical center of the circumambient din.

But the turners woke them up. A row of men, standing each at a bench equipped with a knobbed upright metal post, writhed like damned souls as, muscles bulging through their T-shirts, they whacked the limp inverted footballs over their posts, pushing one point in, and then with savage yet skilled tugging brought the point out through the gap left for the lace-holes and, twisting the impaled, half-actualized football tenaciously about, with more whacking and tugging, brought the other end through, and tossed the result, its thick seams now turned inward, into a gray bucket. The ordeal took less than a minute. The footballs then moved along to a group entirely of women—because, the floor manager shoutingly explained, their hands were small—who inserted the bladders and gave each a whiff of air. The machines that provided air, tall shining canisters such as contain milk in cafeterias, were what had initially struck the dignitary's ears as the sound of lungs, of breathing, of intake on the verge of speech, permeating the mechanical agitation. From the bladder-inserters the footballs passed on to the lacers; these, too, were all men, because of the brute strength required, but their dance of frantic effort was performed sitting down, with a length of thong and a slender hook that became in their gauntleted, bandaged hands a shuttle that with furious speed wove shut the football.

Little remained to complete the industrial process—complete inflation; a computerized weighing to ascertain that the inflated football was within a fraction of an ounce of the regulation weight; a mechanized painting on of the white circles or half-circles at the football tips; a visual inspection and sorting into flawed and flawless; and the packaging of the flawless balls into individual boxes decorated with company slogans and images of athletic heroics.

The dignitary was allowed to hold a football. It felt good, weightless and taut, with that remembered ballistic urgency. In his own high school, thirty-five years ago, he had played second-string end. The occasional catch, but he couldn't stand up to the battering, the blocking and being blocked, the merciless crowd noise, the pressure. Now he felt another sort of pressure; something was expected of him. "Why is it called a pigskin?" he asked the floor manager.

The man's sallow face was slightly plump, with a disagreeable deep dimple in the center of his chin, and an asymmetry to the eyes that would have led an inspector to toss his head into the reject barrel. The rejects, it had been explained, were not thrown out as trash but marketed at a lesser price—to old-fashioned poor boys in patched knickers, the dignitary imagined, and to inner-city high schools on slashed budgets.

The floor manager smiled thinly, as if the dignitary had once again fulfilled his unpleasant expectations. "People always ask that," he said, "and, you know, I've never looked up the answer. They must have been made of pigskin once, but ever since I've been in this business it's been cowhide pure and simple. If you take a look ever at pigskin, it's not at all suitable. No grip on it. No grip at all."

The dignitary nodded politely, but his thoughts and his gaze kept wandering back to the turners, spotlit at the center of the vast factory like a chorus line gone mad, the lack of synchronization in their precise, strenuous movements making it dreadful, each man alone with his demon, his recalcitrant football, wrestling eternally with his individual sins. Each man wore a shirt aggressively stylized, like the costumes of criminals—one T-shirt bearing a big lavender-lidded Madonna, another the slogan BORN TO LOSE, and a third a tie-dye of lichenlike circular overlappings. One man, the only black, had a shaved head, and the whites tended to have hair long in the fashions of the outmoded Sixties, in a pony-tail or straggling to the shoulders. Several had Pancho Villa mustaches, and others displayed blotchy purple tattoos. The strength of these men! How much evening beer must it take to drown these eight hours, to recharge these aching muscles! Not all were in their first youth, but as a group they were younger than the lacers, who bent into their own repetitive torment with a cagier power, with a thrusting crouch, their right arms flailing.

"How much does an experienced worker earn?" the dignitary asked, feeling increasingly dreamlike. Lowering his eyes from the distant row of radiant, revolving turners, he discovered almost at his feet a pool of peace. Next to a striped I-beam pillar a coffee urn had been set up, with Styrofoam cups, and a few metal folding chairs were scattered about; here the workers could take a break. Several women were seated here, among them the lissome pale Art Nouveau beauty whom, a half-hour ago, the dignitary had watched stamping hides into football fourths. Beneath him now she was wearily smoking a cigarette and brushing a wisp of her stubbornly curly blond hair back into her red polka-dot kerchief. In his mind he bent down and asked her to marry him. She looked up, her blue eyes a bit faded and dull and cautious, and, with less surprise and gratitude than he had expected, consented. Her voice exposed the flat rural accent of the region; though not old, she had been knocked about enough to be guarded in her enthusiasm about anything. She had sensed his love, back there at her machine, through all the noise, like a stitch through leather.

They left the factory hand in hand, the inhuman clatter fading behind them, and found a split-level ranch house with aluminum siding, a kind of open combination living/dining room upstairs and a cozy depressed den below it where they put the television set and had a fireplace. They were very happy. She returned to the factory after their honeymoon on a charter flight to Las Vegas, and he loved the way she would bring home on her body every evening the smells not only of sweat and cigarettes and coffee and machine oil but of raw leather. The scent of cowhide, of vast sage-flavored grazing spaces, wafted permanently from her delicate hands. She kept her nails close-clipped, so that her fingers had a grublike and guileless look; he never failed to be stirred under their indolent, tired, fragrant touch. They had two or three kids, to add to the child she had had at seventeen by that bastard of a first husband, and on Saturday nights would weave and shriek their way home bloated with beer and chili in their battered pickup truck. Even into her middle age, when she got dressed up, she had a smudgy-eyed, high-hipped glamour in her satiny turquoise slacks with pegged ankles and slingback spikes, her kinky long hair careless down her touchingly thin back.

Their first years, he sat home with the babies, and now and then went off to fulfill a speaking or consulting engagement that had been contracted for in his old life; but as the invitations and his savings dried up, he succumbed to her offhand but repeated suggestion that he might find work at the factory too. He became—one of the oldest men ever successfully to do so—a turner. The work itself was curiously rejuvenating, and after those first nightmare weeks, when it seemed every night as though he might die of weariness and shoulder pain, his body developed the muscles and his brain the peculiar furious torpor that the job required. His upper body became lumpy with muscle, and he woke each day to the bliss of knowing he didn't have to be polite to anyone. His tattoos spread; he lost his front teeth in a bar fight. His dreams as he lay beside her pale, lightly sweating slenderness were of strenuously turning things inside out and revealing the glory hidden within every pebbled, scarred, tough exterior.

"Strictly piecework," the floor manager was explaining to him, in answer to his question. "If they want to take a break for coffee, they can do it at their own expense."

"And how much, at those rates, can a skilled worker earn?"

These were not questions the man enjoyed answering. He said grudgingly, "Oh, an experienced topflight stitcher on one of the big machines, for example, after the deductions for benefits and withholding, might take home upwards of three hundred a week."

The dignitary made a rapid calculation. He earned four months' worth of such work with a single speech at a big-city chamber of commerce.

The mayor had begun to glance at his watch, and the press photographer had sealed his cameras up in their big-nosed hoods of black plastic. The group gave only cursory attention to the machine, a tall vertical metal cabinet somewhat like a French *pissoir*, wherein footballs were masked and automatically received, with a sharp hiss, their spray-painted circular or semicircular stripes. After the wonders that they had seen, the operation seemed trivial.

Back in the president's office, the silence was eerie. One's head felt light without the helmet and the goggles. The president had put on his suit coat for the little ceremony of saying goodbye. Pink with pleasure, he presented the dignitary with a pair of cufflinks in the shape of footballs—bronze, however, and not gold, like his own. "Was it what you expected?" he asked.

"Not at all. It was much more"—the dignitary searched, trying to find the exact word, for what made him so good (he had been told) at these ceremonious occasions was that extra particle of courtesy he brought, that focused willingness to make a small gem of most the transient event—"*divertissant.*"

The word seemed wasted on the president. "We've pretty well trimmed all the fat out of the operation," the portly man stated. "That's what we're proudest of."

"He loved the turners," the floor manager said, with a chortle on the verge, the dignitary thought, of presumptuousness.

"Most folks do. A lot of them, they can't get over it."

"And the ferocious stitchers," the dignitary said. "And the lovely girl stamping out the big raw hides."

"Everybody plays their part," the president said complacently. "Anybody has an idea how to make the operation more efficient, we encourage that person to speak right up."

The mayor felt constrained to interrupt. "Mr."—he had forgotten the dignitary's name, but covered nicely—"Mister here has to catch a plane over to the Talbotsville airport."

The handshaking began. "It was a pleasure."

"A pleasure for us."

"No, truly. I wouldn't have missed it."

"Well, it shows there's a little more than potato fields out in this part of God's great country."

"Indeed. Much more. And thank *you*, sir," he said with excessive warmth to the rather sour floor manager. "A great tour. You really know your football manufacture. And thank *you*, Mr. Mayor, for working this into your busy schedule."

"My pleasure. Learn something new every time I'm taken through."

"No, no. *My* pleasure." The dignitary found himself shaking the press reporter's hand now, and smiling, and then the photographer's, and then that of an underling who had wandered in with a big square bucket of special souvenir footballs, made with one side of white vellum, for a whole team to sign. "Thank you, a real treat, a *real* treat, thank *you*," he heard himself saying, stamping them out.

THE BELOVED

THOUGH FRANCIS HIMSELF always associated it—his ability to attract love—with a certain trick of his head, a certain alert and listening angle at which he instinctively tilted his narrow skull, it may have been in the beginning, this ability, simply an inability in those around him, an inability to love anyone else but him. The house into which he was born reached back into the youth of the century, the pre-Wilson era of knobbed balusters and framed mottoes and strange pieces of cloth, perhaps one foot by two, whose arabesque patterns of red and gold and blue reminded him of a pen of peacocks seen from above. The colors were exotic, stiff as feathers; the blue had faded to the pallor of ice, and even the red looked cold, like wet clay. Wallpaper glinted in the dark narrow halls high above his head. The house felt old, worn, too warm, closed in, though cornfields were visible from some windows. Perhaps *they* were the pen of peacocks: Francis, his parents, and his mother's parents. They were penned in because they were poor, and they all loved him, Francis suspected, because they had no one else to love.

His grandfather's love seemed to arrive from the greatest distance. He dwelt in a far, Biblical, brown world. He smoked cigars outdoors behind the chicken house. His love had a wordless tang, not disagreeable, of admonition. On each of Francis's birthdays, his grandfather would give him a single dollar bill, removed and unfolded with ceremonial dignity from a wallet worn papery by the rubbing of time, where the child was amazed that wealth still lingered; he imagined that the dollar grew there each spring from a seed left at his previous birthday. It was like manna. His grandfather read an old Bible in leather covers worn fragile as the wallet; for hours each afternoon the old man would sit on the cane-back sofa in the dusk—surrounding walls of trees made the house dark all year; only for the day after a snowstorm did it seem bright—and would dwell in this dry realm, reading, his shuffling feet kicking up on the worn gray carpet little "mice" of fuzz that Mother, the old man's daughter, would complain about in a voice that swooped like the vacuum cleaner. It was the same voice she used when he brought his cigar indoors. Her voice swooped and wanted to eat him; love, Francis saw, was a kind of eating.

As a child he slept in a little room his grandparents had to pass by on their way downstairs. Once, in passing, his grandfather, always the first to arise, squeezed his big toe, which the night had exposed. Awakened by it, Francis never forgot the sensation: the old man's hand dry as a bird's beak, the preying tug that wanted to pluck his toe loose and carry it into the sky. Yet the old man loved him. Between them, the oldest and youngest of the household, there existed a conspiracy of the powerless, a bond of detached amusement; it had been amusing of his grandfather to pinch his toe. Love is comic, in its search for a handle on the body of the beloved. And unexpected: it kindles in our sleep and startles us awake. And it asks no reward: his grandfather had placidly continued down the stairs, with his usual careful sighing and the mingled squeaks of worn wood treads and of old high-top shoes such as babies wear, only black.

His grandmother's love took the form of excessive protectiveness and forced feeding. Once, fed overmuch, he vomited, and the incident, though he knew about it only through his mother's amused retelling (it seemed to mark the moment when she won the child's rearing back from her mother), served to sanction the rebelliousness that underlay his growingly expert acceptance of love. That vomiting was his first "No," and his grandmother was the first to submit to the panicky fury love roused in him. He would beat her; still tiny, he would leap up and his grandmother would bend her already bent back as if to hold him from falling off while he pummelled her sharp shoulder blades with his smarting fists. The cause, as he remembered, was that she would fall asleep while sitting outside the bathroom while he was in it, doing toidy. It was her duty to guard him against ghosts, because she had taught him to believe in ghosts. Muttering in half-German, she had filled the air with phantom dangers—with germs, with likely accidents, with invisible invasions from the outside. Because of her he could never climb a tree and always slept with his windows closed. So he climbed her and relished her high-pitched grunting as his fists struck. Her tousled gray hair seemed to be fleeing her skull in terror; when she turned to shrug him off, her sharp little nose was cruelly nicked by ill-fitting spectacle frames. The certainty of her forgiveness was maddening. In her he first sounded the depths that have no bottom.

His father's love was as high as his grandmother's was deep. There was no word for it but "lordly." It asked nothing, specified nothing, regretted nothing, saw everything. Its center and seat was the high remote head, impeccably combed, which the child customarily viewed in strange perspective, from underneath, and which floated, inaccessible and preoccupied, on the upper limits of his vision. The holy feelings Francis directed toward this far head were complex. He always remembered with a squirm of horror the moment of blasphemy when, walking with his parents after a snowstorm, falling increasingly behind, throwing snowballs almost blindly, he gathered all his strength and threw in the direction of his father's head and struck it. His father, as if in slow motion, turned and presented his profile at the moment the missile closed upon its ear, which then, in memory, turned blood red. Francis had wept and explained and not been blamed. Yet, a few years later, waiting on a gravel path for his father to finish talking to another man, he had experimentally tossed flecks of gravel toward the preoccupied head, seeing how close he could come, not wishing to hit it yet obscurely seeking some impingement. His father asked him to stop and, when he did not, swiftly stepped to him, stooped, and slapped his face. As a blow it was neither hard nor soft; it had a perfect quality of justice, and the child felt confirmed by this condescension. It was the only time his father ever struck him, and it was enough, for what had been in doubt was the possibility that it could happen at all.

His mother, when he was sick in bed with a cold, would apply a vaporish pale-green unguent to his chest. It was at first touch shockingly cold, and then it burned, and its fanning vapors brought tears to his eyes as, her face solicitous and stern, she rubbed the greenish grease into the taut transparent space upheld by his ribs, a space of skin bounded by his nipples and the hollow at the base of his throat. In this hollow she always left, like a supplicatory offering, a final fragrant dab. He did not understand how the grease could penetrate the skin and muscles of his chest to do him any good, but accepted the ministration, as it was given, in faith. Her face, so close to his, was distended like his own face mirrored on the back of a spoon. She seemed involved with him, through the fumes of this rite, in an exchange of guilt and amends. She blamed herself for his frail health. He was often sick, as if he were seeking a truce; for the atmosphere of love into which he had been born was overexciting, like that of a battle. When he came to go to school, he noticed the cheerful ruggedness of the neglected children and the exhausted fragility of the cherished: Marvin, with his wild untruthfulness and chronic anemia, and Hans, who could hardly move across the playground without breaking a bone, and himself, in whom a constant seething irritability would break for relief into fever. As his mother's slow hand, as slow as the something moving in her face, applied the ointment and its fanning vapors burned his eyes, Francis felt himself the focus of a number of lenses, the center of a burning that might consume him. So the child's imagination, flowing toward antidotes, was attracted to images of coolness and indifference— the moon, snow, trees serene in green clouds of their own dreaming, melons, masks, lakes, skyscrapers, mirrors, angels, churches on weekdays, theatres on Sundays.

His mother's books included a limply bound Shakespeare, with a red ribbon marker sewn to the binding; amid these almost transparent pages he discovered a world preferable to his own. Leafing through, one winter afternoon in the endless hour between four and five, he was halted by a line—*O Romeo, Romeo! wherefore art thou Romeo?*—that he had thought was purely a child's joke. He read on, becoming frightened. *Call me but love, and I'll be new baptiz'd . . . My name, dear saint, is hateful to myself . . . The orchard walls are high and hard to climb . . . Thou know'st the mask of night is on my face . . . Dost thou love me? I know thou wilt say "Ay."* These discontinuous fragments, glittering and dark, coalesced in a bewildering lunar brilliance. Fever and a silver chill contended within the child; he had become both voices crying against each other amid the fruit trees. His tight dark home, so crammed with love of him, had broken open, released him into the infinite freedom, the total coolness, of impersonation. As the light in the living room failed, he blindly faced his life, discovering himself to be, to have been since birth, an actor, an excuse for the emotions of others.

In adolescence, Francis showed a preference, which he was to carry with him into fame, for the company of people who did not especially like him—athletes and conventional classroom beauties. He was tolerated, barely, on the fringes of their gatherings. Undersized, uncertain in health, and grotesquely large-featured—his eyes and nose and lips had had the unwholesome flourish of hothouse growth—he added nothing to their court but a jester's loyalty, a happiness in being with them so keen that the dullest felt it and were flattered. Years later, in out-of-the-way bars, in restaurants where no one would recognize him, he would seek again the bliss of those smoky luncheonettes and pine-panelled basement rumpus rooms where, head tilted, he sat alone yet surrounded, accepted yet ignored, free to admire—in the crushing of a beer can, or the tug of plaid cloth across a girl's hips—how life is lived. That life, in the form of a girl, would turn and enwrap him was a possibility that, though intensely imagined, seemed securely remote. *The orchard walls are high and hard to climb.*

The brassy girls he adored barely noticed him. But plainer girls, less insensitized by the clangor of their own beauty, had long observed the inviting tilt of his head, his strange air of both absence and infinite possibility; one of them stepped forward and disclosed to him the treasure he had been accumulating. He never forgot the quality of light in which she first exposed her breasts to his eyes. They had parked during the rain, and while they unfolded for each other through their clothes the moon eluded the clouds and anointed her bare front with the shadows of raindrops still clinging to the windshield. On the windshield a raindrop, too heavy, trembled and broke downward; on the girl's skin an echoing shadow ran down, swerving where her skin swelled. Her glowing body seemed disclosed not only to him; there was a sharing in which he too was somehow generous. He offered himself as a receptacle; she fed him with an impalpable outflowing of herself that became, once accepted, an essential nutrition.

Having this girl, he was no longer allowed idly to watch the others live life. She needed to be tended: kissed, squeezed, rubbed against until she became as pliant as his grandfather's Bible. They would sit on the cellar stairs above the rumpus-room party, their heads in darkness, their feet in the electric glow. Once, abruptly, she pushed him back from feeding on her face; even in darkness she looked pale, listening to motions within herself. She excused herself and stood; light, as she pushed open the door at the head of the cellar stairs, wounded his eyes. Not many minutes later she returned and offered herself to be rubbed. But her hands were cold, her face moist. Her breath had been artificially sweetened by a mouth rinse that tasted pink.

He asked her if she felt sick.

She nodded.

If she had *been* sick.

She touched her mouth self-consciously. Did it show?

No, but didn't she feel queasy still? Wouldn't she rather just sit?

No. She insisted he kiss her lips. On the unobliging stairs she sought to flatten herself against him. Her tainted breath became a mica window through which he looked, frightened, into a furnace. Her body was wet fire. His insides lifted, hoping to hop over disgust. Love is a glutton; it vomits and feasts again. He tried to forgive her; but there was an edge of pleasure, at the end of high school, in his saying goodbye.

"Must you go?"

"To the big city."

"Don't mock me."

Thou know'st the mask of night is on my face.

"You know I never mock."

"You always do. What kind of actor do you want to become?"

"Every kind. Tragical, comical; Caliban, Ariel. Please forget me. I'll fail. I'm nothing. You're well rid of me."

"I love you. I'll die."

"You exaggerate. You'll be fine. You're a fine normal animal."

"Oh, thanks."

"I mean it nicely. I envy you your health."

"My stupidity."

"You see, you saw it all along as a deal, in which you might be cheated."

"If you don't make it, will you come back?"

"Please don't wait."

"Well. I guess that leaves nothing else to say."

Dost thou love me? I know thou wilt say "Ay."

For a time he attended a strange school, where groups of young adults, the women in leotards and the men in tight jeans and black jerseys, stood in circles and watched one another eat imaginary meals, pluck roses and butterflies from the air, climb invisible stairs, and weep at will. Francis admired another student, a small-boned girl with lustreless long blond hair and a flat cat's nose, as if a thumb had depressed it, producing dimples in either cheek. She was magical. She could walk on the bare floor and make you feel pebbles, stairs, deep snow. She could kneel on the floor, cup her hands, drink from a nonexistent spring, and come up with a wet chin. Francis saw why in Christian days actors were superstitiously abhorred. Her private life, the sum of her gestures within actuality, was relatively dim and wan and careless. Rather accidentally, it seemed to Francis, he was at a party with her, then beside her at a bar, then in bed with her. Believing her able to conjure sensations of pleasure as easily as she created illusions for others, he timidly warned her, "I may not please you."

"How could you not?"

In their darkness she was as remote as an audience. He asked, anxious, "How do I feel to you?"

She said, surprised, "You feel beautiful to me," as if his beauty had long ago been generally agreed upon.

It displeased him to discover how totally she was his. A woman's love had first come to him mixed with lunar remoteness; now he was led to understand what a whore means when she confesses to her pimp, "You're under my skin." He could do anything with her, and this abyss, this abnegation, confused his respect for her talent until he perceived that there was no contradiction; self-abnegation was her talent. She was totally open to manipulation; her limp body begged for abuse. He poured nagging scorn into her; he prostituted her to friends. He hit her. She became sallow and heavy-breasted, living with him, and at school he slowly became the magician. He was relieved when they parted. In some way, physically, she had always repelled him. There had always been in the texture of her buttocks a faint and disturbing grittiness, like sand on a damp day at the beach, and a panicky sweatiness in the yellow soles of her little high-arched feet.

His excuse for parting was a small role he had secured in a touring production of *The Importance of Being Earnest*. He had secured it through the young man who played Algernon; Francis played Lane, Algernon's manservant. The curtain went up. The darkness of the audience was dazzling. While a piano was played by a lame old lady in the wings, Francis set tea things on a table, concentrating so hard on not trembling and having them rattle that the rims of china burned crescents into his eyes. Algernon, a muscular, balding young man a shade too phlegmatic for the part, entered, asking, "Did you hear what I was playing, Lane?"

Lane straightened, waiting for the inaudible breeze of the audience's attention to take hold, and said coolly, "I didn't think it polite to listen, sir." Laughter. During the laughter, frozen in the thrilling imitation of death that laughter imposes, Francis was aware of two things the audience could not know: that he, the droll Lane, was shortly to vanish from the play, and that Algernon was his lover.

Francis's homosexual episode was undercut by its element of farce. He could not quite suppress his sense of something inadvertent, like his grandfather's passing attachment to his toe, in the grapplings of another male body for a hold upon his. The experience, at first, of a man's flat-chested muscularity, of the direct and wholly knowledgeable exchange of penile pleasure, was somehow clarifying; there was a purity in being loved against the grain of nature, and an odd slanting height that deepened post-coital sadness into an almost majestic disillusion. But the spoken endearments, the masquerades with makeup and underwear, the fluid and malevolent spread of momentary feminine positions into continuous fillips of gesture and intonation composed a farce that the unremitting self-seriousness of homosexuals rendered outrageous. They dominated the company, and aspired to the dignity of a culture. Francis was especially offended by the tradition, presumably Greek in origin, of philosophic disquisition. Algernon, whose sturdy build and slow calm had reminded Francis of the high-school athletes whose presence had once given him peace, would (in chorus with whatever initiates, in and out of exotic costume, were present in the hotel room) deplore the world, the universal stupidity, the thorough rot, the drastic and titillating stink.

There was a sourness here Francis could not help relating to the sourness of the male rectum. Having hollowed the world, these young men floated loose, contempt their only connection with reality.

Yet it was not easy to leave this weightless world. Long after he had gone "straight," Francis was inwardly bent by the memory of certain poignancies: Algernon's grateful sated sleeping, each breath feathered by a boyish snore; a hermetic outlawry that preserved the troupe of them from conventional contamination and anxiety; a tender black glaze that would come into the other man's eyes when Francis, an increasingly willful mistress, would give a consent; and, above all, the fleshy freedoms, amid a rub of planes satisfyingly solid and flat and rank, that, carried to the porch of pain, could never be reëstablished on the body of a woman, however corrupt. Yet amid these dark planes the actor felt himself going under to what was, essentially, despair.

As he tried to fight free, his lover took it as a personal rejection and turned on him with a woman's spite. Toward the end of the tour, when the director was too faithfully drunk to enforce discipline, Algernon consistently truncated Lane's funniest speech on marriage, which begins, "I believe it *is* a very pleasant state, sir. I have had very little experience of it myself up to the present."

Here Algernon would say (languidly), "I don't know that I am much interested in your family life, Lane," before Lane could enunciate the cap-joke:

"I have only been married once. That was in consequence of a misunderstanding between myself and a young person."

And indeed there proved to be an element of misunderstanding in Francis's marriage. His wife was a tall straight girl with the vaguely blank beauty that dwells unaltered in the Greek statues of Venuses, Apollos, and hermaphrodites. She was the antistrophe of the chorus of the off-Broadway modern-dress *Hippolytus* in which Francis achieved first notice. He was the hero, chosen, over a half-dozen more experienced actors, for a quality about him, a sinister austerity, which the director, a superstitious Hungarian, felt as ominous and appropriate. The reviewers were chilled by the pale and thunderous prig, with a powdery touch of the harlequin, that Francis made of Hippolytus. The audiences, aware of an uncanny tampering at the backs of their minds, applauded with a slightly frightened warmth the slim tuxedoed figure so recently dragged to death by his panicked horses. The formal dress was Francis's suggestion. The director's original inspiration called for business suits (Theseus looked like a gentleman of the audience looking for his seat onstage) and for sack dresses that made Phaedra with the white-clad chorus seem the heavily coiffed manageress of a team of beauticians. Always in his stage career, Francis, given a choice, would favor the formal and stylized, the cool.

Antistrophe, she who stepped forward and cried, "Love is like a flitting bee in the world's garden and for its flowers, destruction is in his breath," was from the Midwest, well-to-do, and twenty-one. Francis, at this turning in his life, was twenty-three and considered gay. Antistrophe, new to New York and its shadowy paths, simply placed herself beside him in the dark passageway one night (the theatre was the basement of a combined Presbyterian church and synagogue, and was entered via a narrow sidewalk striped by a shadow of a fire escape), led him to a brightly lit sandwich shop on Sixth Avenue, drank a milkshake, let him walk her to her apartment on Perry Street, and kissed him good-night in the foyer. Her kiss was like one of those stiff little cupcakes that at birthday parties long ago confidently appeared beside the ice cream. She was tall like a man, but fit him. Her name was Ellen. Moving, night by night, deeper into her, Francis revisited the past, lost landscapes of plain decency where people drove cars, watered gardens, conversed with the mailman, and knew the milkman's son.

But she was conventional only, like an Ibsen stage, in her furniture; her core was a rare sense of truth. In her he found his touchstone, an artistic index he could always consult. Of his Hippolytus, she told him, "You tease us. You dart in and out of him and just when we think we have either him or you you become the other. It makes the death scene very confusing. You seem to be enjoying it too much. There's something mocking in it, something cruel."

The accusation was familiar. "I mock?"

"Up to a point it's nice. You're flirting with us. But after you've flirted you must"—she hesitated, rejecting the coarse obvious words—"go on."

"And can you teach me, to 'go on'?"

She answered his mockery seriously. "Yes."

"I believe you."

She explained, "I can never get very far myself. I'm too big, too inhibited, really. But you, it's just a question of what you want to be." She spoke deliberately, and went directly to the matter of first importance. "How much do you do with other men?"

"Hardly anything any more. I'm attracted physically but repelled intellectually."

She nodded, understanding that what others might have dismissed as

Wildean paradox was his honest understanding of the matter. Encouraged, he dared ask her a question equally direct. "What do you feel toward me, me apart from my talent?"

"It's part of you. I can't separate them."

He saw sadly that the question had been unreal, as he had become unreal; the human object his parents and grandparents had loved was gone, had been transmuted into reputation and performance.

She asked, "And me. What do you feel about *me*?"

He shrugged and said, "I want you and once I have you will probably need you forever." After a moment of consideration she accepted his avoidance of the verb "love," though by this discourtesy he betrayed not so much a passion for precision as a certain plebeian rudeness, like the rough carpentry on the back of an elegant set. He had never taken the time to learn manners, and here too he felt she could help him. She was a lady.

There was a light beneath her skin, a cool light leading him, in the act of love, down toward a total clarity which, when the act was completed, stayed with him as insomnia. In the lucid mental air her love left behind, he felt a visionary excitement. A sense of his own infinite possibilities possessed him; an evil shuffle of masks tormented him. He would wake her and beg for sleep. She would stroke his narrow skull and, as he had taught her, massage his chest, dipping her tongue into the hollow at the base of his throat. In turn he would arrange her long silken hair, bleached in the moonlight, on the pillow to be smoothed and gloated over like a treasure laid out for inventory. Calm and straight as a corpse she would lie under his hands, receding from him. For he was never sure of her love. Her body too often seemed a fine gift carelessly left behind. Their marriage perhaps was too much a contract, too intelligently shaped for their mutual profit. Yet she satisfied the artist in him, through her he could "go on"; and at the ceremony, though it took place in City Hall, he had a full sense, as she confidently stood erect at his side, of the occasion's being sufficiently formal. His successes multiplied. He was invited to Broadway, and stayed. In the next six years, detesting the tedium of long runs and secretly grateful for the plays that folded, Francis became in succession a dope-pusher, in white suit and black sunglasses; a prince in the court of Alfonso the Wise, King of León and Castile; a cuckolded millionaire collecting exotic marine life from the deck of a Mediterranean yacht; a symbolic root-digger speaking in ragged rhyme; the educated miner's son in an adaptation of D. H. Lawrence; Touchstone; Pierre Abélard; an alcoholic pianist; an idealistic Jewish schoolteacher sent to the gas chambers; an effete art-dealer whom the dénouement revealed to be also a homocidal maniac; another cuckolded millionaire; Stephen Foster (*encore* the bottle and piano); Bluntschli in a revival, with inserted Cold War overtones, of Shaw's *Arms and the Man*; and a tainted senator in a timorously fearless play about Washington corruption. Francis regarded most of his vehicles as preposterously feeble. The playwrights he met were bloated with private hysteria and public clichés. The directors were paunchy cads whose artistic consciences and wits had been stupefied by decades of dining in restaurants, at tables of sycophants. The producers, graceful gray men, were bankers and brokers essentially motivated, after years of patient financial accumulation, by the hope of buying an actress or— even better because less conspicuous—an understudy. All the real theatre had moved to the streets, and was brought back indoors by kids just off the streets. Francis felt out of it, a relic; his energy after thirty turned to seduction.

Loving each woman, he discovered, gave him a new shape; some elicited wit from him, others sadness. With some, in bed, he became rampaging, a rhinoceros; with others, insinuant, boneless, an amoeba, ubiquitous and transparent. With all of them, he wearied of the shape they conjured up. For they could not essentially change him any more than we change a mirror by posing before it; when they were gone, nothing remained. Except a handkerchief, a cigarette filter, a wet bathroom floor because one woman had carelessly let the shower curtain hang outside the tub.

The woman who made trouble for him was an over-the-hill director's young second wife, named Patrice. Seeking rejuvenation and reëducation at a blow, the director had found her in a college. She was one of those weirdly both bright and beautiful girls who astound their seminars and intimidate their tutors and even, taking degree after degree, defy time; yet who, once torn from the hothouse of libraries and the company of immortals, darken and go mad. Her lips were painted a red so dark it was black, and in her gestures and stances there was always one limb or angle out of rhythm, awry. Her remarks to Francis were intelligent and merciless:

"On the stage, you don't *move*. Other people, somehow, *are* their bodies; you still live in yours, like a drawbridge operator.

"Your looks hurt you, Francis. Your face has no marks on it. Even lousy actors have some moment when the part coincides with themselves and they fit it, it works. Maybe if you played a Martian, an adolescent Martian . . .

"I've figured out your trouble, Francis. You've never had to face hate. That's why you have no empathy. Empathy equals sympathetic magic equals killing an enemy. Until you've looked at an enemy you've never seen *any*body. That's why Lex is great. Everybody hates him."

Lex was her husband, the famous director. When Francis, intimidated, asked her if she too hated Lex, she snapped back, "Of course. Any real man, you hate sometimes. I could never hate you. Never." So even her confessions came as taunts. He held his head tilted, and she grew frantic. They were in his hotel room; he had asked her there as a courtesy, in the hope that by sleeping with her he would be rid of her. "I wouldn't be here if you were anything at all. If you had even the presence of a fool, I wouldn't be here. You're a ghost, Francis. A spook. Don't touch me. Wait. Please."

He suddenly knew that but for her husband this harsh centrifugal woman was a virgin. She had rushed from the window past him to the bathroom; she returned in her slip. Cravenly kissing those black, black lips, he touched her below, to see if she had left on her underpants. She had not. There was a resilient softness beneath the silken slip, at the center of her, softer than silk; her pussy was so soft he broke the kiss to exclaim "Oh" and wanted to cry. Her softness spun him out fine and taut as shining wire. Afterward, she looked up at him and laughed. "It *is* different," Patrice said.

"Different from what?"

"From with your husband."

Again, later:

"I want to give you a baby."

"How beautiful of you," he murmured. Then there was a small stunned contraction within his chest as he realized, from the complacent quality of her silence, that she meant it literally and, indeed, at the moment, had the means within her. "You mean right now?"

She laughed. Her caressing hand was describing over and over a circle on the small of his back. Her face seemed to glow in the dark, so pale was her skin in contrast with her black hair, her eyebrows, her eyes, her painted lips. She limply wrapped herself around him. "Don't be frightened. I wouldn't trick you into it. I'll do it with your consent."

"Maybe you can't have my consent."

"I'll have it." He was indeed her first lover, and she was touchingly sure of the omnipotence of her surrender.

"I'm married."

"Badly. To a sterile stick. I don't even despise her; isn't that conceited of me?"

"Well, yes."

She laughed again, and it was uncanny to him how her skin, as if electrified by the contrast with her hair, emitted a waxy light. "I love," she said, "the way you pretend to resist me."

"I do resist you."

"If you did, I'd feel it in your body."

"The body and the soul are two different things," he told her. "Didn't you ever go to Sunday school? The body belongs to death, and the soul belongs to God."

"You belong to me. All of you, Francis. All, all. Don't move. If you take yourself out of me, I'll die."

"You exaggerate."

"I *don't* exaggerate. How dare you say that! How dare you mock me! Don't you *know* what you are to me? Don't you *know*?"

"I'm beginning to think I'm too much to you. Hey. Let me up."

Her voice came surely from the darkest depth of her throat. "I'm going to have you, Franky."

Call me but love, and I'll be new baptiz'd.

As once he had felt his will replace the will of another, so now cell by cell he submitted to a tyranny of possession, a helpless and phantasmal tyranny whose perpetrator grew ghostlike, so cold the pallor of her face, so dark the burning of her eyes and lips. He pitied her and, unable to release her from the spell it was his fate to cast, he cried for help by growing careless, leaving clues in his pockets and carrying her scent in his clothes and on his fingertips. His wife seemed deliberately slow to hear this cry. At last one night Ellen brought him a discovered message, an avowal scrawled on a paper napkin to be understood above the noise of a nightclub orchestra; she walked into the room holding it by one corner, like a dead bird by its wingtip.

"Who is this?"

"Nobody. A girl."

"How long have you had this one?"

"Not long. Since I began the new show."

"That's much longer than usual for you, isn't it?"

"Ellen, I'm sorry."

"Not really."

"I'm scared, then. She . . . loves me too much."

His wife smiled; she had grown, he noticed, stiff in their marriage, as if her body were her soul's armor against him. "All by herself! You didn't invite it!"

"I don't know. I don't know why it happens."

"You want me to get you out of it?"

"I don't know. Yes. Please."

"Tell her I know. Tell her it must be ended or I'll get a divorce."

"I can't lie to her. She knows me too well."

"You won't be lying. It's the truth." She turned and spoke with a choral stiffness to the windowless wall of their living room. "It's the simple truth. I'm exhausted. Get rid of this child or I'm through." Inaudibly she gave herself over to weeping.

He found himself frightened of losing his wife, though she had long ceased to love him, or at least to express that love. They had no children, at first by intention, and then through some chemical mystery. But in her presence his feverish sense of being consumed subsided. He was unable to explain it to his mistress; he who could hurl a whisper to the back rows of balconies was unable to convince this intelligent woman that other love existed in the world.

A group of philanthropic citizens, whose generosities were matched by municipal and federal funds, had endowed what was intended to resemble the great repertory theatres of Europe. He was invited to join the company and at Ellen's urging had accepted, though wary of leaving the gambler's strip of Broadway, that cozy jungle where success is oversold and even failure carries a certain panache. The theatre was newly built and, if not acoustically perfect (an elusive old art, acoustics, like violin-making), was visually opulent; he had come to love this theatre, the physical case at last for his jewel, the jewel that he carried inside his tilted head and that only he could not see.

Even here, unforgivably, Patrice waylaid him, bluffing her way, a director's wife, into an unlit side room. Her long hot arms, with their spiralling black hairs, pulled him into her; her black mouth seized his lips; her hand, whose fingertips had a chilly touch, reached into his fly. She led him up, into silver length, to erupt; he sobbed against her open mouth while his mind cried *No*. He tried to explain that her love insulted him, that it was a kind of outpouring of herself which his empty presence made possible. She spoke of him as of a wilderness she was destined to inhabit. Tears shone on her white face in the sharp-edged half-light. The sight of them intensified his appetite for dryness. "Forgive me, forgive me," he said, ceasing to listen to her words, as she had not listened to his. As they parted she touched his chest, dazed. Like a gold thread through their grief ran his pride that he had instructed her, had given her biological conceit a necessary blow, had established, over against nature, another, superior realm.

His chest smarted as if strips of adhesive tape had been torn from it. His mouth was parched. A vapor was affecting his eyes. He walked down a passageway, past the greenroom already alive with the gossip of the extras, Capulets and Montagues, past the closed dressing room of his leading lady. She was the girl with the long dull blond hair and the flat cat's nose. She had survived his desertion to become an actress; she had used him. She had needed to know degradation, to give her voice the necessary shadows. Each night Francis declaimed love into the steady gray gaze of her contempt. Against her resentful body his own grew mockingly light, freed and confirmed as when his father had struck him. The theatre was full. The crowd, dressed formally, male and female alternating, seemed, seen from the height of the stage, an abstract pattern, a pen of peacocks seen from above. The first act, so artificial, passed in a haze of light and verbal glitter; the follow-spot, he felt, never left his eyes and acted as a shield, a mirror interposed between himself and the audience it was so necessary to touch. The moon, perhaps, had come too close; the whiteness of his mistress's skin had dazed his eyes. Her physical extraction from him had left an ache which he feared might be visible through his tights. He left the stage aware that he was fumbling, failing.

His wife was waiting for him in the wings, dressed in an ordinary suit, her brown hair touched with gray. She handed him an envelope on whose face his name emerged from a scrawl of loops. "This is yours," she said.

He knew the handwriting, ill-controlled, the slant inconsistent. His chest contracted. "Where did you get it?"

"The police found it by her bed."

"The poor crazy thing."

Ellen said, "She called me on the phone. She said she was dying and wanted to talk about you. I got her address out of her and called the police. The hospital thinks they reached her in time."

How you exaggerate! The police had already opened the envelope. Her letter was illegible, loops and underlinings spelling love, love in its churning chaotic egotism. He felt disgusted and dizzy; his wife, seeing his reaction in his face, took the letter from him as if redeeming something precious, and turned her back. Turned it forever, he felt.

"Romeo? Wherefore art thou, Romeo?" It was the wing prompter, an envious and sardonic old spinster.

Francis stepped into the light and said, "Can I go forward when my heart is here? Turn back, dull earth, and find thy center out." He hid in the shadows, waited like an animal while two painted young men went through the speeches of Benvolio and Mercutio, and then, coming out of hiding, proclaimed, "He jests at scars that never felt a wound."

An invisible bombardment arose around him—from the motley shadowy wings; from the glaring light troughs framing the black void of the audience; from the space above him, the towering stage house, rigged like a ship, where past and future scenery hung suspended like gigantic gills; from the cardboard façade suspended behind him, where a little cat-nosed face appeared. A ripple of applause expressed surprise from the watching void. His throat like some curved silver weapon released flights of words, *sun, moon, maid, sick,* and the bombardment intensified; he cried out, *stars, spheres, birds, cheek,* and another voice cried out against his: "Ay me!" The light plot, subtle and silent, swirled around them like an eddying of winds; the floor at his feet was chalked with arrows. He tilted his head, as if to receive an obliquely directed blow, in that gesture becoming, helplessly, more himself. *My name, dear saint, is hateful to myself.* He lifted his hand, and it burned before his eyes, bathed in white fire. From all corners, from beyond the footlights, from above the top-most shadows, Francis was bombarded by the certainty that he was—monstrous imposition!—beloved.

THE LENS FACTORY

DAVID KERN, at sixteen, had taken a summer job at the lens factory. Everything seemed huge: the brick factory wall, springing right off the sidewalk, as he entered in the morning; its several football-field-wide floors, flickeringly lit, crammed with the noise and tremor of the machines. Even the space of dirt and weeds behind the factory, where the other workers ate and played quoits for the half-hour allowed, felt enormous to him, as he crossed the diagonal line of shadow into the sunshine where Eddie, a workmate, already sat on a bench made of a plank and cement blocks. David loved these minutes of intermittence from tending his machine, but not completely: there was a pocket of dread within him that he must carry back to the job and even into sleep and out the other side. It made him feel lopsided, this sense of being plucked at by unhappiness.

"How goes it?" Eddie asked him, as David sat beside him. Eddie had been here several years, since dropping out of high school, and David supposed the older boy must have many friends at the factory. But the bench was empty, and Eddie's friendly interest in him seemed unfeigned. When David reported to work three days ago—a Monday, and this was only Wednesday—Eddie had been assigned by the foreman of that part of the floor to show him how to mount the semi-spherical caps of sunglass lenses on the round pivots, how to stack them on the shelved cart when their twenty minutes in the "mud"—the liquid abrasive in its long trough, which stuck under your fingernails and ruined your clothes—was over, and how to keep track of their numbers on the wire overhead. The work seemed simple, yet it was a terrible race to keep the machine from getting ahead, as it scrubbed and chugged away with its row of metal elbows. An inspector in a white shirt came around once every morning and afternoon with his chalk, slashing X's on the dozens of shelved lenses that were ruined, through some error of David's. The timing had to be exact—too little, they weren't polished, and too much, they were "cooked."

"I guess better," David said, unfolding his paper bag and taking out the sandwich of Lebanon baloney his mother had made. She had tucked an apple into his new lunch pail, which made him want to cry, somehow— its Christmassy redness, its country smell. His grandparents' place had an apple tree in the back yard. The apple seemed something he could never get back to, from this abyss he felt he was in, here behind the towering brick factory, sitting on a plank under a scrawny weed tree.

Eddie was smoking a Pall Mall and eating a ten-cent cake, with caramel icing and lemon-yellow insides. He was faintly yellow himself, as if the flickering factory lights had given him their own kind of tan. Smoke and crumbs were mixed in his mouth as he talked. "The thing is to get the rhythm," he said. "The machine has a rhythm and after two weeks here it'll be second nature to you, you won't even have to think what you're doing."

The Lebanon baloney had flecks of spice in it, and these flecks burned in David's stomach, touching the sensitive soreness that was always there now. "What do you think about instead?" he asked the other boy.

Eddie laughed, disclosing more yellow crumbs. "Dirty stuff," he said cheerfully.

David felt invited to ask what dirty stuff, but instead rolled his face away, staring upward into the weed tree (trees of heaven, his mother called them), which had grown surprisingly tall in the shadow of the factory. Its leaves were parallel, like rapid crayon strokes, dark down closer but golden up high, where the sunshine struck. He saw that the tree of heaven was in feeble bloom, with small yellowish-green dirty-looking flowers. David's mind squeezed itself up there as if out of a deep well, high into the tree, where he would never have climbed when he was a child, being shy of heights and this kind of tree being too brittle, too jungle-quick in its growth, to climb anyway. The tree's presence here—a touch of nature, like the apple—seemed a blessing, though. While he was staring off into space, feeling his childhood hovering just above him, like something from which he had just this minute fallen, Eddie's hand had come to rest on his thigh. It was a light, sallow hand, the nails rimmed with dried orange mud, a bit undernourished, like everything else about Eddie. Even Eddie's mind, David imagined, was curled in there like a shrivelled walnut, blackened.

"You're a good kid, Davey," Eddie told him. "You'll get the hang of things."

Nobody called David "Davey." Irritable in his sensitive sad state, he twitched his thigh away from Eddie's consoling hand. He longed to express the horror of life that this job had opened to him, but didn't know quite how to without insulting Eddie, whose life it was. "Yeah, but then so what?" he did say.

"What do you mean, so what?"

"I mean, how do you stand it, day after day, all summer and all? I mean, you don't have any summer."

The other boy blinked, little pink lids and colorless short lashes. "You get as much summer as most people," he argued. "There's weekends, and lots of light hours after four."

Something in the concentrated set of Eddie's thin lips, and the watery way his dull blue eyes stayed on David's face, suggested that the boy was determined not to be insulted. David despaired of expressing how completely the factory seemed to eclipse everything else. He took in breath but there was nothing to say, it was all too big. His comforter saw this and continued for him, "This ain't going to be your life, Davey. You'll do it for the summer and be going back to school. It ain't going to be my life, neither. I'm thinking of joining one of the services, the Navy probably. All kinds of action in the Navy. This city is dead. There's nothing in this city for anybody who wants to be a little different."

It was strange, the way the older boy's voice so softly and insistently went on, embroidering this and saying that, as if searching for a passageway.

"I don't want to be different, exactly," David told him. "I just want room to breathe. When I'm up there with the trough sloshing mud and everything timed to the split-second, it's like I can't breathe."

Eddie lit another cigarette without taking his eyes off of David's face. "You'll breathe," the other boy strangely said. "You'll take lots of breaths before you're done, Davey boy." Puffs of smoke tumbled from his mouth, and he shook his red pack of Pall Malls so one cigarette jumped up for David to take. Eddie had this nimbleness, this sly slippery trickiness, clinging to him like a yellowish film. "You know what 'blow' means?" he asked.

David pretended not to have heard him. He quickly put his paper bag down, with the apple uneaten, and stood up and said, "Think we can get a game of quoits in?" His heart was racing. The entire vacant space here, behind the factory, cut diagonally in two by shadow, felt gathered and focused behind him with a certain pressure, as if the small of his back were blocking the tip of a funnel.

There were two pair of quoits stakes, and both were taken right now, by quartets of men in gray pants and khaki shirts or bib overalls stained and smeared but nowhere near as dirty as David's own dungarees, filthy with dried mud especially around the fly, where he leaned against the trough to change the caps. The clinks of the quoits mixed with eager laughter and yells from the men, and he saw there would not be any free stakes till the end of the break. He had found to his surprise that compared with Eddie and the other boys he was good at quoits, with his country background. He sat down again on the bench, and looked in his paper bag to see if his mother had by any chance put in a cookie he had missed.

Eddie hadn't moved, just sat and smoked. There was a lemon-colored crumb on the edge of his lip, where he couldn't feel it. He asked, "What do you want to be in life, Davey?"

"Oh . . ." He couldn't think, through the pounding blood of his embarrassment at Eddie's earlier question. "Something stupid. Something where you sit at a desk in New York."

"New York's a great town. Not like this town, dead. There's a helluva lot to do in New York."

"How often've you been there?"

It was a tactless, cruel question, it turned out. Eddie's pale color reddened a little. "Once or twice. Penn Station, I couldn't believe it. And the Empire State Building right up the street. And Times Square, all that action. You ever been up that way, Davey?"

He didn't want to hurt Eddie's feelings by saying how often. "A couple times. My parents took me. I have an aunt lives near there."

"Yeah, and what kind of places they take you to? Yankee Stadium? Polo Grounds? Madison Square Garden?"

"I don't know, museums," David said.

"That a fact? Museums? Your folks must be pretty swell to go to museums."

"No, it's just where my aunt likes to takes us. They're free or pretty near, I guess."

Eddie wormed into the idea. "The best things in life are free," he said. "Isn't that what they say? The best things in life are free." There was a suggestion of a tune, the second time, that made his voice croak and pathetically high. "You know what they mean by that, don't you?"

"No. By what?"

"By the best things in life are free." Eddie's hand reappeared on the knee of David's filthy-orange dungarees, but with a smoking cigarette between two of the fingers, which made it less dangerous, somehow. "You know what they mean by the best things, don't you?"

"Air," David offered. "Sunshine." There was now a pressure making his ears ring, and he kept his head bowed, his eyes on his crusty fly, to relieve the pressure.

Eddie laughed in his ear, lightly, with the friendly dried-up delicacy he had, like that of a little old man already, the kind you see shuffling around train stations.

"Naa. They don't mean that. You got to let me show you sometime what they mean."

"O.K.," David said, to say something, to get out of this. He wasn't ready for this, this pressure. He was feeling "cooked." The scabby green door back into the factory, at the low corner of the building as it loomed in its numbing largeness, beyond a blue scattering of cinders to keep the weeds down, seemed reachable only through a tunnel in the transparent air, a tunnel back to the safety of the metal stairs with their waffle pattern, the flickering bluish lights of his floor, his long dirty patient machine waiting for him to bring it to life with the big lever that tied it into the overhead power.

"Davey."

The voice was close and husky and yet far away, from outside the imagined tunnel.

"Was you ever blowed?"

This time when David stood, he accidentally knocked the cigarette from Eddie's hand. "Sorry," he said. The other boy looked up, only mildly surprised and hurt. David discarded Eddie's pale face like a wrapper, forever. He walked rapidly away. The quoits were being clinked into a stack by four men who were finished with their game, but to David's relief there wasn't time to play now, and he wasn't going to be here tomorrow.

FIVE POEMS

Basium XVI

from the Latin of Johannes Secundus (1511–1536)

You star more seductive than silvery Latona
and lovelier than Venus' golden glow—
    give me a hundred kisses,
    give me as many kisses
as Lesbia granted her insatiable poet,
as many as are the erotic enticements,
    the little Cupids, that tease your dear lips
    and infuse your cheeks with rose;
as many as the lives and deaths that your eyes hold,
as the hopes, as the tears, as the joys
    unsleeping obsession sends,
    as many as the sighs of lovers.
Give me as many kisses as the arrows
that the dire winged god has planted in my heart
    and as many as still stand
    collected in his gilded quiver.
Then to these delectations add,
with husky-sweet sibilant whispers and quips,
    laughter, not without friendliness,
    and friendliness, not without nibbling:
in such a way as do Chaonian doves,
trembling and murmuring, rub bill on bill
    while the first warm winds of spring
    begin to melt hard winter.

Love, let your mind go blank. Your eyes aswim
and rolling unseeing, relax against my cheek,
  in my arms, your proud blood drained,
  and beg me to sustain you.
Then I lace my arms around you, you,
your cold breast pressed against my warm one,
  and give you back your life again
  with a long, inflaming kiss,
until my spirit, floundering in turn,
is lost in that small wet mouth of yours.
  Then, sinking within your arms, I beg
  you to gather me up, into you.
And you lace your arms about me, me,
your warm breast caressing my cold one,
  and give me back my life again
  with a long sweet dewy breath.
So: let us seize, light of mine, our life
in its flowering time. For soon infirm old age
  brings all its pathetic cares,
  and illnesses, and death.

Head of a Girl, *at the Met*

Vermeer's girl in your turban and pearl:
I saw you once in The Hague, some sixteen years ago,
and now in New York as part of this visiting show.
You haven't changed, you famous girl,

your lower lip as moist and thoughtful
as the painter's touch could render it, your eyes
resting sideways on mine, their gaze weighted by
that fullness of a woman's eyeball.

I, I have changed a great deal:
hair brown then now gray, heart fresh as red paint
veined now by the crackling of too many days
hung in the harsh sun of the real.

You will outlive me, artful girl,
and with averted head will rest your moment's glance
on centuries of devotees (barring mischance),
the light in your eyes like the light on your pearl.

Cafeteria, Mass. General Hospital

They try to make the places cheerful where
we face our deaths, while sipping
a too-hot paper cup of coffee drawn
from a pseudo-silver urn. At round white tables
while the floor-to-ceiling windows admit
sunshine, fresh grass, some rhododendrons, and
the statue of a naked mother nursing—
O life! Life! We didn't love you enough
even when you were in our arms, humid
and breathing "I love you!"—the doctors
and patients, hard to distinguish, mingle
bright words with the droning monologue
of a cell-phone addict fearful she won't be heard
above the clamor of her evil cells.

An Hour Without Color

An hour without color before snow
a tinge of brown in the oak leaf
a hint of green in the pine: "gray"
is too much to say of what's left
the sea dissolved into white sky
the woods a matted mass webbed with shreds
of last week's faded storm; then
it is snowing, it is now, I see
the particles making a grain across things
half visible half not, sifting
the light from the scene like a thief
who steals what we slowly realize
we can do without, are better off without:
the colors of things afflicting our eyes

Not Cancelled Yet

Some honorary day
if I play my remaining cards right
I might be a postage stamp
but I won't be there to lick me
and licking was what I liked,
in tasty anticipation of
the long dark slither out of the mailbox,
from box to pouch to hand
to bag to box to slot to hand
again: that box is best
whose lid slams open as well as shut,
admitting a parcel of daylight,
the green top of a tree,
and a flickering of fingers, letting go.

Book Chat

HUMOR IN FICTION

THE TITLE OF THIS TALK has been assigned to me; and, though I confess I find it congenial, I confess also that I can hardly imagine a language *less* international than that of written humor. For humor, written or otherwise, operates in the *nuancé* margins of experience and communication; not only is a pun lost in translation from one language to another, but also lost is the rhythm, the slang, and the penumbra of verbal allusion. The great Argentine writer Jorge Luis Borges, in parenthetically discussing the failure of Shakespeare's humor to amuse him, ventured the surprising thought that "humor . . . is an oral genre, a sudden spark in conversation, not a written thing." And, if we reflect upon those occasions when we laugh, we perceive how delicate and complex are the forces giving rise to our reaction, how close to pathos or banality these forces verge, and how difficult it is to describe, later, what, in the heat of conversation or, it may be, in the forward surge of reading, seemed so funny.

The phenomenon of humor, or laughter, has not failed to attract theorists. Henri Bergson located the comic essence in an "encrustation of the mechanical upon the organic." Twins, for example, are humorous because duplication of individuals hints at a mechanical intervention in the species; a man slipping upon a banana peel is comic in that he behaves like a machine, rigidly perpetuating his motion without the foresight and allowances proper to vitality. By Bergson's theory, the comic incident is a misapplication of momentum and the comic character is a monomaniac, which well enough describes the heroes of French farce but does not encompass such a nimble and many-faced comic hero as Shakespeare's Falstaff.

Given on July 1, 1970, in Seoul, South Korea, as part of a weeklong conference, "Humor in Literature East and West," sponsored by International PEN.

Confusingly, just as weeping can express joy as well as sorrow, laughter arises from states of mind that appear not merely various but even opposite: laughter can announce scorn and contempt, but may also be applause. Our laughter at Falstaff, for instance, has much applause and admiration in it, as well as a feeling of superiority, and in literary humor especially there is a necessary ingredient of the genial. Within a comic work we are relaxed in a world of essential safety, where the dangers of death and destruction have been exchanged for mock penalties, for semblances of defeat and punishment that are erased by the next comic scene. The comic character, whether a cat in an animated cartoon or the hero of a classic like *Don Quixote*, is rubbery; he bounces back, and suffers no scars. Contrast the brittle, stony characters of Greek tragedy, who, under the forgiving and mounting pressure of fate's engines, irrevocably shatter.

Sigmund Freud, a few years after Bergson's treatise on laughter and his own epochal work on the interpretation of dreams, attempted to extend the methods of his dream analysis into the analysis of jokes. His book *Wit and Its Relation to the Unconscious* explains jokes and examples of verbal wit, and, by extension, all instances of the comic, in terms of a difference in physical expenditures; the characteristic joke sets up an instant of bewilderment, and laughter follows in the recognition that a kind of sense has been made, but different from what we expected. As Kant said, the comic is "an expectation that has turned to nothing." Certainly jokes, like dreams, do function in a realm liberated from the laws of logic and logical consequence, and there is melancholy profundity in Freud's tentative suggestion that humor, the art of the comic, is an adult attempt to recover "the lost laughter of childhood."

And what might be this original laughter, the laughter of childhood? A recent popular but not uninformative book called, a little provocatively, *The Naked Ape*, discusses, from a zoologist's point of view, the origin of laughter. Desmond Morris first notes that crying is present from birth but laughter does not appear until the third or fourth month of life. It arises in circumstances like these: The mother, holding the child in her lap, pretends to let him drop or does something else startling. The infant's instinctive crying reaction is cancelled by the recognition that he is safe, that the mother is with him, and this cry merges with the parental-recognition gurgle that by this time is part of his vocabulary. In this manner, laughter is born. Many of the games parents instinctively play with infants, for instance—the tossing and clutching, the chasing and tickling—are in fact a systematic daring and scaring, a widening of the circle of safety in which the child feels privileged to laugh. A hundred and fifty years ago, William Hazlitt wrote this on the theory of laughter:

If we hold a mask before our face, and approach a child with this disguise on, it will at first, from the oddity and incongruity of the appearance, be inclined to laugh; if we go nearer to it, steadily, and without saying a word, it will begin to be alarmed, and be half-inclined to cry: if we suddenly take off the mask, it will recover from its fears, and burst out a-laughing; but if, instead of presenting the old well-known countenance, we have concealed a satyr's head or some frightful caricature behind the first mask, the suddenness of the change will not in this case be a source of merriment to it, but will convert its surprise into an agony of consternation, and will make it scream out for help. . . .

The mere suddenness of the transition, the mere baulking our expectations, and turning them abruptly into another channel, seems to give additional liveliness and gaiety to the animal spirits; but the instant the change is not only sudden, but threatens serious consequences, or calls up the shape of danger, terror supersedes our disposition to mirth, and laughter gives place to tears.

Laughter, then, can be construed as a signal of danger passed or dismissed. It occurs within an arena, whether the arms of a mother or the covers of a novel, where the customary threats of life have been suspended. Dreams, jokes, play, and aesthetic pleasures alike mark a truce with the destructive forces of life. The oldest laugh may be the crow of triumph a warrior emits when his enemy is at his feet. We giggle when we are nervous; we scream hilariously when, in the old silent pictures, the comedian totters on the parapet of a skyscraper. The margin of glee in our scream is the knowledge that, being a comedian, he will not fall. The clown, the fool, is traditionally exempt from laws and taboos. Yet his activities, and our laughter, take their point from the backdrop of gravity, of necessary prohibition and actual danger. In literature, comic adventure is woven from the same threads as tragedy and pathos; we laugh within the remittance from seriousness that the artist has momentarily won for us.

This said by way of preface, I would like to read aloud a few passages of "humor in fiction." Let us begin with perhaps the most famous comic episode in Western literature, an incident that has given the English language a phrase, "tilting at windmills." Rather early in Cervantes's *Don Quixote*, the deluded gentleman and his faithful squire Sancho Panza are riding along the plain:

As they were thus discoursing, they discover'd some thirty or forty Wind-mills, that are in that Plain; and as soon as the Knight had spy'd them, Fortune, cry'd he, directs our Affairs better than we our selves could have wish'd: Look yonder, Friend *Sancho*, there are at least thirty outrageous Giants, whom I intend to encounter; and having depriv'd them of Life, we will begin to enrich our selves with their Spoils: For they are lawful Prize; and the Extirpation of that cursed Brood will be an acceptable Service to Heaven. What Giants? quoth *Sancho Pança*. Those whom thou see'st yonder, answer'd Don *Quixote*, with their long-extended Arms; some of that detested Race have Arms of so immense a Size, that sometimes they reach two Leagues in Length. Pray look better, Sir, quoth *Sancho*; those things yonder are no Giants, but Wind-mills, and the Arms you fancy, are their Sails, which being whirl'd about by the Wind, make the Mill go. 'Tis a Sign, cry'd Don *Quixote*, thou art but little acquainted with Adventures! I tell thee, they are Giants; and therefore, if thou art afraid, go aside and say thy Prayers, for I am resolv'd to engage in a dreadful unequal Combat against them all. This said, he clapp'd Spurs to his Horse *Rozinante*, without giving Ear to his Squire *Sancho*, who bawl'd out to him, and assur'd him, that they were Wind-mills, and no Giants. But he was so fully possess'd with a strong Conceit of the contrary, that he did not so much as hear his Squire's Outcry, nor was he sensible of what they were, although he was already very near them: Far from that, Stand, Cowards, cry'd he as loud as he could; stand your Ground, ignoble Creatures, and fly not basely from a single Knight, who dares encounter you all. At the same Time the Wind rising, the Mill-sails began to move, which, when Don *Quixote* spy'd, Base Miscreants, cry'd he, though you move more Arms than the Giant *Briareus*, you shall pay for your Arrogance. He most devoutly recommended himself to his Lady *Dulcinea*, imploring her Assistance in this perilous Adventure; and so covering himself with his Shield, and couching his Lance, he rush'd with *Rozinante*'s utmost Speed upon the first Wind-mill he could come at, and running his Lance into the Sail, the Wind whirl'd it about with such Swiftness, that the Rapidity of the Motion presently broke the Lance into Shivers, and hurl'd away both Knight and Horse along with it, till down he fell rolling a good Way off in the Field. *Sancho Pança* ran as fast as his Ass could drive to help his Master, whom he found lying, and not able to stir, such a Blow he and *Rozinante* had receiv'd. Mercy o'me! cry'd *Sancho*, did not I give your Worship fair Warning? Did not I tell you they were Wind-mills, and that no Body could think otherwise, unless he had also Wind-mills in his Head? Peace, Friend *Sancho*, reply'd Don *Quixote:* There is nothing so subject to the Inconstancy of Fortune as War. I am verily persuaded that cursed Necromancer *Freston*, who carry'd away my Study and my Books, has transform'd these Giants into Wind-mills, to deprive me of the Honour of the Victory, such is his inveterate Malice against me: But in the End, all his pernicious Wiles and Stratagems shall prove ineffectual against the prevailing Edge of my Sword. *Amen*, say I, reply'd *Sancho*; and so heaving him up again upon his Legs once more, the Knight mounted poor *Rozinante*, that was half Shoulder-slipp'd with his Fall.

This episode contains many of the elements that our theorists of the comic would have us look for. Don Quixote's monomania, his determination to see romantic adventures in mundane happenstance, is comic in its rigidity, and admirable in its ingenuity. At first he seems to see the windmills through a cloud, so that sails of wood and canvas take on the appearance of giant human arms; he charges forward despite the shouted warnings of his clear-sighted squire. Then, rebuffed by a whack one sail gives him, and perhaps his vision clarified by his physical closeness to these supposed giants, he reconstructs his delusion upon a new, and invulnerable, ground: his enemy the magician Freston has turned real giants into apparent windmills. All of Sancho's realism is overthrown by sublimely arrogant assertions: "Thou art but little acquainted with Adventures" and "There is nothing so subject to the Inconstancy of Fortune as War." Like some modern statesmen, Don Quixote has constructed from much real information and one wildly false premise an impregnable castle of self-justification; awkward realities are made to argue against themselves, and to reconfirm the malice of the enemy and the nobility of the unreal quest.

His dream does not shatter under reality because the author and Sancho Panza protect him; the author by conferring upon this lean old man a magical stubborn toughness, and Sancho Panza—with a loving and wondering fidelity that is one of the book's masterstrokes—by always rushing forward and picking up the pieces. Don Quixote suffers no ill effects from this adventure; it is Rocinante, his horse, who limps, his shoulder half dislocated by their fall. It is the horse, who cannot reason or go mad but who can suffer, who absorbs and mutely carries off this adventure's residue of pain.

Even this early in the great novel, Cervantes seems indifferent to his stated objective—of burlesquing the pseudo-medieval adventures of Tasso and Ariosto. A cruder author would have hurt his hero severely, or had him spin delusions less plausibly, or accompanied him with a mocking and sardonic squire. Our laughter would have been quicker and sharper, but thinner, and quickly automatic. Satire, as an attack upon an idea or set of ideas, quickly bores us, since the author, manipulating his puppets, makes the same statement over and over. Here, with Cervantes—himself as often battered and disappointed as his hero—our laughter is deepened by a certain ambiguous poetry in the narrative; the windmills are not merely mistaken for giants but somehow *are* giants. The wind, springing up opportunely to turn their giant arms, seems to join the fun; and the knight's unshakable dignity in some sense argues for his delusions, and gives him that air of triumph which is, we noted above, an ancient tributary of laughter.

Cervantes, and Shakespeare, and Rabelais voice the burst of generosity that came over the European spirit in the Renaissance; their exuberant realism yielded, in the so-called Age of Reason, to a less trustful humanism that seeks truth through rational precepts and intellectual controversy. Voltaire wrote *Candide* with a speed that belies its polish and compression, as a kind of pamphleteering attack upon Leibniz and other philosophers who held that evil and suffering are necessary presences in a world in which man can exercise free choice. The uproarious succession of disasters which the author visits upon Candide, his optimistic mentor Dr. Pangloss, and Candide's beloved Cunégonde are not in fact a fair argument against Leibniz's subtle doctrine; they are an underhanded but compelling appeal to our emotional common sense: in the same way, in the same century, Dr. Johnson was to refute Berkeley's subtle subjectivism by kicking a stone and saying, "Thus I refute Berkeley." External facts remain our touchstones for metaphysical truth. Two disastrous earthquakes, in Lima in 1746 and in Lisbon in 1755, deeply impressed Voltaire; they seemed to him a puncture in the deist argument that all is for the best or, as Alexander Pope expressed it, "Whatever is, is right." Here is how Candide and Dr. Pangloss experience the famous Lisbon earthquake:

When they had recovered a little of their strength, they set off towards Lisbon, hoping they had just enough money in their pockets to avoid starvation after escaping the storm.

Scarcely had they reached the town, and were still mourning their benefactor's death, when they felt the earth tremble beneath them. The sea boiled up in the harbour and broke the ships which lay at anchor. Whirlwinds of flame and ashes covered the streets and squares. Houses came crashing down. Roofs toppled to their foundations, and the foundations crumbled. Thirty thousand men, women and children were crushed to death under the ruins.

The sailor chuckled:

"There'll be something worth picking up here," he remarked with an oath.

"What can be the 'sufficient reason' for this phenomenon?" said Pangloss.

"The Day of Judgement has come," cried Candide.

The sailor rushed straight into the midst of the debris and risked his life searching for money. Having found some, he ran off with it to get drunk;

and after sleeping off the effects of the wine, he bought the favours of the first girl of easy virtue he met amongst the ruined houses with the dead and dying all around. Pangloss pulled him by the sleeve and said:

"This will never do, my friend; you are not obeying the universal rule of Reason; you have misjudged the occasion."

"Bloody hell," replied the other. "I am a sailor and was born in Batavia. I have had to trample on the crucifix four times in various trips I've been to Japan. I'm not the man for your Universal Reason!"

Candide had been wounded by splinters of flying masonry and lay helpless in the road, covered with rubble.

"For Heaven's sake," he cried to Pangloss, "fetch me some wine and oil! I am dying."

"This earthquake is nothing new," replied Pangloss; "the town of Lima in America experienced the same shocks last year. The same causes produce the same effects. There is certainly a vein of sulphur running under the earth from Lima to Lisbon."

"Nothing is more likely," said Candide. "But oil and wine, for pity's sake!"

"Likely!" exclaimed the philosopher. "I maintain it's proved!"

Candide lost consciousness, and Pangloss brought him a little water from a fountain close by.

The following day, while creeping amongst the ruins, they found something to eat and recruited their strength. They then set to work with the rest to relieve those inhabitants who had escaped death. Some of the citizens whom they had helped gave them as good a dinner as could be managed after such a disaster. The meal was certainly a sad affair, and the guests wept as they ate; but Pangloss consoled them with the assurance that could not be otherwise:

"For all this," said he, "is a manifestation of the rightness of things, since if there is a volcano at Lisbon it could not be anywhere else. For it is impossible for things not to be where they are, because everything is for the best."

Dr. Pangloss, like Don Quixote, irrepressibly applies the theorems of his *idée fixe* to the incongruous material of life. There is no mistaking the satiric edge, and the author performs his comedy on the edge of pain. Yet we are anesthetized, as it were, and allowed therefore to laugh, by the flitting quickness and neatness of the narrative style. We are told, as if the statistic had been gathered in an instant, that "Thirty thousand men, women and children were crushed to death." The three characters with toylike promptness react in character: the pious and innocent Candide exclaims that the Day of Judgment is near, Dr. Pangloss poses himself a philosophical riddle amid the toppling ruins, and the sailor, cheerfully heartless, seizes the opportunity for theft and lechery. Such stylization preserves the earthquake as an item in an abstract argument and heightens our sense of play. In a sentence, we are told Candide is injured and half buried, but are not asked to dwell upon his condition—Rocinante's limp is more sensuously present. The central figure remains Dr. Pangloss, whose musing in such circumstances approaches heroic detachment and whose lack of pity for Candide is partially redeemed by his equal lack of self-pity. Pangloss's preposterous conclusion of a vein of sulfur running halfway around the world, defended with the stoutness of a Quixote, makes us laugh; and if we look deep into our laughter we detect there:

1.) a sense of superiority to the scientific speculations of the eighteenth century;
2.) a certain pleasure in the image, gaudy and simple as a child's yellow crayon stroke;
3.) applause at the good doctor's unfailing intellectual curiosity;
4.) a kind of hysteria at the frightful fact of calamity and heavenly indifference that Voltaire sets before us;
5.) a confession of pleasurable warmth, which the farcical tempo of the narrative has created in us, and which disposes us to laugh in any case.

Laughter, as we know from its social instances, is infectious and carries a curious momentum; an image, mixed of such incongruities as a man's demand for the oil and wine of the last rites mixed with another man's meditations upon sulfur, trips the trigger of laughter and, recurring (as it does when Pangloss insists, "I maintain it's proved!"), trips it again, harder. Here we touch upon the mystery, in presentation of the comic, of *timing;* in personal presentation, of timing and facial expression. A wrong twist of the face, betraying overeagerness, like an excessive adjective in a sentence, will with mysterious thoroughness defuse a joke and stifle a laugh. The moment of blank bewilderment that Freud describes is somehow sullied. There must be a headlong, clean, economical something, a swift and careless music perhaps descended from the rhythm of ticklings in infancy; no purer example of this comic music exists than *Candide.* Indeed, its example leads us to wonder if any efficient display of energy—an elegant mathematical proof, a well-made young woman briskly walking by—doesn't dispose us to jubilation, to a smile or laugh that is a salute, a shout of greeting to our comrade in life, the *élan vital.*

For all the ruthlessness of its events and the cynical slant of its moral, *Candide* is a crystalline and joyous book, whereas *Huckleberry Finn,* beneath its surface of idyll and slapstick, holds a deep sadness. A bottomless sadness, I would say; for the two European masterworks I have read from both rest upon a faith, an assumption, that, whether or not God is in His heaven and all is right with the world, the significant world is human. Humanity is the measure; humanity crowds even the arid plains of central Spain with its commerce, its conversation, its misplaced confidence. In our American novel we find a world where man is at the margin, a vaguely glimpsed and problematical intruder, no bigger than a cluster of sparks in the immense dark tranquillity of a wilderness.

In looking through *Huckleberry Finn* for a passage to read, I finally settled upon not one of the many comic incidents and dialogues, which seem a bit coarse and trumped up, but upon a descriptive passage that is not comic at all and perhaps not even humorous. But it seemed the worthiest companion to the classic passages I have quoted. Huckleberry Finn, a twelve-year-old boy, and Jim, a runaway slave, are floating down the Mississippi River on a raft. The boy tells the story, and here describes how their days on the river pass:

And afterwards we would watch the lonesomeness of the river, and kind of lazy along, and by-and-by lazy off to sleep. Wake up, by-and-by, and look to see what done it, and maybe see a steamboat, coughing along up stream, so far off towards the other side you couldn't tell nothing about her only whether she was stern-wheel or side-wheel; then for about an hour there wouldn't be nothing to hear nor nothing to see—just solid lonesomeness. Next you'd see a raft sliding by, away off yonder, and maybe a galoot on it chopping, because they're most always doing it on a raft; you'd see the ax flash, and come down—you don't hear nothing; you see that ax go up again, and by the time it's above the man's head, then you hear the *k'chunk!*—it had took all that time to come over the water. So we would put in the day, lazying around, listening to the stillness. Once there was a thick fog, and the rafts and things that went by was beating tin pans so the steamboats wouldn't run over them. A scow or a raft went by so close we could hear them talking and cussing and laughing—heard them plain; but we couldn't see no sign of them; it made you feel crawly, it was like spirits carrying on that way in the air. Jim said he believed it *was* spirits; but I says:

"No, spirits wouldn't say, 'dern the dern fog.'"

Soon as it was night, out we shoved; when we got her out to about the middle, we let her alone, and let her float wherever the current wanted her to; then we lit the pipes, and dangled our legs in the water and talked about all kinds of things—we was always naked, day and night, whenever the mosquitoes would let us—the new clothes Buck's folks made for me was too good to be comfortable, and besides I didn't go much on clothes, nohow.

Sometimes we'd have that whole river all to ourselves for the longest time. Yonder was the banks and the islands, across the water; and maybe a spark—which was a candle in a cabin window—and sometimes on the water you could see a spark or two—on a raft or a scow, you know; and maybe you could hear a fiddle or a song coming over from one of them crafts. It's lovely to live on a raft. We had the sky, up there, all speckled with stars, and we used to lay on our backs and look up at them, and discuss about whether they was made, or only just happened—Jim he allowed they was made, but I allowed they happened; I judged it would have took too long to *make* so many. Jim said the moon could a *laid* them; well, that looked kind of reasonable, so I didn't say nothing against it, because I've seen a frog lay most as many, so of course it could be done. We used to watch the stars that fell, too, and see them streak down. Jim allowed they'd got spoiled and was hove out of the nest.

Once or twice of a night we would see a steamboat slipping along in the dark, and now and then she would belch a whole world of sparks up out of her chimbleys, and they would rain down in the river and look awful pretty; then she would turn a corner and her lights would wink out and her pow-wow shut off and leave the river still again; and by-and-by her waves would get to us, a long time after she was gone, and joggle the raft a bit, and after that you wouldn't hear nothing for you couldn't tell how long, except maybe frogs or something.

I have let this passage run long because, for one thing, I am an American and it is American; for another, it makes its effect by spaciousness. The accumulation of homely yet precise details—the *k'chunk!* of the swung ax that takes time to travel across the width of water—conveys the river to us with the sensual leisureliness so rigorously excluded in *Candide*. The fact that such a beautiful and vivid evocation is expressed by a boy, in a boy's vocabulary, is in itself humorous, though in this passage at least without any flavor of *tour de force*. How strangely expressive are impressionist phrases like "the lonesomeness of the river" and "a whole world of sparks." The lazy breadth of the day gives way to night, and to the comic speculation, by our two heroes as they drift downstream in naked ignorance, that the stars were laid by the moon as a frog lays its spawn of eggs. And from the image of the stars we move to the kindred "world of sparks [belched] up out of her chimbleys" and the sense of human sparks and noises lost in this great dark silence.

Only the fact that this immensity seems benign prevents the underly-ing sadness from drowning us. In Mark Twain, the comic insulation, the shell of safety that lets us laugh, is always very thin, a mere patina of nostalgia. In his boys' books, dreadful things happen—children get lost in a deep cave with a murderous Indian, a boy discovers the body of his dead father in a house floating in a flooded river. Real violence always threat-ens, in a thinly civilized landscape that offers no assurances and no consolation beyond its impervious grandeur and "lonesomeness." Comedy in Twain ceases to be a literary form, or a rhetorical manner that excludes certain resonances of reality, and has become an attitude, a perky, crusty, sharp-eyed verbal approach to things. The improvisation thrust upon America by the unprecedented challenges of the raw land becomes in Twain's style a willingness to tackle anything, any facet of this river scene—the dead fish as well as the singing birds, the tin pans beating in the fog as well as the eternal stars strewn overhead. This indiscriminate poetry will fall upon ears accustomed to more rounded and selective description with the puzzling unexpectedness of a joke; but the joke is in the voice and not in the material. The material is often frightening. We recover, in the stars that may be the moon's frog eggs, the awesome scale of those windmills that may be giants; contrariwise, awe is quite missing from Pangloss's chattery pseudo-rational speculation that Lima and Lisbon are connected by an underground strip of sulfur.

Further on in *Huckleberry Finn*, a steamship engine explodes, and Huck's Aunt Sally says, "Good gracious! Anybody hurt?" Huck answers, "No'm. Killed a nigger." She responds, "Well, it's lucky; because sometimes people do get hurt."

The passage is strikingly like the opening dialogue of Evelyn Waugh's novel *A Handful of Dust*.

> "Was anyone hurt?"
> "No one I am thankful to say," said Mrs Beaver, "except two housemaids who lost their heads and jumped through a glass roof into the paved court."

The Twain dialogue is somewhat incidental, though it does touch upon the book's principal social themes, the brutality of frontier life and the wrongness of slavery. But Waugh begins with his, and human callousness, fostered by the class system but encouraged by greed and lust, is his theme. Again and again, we are startled into laughter because the characters are more flip and diffident and hard-hearted in their responses than we expect. In the shadows of their very English politeness, we keep barking our shins on the furniture of their avarice. The novel concerns sexual love, yet only in its social effects. The one passion we are allowed to feel with the characters is the hero's passionate attachment to Hetton, his huge, ugly, and expensive family estate. Otherwise, everything is masked in offhand conversation and oblique implication. The characters set conscious stock by this manner of expressing themselves:

> "Well," said Reggie, puffing at his cigar. "There's more to it than just money. Perhaps I'd better tell you everything. I hadn't meant to. The truth

is that Beaver is cutting up nasty. He says he can't marry Brenda unless she's properly provided for. Not fair on her, he says. I quite see his point in a way."

"Yes, I see his point," said Tony. "So what your proposal really amounts to is that I should give up Hetton in order to buy Beaver for Brenda."

"It's not how I should have put it," said Reggie.

The other three novels we have read from were all rather picaresque, and could be excerpted easily. Waugh's is a thoroughly modern novel, so interwoven that the full sense, wit, and burden of any passage depends upon a set of prior circumstance that would be tedious to explain. Suffice it to say that Tony is the hero, Brenda is his wife, and Beaver is her lover. In this entire short scene late in the novel, Brenda and Beaver are together:

Dawn broke in London, clear and sweet, dove-grey and honey, with promise of good weather; the lamps in the streets paled and disappeared; the empty streets ran with water, and the rising sun caught it as it bubbled round the hydrants; the men in overalls swung the nozzles of their hoses from side to side and the water jetted and cascaded in a sparkle of light.

"Let's have the window open," said Brenda. "It's stuffy in here."

The waiter drew back the curtains, opened the windows.

"It's quite light," she added.

"After five. Oughtn't we to go to bed?"

"Yes."

"Only another week and then all the parties will be over," said Beaver.

"Yes."

"Well let's go."

"All right. Can you pay? I just haven't any money."

They had come on after the party, for breakfast at a club Daisy had opened. Beaver paid for the kippers and tea. "Eight shillings," he said. "How does Daisy expect to make a success of the place when she charges prices like that?"

"It does seem a lot . . . So you really *are* going to America?"

"I must. Mother has taken the tickets."

"Nothing I've said tonight makes any difference?"

"Darling, don't go on. We've been through all that. You know it's the only thing that *can* happen. Why spoil the last week?"

"You *have* enjoyed the summer, haven't you."

"Of course . . . Well, shall we go?"

"Yes. You needn't bother to see me home."

"Sure you don't mind? It *is* miles out of the way and it's late."

"There's no knowing what I mind."

"Brenda, darling, for heaven's sake . . . It isn't like you to go on like this."

"I never was one for making myself expensive."

What we have witnessed, in this laconic exchange, is the end of an affair, the flickering out of a passion that has uprooted an ancient homestead and overridden a little boy's death. But in this conversation, which ostensibly traces the departure of a tired couple from a restaurant, money is revealed as the backbone of their lives: Beaver's mother has spent the money to buy the tickets to take him away to America; Brenda, with her husband fled and refusing to pay the exorbitant alimony that had been asked, hasn't even enough money to pay for the kippers and tea. Beaver, protesting the price, reveals his stinginess, and exposes his love as a love of her money; and Brenda ironically recognizes this by saying in unacknowledged farewell that she never was one for making herself expensive. He, too caddish even to accompany her home—there seems to be no question now of their going to bed together—is reminded that in this summer of love he has taken her free. The humor in this, as in the texture of *Candide*, is bound up with the economy and energy of the telling. There is also a deflationary aspect, felt not so much in each scene as through the book as a whole: as *Don Quixote* put medieval romances on trial, so Victorian romances are on trial here. We expect, from conditioning by the novels of that Romantic century the nineteenth, adultery to be less cool, more absolute and disastrous than this. The Victorians took a holy and intense view of sex; contrastingly, in one of Waugh's other books, a young lady, after her first sexual experience, compares the experience unfavorably to a trip to the dentist.

By excluding any sympathetic picture of sexual passion, Waugh cuts Brenda off from her own motives, makes her a villainess, and tinctures with nonsense all the action around her; his exclusion provides the insulation that enables us—though rather grimly—to laugh. His dialogue, however, is never only humorous; in this book at least, it is always directed toward the advancement of the action and the delineation of character and milieu. Nor does this method, of unadorned dialogue and skillful indirection—as if the author is, like the characters, somewhat diffident—belong to Waugh alone; it seems especially well suited to depiction of English society and may be found in E. M. Forster and Ivy Compton-Burnett and Henry Green and Anthony Powell. But there is a special Waughian edge, a daring and a savagery, that sets him apart, and with the immortal masters of comic fiction. The scene I have just read is sandwiched between two others set in the South American jungle. While Brenda is winding up her affair in London, Tony has fallen in with an unlikely explorer, a Dr. Messinger, who is still looking for El Dorado in equatorial America. In the scene previous to Brenda's talk with Beaver, Dr. Messinger has frightened away his native bearers and guides by demonstrating a mechanical mouse; in the scene following, the natives return in the night and steal all of his and Tony's weapons and rations, beginning the chain of disasters that will culminate in Tony's being declared dead in England, though in fact he lives as a captive of a jungle lunatic who makes Tony read aloud to him, over and over, the complete works of Charles Dickens. This absurd but horrible life-in-death, strangely terrifying despite its farcical form, is worthy—indeed, is more than worthy—of today's black humorists.

I do not know how much the phrase "black humorists" means to an audience of international poets, essayists, and novelists. But for the last five years in the United States the journalists who invent literary schools have filled the air, and our expectations, with this magic category. Vladimir Nabokov is named as a progenitor, and John Barth and Donald Barthelme are enlisted as contemporary examples. Though their work, initially, was taken as a nihilistic explosion of all accredited social values, today it is linked hopefully with social criticism of the American military involvement in Southeast Asia and the corrupt values that produced it. Humorous fiction is being urged, from some quarters, as one of the means of bringing on a healthy revolution.

Myself, I would not deny that some topical satire is momentarily interesting, and that a little of it achieves the lasting interest of art. But my general impression is that, in literature, other literary modes are the most effectively hit satiric objects, and that, insofar as humor is not an abundance, in the author, of good humor, it testifies to a disenchantment more metaphysical than political. Waugh's disenchantment, for instance, extends to the entire modern world and its materialist premises, which in practice quickly reduce to money-grubbing, snobbery, and selfish sensuality. And Voltaire's real anger is directed beyond the Christian Church and its meliorist apologists, toward a universe that tolerates pain, cruelty, and disaster. Just as we laugh harder at the jokes of someone we trust and like, great humorous authors establish with us, through their evident style and tact and general wisdom and frequent seriousness, a credibility that makes our laughter, when it comes, deep and sincere. However far mechanical theories explain humor, humor cannot be mechanically produced. It is part, in literature as in life, of human exchange; and any attempt to isolate it as a genre will trivialize it.

Just as our tears fatten upon our memories of joy, and our dreams rehearse our waking days, laughter draws strength from the gravity of actual life. The modes of humor in fiction are various, and often lowly; but in the examples I have chosen, humor coexists with the noblest qualities of imagination. These authors do not hasten toward our laughter, and the laughter they prompt does not hasten to pass judgment; rather, the laughter is allied with the wonder that suspends judgment upon the world. We began by discussing the laughter of infants; perhaps one reason we laugh so much in childhood is that so much is unexpected and novel to us, and perhaps fiction revives that laughter by giving us back the world clearer than we have seen it before.

LIVES AND LAURELS

Søren Kierkegaard, 1813–1855

PERHAPS BECAUSE HE LIVED in the toy metropolis of Copenhagen, a little man with a dandy's face and a crooked back strolling zigzag along the
sidewalk, we presume to love him; or perhaps it is his voice—that extraordinary insinuant voice, imperious and tender, rabid and witty—that
excites our devotion. He wrote, in a sense, as a lover, having spurned
marriage, and the torrent of volumes that follows his break with his
fiancée abounds with lovers' stratagems: with flirtatious ambiguities,
elaborate deceits and impersonations, fascinating oscillations of emphasis, all sorts of erotic "display." Apart from his passionate literary production of the 1840s, his life knew few events: his struggle with his father, the
attack by *The Corsair*, the attack upon Christendom. A life of antidotes.
His "aesthetic" holiday of café conversation, brothels, and the Royal
Theatre served as an antidote to the dour household of his theologically
obsessed father. His father died, and Kierkegaard began to write like a
slave. His first title, *Either/Or*, established the note of zigzag and alternation; each pseudonymous "aesthetic" work was accompanied upon publication by "edifying" discourses under his own name. The two campaigns
of publicity in which he was involved—defensive against *The Corsair*,
offensive against the Church—seem thrust and counterthrust in his war
with "the herd." His final, suicidal burst of energy, a public execration of
all earthly manifestations of Christianity including a deathbed rejection
of the Eucharist, was perhaps the subtlest antidote of all—an atoning
reënactment of his father's gesture when, as an eleven-year-old shepherd

Written for *Atlantic Brief Lives*, edited by Louis Kronenberger (1971).

boy on the Jutland heath, Michael Kierkegaard (in the words of his youngest son's journal) "stood upon a hillock and cursed God."

Yet to make of Kierkegaard a case history and to view his ideas—as does Josiah Thompson in *The Lonely Labyrinth*—as maneuvers in a self-administered, and eventually futile, therapy is to excuse ourselves from his truth and his heroism. Heroism not so much of labor (for his was an industrious century) or of personal suffering (for in fact Kierkegaard, though he continually bemoans his mysterious "thorn in the flesh," never impresses us as a martyr; like his slightly younger American contemporary Thoreau, he is a bachelor comfortable among willfully chosen privations), but heroism in facing down the imperious tradition of German idealistic philosophy: "Now if we assume that abstract thought is the highest manifestation of human activity, it follows that philosophy and the philosophers proudly desert existence, leaving the rest of us to face the worst. . . . [Philosophy] is disinterested; but the difficulty inherent in existence constitutes the interest of the existing individual, who is infinitely interested in existing. Abstract thought thus helps me with respect to my immortality by first annihilating me as a particular existing individual and then making me immortal, about as when the doctor in Holbert killed the patient with his medicine—but also expelled the fever."

It is no criticism to say that Kierkegaard is not a systematic philosopher like Hegel; it was his mission to be the anti-Hegel. "I am anything but a devilish good fellow at philosophy," his pseudonym Johannes Climacus admits. "I am a poor, individual, existing man, with sound natural capacities, not without a certain dialectical dexterity, not entirely destitute of education. I have been tried in life's *casibus* and cheerfully appeal to my sufferings." To be human is *inherently* to be a problem; he certified what the Romantics had merely suspected, that sickness is a prerequisite of wisdom: "With the help of the thorn in my foot I spring higher than anyone with sound feet." Philosophy, in his day the monarchial overscience, has become in ours the humblest of semantic inquiries, or else personal testimony. What seems strange is how the atheists Sartre, Camus, and Heidegger have given currency to terms—"the absurd," "the leap," "dread," "despair"—that Kierkegaard coined to pay his way into heaven; but, writing of Christianity as "an actualization of inwardness," Kierkegaard asserted that only two kinds of people could know anything about it, those who accept it and those who "in passion" reject it—"the happy and the unhappy lovers."

It is to would-be believers, above all, that Kierkegaard speaks. Behind all the fireworks and jockeying, the flights of poetry and dramatic imagination, the exegetical brilliance and the casually bestowed abundance of psychological insight, he is conducting, and the religiously inclined reader is desperately following, a search for the "Archimedean point" outside the world from which the world can be lifted, admitting, like a crack of light in a sealed cave, the possibility of faith—that is to say, of escape from death. The assertion that "subjectivity is truth" provides such a point, though a rather slippery one. The concept of "the paradox," all too violently felt as the "crucifixion of intellect," accords with ancient Christian formulae, and gives a certain Promethean aura to alogism. And "the leap" does seem to be the way, both in particle physics and in human affairs, that things move, rather than Hegel's deterministic "mediation."

Although he posited, in *Fear and Trembling*, a "knight of faith," Kierkegaard did not himself become that knight. The theology of his last years is dismaying in its ferocity. And his copious *oeuvre* seems unbalanced, incomplete, subjective to a fault. It remained for Karl Barth to build upon the basis of God's otherness (a concept Kierkegaard phrased, tragically, as "God's inhumanity") an inhabitable theology; it remained for Kafka, though the Dane's journals abound in miniature fables, to develop Kierkegaardian sensations into real fiction, into epic symbols. Kierkegaard, whose emphasis was ever upon "the individual" and who wanted this citation as his epitaph, lives in history not as an author or thinker attached to his work like a footnote, but as a man incarnated in his books, a human knot that refuses to be unravelled, a voice asking to be loved.

F. Scott Fitzgerald, 1896–1940

FITZGERALD should be honored, as a writer, for attempting to describe the American life of his time with all the refinement of European fiction; from imitating the smartness of Shaw and Wells and Compton Mackenzie, he moved to an attempt to absorb the examples of Conrad and Turgenev and Tolstoy and Proust. Not for him an invented American style, brashly experimental like those of Hemingway or Faulkner: unlike theirs, his style is hard to parody, blended as it is of poetry and aperçu, of

---

Contribution to *F. Scott Fitzgerald at 100*, a garland of tributes collected by Jackson R. Bryer (1996).

external detail quickly transmuted to internal sensation. His American characters, from small-town children to uproariously disintegrating sophisticates, receive a respectful and tender attention. He loved Americans and took comfort in their aura; the hero of "Babylon Revisited," returning to Paris after the Crash, finds "the stillness in the Ritz bar . . . strange and portentous. It was not an American bar any more—he felt polite in it, and not as if he owned it. It had gone back into France." The matter of America was much on Fitzgerald's mind, without the braggadocio of Wolfe or Whitman but thoughtfully, in contemplation of a spiritual puzzle. Gatsby balances on the dashboard of his car "with that resourcefulness of movement that is so peculiarly American—that comes, I suppose, with the absence of lifting work or rigid sitting in youth and, even more, with the formless grace of our nervous, sporadic games." Later in the book comes the abrupt observation that "Americans, while occasionally willing to be serfs, have always been obstinate about being peasantry." And so on—the book concludes, a touch thunderously, with its celebrated paean to virgin Long Island, "a fresh, green breast of the new world" wherein man came "face to face for the last time in history with something commensurate to his capacity for wonder." To Henry James's observations of our precious and vulnerable innocence abroad Fitzgerald added notes on our capacity for correspondingly unqualified corruption and despair.

Ernest Hemingway, 1899–1961

IN THE NEAR HALF-CENTURY since Hemingway's shocking suicide by shotgun in 1961, his fame—and did any American writer of the twentieth century enjoy more fame than he?—has attracted denigration, from critics and academics who react, perhaps, more to the man's image than to his works. He whose hero, in *A Farewell to Arms*, is a deserter from World War I, and whose portrait of civil war, in *For Whom the Bell Tolls*, unsparingly reports the atrocities on both sides, is accused of being a lover of violence. His boyhood as a Midwestern doctor's son and his war wounds in Italy at the age of eighteen impressed him with the reality of violence, and his fiction and non-fiction (see *Death in the Afternoon* and

Foreword to *Coffee with Hemingway*, by Kirk Curnutt (2007).

the introduction to his anthology *Men at War*) sought to describe this reality, including the hunter's blood lust; but a fascination is not an endorsement. He is accused of slighting his female characters, yet they— Brett and Catherine and Maria—dominate the canvases of their respective novels, and remain more poignantly, sympathetically, and heroically in the mind than their male lovers do.

Hemingway's apparently simple style, easily parodied, is dismissed as semi-literate when in fact it was a refined and thoughtful product of modernism in its prime; he took English prose and, in Ezra Pound's phrase, made it new. The example of modern painting, above all the scrupulous Post-Impressionism of Cézanne, inspired him; newspaper work honed his powers of distillation; wide reading kept his standards elevated. To be sure, he liked a fiesta, and drank too much, but he reported to his writing stand, with freshly sharpened pencils, each dawn; his writing forms a shimmering paean to our physical existence, to landscape and weather and healthy senses. His stoic hedonism became, in the ruin of conventional pieties left by World War I, a creed for his generation, a laconic lifestyle reflected in popular films, other people's writings, and even common speech.

His first book, published in 1923 in Paris, was titled *Three Stories and Ten Poems:* his short stories, which he effectively stopped producing after collecting them in 1938, are like poems in their concision, polish, and enigmatic abruptness. A sense of life's tragic brevity always lies beneath the surfaces of his taut dialogues and evocations of nature. Only the first two novels, *The Sun Also Rises* (1926) and *A Farewell to Arms* (1929), sustain throughout their length the exquisite economy and freshness of the short stories, though the novella *The Old Man and the Sea* (1952) approached their high quality and helped win the author the Nobel Prize in 1954. In his later years, in shaky physical and mental health, he published almost nothing but wrote steadily, accumulating masses of manuscripts that were mined for a number of posthumous publications, of which the most valuable is a fond memoir of his Paris years, *A Moveable Feast* (1964).

The man was a bearish celebrity when literature still bred celebrities; his work remains a touchstone of artistic ardor and luminously clean prose.

Kurt Vonnegut, 1922–2007

KURT VONNEGUT, JR., was born on Armistice Day, 1922, the third of three children of a distinguished German-American family long established in Indianapolis. It was once my pleasure and privilege to be with Kurt in Indianapolis, and it was wonderful to see how he expanded on that home turf: his smile widened, his gestures widened, and his soft, slow, rueful, considerate manner of speech became even more profoundly Midwestern. His family was locally eminent: Kurt, Sr., and *his* father were architects; Kurt's mother came from a well-to-do line of brewers, the Liebers, creators of Lieber Gold Medal Lager; and Kurt's older brother, Bernard, was a physicist specializing in clouds and thunderstorms. Kurt, Jr., went east to college, to Cornell, and achieved academic probation before being enlisted, at the age of nineteen, to the army.

The army initially sent him to the Carnegie Institute of Technology in Pittsburgh and to the University of Tennessee to study mechanical engineering, but in 1944 he was shipped to Europe with the 106th Infantry Division and soon saw combat in the Battle of the Bulge—in his words, "the largest single defeat of American arms (the Confederacy included) in history." His unit was nearly destroyed, and after several days of wandering behind enemy lines he was captured and sent to a prisoner-of-war camp near Dresden, and assigned, with other prisoners, to make vitamin-enriched malt syrup for pregnant women. The workplace was a slaughterhouse; when, on February 13, 1945, sirens went off, their guards led the prisoners to a meat locker two stories down. That saved their lives; overhead, British and American warplanes carpet-bombed the city, creating a firestorm. He wrote twenty-five years later, in *Slaughterhouse-Five*, "It wasn't safe to come out of the shelter until noon the next day. When the Americans and their guards did come out, the sky was black with smoke. The sun was an angry little pinhead. Dresden was like the moon now, nothing but minerals. The stones were hot. Everybody else in the neighborhood was dead. So it goes." The prisoners were set to work gathering up dead bodies, which he elsewhere described as "seeming pieces of charred firewood two or three feet long—ridiculously small human beings, or jumbo fried grasshoppers, if you will."

He returned from the war to an active and eventually triumphant life.

Read at the dinner meeting of the American Academy of Arts and Letters, November 6, 2007.

He married his childhood sweetheart, Jane Marie Cox. They settled in Chicago. They had three children. In Chicago, Kurt worked as a reporter for the City News Bureau and studied for a master's degree in anthropology at the University of Chicago. His thesis, "Fluctuations Between Good and Evil in Simple Tales," was unanimously rejected by the faculty. In 1947 he moved to Schenectady, New York, taking a job in public relations for General Electric. Three years later he sold a short story to *Collier's* and moved his family to Cape Cod, writing fiction for magazines like *Argosy* and *The Saturday Evening Post*, and, to add to his income, teaching emotionally disturbed children, doing advertising work, and selling Saab automobiles. When, in 1958, Kurt's sister, Alice, and her husband died within a day of each other—she of cancer and he in a train accident—the Vonneguts adopted three of their four boys. Around 1970 he and Jane separated and he moved to New York; in 1979 he married the photographer Jill Krementz, with whom he adopted a daughter, Lily. By this time his novels had made him rich and famous.

Vonnegut was unusual, if not unique, among post-war American writers in having had a primarily scientific education and in acquiring, in the long lead-up to his popular success, experience of the worlds of business and industry. In his first novel, *Player Piano*, an upstate factory and its minions are evoked; in *God Bless You, Mr. Rosewater*, the ups and downs of a Midwestern fortune are traced. Vonnegut was interested in how such things function, and his lawyers and optometrists and housewives may be employed for satiric ends but never with condescension; his fantasies are braced by a respectful practical side. Many males of his writing generation—Mailer, Heller, Salinger, to name three—shared an experience of World War II's combat, but Vonnegut's close witness to the fire-bombing of Dresden and its charred aftermath was, even in those violent times, extraordinary, and it haunted his work in the form of apocalyptic holocausts—in *God Bless You, Mr. Rosewater*, Indianapolis is imagined consumed by fire; in *Cat's Cradle*, the world ends when all water turns to ice; in *Slapstick*, fluctuations in the force of gravity pull down structures all over the globe, and a deserted Manhattan has become Skyscraper National Park.

When, in *Slaughterhouse-Five*, Vonnegut faced his Dresden experience directly, he characteristically garlanded it with an antic science-fiction tale of how our hero, Billy Pilgrim, shaped like a bottle of Coca-Cola, was abducted by space aliens shaped like plumber's helpers with a green eye in the palm of their hand-shaped heads. These Tralfamadorians put Billy in a Tralfamadorian zoo to demonstrate, with another abductee, the gorgeous porn star Montana Wildhack, human mating procedures. With such inventions Vonnegut lightened his hard-won perception that the universe was basically atrocious, a vast sea of cruelty and indifference.

His pessimism is more astringent in early novels like *The Sirens of Titan* and *Mother Night*, before he perfected his mature, aggressively casual style. It seemed to me that Kurt did not always get enough credit for his artistry—for his free flow of invention, for the surreal beauty of his imagery, for the propelling rhythm of his short paragraphs and laconic sentences, a colloquial American style justly ranked with Mark Twain's. His phenomenal success with college students, who were grateful for books about large matters that were easy to read and frequently hilarious, annoyed some critics. His personal charm and persuasiveness as a speaker, toastmaster, and political protester deflected attention, for others, from his vital presence on the page. He was a tall, loose-jointed man, with a splendid head of dark curly hair. He wrote, as I remember, hunched over at a low table, tapping out his space-spanning tales on a small portable. He proceeded deliberately, revising as he went. He smoked cigarettes as if they were good for him, and in one of the last conversations we had, in this very room as it happens, he told me that a recent X-ray had shown his lungs to be as pure as a child's—he was considering offering himself to the tobacco industry as an advertisement. His manner was as gracious and gentle as his books were honest and wry. Everyone who knew Kurt, I think it safe to say, misses him. Indeed, it might be said that the planet misses him.

L. E. Sissman, 1928–1976

ED SISSMAN died last month in Boston, after eleven years of resisting, and rising above, Hodgkin's disease. During those years he wrote copiously, wittily, lovingly of the world he was on the verge of leaving; this magazine published fifty-one of his poems—some of them among the longest we have ever printed—and forty-five book reviews by him. By profession an advertising man, he harbored behind his courtly and faintly owlish manner a poet of the brightest plumage, one whose stream of fancy and verve of phrase could only be termed luxuriant. His reviews and essays showed wide reading, a crisp fund of unexpected information, an avidity for the mundane, an even temper, and a truly benevolent

---

Obituary in *The New Yorker*, April 6, 1976.

nature. He liked smart cars, the suburban life, English novels, old-fashioned meters. He would not want to be remembered as a poet of dying; he had no use for dying—except, perhaps, for the heightened sharpness of vision his "invisible new veil / Of finity" gave him. Though the decade of his illness and the decade of his artistic efflorescence coincided, the coincidence seems more accidental than not. He had long felt impelled to write poetry, and his songs of life—of past adventures remembered, of present scenery apprehended—show no sense of emergency, even when the scenery is a hospital wall. His career and, during his visits to this office, his carriage appeared unhurried. He was forty-eight when he died. One said goodbye to Ed wondering each time if it would be the last time. It marks the quality of the man that this shadow became something pleasant: an extra resonance in the parting smile, a warmth in the handshake. He helped us all, in his work and in his courage, to bear our own mortality.

Raymond Carver, 1938–1988

SOME HARD TIMES are part of every writer's equipment, but Raymond Carver had more than his share. He was born in 1938 in Clatskanie, Oregon, and grew up in Yakima, in the center of the state of Washington. His father filed saws in a sawmill; his mother sometimes worked as a waitress and salesclerk; the family, which included a younger brother, moved from one two-bedroom house to another. The father, Clevie Raymond Carver, had a drinking problem, and would die at the age of fifty-three. When young Junior, as Ray was called, wrote a story about his favorite activity, fishing, and asked his mother to type it up, she went out and rented a typewriter and the two of them amateurishly typed it up and sent it to the circulation department of an outdoor-sports magazine in Boulder. It came back, but Ray's stubborn career as a writer had begun. To his stringent blue-collar beginnings he added the handicap of an early marriage; he was nineteen and his bride sixteen and pregnant. By the time she was eighteen, they had two children. As Carver put it in his interview with *The Paris Review*, "What shall I say at this point? We didn't have any youth. We found ourselves in roles we didn't know how to play. But we did the best we could. Better than that, I want to think." Both these

Read at the dinner meeting of the American Academy and Institute of Arts and Letters, November 3, 1988.

young parents managed, finally, to get college degrees; while acquiring the credits, they worked at such jobs as waitress, night janitor, door-to-door saleswoman, farm worker, and delivery boy, mostly in the state of California. In 1963, Carver saw a story and a poem of his published, when he was an undergraduate at Humboldt State University, in California. Thirteen years were to go by before his first collection, *Will You Please Be Quiet, Please?*, appeared in 1976. To find the space and peace to write, he at times had to resort to sitting in the family car. After over a decade of struggle, in his words, "We were still in a state of penury, we had one bankruptcy behind us, and years of hard work with nothing to show for it except an old car, a rented house, and new creditors on our backs. . . . I more or less gave up, threw in the towel, and took to full-time drinking as a serious pursuit. . . . I made a wasteland out of everything I touched. But I might add that towards the end of the drinking there wasn't much left anyway." He gave up drinking in 1977, and in the same year he and his first wife separated. Ten good years followed, years of recognition, of measured but steady productivity, of a new marital relationship, of teaching positions, grants, and honors, including a Mildred and Harold Strauss Living Award from the Academy-Institute. Then hard luck struck again, in the form of lung cancer, and after one last gallant year of fighting the disease he was dead, at the age of fifty.

And yet, out of this near wreck of a life, Raymond Carver produced stories of exquisite directness, polish, and calm that sit in the mind like perfect porcelain teacups. The clay from which this porcelain comes is American life of a most modest sort, life lived near the poverty line, often in an advanced state of domestic deshabille, among cultural signifiers of an unrelenting bleakness. It is lived out of the range of news, beneath the threshold of any aspiration higher than day-to-day survival, where a good time is an uneasy evening in another couple's living room, a quizzical conversation in a bar, or a moment of instantly regretful sex. The stories are usually in the first person, and the narrator is usually but not always male, and he almost invariably is one of a couple, if not married then very much aware of his vanished half. There is a stoic woundedness in these voices that engages our nervous systems; in his early stories especially, Carver presents domestic life as curiously packed and sinister, as somehow dangerous, as if its meagre scuffed décors were about to tip into darkness. An inexpressible native sorrow wants to well up; the characters suddenly find themselves kneeling and unable to rise, raking the lawn and unable to stop, awake and unable to go to sleep. The later stories recapitulate in less jagged rhythms, at a distanced perspective *The New Yorker's* pages could accommodate, the aboriginal mystery; in the marvellous

"Whoever Was Using This Bed," the hero and his consort, having been awakened at three in the morning, discover an illuminating strangeness by sitting together at the foot of the bed: "We're sitting on the part of the bed where we keep our feet when we sleep. It looks like whoever was using this bed left in a hurry. I know I won't ever look at this bed again without remembering it like this. We're into something now, but I don't know what, exactly."

Of Carver's stories it must be said that they are beautiful. Not since Hemingway, perhaps, has anyone built so lovingly in stacks of plain sentences; Carver was a poet as well as a prose writer, and though the poems could do, perhaps, with a bit less plainness, those frequent stories of his that omit quotation marks look, on the page, like poems. Like Hemingway, he listened to laconic American speech and fished for the tragic consciousness, the ominousness, beneath the gliding skin of plain utterance; in prefacing his collected stories Ray Carver spoke of "trying to learn my craft as a writer, how to be as subtle as a river current." His best stories do move like rivers, as gently and inexorably, with a certain sheen that almost blinds. In our daily misery as he had experienced it he felt something lyrical, and to extract it he revised tirelessly and put himself to school with all the traditional masters of short fiction. His titles— challengingly curt like "Fat," "Feathers," "Vitamins," "Careful," "Sacks," "Boxes," or "Gazebo" or else musically vernacular, as in "Will You Please Be Quiet, Please?," "What We Talk About When We Talk About Love," "The Third Thing That Killed My Father Off," "Where I'm Calling From," and "Nobody Said Anything"—bespeak a consciously literary wit. In person he was ursine, amiable, quietly spoken, and yet impressively precise—a Westerner who weighed his words. His body of work is relatively small, but it displays the loftiest qualities: honesty of vision, integrity of workmanship, and a warm and humane desire to celebrate, to bring the news, as he himself expressed it, from one world to another, in a style that reveals "the fierce pleasure we take in doing it."

FOREWORDS AND AFTERWORDS

Introduction to The Haunted Major, *by Robert Marshall,*
with drawings by Harry Furniss

GOLF is a spooky game. Occult forces are clearly at work as we play. Balls vanish in unaccountable directions, glass walls arise in the direction of the hole, putts run uphill. The phenomena recorded in *The Haunted Major* all ring true, especially in relation to the hapless beginner who is our hero: "I let drive a second time, with the result that the ball took a series of trifling hops and skips like a startled hare, and deposited itself in rough ground some thirty yards off, at an angle of forty-five degrees from the line I had anxiously hoped to take." The "anxiously" is an uncharacteristic admission for Major the Honourable John William Wentworth Gore, 1st Royal Light Hussars, a sublimely self-confident snob and self-proclaimedly "the finest sportsman living." It will take all of golf's devious powers of humiliation to bring him low, and it is one of this little novel's achievements that by the end, boastful cad though he is, we are rooting for him.

Published in 1902, before the literature of golf amounted to much—before Arnold Haultain wrote *The Mystery of Golf,* before Bernard Darwin began his decades of inspired journalism, before P. G. Wodehouse launched his incomparable series of comic golf stories, before Bobby Jones elegantly committed his thoughts on the game to print—*The Haunted Major* provides a classic portrait of a hotly contested match, one hard to top in its violent swings of momentum. Haunting, interestingly, remains a theme of modern golf literature, most impressively in the apparition of the mystical teacher Shivas Irons in Michael Murphy's *Golf in the Kingdom.* And there are lesser texts involving a heavenly replay of the Hogan–Fleck playoff in the 1955 Open, or extraterrestrial tournaments matching up the revenant greats of every era against one another.

None of these spooks are as vivid or vehement as Cardinal Smeaton, whose Scots curses ring in the dazed Major's ears while his transparent bones bedevil his eyes. In truth, we all play golf accompanied by a demon, an inner voice who taunts us and advises us and all too rarely floods us with sensations of golfing grace and power, such as the Major feels when he grips the Bishop's ancient clubs: "My legs and arms tingled as if some strong stimulant were flowing in my veins."

Cardinal Smeaton never existed, but a close approximation did exist in the person of the first Scotsman to be anointed a cardinal, David Beaton (1494–1546). Beaton, educated at the universities of St. Andrews and Glasgow, and then at Paris and Rouen, was the third son of a Fife laird and the nephew of James Beaton, archbishop of St. Andrews, whom David succeeded as archbishop and primate of Scotland in 1539. Beaton was a considerable politician, of the French-alliance persuasion. As the trusted adviser of James V, he dissuaded the monarch from following the anti-papal policy of England's Henry VIII, and he helped arrange the marriage of James and the daughter of Francis I of France.

These were awkward times, however, in which to be a Scots prince of the old church: Protestantism was spreading on the Continent, and George Wishart, a grammar-school master in Montrose, caught the contagion. Accused in Scotland of heresy in 1538, Wishart fled to Europe, but returned in 1544, preaching at his peril and converting John Knox, a former priest and ecclesiastical notary who became a spearhead of the Protestant movement. Beaton was a hard-line enemy of the Reformation and saw to Wishart's arrest, trial, and death by burning in 1546, in St. Andrews. To quote the *Blue Guide to Scotland:* "Beaton watched the burning in comfort from the castle walls. Two months later several friends of Wishart, headed by Norman Leslie, son of the Earl of Rothes, seized the castle, slew Beaton, and hung his corpse over the battlements to prove he was dead." The conspirators held out for two months, during which Beaton's body remained unburied, cast into a dungeon and covered with salt, "to await," as Knox, one of the besieged, explained, "what exsequies his brethren the bishops would prepare for him." The *Encyclopædia Britannica* mildly relates that, "although John Knox and others have exaggerated his cruelty and immorality, both were harmful to the Roman Catholic Church in Scotland, which he tried to preserve by repression rather than by reform."

My encyclopedic sources do not mention Beaton's prowess at golf; but since he had been a university student at St. Andrews, with an uncle established in the cathedral, it is not unlikely he took his whacks at a game already so popular in the fifteenth century that Parliament three times sought to ban it, on the grounds that it was distracting men from doing their archery practice. So the author of *The Haunted Major* may have sound historical reasons for having his ghostly Cardinal claim, "Noo, in ma day, I was unrivalled as a gowfer; there wasna ma equal in the land. Nane o' the coortiers frae Holyrood were fit tae tee a ba' tae me." Smeaton explains his passionate interest in the Major's match by telling him that his opponent, the champion Jim Lindsay, is "a descendant in the straight line o' ane o' my maist determined foes . . . and ony blow that I can deal tae ane o' his kith is a solace to ma hameless and disjasket speerit." It is the *Columbia Encyclopedia* that throws light on this particular dark spot of Scots history. Its entry for "Lindsay, Sir David, c. 1490–c. 1555, Scottish poet," tells us that "as a writer he was a harsh satirist and moralist who directed most of his invective against the Roman Catholic Church. He never formally left the church, but his exposure of its abuses gives him a place second only to that of John Knox in bringing about the Scottish Reformation." The embers of these old fiery quarrels still give off some heat, and the author, in making Beaton so winning a ghost, offers an olive branch, three and a half centuries after bloody events.

Robert Marshall, the author of *The Haunted Major*, is absent from all but the most compendious reference books. He was born in Edinburgh in 1863, attended the universities at St. Andrews and at Edinburgh, and then joined the Duke of Wellington's cavalry regiment, attaining the rank of captain in 1895. He retired in 1898 to become a writer and playwright, and died in 1910, before reaching the age of fifty. That he was a Scotsman might be deduced from the ringing verve of the nearly inscrutable Scots accent he transcribes, from the intimacy shown with the bitter turns of historic religious struggles on Scots soil, and from his satiric creation, in "Jacky" Gore, of so fatuous and arrogant an Englishman. There is a touch of satire, too, in his sketch of the American prize, the rich widow Katherine Clavering Gunter. Her beauty, we are permitted to guess, is ground under some repair: "She is quite beautiful, especially in her photographs"; "I should have thought her face was pale but for two vivid splashes of a most exquisite carmine that glowed, or at all events dwelt, on her cheeks"; "Her wonderful complexion was more ravishing than ever in the soft lamplight . . . and her luxuriant hair, dark underneath, was a mist of ever-changing gold on the top." Nor do the Scots escape, as it were, scot-free: a careful explanation that they are not really dour and stingy leaves us unpersuaded. A national weakness is lightly touched upon by Kirkintulloch when he says it would dishonor his father and mother if he failed to go nightly to the public house, and, any-

way, "I canna sleep if I'm ower sober." Not that the Major's casual consumption of whiskies and brandies, with a golf match hard upon him,
shows any less devotion to fermented spirits.

Americans will be amazed, to the point of doubting the tale's veracity,
when they calculate, as I did, that a round of eighteen holes, with one
player hitting a wealth of imperfect shots, takes from eleven in the morning to one in the afternoon—a mere two hours—and that the afternoon
round, beginning at two-thirty, appears, even with its dramatic and
drawn-out dénouement, to be over in plenty of time to revive the victor
from a faint and treat him to several celebrations, a stiff brandy-and-soda,
and two valedictory interviews, all before he dons dinner dress and goes
a-wooing. As the Scots play it, golf is a brisk walk in natural surroundings
and not a five-hour ordeal in a hand-carved Eden. As those who have
experienced golf in Scotland can attest, religious sensations are not confined to haunted Sunday matches: the skylarks, the breezy breadth of the
treeless links, the blowing tan grass, the plunge and rise of the sandy fairways, and the accretion of lore attached to courses centuries old all
inspire reverent sense of being, as in the Holy Land, *at the source.*

I have played St. Andrews—called St. Magnus here—but once, beginning on a May day near dinnertime and ending in the gloaming between
nine and ten o'clock; my wife walked with me, across the narrow burns
and beside the patches of golden gorse, out to the hook-shaped point and
then back. One hits to a number of the same enormous greens a second
time, at a different pin. I felt tall and ghostly, swinging my thin-bladed
rented clubs, as if my feet were treading air. This was golf as a kind of
sailing voyage, with the sea a constant presence—the sea whence once
came French ships and the winds of reformation.

In St. Andrews there are three sights to see: the golf course and its
solemn Victorian clubhouse; the ruins of the cathedral, by far the largest
in Scotland; and the ruins of the castle where Cardinal Beaton watched
Wishart burn and was then himself slain and preserved in salt. *The
Haunted Major* brings all three together in a curious amalgam of religious
history, Edwardian foppery, and golfing madness, somewhat as the ruddy
color of Kirkintulloch's mustache "suggested equally sunshine, salt
winds, and whisky." There must be, we feel, a connection between the
three salient features of Scotland: the beautiful wildness of much of its
landscape, the austerity of its Presbyterian brand of Protestant Christianity, and its national passion for golf. The Major is an alien amid these barbaric elements, and one of the sources of his narrative's comedy is the
mellifluous innocence of his frequently startled prose; he is the prototyp-
ical colonizer blundering through the tortuous mysteries of the colo-

nized, and the reader feels the pleasure of order restored when he at last seeks out "the best morning train from St Magnus to London."

Harry Furniss's scratchy, suitably hectic drawings have become as wedded to this text as Gluyas Williams's illustrations are to Benchley and Tenniel's to the Alice books. Furniss comes as close to depicting the ineffable as one would wish, and the last two illustrations, of the Cardinal's headstand on the historic railway shed on St. Andrews' seventeenth hole and of his strenuous effort on the eighteenth to blow a putt awry, linger in the mind's eye as emblems of the contortions that golf inflicts on its transported devotees.

Foreword to The Complete Lyrics of Cole Porter, *edited by Robert Kimball*

> You're the top!
> You're the Colosseum.
> You're the top!
> You're the Louvre Museum.
> You're a melody from a symphony by Strauss,
> You're a Bendel bonnet,
> A Shakespeare sonnet,
> You're Mickey Mouse.

COULD THERE BE a love song more American than this?—this consumer's checklist, this breezy catalogue with its climactic, sublimely simple assurance to the beloved that she (or he) is Mickey Mouse. In the succeeding refrains, the Mickey Mouse line becomes "You're cellophane," "You're broccoli," "You're Camembert," "You're Pepsodent," "You're Ovaltine," and "You're stratosphere." Each time, whether we hear the words in the voice of Ethel Merman, who introduced the song fifty years ago in *Anything Goes*, or of Anita O'Day, who made a haunting croaky-voiced recording some decades later, something tender, solemn, nonsensical, and absolute seems to be being said.

The song lyricist's task is to provide excuses for onstage demonstrations of energy and also, at the top of his craft, to provide new phrasings for the ineffable and virtually trite. How many times can the discovery and proclamation that one ersatz creature is in love with another be endured? Infinitely many, as long as real men and women continue to mate: popular composers from generation to generation, if they do not teach us how to love, do lend our romances a certain accent and give our courting rites their milieux—proms, bars, automobiles and their dash-board moons—a tribal background, a background choir of communal experience. In the urbane, top-hat fantasy world wherein Fred Astaire and Cole Porter reign as quintessential performer and creator, love is wry, jokey, casual, and even weary but nonetheless ecstatic: you're Mickey Mouse. Not to mention, "You're romance, / You're the steppes of Russia, / You're the pants on a Roxy usher." One of the delights of this all-inclusive collection that Robert Kimball has assiduously compiled from so many tattered sources consists of following half-recalled lyrics through their many ebullient refrains; we find, for instance, that Porter rhymed "top" not only with the expectable "flop," "pop," "hop," and "stop" but also with the more rakish "blop," "de trop," and "the G.O.P. or GOP."

He brought to the traditional and somewhat standardized tasks of songsmithing a great verbal ingenuity, a brave flexibility and resourceful-ness (how many of these lengthy lyrics were discarded by showtime!), a cosmopolitan's wide expertise in many mundane matters including for-eign lands and tongues, and a spirit that always kept something of colle-giate innocence about it. The decade of the Depression, Porter's creative prime, maintained in its popular culture much of the Twenties' gaiety and bequeathed a surprising amount of it to the war-stricken Forties—the jauntiness of "Shootin' the Works for Uncle Sam" ("North, South, East, West, / All the boys are hep / To do their damndest (darndest) / To defend Miss Liberty's rep") on the eve of Pearl Harbor almost grates, and Porter's wartime musicals quaintly—it seems now—reassure the boys overseas that "Miss Garbo remains as the Hollywood Sphinx, / Monty Woolley's still bathing his beard in his drinks," and that "Café Society still carries on." This lighthearted era was a heyday for light verse: there were book reviews in verse, and sports stories; there were droll ballades and rondeaux and triolets. The plenitudinous newspapers and magazines published Don Marquis, F.P.A., Louis Untermeyer, Arthur Guiterman, Christopher Morley, Dorothy Parker, Ogden Nash, E. B. White, Morris Bishop, and Phyllis McGinley, not to mention such clever curiosities as Newman Levy's rhyming versions of opera plots and David McCord's typographically antic "Sonnets to Baedeker." Song lyricists were of this ingenious company: William Harmon's *Oxford Book of American Light Verse* includes, with poems by all the above-mentioned, lyrics by Porter, Lorenz Hart, Ira Gershwin, Oscar Hammerstein II, and Johnny Mercer. Wit of a specifically literary sort lies behind Porter's sophisticated refer-ences and outrageous rhymes—"trickery / liquor we," "throws a / sub rosa," "presto / West, oh," "Siena / then a," and, famously, from "Night and Day," "hide of me / inside of me" (which Ring Lardner parodied as "rind of me / mind of me" and "tegument / egg you meant"). Light verse seeks, though, to make its trickery seem unforced, and the peculiar grace of the form is well illustrated by the vivid refrain of "My Heart Belongs to Daddy," beginning:

> While tearing off
> A game of golf
> I may make a play for the caddy.
> But when I do
> I don't follow through
> 'Cause my heart belongs to Daddy.

And the next lines follow with another *double entendre* almost as elegant:

> If I invite
> A boy, some night,
> To dine on my fine finnan haddie,
> I just adore
> His asking for more,
> But my heart belongs to Daddy.

The internal rhymes on the second and fifth syllables of the third line are a consummate prosodic trick, repeated without apparent effort, here and then twice more in the second refrain.

Yet how much, it must be asked, of our delight in these particular verses depends upon our memory of the melody, a melody that launched, Mr. Kimball confides in a headnote, the Broadway career of Mary Martin, a melody that has given dozens of thrushes excuse to pucker, pout, and prance, a melody of irresistible momentum and lilt? Very much, must be the honest answer. And where no tune comes to mind to fit the words, they spin themselves a bit vacuously down the page with their "honey / funny / sunny / money" cheer and relentless allusions to half-forgotten celebrities and publicly certified emotional states. Some of the love songs, I fear, put us in mind of that Ira Gershwin lyric that goes (in part):

> Blah, blah, blah your hair,
> Blah, blah, blah your eyes;
> Blah, blah, blah, blah care,
> Blah, blah, blah, blah skies.
> Tra la la la, tra la la la, cottage for two,
> Blah, blah, blah, blah, blah, darling, with you!

Without music, one cannot really read (from Porter's "Why Should I Care?")

> Tra, la, la, la,
> La, la, la, la, la, la,
> Tra, la, la, la,
> La, la, la, la, la, la, la

or the thirty-four "again"s of "I'll Black His Eyes" or the 184 "ha"s of "Riddle-Diddle Me This." Without music, the simple lines of "I Love You" and "True Love" remain banal, daring parodies of banality, indeed; but alloyed with their enchanting tunes, and sung by Bing Crosby (in duet, for the sweet waltz of the second, with the delicate voice of Grace Kelly), the words become gold, affecting and unforgettable. The point scarcely needs making, least of all in the case of a composer like Porter who created his own melodies, that song lyrics are part of a whole, and that reading a book of them is a little like looking at an album of photographs of delicious food. The food looks good, but the proof is in the eating. The proof of Cole Porter's genius was in the stage shows and movies he made his crucial contributions to, and in the dozen or more standards—"Just One of Those Things," "I Get a Kick Out of You," "Begin the Beguine," "In the Still of the Night," "I've Got You Under My Skin," "It's De-Lovely," "From This Moment On," "You'd Be So Nice to Come Home To," "It's All Right with Me," "Night and Day," "My Heart Belongs to Daddy," "You're the Top," etc.—that are woven into the airwaves of these United States and familiar to all who have ears to hear.

Verse, including light verse, makes its own music. The tune is elusive but it requires no stage manager or electronic equipment; it hums and tingles up off the mute page. A light-verse writer is not constrained to extend his inspiration through enough refrains to exhaust the chorus, to shape his syllables toward easy vocalization by a possibly difficult star (Bert Lahr, Mr. Kimball tells us, refused to perform a song because it rhymed "cinema" and "enema"), or to appeal to any store of shared information less vast than the language of its accumulated treasury of allusions. No doubt Cole Porter could have been such a writer, had the immeasurably wider audience for musical comedy not beckoned. Without any orchestral egging-on, we smile at such lines as

> Your effect would be fantastic
> In that pistache Perfolastic

and

> Digging in his fertile glen,
> Goldwyn dug up Anna Sten

and

> Some folks collect paintings,
> Some folks collect stamps,
> Some are amassers
> Of antimacassars
> And other Victorian camps

and

> If a lass in Michigan can,
> If an ass in Astrakhan can,
> If a bass in the Saskatchewan can,
> Baby, you can can-can too.

Porter's transmogrification of Bob Fletcher's original lyric for "Don't Fence Me In" dramatically demonstrates his technical flair. Here is Fletcher's refrain:

> Don't fence me in.
> Give me land, lots of land,
> Stretching miles across the West,
> Let me ride where it's wide,
> For somehow I like it best,
> Don't fence me in.
> I want to see the stars,
> I want to feel the breeze,
> I want to smell the sage
> And hear the cottonwood trees.
> Just turn me loose,
> Let me straddle my old saddle
> Where the shining mountains rise.
> On my cayuse
> I'll go siftin', I'll go driftin'
> Underneath those Western skies.
> I've got to get where
> The West commences,
> I can't stand hobbles,
> I can't stand fences,
> Don't fence me in.

And here is Porter's rewrite:

> Oh, give me land, lots of land under starry skies above,
> Don't fence me in.
> Let me ride thru the wide-open country that I love,

Don't fence me in.
Let me be by myself in the evening breeze,
Listen to the murmur of the cottonwood trees,
Send me off forever, but I ask you, please,
Don't fence me in.
Just turn me loose,
Let me straddle my old saddle underneath the Western skies.
On my cayuse,
Let me wander over yonder till I see the mountains rise.
I want to ride to the ridge where the West commences,
Gaze at the moon till I lose my senses,
Can't look at hobbles and I can't stand fences,
Don't fence me in.

Almost every element in the rather staid, trite source is used in Porter's revision, but wonderfully loosened up with internal rhymes and a certain surreal humor—"Gaze at the moon till I lose my senses" has no corresponding sentiment in the original. True, we can hear the music, jingling and trotting along, and this greatly helps. The more of the music you can hear, the more you are apt to enjoy perusing this monumental omnium-gatherum; but even where the silence of your lonely room remains obdurate, something magical is apt to creep

Like the beat beat beat of the tom-tom
When the jungle shadows fall,
Like the tick tick tock of the stately clock
As it stands against the wall,
Like the drip drip drip of the raindrops
When the sum'r show'r is through.

Afterword to The Luzhin Defense, *by Vladimir Nabokov*

BACK IN THE EXHILARATING DAYS when Nabokov's *oeuvre* in English, stimulated by the best-selling scandal of *Lolita*, was growing at both ends—old works in Russian being translated, new works in English being handed down by the living master from his Swiss retirement—*The New Yorker* devoted a large part of two issues (May 9 and 16, 1964) to *The Luzhin Defense*, as translated by Michael Scammell in collaboration with the author.* Such a serialization was an unprecedented and, as far as I know, unrepeated tribute by the editors of that choosy publication to a work of fiction. And indeed this novel, Nabokov's third, shows him— after the youthful and wistful novella *Mary* and the rather bleak manipulations of *King, Queen, Knave*—entering into his full poetic birthright, that vision which violently combines an ardent nostalgia with an aloof ingenuity, a pale fire of the intellect with an appetite for particulars so fierce and intimate that nearly every sentence has a twist of extra animation.

As he wrote away at the novel in 1929, while living on the Passauer Strasse in Berlin and chasing butterflies in the south of France, he knew he had moved to new heights; he wrote his mother in August, "In three or four days I'll add the last full stops. After that I won't struggle again for a long time with such monstrously difficult themes, but will write something quiet and smooth-flowing. All the same I'm pleased with my Luzhin, but what a complicated, complicated thing!" His wife, Véra, wrote her mother-in-law, "Russian literature has not seen its like." When *Zashchita Luzhina* appeared, in three long installments, in the most distinguished of Russian émigré literary journals, *Sovremennye zapiski*, "V. Sirin," Nabokov's pen name, became unignorable in the small but seething world of émigré letters. The writer Nina Berberova, in her 1969 memoir *The Italics Are Mine*, described her impression after reading the first installment: "A tremendous, mature, sophisticated modern writer was before me; a great Russian writer, like a Phoenix, was born from the fire and ashes of revolution and exile. Our existence from now on acquired a meaning. All my generation were justified. We were saved." And the émigrés' best-known writer, Ivan Bunin, reportedly commented, "This kid has snatched a gun and done away with the whole older generation, myself included."

At the time of writing, Nabokov was thirty, as is Luzhin. Like his hero, the author seems older; few so young could write a novel wherein the autobiographical elements are so cunningly rearranged and transmuted by a fictional design, and the emotional content is so obedient to ingenious commands, and the characterization shows so little of indignation or the shock of discovery. On this last point, it needs to be said—so much

---

*For reasons that can only be conjectured, the book version was given, when published by Putnam in 1964, the truncated and vague title of *The Defense*. This essay was fashioned for the Penguin reprint of 1994, which restored the full and exact title, descriptive of a chess ploy.

has been pointlessly said about Nabokov's "virtuosity," as if he is an illusionist working with stuffed rabbits and hats nobody could wear—that Nabokov's characters live. The humanity that came within his rather narrow field of vision was illuminated by a guarded but genuine compassion. Two characters come to mind, randomly and vividly: Charlotte Haze of *Lolita*, with her blatant bourgeois bohemianism, her ready cigarettes, her Mexican doodads, her touchingly clumsy sexuality, her utterly savage and believable war with her daughter; and Albinus Kretschmar of *Laughter in the Dark*, with his doll-like dignity, his bestial softness, his hobbies, his family feelings, his abject romanticism, his quaint competence. An American housewife and a German businessman, both observed, certainly, from well outside, yet animated from within. How much more, then, can Nabokov do with characters who are Russian, and whose concerns circle close to his own aloof passions!

His foreword, shameless and disdainful in his usual first-person style, specifies, for "hack reviewers" and "persons who move their lips when reading," the forked appeal of "this attractive novel"—the intricate immanence in plot and imagery of chess as a prevailing metaphor, and the weird lovableness of the virtually inert hero. "Of all my Russian books, The [Luzhin] Defense contains and diffuses the greatest 'warmth'—which may seem odd seeing how supremely abstract chess is supposed to be. In point of fact, Luzhin has been found lovable even by those who understand nothing about chess and/or detest all my other books." What makes characters endearing does not admit to such analysis: I would divide Luzhin's charm into (a) the delineation of his childhood, (b) the evocation of his chess prowess.

As to (a), Nabokov always warmed to the subject of children, precocious children—David Krug, Victor Wind, the all-seeing "I" of *Conclusive Evidence* (later entitled *Speak, Memory*), and, most precocious and childlike of all, Dolores Haze. The four chapters devoted to little Luzhin are pure gold, a fascinating extraction of the thread of genius from the tangle of a lonely boy's existence. The child's ominous lethargy; his father's brooding ambitiousness for him; the hints of talent in his heredity; the first gropings, through mathematical and jigsaw puzzles, of his peculiar aptitude toward the light; the bizarre introduction, at the hands of a nameless violinist who tinges the game forever with a somehow cursed musicality, to the bare pieces; his instruction in the rules, ironically counterpointed against an amorous intrigue of which he is oblivious; his rapid climb through a hierarchy of adult opponents—all this is witty, tender, delicate, resonant. By abruptly switching to Luzhin as a chess-sodden adult, Nabokov islands the childhood, frames its naïve brightness, so that, superimposed upon the grown figure, it operates as a kind of heart, as an abruptly doused light reddens the subsequent darkness.

As to (b), Nabokov never shied from characters who excel. In *Pale Fire* he presumed to give us a long poem by an American poet second only to Frost; Adam Krug in *Bend Sinister* is the leading intellectual of his nation; no doubt is left that Fyodor Godunov-Cherdynstev of *The Gift* is truly gifted. Luzhin's "recondite genius" is delineated as if by one who knows—though we know, from Chapter Fourteen of his autobiography, that Nabokov's forte was not tournament play but the "beautiful, complex, and sterile art" of composing chess problems of a "poetico-mathematical type." On its level as a work-epic of chess (as *Moby-Dick* is a work-epic of whaling) *The Luzhin Defense* is splendidly shaped toward the hero's match with Turati, the dashing Italian grandmaster against whose unorthodox attack, "leaving the middle of the board unoccupied by Pawns but exercising a most dangerous influence on the center from the sides," Luzhin's defense is devised. Of Turati physically we are given the briefest glimpses, "rubbing his hands and deeply clearing his throat like a bass singer," but his chess presence is surpassingly vivid. His name, chess experts have told me, echoes that of the famous Czech grandmaster Richard Réti. Turati's opening, as described, resembles Réti's favorite opening, which was called the Réti System. Curiously, the Czech also somewhat resembled Luzhin; he died in 1929, at the age of forty, and in 1926 had married a Russian girl much younger than himself. So, in the hall of mirrors which is chess thought, Luzhin is playing a reflection of himself; small wonder he thinks his way into a nervous breakdown during the tournament, while keen suspense mounts as to whether "the limpidity and lightness of Luzhin's thought would prevail over the Italian's tumultuous fantasy."

Their game, a potential draw which is never completed, draws forth a display of metaphorical brilliance that turns pure thought heroic. Beneath the singing, quivering, trumpeting, humming battlefield of the chessboard, Turati and Luzhin become fabulous monsters groping through unthinkable tunnels:

> Luzhin's thought roamed through entrancing and terrible labyrinths, meeting there now and then the anxious thought of Turati, who sought the same thing as he. . . . Luzhin, preparing an attack for which it was first necessary to explore a maze of variations, where his every step aroused a perilous echo, began a long meditation: he needed, it seemed, to make one last prodigious effort and he would find the secret move leading to victory. Suddenly, something occurred outside his being, a scorching pain—and he let

out a loud cry, shaking his hand stung by the flame of a match, which he had lit and forgotten to apply to his cigarette. The pain immediately passed, but in the fiery gap he had seen something unbearably awesome, the full horror of the abysmal depths of chess.

The game is adjourned, and after such an evocation we have no difficulty in feeling with Luzhin how the chess images that have haunted the fringes of his existence now move into the center and render the real world phantasmal. The metaphors have reversed the terms.

Chess imagery has infiltrated the book from all sides. Nabokov in his foreword preens perhaps unduly on the tiled and parqueted floors, the Knight-like leaps of the plot. His hero's monomania plays tricks with the objective world: "The urns that stood on stone pedestals at the four corners of the terrace threatened one another across their diagonals"; "He sat thinking . . . that with a Knight's move of this lime tree standing on a sunlit slope one could take that telegraph pole over there"; "Luzhin involuntarily put out a hand to remove shadow's King from the threat of light's Pawn." He warily watches the floor, "where a slight movement was taking place perceptible to him alone, an evil differentiation of shadows." Throughout the book glimpses of black and white abound—tuxedos, raspberries and milk, "the white boat on the lake, black with the reflected conifers." Many lamps are lit against the night; Luzhin's father thinks it "strange and awesome . . . to sit on this bright veranda amid the black summer night, across from this boy whose tensed forehead seemed to expand and swell as soon as he bent over the pieces," this boy for whom "the whole world suddenly went dark" when he learned chess and who is to glide, across the alternation of many nights and days, from the oblivion of breakdown into the whiteness of a hospital where the psychiatrist wears "a black Assyrian beard."

The squares on the board can also be construed as chess versus sex. The child maneuvers his own initiation on the blind board of an illicit affair. His father, while he is poring over chess diagrams in the attic, fears that "his son might have been looking for pictures of naked women." Valentinov (!), his sinister "chess father," part manager and part pimp, "fearing lest Luzhin should squander his precious power in releasing by natural means the beneficial inner tension . . . kept him at a distance from women and rejoiced over his chaste moroseness." His marriage, then, is a kind of defensive castling undertaken too late, for the black forces that have put him in check press on irresistibly, past his impotent Queen, toward certain mate. The Luzhin defense becomes abandonment of play. Such a design eminently satisfies Nabokov's exacting criteria of artistic performance, which, in a memorable section in *Conclusive Evidence* concerning butterflies, he relates to the "mysteries of mimicry": "I discovered in nature the non-utilitarian delights that I sought in art. Both were a form of magic, both were a game of intricate enchantment and deception."

However, I am not sure it perfectly works, this chess puzzle pieced out with human characters. In the last third of the book, the author's youth may begin to show; émigré parties, arranged by Mrs. Luhzin, are introduced apparently for no better reason (not a *bad* reason) than that Nabokov was going to such parties at this time. A "mercifully stupid" Leningrad visitor pops up irrelevantly, as a naked index of editorial distaste for the Soviet regime. It is as if Pawns were proliferating to plug a leaky problem. One becomes conscious of rather aimless intricacies: the chronic mention of a one-armed schoolmate (Nabokov's teasing of cripples is not the most sympathetic of his fads) and the somewhat mannered withholding of the hero's first name and patronymic until the last sentences, which then link up with the first. In short, the novel loses inevitability as it needs it most. Suicide, being one experience no writer or reader has quite undergone, requires extra credentials to pass into belief. I can believe in the suicides of Anna Karenina and Emma Bovary as terrible but just—in the sense of "fitting"—events within the worlds the authors have evolved. I am even more willing to believe in Kirillov's suicide in *The Possessed* as the outcome of a philosophic-psychotic mental state explored with frightening empathy. But I am unable to feel Luzhin's descent into an eternity of "dark and pale squares" as anything but the foreordained outcome of an abstract scheme, cutting short a fictional life.

To me, the hero's development seems blocked by something outside the novel, perhaps by the lepidopterist's habit of killing what it loves; how remarkably few, after all, of Nabokov's characters do evade the mounting pin! Certainly his energetic passion for half-concealed symmetries and extended patterns of imagery has here, in a novel about chess, a fitting field of display. Metaphor and matter merge, if not quite as cunningly and persuasively as the master intended, yet astoundingly and beautifully enough. The idyllic boyhood and the lost Russia which Nabokov was to transmute a number of more times in the future receive, in the myopic recollections of his lovable "chess moron," one of their freshest evocations. Every detail of the vanished St. Petersburg is precious as little Luzhin, in Chapter Three, hurries along to the house of his red-haired aunt—the irregular paving-stones of Sergievskaya Street, the "frizzled heads of three waxen ladies with pink nostrils" in a hairdresser's window, the plum-colored house "with naked old men straining to hold up a balcony," the gate's "spurstone showing the white marks of pigeons." The excited precision attached to these images is both that of a boy hastening to his first chess assignation and that of a writer experiencing his still-unfolding powers. This verbal joy, this tender efflorescence of verbal happiness, was to occur again, twenty years later, in the English of *Speak, Memory* and *Pnin*, as Nabokov consolidated his virtuosic control of his adopted language. An innocence of youthful exuberance flavors the Russian tale of Luzhin, along with a matured taste for monstrous difficulty; for those who have yet to enter the unique Nabokovian universe, *The Luzhin Defense* forms an excellent way in.

Introduction to The Best American Short Stories of the Century, *edited by John Updike with Katrina Kenison*

THESE STORIES have been four times selected. First, they were selected for publication, against steep odds. *Story* reports twenty thousand submissions a year, *Ploughshares* 750 a month, *The New Yorker* five hundred a week. Next, published stories—now amounting annually, Katrina Kenison tells us in her foreword, to three thousand, from over three hundred American journals—were sifted for the annual volumes of the *Best American Short Stories of the Year*. The eighty-four volumes since 1915 held a total of two thousand stories; Ms. Kenison read all these and gave me more than two hundred; I asked to read several dozen more. Of this third selection I have selected, with her gracious advice and counsel, these fifty-five—less than one in four. A fathomless ocean of rejection and exclusion surrounds this brave little flotilla, the best of the best.

Certain authors had to be included, that was clear from the outset. An anthology of this century's short fiction that lacked a story by Hemingway, Faulkner, or Fitzgerald would be perversely deficient. Almost as compulsory, I felt, was the female trio of Katherine Anne Porter, Flannery O'Connor, and Eudora Welty. Of post-war writers, there had to be Bellow, Roth, and Malamud, even though only Malamud could be said to have devoted a major portion of his energy to the short story. If John O'Hara and Mary McCarthy—two Irish-Americans with a sociological bent—had been available, I might have included them, but neither ever made a *Best*. Traditionally, in the compilation of this annual short-story collection, excerpts from a larger work are excluded, though some do creep in; among my choices were a pair, by Jack Kerouac and William Goyen, that turned out to be pieces of novels.

Two personal principles, invented for the occasion, guided me. First, I wanted this selection to reflect the century, with each decade given roughly equal weight—what amounted to between six and eight stories per decade. As it turned out, the 1950s, with the last-minute elimination of Peter Taylor's "A Wife of Nashville" and James Baldwin's "Sonny's Blues," were shortchanged, even though it was a healthy decade for short fiction, just before television's fabulations took center stage. My second rule, enforcing the reflection of an American reality, was to exclude any story that did not take place on this continent or deal with characters from the United States or Anglophone Canada. This would seem to exclude little, and yet in Ms. Kenison's selection I encountered a story about Russian soldiery in World War I ("Chautonville," by Will Levington Comfort), another taking place in a polygamous Chinese household ("The Kitchen Gods," by Gulielma Fell Alsop), one involving Gypsies near the Black Sea ("The Death of Murdo," by Konrad Bercovici), a supernatural tale of a woodchopper in New Spain ("The Third Guest," by B. Traven), another of a Czech concert violinist ("The Listener," by John Berry), one set in an African village ("The Hill People," by Elizabeth Marshall), one concerning a magician from nineteenth-century Bratislava ("Eisenheim the Illusionist," by Steven Millhauser), a linked set of Elizabethan epistles dealing with the death of Christopher Marlowe ("A Great Reckoning in a Little Room," by Geoffrey Bush), an astringent account of a Danish semi-orphan ("The Forest," by Ella Leffland), a story beginning "In Munich are many men who look like weasels" ("The Schreuderspitze," by Mark Helprin), several stories of Irish life by Maeve Brennan and Mary Lavin, a lyrical tale of arranged marriage among the Parisian bourgeoisie ("Across the Bridge," by Mavis Gallant), and a deeply feminist, humorously epic account of how a few Latin American women inhabited Antarctica and reached the South Pole some years before Amundsen did ("Sur," by Ursula K. Le Guin). All these are not here. " 'That in Aleppo Once . . . ,' " by Vladimir Nabokov, and "The Shawl," by Cynthia Ozick, *are* here, on the weak excuse that some of their characters are on the way (unknowingly, in Ozick's case) to America.

Immigration is a central strand in America's collective story, and the first two stories in my selection, Benjamin Rosenblatt's "Zelig" and Mary Lerner's "Little Selves," deal with the immigrant experience—Jewish in the first case, Irish in the second. The third, Susan Glaspell's "A Jury of Her Peers," portrays the rural life, one of drudgery and isolation, that was once the common lot and is currently experienced by a mere 1 percent of the population, who feed the rest of us—one of the more remarkable shifts the century has witnessed.

The 1920s, which open here with Sherwood Anderson ("The Other Woman"), are a decade with a distinct personality, fixed between the onset of Prohibition in 1920 and the stock-market crash of 1929 and marked by a new sharpness and vivacity, a jazzy American note, in style and in the arts. The urban minority of Americans that produced most of the writing felt superior if not hostile to what H. L. Mencken called the "booboisie," whose votes had brought on Prohibition, puritanical censorship, the Scopes trial, and Calvin Coolidge. Members of the prospering middle class figure as objects of satire in the fiction of Sinclair Lewis and Ring Lardner, though since both men were sons of the booster-driven Midwest the satire is more affectionate than it first seemed. Lardner's "The Golden Honeymoon" is almost surreal in the circumstantiality of its monologue, a veritable lode of data as to how a certain class of Easterner managed a Florida vacation. The device of the self-incriminating narrator—used here more subtly and gently than in Lardner's better-known "Haircut"—generates a characteriology of American types not to be confused with the author, who may well be sitting at a Paris café table in happy expatriation. Except in stories based on his boyhood, Hemingway couldn't bear to dwell on life in America. It was, for many, a drab, workaday life. The small town or city surrounded by farmland, adrift in a post-Calvinist dreaminess, with the local doctor the closest thing to a hero, is a venue ubiquitous in this period's fiction, not only in Anderson and Lewis but in the "Summit" of Hemingway's chilling yet (with its boy narrator) faintly Penrodian "The Killers," and in the Pittsburgh named in Willa Cather's "Double Birthday," a great city as cozy and in-turned as a Southern hamlet.

Provincial smugness and bewilderment cease to be quite so urgent a theme in the Depression-darkened Thirties. Dorothy Parker's "Here We Are" hovers above its honeymooning couple as if not knowing whether to smile or weep. The heroine of Katherine Anne Porter's "Theft" faces without self-pity the waste of her life amid the passing, predatory contacts of the city. This is a boom period for the short story, a heyday of *Story* and *The American Mercury*. With an exuberant, cocky sweep William Saroyan ("Resurrection of a Life") sums up in a few headlong paragraphs the religious mystery, "somehow deathless," of being alive; William Faulkner ("That Evening Sun Go Down") and Robert Penn Warren ("Christmas Gift") impart to their Southern microcosms the scope and accumulated intensity of a novelist's vision. Faulkner had previously tucked the dénouement of "That Evening Sun" into his 1929 novel, *The Sound and the Fury*. Though he was a staple of *Best American Short Story* collections, represented almost annually in the 1930s, there seemed no avoiding this particular masterpiece, his most anthologized tale, a minimally rhetorical conjuration of impending doom. Fitzgerald's "Crazy Sunday," a knowing, dishevelled tale of Hollywood, took preference, narrowly, over his more familiar "Babylon Revisited," a rueful reprise of the Twenties' expatriate culture. Alexander Godin's "My Dead Brother Comes to America" revisits the experience of immigration in a tone of amplifying remembrance that anticipates magic realism. The longest story in these pages, and perhaps the most melodramatic, is Richard Wright's "Bright and Morning Star," a relic of a painful time when American blacks could see their lone friend and best hope in the Communist Party. The African-American has inhabited, and to a lamentable degree still inhabits, another country within the United States, where most white signposts of security and stability are absent. I have tried to give this country representation, from Jean Toomer's "Blood-Burning Moon" of 1923 to Carolyn Ferrell's "Proper Library" of 1994. Had space permitted, stories by James Baldwin and Ann Petry would have added to the picture's many tints of violence and despair. Even the amiable, detached Ivy Leaguer of James Alan McPherson's "Gold Coast" finds himself, in the end, on the losing side of a racial divide.

I tried not to select stories because they illustrated a theme or portion of the national experience but because they struck me as lively, beautiful, believable, and, in the human news they brought, important. The temptations of the illustrative pulled strongest in the early decades, which were basically historical for me—the times of my fathers. With the 1940s, the times become my own, and the short story takes an inward turn, away from states of society toward states of mind. To an elusive but felt extent, facts become more enigmatic. It is no longer always clear what the author wants us to feel. The short-story writer has gone into competition with the poet, asking the same charged economy of his images as the narrator of *The Waste Land*, whose narrative lay in shards.

Small-town coziness, with its rules and repressions, is absent from the seething but listless town visited by Eudora Welty's travelling salesman in "The Hitch-Hikers." He thinks of himself: "He is free: helpless." Welty, though habitually linked with her fellow-Mississippian Faulkner, here appears more a disciple of Hemingway, and a sister of Flannery O'Connor, the queen of redneck Gothic. Free equals helpless: our American freedom—to thrive, to fail, to hit the road—has a bleak and bitter underside, a *noir* awareness of ultimate pointlessness that haunts as well the big-city protagonists of Jean Stafford's "The Interior Castle" and E. B. White's "The Second Tree from the Corner." White's story, incidentally, marks the earliest appearance in my selection of *The New Yorker*, which was founded in 1925. Its editors, White's wife, Katharine, foremost, sought for its fiction a light, quick, unforced, casual quality that was slow to catch on with *Best American Short Stories* and that, however telling in its magazine setting, stacks up as slight against earthier, more strenuous stories. *The New Yorker* might have run, but didn't, Elizabeth Bishop's crystalline "The Farmer's Children," an almost unbearably brilliant fable in which farm machinery and Canadian cold become emissaries of an infernal universe; only a poet of genius and a child of misery could have coined this set of wounding, glittering images.

All was not *noir:* from the bleakest of bases, Paul Horgan's "The Peach Stone" builds to a redemptive affirmation, and Vladimir Nabokov, portraying the refugee chaos and panic on the edge of Hitler's war, imports into English an early sample of his unique legerdemain. It surprised me that World War II, that all-consuming paroxysm, left so meagre a trace in the fiction of this decade, as selected by others. Perhaps it takes time for great events to sift into art; however, I remember magazines of the Forties as being full of stories from the camps and the fronts—many of them no doubt too sentimental and jocular for our taste, but functioning as bulletins to the home front. On request, Ms. Kenison came up with several, including Edward Fenton's harrowing "Burial in the Desert," which depicts the North African campaign's harvest of corpses. In the end only Martha Gellhorn's account of an unsatisfactory flirtation, "Miami–New York," conveyed to me the feel of wartime America—the pervasive dislocation that included erotic opportunity, constant weariness, and contagious recklessness.

The Fifties, though underrepresented, are represented handsomely, with two of the century's supreme masters of the short story, John Cheever and Flannery O'Connor. They occupied different parts of one country, of the society, and of the literary world, yet were similar in the authority with which they swiftly built their fictional castles right on the edge of the absurd. They wrote with an inspired compression and heightened clarity; their prose brooked no contradiction or timid withholding of belief. Both were religious—O'Connor, fated to die young, fiercely so—and transcendent currents, perhaps, enabled them to light up their characters like paper lanterns, to impart an electric momentum to their narratives, and to situate human misadventure in a crackling moral context. Both "Greenleaf" and "The Country Husband" display animals—a bull, a dog—as spiritual presences; J. F. Powers's "Death of a Favorite" is told by a cat. The effect is not frivolous. For Powers, like O'Connor a Catholic, the mundane, heavily politicized celibate life of male priests was a serious and all but exclusive obsession. Few story-writers of high merit have staked so narrow a territory. And why, the reader may ask, with so many thoroughly crafted works to choose from, have I included a thinly fictionalized piece that drifts off into ellipses and appeared in the ephemeral, chichi *Flair*? Well, there are some grave turnings caught in the courtly diffidence of Tennessee Williams's "The Resemblance Between a Violin Case and a Coffin." The narrator, though fearing "that this story will seem to be losing itself like a path that has climbed a hill and then lost itself in an overgrowth of brambles," comes to the double realization that his sister is mentally ill and that he is gay. Overall, there were fewer stories of gay experience than I had expected—not many were written, I think, before 1970 or so—but more about music and its performance: Phillip Lopate's "The Chamber Music Evening" and Charles Baxter's "Harmony of the World" were especially fine and heartfelt, and it pained me to lack space for them.

The Sixties, at least until President Kennedy was assassinated in 1963 and perhaps until President Johnson deepened our Vietnam commitment in 1965, were a scarcely distinguishable extension of the Fifties. In any case, while looking to fiction to mirror its time, we must remember that writers generally write through a number of decades and gather their formative impressions in decades earlier still. Saul Bellow's world, for example, remains essentially a Thirties world of scramble and survival. "The Ledge," by Lawrence Sargent Hall, is timeless—a naturalistic anecdote terrible in its tidal simplicity and inexorability, fatally weighted in every detail. Philip Roth's "Defender of the Faith" looks back to the time of World War II, as does Bernard Malamud's "The German Refugee." Roth's story, written by a man too young to have served, has the authentic khaki texture and unfolds with a layered irony that would have been hard to muster in 1945. The Malamud was chosen, after some dithering, over his famous "The Magic Barrel"; less fantastic, beginning like a small anecdote, "The German Refugee" ends surprisingly and powerfully, with Malamud's sense of Jewishness as a mystical force founded on suffering. Jewishness! What would post-war American fiction be without it—its color, its sharp eye, its colloquial verve, its comic passions, its exuberant plaintiveness? Stanley Elkin rarely knew when to stop, and "Criers and Kibitzers, Kibitzers and Criers" could be shorter, beginning with its title. But it gives us what seldom gets into fiction, the taste and texture of doing business, the daily mercenary pressures that compete with even the deepest personal grief for a man's attention. No one could strike the Hebraic ethnic note more purely, with a more silvery touch, than the Yiddish writer Isaac Bashevis Singer. "The Key" fashions a religious epiphany, adorned with heavenly omens, from a distrustful old lady's inadvertent night on the town. We are reminded of Chagall and Bruno Schulz and the midnight ordeals of the Old Testament.

Scanning the Sixties stories for signs of revolution, we wonder if the grotesque hero of Joyce Carol Oates's "Where Are You Going, Where Have You Been?"—a misshapen yet irresistible troll out of a youth culture that won't quit—might be taken as the call of the counterculture, luring the Fifties' restless Connies out from their cramping domestic security and onto the road. The story is dedicated to Bob Dylan. Fifteen years of civil-rights agitation and selective advancement lie behind the educated, self-pampered narrator of McPherson's "Gold Coast," who for a time moved smoothly—"I only had to be myself, which pleased me"— through a multiracial world. And could Mary Ladd Gavell's airy, melancholy pastiche, "The Rotifer," leaping so gracefully from the microscopic to the historic to the contemporarily romantic, have been composed ten years earlier, without the examples of Barthelme's pastiches or Salinger's interloping authorial voice? This gem was Gavell's only published story; the managing editor of the magazine *Psychiatry*, she died in 1967 at the age of forty-eight, and the magazine ran the story as a memorial.

Something of Gavell's mulling, quizzical approach can be heard in the next decade's "How to Win," by Rosellen Brown, and "Roses, Rhododendron," by Alice Adams. There are the facts—a dysfunctional child, a girlhood friendship—and there is the female mind that views these facts with a certain philosophical élan. This is feminism in literary action, the contemplative end of a continuum that includes this era's angry confessional memoirs. When Lardner or Parker deployed the first person, it was apt to be an exercise in dramatic irony: we knew more than the crass and innocent narrator. Now the first person is deployed in earnest, for lack of a trustworthy other; the writer and reader are partners in a therapeutic search that will be, we know, inconclusive. Harold Brodkey's "Verona: A Young Woman Speaks" is an exercise of quite another kind: an attempt to plumb the depths, to portray a bliss at life's root, to express the never hitherto quite expressed, at a point where family complication and shining white Alps and "miraculously deep" blue shadows converge. If Brodkey sought, through the laborious dissection of sensations, depths, Donald Barthelme and Ann Beattie and Raymond Carver offer surfaces—uninflected dialogue, a bluntly notational (if not, as with Barthelme, hilariously absurdist) manner of description. No writer ever gratefully claimed the title of "minimalist," yet the term "minimalism," borrowed from the art world, did identify something new, or something new since the Thirties' rampant imitation of Hemingway—a withdrawal of authorial guidance, an existential determination to let things speak out of their own silence. Such writing expressed post-Vietnam burnout much as Hemingway spoke for the disillusioned mood after World War I. The reader's hunger for meaning and *gloire* is put on starvation rations; the nullity of quiddity is matched by the banality of normal conversation. Beattie was the first to put forth the no-frills, somewhat faux-naïve style (Martha Foley shunned her early efforts, leaving us with only the later, not entirely typical, but still dispassionate "Janus"); Carver ("Where I'm Calling From") became the darling of the college crowd, and Barthelme ("A City of Churches") of the New York intelligentsia. English style needs a periodic chastening, and minimalism gave college instructors in the proliferating writing courses a teachable ideal: keep it clean, keep it concrete. As William Carlos Williams immortally put it, "No ideas but in things." The dictum is congenial, bespeaking no-nonsense American pragmatism.

But ideas exist in human heads, and the more baroque possibilities of language, conceptualization, and a companionable authorial voice will not go away. Who would deny "A Silver Dish" its tumbling richness, as with the usual Bellovian superabundance of characterization, a kind of urban hurry and crowding, the master pursues his usual theme, the vagaries of human vitality? "That was how he was"—the story's last sentence shrugs in plain wonder at life, its barbarities and family feeling. "Do they still have such winter storms in Chicago as they used to have?" An epic trolley-car ride in a blizzard serves as an image of our brave human pertinacity. Cynthia Ozick is a baroque artist of the new generation: her brief, desolating "The Shawl," which comes as close to the reality of the death camps as imagination can take us, should be read in conjunction with its expansive American sequel "Rosa," set in a surreal Florida of Jewish retirees. My own story, "Gesturing," seemed of the several available to offer the most graceful weave, mingling the image of a defenestrating skyscraper with those from a somewhat gaily collapsing marriage. Marriages and relationships, as the century progresses, are on ever shakier ground, with fewer and fewer communal alternates like the band of farm wives in "A Jury of Her Peers" or the Communist brotherhood of "Bright and Morning Star." Domestic life, with piped-in entertainment and takeout meals, is our scarcely escapable mode of living, though the urge to escape is widely chronicled.

The health of the short story? Its champions claim that as many stories are published as ever. But there is a difference, in a consumer society, between something we have to have and something that is nice to have around. Few magazines still pay the kind of fees that kept Scott Fitzgerald in champagne. If *The New Yorker* published eleven of my last twenty selections, one reason may be that it had less and less competition as a market. Whatever statistics show, my firm impression is that in my lifetime the importance of short fiction as a news-bearing medium—bringing Americans news of how they live, and why—has diminished. In reaction to this diminishment, short-story writers, called upon less often, seem to be trying to get more and more into each opportunity to perform. Alice Munro, ever more a panoramist, gets into "Meneseteung" an entire late-Victorian Ontario town, and a woman's entire life with it. Susan Sontag gets an entire microcosm of New York's artistic crowd into "The Way We Live Now," as a circle of friends reacts with gales of gossip, like a hive of stirred-up bees, to the blighting of one of their number by a mysterious disease that, though unnamed, must be AIDS. Tim O'Brien gets the Vietnam War, its soldiers and their materiel, into "The Things They Carried"; O'Brien's plain, itemizing style bears a trace of minimalism, but the scope of his topic, as First Lieutenant Jimmy Cross learns to "dispense with love," moves him into maximal territory.

In a short-story world that has lost many potential practitioners to the rewards of television sitcoms and the gambler's odds of the novel, Lorrie Moore and Thom Jones have emerged as strong voices, at home in a medium length that gives them space to express (not without some gaudy gallows humor) the smoldering rage of the radically discontented female and of the barely tamed, battle-loving male, respectively. The image that ends "You're Ugly, Too"—the heroine's nearly consummated desire to push over the edge of a skyscraper a man dressed, in a marked-up body stocking, as a naked woman—holds worlds of conflicted contemporary female feeling. Jones, a celebrant of pugilists, soldiers, and men on pills, in "I Want to Live!" tells in clairvoyant, appalling detail of a woman's descent, medicine by medicine, into the last stages of cancer. In Alice Elliott Dark's "In the Gloaming," a mother tends her son as he dies of AIDS, and in doing so reclaims the maternal bond; few of these stories are more quietly modulated and more moving than this one.

A quality of meltdown pervades the last selections here, which may reflect a *fin-de-siècle* desperation—a fear that our options are exhausted—or may reflect my own difficulties in choosing them. "Proper Library," by Carolyn Ferrell, gives us one of those shifting, precarious black households of such concern to legislators and social workers and moralists, and from the viewpoint of an especially unpromising member of it, a none-too-sharp-witted boy coping with homosexual desires. Yet a sense of human connection and striving comes through: "Please give me a chance." The hero of Gish Jen's "Birthmates" belongs to a group, Asian-Americans, that has lately found its English voice. He is near the end of his rope, and being in the thick of the computer revolution doesn't help him make a connection where it counts. "Soon," by Pam Durban, takes us back to the turn of the century and a botched operation on a little girl's eyes, and beyond that deep into the previous century, when one of those propertied Protestant lines established its stake in the New World; now that stake is mostly memory in an old woman's mind. And Annie Proulx's "The Half-Skinned Steer," taken from *The Best American Short Stories 1998*, revisits the West, the West that has seemed to this country the essence of itself. An elderly former rancher finds it empty and murderous. I would have liked to finish this volume with a choice less dark, with an image less cruel and baleful than that of a half-skinned steer, but the American experience, story after story insisted, has been brutal and hard.* The continent has demanded a price from its takers, let alone from those who surrendered it. I regret that no story about Native Americans could be worked into the table of contents; the closest was James Ferry's "Dancing Ducks and Talking Anus," updating a cult of pain that was here before the white man.

As I picked my way through the selecting, I was always alert for stories that showed what William Dean Howells called "the more smiling aspects of life, which are the more American." A number of lighter stories I had thought of including—"The Girl with Flaxen Hair," by Manuel Komroff; "Your Place Is Empty," by Anne Tyler—had to yield to the pressure of weightier or more aggressive competitors. But one story that did survive—and the only one of my final selection not yet mentioned—is the delicious trifle "Wild Plums," by Grace Stone Coates, published in *The Frontier* in 1929. In it, a child tugs against her parents' puritanical injunctions, hardened by immigrant caution and rural class-consciousness. The obedient child, it seems, is being barred from the experience of life itself. A veteran short-story reader dreads the worst, rendered with some dying fall and bitter moral. But the outcome is in fact like "wild honey, holding the warmth of sand that sun had fingered, and the mystery of water under leaning boughs." A story exceedingly simple, and unexpectedly benign, but not false for that, nor less American than the rest.

---

*To take the century down to the wire, a story from the 1999 selection was added to the paperback edition. Pam Houston's "The Best Girlfriend You Never Had" depicts a circle of friends drifting toward the millennium unfulfilled, wanting love, wanting more. The narrating heroine, like the protagonists of the first tales in this anthology, is an immigrant, crossing not the Atlantic but the well-worn and weary continent, toward San Francisco and "something like a real life." Out of dreams, reality—and vice versa.

WORKS AND DAYS

The Changeling

EDITH WHARTON, by Hermione Lee. 869 pp. Knopf, 2007.

The life of Edith Wharton is not an inspiriting rags-to-riches saga, nor is it a cautionary tale of riches to rags—riches to riches, rather. Born Edith Newbold Jones, in January of 1862, into one of the leading families of New York—the phrase "keeping up with the Joneses" is said to have originated with reference to her great-aunts Mary and Rebecca Jones, who shocked the rest of their staid society by building a mansion north of Fifty-seventh Street, unthinkably uptown in the nineteenth century— the author maintained multiple establishments and travelled in the highest style, with a host of servants, augmenting her several inheritances by writing best-selling fiction. In the Depression year of 1936, when two thousand dollars was a good annual income, her writing earned her $130,000, much of it from plays adapted from her works. Yet her well-padded, auspiciously sponsored life was not an easy one. The aristocratic social set into which she was born expected its women to be ornamental, well-sheltered, intellectually idle agents of their interwoven clans, whereas Edith was an awkward, red-haired bookworm and dreamer, teased by her two older brothers about her big hands and feet and out of sympathy with her intensely conventional mother, née Lucretia Stevens Rhinelander—a mother-daughter disharmony that rankled in Edith's fiction to the end. She felt like a changeling, writing, in a last, unfinished effort of autobiography, "Life and I," that her parents "were beginning to regard me with fear, like some pale predestined child who disappears at night to dance with 'the little people.'"

In truth, some of her imaginative activity was alarming, as she describes it; from the age of four or five she would march up and down the house with a book in hand, pretending to read aloud words that she concocted in an "'ecstasy' of invention." In "Life and I," she writes of "the rapture of finding myself again in my own rich world of dreams" and of "the ecstasy which transported my little body." Her mother disapproved and attempted to distract her with suitable playmates; her father's library was the site of her reading pleasure, as she lay stretched out on the rug. George Frederic Jones had graduated from Columbia College, sat on charitable boards, and inherited enough money to keep up (just barely) with his wife's expenditures. Thrift and a dip in the family fortune prompted him to move the family to Italy and France, with their dollar-friendly economies, between 1866 and 1872; Edith returned, at the age of ten, knowing French, Italian, and German, and with a lifelong love of Europe.

In 1881, the family went again to Europe, this time for the father's health; he and Edith saw sights in Italy with Ruskin's writing as their guide. But George Frederic Jones died the following year, in Cannes, at the age of sixty-one, when Edith was twenty. She gave him credit for her bookish, culturally voracious side, though in her memoir, *A Backward Glance*, she credits her mother with arranging the private printing of her first book, *Verses*, when Edith was sixteen. Others remembered it as her father's idea, and on her deathbed she assigned her father credit. In 1905, when *The House of Mirth* was published, to great success and acclaim, she wrote to a friend, "I often think of Papa, and wish he could have been here to encourage me with my work." Yet, had he lived, her unhappy married life, and her eventual blooming into one of the twentieth century's finest American writers, might well have taken other turns, to posterity's loss. The upper crust builds thick inhibitions around its would-be writers; a live father and a more compatible husband might have kept Wharton's rather dour, frequently satiric genius sealed in a carapace of good manners and amateurish diffidence.

As Wharton's reputation gradually emerged, after her death, in 1937, from under the cloud of her late, commercially successful but critically denigrated novels and the impression they reinforced of a facile, popular "lady novelist," she has not lacked for biographical and critical attention. Her literary executor, Gaillard Lapsley, a conservative Cambridge historian, sold her manuscripts and letters to Yale, embargoing "anything of a biographical sort" for thirty years. However, in the mid-1940s he invited Percy Lubbock, another Cambridge scholar whom Wharton had met through Henry James, to compose a memoir of her, which to some other of her acquaintances seemed a poor caricature. The embargo was lifted in 1968, and Louis Auchincloss's friendly, elegantly illustrated brief biography, *Edith Wharton: A Woman in Her Time*, followed, in 1971. As early as 1966, a number of eminent American writers, including Edmund Wilson, Leon Edel, and Alfred Kazin, had been considered by the custodians of the Wharton lode for the authorized biography; the Yale professor R. W. B. Lewis was chosen. His *Edith Wharton: A Biography* came out in 1975, winning the Pulitzer Prize, and it remains, more than thirty years later, the gold standard—the Wharton biography that most people have read. Now an equally long and territorially similar biography, simply titled *Edith Wharton*, has been produced by Hermione Lee, the first female Goldsmiths' Professor of English Literature at Oxford and the author of book-length studies of Elizabeth Bowen, Willa Cather, and Philip Roth, and of a greatly admired, nearly nine-hundred-page biography of Virginia Woolf. The reader peruses her biography of Wharton, watchful for the ways in which it differs from, and improves on, Lewis's.

Lee tells us that her Wharton "makes use of the recent publication of her letters to Léon Bélugou and Louis Bromfield, draws on a large scatter of unpublished letters . . . and follows her trail more closely in France, Italy, and England." These are real additions to the record, but nothing on the sensational order of the revelations that Lewis's biography contained: an account of Wharton's passionate affair, from 1908 to 1910, with the hitherto obscure journalist Morton Fullerton; the publication, in an appendix, of an enthusiastically pornographic fragment of an unfinished story titled "Beatrice Palmato"; and the inclusion, complete, in Lewis's text of a long, long-lined poem, "Terminus," addressed to Fullerton in the hot wake of his embraces in the Charing Cross Hotel.

Lewis, surveying his task in a prefatory chapter, accentuates the positive:

> If Edith Wharton did look forward rather fearfully to being given biographical treatment, she also took pains to see that the biographer would have at his disposal as complete a record as possible. . . . [She] destroyed relatively little and destroyed selectively—most notably, the letters she had written Walter Van Rensselaer Berry and the majority of letters Berry had written to her over the years. She left behind, meanwhile, a number of extraordinarily revealing documents: diaries, unpublished poems, fragments of autobiography, unfinished stories, which, to speak personally, shook to pieces most of the preconceptions with which I came to this work.

His impression of her as "rather too much of the *grande dame* . . . whose private life was a narrow one, who was cool and even abrasive in her outward relationships, and puritanically repressed within," was supplanted by "a picture of a woman hardly recognizable alongside the Edith Wharton of legend. There was, after all, a fund of passion and of laughter in her, and almost unbelievable energy. There was genuine daring of both a personal and a literary variety." Lee, looking at the same archives, sees a glass half empty, a fund of suppression and silence:

> Wharton's life story often feels like a cover story, with tremendously articulate activity on the surface, and secrets and silences below. This is partly due to the missing bits in the archive, missing because she—or someone else—deliberately made away with them. There is no remaining correspondence with her parents or her brothers, and hardly any of their own documents. There are only a few letters from the most important person in her life, Walter Berry: she destroyed most of his letters to her, and managed, also, to retrieve and make away with hers to him; only four of these slipped through the cull. There are very few of her many letters, some of them extremely personal, to Henry James: he burnt them. . . . There are only three painful letters from her husband, and few traces of him. There are no letters from her lover, Morton Fullerton, though hers to him came to light many years after her death (how she would have hated it). Her published autobiography is selective and evasive. . . . Reserve and concealment are everywhere in her fiction.

It is not that Lee is disapproving of Wharton, or fails to do justice to her exemplary qualities, her intelligence and artistry and the triumphant energy and will invested in the passage from the ugly upper-class duckling to the literary queen with her posh leather-bound library, her splendid gardens, her international fame. But something slightly heavy and lustreless weighs on the big pages as Lee inventories the many members of Wharton's extensive acquaintance and tracks her avid travels through the American Northeast and Europe and North Africa; each page begins to loom as a cliff that the reader must scale upside down, top to bottom.

Just a few glances into Lee's lauded biography of Virginia Woolf suggest an animating difference: she loves Virginia Woolf, or—to put it less heatedly—her life and her subject's touch. In an afterword called "Biographer," Lee joyfully outlines her contacts with Woolf—her discovery, when she was eight or nine and sleeping over at a friend's house, of a Penguin edition of *The Waves* on her bedside table, and her feeling that "I had happened on a secret language which belonged to me"; her exploration of a London whose place-names and vistas Woolf had experienced decades before; her sense, as she began to seek interviews ("to be met, on the whole, with kind but wearied civility"), that she was moving toward a person who "was at once locked in past, distant history, and touchably close." The starchy Joneses, with their ritual transatlantic reach toward the seats of real culture, their naïve and monotonous snobbery, their strange mixture of religiosity and materialism, their unforgiving family quarrels, do not invite touching. Lee, in praising Wharton's artistry, keeps using the word "ruthless": *Ethan Frome* unfolds with "brilliant, ruthless speed"; *The Age of Innocence* uses "her entire family network, and every vase, net curtain and picture-frame in the Jones household, in the most ruthless and lavish way"; and the short story "Roman Fever" is an "impeccable, ruthless masterpiece."

As Lee's Anglicisms—"unpicks," "incomers," "cod reviews," "playing up" (for "acting up"), "left in store" (for "left in storage")—remind us, she is, no matter how many visiting fellowships have brought her to these shores and how many American authors she has mastered, an alien, to whom America, for all its allurements, has something fathomless and blank about it. On no authority, it seems, other than her own intuition, Lee tells us that when Edith Jones first returned to New York, it "seemed to the ten-year-old, after six years in Europe, startlingly ugly and drab, and . . . from this moment on she felt like an exile in America." Returning at age forty-one, in 1903, to the Mount, the stately home she had built in fashionable Lenox, in the Berkshires of Massachusetts, the proprietress did write to her friend Sally Norton of "the wild, disheveled, backwoods look of everything when one first comes home." But it was the backwoods people, their dishevelled and sparse culture, their "complete mental starvation," that made Wharton an expatriate. Lee explores, in the vast tracts of the novelist's writings, her annotations in her own beloved books, and reports:

> Santayana, whom she greatly admired, gets one annotation in *The Life of Reason*. Next to this remark—"In some nations everybody is by nature so astute, versatile, and sympathetic that education hardly makes any difference in manners or mind"—she writes "France."

Lee is very good on Wharton in France. The Rue de Varenne, its *hôtels particuliers* dating back to the eighteenth century and "packed tight with ancient families," was, with several changes of address, where Wharton lived from 1907 to 1920; here, in the aristocratic Faubourg Saint-Germain, she wrote a great deal of American fiction, including *Ethan Frome*, which was begun—surprisingly—as an exercise in French. For four strenuous years, she founded and directed a number of charities for those who, like Belgian children, were displaced and deprived by the First World War. For her tireless work, which nearly broke her health, she was made a Chevalier de l'Ordre National de la Légion d'Honneur; "Mme Warthon" was cited as one "*qui a toujours eu pour la France le sentiment qu'on donne à une seconde patrie.*" Another honor from her second country, the Prix de Vertu, was bestowed in a speech that claimed, of her writings, "*Jamais la France n'a été mieux comprise ni mieux aimée*"—France has never been better understood or better loved. Wharton's spoken French, we are told, was grammatically faultless but pronounced with a strong "English" accent. Her love letters to Fullerton switch back and forth between French and English, and Lee says, "Sometimes French seems to be the only possible language for what she wants to say: '*Si tu veux que nous nous aimions encore, aimons nous. J'aurais toujours le temps d'être triste après*—'" Lee herself seems at home in the language, and leaves half her French quotations untranslated, setting the reader a salutary test.

After the war, Wharton tired of Paris, writing to Bernard Berenson, "Paris is simply awful—a kind of continuous earth-quake of motor-busses, trams, lorries, taxis & other howling & swooping & colliding engines, with hundreds & thousands of U.S. citizens rushing about in them." By 1917, she had found a likely house, a half-hour from Paris, in the village of Saint-Brice, in the area of Fontainebleau; the dilapidated house had a romantic past as a *maison de plaisance*, a rural retreat occupied by a dashing Venetian family whose eldest daughter, a flaxen-haired beauty with the stage name of Mademoiselle Colombe, was the mistress of, successively, an Irish nobleman and the keeper of the king's finances. Wharton named the place Pavillon Colombe and, after extensive interior renovations and a start at turning its forested seven acres into a garden, had moved in by 1920. At the same time, vacationing in the south of France, she found in the town of Hyères an empty house, built into the ruined walls of the town's medieval castle, that she arranged to rent on a long lease, renaming the place Sainte-Claire-du-Château. Here, to create a garden, she needed to build terraces, haul in soil, construct pergolas and paths, and develop irrigation; the results, imperilled by the region's sharp frosts, droughts, and violent rains, were what Lee calls a "dramatic and enchanting" garden, described, when the house was sold after her death, as "among the most celebrated in France." The biographer draws a pleasing parallel between gardening and novel-writing:

> The mixture of disciplined structure and imaginative freedom, the rework-ing of traditions into a new idea, the ruthless [that word again!] elimination of dull, incongruous or surplus materials, and the creation of a dramatic narrative, all come to mind—not to mention patience, stamina, and atten-tiveness. John Hugh Smith reported to Lubbock, in 1938, that "she told me that she thought her gardens were better than her books."

Lee is at her best with Wharton's books. Her close and ingenious expli-
cations reveal formal patterns of design and persuasive, sometimes subtle
connections with Wharton's experiences; as with most authors, her life
was her ultimate subject, whether she was projecting her imprisoning
marriage and thwarted romance into the rural misery of *Ethan Frome* or
using her own broad experience of authorship in the wide-ranging satire
of *Hudson River Bracketed*. Lee gives the later, critically shunned novels
respectful readings, and is keen enough on the short stories to rouse guilt
in a susceptible breast over their less-than-canonical status. On the three
full-length novels (all with "of" in their titles) at the heart of Wharton's
enduring accomplishment, Lee is wise, fresh, and generous, though in
my own taste she ranks *The Custom of the Country* too highly as "her
greatest book" (not to mention "her most ruthless, harsh and ebullient"),
and slightly underplays the tragic impact of *The Age of Innocence*, even
"though, as usual, personal emotions are carefully distanced and dressed
up." Lee spells out "the qualities that make Wharton a great writer—her
mixture of harshly detached, meticulously perceptive, disabused realism,
with a language of poignant feeling and deep passion, and her setting of
the most confined of private lives in a thick, complex network of social
forces." The biography's penultimate chapter, "A Private Library," movingly describes Wharton's wide reading (her favorite author was Goethe,
read in German) and earnest study—from her lonely girlhood on, she
consumed volumes of anthropology and Darwinism, history and philosophy. Her inexorable naturalism was acquired via books as well as by bitter
experience.

She wrote, famously, in bed, tossing her handwritten pages onto the
floor for her secretary to type, and balanced her writing desk on her
knees with an inkpot in it and a pet Pekinese dog on the bed with her. She
lived into modern times, long enough to vote for Roosevelt once and
then, deeming him too "socialist," not again. But she was not a modernist, though well aware of changing fashions; her young friends could
not convince her of the virtues of *Ulysses*, which she called "a turgid welter of schoolboy pornography (the rudest schoolboy kind) & unformed &
unimportant drivel. . . . The same applies to Eliot." Dreams, delirium,
and ghosts figure in her fiction, but not a programmatic, fragmentary
surrealism. Asked about the role of the unconscious in creating fiction,
she sounds somewhat French, somewhat starchy, and quite sensible:

> I do not think I can get any nearer than this to the sources of my story-
> telling; I can only say that the process, though it takes place in some secret

region on the sheer edge of consciousness, is always illuminated by the full light of my critical attention.

The full light was not necessarily a harsh one. Her fiction shows a striking empathy with the losers of the world, without her wanting to be one of them. In the dreariest days of her dying marriage to Teddy Wharton, when she felt herself locked up in a *prison de suie* ("prison of soot"), she wrote Berenson, "You mustn't think there haven't been bits of blue sky all the same; there always are with *me*; I can hardly ever wholly stop having a good time!"

Back-Chat, Funny Cracks

FLANN O'BRIEN: *The Complete Novels*, with an introduction by Keith Donohue. 787 pp. Everyman's Library, 2007.

Begob, and the truth would not be played false were a frank man to say that Flann O'Brien, born Brian O'Nolan in Strabane, Ulster, in 1911, and known as Myles na gCopaleen to the readers of his long-standing column "Cruiskeen Lawn" in the *Irish Times*, when acting as a novelist proffered a mixed bag of blessings and their opposite. Such a pained reflection has been given rise to by a thorough if at intervals dozy reading of *The Complete Novels* by the above-named, as published by Everyman's Library in its fine format, no fewer than 824 pages (counting the front matter) of wee Bembo type bound in glorious red covers with a sewn-in bookmark of golden fabric. On the jacket the author is obscured by his dark hat and his black-rimmed glasses and his own hand at his mouth, and, to be sure, Flann/Brian/Myles, where many an author not only rejoices in his face on his jacket but sets his personal facts in the forefront of his prose, engaged in a significant effort of self-concealment, of pseudonymity lurking behind a prose greatly melodious and garrulous in its confident manner. The front flap of the same jacket states him to be "along with Joyce and Beckett . . . part of the holy trinity of modern Irish literature," which rings strangely of one who disparaged the Holy Trinity, discounting with considerable scholarly fury in his final novel, *The Dalkey Archive*, the very notion of the Holy Ghost, as having been heedlessly foisted upon the Christian Creed by the Council of Alexandria in the year 362. The man was ingenious and learned like Jim Joyce, and like

Sam Beckett gave the reader a sweet dose of hopelessness, but unlike either of these worthies did not arrive at what we might call artistic resolution. His novels begin with a swoop and a song but end in an uncomfortable murk and with an air of impatience.

The first, *At Swim-Two-Birds* (1939), is the best known and the most rigorously confusing—confusing even the compendium's introducer, Keith Donohue, who describes it as "a mock-heroic novel about a man named Orlick Trellis," when in fact Orlick is the relatively incidental son of *Dermot* Trellis, a bedridden author introduced, on page 31, as "writing a book on sin and the wages attaching thereto." In equipping himself for this mighty task he "has bought a ream of ruled foolscap" and "is compelling all his characters to live with him in the Red Swan Hotel so that he can keep an eye on them." Dermot Trellis is enough captivated by the beauty of Sheila Lamont, a character he has invented to illustrate female virtue, "that he so far forgets himself as to assault her himself." Not only assaults: he impregnates her. Their child is Orlick, who, after an education in the home of the Pooka MacPhellimey—one of several figures from Irish legend that have materialized in the narrative—becomes a writer himself, coached by three idlers called Shanahan, Furriskey, and Antony Lamont, the abused woman's brother, all of them intent upon indicting and punishing, by way of Orlick's fledgling fiction, his father's perfidy. The elder Trellis is kept immobilized in his bed by surreptitiously drug-induced sleep while his characters, including a number of American cowboys recruited from the novels of one William Tracy, run wild. At least, that's what I think is happening.

The manuscript keeps restarting itself, repeating whole paragraphs at a time, and the only segments of Irish life that savor of actual experience are the unnamed narrator's passing conversations with his sententious uncle and with his flippant acquaintances at University College, Dublin. It is this unnamed narrator, easily confused with the young Flann O'Brien, who is composing this many-levelled travesty of a novel. Graham Greene called *At Swim-Two-Birds* "one of the best books of our century. A book in a thousand . . . in the line of *Ulysses* and *Tristram Shandy*." The *Chicago Tribune* said, more cagily, that it is "of such staggering originality that it baffles description and very nearly beggars our sense of delight." All of O'Brien's novels of nearly beggared delight convey what Donohue calls his "disdain for certain, clear meaning and interpretation."

Disdainful though it is, *At Swim-Two-Birds* can be wonderfully written, with an offhand lilt that twists the drab ordinary into a peculiar precision:

On wet days there would be an unpleasant odour of dampness, an aroma of overcoats dried by body-heat.

Now listen, said Shanahan clearing the way with small coughs.

It was an early-morning street, its quiet distances still small secrets shared by night with day.

Like the overbearing master of the Dublin quotidian, James Joyce, O'Brien is not afraid to bore the reader. Pages go by in alcoholic discussion of the relative merits of various musical instruments ("The fiddle is the man, said Shanahan") and the elusive quality of "kangaroolity." A mock-heroic fustian inflates the prose:

A learning and an erudition boundless in its universality, an affection phenomenal in its intensity and a quiet sympathy with the innumerable little failings of our common humanity—these were the sterling qualities that made Mr John Furriskey a man among men and endeared him to the world and his wife.

If this tone was inspired by the many mock-heroic passages in *Ulysses*, O'Brien's impudent introduction of Finn MacCool, the Pooka MacPhellimey, and the invisible Good Fairy ("I am like a point in Euclid, explained the Good Fairy, position but no magnitude, you know") into the cast of *At Swim-Two-Birds* may allude to the background of archaic myth in *Finnegans Wake*, which was also published in 1939 but, starting in 1924, was heralded by advance excerpts, under the title *Work in Progress*, in various French- and English-language publications, and was surely known to O'Brien. Joyce cast a heavy shadow on the younger writer's mind, being often invoked in O'Brien's newspaper column and emerging as a character in his last novel.

O'Brien's next novel, *The Third Policeman*, widely regarded as his best, was rejected, in 1940, by his publisher, Longmans, Green & Co., and consigned to a drawer, where it waited until the year after the author's death, in 1966, for its publication. Read in sequence, as following hard upon *At Swim-Two-Birds*, it can be appreciated as equally fantastic and original but more coherent, with a story line that rouses suspense and comes, in irregular fashion, full-circle. In its heterodox way, it tells a tale of hell and of a murderer's proper punishment. *The Complete Novels* includes a diffidently exuberant letter that O'Brien wrote to William Saroyan, another free literary spirit of the time:

When you get to the end of this book you realize that my hero or main character (he's a heel and a killer) has been dead throughout the book and that all the queer ghastly things which have been happening to him are happening in a sort of hell which he earned for the killing. . . . I think the idea of a man being dead all the time is pretty new. When you are writing about the world of the dead—and the damned—where none of the rules and laws (not even the law of gravity) holds good, there is any amount of scope for back-chat and funny cracks.

His narrator, again nameless, is persuaded, by the deceiving scoundrel John Divney, to commit robbery and murder so gradually ("Three further months passed before I could bring myself to agree to the proposal and three months more before I openly admitted to Divney that my misgivings were at an end"), and so ingenuously accepts the consequent terrors and perils, that he doesn't seem a heel at all; he seems as innocent as Alice in Wonderland or one of Kafka's heroes, gamely trying to puzzle through a bizarre and bewildering world. We identify with him, to a degree rarely permitted by O'Brien, who, even in his rambling, personal daily column, maintained a certain brusque distance from the reader. (Toward the end of *The Dalkey Archive*, a character delivers what feels like the author's own credo of authorship: "One must write outside oneself. I'm fed up with writers who put a fictional gloss over their own squabbles and troubles. It's a form of conceit, and usually it's very tedious.")

The protagonist of *The Third Policeman* occupies the stage continuously, without the subplots and compounded fictions of *At Swim-Two-Birds*. His voice is confiding, making us privy to his musings as he moves through a rural landscape redolent of a prehistoric past:

The road was narrow, white, old, hard and scarred with shadow. It ran away westwards in the mist of the early morning, running cunningly through the little hills and going to some trouble to visit tiny towns which were not, strictly speaking, on its way. It was possibly one of the oldest roads in the world. I found it hard to think of a time when there was no road there because the trees and the tall hills and the fine views of bogland had been arranged by wise hands for the pleasing picture they made when looked at from the road. Without a road to have them looked at from they would have a somewhat aimless if not a futile aspect.

From this recurrent image of a road he drops into evoking the thought of his intellectual idol, the "physicist, ballistician, philosopher and psychologist" called de Selby. A number of footnotes quoting the de Selby scholars Le Fournier, Hatchjaw, Bassett, Kraus, Le Clerque, and Henderson reveal their subject to have been less a savant than an idiot, who fell asleep in meetings of learned societies and even "when walking in crowded thoroughfares," who could not distinguish men from women, who believed that night comes because of the day's accretions of dirty air, and who left behind a closely handwritten two-thousand-page Codex of which not one word is legible. De Selby is a vivid comic invention, perpetrated by O'Brien with pedantic gusto, and the narrator's loyalty to this preposterous wizard adds to his sympathetic qualities.

Policemen—courteous, overweight, and menacing—and bicycles figure prominently among the figments of *The Third Policeman*. Perhaps the most erotic passage in O'Brien's fiction concerns a bicycle that nuzzles up to our hero in a moment of need:

> How can I convey the perfection of my comfort on the bicycle, the completeness of my union with her, the sweet responses she gave me at every particle of her frame? . . . She moved beneath me with agile sympathy in a swift, airy stride, finding smooth ways among the stony tracks, swaying and bending skilfully to match my changing attitudes, even accommodating her left pedal patiently to the awkward working of my wooden leg.

The wooden leg attracts fourteen men with the same affliction; they try to rescue him from the policemen, who have led the narrator through a subterranean realm of circular corridors and metal doors not dissimilar to one of Beckett's carefully mapped hells. Ovenlike cabinets produce objects that defy description ("I can only say that these objects, not one of which resembled the other, were of no known dimensions"), as well as a half-ton block of gold and a host of other wish fulfillments. Surreal though all this is, the reader cares about what happens next because it promises, unlike events in *At Swim-Two-Birds*, to be connected to what went before and what will come. Into this weird fable of guilt and flight O'Brien has inserted some curious truths (bicycles are never mounted from the right) and some ineffable sentences:

> Birds were audible in the secrecy of the bigger trees, changing branches and conversing not tumultuously.

> MacCruiskeen lit a match for our cigarettes and then threw it carelessly on the plate floor where it lay looking very much important and alone.

> The long evening had made its way into the barrack through the windows, creating mysteries everywhere, erasing the seam between one thing and another, lengthening out the floors and either thinning the air or putting some refinement on my ear enabling me to hear for the first time the clicking of a cheap clock from the kitchen.

The rather systematic French absurdism of Jarry and Queneau takes on the twilit shimmer of a Celtic fairy tale. Yet the book, for all its shape-shifting comedy, has a heft of despair to it, an honest nihilism, as expressed by Martin Finnucane, an unrepentant robber. Asked by our narrator if he has any objections to life, he answers, "Is it life? . . . I would rather be without it . . . for there is a queer small utility in it. You cannot eat it or drink it or smoke it in your pipe, it does not keep the rain out and it is a poor armful in the dark. . . . It is a great mistake and a thing better done without, like bed-jars and foreign bacon."

O'Brien, who spoke Irish Gaelic in his childhood home, wrote his next extended fiction, *An Béal Bocht*, in Gaelic, in 1941; in 1973, it was trans-lated, by Patrick C. Power, into a spirited imitation of O'Brien's English as *The Poor Mouth: A Bad Story About the Hard Life*. Less than a hundred pages long, the tale has the advantage of a relatively clear, if extravagant, story line and a distinct satiric point—i.e., that the Irish Republic's offi-cial cherishing of the nearly extinct Gaelic language ignores the miser-able poverty of its surviving speakers, the rain-battered peasantry of the countryside. In one episode, government orators at a Gaelic *feis* parrot and praise the venerable language while in their audience "many Gaels collapsed from hunger and from the strain of listening." In another, a folklorist from Dublin, visiting O'Brien's fictional Gaeltacht area of Corkadoragha, and frustrated by the drunken taciturnity of an assembly of local males, records the muttering of a pig under the impression that it is Gaelic: "He understood that good Gaelic is difficult but that the best Gaelic of all is well-nigh unintelligible." Parodying sentimental novels and memoirs in modern Gaelic by such authors as Tomás Ó Criomhthain and Séamas Ó Grianna, O'Brien protests on behalf of a depressed Irish population: "In one way or another, life was passing us by and we were suffering misery, sometimes having a potato and at other times having nothing in our mouths but sweet words of Gaelic." His hero, young Bonaparte O'Coonassa, does find, in an abysmal cave inhabited by a her-mit, a hoard of gold coins, but the cave also holds a stream of yellow water that, in a scene of alcoholic revelation with counterparts in every novel by this author, turns out to be whiskey:

> Amazement surged up in my head until it injured me. I went to the well on my knees, to the place where the yellow water was bursting up, and con-sumed enough to set every bone a-tremble.

Had *The Third Policeman* made its way to print in 1940, there is no telling what further novels O'Brien might have written. As it was, he devoted his contrarian instincts and bristling erudition (he knew a startling amount about steam engines, and could toss off sentences in Greek, Latin, French, German, and Italian) to his column in the *Irish Times*, busying himself as well with plays and television scripts.

Not until 1961 did he publish another novel, *The Hard Life: An Exegesis of Squalor*. He dedicated "this misterpiece" to Graham Greene, "whose own forms of gloom I admire," and chose as his epigraph the *pensée* of Pascal's that blames all the trouble of the world on people ever leaving their rooms. Donohue's introduction relates the novel's Dublin milieu and its relatively conservative artistry to the author's twenty-year stint of churning out newspaper copy as Myles na gCopaleen. He likens its humdrum setting and mood to Joyce's *Dubliners*, and errs by claiming that the action ends in 1904, the year of Bloomsday—its climactic death comes in 1910. "Oddly oblique," he concludes, "*The Hard Life* reads as . . . a rather mild attack on the pretenses of Catholicism and an already vanishing social order."

Oblique it is: there is nothing especially hard or squalid about the situation of the two orphaned brothers, Manus and Finbarr, who grow up under the care of their deceased mother's half-brother Mr. Collopy and his daughter, Miss Annie. The boys are fed, sheltered, clothed, and sent to school. Mr. Collopy has for a friend an immigrant German Jesuit, Father Kurt Fahrt, and for a cause he leads a campaign to provide adequate public rest rooms for the good women of Dublin. In their evening conversations, he baits Father Fahrt about the Jesuits, but the priest makes peaceable replies and—a traditional Irish courtesy—accepts another drink. Possibly infuriated by his characters' refusal to kindle a fire under the novel, O'Brien consigns them all to a flagrantly farfetched encounter in Rome with the Pope, arranged by Manus, who has left Ireland to pursue, with some success, a host of elaborate and fraudulent schemes. The dialogue with the Pope, who speaks a scrupulously transcribed mixture of Latin and Italian, and the unwieldy decline of Mr. Collopy, who becomes prodigiously, fatally heavy through faithful ingestion of Gravid Water as prescribed and supplied by his former ward, do raise smiles and even laughter in the indulgent reader; yet the theme of being poisoned, proposed by an author whose health was sinking, in early middle age, into a morass of uremia, pleurisy, sycosis, neuralgia, anemia, and liver cancer, is not that funny. Like *The Poor Mouth*, *The Hard Life* drips with disgust, but it feels too autobiographical to direct the disgust outward onto objective correlatives. It ends when Finbarr, the relatively inert and passive narrator, abruptly undergoes a violent purge:

In a daze I lifted my own glass and without knowing what I was doing did exactly what the brother did, drained the glass in one vast swallow. Then I walked quickly but did not run to the lavatory. There, everything inside me came up in a tidal surge of vomit.

The Dalkey Archive, published in 1964, has lent its name to the avant-garde publishing house that keeps Flann O'Brien in print in this country. It is the only one of his novels (but for the unfinished *Slattery's Sago Saga*) to be written in the third person. The opening pages, evoking the village of Dalkey, are promising ("It is an unlikely town, huddled, quiet, pretending to be asleep. Its streets are narrow, not quite self-evident as streets and with meetings which seem accidental. Small shops look closed but are open"), and, toward the end, a penetrating poignance colors the portrait of an imagined James Joyce who quietly tends bar south of Dublin and attends Mass daily, who did not die in Switzerland but lived on, disowning *Ulysses* as a "dirty book" and forgetting *Finnegans Wake* entirely. He has shed his voracious genius and emerged as a decent, mild old man with bad eyesight who timidly dreams of becoming a Jesuit. O'Brien had Oedipal feelings about Joyce, and this conjuration momentarily steals the show. The adventures of Mick Shaughnessy, a civil servant with a girlfriend called Mary and a self-assigned mission to save the world from a four-gallon metal cask of oxygen-eating chemicals, fail to engage both the writer and the reader. De Selby has been salvaged from the unpublished manuscript of *The Third Policeman* but is presented with nothing like the brio of that book's footnotes. The rejected novel's bicycle-mad policemen, and its "fine views of bogland," are transplanted nearly intact. Even its road magic is remembered:

> The cracking of your feet on the road makes a certain amount of road come up into you. When a man dies they say he returns to clay funereally but too much walking fills you up with clay far sooner (or buries bits of you along the road) and brings your death halfway to meet you.

However, as is said of one loquacious character, "his fancies were usually amusing but not so good when they were meaningless." Whatever meaning O'Brien set out with on this particular road has been left scattered along the wayside. He said of *The Dalkey Archive* that it was "not a novel" but "really an essay in extreme derision of literary attitudes and people, and one pervasive fault is absence of emphasis, in certain places, to help the reader." It was too late, perhaps, to think of helping the reader, though O'Brien provides passages of synopsis to keep the events, and non-events, straight. But orthodox narration was never his forte; at his

best he went where he would, at a blithe speed, and carried the reader—
a dazzle of verbal dust in his eyes—along.

Imperishable Maxwell

WILLIAM MAXWELL: *Early Novels and Stories*, edited by Christopher Carduff. 997 pp. The Library of America, 2008.

WILLIAM MAXWELL: *Later Novels and Stories*, edited by Christopher Carduff. 994 pp. The Library of America, 2008.

To those who knew him, William Maxwell as a person—soft-spoken yet incisive, moist-eyed yet dry-voiced, witty yet infallibly tactful— threatened to overshadow Maxwell as a writer. We aspiring authors who enjoyed his unstinting editorial attention and gracious company tended to forget that, for four days of the week, he stayed at home and wrote, reporting to the typewriter straight from breakfast, often clad in bathrobe and slippers. He had finished two novels, the second of them a Book-of-the-Month Club selection, before finding, in 1936, employment at *The New Yorker*, where he remained, with a few interruptions, as an editor until 1975; he continued as a contributor until 1999, when he was ninety-one years old and in his last year of life. Now his writing is what we still have of him, and it warms the heart to hold almost all of his fiction in two sizable, relatively imperishable Library of America volumes, timed to be published a hundred years after his birth, in Lincoln, Illinois. The books have been scrupulously edited by Christopher Carduff; his "Note on the Texts" is exceptionally full, tracing Maxwell's earlier novels through their several revisions, and his twenty-nine pages labelled "Chronology" approach the intimacy and interest of a fulllength biography. For the year 1945, for instance, we read:

> In June, Maxwell ends therapy with [Theodor] Reik, upon whose couch, he says, "the whole first part of my life fell away, and I had a feeling of starting again."

Three years later: "In fall 1948, Maxwell, dismayed by poor sales of new novel and by lack of enthusiasm at Harper's, returns to *The New Yorker* on part-time basis." Abrupt details supply, in Carduff's notes, a sense of drama largely absent from Barbara Burkhardt's stately, exegetical *William*

Maxwell: A Literary Life (2005). Carduff's Chronology entry for 1950 reads:

> Struggles to imagine opening scene of book about France, but is undecided whether material would be better treated in first or third person, as fiction or as straightforward travel memoir. In fall he and Emily, after five years' trying to conceive a child, attempt to adopt, but Maxwell's age, 42, presents bureaucratic difficulties.

People already well acquainted with Maxwell's work will be fascinated to read, at the outset of the first Library of America volume—*Early Novels and Stories*—the author's first novel, *Bright Center of Heaven* (1934), which Maxwell, after a sold-out edition of a thousand volumes and a largely unsold second printing of another thousand, in effect suppressed. In 1958, when his new publisher, Alfred A. Knopf, undertook to reprint in its Vintage paperback line three earlier novels, Maxwell declined the offer to include *Bright Center of Heaven*, finding it, upon rereading, "hopelessly imitative" and "stuck fast in its period." In a *Paris Review* interview, he said, "My first novel . . . is a compendium of all the writers I loved and admired." Virginia Woolf's *To the Lighthouse*, especially, is imitated in the drifting weave of action and interior reflection, and in the rhythms, paced by commas, of the long descriptive sentences. Ten years after the novel's publication, he reread it and wrote, "I . . . discovered to my horror that I had lifted a character—the homesick servant girl—lock, stock, and barrel from *To the Lighthouse*." But these borrowings do not taint the peculiarly American innocence of the setting—Meadowland, an informal artists' colony in rural Wisconsin—or the indigenous ebullience borrowed from the Midwestern novelist Zona Gale. Meadowland was based upon Bonnie Oaks, a hospitable farm near Portage, Wisconsin, where Maxwell spent a number of summer months and one winter. Gale lived nearby, and, in many conversations, she shared with the young Maxwell her belief that artists should find "excitement in the presence of life" and bring out "the mysterious beauty of the commonplace" and the "brighter" aspect of reality.

Brightness is everywhere, indoors and out, in his first novel. With a confident empathy the twenty-five-year-old author moves among a dozen residents and guests at the place. We partake of the interior sensations of the owner, a widow battling mental confusion, and of her two adolescent sons, and of a young woman sleeplessly coping with an unintended pregnancy, and of her oblivious, bookish lover, and of a crusty hired hand left over from the days when this was a serious farm, and of a concert pianist as she practices her drills, and of a painter wrestling with the abstract qualities of two oranges and an oil can, and of a "pestilential and garrulous youth" with no discernible artistic dedication, and of a homesick German cook, and of a sickly Southern spinster, and—the focus of the novel's suspense—of a Harvard-educated black lecturer, an ardent advocate of racial equality. Though critics have found fault with the black character, he seemed to me plausible and complex enough— the earliest of Maxwell's many honorable attempts to portray African-Americans.

Bright Center of Heaven gives those of us who knew him as the mature master of a deliberately low-key prose a new Maxwell—bolder, more overtly poetical, more metaphysical, and frequently surreal. The book's title comes from a bizarre vision entertained by Amelia, the racist Southern spinster, as she sits, stunned into muteness, at the dinner table with a black guest: "The candles soared toward a heaven of blue and white larkspur, and in the bright center of heaven Amelia saw a great black face with gold-rimmed glasses." Her sense of outrage finds another expression in her suddenly hearty appetite, where she has previously been a picky, invalid eater. Nothing is predictable at this social occasion, which ends when the black visitor, Jefferson Carter, batters his way out of a screened tent where the postprandial discussion, despite the liberal dispositions of the white participants, has irritated him into a rage. "These seven people," he thinks, "had no meaning beyond themselves, which was to say that they had no meaning at all. They did not express the life of the nation. They had no visible work. They were all drones and winter would find them dead."

The mural scale of the indictment (in an aggrieved mind) is one that Maxwell did not strive for again. The novel, though not long, is ambitious in the reach of its human diversity and the extravagance of its metaphors. Emotional nuances are reified into audible objects:

> "Merry sunshine, Amelia!" Mrs. West's voice flew toward her husband's half-sister like a volley of silver arrows, intending to undo with their brightness the work of years of indigestion. The arrows struck harmlessly against the breastplate and the helmet. They fell with a clatter at Amelia's feet.

A page later: "Amelia, too scandalized for speech, wrapped her disapproval round her and laid the folds of it at her feet." These overanimations are eddies in the "bright confusion" of this long day in the upper Midwest. Myth leaks into the humdrum: Whitey, the younger of Mrs. West's sons, "is the family Ariel." When Mrs. West takes a hurried hand in the preparation of lunch, "the air about her grew bright with the combat" and the cook surveys the mess in the kitchen "without expression save for the utterly dead look of one who sees her sons slain by the invader, her daughters violated, and her house pulled down about her head." A palpable modernist influence, aside from the subtle, quirky domestic realism of Woolf and E. M. Forster, is that of James Joyce, particularly of *Ulysses*, which explodes as it progresses into a cosmic inclusiveness. A day in Dublin, a day in Wisconsin are alike sufficient samplings of humanity—random test cores plumbing the depths of existence. Homeric metaphors give epic magnitude to an eighteen-year-old boy's labor of unrequited love:

> As a mountain-climber is sometimes startled at the sight of one small flower growing miraculously out of the bare rock, and stops to gaze at its petals, white veined with blue, and at its yellow-and-blue center; and then the mountain-climber goes on up the precipitous wall of rock with less of weariness in his knees and a lighter pack on his back, so did the flower of Thorn's small hope refresh him and make the weight of his hurt feelings less burdensome to him.

An achieved and reciprocated love demands an even wider verbal stretch: "Beyond the shadow of all doubt she was certain that if he let go, if he took his hands from her face even for a second, she would fall headlong. She would be bruised and battered against ten thousand unnamed stars." The "heaventree of stars" that hangs over Leopold Bloom at day's end is glimpsed from another longitude.

In his next novel, *They Came Like Swallows* (1937), Maxwell subdues his figurative language to describe the most momentous event of his life: his mother's sudden death in the flu epidemic of 1918–19, after childbirth, at the age of thirty-seven. "My childhood came to an end at that moment," he later wrote. "The worst that could happen had happened, and the shine went out of everything." Modest specifics, clearly rendered, replace the sometimes florid style of the first novel. The voice and form did not come easily: Carduff's Chronology tells us, of the year 1935, "Plans autobiographical novel about death of his mother; writes seven drafts of the opening section but is happy with none of them." The work was completed with the help of the MacDowell Colony, in New Hampshire, and a patron in Urbana, who gave him, in exchange for grading papers, four dollars a month, room and board, and privacy. "Without this arrangement," he later said, "I doubt very much that the book would ever have been finished or that I would have continued to be a writer." He also credited his friend Robert Fitzgerald, the poet and translator, with persuading him that "life was tragic" and "literature was serious business."

The novel is not simply autobiographical; the lies of fiction were employed to get at the nearly unbearable heart of truth. Maxwell was ten when the flu seized his family and his mother died; his alter ego in the novel, Bunny, is eight. The subtracted two years sharpen the child's vulnerability and simplify his picture of events. He does not understand, for instance, that his mother is pregnant, even though other characters can see that she plainly is, and he has no grasp of pregnancy's timetable. Nor does the novel, divided into three parts, confine itself to his point of view; the actual death and its immediate aftermath are shown as perceived by Bunny's rough-and-tumble thirteen-year-old brother, Robert, and by his similarly masculine, unsympathetic father. If Bunny's section, titled "Whose Angel Child," is one of Maxwell's most brilliant transformations of memory, the next two, told from well beyond Bunny's point of view, testify to the author's powers of imagination.

Bunny, the angel child embodying the helpless infantile dependence upon maternal nurture that never totally leaves us, is, from his older brother's point of view, a tyrannical rival. When Robert prepares to say goodbye to their mother, who is heading off to what will prove to be a fatal hospital stay, "he started toward her, but Bunny was there first, tugging at her and sobbing wildly into her neck." As she comforts her younger son, her husband impatiently consults his watch, and Robert never does get to say his farewell. A few minutes later, Bunny is busy courting the good will of his new caretaker, Aunt Clara:

> Although his face was streaked with tears, Bunny was pleased with himself. Robert recognized the symptoms. And he saw that Bunny was making up to Aunt Clara—starting up the stairs in front of her as if she were the one person that he liked and depended on. Just as he did to Irene, or to Sophie, or to anybody who happened to be around and could get him what he wanted.

In the third section, the briefest, Clara returns Bunny to his grief-stricken father, James Morison, and the tearful child looms as a puzzling responsibility; he tells him, "There, there. You mustn't, son. You mustn't take on so. You'll be sick," and struggles "with the large buttons on the child's coat." Having determined in his daze of grief to sell the house and give the children to one of their aunts, so "there would be no trace . . . anywhere" of his dead wife, Elizabeth, he "turned to the doorway, and saw Bunny staring at him with Elizabeth's frightened eyes." The network of family connection reclaims him.

The social context of these private events is never lost sight of; the novel is not only about the mother's death but about Aunt Irene's broken marriage, and Robert's amputated leg, and the pious unction of Aunt Clara and her husband, Wilfred. Irrelevancies, including the terms of the First World War armistice, keep intruding. In the depths of his sorrow, "James caught a glimpse of a pocket knife: Wilfred was going to pare his finger nails." The widower wanders out into the snowy midnight, where the bizarre apparition of Crazy Jake, the local junk collector making his rounds, comes to James as a revelatory call back to life. The novel, like its predecessor, is somewhat supernatural; human awareness animates the inanimate ("All the lines and surfaces of the room bent toward his mother, so that when he looked at the pattern of the rug he saw it necessarily in relation to the toe of her shoe") and comforts the bereaved with intimations of a persisting ghost.

Novel after novel, the reconciliation of art and actuality continued to present stimulating difficulties for Maxwell. In describing, in *The New Yorker*, his friend the poet Louise Bogan, upon her death, in 1970, he said, "In whatever she wrote, the line of truth was exactly superimposed on the line of feeling": such an exacting superimposition represented his ideal. It was Bogan who, when, in 1940, he showed her a short story about two boys who meet at the school swimming pool, suggested that what he had written was the first chapter of a novel. As he worked for more than four years on the novel, she provided her responses to each new installment and at the end gave the work in progress its eventual title, *The Folded Leaf* (1945). Carduff's Note on the Texts relates that Maxwell in 1943 was "still struggling with the material" so noticeably that *The New Yorker* gave him five months' leave at full pay so that he could finish up; even then, it took several more drafts.

The core of the recalcitrant material was the second-most-traumatic event of his young life: he attempted suicide at the age of nineteen, while a sophomore at the University of Illinois. According to Carduff's Chronology, Maxwell had been courting a professor's daughter, Margaret Guild, and he introduced her to his Chicago high-school friend Jack Scully. When Jack and Margaret became lovers, Maxwell later recounted, "I thought I didn't want to live any more and cut my throat and wrists with a straight-edged razor." As the novel describes it, it is not the girl but the male friend whose defection pushes the slight, physically underdeveloped protagonist, Lymie Peters, into despair. In *The Folded Leaf* Maxwell describes, with a candor then rare in American fiction, homosexual passion. Swimming-pool and locker-room nudity leads to frenzied tussling, a bawdy frat initiation, a shared bed, a relationship anxiously servile on one side and gruffly commanding on the other, and, in the culminating reconciliation, a kiss on the lips. Though the physical beauty of the gruff partner, Spud, is repeatedly extolled, no description of physical interaction is more graphic than this:

> Lymie slept on his right side and Spud curled against him, with his fists in the hollow of Lymie's back. In five minutes the whole bed was warmed and Spud was sound asleep. It took Lymie longer, as a rule. He lay there, relaxed and drowsy, aware of the cold outside the covers and of the warmth coming to him from Spud, and Spud's odor, which was not stale or sweaty or like the odor of any other person. Then he moved his right foot until the outer part of the instep came in contact with Spud's bare toes, and from this one point of reality he swung out safely into darkness, into no sharing whatever.

Looking back, with more than a year of psychoanalysis with Theodor Reik behind him, Maxwell ascribed his suicide attempt to reading too much Walter de la Mare, which gave him a "poetic idea of life after death," a life in which he would be reunited with his mother. A debonair note penned from his hospital bed readily accepted a female fellow-student's invitation to a dance and referred to his attempt as "having failed to discover whether the moon really was made of green cheese." But the italicized section in *The Folded Leaf*, in which Lymie recalls swallowing iodine and then, as his stomach-ache recedes, trying to slash his way through his blood's insistent congealing, is the most harrowing page Maxwell ever wrote. Shirley Hazzard, in her eloquent tribute to Maxwell after his death, thought that his near suicide was "a spectral presence in Bill's equilibrium and in his greatest pleasures."

Bogan's advice to make a novel of his vignette of two boys meeting in a swimming pool led him, it may be, to pad the slender basic story with too many details of college life and ruminations, influenced by Frazer's *Golden Bough*, on tribal rites. His brave leap into sexual honesty was achieved with little assistance from his British models; Forster vaguely urged the male principals of *A Passage to India* to achieve Anglo-Indian connection, but left his novel about a homosexual affair, *Maurice*, unpublished at his death, and Virginia Woolf transmuted her androgyny into the mannered ingenuities of *Orlando*.

In 1945, the same year that *The Folded Leaf* was published—in a healthy total of two hundred thousand copies—Maxwell married Emily Gilman Noyes, a recent Smith graduate who had come to *The New Yorker* to interview for a possible job. She was, as those of us who knew them remember, his beautiful counterpart, with equally luminous dark eyes and the same enchanted aura of a truly rare creature. They died a week apart, after fifty-five years of marriage. As the first fruit of his happiness,

Maxwell began writing a novel for which Emily provided the title, *Time Will Darken It* (1948). It was not easy to work at it while carrying on his editorial duties, but it flowed:

> I seemed to have no more choice about this than one has about the background of a dream. . . . A set of characters seized me, and ran off with me. My function was simply to record what they said and did, rather than shape the goings on.

The events take place in a house just like Maxwell's childhood home, and deal with men and women based upon his kin, from Illinois and Mississippi. There is no character, no Bunny or Lymie, who can be readily identified with the author. An unprecedented reliance on dialogue, and the interjections of an exceptionally relaxed narrator, move the plot smoothly along. The plot is not easy to remember; there is a stove explosion in it, induced by kerosene, and a baby, but "the mysterious beauty of the commonplace" blurs individual incidents. Maxwell (who once said to me, "Plot, shmot") is ready to dispense with the contrivances of fiction altogether.

The second Library of America volume, *Later Novels and Stories*, shows Maxwell the person and Maxwell the writer becoming indistinguishable. It opens with the long anti-novel *The Château* (1961), based closely upon a trip to France that he and Emily took in 1948. A very thinly disguised couple, Harold and Barbara Rhodes, encounter the felicities and opacities of a foreign language and society. An appended section, "Some Explanations," rather impudently offers to clear up a few mysteries: "But if you really want to know why something happened, if explanations are what you care about, it is usually possible to come up with one. If necessary, it can be fabricated." The book gave him no end of trouble, though its inspiration—a tribute to the beauty of France and his happiness there—was instant: a preface to a later edition of *The Château* declared that, upon returning to America, "with my hat still on my head [I] sat down to my typewriter and wrote a page of notes for a novel. . . . For the next ten years I lived in my own private France, which I tried painstakingly to make real to the reader. It was my way of not coming home." He filled a carton with "unreadable" versions and enlisted the sometimes chastening advice of friends like Frank O'Connor, the Irish short-story writer, and Francis Steegmuller, the eminent scholar and translator from the French.

Maxwell's long period of painstaking struggle included his move from Harper & Brothers, then the usual publisher for *New Yorker* contributors, to Alfred A. Knopf, at the founder's invitation. Knopf's editor-in-chief, Harold Strauss, didn't much like the novel and wanted the second part cut, and might have prevailed had not Knopf himself intervened, genially telling his new author, "Have it whatever way you want." The book was assigned to the editor Judith Jones, a kindred spirit who edited Maxwell's volumes for Knopf until his death. *The Château* continued to give him trouble even after its publication. One difficulty, which had inhibited its writing, concerned the possible reaction of the French family portrayed in its gossamer fiction. He refused to let the book be published not only in France but in England, because "English books would get across the channel so easily." Nevertheless, his French friends did eventually discover the book, and one of its purported victims, who figured in it as a deaf old lady, told him, not unkindly, when, later, he visited her in Paris, "You were very naughty to write that book. Because you didn't speak French, you didn't understand things." Her son-in-law, overhearing this remark, contradicted it, saying, "He got everything right." Yet, when, later still, Maxwell attempted to obtain the family's permission to publish the book in France, word came back: "No, not now. Not ever."

It is good to be reminded, upon rereading, how delicious and dead-on *The Château* is. All the embarrassments and gratifications of European travel are preserved in the amber of Maxwell's much-pondered, seemingly casual prose. How familiar is the intimidating breakfast that greets the Rhodeses on their first morning in the handsome but chilly château, near Blois, which has been converted to a guesthouse:

> Talking in subdued tones, they discovered the china pitcher of coffee under a quilted cozy, and, under a large quilted pad, slices of bread that were hard as a rock and burned black around the edges from being toasted over a gas burner. The dining-room windows offered a prospect of wet gravel, long grass bent over by the weight of the rain, and dripping pine branches. The coffee was tepid.

It is 1948. Sugar is still rationed; war damage is still evident; blackout paper lingers on some of the château's windows; bicycles, cigarettes, and Citroëns are in short supply. France is wounded and poor and (a word that keeps cropping up in considerations of Maxwell) vulnerable. The Rhodeses in their innocence are in the first wave of tourists, and Harold, alternately ecstatic and wary, begins "to feel as if an unlimited amount of kindness had been deposited somewhere to his account and he had only to draw on it." He worries why this is, asking his hostess, "Are French people always kind and helpful to foreigners?" Rather hypochondriacally, he wonders how they would have been received had they come before the Marshall Plan was announced, but reassures himself that "the kindness he had met with everywhere was genuine." Harold is thirty-four, six years younger than Maxwell was in 1948, while Barbara is about Emily's age, the mid-twenties. The youthful intensity that Harold brings to even momentary relationships was a recognizable trait of his creator, who tells us of his hero:

> On meeting someone who interests him he goes toward that person unhesitatingly, as if this were the one moment they would ever have together, their one chance of knowing each other. . . . He lets the other person know, by the way he listens, by the sympathetic look in his brown eyes, that he wants to know everything; and at the same time the other person has the reassuring suspicion that Harold Rhodes will not ask questions it would be embarrassing to have to answer. He tries to attach people to him, not so that he can use them or so that they will add to his importance but only because he wants them to be a part of his life.

As if to relate more closely to the reader, to attach him or her more tightly to him, Maxwell grew increasingly impatient with the disguises and falsifications—the *pretenses*—of fiction. The busily omniscient modernist author of *Bright Center of Heaven* and *They Came Like Swallows* becomes, in the "Some Explanations" section of *The Château*, a postmodern exponent of unknowability: we are mysteries to one another, and an honest narrative retains its puzzles. His novella *So Long, See You Tomorrow* (1980) is the triumphant culmination of this approach, winning Maxwell—whose distinctive career had been unduly shy of awards—the Howells Medal from the American Academy of Arts and Letters, for the best novel of the previous five years. In his amusing acceptance speech, Maxwell made much of the fact that the box handed him, ostensibly containing the medal, was in fact empty, a precaution taken because at a previous occasion a freshly presented medal had been accidentally dropped and damaged. With a similarly disarming admission, he announced to the reader that the central story of *So Long, See You Tomorrow*—a vivid tale, based on childhood memories and a few photostatted stories from the local newspaper, of farm-country adultery, leading to double separation, murder, and suicide—was a fabrication:

> If any part of the following mixture of truth and fiction strikes the reader as unconvincing, he has my permission to disregard it. I would be content to stick to the facts if there were any.

On an early page, he calls his work a "memoir—if that's the right name for it." Maxwell knew, slightly and briefly, the boy identified as Cletus

Smith, a son of the murderer; years after the scandal, he spotted him in the corridor of a big Chicago high school and, shocked by surprise, said nothing to him. This failure haunted him; he never saw Cletus again. Giving this confession a context, he tells the reader the personal story already reflected in his fiction—his mother's death, the dishevelment of grief that followed, and the move with his father and stepmother to Chicago, leaving the idyll of his boyhood in Lincoln behind. This basic autobiography is imparted with a fresh stylistic firmness, a bluntness not possible when his near kin were alive, and a note of grievance not struck before: Why did nobody protect him from the brutal bullying by stronger children to which he was subjected as a delicate child? Why did neither his father nor his older brother talk to him about his mother's death? He describes his inability to master the piano, which his omni-competent father played with ease and pleasure, as "a small plot of ground on which I could oppose my father without being actively disobe-dient." His music teacher, we learn, was the go-between for the love let-ters his father received from the woman who became his second wife, and his son was enlisted to deliver them; he retrospectively marvels at this. As young teen-agers, he and Cletus, now living in Lincoln with his mother, meet to play, a bit dangerously, in the open framework of the new house that Maxwell's father is building on the edge of town, an emblematic framework that the narrator, now an elderly New York sophisticate, rediscovers in Alberto Giacometti's sculpture *The Palace at 4 A.M.*, at the Museum of Modern Art.

In the tragic romance that Maxwell, in our plain sight, invents, he shows, for a boy reared in a small city, a persuasive feel for the hard daily life of tenant farmers in the black-earth countryside around Lincoln; the bleak tale-within-a-tale of friendship and love gone miserably awry earns him a place as a prairie novelist in the naturalist Midwestern vein of Willa Cather and Hamlin Garland. The editors at *The New Yorker*, which printed *So Long, See You Tomorrow* in two installments, objected to the articulated thoughts of a dog, Trixie, belonging to Cletus's family, but Maxwell, as with the second section of *The Château*, got his way. The dog's thoughts, which are not complex, are one with his creator's lifelong habit of personifying furniture, objects, and rooms, sometimes giving them words to speak, within the wide discourse of things that present themselves to human awareness. His tender anthropomorphism here descends even upon a lowly ant, as Cletus "with a stick . . . drew crosses in the dirt, making life difficult for an ant who had business in that patch of bare ground."

The fault, if any, with *So Long, See You Tomorrow* lies in the device of the self-conscious, conspicuously confiding author: when the author becomes the main character, the other characters appear secondary, and their actions and decisions become ripples within the central feat of storytelling itself. Cletus hardly exists compared with the boy the narrator once was; remembering the two boys testing their equilibrium in the half-built house, Maxwell writes, "It occurs to me now that he was not very different from an imaginary playmate." When he searches his high-school yearbook for any image or mention of Cletus, he finds none, as if the character were fictional after all. The contract between writer and reader, which calls for a willing suspension of disbelief, has been quietly abrogated. When the author casts off his cloak of invisibility, and a novel is no longer (as Stendhal put it) "a mirror that strolls along a highway" but one that strolls down Memory Lane, he stands in front of the curtain either as a memoirist or as a fabulist exulting in the magic of make-believe; Maxwell in his shorter late works was now one and then the other.

Those already well acquainted with Maxwell's work will surely find something new and delightful in the forty fabulous "improvisations" that the editor has assembled from the twenty-one that Maxwell included in *All the Days and Nights: The Collected Stories* (1995) and nineteen published in sundry places between 1957 and 1999. The earliest of them all, "The Woodworker," was written in 1946, as a Christmas present for Emily. In a National Public Radio interview in 1995, he explained the genesis of this improvisatory mode:

> Actually, they began because my wife liked to have me tell her stories when we were in bed in the dark before we were falling asleep. And I didn't know where they came from, but I just said whatever came into my head and sometimes I would fall asleep in the middle of a story and she would shake me and say, "What happened next?" And I would struggle back into consciousness and tell her what happened next. And then I began to write them for occasions, for Christmas and birthdays. . . . And I would sit down at the typewriter and empty my mind entirely and see what came out on the typewriter, and something always did. And from the first sentence a story just unfolded.

His time in psychoanalysis possibly contributed to such easy and trusting access to the wellsprings of narration; certainly the tales, in their playful fairy-tale manner, tap into his deepest sensations and moral convictions, with no hint of preachiness. The last three in the volume, for instance — "The Dancing," "The Education of Her Majesty the Queen," and "Newton's Law"—are moving parables of marital fidelity, of altruism, and of death's heavy approach, respectively. There is a sparkle to these fairy tales that reminds us of *Bright Center of Heaven*, with its rueful comedy of brightness. Whereas Maxwell, according to Carduff's Chronology, before embarking on his book-length essay about his family history in *Ancestors* (1971), reread E. B. White for stylistic inspiration, his fables suggest Thurber's, and Thurber's faux-medieval children's books, fleshed out with a novelist's superior interest in human circumstances.

Maxwell's sublimely diffident and benign little essay "Nearing Ninety" touches on the pleasures of remembering:

> I have liked remembering almost as much as I have liked living. But now it is different, I have to be careful. I can ruin a night's sleep by suddenly, in the dark, thinking about some particular time in my life. Before I can stop myself, it is as if I had driven a mineshaft down through layers and layers of the past and must explore, relive, remember, reconsider, until daylight delivers me.

"A Final Report" (1963), inventorying the estate of Aunty Donald, a female neighbor who used to carry the author as a frail infant on a pillow, was the first short story that posed as a reminiscence and called the fictional Draperville Lincoln. He said, "I found I could use the first person without being long-winded or boring, and at the same time deal with experiences that were not improved by invention of any kind." Pieces of fiction closely portraying his father and his older brother followed—the latter, "A Game of Chess," signed with the pseudonym Gifford Brown to protect his brother's feelings. The marvellous very short story "Love" (1983) commemorated Miss Vera Brown, his fifth-grade teacher, whom all her students loved, and who died of tuberculosis at the age of twenty-three. The longer "Billie Dyer" (1989) drew liberally upon historical research in its portrait of a Lincoln black man who became a prominent physician in Kansas City and appeared as one of Ten Most Distinguished Men in Lincoln's centennial pageant, in 1953. The story gave its title to a collection of fictionalized memoirs, including among the subjects Maxwell's father's friends, his mother's brother Ted, his own brother Hap as a child, and William Dyer's sister Hattie, who had cared for Maxwell's Grandmother Blinn and then worked for the Maxwells for five years. In the story "The Front and the Back Parts of the House," Maxwell tells how, on a return visit home, he found Hattie in his Aunt Annette's kitchen and impulsively put his arms around her: "There was no response. Any more than if I had hugged a wooden post." He later traced the snub to an invented black drunk, in *Time Will Darken It*, whom Hattie took as a portrait of her husband. He was not, but Maxwell did believe, ever more strongly, that reality was the best fiction. In that same recollection, he says in an aside that even when the author imposes the disguise of a name on characters, actual names "are so much more convincing than the names he invents for them." Apropos of "Billie Dyer," he told an interviewer, "For me, 'fiction' lies not in whether a thing, the thing I am writing about, actually happened, but in the form of the writing . . . a story, which has a shape, a controlled effect, a satisfying conclusion—something that is, or attempts to be, a work of art."

He lived for art, its appreciation as well as its creation. In "Nearing Ninety," he likened death to lying down for a pleasant afternoon nap and found "unbearable" only the thought that "when people are dead they don't read books." His shapely, lively, gently rigorous memoirs, out of the abundance of heartfelt writing he bestowed on posterity, are most like being with Bill in life, at lunch in midtown or at home in the East Eighties, as he intently listened, and listened, and then said, in his soft dry voice, exactly the right thing.

Basically Decent

CHEEVER: *A Life*, by Blake Bailey. 779 pp. Knopf, 2009.

On the one hand, Blake Bailey's biography of John Cheever is a triumph of thorough research and unblinkered appraisal—a nearly eight-hundred-page labor of, if not love, faithful adherence. Cheever, the author of five novels and of many—121—of the most brilliant and memorable short stories *The New Yorker* has ever printed, died in 1982, at the age of seventy, and in the years since an unusually full and frank wealth of biographical material has accumulated: a memoiristic biography, *Home Before Dark* (1984), by his daughter, Susan; a collection of letters, edited and annotated by his son Benjamin (1988); a four-hundred-page biography by Scott Donaldson (1988); and, an embarrassment of riches and a *richesse* of embarrassment, the forty-three hundred pages, mostly typed single-space, of Cheever's private journals, stored at Harvard's Houghton Library and mined, by Robert Gottlieb, for six excerpts published in *The New Yorker* between August of 1990 and August of 1991. Bailey estimates himself to be one of possibly ten persons to have read through the journals, which he calls "a monument of tragicomic solipsism." His investigations have been tireless: from the murky details of Cheever's indubitably

Yankee ancestry and his career at Thayer Academy right through to the confidential lab reports on his terminal cancer, Bailey distills facts from the impressionistic version of reality that Cheever spun around himself. Of a certain Dr. Schulman, whose divulgences to his patient may have been less than candid, Bailey informs us in a footnote, "I'd very much like to hear Schulman's side of the story, but he died several years ago in a head-on collision," and of an aspiring writer assured by Cheever that he should submit his novel to a New York publisher "and they'll publish it right away," we learn in parenthesis, "'I never got it published,' the author reported thirty years later."

On the other hand, all this biographer's zeal makes a heavy, dispiriting read, to the point where even I, a reader often enraptured by Cheever's prose and an acquaintance who generally enjoyed his lively company, wanted the narrative, pursued in methodical chapters that tick past year after year, to hurry through the menacing miasma of a life which, for all the sparkle of its creative moments, brought so little happiness to its possessor and to those around him. The biography's valedictory pages are rather stunningly anticlimactic. Though *The Wapshot Chronicle* and *Falconer* appear on best-novels-of-the-century lists, "neither novel (nor any of Cheever's others) is read much anymore." "Academics tend to throw up their hands: Cheever is hardly taught at all in the classroom, where reputations are perpetuated." In Ossining, New York, where he lived for decades as the town's most prominent citizen, a move to name a short street after him was turned down at a town meeting, and only the main reading room of the public library honors his memory. The joy of the physical world, so often extolled in his fiction, and the triumph of his rise from an impoverished young immigrant to New York City to star literary status afforded him, it seems, far from enough comfort. Max Zimmer, the chief of the male acolytes and servitors brought into Cheever's life by his belated homosexual acknowledgment and by his gradually increasing debility, said at the time, "If there's someone who never loved himself, it was John." Twenty-five years later, Max, married and with a family, and having turned his literary ambitions into a livelihood as a technical writer, summed up his former mentor:

> He was extraordinarily blessed by anyone's standards . . . but he liked to say that all he had in life was an old dog. There was his despair. And then there was his inability to comprehend the despair and self-negation he inflicted on others.

Gottlieb, who as head of Knopf published two best-sellers (*The Stories of John Cheever, Falconer*) that at last gave Cheever the financial ease that had always eluded him, said, of his editorial selection from the journals, "There were . . . those who thought, 'Why are you doing this stuff? I don't want to read one more *word* about this dopey alcoholic fag.'"

The basic psychoanalysis of John Cheever has been amply delivered: the unwanted late child, threatened by his father's demand that the pregnancy be aborted; the smaller, sensitive brother of a larger, apparently successful brother; the helpless witness of his family's descent from prosperity to a poverty of which his mother's gift shop, in downtown Quincy, was a humiliating symbol; the homosexual yearnings suppressed in favor of mock-aristocratic respectability and an idealized domestic life; the fearfully copious drinking, bred of shyness and insecurity; and the eventual nick-of-time sobriety, with its attendant recognition of his homosexuality. Repression and expression: twin causes of complication and disharmony with others. Only dogs, usually old and feeble, didn't let him down.

Bailey's massive accounting did introduce, to me, some new paths of meditation upon Cheever's paradoxical character. In the mid-1930s, when he was selling a story now and then to various magazines and, as a protégé of Yaddo's Elizabeth Ames, running a launch on Lake George, he had an affair with Lila Refregier, the wife of a friend. "[I] always hoped that something, the love of a beautiful woman, would cure my ailments. I thought that Lila would lead me away from my jumpy past," he wrote in his journal in 1967. She, many years later, remembered him as "such a nice person, a basically decent person, with something in him that kept him from being completely decent." What was this something? What were his "ailments"? None of us are completely decent, but for decades he brought to social intercourse the impatience of an incorrigible alcoholic, his inmost attention focused on the next drink. He could be whimsically gracious to visiting strangers, but also shockingly rude; a friend from the Iowa Writers' Workshop recalled how Cheever got drunk before a scheduled meeting with some local Christian Scientists—"This was a big event for these people, and he just treated them like dirt." As a parent, he could be loving and companionable but was also sharply sarcastic and, in what he confided to his children, merciless. With the two oldest, Susan and Benjamin, he made no secret of his disappointments. Susan, who resembled him in her compulsions, wild streak, and intelligence, was overweight in spite of both parents' relentless nagging; she told Bailey, "In many ways I was a tremendous disappointment to them, I'm *proud* to say, and hope I've continued to be, since what they wanted me to be is pretty empty." Ben, when he came to read his father's confessional journals, was dismayed by how little he and his siblings figured in them; he underwent, during his first marriage, a period of determined estrangement. Federico, the youngest child and the only one not a writer (he became a law professor), attempted to be his father's caretaker in the worst days of Cheever's alcoholic decline, and takes the most level and dispassionate view of the fabulist as essentially clueless in the real world: "He was always at sea. He didn't understand how the world worked. He was forever being cheated by tradesmen. . . . He had no profession. He'd spent his entire career as a writer." Federico, known in the family as Fred, insisted, "No one, absolutely no one, shared his life with him. There was no one from whom he could get honest advice."

Certainly Cheever's voluminous harping, in his journals, on the sexual non-responsiveness of his wife, Mary, is obtuse and less than decent in perceiving no link between Mary's coolness and his daily drunkenness. Her attempts to get herself a separate life, through poetry and teaching and new associations, were transformed, in one of the last of his stories that could be called masterly, "The Ocean," into the high-voiced (Mary's distinct trait) heroine's attempt to poison her loving husband, and, in a later story published in *Esquire*, "The Fourth Alarm," into a wife's enthusiastic enlistment in the cast of an all-nude *Oh! Calcutta!*–like revue. Gleeful nudity was really his own thing; even while casting off his own sexual fetters, he remained prim and censorious toward others. There was, between his shadowy "proclivities" and his luminous work, an almost organic disconnect. We learn, in Bailey's biography, that Cheever, while in the Army in 1942, scored too low on the IQ test that would have qualified him for Officer Candidate School. He asked Mary to send him a book "on easy ways to get a high IQ," so he could raise himself "out of the moron class," but when he took the test a year later he still fell short of the requisite score of 110. He never rose above the rank of technical sergeant. His lack of formal education and of mathematics in general was surely a cause, but, still, it startles us that this impressively agile writer, with a prodigious memory that allowed him to recite a finished story verbatim, scored so averagely. Nor did he improve with age and celebrity; Smithers, the New York City sanatorium where he finally dried out, in 1975, had him upon admittance take "the abbreviated Shipley IQ test (scoring, as ever, in the high-average range)." A pre-Smithers CAT scan had disclosed "severe atrophy of the brain," which is cited as the possible cause of his intermittent spells of musical hallucination and "otherness." "I am in a bell jar or worse since I seem to respond to nothing that I see," he wrote. "I remember being as depressed in Rome. A cigarette butt in a cup, a formation of dust under a table seemed to represent the utter futility of staying alive."

John once said to me that a psychiatrist he was then seeing told him he was fascinated by criminality. He volunteered in 1971 to teach a course on the short story to inmates at Sing Sing. He befriended some of the inmates, especially a "pale, emaciated white man" and "serious loser" (son Fred's term) named Donald Lang, whom Cheever continued to associate with after his release. It was Lang who, hostilely, wondered "where a little shit like you gets the balls to come in here": even at the time of the prisoner riots at Attica, Cheever remained blithe, and later told an interviewer, "If the cons and I were lined up against a guard, I was all with the cons." The sinister power of many of his early stories entails an identification with criminality. In "Goodbye, My Brother," a story that ends with the idyllic vision of two women emerging from the sea, "naked, unshy, beautiful, and full of grace," the protagonist clubs his brother unconscious with a saltwater-soaked root. In "The Enormous Radio," the wife of a Sutton Place couple introduced as "the kind of people who seem to strike that satisfactory average of income, endeavor, and respectability that is reached by the statistical reports in college alumni bulletins" turns out, in her husband's furious accusations, to be guilty of stealing her sister's inheritance and going off to have an abortion as coolly as if she were going to Nassau. The central character of "Torch Song" feeds her morbid soul on a series of ailing, abusive lovers; the wronged secretary in "The Five-Forty-eight" boards a commuter train with her former employer and pulls a gun on him, forcing him, at his station, to kneel down and put his face in the dirt; the hero of "The House-breaker of Shady Hill" enters an affluent neighbor's house and steals his fat wallet. All these depths open up in conventional social scenery, sketched with a fond and lively eye for realistic detail.

Like Kafka and Kierkegaard, Cheever felt his own existence as a kind of mistake, a sin. His homosexuality, furtively explored in his boyhood but then suppressed in an apparently perfect marriage to bright, pretty Mary Winternitz (she was even the perfect size for him), seemed criminal; in his last years, he marvelled at the insouciance with which younger men, among them Allan Gurganus, accepted their own. Cheever's father, Frederick, a crusty Yankee shoe salesman, was—like his namesake, John's older brother—a vigorous participant in virile sports; he feared that with John he had "sired a fruit." As an adult, John "flung himself into icy pools and skated with a masculine swagger," and cultivated the reputation of a womanizer. In turn, he worried at Ben with suspicions that the boy had homosexual tendencies. Yet, in one of the least coherent of Cheever's late stories, "The Leaves, the Lion-Fish, and the Bear" (published in *Esquire* in 1974, and in a limited edition, by Sylvester & Orphanos, in 1980), he most nakedly sought to convince himself, and the reader, that male homosexuality is innocent, of a piece with his beloved world of light and air and female beauty. Two men, Estabrook and Stark, are brought together in a motel room in a snowstorm, drink four whiskeys each, and make love: "They were both inexperienced but they reverted passionately to the sexual horseplay of adolescence." In the morning,

> The ungainliness of two grown, drunken and naked men in one another's arms was manifest but Estabrook felt that he looked wonderfully on to some revelation of how lonely and unnatural man is and how deep and well-concealed are his confusions. Estabrook knew that he had done that, which by his lights he should not have done but he felt no remorse at all—he felt instead a kind of joy at seeing this much of himself and of another. There were no concealments at that hour. These men were what they were—bewildered, naked, carnal and content—and instead of freeing himself from Stark's embrace he put both arms around the stranger and drew him closer. . . . Estabrook was astonished to find that he could convince himself he had merely discovered something about himself and his kind. When he returned home at the end of the week, his wife looked as lovely as ever—lovelier—and lovely were the landscapes he beheld.

"How lonely and unnatural man is and how deep and well-concealed are his confusions"—no wonder Cheever's fiction is slighted in academia while Fitzgerald's collegiate romanticism is assigned. Cheever's characters are adult, full of adult darkness, corruption, and confusion. They are desirous, conflicted, alone, adrift. They do not achieve the crystalline stoicism, the defiant willed courage, of Hemingway's. Cheever was not a stoic; he was for most of his adult life a regular, indeed compulsive, communicant at Episcopal morning Mass. His errant protagonists move, in their fragile suburban simulacra of paradise, from one island of momentary happiness to the imperilled next. Johnny Hake, the housebreaker of Shady Hill, confides before revealing his turn to crime, "We have a nice house with a garden and a place outside for cooking meat, and on summer nights, sitting there with the kids and looking into the front of Christina's dress as she bends over to salt the steaks, or just gazing at the lights in heaven, I am as thrilled as I am thrilled by more hardy and dangerous pursuits, and I guess this is what is meant by the pain and sweetness of life." That is about as good as it gets in Cheeverland, and such glimmers of grace and well-being are all but smothered in Blake Bailey's painstaking chronology of a tormented man's daily struggle with himself.

FICTION NOW

Hugger-Mugger

THE MISSION SONG, by John le Carré. 339 pp. Little, Brown, 2006.

FORGETFULNESS, by Ward Just. 258 pp. Houghton Mifflin, 2006.

Hugger-mugger is part of life, especially under modern political conditions. For decades, it had its capital in the Kremlin and the inner councils of Beijing; now it gathers thickly but elusively in the alleys of Baghdad and the mountains of Pakistan and Afghanistan. Many outside the borders of the United States, and many within those borders, place its originating center in Washington, D.C.; there, as Robert Lowell wrote decades ago in his poem "July in Washington," "The stiff spokes of this wheel / touch the sore spots of the earth." John le Carré, the leading fictional dramatizer of the clandestine struggle between the capitalist West and the Communist bloc, maintains a brisk trade in hugger-mugger, searching in each new novel for a fresh locale, a newly sore spot. In *Our Game* (1995), it was the small, mostly Muslim republic of Ingushetia, striving for freedom from Russia, that huge remnant of the defunct Soviet Union; in *The Tailor of Panama* (1996), it was the bedevilled isthmus to our south; in *Single & Single* (1999), the financial underworld of the new Russian states; in *The Constant Gardener* (2000), perfidy in Kenya by the pharmaceutical industry. In *Absolute Friends* (2003), the sore spot became le Carré's fury at the American and British intervention in Iraq. Now, in *The Mission Song*, he has turned to Joseph Conrad's old heart of darkness itself, upriver on the Congo. The genocidal ethnic strife in neighboring Rwanda has spilled over the flagrantly porous eastern borders of the Democratic Republic of Congo, and a murderous mixture of refugee Rwandan *génocidaires*, warlord armies, meddlers from Uganda and Burundi, and mercenaries of many stripes prolongs and complicates a conflict that has claimed, since its commencement, in 1998, four million Congolese lives, most of them women and children, from war-related violence, hunger, and disease. At stake is eastern Congo's mineral wealth—copper, gold, diamonds, uranium, potential oil, and coltan, short for columbite-tantalite, described in *The Mission Song* as "a highly precious metal once found exclusively in the Eastern Congo." The definition, provided by the novel's narrator, colloquially continues, "If you were unwise enough to dismantle your cell phone, you would find an essential speck of it among the debris. For decades the United States has held strategic stockpiles of the stuff, a fact my clients learned to their cost when the Pentagon dumped tons of it on the world market." There's hugger-mugger for you.

Into the miserable chaos of eastern Congo le Carré's imagination projects the Syndicate, a neo-colonial group of capitalist entrepreneurs, headed by one Lord Brinkley and, though ostensibly multinational, English in its visible functionaries; it intends to enlist three leading warlords, colorfully sketched, in a coup that will establish in power, before destabilizing elections take place, a "self-proclaimed Congolese saviour chap, an ex-professor of something," called the Mwangaza. To this purpose—benign, mind you, "democracy at the end of a gun barrel" designed to "give the People a fair slice of the cake for once, and let peace break out," as well as assure the Syndicate its own more than fair slice— a conference is held on a nameless island in a northern sea. An interpreter is needed, and that brings in our narrator, Bruno Salvador, Salvo for short, the Congolese love child of an amorous mission priest of Irish-Norman descent and a village headman's beautiful daughter. She, a few months after giving birth to Salvo, "crept back to her kin and family, who weeks afterwards were massacred in their entirety by an aberrant tribe, right down to my last grandparent, uncle, cousin, distant aunt and half-brother or sister."

Salvo's voice is jaunty, as well it might be, since, thanks to his irregular upbringing in the care of missionaries, he learned not just Swahili and French but Lingala, Bemba, Shi, Kinyarwanda, and sundry other languages of Central Africa. Many of these come into play at the conference, which takes up about half of the novel. The Syndicate hosts plant electronic eavesdropping equipment in their guests' quarters, enriching the hugger-mugger. Salvo later explains it to Lord Brinkley, who seems as much in the dark as he is:

"The whole island was bugged, sir. Even the gazebo on the hilltop was bugged. Whenever Philip reckoned we'd reached a critical moment in negotiations, he'd call a recess, and I'd dive down to the boiler room and listen in, and relay the gist to Sam upstairs so that Philip and Maxie would be ahead of the game next time we convened. And take advice from the Syndicate and Philip's friends over the sat-phone when they needed it. Which was how we focussed on Haj. He did. Philip. Well, with Tabizi's help, I suppose. I was the unwitting instrument."

Hugger-mugger takes a lot of explaining, a lot of diagramming. An additional trouble with it, which keeps the suspense thriller, however skillful and polished, a subgenre, is that the novelist, manipulating his human counters on the board, must keep them somewhat blank, with selective disclosure of their inner lives, lest the killer or mole or whatever be prematurely unmasked. Even the most intimate human matters are turned into diagrams. Salvo's love, Hannah (not to be confused with his wife, Penelope), is thus addressed by an Americanized friend, Baptiste:

"Let's do facts. Here are the facts. Your friend here fucks you, right? Your friend's friend knows he fucks you, so he comes to your friend. And he tells your friend a story, which your friend repeats to you because he's fucking you. You are rightly incensed by this story, so you bring your friend who is fucking you to me, so that he can tell it all over again, which is what your friend's friend reckoned would happen all along. We call that *disinformation*."

Between information and disinformation, characters don't have much breathing room. We like Salvo well enough. He is humorous, for one thing, which is rare in this solemn shadow world of closed mouths and gritted teeth. With his interpreter's ear, he discriminates among varieties of spoken English, from "your Blairite wannabe-classless slur or your high-Tory curdled cockney" to "your Caribbean melody" and "the goneaway vowels" of his late father's Irish brogue. Finding himself thinking licentiously of another female hours after his inaugural orgy with Hannah, he excuses himself with the poetic thought "When Hannah has lit your lamp for you, it's natural to see other women in its rays." The reader in a mild way wants him, married to a faithless and ambitious white journalist, to find happiness with his pure-black* Hannah, an idealistic nurse and fellow-native of eastern Congo. The dandified, French-educated Haj, another such native, calls Salvo a "zebra," and *The Mission Song*

---

*When they hold hands for the first time, Salvo dotingly observes, "Here they are, my half-brown, half-Congolese hand and Hannah's authentic all-black version, with its pinky-white palm and fingernails." Later, she describes herself as "black-black."

neatly resolves for the biracial interpreter the quandary, in his half-English condition, of which stripe to settle on.

But the novel's resolutions, romantic and political, are achieved at an emotional distance, behind a thick protective layer of thriller awareness and thriller expectations. Le Carré has researched his chosen venue diligently (his acknowledgments thank "Jason Stearns of the International Crisis Group for his unique expertise and guidance during my brief visit to the Eastern Congo") and delivered an entertainment whose foremost passion is a commendable indignation over the sufferings of a large African population at the hands of berserk militias, corrupt if not altogether absent government, and, from the West, cold corporate greed. *The Mission Song* illuminates with animated personifications a portion of the globe's daily misery that tends to be, in American news, at least, murky and abstract. We are pleasantly surprised to learn, in a letter written by Haj to our hero from his flowery estate in Bukavu, on Lake Kivu, that the heart of darkness is not altogether dark: "The Goma cheese is still okay, the lights go out for three hours a day, but nobody puts out the lights on the fishing boats at night."

Forgetfulness, Ward Just's fifteenth novel, from its first pages drops the reader into a level deeper than animated news reports, into the wandering mind of a middle-aged Frenchwoman while she lies freezing and disabled by a broken ankle on the darkening slope of a mountain in the Pyrenees. Not that Just, a former war correspondent who has lived in many countries and at present divides his time between Paris and Martha's Vineyard, is unaware of the news: his publisher advertises that the novel "mixes the immediacy of the headlines with the moral and emotional intricacy of a le Carré novel." His immobilized heroine, Florette, who is married to an American painter, Thomas Railles, and lives with him in an Aquitaine village, St. Michel du Valcabrère, at the base of the mountain, allows her thoughts, "blown this way and that," to touch on overheard conversations between Thomas and two old American friends as they excitedly talk politics:

> Capitalism's responsibility for the turbulence of the modern world, its heedlessness and chaos, its savagery, its utter self-absorption, capitalism the canary in the mine-shaft. But it's what we have, isn't it? No turning the clocks back. Against the jihadists, we have capitalism. Will money trump faith?

It is Florette's misfortune, on a walk undertaken to get away for an hour from the conversation of these men, not only to have broken her ankle but to have fallen into the hands of four strangers, "dubious men who did not belong here." For a time, they carry her, with difficulty, down the slick, winding trail in a handy stretcher, but, as darkness closes in and snowflakes begin to fall, they change their minds, put her down on the cold ground, and, smoking many Gitanes, debate their situation in their inscrutable language. The author gives not only her interior monologue but some of the thoughts of the men as well—"None of this—the weather, their slow progress—was to their advantage. The rescue of the American woman was an error* and they would pay for it." While Florette speculates, dozes, and dreamily entertains memories, the reality of her worsening situation bears down upon the reader. Her mind keeps touching on the fact that she needs to pee, and when, as she euphorically pictures her rescue by Thomas and the villagers, her bladder lets go— "She peed and peed some more, such a strange sensation lying on her back but so welcome"—the release signals an end. It is a terrific scene, and Just's novel throughout, as it wanders and even maunders, has the electric potential of being terrific, with the kind of terrific that sneaks up out of the mundane. Compared with le Carré's, its slower, thicker prose seeks to drag visceral recognitions from us, keeping us alert and tense.

The fatal mountain, its lower slopes continuous with the Railleses' back yard, is called Big Papa, and Hemingway's influence on Just is hard to miss. The flatly declarative tone, both burnt-out and faintly pugnacious, has sudden recourse to the second person, like a jabbing finger: "Thomas . . . tried to remember the exact spot on the mountain where they had had their picnic but he could not; it was so long ago and all mountains looked the same when you were on them." Clauses are strung together bluntly, without fear of contradiction: "The mountain would always be in his vision when he was working unless he chose to turn his easel to the wall, and still he would be unable to forget, and he was a man who forgot things all the time." Thomas shares Hemingway's café vision of Europe, a sense that the restless American search for a good place finds its ease here:

> Thomas ordered a glass of wine and a dozen oysters and sat back to collect his thoughts. But he was unable to gather them coherently so he contented

---

*They deduce, wrongly, that she is American because in pleading with them she uses the word "Please." Also, in their minds, "It was well known that Americans were complainers when fate went against them. Americans believed they occupied a unique place in the world, a place under God's special benevolence. And if God was absent, anyone would do. The women were no better than the men. Wherever they went in the world they expected cooperation, and if they did not get it they complained."

himself watching the show, the bar arguments and laughter and the young lovers at the corner table who were making plans for the evening. His attention was noticed because the young woman caught Thomas's eye and winked; he tipped a glass in her direction. The *patron* continued to pull the porcelain handles, glass after glass.

Yet an American cozy in Paris is still an alien, and *Forgetfulness* strikes the theme of aliens early and often. The pain in Florette's leg is "migrating, an unwelcome undocumented alien." She is an alien in the realm of the mountain gods, who are "especially vengeful toward women who invaded their domain, careless uninvited intruders who did not know their rightful place in the world." The leader of her halfhearted rescuers, with his soft, coarse voice, reminds her of her crazily brutal father, of whom her mother explained, "He is an alien." North Africans in Europe, Hispanics in Thomas's once German-dominated hometown of LaBarre, Wisconsin, Slovenian bears imported to replace the extinct bears of the Pyrenees, solitary Englishmen in remotest France, like Thomas's 106-year-old neighbor St. John Granger—all are aliens. St. John Granger's great-niece, come from Pennsylvania to collect her inheritance, says to Thomas pointedly, "I have never understood people who choose to live outside their own country. Why is it important to them to live among strangers, speaking a foreign tongue, eternally on the outside of things. Who do they think they're kidding? It's like trying to escape your own shadow, except every time you look over your shoulder it's there." Thomas (whose career in portraiture specializes in strangers: "Strangers were his métier, fifteen minutes' acquaintance and a series of snapshots all he required") spends the novel looking over the shoulder at his past, with substantial doses of alcohol to clarify the view.

Forgetfulness is a portrait of loss and grief, as not only does Thomas's wife disappear but his two boyhood buddies from LaBarre, Russ Conlon and Bernhard Sindelar, cease to be vital presences in his life. He drifts irresolutely to America, where he rents a small house on a Maine island attached to the mainland by an irregular ferry. When Bernhard visits him, it is as an alien from a distasteful world of hugger-mugger: he has become the managing director of a security firm that supplies "ex–Special Forces, ex-SAS, ex–Foreign Legion, ex–Wehrmacht, ex-cops, ex–Chicago goons, Los Angeles shamuses" to whoever can pay for them. Bernhard and Russ both, after college, were recruited by the government for overseas intelligence work, as NOCs, under "non-official cover." From their feast of clandestine activity, they sometimes let fall crumbs, "odd jobs"— "the small change of snooping"—in Thomas's way; the roving painter found the work congenial, "the technique similar to portraiture, slipping into an alter ego," but the enchantment has long worn off. To Bernhard, espionage work was "coherence," a calling; "only chaos was inadmissible." While still in government service, he availed himself of French contacts to locate the four men who carried Florette halfway down Big Papa, and he invites Thomas to witness their interrogation in Le Havre. Here the reader, looking with the painter through the two-way mirror, becomes an alien, in the unfamiliar world of officially condoned torture, the vigorously applied leather bastinado and the cruelly languid inquisition:

> So, the Frenchman repeated, his voice light, almost cheerful. He turned his head to look at the clock . . . and Thomas noticed that it read five. The Frenchman looked at it for a minute or more, giving the impression that time was infinite. . . . Now he lowered his eyes to the file and began to read once again, except his posture was confidential, an attitude approaching intimacy. He had put his foot on the chair, leaning forward with the file in his thick hands, wetting his thumb again and again as he turned the mysterious pages.

Mysterious also is the liking that the inquisitor, Antoine, takes to surly Thomas, and the permission he grants him to spend two hours alone with the head suspect, a terrorist or smuggler who at last confirms, from his own angle, what we have already seen from Florette's. After this anticlimax of a climactic encounter, the novel and its hero's actions subside into incoherence: "He had lost the rhyme and melody of feelings. . . . Thomas believed he had made a mistake in Le Havre but he didn't know what it was. He imagined the mistake was some form of Lebenslüge. But what was the lie that allowed him to live? He wondered if the lie was his refusal to have blood on his hands. So the interrogation at Le Havre, too, was unresolved and marked by doubt."

Numerous threads are tugged—Thomas drinks more and has taken up smoking again; his doctor warns him he is headed for heart trouble; he walks the two miles from the village to his home in a cataclysmic thunderstorm and is blown into a ditch; he has farewell drinks with Granger's pro-Bush heir and her cell-phone-addicted husband, who have sold the house; he returns to America for the first time in ten years; he visits LaBarre, finds his family's house and everyone he knew gone, and is advised to get out of town; he spends time in New York with Russ, who has turned to writing short stories—but none of these threads pull Just's wide weave of incident and rumination tight. There are reverberant, dead-on patches of writing—the interrogation; the thunderstorm; riffs on billiards and churches and old jazz records and Billie Holiday; Thomas's memories of small-town life and of his father, a chain-smoking doctor, and of his first model and passionate lover, Karen, and his first New York show, where his churchly mother met Karen nude on canvas and in the tipsy flesh—but what Thomas makes of his retrospect and intends to do with the rest of his life is left in the Maine fog. The reader at this point could use a little of le Carré's well-crafted intricacy and tidy professional closure. Ward Just and his hero just fade away, somewhat like the Washington masters of hugger-mugger when jargon-prone Bernhard returns for a conference, "a general review of current operations with special attention to methods and sources, connecting dots while they walked back the cat, a dispirited and dispiriting exercise. Morale was terrible, the fudge factory's bureaucracy nervously broken down without energy enough for rebellion. Congress was asniff, the Pentagon frightened, and the White House in deep prayer." Well, such is life when hugger-mugger palls.

Classics Galore

Ten Days in the Hills, by Jane Smiley. 449 pp. Knopf, 2007.

Jane Smiley's capacious new novel does not give the reader a warm welcome—the first chapter is cloying and confusing—but accommodates him amply enough so that at the end, 450 pages later, he is reluctant to leave. The ten chapters are named for ten successive days; the first, "DAY ONE • Monday, March 24, 2003," comes five days after the U.S.-led coalition initiated the second Gulf War. More than seven thousand miles from Baghdad, in Pacific Palisades, California, within sight of the Getty Center shining on its hill, a woman simply called Elena awakes, full of memories of last night's Academy Awards ceremony, which she attended with her lover, Max, a well-known, if recently idle, director whose name is Nathan Maxwell, Anglicized (it is thought) from Milstein. She is fifty, he is fifty-eight. They met "in the cheese section at Gelson's last Easter, when Max was buying a Piave and Elena was buying a Gruyère de Comté and their hands touched as they both reached for the Époisses." They are still reaching for happiness together, and the reader is thrust into the middle of their mutual fascination. Max expresses the desire to make a movie, on the model of *My Dinner with André*, called *My Lovemaking with Elena*. She contemplates his penis, fondly dubbed the

Big Classic after they searched for its match in a dildo shop: "It lay over to the side, not a straight, evenly shaped sausage, but more of a baguette, bulging comfortably in the middle and then narrowing just below the cap." Physical facts and sensations are not stinted in the novel; as in *My Dinner with André*, there is no apparent hurry. He kisses her:

> The sensation of his lips on hers flowered along her cranial nerves, which she imagined fanning outward from her lips over and around her head like a spiderweb, and within that web was a darkness whose life she could better sense when her eyes were closed. When her eyes were open, she was all surface, facing the world. When her eyes were closed, she was all hollow, facing inward.

Similarly biform, each chapter is roughly half talk and half sex. The sexual descriptions set a new mark for explicitness in a work of non-pornographic intent. Smiley works in close focus, and from a male as well as a female point of view. A differently placed kiss:

> He kissed her again, and then pulled her labia into his mouth and ran his tongue over them. He could feel her clitoris begin to touch his upper lip. . . . Suddenly she shivered and cried out, and the aroma of her sex mushroomed around him, tangy and rich and erotic. "Ah ah ah ah ooh!" she said, and a moment later pushed his head away.

The talk, when the characters come up for air, ranges widely but keeps reverting to the Iraq war and the movie business. The acknowledgments at the book's end thank "every director and commentator on every DVD who bothered to add 'Special Features,'" and there can be no doubt that Smiley, whose previous novels have abundantly shared information on farming, horses, real estate, and medieval Scandinavian settlements in Greenland, has done her DVD research with characteristic thoroughness. Movies—classic and obscure, real and imaginary—pepper the conversation as Max's house suddenly fills up with guests. Realizing that his lovemaking with Elena this morning will be, thanks to the Big Classic's curious lack of coöperation, all foreplay, he ventures to the bathroom and reports, "The house is full of people." "How many people?" Elena asks. "Do we know them?" He answers, "Stoney, Charlie, Delphine, Cassie, Isabel, and Simon." Two more guests, the actress and singer Zoe Cunningham and her lover and guru, Paul Schmidt, show up and invite themselves to stay, which brings to a tidy ten the cast of this modern-day *Decameron*.

Of the ten, Max is a reputable director, Zoe a famous star, and Stoney

Whipple an agent, the relatively laid-back son of the legendary, recently deceased agent Jerry Whipple, born Hillel Goldman. The others are linked by kinship or friendship to these workers in the film industry: Delphine is Zoe's mother; Cassie Marshall, "notoriously well connected," runs an art gallery and is Delphine's best friend; Simon McCracken is Elena's twenty-year-old son by a former conjunction; Isabel is Max and Zoe's twenty-three-year-old daughter by their previous marriage to each other. Charlie Mannheim, the least Hollywood-flavored of the lot, has been Max's buddy since they were boys in New Jersey. He still lives in New Jersey, though he no longer works for the Pepsi-Cola corporation, and is separated from his wife, who bore him five children. The group has some ethnic diversity: Elena is a Midwesterner of Scandinavian blood, and Delphine a black Jamaican, which makes Zoe and Isabel, though both had white fathers, women of color. Isabel, as it happens, has been surreptitiously sleeping with Stoney since she was sixteen, and Paul, in a coincidence that doesn't go anywhere, was bullied as a child by Max, who doesn't recognize him behind his luxuriant guru's beard.

In their ten days of living together, the ten characters generate more chatter than drama. Simon impulsively, meaning no harm, punches Paul and knocks him off a kitchen barstool. Zoe, again impulsively, sleeps with Simon; when she blithely confesses to a displeased Paul, he asks, in good therapeutic manner, "Does that seem to you to have been appropriate?" She answers, "I don't know. It was fun. He's nice. I realize he punched you, but I'd sort of forgotten about that by the late afternoon." Charlie, feeling out of place, supports the Administration's position on Iraq and watches Isabel and Stoney copulate beside a swimming pool, then joins them in conversation about his pills (twenty-one a day), the herbal cure for his high PSA, and his negative take on Isabel's mother's hairy new lover. Some of this behavior teeters on the edge of the acceptable, but Smiley has put herself on the edge of acceptable novel-writing, replacing plot and suspense with something freer and more lifelike—casual talk, generally inconsequential but creating a lattice of cross-purpose in which emotions and attractions extend their tendrils.

When, in the seventh chapter, the house party moves, entire, higher into the hills, to a preposterously palatial Bel Air mansion being remodelled by a Russian plutocrat called Mike, who wants Max to make a movie of Gogol's violent, somewhat anti-Semitic historical tale *Taras Bulba*, things get a bit more eventful: children and parents have it out; lovers part or confirm their unions; and the mansion's two maids, Russians named Monique and Marya, interact with the guests. The funniest, most outrageous, and most revelatory sex scene occurs when Monique, a thirty-three-year-old beauty, emerges from a secret corridor into Charlie's bedroom. Bored with her life in the uncompleted palace, she has sized up the ten strangers and "thought I might find some entertainment among you." Also, Charlie patted her derrière while she was serving dinner, and in revenge she playfully spanks him. Fussy about his sleep, obsessed with his many medications, he grumpily resists her impudent provocations, declining an invitation to spank her in turn. When she tells him that, in her view, "most Americans are narrow-minded, ignorant, and provincial," he feels his face go red, and she quickly says, "So now are you ready to spank me? I have insulted your country; Americans hate that sort of thing." Monique is of a type rather new to American fiction's provinces, a post-Communist Russian, saucily enriching the free world with her native energy and bluntness. Finding hypochondriacal Charlie unresponsive, she demonstrates the successful use of a vibrator and admits to adoring her fellow-maid Marya's breasts:

> "Just today, while you in the dining room were eating your main course, we went into the pantry while Raphael wasn't looking, and I opened her shirt, which has snaps, you see, and then her bra, which has a front hook, and I sucked her tits like mad and also squatted down and brought myself. That's why we were a little late picking up the plates. I didn't even have time to wash my hands. . . ."

So much blithe sluttiness does at last excite the aging American, yet when he consummates his arousal in her body she sulks, saying, "I think penetration is going a little far." Charlie replies with American pragmatism, "There's nothing you can do about it now." Monique admits, "Your attitude seems quite strange to me." The twists of libido are wound into a cultural exchange, and the anatomy of our inward hollows is illuminated to surprising and comic effect.

Male arousal (not female, which seems to be pretty constant) is a main theme. Max's impotence on Day One has something to do with the Iraq war and Elena's furious, irrepressibly vocal dislike of it: "She had been wondering whether it was time to make that behavioral connection— war–angry woman–impotence—that would show that the failure was her fault." His potency revives ("It felt like he was entering her up to her throat, that's how big he was") on Day Nine, with the stimulus of a video camera handheld by her. The camera is symbolic, perhaps, of the return of his creative vocation. He is turned on, after much sensible reluctance, by the prospect of directing a remake of *Taras Bulba;* a previous film version came out in 1962, starring Yul Brynner.

* * *

The Iraq war, in its opening and apparently triumphant weeks, is analogous to the Black Death, which forms the background of *The Decameron*. Having evoked the full horror of the collapse of civil order in fourteenth-century Florence, Boccaccio conjures up an idyll of civilized society in the nearby countryside. His ten refugees from the city—seven women and three men (unlike the five and five of *Ten Days in the Hills*, and with no overt sexual interaction)—establish a model of decorous mutual entertainment, ten stories each for ten days, each day ruled by a rotating moderator, a "king" or a "queen." With the aid of servants conveniently brought along, all is delight and abundance and beauty, though some of the narratives are cruel and bawdy. Smiley's brief essay on *The Decameron* in her previous book, *Thirteen Ways of Looking at the Novel* (2005), couldn't be more admiring:

> The ten young people form a perfect comic society, surrounded by beauty and abundance that they can fully appreciate. . . . The treasury of detail in *The Decameron* defies analysis, or even sufficient appreciation. The reader . . . can only appreciate each brilliant turn of phrase or each exquisite irony or each perfect set piece and then move on to the next, allowing them, afterward, to coexist imperfectly but delightfully in the memory, until her enjoyment is renewed with another reading.

Ten Days in the Hills, unable to subdue its modern matter to a late-medieval courtliness and formality, strives for, and to an impressive extent achieves, a kindred richness. *Thirteen Ways of Looking at the Novel*, a lavish trove of sharp perceptions and firm opinions, includes the author's vision of her next novel—that is, the present one, foreseen as "spherical and self-contained, but jammed with things, like a spaceship made of Venetian glass, shining, intricate, and full of colors." The novel's pampered, restless Hollywood types, sheltered in two luxurious houses, the second of which is shot through with Byzantine fantasy, regale one another with stories from their lives, or found in the newspapers, and end each day, as people do in Hollywood, with a privately screened movie. Art of a sort is always on their minds, and their conversation and copulation possess, against the background of a distant tactical war, the benign glow of peaceful activity.

Smiley's introduction to *Thirteen Ways of Looking at the Novel* contains some abruptly confessional sentences. She tells us that in 2001, when she turned fifty-two and the World Trade Center was destroyed, she became stuck two-thirds of the way through a novel called *Good Faith*. Her dutiful, efficient life—"no drinking, no drugs, personal modesty and charm, good behavior on as many fronts as I could manage, a public life of agree-ability and professionalism"—foundered on fear, "fear of anthrax, fear of nuclear terrorism, fear of flying, fear of the future." At the same time, her "lover and partner" was diagnosed with heart disease and underwent some procedures that made her fear that she "would be bereft of his phys-ical presence," a gingerly phrasing that hints at religious belief: "I tried to remind myself of the illusory nature of the world and my conviction that death is a transition, not an end, to discipline my fears."

In *Ten Days in the Hills*, the yoga adept and holy man Paul assures the others of the illusory nature of the world, and Elena, pondering her lover's impotence, hypothesizes that he can love her "only if who she was was not so potent and concentrated as to irradiate him with the full inten-sity of her fears." Of these many characters, Smiley most fully inhabits Elena, but she seems to approve most fully of Zoe, who emerges in the novel's last pages as its heroine. Zoe, an indifferent mother and a fickle lover, at the age of forty-three still dominates any room she enters, and is possessed of a sublime carelessness. Stoney observes:

> Deep in her heart . . . she didn't care about men and her effect on them, or else she didn't care about her effect on anyone, men or women. . . . While Zoe was talking vivaciously, being friendly and affectionate and entertain-ing, and even seductive, Stoney saw that it meant nothing. . . . There was nothing she wanted even from her mother.

(Zoe and her non-attached guru are a good match, and their bodies know it. She and Max, for all their glamour, weren't: "Their bodies didn't get along. Where his eye was, there was her elbow. When he was awake, she was asleep. When she was awake, he was snoring. . . . They could not walk in step, and often didn't hear what each other said, even though they both had resonant voices.") Zoe's uncanny indifference helps her in negotiations: "They think they have to make her care, and of course they think the way to do that is money and perks and points and stuff. But she doesn't really seem to care about that, either, so they offer more." In the novel's last pages, when she has returned to her own home, we learn that "what she really liked, in the end, was a little stage in a little club, with Tony at the piano and good acoustics." She cares about singing, and, moved by hearing her singing in her room, the Russian staff in Mike's house has smuggled into the trunk of her car a painting that looks as serene and tender as a Vermeer but is more likely by "a woman of the period named Judith Leyster." In it, a young girl looks up from playing the recorder, about to smile, happy "in spite of deaths, in spite of the plagues and the fires and the massacres and the genocides and the clashes of armies and civilizations."

Smiley's raunchy survey of the human condition comes down to an endorsement of art and the relatively selfless, guileless artist. Her own art often warms itself at other works: in *A Thousand Acres*, she needed *King Lear* to get at all she knew about Iowa and farm life; *Ten Days in the Hills* not only channels *The Decameron* but holds an odd ghost of what is passingly alluded to as "the siege of Troy." Elena/Helen, mated with Max/Menelaus, is abducted, spiritually speaking, by Paul/Paris; the tenuous parallel helps explain the two peripheral women, Cassie and Delphine, who, like Cassandra and the Delphic oracle, can do little but offer ignored wisdom. Even if this ghost of a myth exists only in the critic's eye, two books discussed in *Thirteen Ways of Looking at the Novel*—*Taras Bulba* and *Uncle Tom's Cabin*—do figure in our Hollywood talkfest, and our hostess is herself a writer: Elena is composing, amid the mess of human imprecision, a tome with the schoolmarmish title *Here's How: To Do EVERYTHING Correctly!* In such an oblique self-parody, one can see the author smile.

A Boston Fable

RUN, by Ann Patchett. 295 pp. HarperCollins, 2007.

Ann Patchett has not rushed to follow up her breakthrough novel, *Bel Canto* (2001), which promoted her from private to major in the embattled ranks of literary novelists. Before *Bel Canto*, she had been admired but obscure, a veteran of academic postings and the grant wars. Her arresting, elegant thriller cast a hostage crisis in a nameless Latin American capital as an operatic illustration of the well-known truism that captives and captors tend, as the days of mutual exposure draw on, to develop solidarity with one another. Patchett's customarily benign view of human nature took on global import within the besieged mansion of a Peru-like nation's Vice-President. A lavish party—designed by the government to court the Japanese industrialist Mr. Hosokawa, with a special performance by the internationally esteemed lyric soprano Roxane Coss, whom he has long loved from afar—is invaded by a tiny army of terrorists, consisting of three revolutionary "generals" and fifteen youthful recruits from the impoverished countryside. Their hope is to kidnap the President, but he does not attend. The coup thus fails at the outset; negotiations drag on while government forces tunnel beneath the mansion and, in the barricaded cohabitation of hostages and hostage-takers, the ill-educated young rebels, exposed to the international array of refined party guests, reveal great talents for singing, chess, and romance. Two of the peasant soldiers turn out to be female, and a Mozartean weave of amorous attraction, lessons in literacy, and companionable soccer games unfurls before the tragic dénouement. One revolutionary ends thus: "A pain exploded up high in her chest and spit her out of this terrible world."

But this terrible world also holds art and love; of the book's many rave reviews, one called *Bel Canto* "the most romantic novel in years" and another promised readers that they would experience "a strange yearning to be kidnapped." The sole complaint about the saga that this reader heard was a protest, from a rigorous Jewish critic, that terrorists weren't really so nice. But Patchett's point, not only in this novel but in her well-regarded earlier three, seems to be that everybody is nice, given half a chance. In the pessimistic halls of literary fiction, she speaks up, gently but firmly, for human potential. *Bel Canto* sold moderately in hardcover, but hearty paperback sales and a sprinkling of prizes, including the PEN/Faulkner, put a conspicuous shine on a rare achievement, a captivating blend of political drama and aesthetic passion.

She followed it not with another novel but with a curiously loving memoir, *Truth & Beauty* (2004), describing her enduring relationship with a friend made in college and the Iowa Writers' Workshop, Lucy Grealy. Grealy had lost much of her jaw to childhood cancer and endured chemotherapy, radiation, and reconstructive surgery that still left her facially deformed. The success won by her first book, *Autobiography of a Face*, was dissipated in pills, drink, promiscuity, a funked novel contract, and, finally, heroin addiction, before her death, in 2002, at the age of thirty-nine. "I'm such a fuckup," she whispered in Patchett's ear at one of her many low points. The author achieved, silhouetted against this brightly lit portrait of a heedless life, a self-portrait, that of a tender-hearted, even-tempered, calmly dedicated artist who, as Grealy put it, is "always going to be fine." This somewhat dismissive reassurance ("It's your blessing and your curse") is offered when Patchett tries to interrupt the other woman's spectacular litany of misfortunes with some of her own troubles. Grealy, in the course of her self-destruction, diagnoses Patchett's tenacious attachment to her: "At least I can make you feel like a saint. That's what you've always wanted." Stung, Patchett retorts, "That's a terrible thing to say," but her works, habitually trafficking in the numinous and the magical, do show a loyalty to her Catholic upbringing.

Her masterly first novel, *The Patron Saint of Liars* (1992), tells of a pregnant young woman who flees her harmless husband and finds refuge in a Catholic home for unwed mothers, and her latest, *Run*, begins and ends with a holy statue, a painted rosewood carving of a red-haired Mary stolen from an Irish church in the mid-nineteenth century and brought to Boston by the descendants of the thief and his wife, who strikingly resembled the sacred image.

Compared with *Bel Canto*, as it must be, *Run* is a tricky and flimsy work, a stylized fable of families, of parenting and vocations and race, set in a Boston and a Cambridge that, though accurately enough mapped by a former fellow at Radcliffe's Bunting Institute, do not feel as solid underfoot, as welcoming to the roots of imagination, as, say, the Kentucky of *The Patron Saint of Liars* or the Los Angeles of *The Magician's Assistant* (1997). Primed for commercial success, the book seems overdesigned, sprinkled with ornamental snowflakes and lowercase headings, and the novel feels overplotted. The plot, indeed, is so dense, artfully leading us from one point of suspense to the next, that the reviewer can scarcely venture a summary without betraying some of its carefully hoarded and deployed mysteries.

It all takes place in twenty-four hours, during a New England snowstorm and its chilly, sunny aftermath, except for a last chapter in Baltimore five years later. Bernard Doyle, a Boston lawyer, politician, and former mayor, and his late wife, Bernadette, conceived one son, Sullivan, and, failing to produce another, adopted two black boys, Tip and Teddy, who are twenty-one and twenty at the time of the snowstorm. While, in this blinding storm, after the three Doyles have attended a talk in Cambridge by Jesse Jackson, the widower and Tip are arguing about the young man's lack of interest in politics and his obsessive interest in the million-plus dead fish preserved in Harvard's Museum of Comparative Zoology, Tip steps off a curb and an unknown black woman pushes him out of the path of an oncoming SUV that he has failed to notice. He gets away with a sprained ankle and a slight fracture of the fibula; the woman takes the brunt of the hit and sustains a broken hip, wrist, and rib, a concussion, and other injuries. Her eleven-year-old daughter, Kenya, gathers up her mother's possessions in the snow, accompanies her and the Doyles to Mount Auburn Hospital, and, though she wants to stay there with her mother, is persuaded to spend the night with the Doyles in their home in Boston's South End. Arriving, they discover that Sullivan has unexpectedly returned from Africa, where he has been for years, distributing antiretroviral drugs to the HIV-positive.

Even so brief a summary reveals a certain playfully schematic quality to the author's design: Tip and Teddy carry the names of New England's most popular recent politicians; Kenya bears one geographical name, and her mother, it turns out, is called Tennessee Moser; Sullivan, a scoffer, shares his name with his mother's uncle, Father John Sullivan, who, in his infirm last days in the old priests' home Regina Cleri, is besieged by ailing persons who believe, not entirely wrongly, that his touch has miraculous healing powers. Like Sister Evangeline in *The Patron Saint of Liars*, he is one of Patchett's holy clairvoyants;* though his appearances in *Run* are few, he is among the novel's more entertaining and persuasive characters. The kinship panorama, in a text that even with generous leading comes to fewer than three hundred pages, spreads itself thin: Teddy and Tip, physically hard to distinguish, are built around rather abstract traits—a religious, do-gooding streak and a categorizing scientific bent, respectively. Sullivan, whose bad behavior somehow cost his father his political career, behaves, as the reader sees him, with a spontaneous warmth and relational ability that make his black brothers look shy and stiff. Confined to a day's crowded comings and goings by foot and taxi in the snowbound streets, the novel relies heavily on retrospect and reminiscence—a lot of telling in proportion to the showing. Its willfully controlled mysteries keep us reading—what is the grudge between Sullivan and his father? what happened in Africa? who was the black woman who saved Tip's life? why were she and her child out so late in Cambridge? who is the other black woman she talks to in her delirium, also named Tennessee?—but even the most pliant reader can get to feeling manipulated. To be sure, no narrative divulges its facts all at once, but this one seems more of a tease than its earnest themes warrant.

Race—race in greater Boston, the birthplace of abolitionism yet within memory the site of some ugly anti-integration scuffles—is a muted issue in *Run*. Its live nerve is touched only in a stray sentence or two. Tip, at the Jesse Jackson speech, observes that the audience holds a majority of blacks: he, a black male raised with white advantages, "would have said it made no difference to him, when in fact that alertness he always carried in his neck, the alertness that stayed with him so consistently he never even noticed it anymore, temporarily released its grip and disappeared." The theme of political engagement, so natural an undercurrent in *Bel Canto*, here intrudes awkwardly in the form of fragments of famous speeches, from Eugene Debs to Martin Luther King; Doyle,

---

*Not the only similarity with her first, fuller novel: both involve benevolent Catholic institutions (for unwed mothers, for retired priests), contain an absent (dead or aloof) mother, and end with a young heroine in the dark as to the identity of one parent.

obsessed with politics, had demanded that Tip and Teddy memorize them.

The theme dearest to Patchett, of vocation or, in religious terms, calling, is somewhat precariously carried by the central figure of Kenya, an eleven-year-old slightly too good to be true. She has the wit to gather up her mother's wide-flung possessions in a snowstorm; when Tip, walking too far on crutches, comes down with hypothermia, she successfully applies her Girl Scout lessons in its treatment; and in her budding relations with the Doyles she shows a preternatural poise, lucidity, and courage. Her vocation is to run—hence the novel's stark title. She speeds around Harvard's Gordon Track, not only outracing the few others on it but stopping them dead: "All the other runners on the track had stopped now, the way dancers will stop when the soloist steps forward to dominate the floor." She is running, Patchett tells us, to outrun "the sight of her mother being hit by the car . . . and the girl at the front desk intimating that Kenya was not a person to be on this track." She outruns even her own niceness, meditating, "Nobody who was very, very nice would ever work this hard to take something they wanted only for themselves. Nice girls did not demand that everyone stop what they were doing and look at them but that was exactly what she asked for and what she got."

Yet the liberal, brotherly, quickly loving environment in which she finds herself offers not much more resistance to her running than air. Even at the outset of her ordeal of transformation, she finds that "people treat you nicely when you come to the emergency room in a police car." The people Kenya encounters in this novel are generally nice, and become nicer. Perhaps, in the diversity-positive twenty-first century, an African-American child encounters less resistance to her progress than used to be common; or perhaps Ann Patchett in her own niceness gives us the world as it should be, rather than as the dirty, abrasive place it is. As realism, her novel is pale; but as a metaphoric representation of growth it transcends its sentimentality. When Kenya awakes for the first time on the sunstruck top floor of the Doyle house, the waves of imagery express not just one eleven-year-old's arrival in a brighter, more affluent place but the civilized enlightenment whose glories should be available to all:

> She could do nothing but take in the light. It had never occurred to her before that all the places she had slept in her life had been dark, that her own apartment had never seen a minute of this kind of sun. Even in the middle of the day, every corner hung tight to its shadows and spread a dimness over the ceiling and walls. . . . But in the light that soaked this room a girl could read the spines of the books on the very top shelf. "*The Double Helix*," she said aloud. "*A Separate Peace.*" She stretched her arms down the

comforter and admired them. She spread her fingers wide apart and took her fingernails under consideration. Every bit of her was straight and strong and beautiful in this light. She glowed.

Nan, American Man

A FREE LIFE, by Ha Jin. 660 pp. Pantheon, 2007.

A critic cannot but be impressed by the courage and intellect of the Chinese-American writer Ha Jin. Born in 1956 of parents who were both military doctors, he volunteered for the People's Liberation Army at the age of fourteen and served five and a half years, near the northeast border with Russia. He began to take a keen interest in reading in his late teens, by which time the Cultural Revolution (1966–76) had closed down China's educational institutions and made any books but Mao's "little red book" suspect. In 1977, Heilongjiang University, in Harbin, admitted Ha Jin but assigned him to study English, even though it was his last choice on a list of preferences. After receiving a master's degree in American literature from Shandong University, in 1984, he came to the United States to do graduate work at Brandeis University. His plans to return to China as a teacher or a translator were changed by the Tiananmen Square massacre, in 1989: he decided to stay in America and to try to become a writer in English. A year later, he published his first book of poems, *Between Silences;* during the 1990s, he published five more volumes in English, including two collections of short stories, one of which, *Ocean of Words* (1996), won the PEN/Hemingway Award and the other, *Under the Red Flag* (1997), received the Flannery O'Connor Award for Short Fiction. His busy decade—in the course of which he was hired, in 1993, by Emory University, in Atlanta, as an instructor in poetry—was capped by a first novel, *Waiting*, which received the 1999 National Book Award and the 2000 PEN/Faulkner. His prize-winning command of English has a few precedents, notably Conrad and Nabokov, but neither made the leap out of a language as remote from the Indo-European group, in grammar and vocabulary, in scriptural practice and literary tradition, as Mandarin.

Waiting is impeccably written, in a sober prose that does nothing to call attention to itself and yet capably delivers images, characters, sensations, feelings, and even, in a basically oppressive and static situation, bits of comedy and glimpses of natural beauty. The very modesty of the tone strengthens the reader's belief that this is how private lives were conducted amid the convulsions of the Cultural Revolution, as ancient customs worked with a fear-ridden Communist bureaucracy to stifle normal human appetites. Every simple, bleak detail has the fascination of the hitherto unknown; not a word of Ha Jin's hard-won English seems out of place or wasted. And the first-person, rather documentary prose of a subsequent prize-winning novel, *War Trash* (2004), flows as smoothly.

His new novel, *A Free Life*, is a relatively lumpy and uncomfortable work, of which a first draft, he confides in a brief afterword, was completed in the year 2000. In an interview that same year, with Book reporter.com, he declared, "I plan to write at least two books about the American immigrant experience, but not my own story." However, his dedication to *A Free Life* reads, "To Lisha and Wen, who lived this book"; Lisha and Wen are the names of Ha Jin's wife and son. Nan Wu, the hero of *A Free Life*, also has a wife and son, Pingping and Taotao, and shares with Lin Kong, the protagonist of *Waiting*, a cautious, bookish nature and a nagging indecision in regard to a basic emotional choice. Lin, a military doctor, vacillates between a homely wife, chosen by his parents, back in his village, and a nurse in the hospital where he is posted; Nan, a graduate student adrift in America, cannot stop longing for an adored early love, Beina, who spurned him. Ha Jin, not an author averse to flat statement, spells out on an early page the dilemmas facing his hero, as he welcomes his six-year-old son to the United States:

> He was uncertain of his future and what to do about his life, not to mention his marriage. The truth was that he just didn't love his wife that much, and she knew it. Pingping knew he was still enamored of his ex-girlfriend, Beina, though that woman was far away in China. It seemed very likely to Nan that Pingping might walk out on him one of these days. Yet now he was all the more convinced that they must live in this country to let their son grow into an American. He must make sure that Taotao would stay out of the cycle of violence that had beset their native land for centuries. The boy must be spared the endless, gratuitous suffering to which the Chinese were as accustomed as if their whole existence depended on it.

As Nan's search for security takes him from Massachusetts to New York City and then to the Atlanta area, he encounters a colorful variety of Chinese expatriates and relatively native Americans, and copes with a series of lowly jobs, but the reader follows him for more than 650 pages in pursuit of resolutions to the issues posed in the sentences above. Will Nan get over Beina? Will he start to write poetry in English? Will Pingping ever be loved by Nan as she deserves? What kind of American will Tao-tao become? Will the Wus get to own two cars and pay off their mort-gage? It's a long trudge, but, then, so is assimilation.

In an interview with Powell's Books, Ha Jin said that "the core of the immigrant experience" was "how to learn the language—or give up learning the language!—but without the absolute mastery of the language, which is impossible for an immigrant." A striking typographical device conveys the inside and outside of the linguistic problem. Conversations in Mandarin are rendered in italicized English, and we observe Nan's brain and tongue functioning at a sophisticated level. When he applies to an Italian-American supervisor called Don for the job of night watchman at a factory in Watertown, we hear him speak as he sounds to Americans:

> "I worked for one and a half years at zer Waltham Medical Center, as a cahstodian. Here's recommendation by my former bawss. . . . My bawss was sacked, so we got laid all together."
>
> "You got what?" Don asked with a start. A young secretary at another desk tittered and turned her pallid face toward the two men.
>
> Realizing he'd left out the adverb "off," Nan amended, "Sorry, sorry, they used anozzer company, so we all got laid off."

And Nan's English isn't that bad; how else do you pronounce "boss"? But he is tripped up here by a peculiarity of English that Dr. Johnson noted in the preface to his dictionary:

> There is [a] kind of composition more frequent in our language than perhaps in any other, from which arises to foreigners the greatest difficulty. We modify the signification of many verbs by a particle subjoined; as to *come off* [and] innumerable expressions of the same kind, of which some appear wildly irregular, being so far distant from the sense of the simple words, that no sagacity will be able to trace the steps by which they arrived at the present use.

Nan agrees: "Compared with written Chinese, English was indeed a language of common people, despite being hard to master, its grammatical rules too loose and its idioms defying logic." Elsewhere, becoming a handy American householder, he thinks, "Now he loved hand tools—oh, the infinite varieties of American tools, each designed for one purpose, just like the vast English vocabulary, each word denoting precisely one thing or one idea." This exacting language is "like a body of water in which he had to learn how to swim and breathe, even though he'd feel out of his element whenever he used it."

Reaching to encompass the American scene, Ha Jin's English in *A Free Life* shows more small solecisms than in his Chinese novels. We get a character "licking his compressed teeth," a tennis court "studded with yellow balls," "a giant disk [the sun] flaming a good part of the eastern sky," "the lobby was swarmed with people," a victim of violence "booted half to death," eyes that "shone with a stiff light like a crazed man's," a "hilly gravel road filled with doglegs," a swimmer "crawl-stroking to the shore." Complicated facial maneuvers challenge our ability to visualize: "Unconsciously she combed her upper lip with her teeth"; "His eyebrows were tilting as he kept pushing his flat nose with his knuckle"; "His eyes turned rhomboidal and his face nearly purple." Metaphorical overload can occur: "In his arms, she was like a meatball with love handles." Some expressions feel translated from the Mandarin: Pingping says, "You shouldn't have mixed our decision with his fault," and Nan thinks, "If his wife had been of two hearts with him, this family would have fallen apart long ago." Rare words wander in from the hinterlands of the English dictionary: "a short-haired barmaid in a lavender skong," "It was mizzling," "empleomaniac." Taotao's vocabulary has grown to the point where he exclaims, in the midst of a family tussle, "Ow! Don't break my humerus!" Anxiously, Nan keeps seeking verdicts on his use of English: one consultant pronounces it "fluid, elegant, and slightly old-fashioned," whereas another, an editor of a little magazine called *Arrows*, testily tells him, "The way you use the language is too clumsy. For a native speaker like myself, it almost amounts to an insult."

Unfortunately, the novel rarely gathers the kind of momentum that lets us overlook its language. The processes that Ha Jin is concerned to describe—survival and adjustment in an alien land, the firming up of a literary vocation, the emergence of marital and family harmony after the shocks of transplantation—are incremental, breaking into many small chapters but yielding few dramatic crises. The central action consists of the Wus' decision to buy a small Chinese restaurant, the Gold Wok, in a half-deserted mall northeast of Atlanta, and their recipes (foreshadowed by some knowledgeable descriptions of food preparation in *Waiting*) for success. The sheaf of the fictional Nan Wu's poems at the very end is meant to serve, like Zhivago's at the end of Pasternak's *Doctor Zhivago*, as the narrative's climax and triumph. Of the other Chinese literary aspirants Nan meets in the United States, he alone commits to English-language production; the others, after their overseas adventures, return to the Chinese mainland and the constraints and rewards there. One returnee, Danning Meng, achieves official approval and financial security, but tells Nan, when the expatriate visits:

The higher-ups want us to write about dead people and ancient events because this is a way to make us less subversive and more inconsequential. It's their means of containing China's creative energy and talents. The saddest part is that in this way we can produce only transient work.

Bao Yuan, who employs Nan for a time on his short-lived Mandarin quarterly in New York, *New Lines*, becomes a painter and makes an American splash, establishing himself in a studio near Nashville with students and a rich patron, but Nan, nothing if not critical, "could find little originality in these paintings" and distrusts the American sunniness and exuberance that have replaced Bao's old "depressive agitation, the jaundiced view of the world, and the dark despair." Sure enough, Bao's paintings bring less and less money, though he turns them out ever faster. When last seen, he has taken a Chinese bride, a factory owner's daughter, and cranked out a series of bad paintings of Shanghai: "Obviously Bao, cashing in on his success, had diffused his energy and lost his creative center. This troubled Nan." Not that Nan's American friend, the poet Dick Harrison, is any more of an inspiration, scrambling up the rickety ladder of grants and workshops and prizes and influential acquaintances that enable ascent in a capitalist versifier's thoroughly academic career.

Ha Jin's description of American life—laborious, money-mad, philistine, and cheesy (there is apparently no cheese in China)—is not apt to trigger a wave of immigration. Asked the difference between China and America, Nan says, "In China every day I wanted to jump up and fight wiz someone. . . . Zere you have to fight to survive, but here I don't want to fight wiz anyone, as eef I lost my spirit." To himself, he thinks, "The louder I shout, the bigger a fool I'll make of myself. I feel like a crippled man here." Nevertheless, he elects to stay, in this "lonesome, unfathomable, overwhelming land." The Wus strive less to let America in than to squeeze China out—"squeeze every bit of it out of themselves!" Nan tells Danning, "*I spit at China, because it treats its citizens like gullible children and always prevents them from growing up into real individuals. It demands nothing but obedience.*"

Toward the end of *A Free Life*, our hero wins, in a supermarket raffle, an airline ticket from Atlanta to Beijing and back. He visits his parents and sees signs of the new prosperity but is unmoved: "He wondered why so many overseas Chinese would retire to this mad country where you had to bribe and feast others to get anything done. Clearly a person like him wouldn't be able to survive here. Now he wanted all the more to live and die in America." The flight reminds him of his first flight, in 1985, to America, and how he and his fellow travelers, most of whom were students, had been nauseated by a certain smell in the plane—so much so that it made some of them unable to swallow the in-flight meal of Parmesan chicken served in a plastic dish. It was a typical American odor that sickened some new arrivals. Everywhere in the United States there was this sweetish smell, like a kind of chemical, especially in the supermarket, where even vegetables and fruits had it. Then one day in the following week Nan suddenly found that his nose could no longer detect it.

His assimilation had begun.

An Upstate Saga

AMERICA AMERICA, by Ethan Canin. 458 pp. Random House, 2008.

From the first pages of Ethan Canin's new novel, *America America*, we feel in safe hands; the prospects are panoramic, and the prose, in the author's preferred first-person mode ("It's easier to write when you have a voice," he has said), is ruminative, ominous, and all set to confide a story. The narrator, Corey Sifter, is a fifty-year-old journalist and the publisher of the *Speaker-Sentinel*, a surviving independent newspaper in a town called Saline, an hour south of Buffalo and twenty miles east of Lake Erie. Corey has just attended, on a Saturday in late September 2006, as "the smell of rotting apples was drifting up from the meadow," the funeral of Senator Henry Bonwiller, a local product who in 1972 made a strong but thwarted run at the Democratic nomination for the Presidency of the United States. Bonwiller was eighty-nine, and had been out of politics for twenty-eight years. The funeral is well attended, though hints of two old scandals, alluded to as "Anodyne Energy" and "Silverton Orchards," shadow the graveside tributes to "the greatest liberal member of the United States Congress since Sam Rayburn." One elderly couple linger as the sod is being laid on Bonwiller's grave, and the man, with a carved cane and "that certain kind of roughly determined American face that you see less and less often around here," kneels and weeps. Corey recognizes him: "There was no one else alive now who knew." Thereby hangs the tale.

And a complicated, many-layered epic of class, politics, sex, death, and social history it is, shuttling between the twenty-first-century present and the crowded events of 1971–72, with thorough retrospectives of the narrator's education and romantic life and the region's development as the fiefdom of a single family, the Metareys. Eoghan Metarey and his father were penniless Scots immigrants who in 1890 opened a hardware store and by 1900 held a firm grip on the area's wealth of hardwood forests and granite and limestone quarries. Eoghan and his younger son, Liam, successively administered the family fortune out of a "twenty-four-room brick and stone Edwardian manor" called Aberdeen West, which occupied "the apex of a hundred-thousand-acre triangle of land." Not only that, but the streets and houses of Saline ("which if you're an old-timer rhymes with *malign*, and if you're a newcomer, with *machine*") were "almost entirely built and owned" by the Metareys. At sixteen, Corey, the son of a self-educated and well-regarded plumber, is summoned by Liam to come and work at Aberdeen West. (An unassuming tycoon, Liam comes knocking at the Sifters' back porch; his wife shops locally and his two daughters attend the local high school, "like all the rest of us.") Corey's story becomes part *David Copperfield* and part *An American Tragedy*, with less suspense than either. We know from the outset that Corey has survived and prospered, and how much tragedy can attach to a senator who lives to be eighty-nine?

Like Dickens, Canin has an unabashed fantastic streak. *Emperor of the Air* (1988), his first and best-known book, a collection of delicately soulful short stories, contains much weird behavior: a mild-mannered retired high-school teacher creeps into the night to poison his neighbor's trees with a jar of voracious red insects; another retiree stares at fish in the local aquarium all day and reads poetry while his wife hallucinates that a man is at her window; two adult sisters cope with their mother's incorrigible shoplifting; a boy stows away in the trunk of his golf-mad father's car and shouts out during the man's backseat lovemaking. As in Sherwood Anderson's *Winesburg, Ohio*, unfulfilled longings twist conformity out of shape. In *America America*, Christian Metarey, one of the teen-age sisters, appears on the roof outside Corey's window and, climbing by moonlight, leads him eighty feet up into a giant pine tree, and, toward the end of the novel, Corey's father, nearing ninety, bends down and with a key scratches two sentences by Karl Marx into the wet concrete of a huge mall under construction. Such actions seem more emblematic than plausible. The characters, especially young and innocent Corey, struggle through a fog of imperfect and fitful revelation; after thirty years of hindsight, the narrator is still groping to understand the novel's central events.

How unambiguously, in contrast, Dreiser moves in inexorable, laboriously detailed linear fashion through the interlocking steps of his own upstate tragedy, shining a glaring light of sympathy upon the motives, intentions, and hopes not only of his principals but of the secondary characters who enforce society's unforgiving will—the doctor who denies Roberta an abortion, the district attorney who leads the hunt for Clyde and then his legal prosecution, the clergyman whom Clyde's mother sends to her condemned son in a vain quest for a mitigating circumstance that will save his life. A ponderous weight of authorial omniscience and compassion conveys the reality—single, one-shot, claustrophobically limited—of life itself. So, too, with the other naturalists, from Jack London to Edith Wharton, of a century ago. Canin, contrariwise, pieces together, in mostly short takes, an airy collage of imperfect memory and fleeting impression, as Corey's recollection of a bygone misfortune, half-comprehendingly witnessed in his adolescence, keeps reverting to pleased contemplation of his bourgeois present.

Of the book's many strands, it is Corey's boyhood in worker housing, under the protection of his two admirable parents and the patronage of the Metareys, that comes across most warmly, and the political strand, generating national headlines, that seems thinnest and least persuasive. Canin carefully wedges his fictional Senator Bonwiller into an election year, 1972, when, in fact, a Democratic field including a fading Hubert Humphrey, an allegedly weepy Edmund Muskie, and a glowering George Wallace yielded the nomination to George McGovern, who lost to an incumbent Richard Nixon in one of the worst defeats in the history of Presidential contests. Nixon, who figures in this novel as a sinister background of fathomless conspiracy, was a touching character in Canin's short story "Vins Fins," which appeared in *The New Yorker* and presented political drama as it usually is, surreally fighting for our attention in a stew of personal and domestic happenstance. Born in 1960, Canin has done his homework. To verify Bonwiller's substance as a near President, he lists the notables in attendance at a campaign reception at Aberdeen West:

George Meany was there, and Carl Stokes, and Averell Harriman, and Senator Kennedy and Senator Mansfield and even Senator Humphrey. So were Arthur Schlesinger and Betty Friedan, and the famous young journalist David Halberstam, who'd just written a book called *The Best and the Brightest.* . . . G. V. Trawbridge [fictional] was in the crowd, too, and I assume now that both men must have agreed to take everything on deep background. I saw Daniel Patrick Moynihan and Shirley Chisholm, also, and even though now I can remember all these names and faces so clearly, the truth is that on the afternoon itself all but Trawbridge and Humphrey and Kennedy had to be pointed out to me. . . . But I can also say that without any prompting I sensed instantly that there was a new sort of stature in the room.

Though it gives an old-timer like me pleasure to picture George Meany and Betty Friedan in affable discourse, to anyone under forty these names can't spark much electricity and, in any case, paradoxically weaken Aberdeen West's claims on the imagination. Corey, with a brand-new driver's license in his pocket, drives Bonwiller around, but the Senator, away from a microphone, is taciturn and, until his downfall, remains pretty much a cipher. Though Corey's father remembers him as "the best friend the working men of this country have ever had," it is hard to believe that Liam Metarey, committing his heart and resources to the campaign, does not see the feet of clay so easily visible to, among others, his daughter Clara.

In Corey's perspective, his patron and mentor, for all his generosity, also remains a bit remote and blank, coming to life mainly in this endearing glimpse:

> If anything broke, anywhere on the estate, he tried to fix it himself; and if he couldn't fix it, he dismantled it, salvaging it for parts, which he filed in the work barn in a ceiling-high collection of labeled drawers—themselves salvaged, it seemed, from some country auction. It was as though he were two men: the Liam Metarey who owned a third of Carrol Township and spoke with the governor just about every week, and another man entirely—a determined, hardscrabble Scotsman trying to scrape out a living on rocky land. His toolshed looked like the barn of an ingenious and frugal farmer.

This paternalistic tinkerer presides over a considerably dishevelled household—a wife who drinks and flies a biplane, a son who quits school and enters the Vietnam-era military, and two daughters who compete for Corey's attention in contrasting, though equally unbalanced, styles. But their collective eccentricities feel halfhearted and joyless compared with those in *Emperor of the Air*, especially those of the family in "American Beauty," whose jaunty dysfunction carries on guilt-free, with no burden of dynastic responsibility or need to further a novel's plot. In Carrol Township, their bohemian ilk, the Millburys, dwell in the "failed farmland" ten miles north of Saline, in a trailer on the edge of a bog; the man of the house has dropped out of a job as a chemist at DuPont, the mother paints, all six children are homeschooled, and, to make ends meet, the family grows and sells raspberries and blueberries. However, a daughter, Trieste, is bright enough to win an internship with the *Speaker-Sentinel*, and, cantankerous and ill-dressed as she is, gives the newspaper's publisher an opportunity for mentorship and, guardedly, friendship. Their conversations, often about the ancient Bonwiller affair, form another of the book's strands, though Trieste is less a character than a case study: "I could hear in her northern hillbilly voice what I later came to learn was her father's social opposition. A thin flow of bile mixed with a radical amusement and a fierce, uncooked intelligence, nourished over decades of contemplation. Class upon class."

The novel's best characters, the ones we come to know well enough to care about, are women: the narrator's concerned, loving mother, and the Senator's mistress and victim, JoEllen Charney. "Victim" only in a sense: it is someone else, it turns out, who allows this inconvenient female—like Dreiser's Clyde Griffiths with Roberta Alden—to die. Corey sees her only once, waiting alone in a restaurant, "a young woman in a flowered hat and dark glasses who looked like what I imagined a schoolteacher on vacation might look like." Among the male characters, Corey's father grows another dimension as a widower, and his former neighbor and best friend, Mr. McGowar, whose voice has been destroyed by fifty years of inhaling stone dust, makes a big splash on the page with the words he writes out in capital letters. One thinks of what an Upton Sinclair would have made of Mr. McGowar—a handicapped former quarryman, a symbol of industry's pitiless exploitation—but Canin plays his phonetic misspellings for laughs and lets him live cheerfully to the age (at last sighting) of ninety-five.

Canin writes *America America* in various tenses—present and past—and styles, from staccato to stentorian. Much of the second half of the book feels like an after-dinner speech, a rumbling aftermath of Bonwiller's "tumble," studded with reverberant quotations, including Auden's "Musée des Beaux Arts" in its totality. The staccato style, sometimes merely hasty and melodramatic, is effectively internalized as Corey's mother suddenly collapses and dies:

> Then comes the first blow. The feeling in her arm dropping away. A shudder over the shoulder and scalp. Then the swooning. The floor pitching. She tries to right herself. Grabs the counter. Use the other arm, silly. Lift! Silly girl! Up, Anna Bainbridge. Up! The floor, wrapping her. All over, how can it do that? Cheeks on the cold linoleum. Funny, funny! God, it's turning me over. The black and white. The squares. A wave turning me over.

Bainbridge was her maiden name, not to be confused with the names of G. V. Trawbridge and Corey's prep-school roommate, Astor Highbridge—a nice guy in spite of his tony moniker.

Though his fictions often deal with distracted goof-offs, Canin knows the world of hard work. He itemizes practical procedures and labels humble implements: "buck knives," "compression nuts," "a slider" (to carry a man under a car), an "old Rockwell impact wrench," a "drip line," "wash trays." Newspapers are "arranged on café sticks in the library," and the Metarey sisters have the family dog "stretched out on their laps like a white stadium blanket they were sharing." Commanding, throughout, an impressive geographical range of reference, Canin brings this once wild, winter-bitten region to life with the eye of a native:

> The terrain is really quite beautiful here, a run of shallow, overlapping hills that are staggered from the glacier's first track through the basin, the low horizon striped by the shadows of their intersecting valleys.

When the bulldozers move in, we mourn the felling of the Metareys' age-old oaks as if they were a New World cherry orchard. Corruption and change are what the novel is about, and the hazards of being taken up by the rich. Out of loyalty to the Metareys, Corey lies that he has never seen Bonwiller take a drink; to conceal the damage to a drunkenly driven car, Bonwiller and Liam Metarey, that benign benefactor, involve the boy in a deliberate crash in which he could have been seriously injured. "Nasty sport" is how Corey's wife sums up the Metareys' meddling in his life. And his subsequent rise in social status may not be on merit alone: he has married money. "The history of riches is always sordid," he declares to the reader, and is informed by his father that progress is "always half criminal." As for journalism, he concludes that "undifferentiated silt-panning for truth serves the citizenry only slightly better than a crooked disregard for it." Maybe the reader isn't in such safe hands after all. *America America* doesn't quite earn its grand, double-barrelled title, but its reach is wide and its touch often masterly.

Relative Strangers

THE STORY OF A MARRIAGE, by Andrew Sean Greer. 195 pp. Farrar, Straus & Giroux, 2008.

Andrew Sean Greer's 2004 novel, *The Confessions of Max Tivoli*, quite brilliantly fulfilled the difficult task it set itself—to show the life of a man born old, who over the decades grows backward into infancy and, finally, nonexistence. This narrative feat had been attempted before, by Scott Fitzgerald and Gabriel Brownstein, but never at such length or with such loving ingenuity. At every turn of Max Tivoli's wrong-way life, his predicaments and discoveries light up the human condition as the odd thing it is and, in addition, give us vivid glimpses of San Francisco's colorful past as it evolves toward the present. The novel is magical; but such a success holds for the novelist a temptation to cast himself as a magician and stuff his sleeves for every performance onstage. The great Nabokov did something like this, out of loyalty to illusion and deception as aesthetic ideals, but Greer is possessed by a serious tenderness that asks the reader's indulgence in a way that the aloof Russian would have scorned. Greer's new novel, *The Story of a Marriage*, announces its basic illusion on the first page:

> We think we know the ones we love.
> Our husbands, our wives . . . We think we love them. But what we love turns out to be a poor translation, a translation we ourselves have made, from a language we barely know. . . . One morning we awaken. Beside us, that familiar sleeping body in the bed: a new kind of stranger.

Presto, change-o. The plot meant to illustrate these ruminations is so tricky, so full of pregnant pauses and delayed revelations, that to discuss it at all is to risk giving it all away. The narrator, who reveals herself as female on the second page, when she speaks of her husband, does not let the reader know until page 48 that she is African-American. The news at this point is startling, but, in retrospect, it explains a certain tense reserve in her voice, an embattled, extra-keen awareness of the passing pedestrians and car headlights in the neighborhood of Ocean Beach, north of San Francisco. Hers, it turns out, at this juncture in the early 1950s, is the only black family, across the street from the only Jews. Perhaps her name, Pearl, was a tip-off, or the skimming mention of her eating in "a special area of a department-store lunchroom, after being turned away by two others," but this reader was taken by surprise. Mysteries cling to some fraught asides and constrained locutions in Pearl's tale. "Pearlie, I need you to marry me" is Holland Cook's way of proposing marriage, and "Let me take care of you" her inspired way of announcing her availability. A shadow, a rumor, of disability hangs over the groom from the start, though everyone agrees that he is an attractive, amiable man.

Pearl and Holland were children together in Kentucky, and began to walk home from school hand in hand as teen-agers. In 1943, Pearl helps Holland's mother protect the young man from the draft, tutoring him and bringing him fond but chaste companionship in the farmhouse room where he is hidden. An illness blows his cover—Pearl goes for the doctor, who is not the one to report him to the police. The draft officer, failing to elicit any philosophical beliefs that would justify draft evasion, gruffly releases him, saying, "Boy, I can't put down that you're just a goddamn

Negro coward. I can't have that in my district." Holland is drafted, and is
severely burned when his transport ship is sunk. Meanwhile, Pearl has
been enlisted by a Mr. Pinker to be a factory worker on the West Coast
and to spy on her fellow-employees ("Be a finker . . . for Mr. Pinker!").
She complies, and then becomes a WAVE. When, shortly after the war,
she spots Holland on a Bay Area park bench, she is "startled to see such
despair on his square handsome face." On his side, he doesn't even recognize her. As she pursues the relationship, he warns her, "You don't know
me, not really."

Nevertheless, they marry. They have a child, Sonny, who contracted
polio and must wear leg braces. Holland is a caring father but a moody
husband, frequently away on business. At home, he sleeps in his own bedroom. In deference to his supposed fragility, Pearl pampers him to the
remarkable extent of clipping disturbing items from the newspaper. But
all seems relatively well in Ocean Beach until, in 1953, an elegantly
dressed white man, with a broken nose and "sapphirine" blue eyes, rings
at the door; he introduces himself to Pearl as Buzz Drumer and, before
long, tells her that he and Holland met in an Army hospital and fell in
love. Buzz has come to get his former lover back. He is rich, and offers to
recompense Pearl if she conspires with him in his lovelorn plan to carry
Holland off. She hates the idea, but feels helpless: "I did not know how to
fight a white man; I was born without that muscle."

So the novel settles in as a murky triangle and a historical study of how
American blacks, gays, and pacifists fared "in tragic times"—that is,
between 1943 and 1953. Greer was born in 1970. Though there is no dis-
puting the contemporary facts and news stories—the Second World
War, rationing, harsh government treatment of conscientious objectors
("conchies"), racial discrimination, homophobia, Cold War militancy,
McCarthyism, the Rosenbergs, air-raid drills, Korea—with which Greer
sketches the background of his story, this background has a papery feel to
it. I was put in mind of Henry James's ringing admonitions, in 1901, to
Sarah Orne Jewett on the subject of "historical" fiction:

> You may multiply the little facts that can be got from pictures and docu-
> ments, relics and prints, as much as you like—*the* real thing is almost
> impossible to do, and in its essence the whole effect is as nought. . . . You
> have to *think* with your modern apparatus a man, a woman—or rather
> fifty—whose own thinking was intensely otherwise conditioned, you have
> to simplify back by an amazing *tour de force*—and even then it's all humbug.

Whose own thinking was intensely otherwise conditioned: in indicting, however lightly, the hard-hearted prejudices and dispositions of an earlier

time, a writer emphasizes that he has transcended them. He invisibly substitutes his own (in favor of, say, love, tolerance, and peace), with their
own possibly less-than-eternal shelf life. A merely diagrammatic situation emerges. Greer is so tactful, so respectful, in his portrait of the colored Cook family that they seem colorless. His crucial invention, Buzz
Drumer, a homosexual passionate enough to sacrifice his fortune for a
bygone conquest, is oddly unpersuasive as gay; he is so politely and persistently attentive to Pearl that he is mistaken for her lover. Questions of
plausibility arise. Would one male American really try, in 1953, to buy
another from his wife? Would she, even if a daughter of the Jim Crow
South, so docilely entertain the proposition? Would any couple be as
radically noncommunicative as Pearl and Holland? And would even a
woman who (as Holland admiringly says) "talked like a book" tell her
story with such meanders of metaphor as:

> You cannot go around in grief and panic every day; people will not let you,
> they will coax you with tea and tell you to move on, bake cakes and paint
> walls. You can hardly blame them; after all, we learned long ago that
> the world would fall apart and the cities would be left to the animals and
> the clambering vines if grief, like a mad king, were allowed to ascend the
> throne.

Greer is a prose writer who works on the edge of the overcooked, and
there is nothing wrong with that—better that than raw—but can we
believe in these highly seasoned sentences as passing through Pearl's
mind?

> A crowd of untended roses lay bruised and blue in the dusk, alongside
> daylilies caught in the act of closing for the night. In one, a tardy bee
> engrossed herself among the shutting petals. Perhaps she would linger too
> late, become trapped in the mindless flower, struggling in there all night,
> exhausting herself to death in that pollened room.

A bit too artfully, Greer spices up the narrative by making parts of it,
while we watch, vanish: a crucial question is interrupted by an air-raid
alarm and left unanswered; a "rain-soaked Holland" appears to Pearl in a
dream "with a single word on his lips," which we never hear; Buzz gives
his central revelation and proposal—a speech "pieced . . . together over
the years, practiced . . . over and over in his bachelor's rooms downtown"—in brief paraphrase. On page 79, a soda jerk, William Platt, mut-
ters "an ugly term" as Pearl leaves a drugstore; on page 144 we learn that
the term was "nigger." When Pearl hears that a training accident has
affected Platt instead of her husband, she mumbles "something before I

burst into tears"; we have only to turn the page to discover that the mumbled phrase was "*Thank God.*" It is Buzz Drumer's shame, perhaps, that delays the explanation for his missing little-finger joint—noticed when Pearl meets him on page 22—until page 156. It is involuntary memory that leads Pearl, while dancing with a man who hums along with the tune, to fish for "something that was gone the instant I felt it," and that turns out to be the memory of young Holland, back in Kentucky, "humming in my ear as he lay beside me on the bed." The author more than once evokes the magician's art, tempting us to equate legerdemain with storytelling and the course of love: "to place the gleaming coin on the heartline of your hand, close it in a fist, and—presto!—a moment later the fingers open on barren palm."

The Confessions of Max Tivoli was a beautiful stunt, a defiance of actual gravity that needed, to hold it down, all the trinkets of realism, of period detail and solemn aphorism that Greer could provide. *The Story of a Marriage*, taking up the ambiguities of intimacy and bisexuality, is a less unusual human story, that of "changeling boys . . . and the poor girls who someday would love them." Women loving gay men in vain crop up not infrequently in today's fiction—in Ann Patchett's *The Magician's Assistant* and Thomas Mallon's *Fellow Travelers*, for instance—and scarcely need the complications of race and mid-twentieth-century mores to heighten their predicament. Greer overestimated, perhaps, his theme's fragile strangeness, and armored it in the equivalent of the painstakingly provided Fifties cars and clothes and background music of *Far from Heaven*, a blue-lit mock-weeper of a movie. The industriously unearthed details of how West Coast soda jerks used to concoct a "Suicide" or of how truly precarious amusement-park rides used to be are fascinating in themselves but marginal to his tale of divided loyalties and dangerous affections.

The Story of a Marriage is a sentimental, overwritten, overcalculated novel that nevertheless proves moving in the end, pulling all its prevarications and flourishes into an affirmation of the unideal everyday as it was experienced fifty years ago and, possibly, as it is even now. Looking back, Pearl decrees, "The way we lived would not do, would not hold"; the improvements in overt racial and sexual attitudes, the lessening of received prohibitions and discriminations, need just a glance at our national campaigns and headliners to be confirmed. But even in benighted yesteryear, life had to be lived, on the terms available. Greer's instincts vote, in the end, for the unmagical and enduring, for the brightness of—to give away the novel's last two words—"startling day."

Dreamy Wilderness

A Mercy, by Toni Morrison. 167 pp. Knopf, 2008.

Toni Morrison has a habit, perhaps traceable to the pernicious influence of William Faulkner, of plunging into the narrative before the reader has a clue to what is going on. Her newest novel, *A Mercy*, begins with some kind of confession from an unnamed voice, which reassures the reader:

> Don't be afraid. My telling can't hurt you in spite of what I have done and I promise to lie quietly in the dark—weeping perhaps or occasionally seeing the blood once more—but I will never again unfold my limbs to rise up and bare teeth.

We are not totally reassured. What blood? What have you (there in the dark) done? The darkness does not quickly lift: "You can think what I tell you a confession, if you like, but one full of curiosities familiar only in dreams and during those moments when a dog's profile plays in the steam of a kettle." A dog's profile does what? "That night"—what night?—"I see a minha mãe standing hand in hand with her little boy, my shoes jamming the pocket of her apron. Other signs need more time to understand."

"Minha mãe," research reveals, is Portuguese for "my mother," and in time we come to comprehend that it is 1690 in Virginia, and that the narrator is a sixteen-year-old black girl called Florens, who was, at her mother's plea, impulsively adopted, eight years ago, by a white proprietor ("Sir" to Florens), in partial settlement of a debt owed him by an insolvent slave owner from Portugal called "Senhor." This adoption constitutes the "mercy" of the novel's title. It landed Florens in a tobacco-growing homestead populated by Sir, known to the wider world as Jacob Vaark; his wife, Rebekka, a hardy and good-natured London native the servants call "Mistress"; Lina, short for Messalina, a Native American whose people have been decimated by a plague, and who was sold to Jacob by the Presbyterians who rescued her; and Sorrow, a "mongrelized" young woman, possibly a sea captain's daughter, who survived a shipwreck and was named Sorrow by a sawyer's wife who cared for her until passing her on to the hospitable Sir and Mistress.

When Sir dies, this household becomes a typical Toni Morrison collection of "unmastered women," each spinning "her own web of thoughts unavailable to anyone else." Their vulnerable isolation is mitigated but not wholly relieved by the presence of Scully and Willard, two indentured laborers, homosexual and white, whom Sir hired to work on his quixotically ambitious mansion. After Sir's death, they continue to work for the widow's pay. With amiable competence the two men deliver a child that Sorrow, who watched Lina drown her first-born, has conceived. The infant safely born, Sorrow, long addled in the head by her shipboard traumas and her illusion of an advisory companion called Twin, regains focus and, to cap this saga of freighted names, renames herself:

> She had looked into her daughter's eyes; saw in them the gray glisten of a winter sea while a ship sailed by-the-lee. "I am your mother," she said. "My name is Complete."

From her first novel, *The Bluest Eye* (1970), Morrison has worked, in line with the celebrated Faulknerian dictum that the past is not past, in a historical vein. *The Bluest Eye*, bristling with Sixties literary trickiness and protest, takes place in 1940–41, and includes an impressionistic map of black flight from the South during the Depression; stepping momentarily into the present, the author offers a retrospective history of the structure "on the southeast corner of Broadway and Thirty-fifth Street in Lorain, Ohio," which for the time of the narrative was occupied by the doomed and desperate family of the thorough loser Cholly Breedlove. *Sula* (1974) opens with an elegiac sketch of a black neighborhood called the Bottom and dates its chapters from 1919 to 1965. *Song of Solomon* (1977) begins four years after Lindbergh's 1927 transatlantic flight, and *Beloved* (1987) takes place a few years after the Civil War. The shorter novels that have followed—*Jazz* (1992), *Paradise* (1997), and *Love* (2003)—share a reminiscing narrator and a sense of the bygone as reverie, a dream that it is a struggle to remember and piece together.

A Mercy takes us deeper into the bygone than any of Morrison's previous novels, into a Southern seaboard still up for grabs: "1682 and Virginia was still a mess." Indian tribes haunt the endless forest; the colonial claims of the Swedes and the Dutch have been recently repelled, and "from one year to another any stretch might be claimed by a church, controlled by a Company or become the private property of a royal's gift to a son or a favorite." Jacob Vaark, coming from England to take possession of 120 acres bequeathed to him by an uncle he never met, rides from Chesapeake Bay into "Maryland which, at the moment, belonged to the king. Entirely." The advantage of this private ownership is that the province allows trade with foreign markets, and Vaark is more trader than farmer at heart. The disadvantage is that "the palatinate was Romish to the core. Priests strode openly in its towns; their temples menaced its squares; their sinister missions cropped up at the edge of native villages." His claim lies in Protestant Virginia, "seven miles from a hamlet founded by Separatists" who "had bolted from their brethren over the question of the Chosen versus the universal nature of salvation."

In *A Mercy*, Morrison's epic sense of place and time overshadows her depiction of people; she does better at finding poetry in this raw, scrappy colonial world than in populating another installment of her noble and necessary fictional project of exposing the infamies of slavery and the hardships of being African-American. The white characters in *A Mercy* come to life more readily than the black, and they less ambiguously dramatize America's discovery and settlement. When Vaark strides ashore through the Chesapeake surf, he is Adam treading the edge of an immense Eden:

> Fog, Atlantic and reeking of plant life, blanketed the bay and slowed him. . . . Unlike the English fogs he had known since he could walk . . . this one was sun fired, turning the world into thick, hot gold. Penetrating it was like struggling through a dream.

When Rebekka sails to join him, the indignities of steerage are made vivid—she says, "I shat among strangers for six weeks to get to this land"—as are the squalor and the gory public executions of the London she is escaping:

> The intermittent skirmishes of men against men, arrows against powder, fire against hatchet that she heard of could not match the gore of what she had seen since childhood. The pile of frisky, still living entrails held before the felon's eyes then thrown into a bucket and tossed into the Thames; fingers trembling for a lost torso; the hair of a woman guilty of mayhem bright with flame.

When she disembarks in the New World, "the absence of city and shipboard stench rocked her into a kind of drunkenness that it took years to sober up from and take sweet air for granted. Rain itself became a brand-new thing: clean, sootless water falling from the sky."

In so keenly relished a near-virgin environment, the diverse "unmastered women" blend into the moonlit trees like guilty phantoms in Hawthorne. Rebekka, who had disembarked as a "plump, comely and capable" young woman, becomes Mistress, and, after gamely coping with the wilderness, the deaths of three infant children and of a five-year-old daughter, and her husband's untimely dying, takes to her bed in despair:

"The wide untrammeled space that once thrilled her became vacancy. A commanding and oppressive absence." She falls ill, and orders Florens to find a free black man she thinks might cure her, a blacksmith once hired by Jacob to help build "the grandest house in the whole region"—an unfinished mansion that becomes haunted by its dead master. Florens, travelling alone through the forest primeval, finds the blacksmith living in a cabin, where he has taken in a small male foundling. He returns to Mistress and effects a talking cure: he is asked, "Am I dying?" and answers, "No. The sickness is dead, not you." Back in the cabin, Florens proves to be a poor babysitter for the foundling and injures his arm. The blacksmith, who had been her lover, is displeased.

Much has been made of Florens's love for the blacksmith:

> The shine of water runs down your spine and I have shock at myself for wanting to lick there. I run away into the cowshed to stop this thing from happening inside me. Nothing stops it. There is only you. Nothing outside of you. My eyes not my stomach are the hungry parts of me. There will never be enough time to look how you move.

Alternating chapters take up her stream of consciousness during the hazardous journey to deliver Mistress's message and reunite with the blacksmith. Morrison has invented for her feverish mind a compressed, anti-grammatical diction unlike any recorded patois: "Both times are full of danger and I am expel. . . . With you my body is pleasure is safe is belonging. I can never not have you have me. . . . I dream a dream that dreams back at me." But the blacksmith rebuffs her love in his own firm diction: "Own yourself, woman, and leave us be. . . . You are nothing but wilderness. No constraint. No mind." This rejection and her subsequent violence are the bitter fruit, then, of the mercy that Jacob Vaark showed her when she was eight years old.

On the book's last pages, Florens's mother somehow returns, as a disembodied voice, and recounts her enslavement in Africa ("The men guarding we and selling we are black"), the Middle Passage in "a house made to float on the sea," her arrival in the hot sun and cane fields of Barbados, and her "breaking in"—her rape—by white men who apologize and give her an orange as consolation. Florens and her brother resulted, and the moment of Vaark's mercy is recalled, but, in view of the dismal outcome, to sadly little point. Of the other characters, Lina remains a stoic source of domestic order and a nurturing substitute mother to Florens when she is docile, before love turns her feral. Sorrow/Complete is, in this household of orphans, the hardest to picture, her color included. By her own account, she had always lived on a ship and was brought to land by "mermaids. I mean whales." The insemination that produced her two pregnancies is mysterious, at least to me. She seems less a participant in the action than a visitor from the Land of Allegory, a "curly-haired goose girl" whose only human skills are sewing, acquired on shipboard, and, eventually, motherhood.

In the dark stew of seventeenth-century America, procreation seems the one intelligible process available to slave, servant, and mistress, and love and disease threaten to make martyrs of them all. Motherhood is so powerful a force in Morrison's universe as to be partly malevolent; its untidy agents, menstruation and sex and birth, come with a menacing difficulty. This author's early novels were breakthroughs into the experience of African-Americans as refracted in the poetic and indignant perceptions of a black woman from Lorain, Ohio; as Morrison moves deeper into a more visionary realism, a betranced pessimism saps her plots of the urgency that hope imparts to human adventures. *A Mercy* begins where it ends, with a white man casually answering a slave mother's plea, but he dies, and she fades into slavery's myriads, and the child goes mad with love. Varied and authoritative and frequently beautiful though the language is, it circles around a vision, both turgid and static, of a new world turning old, and poisoned from the start.

AMERICANA

Famous Aimee

AIMEE SEMPLE MCPHERSON AND THE RESURRECTION OF CHRISTIAN AMERICA, by Matthew Avery Sutton. 351 pp. Harvard University Press, 2007.

The name of Aimee Semple McPherson resonates faintly now—a rather comical run of syllables compounded of a first name bestowed by a rapt young mother, Minnie Kennedy, in an Ontario farmhouse in 1890, and the last names of Aimee's first two husbands, Robert Semple and Harold McPherson. Yet in the 1920s and 1930s she was one of the most famous women in America—for a time, the most famous, according to one biographer. After running away from her second husband, in 1915, she became a full-time revival preacher, in a white dress and a military cape. She not only preached, she healed, having herself experienced a broken ankle and torn ligaments abruptly repaired by prayer. She wrote:

> I suddenly felt as if a shock of electricity had struck my foot. It flowed through my whole body, causing me to shake and tremble under the power of God. Instantaneously my foot was perfectly healed.

Between 1916 and 1923, Sister Aimee, as she called herself, travelled the glory trail coast to coast six times and preached in more than a hundred cities. She and her mother arrived in Los Angeles in 1918, and within a few years she decided to build an inexpensive wooden tabernacle there, for local meetings; on New Year's Day of 1923, she dedicated the Angelus Temple, near Echo Park, at the corner of Sunset and Glendale boulevards. It seated more than five thousand, was topped by a rotating lighted cross visible from fifty miles away, and became, thanks to McPherson's eloquence, fervor, and theatrical flair, a leading Los Angeles institution and tourist attraction. She extended her ministry with an evangelical newspaper, *The Bridal Call*, and, beginning in 1924, with foresighted employment of a novel medium, radio, broadcasting sermons and services over her own station, KFSG (Kall Four Square Gospel).

National celebrity followed upon a series of newsworthy personal scandals, of which the most headlined, in 1926, involved her disappearance from Venice Beach and her reappearance, five weeks later, in a Mexican border town. She claimed to have been kidnapped by a trio of malefactors named Steve, Jake, and Mexicali Rose; she escaped, she said, from an isolated shack by sawing through her bonds with the jagged edge of a syrup can and walking for seventeen hours across the desert. For all its suspect details (she emerged from her desert ordeal neither sunburned nor dehydrated, wearing unscuffed shoes and a watch that she had not taken with her to the beach), she stuck to her story through a number of hearings and trials. An alternative story, which the newspapers were quick to air, held that she had spent the missing five weeks trysting in Carmel or elsewhere with Kenneth Gladstone Ormiston, the handsome, dapper, and married radio engineer who had been in charge of KFSG's operations. He and Aimee had daily technical exchanges, which some eavesdroppers considered suspiciously friendly, if not raucous, in tone. The Los Angeles district attorney investigated the alleged abduction and then had her arrested, along with her mother and Ormiston, on charges of "corruption of public morals, obstruction of justice, and conspiracy to manufacture evidence." The public and the press couldn't get enough of the trial—grandstands were erected in municipal court—though in the end all charges were dismissed. McPherson's Foursquare Gospel continued to be rousingly proclaimed at the Angelus Temple, and her thousands of devotees remained loyal during the furor, but her reputation had taken on a taint, a fascinating hint of sexual errancy, that lasted until her death. She was only fifty-three when she died, of a probably accidental overdose of barbiturates, in 1944.

Her fame and her aura transcended those of a religious figure; she consorted with Hollywood stars as an equal and charmed even H. L. Mencken, no booster of evangels. (He felt, with reason, that she was persecuted by the Babbitts and official bullies of Los Angeles.) The International Church of the Foursquare Gospel, spawned by the Angelus Temple, which at her death included 410 churches, two hundred mission stations, and about twenty-nine thousand members, has come to involve, under the leadership of her son, Rolf, and his successors, more than twenty-five thousand churches, a membership approaching two million, and a third of a billion dollars in funds. The story of her life, which she dramatized in a number of high-flown and breathlessly candid memoirs and sermons, was retold by two biographers in the early Nineties, Edith Blumhofer and Daniel Mark Epstein, and is now told again, with a determined sociological thrust, by Matthew Avery Sutton, in *Aimee Semple McPherson and the Resurrection of Christian America.*

Sutton, in three copious pages of acknowledgments, records that his uncle is a "longtime Foursquare minister" and that his grandmother's life was "a testament to the power of the Foursquare gospel." Though he maintains in his prose the dispassionate scholarly demeanor befitting a publication of the Harvard University Press, his conclusion amounts, sixty years after her death, to a reselling of Sister Aimee: "From her location in Hollywood, Aimee Semple McPherson reshaped and redefined the old-time religion in the United States, in effect resurrecting Christian America." Sutton's reaching for such a high estimate of his subject's historical importance slights the aspects of her personal story that would feed and deepen a psychological portrait. He mentions Blumhofer's emphasis on "the evangelist's Canadian roots and the religious context in which she matured," as if to admit that his own emphasis is elsewhere.

Sutton begins by describing a 1934 pageant that finds her magic in full flower, and then flashes back to the opening of her spectacular megachurch. Her formative years, up to her marriage to Robert Semple and his death, in Hong Kong, from dysentery and malaria contracted on the Chinese mainland, are covered in three brisk pages, whereas Epstein's biography, *Sister Aimee*, takes nearly seventy pages to reach the same point. We learn that she was a headstrong, clever, religiously troubled, and not always manageable girl, the only child of an orphan mother greatly attached to the brassy, egalitarian, and unconventional Salvation Army. Minnie Kennedy, married at fifteen to a man of fifty, had prayed for a daughter, and Aimee was raised with the maternal indulgence and high hopes more usually bestowed on a son. Mother and daughter were alike ambitious, and when Aimee found her religious vocation Minnie went with her and managed everything, including the finances. Neither was cut out for marital subservience; Aimee was to write that her mother was early "compelled to acknowledge that she was caught in the devil's net," though James Kennedy—a devout Methodist, a choir director— was, by all outward signs, a kind and steady husband.

To the heady blend of her parents' different versions of Christian devotion was added Aimee's exposure to Darwinism and her exploration of such worldly delights and theatrics as rural Ontario provided. She was rescued from worldliness by love at first sight with a tall Irish-immigrant evangelist, Robert Semple, who introduced her to a radical new religious movement, Pentecostalism. Its hallmarks were faith healing, the millennial belief that the Second Coming was imminent, and glossolalia, or speaking in tongues. After days of self-torment, sleeping and eating little but praying almost continuously, Aimee managed this last sign of inner baptism. She described the experience in her writings as a battering "through a thick stone wall that was growing as thin as tissue paper," and then as a "floating upon the billowing clouds of glory." Paraphrasing the Biblical account of Pentecost, in Acts 2:4, she declared, "Then suddenly, out of my innermost being flowed rivers of praise in other tongues as the Spirit gave utterance." Of her romance with Semple, Epstein says, "At last she had broken through to him." They married six months later and went as missionaries to China. Her husband, on their ill-fated mission, witnessed what she herself calls hysterics. Horrified by an odorous Hindu cremation occurring on the street below their windows, she began screaming. When Semple tried to comfort her, she relates:

> His sympathetic caress touched the match to the pent-up powder keg of my emotions, and immediately I was in the grasp of violent hysterics. It seemed as I listened to the high-pitched wails and wild laughter that came from my heart that the screams came from another person entirely.

She was no stranger to out-of-body sensations. Earlier that year, en route to China, she had been unexpectedly called upon to preach in Royal Albert Hall, and, as she described it, her hour of impressive oratory came entirely from her subconscious, like speaking in tongues, only the tongue this time was English. Throughout the pressure-laden decades of her success, she suffered lapses of discipline and nervous breakdowns that led to extended periods of seclusion. She was a woman on the edge, and fascinating as such.

Though her recoil from Darwinism into Pentecostal doctrine, as presented by a love object, and "good old-fashioned fundamentalism" could be said to be regressive, Sutton's biography finds much that was progressive and liberal in her social programs at the Angelus Temple. In 1927, she established a temple commissary that, as the Depression settled in, emerged as "one of the region's most effective and inclusive welfare institutions." According to Epstein:

> When the schools stopped feeding children free lunches, Aimee took over the program. When city welfare agencies staggered under the load of beggars, the women of Angelus Temple sewed quilts and baked loaves of bread by the thousands. When bread lines stretched for city blocks . . . Angelus Temple was the only place *anyone* could get a meal, clothing, and blankets, no questions asked.

She brushed aside the distinction between the "deserving" and the "undeserving" poor, and that between legal and illegal residents. One Mexican, the actor Anthony Quinn, who as a teen-ager acted as a translator for her, told an interviewer, "During the Depression . . . the one human being that never asked you what your nationality was, what you believed in and so forth, was Aimee Semple McPherson. All you had to do was pick up the phone and say, 'I'm hungry,' and within an hour there'd be a food basket there for you. . . . She literally kept most of that Mexican community . . . alive." In an era when anti-black racism was freely expressed, not least loudly by fundamentalist white Protestants, she persistently tried to make "interracial revival a reality at Angelus Temple," bringing a series of black leaders to its pulpit and welcoming into the congregation poor Southern blacks who had recently immigrated to a Los Angeles of increasing racial tensions. The same week of the Detroit race riots, in June of 1943, McPherson publicly converted the notorious black former heavyweight champion Jack Johnson on the Temple stage, and embraced him "as he raised his hand in worship."

Nor, herself a feminist symbol, though not a member of any feminist organization, did she neglect the cause of gender equality. She graduated female preachers from her LIFE Bible College, ordaining many in Foursquare churches. Confronted with Saint Paul's admonition "Let your women keep silence in the churches," she offered the exegesis that he was referring not to preaching or prophesying but to "chatter," as the segregated women in the ancient church tended their babies. The Pauline text she preferred to cite was Galatians 3:28: "There is no longer male nor female, bond nor free, Jew nor Gentile, for we are all equal in Jesus Christ." On a supernatural plane, she envisioned Pentecost as a great melting: "Saints who were once smelted together in the fires of Pentecost are being re-united, re-welded, and rejuvenated." Closer to earth and the contemporary financial crisis, her commissary gave young mothers complete layettes and provided a day nursery for the children of working mothers, amid complaints that working women threatened "family values."

The Ontario farm girl, without disavowing fundamentalism's conservative, nativist strain, had a number of surprises in her, including a bold curiosity. Challenged by some college students in 1934 with the assertions that "the teachings of the Nazarene have outlived their usefulness" and that "cold reasoning is the new savior of the world," she embarked on a world tour that took her not only into the presence of leaders like Mussolini and Gandhi but, to quote Epstein, to "the floating brothels on the

Cantonese River, the infamous Flower Boats to which impoverished fathers sold their blind daughters for food. She also visited a harem and a leper colony. Her book contains many images of women enslaved or victimized." Sister Aimee's own image—flamboyant, brave, brassy, neurotically fragile—defied contemporary attempts to pin it down. After her sudden death, her most vehement critic among the Los Angeles clergy, Robert Shuler, wrote admiringly in *The Methodist Challenge* of her appeal to "the people—the hungry-hearted people," and, while he admitted that he could "never understand why God used Aimee," also admitted that the army of preachers and workers she left behind was "nearer akin to the army with which Wesley started than we Methodists would rejoice to concede." From a standpoint outside Christianity, the distinction between mainstream Protestantism and marginal movements like Pentecostalism and the Salvation Army appears less significant than it does from within; all shades of the Christian religion derive from the same sketchy Gospel accounts of a charismatic miracle worker and a cosmic narrative wildly different from what science shows. Pentecostalism is unusual primarily in its expectation of present-day miracles—faith healing, talking in tongues—like those reported in Acts. But any version of Christianity must resort, in the end, to an assertion of faith, to fundamentalism of a sort, be it as simple as shouts of assent at a revival meeting or as pondered and impressively phrased as Karl Barth's neo-orthodoxy.

Sutton's attempt to carve out a pivotal role for McPherson in the amorphous seethe of twentieth-century Christianity in America itself seems mostly a matter of assertion, rather than a demonstrable thesis. She was, we do not doubt, "a superstar who, though dogged by scandal, was adored by her followers, large segments of the press, and the increasingly secular American public." But "increasingly secular" may be the most telling phrase. There was a tide of irreligion that she could not stem. Her scandals, her mercenary bent and vanity, and her eventually rampant worldliness hurt her cause. In 1927, she rattled teacups by bobbing her trademark long auburn hair; she slimmed down her stocky figure, shopped for clothes in Paris, and was caught trying to smuggle some past U.S. Customs. Sutton owns up to "her predominantly negative image in American popular culture." Can it be true, even taking into account the growth of the Foursquare denomination, that "religion in the United States reaped the benefit of her popularity"? It might as well be said that the film industry reaped a benefit from Marilyn Monroe's popularity; she, too, captivated the "hungry-hearted," and vanished in a haze of self-medication and aborted relationships.

McPherson's hope that, as she wrote, "romance and Religion can walk hand in hand, and love and faith can find room in the heart of a woman," produced, after her divorce from the lingeringly loyal McPherson, another terminated marriage, this time to the three-hundred-pound David Hutton, whom she had hired to sing the part of the Pharaoh in her sacred opera *The Iron Furnace*. The marriage gave her a few happy months, but foundered when Hutton was sued by a massage nurse for breach of promise. McPherson and her strong-willed mother had already become permanently estranged, and before her death Aimee suffered a heavily publicized, litigious break with her daughter, Roberta. Like many another enchantress of the public, she attained few and fleeting private satisfactions. Her personal story is so arresting, poignant, and fantastic that the reader resents Sutton's muffling it in portentous generalizations:

> Whether she intended to or not, McPherson embodied the changing norms regarding women's sexuality, fashions, and bodies in that era.

> In effect, McPherson was redefining the relationship between conservative Protestantism and American culture by working to harness the religious potential of the new mass media.

The reality of her, gone from the scene for most of a century, emerges affectingly not in sociological boasts but in anecdotes that take her as she came. In 1927, a month after the charges against her were dismissed in Los Angeles, she arrived in New York in furs and a yellow suit, and was taken to a prime watering spot of the Roaring Twenties, Texas Guinan's speakeasy, on Fifty-fourth Street. A reporter called out, with whatever sardonic intent, that she should be invited to speak. Guinan agreed, and, as Epstein tells it, "Aimee, demure, dignified, stone sober . . . left her table and stood in the center of the dance floor, smiling until everyone was quiet." Then she said:

> Behind all these beautiful clothes, behind these good times, in the midst of your lovely buildings and shops and pleasures, there is another life. There is something on the other side. "What shall it profit a man if he gain the whole world, and lose his own soul?" With all your getting and playing and good times, do not forget you have a Lord. Take Him into your hearts.

And that was all—a miniature masterpiece of the evangelist's art, silencing a boozy crowd in no mood to hear it. Epstein writes, "All at once they applauded, and Tex put her arm around Aimee. The clapping went on for much longer than her speech had taken."

Laissez-faire Is More

THE FORGOTTEN MAN: *A New History of the Great Depression*, by Amity Shlaes. 464 pp. HarperCollins, 2007.

As the generations that experienced the Great Depression, even the youngest of them, die off, the period passes into the care of historians. There is a danger, at this remove in time, of Depression nostalgia. T. H. Watkins's *The Great Depression: America in the 1930s*, an illustrated print companion to 1993's public-television series of the same name, concludes on a ringing upbeat note:

> In the end, the world of the Great Depression, molded by fear, uncertainty, determination, and a wondrous bravery, gave us the world of our own present hope—and if we shape our world half as well as did the men and women of the 1930s, we will have gone a long way toward honoring our own obligation to the future.

David M. Kennedy's mammoth *Freedom from Fear: The American People in Depression and War, 1929–1945* won its author the Pulitzer Prize for the year 2000 and, from the *Boston Globe*, the encomium "This is modern America's story—modern America's most thrilling, most irresistible, and most significant story." If not as thrilling and oft-told as that of American involvement in the Second World War, the decade that preceded the war has received ample attention, from Studs Terkel's book of colloquial, sometimes searing interviews, *Hard Times* (1970), to the tables and hardcore economics of Ben S. Bernanke's *Essays on the Great Depression* (2000). Now we have, in a sprightly contrarian mood, *The Forgotten Man: A New History of the Great Depression*, by Amity Shlaes, a syndicated columnist for Bloomberg News and a former member of the editorial board of the *Wall Street Journal*.

Where the words "new history" appear, revisionism will follow. Shlaes's introduction tells us, "It is time to revisit the late 1920s and the 1930s. Then we see that neither the standard history nor the standard rebuttal entirely captures the realities of the period." With a degree of divulgence rare in an introduction, Shlaes lays out her thesis. "The standard history of the Great Depression" is pro-Roosevelt, and is wrong:

> The same history teaches that the New Deal was the period in which Americans learned that government spending was important to recoveries. . . . The attitude is that the New Deal is the best model we have for

what government must do for weak members of society, in both times of crisis and times of stability. . . . The New Dealers displayed a sort of dynamism from which today's moribund politicians might learn. . . . FDR saved the country in peace, and then he saved it in war. Or so the story line goes.

Shlaes's story line proposes instead that the 1920s, far from "a period of false growth and low morals," were "a great decade of true economic gains" whose "faith in laissez-faire" was justified. "American capitalism did not break in 1929. The crash did not cause the Depression. It was a necessary correction of a too-high stock market, but not a necessary disaster." The crash preceded an underlying problem, deflation, caused by not enough money in circulation as banks failed and shut their doors; a number of dollar-starved communities—Salt Lake City; Ventura, California; Yellow Springs, Ohio—issued their own scrip, while Presidents Hoover and then Roosevelt supported policies, like the gold standard, aimed at a nonexistent inflation. There were multiple contributing factors: the stingy Federal Reserve; the "disastrous" Smoot-Hawley Tariff, which discouraged foreign trade; higher taxes imposed on a staggering citizenry; freaks of weather like floods and the drought-induced Dust Bowl. But the gravest problem, as Shlaes sees it, was government "intervention, the lack of faith in the marketplace." Both Presidents tried to lift wages, when letting them sink would have liberated businesses to start hiring and resume business as usual. Business knows best.

Hoover, contrary to his popular image as a do-nothing President who hid from the Depression on fly-fishing retreats to his Appalachian camp on Virginia's Rapidan River, was a dynamo, a world-travelling free-lance engineer and humanitarian from the West; he had risen to the highest office after energetically performing as Secretary of Commerce for Presidents Harding and Coolidge. "By personality an intervener," he favored government intervention, as long as it didn't violate his sense of the Constitution, and sought control over economic events that would, according to Shlaes, have gone better if left alone. She draws an arresting parallel:

Hoover and Roosevelt were alike in several regards. Both preferred to control events and people. Both underestimated the strength of the American economy. Both doubted its ability to right itself in a storm. Hoover mistrusted the stock market. Roosevelt mistrusted it more. Roosevelt offered rhetorical optimism, but pessimism underlay his policies. Though Americans associated Roosevelt with bounty, his insistent emphasis on sharing—rationing, almost—betrayed a conviction that the country had entered a permanent era of scarcity. Both presidents overestimated the value of government planning. Hoover, the Quaker, favored the community over the individual. Roosevelt, the Episcopalian, found laissez-faire economics immoral and disturbingly un-Christian.

In the parade of individuals—some still well known, most now faded into obscurity, almost all of them male public servants—with which, in the 370 pages that follow the introduction, Shlaes pursues her thesis through the Thirties, few heroes emerge, and the most highly placed two are not apt to figure in many liberal pantheons: Calvin Coolidge and Andrew Mellon. Coolidge, who sardonically called Hoover a "wonder boy" and who memorably stated, "The chief business of the American people is business," is presented as a kind of Zen saint, a pillar of inaction: "Coolidge had long ago determined that the world would do better if he involved himself less. [He] believed that the work of life lay in holding back and shutting out. He conducted his official life according to his own version of the doctor's Hippocratic Oath—first, do no harm." Shlaes hails his decision to leave the Presidency after five and a half years (thus ducking the crash and its consequences) as "another of Coolidge's acts of refraining, his last and greatest."

Andrew Mellon, the Pittsburgh venture capitalist who served Harding, Coolidge, and Hoover as Secretary of the Treasury, presented an even more reserved personality: "More than Coolidge, he hid from newspapermen, even when he had good news." His principal agenda was lowering taxes; he urged thrift, investment in the private sector, and patience. He figures in John Kenneth Galbraith's entertaining and mordant history *The Great Crash, 1929* (1954) as "a passionate advocate of inaction" and the official who, in the month before the Crash, assured the public, "There is no cause for worry. The high tide of prosperity will continue." Shlaes views government inaction as generally a beneficial thing, and underlines Mellon's honorableness, private generosity, and public spirit as well as the business acumen that enabled him, exploiting the possibilities of Pittsburgh somewhat later than Carnegie and Frick, to assemble a financial empire. In 1934, the Roosevelt Administration prosecuted him for underpaying his taxes by several million dollars in 1931. At the same time, Mellon was firming up plans to donate to the government his priceless art collection and to construct on the Mall a great National Gallery—imagined first as limestone but then promoted to marble. After Roosevelt's crushing victory over Alf Landon, in 1936, Mellon in a brief, personal letter approached the President with his offer to "the people of the United States." The gift met rapid acceptance, although Mellon, who died in 1937, did not live to see the gallery's completion or his exoneration on the count of tax evasion, four months after his death. As Shlaes reads these events, Mellon put his money where his mouth was, demonstrating, in a time of overactive federal government, the power and generosity of the private sector. As she concludes the chapter "Mellon's Gift," her admiration generates a rough-hewn prose couplet: "Mellon might be correct about the Depression being a bad quarter hour. History alone would tell whose edifice had the more enduring power."

She gives Roosevelt a mixed and skeptical report. He was more charming, she has to admit, than Hoover:

> Roosevelt by contrast had a wonderful temperament, and could get along, when he felt like it, with even his worst opponent. His calls for courage, his Fireside Chats, all were intensely important. . . . In the darkness, Roosevelt's voice seemed to shine.

He had the good fortune to be "a great radio speaker born into the era of radio." As an experimenter with the economy, however, he was capricious and vacillating. In his manipulations of gold and the gold standard, according to Shlaes, "FDR's playfulness was at its most destructive." This was no time for playfulness: "Focusing on the fun of experiments neglected the question of whether unceasing experimentation might frighten business into terrified inaction." The plethora of ambitious programs and agencies perpetrated in the first hundred days of the New Deal seemed aimed more at creating a sensation of activity than at achieving feasible objectives: "Americans must know Washington was doing something. If there were contradictions between experiments and within them, well, that did not matter." Shlaes, in a bold stroke of psychologizing, lays the hyperactivity to "the restlessness of the invalid." She goes on, "Like an invalid, the country took pleasure in the very thought of motion." More ominous was Roosevelt's totalitarian tendency: "His remedies were on a greater scale and often inspired by socialist or fascist models abroad."

One of Shlaes's chapter-length detours deals with a junket that, in 1927, on the good ship *President Roosevelt* (named after Theodore), carried a self-designated "unofficial American trade-union delegation" to investigate and report on conditions in the Soviet Union. A number of these junketeers—the Columbia economist Rexford Guy Tugwell, the economic commentator Stuart Chase, the Chicago labor scholar Paul Douglas—were to become significant supporters of and participants in the New Deal. Toward the end of the junket, this progressive delegation was granted an interview—"A small pockmarked man met them in a cloakroom; Douglas assumed it was an attendant"—with Joseph Stalin, who conversed and answered their questions for more than six hours.

Stalin was not wasting his time; wooing susceptible Americans might lead to unofficial U.S. approval if not official recognition of the Soviet Union. Stuart Chase upon his return wrote, "*Laissez-faire* rides well on covered wagons, not so well on conveyor belts and cement roads." Collectivism was the inevitable direction. After all, Chase wrote, "why should Russians have all the fun remaking a world?" The poisoned chalice was passed around. Shlaes names New Dealers with Communist connections— Lauchlin Currie, Harry Dexter White—and supposed spies such as Lee Pressman and Alger Hiss, who "duped colleagues in government repeatedly." But "few New Dealers were spies or even communists," she reassures the reader. "The problem was their naïveté about the economic value of Soviet-style or European-style collectivism—and the fact that they forced such collectivism upon their own country."

Another chapter, "The Chicken Versus the Eagle," takes us through the legal case of a Brooklyn band of brothers, the Schechters, whose name means "ritual butcher" in Yiddish, and whose business was the marketing of kosher chickens. In 1934, Roosevelt's Justice Department prosecuted them under the National Recovery Administration's Code of Fair Competition for the Live Poultry Industry of the Metropolitan Area in and About the City of New York, "a lengthy and forbidding document." The code forbade, among other deleterious practices, so-called straight killing, which meant that "customers might select a coop or a half coop of chickens for purchase, but they did not 'have the right to make any selection of particular birds.'" Not only did the code unleash upon their business a plague of ignorant and imperious government inspectors, the Schechters argued, but "they were busting in on an intimate private relationship: that of the small businessman with his customer." In their first trial, the chicken vendors were found guilty, fined, and sentenced to jail, and the circuit court rejected their appeal; but the Supreme Court, handing down judgment in 1935 in *Schechter Poultry Corp.* v. *United States*, unanimously ruled that "the NRA had abused the Schechters, and other businesses, through unconstitutional 'coercive exercise of the law-making powers.'" The London *Express* ran the headline "AMERICA STUNNED! ROOSEVELT'S WORK KILLED IN 20 MINUTES." In response, Roosevelt gave an uncharacteristically intemperate press conference, accusing the Supreme Court of wanting to revert to "the horse and buggy age."

The Schechter case spelled the death of the NRA. Dozens of lawsuits and injunctions besieged such New Deal structures as the Tennessee Valley Authority, the Administration's showpiece intervention in the utility industry; and the President, flush with his landslide reëlection in 1936, blatantly overplayed his hand by initiating legislation that would have added a new appointee to the Supreme Court for every justice over the age of seventy—a measure plainly aimed at the elderly core of judicial resistance to his revolution. The court bill failed ("dead as a salt mackerel shining beneath the pale moonlight," a Mississippi newspaper gloated), and the Depression slogged on, ending only in 1940, as the government decisively hiked defense spending. Roosevelt's extensive and not especially effectual attempts at collectivism prepared the ground for, it might be said, the most truly collective war effort the nation has ever known, with virtually unresisted conscription, dizzyingly raised taxes, severe rationing, price controls, and patriotic participation by every class of citizen.

Shlaes's Thirties chronicle, with its abrupt hopping, chapter to chapter, from one sideshow to another, is not easy to follow. Government officials blend into a gray mass; non-government notables like the black religious preacher Father Divine and the alcoholic co-founder of Alcoholics Anonymous, Bill Wilson, are dwelt upon to no apparent point except to illustrate the value of self-help and problem-solving without government aid. Many pages toward the end are devoted to building up Wendell Willkie—a man risen from the world of business, like Hoover (and like him called a "wonder boy")—as a sympathetic, charismatic anti-Roosevelt, but it all comes to anticlimax with Roosevelt's easy electoral victory, for an unprecedented third term, in 1940. Willkie in his campaign indicted the President's "philosophy of distributed scarcity" and asserted that it was only "from weakness that people reach for dictators and concentrated government power." These seem to be Amity Shlaes's views also, but in 1940 there was no breaking the bond between Franklin Roosevelt and the bulk of the American people. *Time*, which had backed Willkie, summed it up: "Whether Mr. Roosevelt is Moses or Lucifer, he is a leader."

The Depression was a good time in which to be a sheltered only child. The small town around me didn't change; horse-drawn farm wagons mingled the clip-clop of horseshoes with the swish of automobile tires. The vacant lots remained vacant; shoppers and workers were carried to the nearby city (Reading, Pennsylvania, with its Socialist mayor) on the same swaying, sparking trolley cars; the movies and radio were never more innocently entertaining; the schools were safe and tidy, with girls and boys segregated at recess on the asphalt playground; nickels and pennies counted for something; Major League baseball had two symmetrical leagues of eight teams, with five cities fielding two teams each, as they had for years. A child did not know that change and expansion were the norm for a thriving economy. But the two men of my snug household, my father and my maternal grandfather, had both taken deep economic wounds: my grandfather had lost almost all his investments in the stock-market crash, and my father had been laid off from his job as a happily peripatetic telephone lineman. He endured a long interval of odd jobs and no job, with summer stints on local WPA projects. Fortunately, the town school board eventually hired him, for twelve hundred dollars a year, as a math teacher. The job saved him for respectability, but he never forgot the trauma of being out of work with an infant son and no home of his own, in a world with no economic safety net, just breadlines. Hoover in his obtuse aloofness later wrote of the crisis, "Many persons left their jobs for the more profitable one of selling apples." Shlaes's account of economic-philosophy wars *en haut* in Washington could have done with a little of the gritty testimony Studs Terkel collected, for instance that of Peggy Terry, who remembered of a soup line:

> "So we'd ask the guy that was ladling out the soup into the buckets—everybody had to bring their own bucket to get the soup—he'd dip the greasy, watery stuff off the top. So we'd ask him to please dip down to get some meat and potatoes from the bottom of the kettle. But he wouldn't do it."

My father had been reared a Republican, but he switched parties to vote for Roosevelt and never switched back. His memory of being abandoned by society and big business never left him and, for all his paternal kindness and humorousness, communicated itself to me, along with his preference for the political party that offered "the forgotten man" the better break. Roosevelt made such people feel less alone. The "impression of recovery"—the impression that a President was bending the old rules and, drawing upon his own courage and flamboyance in adversity and illness, stirring things up on behalf of the down-and-out—mattered more than any miscalculations in the moot mathematics of economics. Business, of which Shlaes is so solicitous, is basically merciless, geared to maximize profit. Government is ultimately a human transaction, and Roosevelt put a cheerful, defiant, caring face on government at a time when faith in democracy was ebbing throughout the Western world. For this inspirational feat he is the twentieth century's greatest President, to rank with Lincoln and Washington as symbolic figures for a nation to live by.

Makeup and Make-Believe

MAX FACTOR: *The Man Who Changed the Faces of the World,* by Fred E. Basten. 172 pp. Arcade, 2008.

The happy story of Max Factor, as enthusiastically told by Fred E. Basten, begins, like a movie, at a high-energy moment of extreme peril:

> On a winter night in February 1904, twenty-seven-year-old Max Faktor huddled with his wife and three young children in a Russian forest, frightened more for the family he had kept secret for nearly five years than of the wind and snow or even the approaching czar's men calling his name. Only days earlier, Max Faktor was a favorite of the royal family and was esteemed by the royal court. Now he was being hunted as a fugitive.

The little ("barely five feet tall") Polish Jew's involvement with the czar had advanced with the quick progressions of a fairy tale. One of ten children born to a worker in the textile mills of Łódź, he was reared by his siblings and had scant formal education. At the age of seven, he was set to selling oranges, peanuts, and candy in the lobby of Łódź's Czarina Theatre; he later called this his "introduction to the world of make-believe." At the age of eight, he worked as an apothecary's assistant, learning some chemistry; at just nine, he became an apprentice to the city's leading wigmaker and cosmetician. Within four years, he was proficient enough to join the staff of the Berlin hair stylist Anton, and by the age of fourteen he had moved on to Moscow, where he worked for Korpo, the cosmetician to the Imperial Russian Grand Opera. At his eighteenth birthday, Faktor was obliged to serve four years in the Russian Army; he was picked for the Hospital Corps, and took up nurse's duties. "I did not like it but I learned much," he later said.

Discharged at twenty-two, he opened a small shop in the Moscow suburb of R'azan, "making and selling his own creams, rouges, fragrances, and wigs." According to Basten, a member of a passing theatrical troupe stopped in on the way to a performance before the imperial family, and, "within weeks, Max's business took a royal upswing in sales and he was adopted by the summer court." The courtiers adopted him so thoroughly that he had little time left for his own shop—"All my attention," he remembered, "went to their individual needs by showing them how to enhance their good points and conceal the less good." The aristocrats paid well and introduced him to their luxurious world but were possessive: he could not leave the court unescorted and was limited to brief weekly visits to his shop; he had to marry on the sly, and fathered three children in five years. Meanwhile, anti-Semitism was on the rise in Russia; in 1903, Czar Nicholas II "ordered a siege on the Jews he so feared and hated, and burned down their villages." Max longed for America, where a brother and an uncle had settled in St. Louis, with its impending World's Fair.

A friendly general noticed the court beautician's downcast mood and, being told of Max's secret family, arranged for his escape. Before an interview with the general's personal physician, Max covered himself with yellowish makeup—an especially fairy-tale touch. His sickly appearance won him an official recommendation for three recuperative months in Karlsbad, a spa in far-off Bohemia to which court members often repaired. Russian guards accompanied him, however, so he continually faked a limp; as he hobbled into the main square of Karlsbad, whom should he find huddled at the fountain but his wife, Esther, and their three children! In a twinkling, they disappeared into the Bohemian (not Russian, as in the opening paragraph) forest and, walking mostly at night, travelled "seemingly endless miles"—hundreds and hundreds, it must have been, to the nearest seacoast—"until they reached a clearing in the woods. Ahead was a seaport where the steamship *Molka III* was boarding for America. Max happily paid the fare. Money was not a problem. Over the years, he had saved nearly $40,000, which he carried with him in a pouch." No passports were required then, in the flood tide of immigration. A customs official misspelled "Faktor" as "Factor."

America was not without difficulties for Max and his magic pouch: his English was nonexistent at first, and remained heavily accented; an English-speaking partner who helped him set up shop at the fair in St. Louis absconded with the funds; his wife, less than two years after giving birth to their fourth child, dropped dead on a sidewalk; he sent to Russia for a second wife, and she, Helen, after bearing him his fifth offspring, proved to be so temperamental that he had to divorce her. However, he had opened a barbershop in St. Louis, and it prospered; in 1908, he married a neighbor, Jennie Cook, and headed to California to try his luck supplying cosmetics and hairpieces to a new brand of entertainment, the motion pictures. In those days, one-reelers were being shot all over Los Angeles, under tirelessly blue skies, and Max, from his little shop on the edge of downtown ("Max Factor's Antiseptic Hair Store. Toupees made-to-order. High-grade work"), spotted some "ghoulish" people passing by. He followed them to an empty lot where a bar brawl was being staged and filmed. Max was curious about what they had on their faces:

Some were using stage make-up, while others wore concoctions they had made themselves: odd mixtures of Vaseline and flour, lard and cornstarch, or cold cream and paprika. The more adventurous had even tried ground brick dust mixed with Vaseline or lard to get a flesh-colored look.

Such pastes, applied an eighth of an inch thick, formed a mask that cracked under the stress of facial expression; this didn't matter at the distances of a live theatre, but in film close-ups even hairline cracks showed. In 1914, working in his shop's laboratory, Factor created "a greasepaint in cream rather than stick form, ultra-thin in consistency, completely flexible on the skin, and produced in twelve precisely graduated shades." The silent-film comedians—Chaplin, Keaton, Fatty Arbuckle—were the first to try it, and "returned not only to give Max their enthusiastic approval but to have him personally apply the new make-up."

Then there were wigs. Max persuaded Cecil B. DeMille, in town to direct the large-scale Western *The Squaw Man*, that wigs and hairpieces painstakingly formed of real human hair (135,168 individually knotted strands went into an average Max Factor wig, with sixty thousand in a full beard and a mere seven thousand in a false mustache) were more photogenic than "clumsy substitutes such as straw, mattress stuffing, excelsior, Spanish moss, wool, tobacco leaves, even mohair stuffing from Model-T Fords!" DeMille admired Factor's wigs but said he couldn't afford them, and suggested renting them. The deposit needed to safeguard the costly wigs posed a sticking point, which Factor, resorting not for the last time to his brood of useful children, circumvented by waiving the deposit and having DeMille hire his three sons as Indian extras, paying them three dollars a day; at the end of each day, they collected their father's wigs or had their pay docked. By 1916, Max Factor & Company was booming enough to move to larger quarters, in the prestigious Pantages Building, "at the center of it all."

Triumph followed triumph. As Basten—a former assistant in the company's public-relations department—tells it, Max devised false eyelashes for Phyllis Haver, who was tired of having pies smashed in her face and wanted to move up to vamp roles. He created a yellow makeup to lighten Rudolph Valentino's skin so that the actor, who ground pigments to help speed up the process, could escape bit parts as a swarthy villain. Max brought the tempestuous Pola Negri to heel by shouting back at her in their native Polish. When he outgrew his space in the Pantages Building, he moved to a new store, on South Hill Street, and called it the House of Make-Up. The theatrical term "make-up"—Max always insisted on the hyphen—had been considered risqué, but at the urging of his son Frank he began applying it to his products, and it swept the world. Snubbed when he visited the German offices of Leichner, for whose stick grease-paint he had been a longtime American distributor, he cabled his sons, "Start selling greasepaint in tubes," and the tubes were, of course, another triumph. For Douglas Fairbanks's sweaty exertions, Max invented "the first perspiration-proof body make-up" and then "devised the reverse—cinematic sweat—by simply combining equal parts of water with mineral oil." For M-G-M's production of *Ben-Hur*, he and his staff conjured up more than six hundred gallons of light-olive makeup to match the army of pale local extras to the darker extras already filmed in Italy. He conquered the persistent problem of lip pomade's melting under the hot studio lights by firmly pressing two thumbprints onto the actress's upper lip and then one thumbprint on her lower lip, thus single-handedly creating the sensational new look of "bee-stung" lips. For Joan Crawford, he created "the smear."

There seemed no limit to the labors that Hollywood could set before this diminutive Hercules. Each technical advance in cinematic art posed a fresh problem in makeup. When, in the late Twenties, sound came in, the microphones "picked up the noisy sputter of the carbon arc lights—the standard film lighting used . . . for fifteen years." The new tungsten lamps were quiet but also much hotter, and provided a softer light. "The old Orthochromatic film, which had been used since the birth of the film industry, was not sensitive enough to properly record faces under the new lighting." And so:

> The old film was replaced by super-sensitive, faster Panchromatic film, but it made faces appear noticeably darker, as if in shadow. The new film made every item in the Max Factor make-up line for motion pictures instantly obsolete.

Max to his own rescue! He and Frank labored for months

> to test and perfect an entirely new formulation in a wider-than-ever range of shades that reflected the correct degree of light required by the sensitive new film. It had only one drawback. Because it was designed for black-and-white film, it looked bizarre in real life. For example, actresses wore dark brown lipstick, which photographed as red on film.

This new panchromatic makeup was, Frank admitted, "horrifying to look at" in daylight. For its invention, Max Factor was presented with a special certificate by the Academy of Motion Picture Arts and Sciences, in recognition of his contribution to "Incandescent Illumination Research." Frank recalled, "I had never seen my father simultaneously so happy and so on the verge of tears."

Dr. Herbert Kalmus, an MIT graduate, had been developing Technicolor film since 1912; its first successful two-color (red and green) version was employed throughout the Douglas Fairbanks feature *The Black Pirate*, in 1926, and its full three-color form was displayed in Disney cartoons of the early Thirties and an otherwise undistinguished live-action two-reeler, *La Cucaracha*, in 1934. Everybody who viewed Technicolor, including Kalmus and Max, "realized something was wrong":

> Filmmakers were using Max Factor's Panchromatic make-up, created for black-and-white film. . . . Although thin and transparent, its greasepaint base left a slight sheen on the skin, which reflected surrounding colors. If an actor was standing near red drapes, for example, his face would have a red cast.

Bette Davis, Carole Lombard, Joan Crawford, Greta Garbo, Norma Shearer, and Claudette Colbert were among the stars who refused to appear in so unflattering a light. It may have been while brooding upon this rebellion that Max stepped from a curb and was hit by a delivery truck. While he was laid up, Frank hustled back and forth between the Factor labs and the Technicolor company, and, by the time his father was back, walking with a cane, had the reflective problem nearly licked. "Together," Basten relates,

> they improved the original formula until the make-up was more porous, allowing air to penetrate it and the skin to breathe. They also overcame its slight tendency toward flakiness, so that no particles were shed after the make-up was applied. . . . The new make-up, which the Factors called the "T-D" series, was in a solid cake form. When applied with a damp sponge, it offered a transparent matte finish while concealing small skin blemishes and imperfections. The project was enormously complex, as Max admitted in a press release.

The fully refined preparation, its name changed to Pan-Cake, for its panlike container and its cakelike form, was perhaps Max Factor's greatest invention; not only did it make Technicolor visually palatable but women on the set kept stealing it off the shelves for personal use. Based upon the spectroscopic perception that skin holds a multitude of tints yet is "essentially a translucent covering with relatively little color of its own," Pan-Cake was too dark to be worn successfully at night. Max at first resisted the popular demand that it be produced in lighter shades, saying that it was made for the movies and there was only enough of it for them, but Frank saw to its wide commercial release; it "immediately became the fastest- and largest-selling single make-up item in the history of cosmetics," outselling all sixty-five of the imitations advertising themselves with the now magic word "cake."

It was not long after this that Max, in Europe with his son Davis pursuing some of the possibilities that his company's international success had created, received a death threat (modestly demanding two hundred dollars, or else) that unnerved him and prompted his return home; he died in his bed in 1938, at the early age of sixty-one. Max Factor & Company did not die with him; Frank even legally changed his name to Max to smooth over the transition. Under its new Max, the company supplied the copper-green makeup that Margaret Hamilton wore as the Wicked Witch of the West in *The Wizard of Oz*, as well as the color of the Munchkins and the six horses that flash by in the Horse of a Different Color sequence. For the masses, it produced Tru-Color, "the world's first perfect lipstick . . . non-drying but indelible," its mettle proved in many an ordeal at the Kissing Machine—a device with rubber lips, a crank, and a pressure gauge. But Basten's idolizing tome loses steam once its dapper, ambidextrous (he could apply makeup with either hand), chemically resourceful hero passes from its narrative.

The company survived to develop makeup for television, but its glory days were with the golden age of the movie studios, when the stars used to provide product endorsements for as little as a dollar. Their glamour rubbed off on Max Factor, and vice versa. As the nation's cinema palaces emptied and the fading studios cut their costs, Factors started to drift out of the executive ranks of what had been, ever since Max's boys became "Jewish Indians" to protect hired wigs, a family firm. Its stock began to trade on the New York Stock Exchange in the early Sixties, shortly after it acquired the French company Parfums Corday; in 1973, it was itself acquired, by the Norton Simon conglomerate, which ten years later was taken over by Esmark, which a year later merged with Beatrice Companies, which made Max Factor part of its International Playtex division and moved its headquarters to Stamford, Connecticut. This left high and dry in Hollywood the Max Factor Make-Up Studio, a palatial Art Deco showpiece with offices and labs and makeup rooms (for brunettes, blondes, redheads, and "brownettes"), whose opening, in 1935, as floodlights probed the skies and stars from Betty Grable to Bela Lugosi signed a parchment Scroll of Fame, had been the crowning glory of Max Factor's ascent. Now the building, restored after some thin times, survives as Donelle Dadigan's Hollywood History Museum, Ms. Dadigan being a

"Beverly Hills real estate developer and passionate Hollywood memorabilia collector." But of course all the memorabilia in the world won't
bring back Max Factor's Hollywood or—and who would mourn?—the
innocence of a cultural climate where makeup was a shameful secret,
associated with sexual prostitution and stage performers.

This biography foregrounds its central figure in almost total isolation
from the history of cosmetics and the beauty industry—topics of lively
interest to contemporary social historians, almost all of them female, as it
happens. In the slim and frivolously titled *Read My Lips: A Cultural History of Lipstick* (1998), by Meg Cohen Ragas and Karen Kozlowski, we
learn that an ancient Egyptian papyrus shows a woman applying lip
rouge. *Inventing Beauty* (2004), by Teresa Riordan, points out that as
photography became, from 1870 to 1900, more popular so, too, did cosmetics, and that, "as the Depression deepened, cosmetics sales climbed
steadily," and that, in the 1950s and 1960s, the proliferation of synthetic
compounds freed cosmetics from the drawbacks of naturally viscid and
odorous oils and solvents. Riordan illustrates her text with patent appli-
cations of beauty enhancers right out of a torturer's manual. *Hope in a
Jar: The Making of America's Beauty Culture* (1998), by Kathy Peiss,
counters arguments, raised with special vehemence in the countercul-
tural Sixties, against the beauty industry's manipulation and trivialization
of women by pointing out that it gave multitudes of needy women
respectable employment as beauticians, manicurists, and saleswomen, as
well as enabling some entrepreneurs, like Elizabeth Arden and Helena
Rubinstein, and the African-American Annie Turnbo Malone and
Madam C. J. Walker, who manufactured hair-care products, to head up
successful corporations. Max Factor, Peiss asserts, became a factor in this
female-dominated industry by shunning the air of foppish effeminacy
that since the eighteenth century had attached to male hairdressers:
"Photographs of Factor show him simultaneously as makeup artist,
chemist, and father figure." To preserve this solemn image his publicists
discouraged him from giving, in his comically strong accent, interviews.

Sally Pointer's *The Artifice of Beauty: A History and Practical Guide to
Perfumes and Cosmetics* (2005) offers a thorough and harrowing history of
cosmetics, going back to the first prehistoric traces of red ochre found in
graves. The reader puts the book down convinced of the incorrigible
human, and particularly feminine, appetite for beauty aids. Pointer
quotes eight apt lines by George Gascoigne, in his blank-verse satire of
1576, "The Steele Glas":

> Behold, behold, they neuer stande content,
> With God, with kinde, with any helpe of Arte,
> But curle their locks, with bodkins and with braids,
> But dye their heare, with sundry subtill sleights,
> But paint and slicke, til fayrest face be foule,
> But bumbast, bolster, frisle, and perfume:
> They marre with muske, the balme which nature made,
> And dig for death, in dellicatest dishes.

Even as Gascoigne wrote, his monarch, Elizabeth I, was poisoning her complexion with ceruse, a lead-based skin whitener used in ancient Rome and revived in the Renaissance. Ceruse persisted into the eighteenth century as an ingredient in potent "wash balls," long after many a woman of fashion had died of such toxins. The contemporary barbarism of piercing (eyebrow, tongue, navel) was preceded in the 1890s by a craze for nipple rings; a contemporary wearer wrote that "many ladies are ready to bear the passing pain for the sake of love."

For the sake of love, broadly speaking, American women in the early twentieth century, overcoming puritan scruples enforced by male employers, husbands, editorial writers, and legislators (in Kansas in 1915 a law was proposed making it illegal for women under the age of forty-four to wear cosmetics "for the purpose of creating a false impression"), began to paint themselves. Movies enhanced by Max Factor makeup were not alone to blame, but they did help legitimatize artifice and its false impressions. Their heightened images spoke to women of an attainable better self. As I remember it, years ago a scientific study, which electronically tracked eyeball movement, demonstrated that, during the showing of a motion picture, the eyes of the men in the audience followed the woman on the screen. But so did the eyes of the women.

Sparky from St. Paul

SCHULZ AND PEANUTS: *A Biography*, by David Michaelis. 655 pp. Harper-Collins, 2007.

There is much to enjoy and admire in *Schulz and Peanuts*, a biography of Charles Schulz by David Michaelis. The basic story, of how a not conspicuously gifted but very determined barber's son from St. Paul, Minnesota, rose to become the richest cartoonist of all time, warms the heart in traditional American fashion. Michaelis, whose previous biography concerned the dynasty-founding illustrator N. C. Wyeth, never met Schulz but has interviewed almost everyone still alive who brushed against the lonely, self-contained creator of *Peanuts*, and has taken good advantage of the superabundant interviews that the cartoonist, jealous of his privacy though he was, gave to reporters:

> Charles Schulz's commitment to newspapers was second only to cartooning itself. He saw it as his obligation to give an interview to every editor who sent out a reporter, no matter how large or small or distant the paper. Across five decades he spoke through the press about his life and *Peanuts*, and in answering what were often the same old questions week after week, year after year, he charted major and minor shifts in his beliefs and opinions, all the while accumulating a vast treasury of commentary about his personality and character.

His character was made in Minnesota, and Michaelis has an evocative feel for such period Americana as the ecclesiastical profile of a mid-century Midwestern city:

> Veterans coming home to any midland city found the principal Christian denominations clearly marked: the Episcopalian parish church evoked Anglican tradition in its lavish half-timbering; the Catholic cathedral's domed basilica proclaimed its place in a universal order; Lutheranism showed its stolid presence in brick churches quietly displaying modest, useful banners announcing bingo and bake sales, their pinnacled bell towers culminating in tall Gothic spires; the Methodist and Presbyterian churches, the one built of stone, the other of wood, each thrust a tall white steeple over opposite corners of a well-tended thoroughfare, invariably Church Street.

Amid all this denominational pomp, Michaelis goes on to say, "the Church of God had no defining style or architectural tradition. It barely announced itself." It was to this colorless permutation of Christianity, founded in Indiana in 1881, that the young Schulz attached himself, becoming a tithing pillar and part-time preacher. In the raffish, New York City–centered brotherhood of cartoonists, he was an antisocial, tee-totalling, non-smoking oddity. He had never gone to an art school, learning his trade as a student at and then instructor for a Minneapolis learn-by-mail outfit called Art Instruction. *Peanuts* was launched, in 1950, in a squat, space-saving format and under an enigmatic title imposed, to Schulz's lifelong indignation, by the syndicate heads. That same year, his nomination to the National Cartoonists Society was blocked by Otto Soglow, the membership-committee chairman, on the ground that no member—not even his nominator, Mort Walker, of *Beetle Bailey* fame—had ever met him. In 1954, while *Peanuts* was taking off with the public and setting new standards of minimalist subtlety and quiet daring, Schulz came east to the society's awards dinner on the rumor that the coveted Reuben, already bestowed upon Walker and *Dennis the Menace*'s Hank Ketcham, would go to him. Instead, the sports cartoonist Willard Mullin received it. Schulz left without a word of farewell to his tablemates and claimed, back in Minneapolis, that he had been treated like "someone's poor relative."

The pervasive magic of syndicated cartooning in the twentieth century is knowingly sketched by Michaelis, not only in historical terms, from *The Yellow Kid* and *Happy Hooligan* on up through *Gasoline Alley* and *Blondie* and *Joe Palooka* and *Li'l Abner* and—the first strip to captivate intellectuals—*Krazy Kat*, but as experienced by the aspiring young Schulz. Born in 1922, he doted on the comic pages, copying *Popeye* and *Tim Tyler's Luck* on his father's shirt cardboards. When, in the Depression years, he earned nine dollars a week as a grocery-store clerk, he was enabled "to work with Bristol board and Higgins India ink and Craftint doubletone." The arcana of the cartoonist's trade were dazzlingly displayed, Michaelis relates, in a 1934 exhibition of comic-strip art at the St. Paul Public Library:

> Here hung several hundred lengths of layered illustration board stroked in dense ink more purely black and warmly alive than the engraving process allowed for. . . . Outside the panels, cryptic instructions had been penciled in the margin; sky-blue arrows aimed to catch an editor's eye. Inside the panels, there were unexpected traces of effort: accidental blots, glue stains and tape bits, strips of paper pasted to correct mistakes in lettering, unerased letters, registration marks, residues of white gouache, pentimenti reversing all kinds of slips and false starts—a whole unseen world of reasoning and revision had passed over the drawing board before mechanical reproduction reduced and tightened the lines.

And yet, for all the biographer's animation of the professional and geographical environments that shaped Schulz, he remains somewhat blank and hard to like, with a "cold, untrusting side." An only child, he was a second-generation American on both his German father's side and his Norwegian mother's. Though he signed his strips simply "Schulz" and inherited his father's work ethic, neatness, and devoted pride of profession, he said, "I always regarded myself really as being Norwegian and not German." Yet his mother's hard-drinking, violent-tempered brothers frightened him at Sunday family get-togethers. Though German immigrants gravitated to the cities and brought cultural institutions with them, the Norwegians, according to the Minnesotan Sinclair Lewis, "brought nothing new"; they clung to their family farms and clannishly intermarried. Neither ethnic group offered much encouragement to artistic aspirations, or lofty aspirations of any sort: "Don't get a big head" was a mantra of the upper Midwest; the big-headed tots of *Peanuts* emerged as a defiance. Nor was display of the heart prominent; there was not much touching, Michaelis notices, in family photographs or in Schulz's memory. When Sparky—as he was called all his life, nicknamed in infancy after the racehorse Spark Plug in the comic strip *Barney Google*—returned from the Second World War, in which he had seen overseas combat, he entered his father's barbershop and the haircut in progress continued. "No one gave me a hug," the young veteran recalled. "We didn't have any party. . . . That was it." In turn, Schulz was gingerly with his own children and shied from physical affection; his cousin Patty testified, "Hugging him was like hugging a tree—he never moved." At the outset of his wartime service, in 1943, he came home on a day pass to say goodbye to his mother, who was painfully dying of metastasized cervical cancer. In Michaelis's telling: "He said he guessed it was time to go. . . . She turned her gaze as best she could—it was a struggle to move at all. 'Well,' she said. 'Good-bye, Sparky. We'll probably never see each other again.'" A bleaker deathbed blessing has seldom been recorded.

The *Peanuts* empire early and late included bound volumes of the strips, and for some of them, notably the wide-format *Peanuts Jubilee* (1975), Schulz provided, in an economical, unassuming prose, pieces of autobiography between selections of reprinted *Peanuts*. His own version of his mother's farewell reads slightly softer than the version above: "Yes, I suppose we should say good-bye because we probably never will see each other again." In another spot he dips into his uncanny childhood sense of himself:

> When I was small, I believed that my face was so bland that people would not recognize me if they saw me some place other than where they normally would. I was sincerely surprised if I happened to be in the downtown area of St. Paul, shopping with my mother, and we would bump into a fellow student at school, or a teacher, and they recognized me. I thought that my ordinary appearance was a perfect disguise. It was this weird kind of thinking that prompted Charlie Brown's round, ordinary face.

Later in the same section, he writes, "Charlie Brown has to be the one who suffers, because he is a caricature of the average person. Most of us are much more acquainted with losing than we are with winning." This from a man who was making four million dollars in 1975 and was to receive, in the twenty-five years ahead, as much as sixty-two million a year, from the proceeds of the world's most widely syndicated strip and of shrewdly managed licenses for merchandise (clothing, books, toys, greeting cards), advertising (cameras, cars, cupcakes, life insurance), translations (Arabic, Basque, Malay, Tlingit, Welsh), animated television specials, and the musical comedy *You're a Good Man, Charlie Brown*, which went through forty thousand productions, involving 240,000 different performers. Behind the bland face a fiercely competitive spirit blazed; as Snoopy challenged Charlie Brown for the starring role in the strip, his creator bragged, "He is the most recognized character in the world, much more so than Mickey Mouse"—a gratuitous put-down of his mightiest predecessor in multimedia self-exploitation, Walt Disney.

Though short and slight as a boy, Schulz was a passionate athlete, living for after-school baseball games and ranking second on the high-school golf team. As an adult he held a low handicap (Michaelis, an apparent stranger to the terminology, calls Schulz "a scratch golfer, with a five handicap") and played in the Crosby Invitational until midlife agoraphobia curtailed his travels. In an attempt to re-create Minnesotan pleasures in northern California, Schulz and his first wife, the enterprising Joyce née Halverson, constructed an elaborate skating rink, the Redwood Empire Ice Arena, and there, while Schulz was playing on a hockey team opposing that of his son Monte, "Monte danced away from Sparky during a play, whereupon father slashed son across the backs of his legs so hard that Monte had trouble walking to the locker room." Still mentally smarting years afterward, Monte told Michaelis, "He really injured my leg—an unbelievable welt," and did not recall "that his father apologized until two days later." Nor did Sparky, in Michaelis's account, "express remorse or show sympathy" when, in 1970, Joyce discovered, through a telltale phone bill, his affair with Tracey Claudius, a twenty-five-year-old employee of the Fairchild Semiconductor Corporation who had tagged along on one of Schulz's innumerable interviews. Interviewed herself years later, Tracey delivered a thoughtful appraisal of her former lover: "He . . . never got over himself. I guess no one had made him the center of the world, so he became the center of his own world." His own self-appraisal put it, "It took me a long time to become a human being."

"She's something and I'm nothing," Charlie Brown says of the object of his hopeless romantic longing, the Little Red-Haired Girl. The young Schulz was invincibly chaste and shy. In 1941, when he was nineteen and working long night hours in an alcove in his parents' attic at gag "roughs" that *Collier's* and *The Saturday Evening Post* faithfully rejected, his mother, earthy, vivacious Dena, suggested that his gags perhaps weren't "smutty" enough. He later confessed, "I couldn't have drawn a 'smutty' cartoon if I had tried." He couldn't even say "damn" or "hell," as his prim father occasionally did. "Maybe there's some kind of a fatal flaw," he speculated. When, in 1950, a red-haired girl did stir him to pursuit and proposal, she married a virgin. Joyce herself had married before, at the age of nineteen; her first groom was a New Mexico cowboy who got her pregnant and deserted her so promptly that the child, a girl, was born back in Minneapolis. Michaelis writes, "When Sparky met her at the party, Joyce was twenty-two years old, divorced, with a baby and a curfew." Both she and his second wife, Jean, are still alive, so they are glimpsed through a mist of discretion. He and Joyce divorced in 1973, after twenty-two years and four more children; from start to finish, she was characterized by friends as "the dynamo of the duo"—brassy where he was wispy, venturesome where he was stay-at-home. She got him, against his inclinations, out of St. Paul—first, abortively, to Colorado Springs, and then, lastingly, to California—which was likely to the good, since he then had to reimagine his childhood instead of merely relive it. (Joyce's explanation of why they returned from Colorado after only nine months was that "Sparky couldn't handle being away from his dad.")

Joyce lives in his comic strips, Michaelis claims, as Charlie Brown's relentless tormentor Lucy Van Pelt. An Art Instruction colleague of Schulz's is quoted: "She and Sparky were a fun couple . . . but there were times when she was pretty nasty to him." To be fair, his passivity and his preoccupation with his strip might have been maddening. Both wanted more than they were getting. In the years of their marriage, he had become a handsome man—slim, fit, silver-haired—as well as a hugely rich national celebrity, and women were beginning to pick up signals. Jean Clyde, sixteen years younger than he, took her daughter to the arena three times a week, and strode through the coffee shop called the Warm Puppy,* where Schulz, informally separated from Joyce at this point, daily had his breakfast. Jean—"intelligent and, among the women in Charles Schulz's life, comparatively well educated"—was the daughter of English parents; she had been brought up by her mother on a southern-California avocado ranch, and was the wife of a guitar-playing journalist who had turned to dealing in real estate. Though married to others when they met, Schulz and Jean were divorced and wed within the next year.

---

*"Happiness is a warm puppy"—Lucy Van Pelt, in a strip dated April 25, 1960.

They moved into what had been a bishop's residence, complete with prayer grotto.

Schulz's own religiosity seems to have quietly faded in the California sunshine, though he continued to contribute a cartoon panel to the Church of God magazine and for a time taught Methodist Sunday school in Sebastopol. His manifold newspaper interviews trace a gradual withdrawal: "I'm not an orthodox believer, and I'm becoming less of one all the time." Robert Short, the author of the immensely successful *The Gospel According to Peanuts* (1964), admitted, "Sparky . . . could sound like the conservatives, but . . . there was always this very humanistic liberal strain that was beneath the surface." In Schulz's strip, the Great Pumpkin episodes verge on travesty if not blasphemy, and in his life he diffidently accepted his children's lack of interest in Sunday school. His daughter Amy, who eventually became a Mormon, complained, "He never read [the Scriptures] to us kids and he never took us to church. He didn't share it with us."

Jean turned Schulz from a golfer into a tennis player. Whereas Joyce had worked off her leftover energy by going on building sprees (she married their contractor a day after the divorce came through), Jean flew airplanes with her mother and travelled the world with her two children by Mr. Clyde. She saw her new, aging husband through a quadruple heart bypass in 1981 that momentarily left Schulz's precise, dashing pen lines slightly shaky, and then through the colon cancer that carried him off, early in the year 2000, at the age of seventy-seven. His obituary appeared in Sunday papers the very same day as his last strip. "In the moment of ceasing to be a cartoonist, he ceased to be," Michaelis writes. For almost exactly fifty years, he had produced the strip alone—its ideas, its lettering, its every mark on Bristol board were his. Even the mechanical-appearing bars of Beethoven that appear behind Schroeder at his toy piano were hand-drawn by the cartoonist. "I work completely alone," he insisted. Amy recalled, "Were we his everything? No. His strip was his everything."

Michaelis secured permission to reproduce 240 images from the 17,897 *Peanuts* strips to illustrate how often they were closely derived from Schulz's life. Charlie Brown's insecurity, his longings, his baseball games, his barber father all go back to St. Paul. Snoopy is closely based upon an abnormally clever dog from Schulz's childhood called Spike; as Dena was dying, she said that if they ever had another dog they should name him Snoopy—*snupi* being a Norwegian term of endearment. The beagle's fantasies of the French Foreign Legion and of being a World

War I flying ace were based on Thirties movies that Schulz had imbibed as a boy in St. Paul's Park Theatre. Closer to adulthood, his affair with Tracey Claudius left blatant traces in the strip. Snoopy, typing away on the roof of his doghouse, parodied Schulz's own feverish love letters. In one of them, he wrote Tracey, "Dark hair and a perfect nose. Soft hands that are sometimes cool and sometimes warm"; Snoopy, lying dreamily on his doghouse roof, thinks, "She had the softest paws. . . . * sigh *." Joyce's discovery of his surreptitious phone calls showed up, Snoopyized, in the strip, as did Schulz's receipt of the summons in the divorce case she subsequently initiated. Snoopy, as Michaelis points out, is a grown-up, with a sex life—at the Daisy Hill Puppy Farm—and adult possessions, including a pool table, a stereo, and a van Gogh, somehow crammed into his doghouse. Episodes involving him come to reflect the psychedelic Sixties and are relatively free of the backbiting and unrequited love sadly common in the strip's population of children. Snoopy acquires a set of disreputable relatives based upon the male Halversons, and there are desert intervals (reminiscent of *Krazy Kat*'s surreal habitat) derived from the Schulz family's brief, ill-fated attempt to transplant itself, in 1929–31, to Needles, in the Mojave region of California.

Peanuts, of course, was more than a running autobiographical tease, as the reader can reassure himself by leafing through the lavish *Peanuts Jubilee* or its less lavish, rather jumbled successor, twenty-five years later, *Peanuts: A Golden Celebration*. The elegant economy of the drawing and the wild inventiveness of such pictorial devices as the towering pitcher's mound and the impossible perspective of Snoopy's doghouse keep the repetitiveness, talkiness, and melancholy of the strip a few buoyant inches off the ground, and save it from being fey. With the introduction, in 1970, of Snoopy's friend the tiny yellow bird Woodstock, Schulz gave himself access to a whole fresh realm of tenderness; a sort of parenthood at last crept into the strip, where human parents are invisible. And yet, in the end, it was the woeful personal undercurrent—the frozen memory of a grade-school loser's unshakable existential angst, a child alone behind his unrecognizably bland face—that set *Peanuts* apart and attracted the devoted loyalty of millions, including future celebrants like the artists Chip Kidd and Chris Ware and writers like Jonathan Lethem and Jonathan Franzen. As Schulz said, most of us are better acquainted with losing than with winning. *Peanuts* was a unique creation, a comic strip at bottom tragic.

Gallery Tours

OLD MASTERS

A Wistful Würzburger

TILMAN RIEMENSCHNEIDER: *Master Sculptor of the Late Middle Ages*, at the Metropolitan Museum of Art, New York, February 10–May 14, 2000.

The Metropolitan Museum's current exhibition of the sculpture of Tilman Riemenschneider and some contemporaries is, I would guess, the most exquisite package to arrive on these shores from pre-modern Northern Europe since the Vermeer show at Washington's National Gallery in 1995. As with the Vermeer, there is a problem of seeing. The Vermeer paintings, though most of the twenty-three had walls to themselves, were hard to glimpse through the scrum of art lovers in front of each; and, once a view had been obtained, it was hard to maintain it for more than a moment in the press of bodies. The Riemenschneider exhibit is besieged by no such throngs, but its elements, ingeniously mounted through seven spacious chambers, pose in acute form the perennial visual problem of sculpture: from what angle is it best, or most appropriately, viewed?

A color reproduction of a painting gives us, as precisely as the printer's process can manage, the thing itself, minus only the (not inconsiderable) qualities of its texture and scale. Sculpture, however, exists in three dimensions, and in variable light, so that no photograph can be definitive for more than one moment, usually a frontal and evenly lit moment, in a potentially infinite array of appearances. Most of these pieces were designed as aids to worship, mounted in churches at some height above the congregation and to be seen, dramatically shadowed, in the trembling soft glow of candlelight. Is it proper to approach, as I did in hopes of duplicating a supplicant's aesthetic sensations, a large limewood representation of the Virgin and Child, raised on the museum wall to place her feet level with my eyes, so closely that, looking upward, I created steep perspectives wherein hands, drapery, and the two holy heads achieved a dramatic, foreshortened conjunction? Was it legitimate to admire, from the side, in the *Seated Virgin and Child* attributed to Michel Erhart, the way the Christ Child's tiny uplifted right arm is freestanding in the narrow slot of space between his mother's abdomen and her arm, which thrusts into the Man-God's mouth one of the world's earliest (c. 1480) representations of a pacifier? More urgently still, did it deviate from permissible connoisseurship to look *behind* the wooden tableaux that predominate in Riemenschneider's late work, and to see, with a perverse thrill, that the figures so impressive and finely worked from the front are hollowed out like huge salad bowls, figures five feet high but hardly more than six inches deep? Riemenschneider, we feel, somehow tricked his public with such august *trompe l'oeil*, but the modern museumgoer sneaks behind the altarpiece and catches him out.

In his 1955 Mellon Lectures for the Fine Arts, *The Art of Sculpture*, Herbert Read claimed that sculpture appeals to the "haptic" sense. The word, scarcely heard of in 1955, can now be found in dictionaries, defined as "related to or based on the sense of touch." Read employed it in a subtler sense, closer to its parent Greek *haptikon*, "to lay hold of": the forms of sculpture arouse in the viewer "tactile impressions" which translate into semiconscious "bodily sensations," a virtually muscular apprehension of the object's dynamic mass and weight. Riemenschneider is a disconcerting sculptor in that his career evolved toward weightlessness, in the form of large altarpieces like bas-reliefs without the grounding panel of wood or stone.

Born around 1460, he appears on the records of Würzburg, in Franconia, in 1483, as a journeyman, having evidently received training elsewhere. Fourteen months later, in early 1485, he received his citizenship in this, the smallest (at six or seven thousand souls) of the three centers of woodcarving, the other two being Nuremberg and Ulm. An early Annunciation in alabaster, dated circa 1485, is displayed with another, anonymous, alabaster Annunciation, produced in Würzburg in 1484, and, though the comparison is meant to be in Riemenschneider's favor, the anonymous work distinctly makes the stronger appeal to our haptic sense: the figures are palpably blocks of stone, the faces rather lightly nicked by their features, whereas the Riemenschneider Gabriel's robes swirl and the Virgin's cup her torso like a crumpled chalice. The hair of both Riemenschneider figures is wonderfully dematerialized; the angel's long locks curl around deeply drilled vortices and the Virgin's long strands ripple in their gilt like slender snakes. The alabaster is subverted

Riemenschneider, Saint Barbara, *c. 1485–90. Alabaster with traces of polychromy.*

to animation and lightness; spirituality tugs at the relatively chunky figures. In another early alabaster, of Saint Barbara (c. 1485–90), the characteristic Riemenschneiderish expression—mournful eyes drooping
down at the outer corners and underlined with at least one crease; lips
pressed together with pensive, determined dents at the downturned
corners—is already in place.

Throughout the exhibition, regrettably, I was instinctively attracted to the statues that were *not* Riemenschneider's: the two finely carved Virgin and Childs attributed to Niclaus Gerhaert von Leiden, especially the superb small boxwood piece, whose tight grain permits the most uncannily delicate carving of the show; the faintly Romanesque, round-eyed applewood carving *Virgin and Child on the Crescent Moon*, attributed merely to "Strasbourg(?)"; the good-humored, even humorous sandstone *Saint Anne with the Virgin and the Christ Child*, also from Strasbourg; and, from 1516, the robust, theatrical *Archangel Raphael and the Young Tobias* by Veit Stoss, described by the catalogue as "Riemenschneider's most important contemporary and . . . often seen as his polar opposite." All of these works have a certain earthiness, an aura of good cheer, that is not prominent among Riemenschneider's beautiful qualities.

In Till-Holger Borchert's instructive catalogue essay on Riemenschneider's "shifting critical fortune" in Germany, it is noteworthy that Riemenschneider's name emerged from the multitude of late-Gothic sculptors only in the nineteenth century, and that a Weimar Republic exponent of "the autonomous entelechy of German art," Wilhelm Pinder, found Riemenschneider "dried up" and "senile" compared to what Borchert terms the "expressionist modernity of a Veit Stoss." Pinder, who became a Nazi supporter,* admired Veit Stoss's unbending, pugnacious character and saw Riemenschneider's prolific production as having corrupted all of Lower Franconia, blaming "this gentle tyrant" for "the destruction of the individuality of an entire artistic region."

Such cultural politicizing was encouraged by the political content of Riemenschneider's life. A prominent artist-burgher, he was several times elected to the Würzburg municipal council, and served as mayor in 1520–21. During the Peasants' Revolt of 1525, aimed at the Catholic nobility and especially violent in Franconia, he was on the municipal council which refused to allow Würzburg's prince-bishop, Konrad von Thüngen, to gather all his troops in the city. After the rebellion was crushed, Riemenschneider was dismissed from the council, jailed for two months, and, it is said, tortured. Though he lived for six more years, until 1531, no new sculpture appeared under his name; his resistance to the prince-bishop apparently cost him the state's indispensable patronage. In

---

*In his foreword to his 1939 volume *Art in the Age of Dürer*, he wrote: "This book appears before a Germany that is once again forced to fight for its life and challenged to even greater victory. . . . The author, who is no longer able to participate personally in this second great war, hopes for a small consolation from this minor contribution to the fortification of the German nation: that its perusal may, in a small way, serve to inspire action."

1945, speaking at the Library of Congress in the immediate wake of Allied victory, Thomas Mann cited Riemenschneider (in contrast to Martin Luther) as a good German who had resisted authority for the sake of "freedom and justice," which were "more important to him than art and peace of mind." At the same time, the artist's popularity within Hitler's Third Reich was second only to Dürer's, though the leading expert on Riemenschneider, Justus Bier, was a Jew and had been forced to emigrate in 1936. In the years of Communist rule in East Germany, Riemenschneider was cherished as a hero of "early civic revolution" and thus as a forerunner of German socialism.

His tardy emergence as a star of late-Gothic limewood sculpture, the popularity that overrode scholarly antagonism, and the uneasy feeling among explicators of German culture that he was somehow not quite German enough: these derive, it may be, from the sculptor's curious tenderness, a preoccupied dreaminess that sets him apart from what Georg Dehio, in his Weimar-era *History of German Art*, called "the simple efficiency of our nation." To him Riemenschneider seemed to "make a concession to beauty, with ethical and artistic sincerity, which was unexpected for German art of that time." A Netherlandish influence, by way of Strasbourg, has been proposed to explain the strangeness.

What we seem to have, most conspicuously in Riemenschneider's large male figures, is an attempt to express spirituality while acknowledging the heightened awareness of human individuality that came with the Renaissance. The faces on the High Gothic portal figures of the Chartres, Amiens, and Reims cathedrals, though individual, are relatively smooth; only beards and a few forehead wrinkles age them, their eyes are unnaturally far forward in their faces, and there is a tendency, vivid at Amiens, to a dreamy smile. They stare over our heads toward a glory close at hand; Riemenschneider's socketed eyes, with their creased lids, also stare over our heads, but at something farther away. The figures from Strasbourg in this show, the applewood Virgin especially, still have the round Gothic stare, whereas the eyes, say, of Mark from the Münnerstadt altarpiece (1490–92) and of the *Seated Bishop* (c. 1495–1500) usually displayed at the Cloisters, are weeping eyes—eyes weeping, unlike those of the crucified Christ from Darmstadt or the left-hand woman of the *Mourning Women* (c. 1510) from Stuttgart, without an immediate reason to weep.

Riemenschneider's figures are deeper sunk in the mire of this world than the Gothic statues, and their aspirations to rise above it leave them little margin for smiling. Of course, the medium of limewood permitted him greater precision in carving than limestone afforded the Gothic sculptors; his virtuosity extends itself in the bumps and sags of aging faces, such as those of the Cloisters bishop, the wonderful Saint Matthias from Berlin (c. 1500–5), Zebedee from the Victoria and Albert (c. 1505–10), the Saint Anne from Munich (c. 1505–10), Nicodemus in the big Lamentation from Grossostheim (1515), and the unignorable fat man at Simon's table in one of the relief panels from the Münnerstadt altarpiece.

Such fleshy realism, in the younger figures, can become sensual; the throats and hands of his Virgins, the only exposed flesh save for their faces, are attentively rendered. Their hands, with their manneristically extended fingers and sometimes grotesquely elongated thumbs (see that of the 1495 Virgin from Cologne), have been much praised, but I was struck by the delicately muscled throat of the Virgin from Boston's Museum of Fine Arts (1490–95) and by those of two female saints brought forth, for this exhibit, from private ownership: That of Saint Catherine shows its delicate rings of fat; the Virgin from Hamburg (c. 1503–5) has enough soft flesh under her dimpled chin to remind us

Riemenschneider, Virgin and Child (Hamburg), *c. 1503–5. Limewood.*

that chucking beneath the chin was a favored medieval form of sexual play. It is this Virgin, incidentally, who is most successfully united with the Child—holding him securely but up for display, turned to face his cosmic audience.

Riemenschneider, it is known, had four wives—two called Anna and two called Margarete—and his females, with their snug small bosoms and outthrust abdomens, are executed with a confident verve. The S-shaped pose, with a hip cocked to take the weight of a holy child or ponderous holy book held in a curved arm, is iconically standard, and a pose not given this swing would be too, well, wooden. Still, Riemenschneider's female statues made me wonder if the emphasis, by posture and costume both, on a woman's belly wasn't a medieval equivalent of the valorized bosom and derrière of modern fashion: the visual signalling of a gender characteristic, heightened in these Gothic carvings by deep, often oval drapery folds leading the eye up from the peeping feet to the area of the womb.

The uses of sculpture in a culture with no direct connection to classical humanist art are somewhat problematic. How lovely should a Virgin be? Some of Riemenschneider's—the one in the three-person fragment from an Adoration in Nuremberg (1485–90) and the late studio piece carved from an inferior piece of limewood (1521–22)—are very lovely, or are made to seem so in the catalogue photographs. Their real presence is less striking, less glamorous. As I say, the statues are generally mounted high, and their gazes search the space over our heads. Their realism aims to take us to the edge of an immaterial realm. Small statuettes for private worship arose in the late-medieval period, as part of the privatizing of religious experience that would flower, or collapse, into Protestantism. These figures, fanatical in their detailed working, were designed to be tactilely cherished: a contemporary book of devotions instructs the worshipper, "Kiss the beautiful little feet of the infant Jesus who lies in the manger and beg his mother to let you hold him for a while."

Does color add to the seductive persuasiveness of statuary? The Middle Ages thought so, at least in its church interiors, as we can see in Catholic churches to this day. Riemenschneider is associated with the shift to uncolored carving; if not the originator of it, he was an early convert. Most of the items in the exhibition are monochromatic wood, which does not mean that they were always so. Fashions changed: some works which Riemenschneider intended to be without paint looked so bare to their public that paint was soon added, whereas the nineteenth century so strongly preferred "honesty toward the material" that it stripped statues of paint which the centuries had left shabby in any case. The polychroming was not done in the sculptor's studio, but by a separate guild; the application of glazes, pastes, gilding, and sizing was a complex, gluey affair and filled in the finest details of the carving. The presence of very fine carving and textural stamping indicates that the sculptor intended the work to go unpainted. The few colored pieces at the Metropolitan show confirmed this twenty-first-century viewer's prejudice that paint makes the statue *less* persuasive—more toylike, more visually brittle, more clearly "off." Uncolored, of one natural substance, the statues occupy a realm of their own rather than enjoy a second-rate, inanimate status within ours. Mimesis does best with a restricted set of tools. Just as black-and-white movies had a stylized finality before the onset of Technicolor, so statuary in abandoning color became both more intimate and more impressive. Images self-professedly from the hand of man extract from us a leap like the leap of empathy; we are no longer children to be fooled into idolatry, into thinking a tinted simulacrum is inhabited by an actual spirit.

Yet something is lost in the sophistication. The representational statues we most trust are those which, in marble or metal, seem solid enough, sturdy enough in the round, to receive a spirit if one were, in answer to a Pygmalion's prayer, to descend. For that reason, we like to see the backs finished; Riemenschneider's little pearwood Adam from Vienna (1495–1500) is in fact least gawky when viewed from the back. A statue should exist in God's circumambient eye; there is a savor of bad faith to not-quite-three-dimensional fabrications designed, with careful distortions, to present a satisfactory illusion—stage sets within the holy theatre of the Mass. Of course, church interiors were to become more theatrical yet, in the Baroque spectaculars that accompanied the Counter-Reformation—a spillage of marble statues above the columns and a painted cupola receding straight up to heaven in a flurry of pink *putti* bottoms.

It occurred to me that my unease with mild, melancholy, masterful Riemenschneider had a Protestant accent, a touch of puritanical iconoclasm. Iconoclasm, and a whitewashed starkness of church interiors, was to follow Luther's revolution in Northern Europe. Most of what made the objects of Christian faith concrete—holy relics, indulgences, idol-like images—were renounced. The crucifix became a symbolic cross, without a man on it. Riemenschneider participated in this sublimating, though he died a Catholic—his tombstone portrait has a rosary in its hand. But his saints and gods represent an anxious humanity, a citizenry possessed by the invisible but not bodying it forth. They wear no halos, even in carved low reliefs, as from the Münnerstadt altarpiece, where it would have posed no mechanical problem to impose them. The exemplars of the new faith are heroic inwardly, their struggles and ardor written on their faces in a calligraphy of wrinkles and careworn resolve. When transcendent worth can wear no outward sign, the interesting amorphousness of democracy descends. In these galleries of complex visages and deeply carved, agitated draperies we feel the feudal hierarchies (though still puissant enough to jail and torture Riemenschneider and end his career) slipping away, ebbing from nations and the heavens, leaving mankind as we see it here—heroic, wistful, and willing to "make a concession to beauty."

Singular in Everything

EL GRECO, at the Metropolitan Museum of Art, New York, October 7, 2003–January 11, 2004.

The strangeness begins with his name, which was properly Doménikos Theotokópoulos; he always signed his works thus, often in Greek characters, but in Italy he was called Il Greco, and in Spain Domenico Greco or El Griego. The solecism "El Greco" is what stuck. Born in Crete, trained in Italy, he found recognition and employment only in Toledo, the capital of the Spanish Counter-Reformation, teeming with Neoplatonists and idealistic priests burning to take back Europe from the Protestants or, that hope failing, to make an implacable stand in the Spanish heartland. In Toledo, in his mid-thirties, he found himself, and was indulged. The king in Madrid, the conscientious and grimly pious Philip II, spurned the immigrant painter's efforts to become one of the decorators of his pet project, the gigantic Monastery of San Lorenzo de El Escorial. The king had ordered the prior to equip El Greco with materials, "especially ultramarine," for a commission on the martyrdom of Saint Maurice, but rejected the finished work, on grounds that modern critics speculate about: perhaps Philip didn't like the contemporary portraits the painter had included, or the fact that the martyrdom itself is relegated to the middle background. El Greco, undoubtedly pious, set exalted fees, inaugurated many financial disputes, and operated on the edge of the iconographically permissible. His admirer Francisco Pacheco, who was to become the teacher of Velázquez, found that "El Greco made statements that were paradoxical and contrary to received opinion." In his *Arte de la pintura*, Pacheco wrote that the Greek was "singular in everything, as he was in painting."

Had El Greco not invented himself, no one like him need have existed. Dutch genre painting might not have produced a Vermeer, or Venetian art a Titian, but the many close approaches would make a gap hard for even the most intuitive art historian to notice. El Greco, on the sparser cultural ground of Spain, looms as a brilliant anomaly, with a large work-shop but no followers, and his antecedents in Italian mannerism flamboy-antly consumed within his peculiar ardor. Yet his name didn't cross the Pyrenees during his lifetime (1541–1614), and it wasn't until the nine-teenth century (as in the case of Vermeer) that his reputation as a master took shape. Delacroix and John Singer Sargent owned copies of El Greco's works; Cézanne did a copy of one, *A Lady in a Fur Wrap* (late 1570s). In the twentieth century, the homage becomes passionate, at the expense of Velázquez: the Met quotes on the exhibit's walls Picasso ("Velázquez! What does everybody see in Velázquez these days? I prefer El Greco a thousand times more. He was really a painter") and Matisse ("When I saw [Velázquez's] work in Madrid, to my eyes it was like ice! Velázquez isn't my painter: Goya, rather, or El Greco"). Jackson Pollock listed El Greco among his five favorite painters, and in his groping apprentice years copied into his notebooks rather Cubistic analyses of details in El Greco reproductions, focusing on the linear rhythms of the drapery; five pages are on display in the Met's gallery of drawings, a few steps from the six second-floor rooms where some eighty works by El Greco are proudly on display.

On the day of the preview for reporters and special friends of the museum, a mellifluous, mutually congratulatory speechifying from the various experts, directors, curators, and financial powers responsible for the show—the first major retrospective in this country since 1982—drowned out any concern that, for the twenty-first-century art public, these large, lurid, hyper-Catholic canvases, with their tormented compo-sitions and insipidly pretty, pasty faces, might reawaken the qualms of Philip II and seem *too* singular, and even—dare I say?—repellent.

In 1983, the cleaning of an icon kept in the Holy Cathedral of the Dor-mition of the Virgin, on the island of Syros, Greece, uncovered the name of Doménikos Theotokópoulos, and this small but ambitious painted panel, containing many figures in a partially gilded tableau, together with a damaged representation from an Athens museum of Saint Luke as him-self an icon painter, reminds us, at the exhibition's outset, that El Greco began as a producer of holy artifacts, of icons still Byzantine in their rigid postures, zigzag clothing folds, and rudimentary perspective, though some attempt to render depth in the Italian manner was made. Crete at that time was a possession of the Venetian Republic; it was to Venice, and then Rome, that he travelled in his mid-twenties, studying the work of Titian and Tintoretto, Correggio and Parmigianino, and reading Vasari's *Lives*. He retained, however, an icon maker's way of thoroughly using his space and of resorting to stark white highlights, which give fabric in even his later work a coarse and implausible shine; white outlines impart to the cityscape of his magnificent *View of Toledo* (c. 1597–99) its spectral ghost-liness. All his life, except for his secular portraits and the celebrated *View*, he produced religious images designed to be seen in a church's dim candlelight, at some distance; in such settings his garish colors and failure to provide High Renaissance perspective were virtues of a sort. His most striking invention, his flattened space, with a twisting, gray, close back-ground spilling down from explosive skies, suits a church niche and the abstracted glance of worshippers. Roger Fry in 1920 wrote of El Greco's "peculiar power of creating, as it were, a new kind of space, a space of which we have no actual experience, but which we accept as peculiarly enhancing the emotional tone of the scene." It permits, Fry went on to observe, the large figures to "seem to move freely in a vaster space than any actual scene of such dimensions would allow."

As the viewer moves through the early rooms, holding works from the 1560s and 1570s, he painfully feels the painter's struggle with Italianate perspective, its large colorful crowds distributed over receding marmo-real vistas. His several treatments of *Christ Healing the Blind* and *The Purification of the Temple* never achieve persuasiveness or the stage-front drama that would become characteristic. The second tableau, with its agitated knot of figures being whipped by a Christ athletically up on one foot, was more congenial to El Greco's sense of concentrated action, and versions are displayed from as late as (roughly) 1600 and 1610. In the lat-ter, grotesque elongation stretches Christ to an ineffectual slenderness, his whip all but hidden by his upraised hand; the arch giving in other ver-sions onto an outdoor street has been sealed shut; a wildly gesticulating woman and cherub have been added, out of scale, to the extreme left edge; and, higher up on this edge, a marble nude (Adam?) threatens to shimmy right out of his niche.

As El Greco settled more securely into his visionary mode of attenu-ated anatomy and surreally compressed space, he arrived at a nervous, crumbly brushwork, a dashing dry treatment conspicuous in the mon-strously ungainly *Laocoön* of the early 1610s and the fine, rather homo-erotically charged portrait of the poet-priest Fray Hortensio Félix Paravicino (c. 1609). En route to this furry and electric texture his brush-strokes worry in a wormy way at forms that don't really engage him. The two *Pietàs* of the 1570s echo the triangular monumentality of Michelangelo's unfinished sculpture (probably known to the painter through an engraving) without Michelangelesque solidity; the bodies have the weight and tint of chalk while the sky looms in broad slabs, one of which, in the *Pietà* of 1575, actually eclipses, by a feat of vaporous occlusion, the tops of Calvary's three crosses. Other unpleasant, primitive representations, all from the early 1570s, include *The Adoration of the Shepherds*, as Stygian as a cellar; *Saint Francis Receiving the Stigmata*, a golden landscape with a leaden flow and a nonplussed saint; and *Mount Sinai*, tall brown heaps suggesting towers of excrement or mourners wrapped in mud, dabbled with tiny figures and constructions feebly adapted from a woodcut by Titian. El Greco did not have an easy time converting himself from the brittle, formal style of Eastern Christianity to the physical realism of the West.

This triumphant physical realism, of which Michelangelo was the epitome, posed a problem for religious representation: the more vividly anatomical and muscular the figures became, the less spiritual they seemed. Michelangelo's drawing of a fully fleshed Christ floating up out of the tomb, and his sculpture of the beautiful young body lying in the Virgin's broad lap, were as far as visual humanism could be stretched to illustrate the Christian story; the broad-chested frontal nude, with penis, hurling judgment out upon mankind on the great wall of the Sistine Chapel may have been godlike, but he wasn't the meek, conflicted Jesus of the Gospels or the hieratically stiff deity of medieval tympana showing the Last Judgment. How to get past all this more precisely limned sinew and muscle and keep a grip on heaven, on the immaterial other world? Raphael and Leonardo softened their anatomical mastery with sweet, half-smiling facial expressions, and Pontormo, whom Michelangelo had commended as a successor, brilliantly bestowed an impossible lightness upon his figures, so that in his pastel-colored *Transportation of Christ* (c. 1527–28) the foreground figures carrying Christ's dead weight support themselves on a few unbending toes.

El Greco, in the ambitious *Adoration of the Name of Jesus* (c. 1577–79), hasn't yet solved the problem of weight for himself; the sharklike mouth of a teeming hell, the countless heads of the redeemed like a roadway of round cobblestones, the sickly-white profile of Philip II (who was still being courted by the painter) are dutiful renditions, filled in without flair. The sky above, however, populated by baroquely foreshortened angels kneeling on rock-solid clouds, composes more happily, inviting the eye to travel toward the mystic name. In his much-admired signature piece, *The Burial of the Count of Orgaz* (1586–88), still in Toledo but prominent in the catalogue, the heavenly upper half is more persuasive than the overly literal, face-by-face depiction of the funeral ceremony. Even in the clumsy *Saint Francis Receiving the Stigmata*, the free-flowing clouds attract our eye. El Greco was at home in the clouds, their visual tumult and their release from the spatial confinements of gravity. His jagged skies feel on the verge of lightning and of the darkness that preceded the veil of the temple being split in two.

At the Met, in the third chamber, our eyes greet at last a masterpiece, *echt* El Greco: *The Crucifixion with Two Donors* (c. 1580). A slender silvery flame of skin, Christ rolls his eyes and his nail-pierced hands upward; he is flying, against a background of black cloud, leaving below the two reverent donors, only their torsos in view as they stand on the unseen earth. Against precedent (as the catalogue essay points out), there is no trace of landscape. Nor are there the usual mourners, or attending angels, or any sense, as there is in the Michelangelo chalk drawing *The Crucifixion* (1538–41), of any pain or muscular resistance, or, as in a Cellini marble sculpture (1556–62), of sagged weight, relaxed in the surrender of death. This Christ spectacularly lives, in a transmaterial realm of blanched flesh lit from within, closely looming skies, and minimal terrestrial traces. To this sublime realm belong the paired portraits *Mary Magdalene in Penitence* and *Saint Peter in Penitence*, the rather epicene *Christ Carrying the Cross* (the catalogue points out that the cross seems weightless and "the eloquently drawn hands . . . do not so much grasp as delicately embrace" it), the stagy but eloquent *Saint Dominic in Prayer*, and *The Holy Family*, marred by one of the ugliest Christ children ever shown mouthing a breast. All are dated in the 1580s.

In the twenty-five years left to him, El Greco extended his brand of mannerism deeper into the individuality and eccentricity that endears him, with his distortions, nervous brushwork, and unmodulated sharp colors, to the modern spirit. Soaring operatic concoctions like *The Annunciation* (c. 1597–1600) and *The Virgin of the Immaculate Conception* (1608–13) are in their way stupendous, though the vapid expressions and pointy noses of his long-necked females give their cosmic occasions a flavor of Watteauesque fête. *The Resurrection* (late 1590s), very narrow for its height, has a slender, red-bearded Christ whose levitation out of the tomb knocks a crowd of Roman soldiers clad in skintight monochrome tunics flat on their backs; the viewer could more easily assimilate the wild tumble of limbs if Christ were not wearing a slight smirk and gesturing like a debonair stuntman saying, "What do you think of *that*!"

The Adoration of the Shepherds, in its version of 1612–14, is one of the last paintings from El Greco's hand and ingeniously uses the tiny body of the newborn Jesus as the main source of illumination, so that all the witnesses, including two angels and a flock of cherubs above, bask in its glow; the ingenious conception loses the intimacy of the manger. In such details as the arm of the tallest shepherd here, and the side figures of *Lao-*

El Greco, The Crucifixion with Two Donors, *c. 1580. Oil on canvas.*

coön, and, most boldly, the spectral nudes of *The Opening of the Fifth Seal* (1608–14), anatomical truth is brushed aside; these wavery limbs and dwindled heads have less to do with the human body than with an *idea* of bodies, whose basic reality lies behind or beyond their appearance: white shadows in a cave where flares of neon color patch a basic *grisaille*. Stiff and shiny robes, smeared with white shine, take on the self-importance of clerical vestments—see the left-hand figure in *The Opening of the Fifth Seal*, the hasty *Marriage of the Virgin* (c. 1613–14), and the nearly Daliesque *Visitation* (early 1610s), which seems less the meeting of two women than of two hooded robes.

Then there are the portraits, some of them superb: the much-reproduced bespectacled cardinal of 1600–1; the agreeably misty, wispy *Elderly Gentleman* (late 1580s or 1590s); the stabbing, near-pointillistic *Antonio de Covarrubias* (about 1600); the early *Giulio Clovio* (c. 1571–72), with a golden crust of facial rework *à la* Rembrandt; the gallant yet fragile *Nobleman with His Hand on His Chest* (c. 1583–85); and the startling *Lady in a Fur Wrap* (late 1570s), a fur-clad, ivory-faced beauty staring out with her huge dark eyes at the painter as if to recall him from otherworldly visions. Indeed, the authenticity of the attribution to El Greco has been questioned. She is the only female in this sober room of black-suited grandees and robed, rueful clerics. Perhaps for this reason, a woman in the crowd of previewers confided, "This to me is the deadest room in the show." With its submission to close observation and its concern with individual personality the room was the least El Grecoesque; like the religious paintings of Goya, the portraits remind us that their visionary creator was also a practitioner, a professional adept.

In another passing comment, an acquaintance, a distinguished painter and caricaturist, told me that he, though an atheist, now found himself, after this show, willing to be converted. Was my own relative lack of enthusiasm, I wondered, a product of a stubborn, hard-shell Protestantism? The catalogue, in its essay by David Davies, briskly sketches the Catholic Counter-Reformation, whose main cause, of course, was the Protestant Reformation. Luther and, more rigorously, Calvin dismissed a vast intercessory apparatus that included the Pope, the supernatural role of the priest during Mass, the transubstantive nature of the Eucharist, confession, absolution, and the selling of indulgences to lessen a sinner's posthumous term in purgatory. In place of all this, Protestantism substituted *sola fide*, the Holy Bible, long sermons, and bare church walls. Roman Catholicism answered with its own simplifications and inwardness, notably a concentration upon mystical union with God through Christ. "Thus," Davies writes, "the narrative cycle of Christ's life was subordinated to the specifically salvific, to the achievement of salvation. Scenes of his infancy, passion and resurrection, rather than of his ministry, predominated in Catholic prayers and writings." When Christendom split in two, both sides sought higher, purer ground in subjective experience, as the tide of materialism—with it, science and atheism— inexorably rose, claiming the universe.

In Spain, the union with Christ took on erotic qualities derived, in part, from the love poetry of the Moors. Saint John of the Cross, the greatest of the Counter-Reformation poets, wrote of a night where, "inflamed by love's desires," he ventured out to a rendezvous *"Amado con Amada, Amada en el Amado transformada,"* which my English translation, without the convenience of genderized nouns, renders as "Lover with Mistress, the Mistress transformed into the Lover!" Something of this ecstatic androgyny permeates El Greco's images of Christ, with their long-fingered hands, airy gestures, and fine-grained pallor. What I miss in them is a sense of God Incarnate, a walking-around Jesus, a man among others, as we see in Giotto and Titian, in Rembrandt's etchings and Dürer's woodcuts. El Greco's divine personages, once he has reached his stylistic maturity, are like movie stars, perfect and untouchable. His Baby Jesus is a lightbulb. His art has the slickness of any art that doesn't subject itself to a constant reality check.

El Greco solved, in singular fashion, the problem of weight. His supernatural bodies lift free of gravity, but at a cost: they seem insubstantial— too smooth, too rapt, too willowy, too elongated. They exist, but up there, in another world, with little of, say, Giovanni Bellini's calm, gem-bright practicality of draftsmanship. True to his origins as an icon painter, El Greco provides votive images, images that draw our attention out of ourselves, in an aspiring direction. But only occasionally—as in the fiery, frowning, famous *Saint Jerome as a Scholar* (c. 1600–14), or in the freely painted canvas of a gaunt, yellow-robed *Saint Peter* (early 1610s), with his loosely held keys to the kingdom, his bony other hand, his touching little bare feet, and his rueful oblique gaze—do we feel the pinch of the human bind.

More Light on Delft

PIETER DE HOOCH, 1629–1684, at the Wadsworth Atheneum, Hartford, Connecticut, December 17, 1998–February 27, 1999.

Pieter de Hooch, though often cited in lists of Dutch painters, was never the exclusive subject of a show until one this fall, which enjoyed record-breaking attendance in its ten weeks at London's Dulwich Picture Gallery before coming, with the winter, to the Wadsworth Atheneum in Hartford. His reputation has long been associated with that of his contemporary Vermeer. When, in 1765, a painting of his was offered for sale in Amsterdam, it was described as *"zoo goet als de Delfze van der Meer"*—"as good as Vermeer of Delft"—and the nineteenth-century French critic Théophile Thoré, in reviving Vermeer's reputation, attributed to him five paintings by de Hooch. It is true that both painters portray intimate domestic interiors of a modest scale and quiet mood, but de Hooch suffers cruelly from the comparison. His brushstrokes are scratchy, his colors brownish and murky, and his compositions haphazard when viewed with Vermeer's pellucid and exquisitely rigorous canvases in mind. Compared with Vermeer, de Hooch does not draw well, let alone paint with the younger man's serene rapture of weightless touch and opalescent color. For Vermeer, as for very few artists prior to the Impressionists, painting is not just the method but the subject, a topic explored in such dazzling visual essays as the reflections on a brass water pitcher and basin, the shadows falling across the shallow ridges of an unscrolled map, the photographically exact yet rather freely brushed pattern of a folded and foreshortened Oriental rug, the liquid spill of a lacemaker's red and white threads, the cool folds and dimples of a silk skirt, the delicately muted and flattened colors of a picture on a wall—a picture within a picture to tell us that this too is a picture. The science of perspective and the invention of the *camera obscura* opened to Vermeer, in this era of burgeoning astronomy and microscopy, a world of optical truth to which both the painter and his human subjects are in a sense transitory visitors, accessories to the transcendent process whereby light defines objects.

With de Hooch the topic is less the seeing than what we see—homely Dutch folk and their furniture, their rooms, the cityscape glimpsed over their shoulders. Thirty-eight of his paintings fill two big rooms of the Wadsworth (it and the Dulwich Gallery, the catalogue proudly points out, are equally venerable—"the first public museums to open in their respective countries"), and they reveal not only where de Hooch falls short of Vermeer but where he goes beyond him, providing what Vermeer in his great rarefaction does not. Children, for one thing. Though Vermeer had at least eleven, not a single child appears in a painting by him, perhaps because children could not remain still long enough. On the other hand, a high proportion of the de Hooch canvases on display at Hartford contain children—a bit stiffly and incidentally in *Mother and Child with a Serving Woman Sweeping* (c. 1655–57), *Two Women and a Child in a Courtyard* (c. 1657–58), and *A Woman and Child in a Bleaching Ground* (c. 1657–59), and with an affecting tenderness and concentration in *Woman and Child in an Interior* (c. 1658) and *A Woman with a Baby in Her Lap, and a Small Child* (1658). The tiny hands in the latter—the baby's curled in drowsy relaxation on its mother's lap, the child's grasped around a complaisantly limp lapdog—are painted with a tactful skill de Hooch brought rarely to human anatomy. The sunlight caught in the backlit woolly hair of the child in *The Bedroom* (c. 1658–60) is one of de Hooch's most admired effects, tellingly enlarged in the catalogue, and *A Mother and Child with Its Head in Her Lap* (c. 1658–60), showing the mother searching her docile child's head for lice, is one of his most loved and atmospheric interiors. He does not let us forget that a focus of these

De Hooch, A Mother and Child with Its Head in Her Lap, *c. 1658–60. Oil on canvas.*

cozy, clean, sun-washed Dutch interiors is the nurture and protection of children; it is their pets and toys (including a *colf* club and ball) that interrupt the swept severity of the tile floors.

All these paintings—and the bulk of de Hooch's best—come from the period when, by the spotty records, he lived in Delft. Born in Rotterdam in 1629, he learned and practiced his trade there until his marriage to a Delft woman in 1654 cemented his move to that city, a venerable and economically declining center of tapestry ateliers, breweries, and delftware factories. This modest town of twenty thousand people housed, during the 1650s, a boom in genre painting, including such artists as Gerard ter Borch, Carel Fabritius, and Jan Steen, as well as Vermeer and de Hooch. Though no records remain of interactions between the latter two, it seems unlikely that in circles so small there were none. De Hooch, three years older, may have influenced Vermeer to turn from the large mythological subjects of his earliest canvases to smaller-scaled realism. Around 1660, de Hooch moved from Delft to the metropolis of Amsterdam, where the patronage was richer, and his paintings became more elaborate and ostentatiously refined.

But while in Delft he captured qualities excluded from Vermeer's paradise of jewel-like moments. The son of a bricklayer, de Hooch gives us the textures underfoot. The floor tiles, arrestingly smoothed to a pattern of alternating black and white in Vermeer, in de Hooch paintings wear their uneven glazing, their raised edges catching the light. His bricked courtyards have the slight wave of uneven earth beneath, and his whitewashed walls bear cracks and rough patches. When de Hooch gets to Amsterdam, he exults in walls of gilt leather, whose embossed and glinting arabesques, in such ambitious canvases as *A Party of Figures Around a Table* (c. 1663–65) and *Merry Company* (c. 1663–65), all but overpower the rather pallidly projected merry companies. The human figures in the Amsterdam pictures in general lack the warmth of individuality, as if he did not know them the way he did his neighbors in Delft; he visits their houses as a social inferior and is encouraged to focus on their conspicuous possessions. *A Seated Couple with a Standing Woman in a Garden* (c. 1663–65) strikingly highlights the sunstruck façade of a small Amsterdam house—brick by brick and pane by pane, vivid as an architect's projection—and leaves the tête-à-tête in shadow and its flirting couple virtually faceless. De Hooch's sense of human drama is vague and elastic enough, frequent *pentimenti* reveal, to permit him to paint people in and out quite late in the stages of composition. In *A Woman Drinking with Two Men, and a Serving Woman* (c. 1658), the serving woman was added to fill the unpopulated right half of the canvas after the completion of the floor tiles, which show through her feet and skirt; in *A Music Party in a Hall* (c. 1663–65), a black servant attending a viola-da-gamba player was painted out, leaving a wineglass being passed between them suspended in an awkward toast. Even if de Hooch did not execute these later revisions, something unresolved in his initial composition opened the way for the muddle. Some of his figures have a Magritte-like air of floating disconnection. The viewer is frequently struck by vacuously dark stretches in his canvases, whose occupants seem semi-lost in spaces too big for them.

Perhaps space is the secret topic that concerned de Hooch. If Vermeer was the much superior director of human drama, even when only one woman is on the canvas, de Hooch gives us an aspect of Delft that Vermeer, save in his two great cityscapes, reduces to a creamy light evenly streaming through a window: the outdoors. De Hooch's sunlight is tawny, one with his orange tiles, baked bricks, and varnished cabinets. He takes us out into the paved courtyards where much of Delft's domestic work was done; he shows us a dirt alley blanketed with laundry (*A Woman and Child in a Bleaching Ground*) and depicts the makeshift wooden sheds and lattices that pieced out this city of brick and tile (*A Courtyard in Delft with a Woman and Child*, 1658). Further, his interiors have long perspectives, one room opening into another where a window in turn affords a glimpse of sunlit scenery. The two of his paintings with children already mentioned as most affecting share this layout, and in the slightly later *Bedroom* the interplay between outdoor and indoor illumination approaches the virtuosic. There is the child's hair and figure, backlit by the daylight of a vista seen through two doorways, and there is a tawny double window on the left, illumining the mother on the left, planting a rectangular highlight on a chamberpot at her feet, and drawing a trapezoidal shadow from the painting above the doorway. The watery band of light—a ghost refraction—thrown diagonally through the window is well observed, and possibly never before registered in any painting.

The sense of healthy interchange between outdoors and indoors, between leafy growths and buffed artifacts, helps to create the airy intimacy of *A Mother and Child with Its Head in Her Lap*, where open doors on the left disclose a sunny exterior and open curtains on the right a pillowed bed—a stereoscope of housed comfort. (*A Courtyard in Delft with a Woman and Child* offers an even more distinctly double view, as if each eye is being offered a separate channel.) In his Amsterdam phase, the far doorway giving onto a sunny vista became a compulsive de Hooch signature; in one painting of the magnificent new town-hall interior (*The Interior of the Burgomasters' Council Chamber in the Amsterdam Town Hall with Visitors*, c. 1663–65), he violated the actual design to create such a motif, and in another (*A Couple Walking in the Citizens' Hall of the Amsterdam Town Hall*, c. 1663–65) a nineteenth-century restorer did it for him, adding an imaginary room with checkerboard floor and bright window to make the painting, presumably, more de Hoochian. But the distinguished passage of this painting is the beautifully hovering patch of sunshine which, falling through an unseen window, splashes the base of a great pilaster and bounces—it or a brother beam—across the chests of the strolling couple. Two Amsterdam paintings not in the show but reproduced in the catalogue, *Woman Lacing Her Bodice Beside a Cradle* (c. 1661–63) and *A Boy Handing a Woman a Basket in a Doorway* (c. 1660–63), show his indoor-outdoor fugue to exquisite, enamelled effect. Such canvases, though more dryly detailed than any by Vermeer, have been lifted above the anecdotal interest of genre scenes to a plane of pure painting—"pure" for lack of a juster word to denote painting as disinterested exploration and meditation. The splash of golden light adds almost nothing to the republican splendor of the town hall or the picturesque character of the couple; it adds a good deal to our sense of time and of the universe.

What a curious thing, after all, genre painting is, beginning with the name—an inexpressive term, the French word for "sort" or "type," first

De Hooch, A Merry Company with Two Men and Two Women (*detail*), *c. 1657–58. Oil on panel.*

used in English, according to the OED, in 1849 to designate paintings of ordinary life. Though examples can be found in French painting (Chardin) and American (Winslow Homer, the Ashcanners), the supreme examples belong to the Dutch seventeenth century. The emergent middle class holds up the mirror to itself in saucy eclipse of all those gods and kings who formerly held a monopoly on glorification. A school arises that abandons the religious and mythological subjects which have hitherto formed the nearly exclusive matter of European painting and substitutes, with a vengeance, the daily ordinary, including such ignoble scenes as soldiers getting drunk in a brothel and mothers wiping their infants' shitty bottoms. Its genealogy can be traced from late-medieval calendar illustrations through the scenes of peasant life by Pieter Brueghel the Elder; but a crucial transition, I think, exists in the Biblical scenes by Caravaggio and Rembrandt and (a bit later) de La Tour that garbed the incidents of Holy Scripture in the particularized faces and intimate gestures of a neighborhood household. These Bible people are people we know: a Protestant assertion that brings the sublime down to earth. Dutch genre painting, according to Peter C. Sutton's excellent, comprehensive catalogue text, began in the sixteenth century with frankly cautionary illustrations of intemperance and brothel revelry. With gusto Jan Steen depicted *The Effects of Intemperance, The Drunken Couple, The Disreputable Woman, The Disorderly Household.* The debauches of the Prodigal Son and of Lot with his daughters came in for pointed illustration. Soldiers, a constant Dutch presence in these decades of the Eighty Years' War, were a favorite topic for "guardroom" paintings that showed them as tipsy and lusty—no military *gloire* here.

De Hooch began with brownish, stilted, claustral depictions of "merry company"—rest and recreation, it was called in later days. A sinister though increasingly vague atmosphere of sexual negotiation dominates. In *A Merry Company with Two Men and Two Women* (c. 1657–58) the painter startles us with, near the center of the canvas, in a quartet of otherwise averted or cursory faces, a woman's face, sunlit, of vivid expectancy and alertness. Her wrist is being clasped by the man across the table from her, so it is clear enough what she is being alert and expectant about; but here, in a room whose shape and lighting could be straight from Vermeer, de Hooch goes further than he has to and gives us a brilliant, dramatic exploration of a live person—a kind of painterly grace has descended on this hyperanimated woman of dubious virtue. Something of the same abrupt brilliance returns in a late painting of his Amsterdam period, *A Man Reading a Letter to a Woman* (c. 1670–74). Her red dress and gold skirt attract the sun, but our attention is held by the complex expression on her listening face, patient yet skeptical. The genius of genre painting was that, unlike more hierarchical and stylized and reverent modes, it posed no deflecting alternative to reality.

Rather, it insisted on it—the mundane quotidian in its ambiguous, charged stillness. And, just as sunlight broke through the leaded windows into the whitewashed rooms, a freshly felt glory infused representation. The Dutch virtues—a fierce cleanness and orderliness in the face of threats from monarchal empires and the unruly sea—idealized the patient rounds of daily housekeeping. How central a sense of shelter was to the beauty of Dutch genre painting is indicated by the drab sunlessness of de Hooch's outdoor paintings of women doing laundry or of families posing for a portrait: there was too much naked light for him; he could not form defining shadows or highlights. His Amsterdam pictures get darker and darker, framing a few spotlit figures. Circumambient light seen from inside, and experienced within: that is de Hooch's settled manner, and a metaphor for Protestantism's new version of religious experience.

Plain and Simplified

CHARDIN, at the Metropolitan Museum of Art, New York, June 27–September 3, 2000.

The elegant Chardin show at the Met has been travelling through the turnover of centuries, beginning in Paris last fall, advancing to Düsseldorf and London, and arriving in the New World with an air of triumph. Chardin, whose life stretched from 1699 to 1779, has come to outrank, to modern taste, Watteau and Fragonard at the earlier, rococo end of his century and David at the other, neoclassical end. André Malraux, fifty years ago in *The Voices of Silence*, delivered this judgment: "Chardin is not a minor eighteenth-century master who was more delicate than his rivals; like Corot he is a subtly imperious *simplifier*. His quiet talent demolished the baroque still-life of Holland and made decorators out of his contemporaries; in France, nothing can rival his work, from the death of Watteau to the Revolution." Chardin's eloquent literary champions range from the *philosophe* Diderot, who said of the painter's work that "it is nature itself," to Proust, who in a study of Chardin unpublished during his lifetime wrote that, "having understood the life of his painting you will have discovered the beauty of life." Chardin's later admirers include

Manet, Cézanne, van Gogh, Giacometti, Francis Ponge, Julien Green, Lucian Freud, the brothers Goncourt, Vermeer's rediscoverer Théophile Thoré, and a host of modern critics whose detailed appreciations are surveyed by Colin B. Bailey in his catalogue essay on recent writings on Chardin. The French painter, whose repute and income during his lifetime, while not insignificant, were unspectacular, has been enlisted in the exalted company of Vermeer and Cézanne, the purest of pure painters, whose genre scenes and still lifes, respectively, both impeccably serve and mystically transcend their subjects.

Made expectant by rumors of this high regard, the visitor to the eight galleries the Metropolitan has devoted to Chardin may be surprised (especially if he or she has come from the bright and lively show of modern Paris paintings on the floor below) by the rather relentless brownness of Chardin's canvases, their skyless subterranean cast; they seem, most of them, rendered with an ascetic palette more Spanish than French. Some of the colors may have sunk: the orange in *Rabbit with Red Partridge and Seville Orange* (1728–29) is a half-ghost; the plums in *Bowl of Plums, a Peach and Water Pitcher* (1728–30) are likewise chalky and unfleshed; and the dead thrush in *Wild Rabbit with Game Bag, Powder Flask, Thrush and Lark* (c. 1730) is a transparent sketch in white and gray. These early still lifes were almost all arranged on the same stone ledge, before an olive-drab stone wall rendered with a fury of broad brushing and scrubby blotches that anticipates Abstract Expressionism—for example, in the two identically sized canvases from the Staatliche Kunsthalle in Karlsruhe, one dated 1728 and the other estimated to be from the same year.

Rabbit fur ("Poor bunnies," a female museumgoer murmured in passing) functioned for Chardin much as reflections in water did for the Impressionists, as a goad to innovation in technique. According to the posthumous biographical essay by Charles-Nicolas Cochin:

> He had never attempted to paint fur before. He realised that he should not paint it hair by hair, or reproduce it in detail. "Here is an object which I must aim to reproduce," he said to himself. "In order to concentrate my mind on reproducing it faithfully I must forget everything I have seen, and even forget the way such objects have been treated by others. I must place it at such a distance that I cannot see the details. I must work at representing the general mass as accurately as possible, the shades and colours, the contours, the effects of light and shade."*

---

*Quoted by Pierre Rosenberg in his catalogue essay. This and all subsequent quotations from the catalogue, edited by Monsieur Rosenberg for the Réunion des Musées Nationaux, Paris, are translated from the French by Caroline Beamish.

His rabbit fur explodes in flurries of dry brushstrokes; the limpness of death erases anatomy and almost returns these fruits of the hunt to the mottled background of stone. Rabbit fur taught Chardin a certain atmospheric mistiness that carried over into his depictions of fruit. His peaches and plums look furry, whereas the cats with which he decorated his early, larger still lifes do not.

Chardin's name was made, when he was twenty-six or so, with the large-scale *Ray* (1725–26), a still-startling *nature morte* dominated by a partially eviscerated ray or skate, whose gills and eyes do an eerie imitation of a smiling, pin-headed man. The surrealism was, I believe, unintentional, but the glistening, arrestingly detailed inner flesh was thoroughly meant. *The Ray*, when displayed at the 1728 Exposition de la Jeunesse, made a sensation, and it, along with the even more ambitious, heaped *Buffet* (1728), led to his shortcut admission, the same year, to the Académie Royale de Peinture et de Sculpture. The Académie bestowed upon its members the right to exhibit at the annual Salon, which was attended by the king and the fashionable public. Hitherto, Chardin, a cabinetmaker's son who lacked the classical education necessary to study at the Académie Royale, had belonged to the run-down, maverick Académie de Saint-Luc. Henceforth, he had the status of a master painter, and the credentials for professional success.

Art as practiced in the *ancien régime* was a hierarchical department of the idealized monarchy. Four genres of painting were recognized—in order of importance, history painting, portraiture, scenes from ordinary life (genre painting), and still life. With an almost comical strictness their subjects presented a dwindling in social rank: kings and rulers and religious beings were the subjects of the first, the aristocracy and upper bourgeoisie of the second, the common people and servant class of the third, and lowly objects, edible or not, of the fourth. Chardin showed his character by steadfastly sticking, for five years after 1728, to the lowest of the genres, deepening and varying still life and shedding the virtuosic precision and crowding of his seventeenth-century Dutch and Flemish predecessors.

Two paintings of hares from around 1730 achieve, with their more elongate lapine bodies, striking gestural drama on the canvases. All supporting details are forsworn but the game bag and powder flask, instrumental in the chase; nails stretch a single hind leg to the top of the canvas; the colors all revolve close to the fur's grayish brown. This single-subject minimalism makes a violent effect congruent with dashing streaks and stabs of Chardin's brush. The merest dry dabble of red shows blood leaked from the creature's nose or drying in its crotch, reinforcing the

Chardin, A Mallard Drake Hanging on a Wall and a Seville Orange, *1728–30. Oil on canvas.*

hint of crucifixion. A viewer should of course not bring modern squeamishness to Chardin's depiction of game, ubiquitous and indispensable in this era; yet the limp weight of death figures as a psychological factor as well as the occasion for a baroque diagonal. *A Mallard Drake Hanging on a Wall and a Seville Orange* (1728–30) shows the feathered body hanging with an askew plump weight from one foot, and extends Chardin's usual browns and whites into black, which forcefully outlines the bird's red bill, seen from beneath, as well as tipping the tail and wings. The shadows on the wall—Chardin's shadows, and the theories of shadow and perception common in the eighteenth century, were the topic of a recent book by the searching theorist of representation Michael Baxandall*—are especially

---

Shadows and Enlightenment (Yale University Press, 1995).

shuddering, like echoes of the drake's vanished animation. This "majestic" (as the wall caption rightly says) bird reappears, along with one of the hares, in the large *Water Spaniel* (1730), a commissioned piece that also includes a rifle. According to Cochin, Chardin when a student was told by his teacher, Noël-Nicolas Coypel, to paint a rifle, and discovered in the exercise that "the colours and effects of light presented by nature are difficult to achieve; the reflections that this experiment gave rise to helped to make him what he later became." Given the importance of "the colours and effects of light presented by nature," the exact duplication within one painting of figures lifted from others surprises us, and bares a gap between Chardin's sense of the artist's craft and our own. He commonly duplicated genre paintings and sold them again—one of the more popular, *The Return from Market* (1738), no fewer than four times. The borrowed bodies in *Water Spaniel*, it should be said, are brighter than in the originals, and indeed look spotlit. One of the last Chardins to depict a living animal, this ambitious work is the only one in this show to occupy an outdoor setting; with a curious bush and stage-flat clouds, it looks very artificial.

On the other hand, some of the early still lifes seem crude. Two small canvases, loaned from museums in Bordeaux and Houston, both date from 1730 and involve chunks of mutton dangling above an array of utensils and vegetables. Both are painted with short quick strokes and dabbled highlights of white; the meat is scarcely recognizable as such, and an inky darkness underlies the scrubbed-looking spots of color. The Bordeaux canvas, which was not discovered until 1969, appears scarcely finished. He was experimenting with texture; in *Still Life with Ray and Basket of Onions* (which he reproduced at least six times), the brushstrokes are noticeably dry and granular, even those defining the smooth eggs. (One worries, in fact, about the chemistry of Chardin's underpainting and his notoriously patient way of letting his works ripen; some of his figural canvases, like *Girl with Shuttlecock*, 1737, and *The Morning Toilet*, 1741, are cruelly crackled, and parts of *Domestic Pleasures*, 1745–46, are alligatored like a Ryder.) In searching out visual truth among humble objects, Chardin disdained *trompe-l'oeil* smoothness; in *Musical Instruments and Basket of Fruit* (1732), one of a pair of "overdoors" commissioned for the Paris residence of the Comte de Rothenbourg, the basket and a leaning guitar both shrug, in a Cézannesque manner, at correct perspective, and the musical notation on two crumpled sheets is rendered as lyrical scribbles—what, instead, would a Flemish precisionist have carefully made of those bars of notes!

According to a tale in a 1749 article on Chardin by Pierre-Jean Mariette, a dealer in prints, the painter was executing, for a firescreen, a picture of a saveloy (a highly seasoned sausage) on a dish. When he endeavored to persuade a friend, Joseph Aved, a portrait painter, to accept four hundred *livres* for a portrait, Aved replied that he would, "if a portrait was as easy to do as a saveloy." Chardin reflected on this friendly sneer, and turned, around 1732, from still life to the next step up in the ladder of genres, the painting of scenes from ordinary life. The earliest surviving example, *Woman Sealing a Letter* (1733), is rather gloomy and cluttered, and its setting and costumes border on the luxurious; it was quickly followed, however, by *The Washerwoman* (1733), which takes us to the servants' quarters. The little capped ragamuffin blowing soap bubbles feels lifted from a cozily dishevelled Dutch interior, but the washerwoman herself, glancing wistfully toward the painting's left edge, feels French, and in her ambiguous, abstracted attitude typically Chardinesque.

His attempts at facial animation are halfhearted at best, and his human interactions lukewarm, and yet for all their indifference to signs of conventional charm the paintings were turned into popular engravings; an array of these, taken from the Met's collection, occupies the last room of the exhibition, and it is striking how the engravers sharpened the poignance and heightened the little actions, including rhyming verses to drive home a moral that is scarcely there. The innocuous servant girl, for instance, in *The Return from Market* was charged with these verses by the engraver, François-Bernard Lépicié:

> From your look, my dear young girl,
> I calculate that, recklessly,
> You borrow from the housekeeping
> The cash you need to clothe yourself.

The gentle housekeeping tensions in *The Governess* (1739), between a dapper boy with downcast mien and a servant brushing his tricorn hat; the tender vanities of *The Morning Toilet*, as a mother primps a docile small girl who sneaks a look into the mirror; the domestic pieties of *Saying Grace* (1740 and 1744): all these were made much of, by the engravers, their caption devisers, and contemporary commentators. A late and especially sensitive sentimental anatomist was Proust, who observed in *Saying Grace* "the contented hands of the woman setting the table and the ancient tablecloth and the plates still intact after so many years and whose smooth firmness she has felt the resistance of always in the same spot between her careful hands." Such emotional content is not necessarily absent from the works: Chardin himself said, according to Cochin's account, "You use colours, but you paint with your feelings."

Chardin, Saying Grace, *1740. Oil on canvas.*

Yet comparison of print and painting often shows the print to have crisply heightened a mood cool and enigmatic in the original: one's eye in the painted *Morning Toilet* goes less to the little girl's glance than to the dashingly painted shoe peeping out from the mother's dress, the lovingly highlighted silver jug so solidly situated on the floor, and the gilded book resting on the red stool in the foreground.

The single or dominant figures in many of the genre canvases are painted as if they are objects in a still life, with no more or less attention than Chardin gives to a bunch of onions or a copper pot. The copper pot in *The Scullery Maid* (c. 1738) steals the show, and the figure in *The Cellar Boy* (1736–38) serves, stiffly, as the mustering-point for various large containers. These servants' faces are expressionless, and those displayed in *The Turnip Peeler* (1738) and the much-duplicated *Return from Market* are, one could say by a sympathetic stretch, reflective, insofar as lives of drudgery permit reflection. Vermeer's women seem in comparison engaged by their tasks, quietly smiling as a hum of secluded peace encloses them.

Strikingly absent from Chardin's genre paintings is any hint of the erotic, even as a flirtatious possibility; his masterpieces of human representation have solitary children as their subjects. Three of these—*Girl with Shuttlecock*, *The House of Cards* (c. 1737), and *Child with a Top* (1737–38)—are arrayed on one wall of the exhibit, with a fourth, *The Young Draughtsman* (1737), near at hand. The viewer comes rapturously upon these celebrated signature pieces, in which Chardin's particular innocence and simplicity achieve a human scale both majestic and intimate. The heads are doll-like in their smooth roundness and rosy glow and unshakable calm; the consummate tranquillity of his best still lifes informs their rendering, which is generally smooth, without much of that artful scumble which reminds one (in, say, *The Cellar Boy* and *The Return from Market*) of amiably rough Wyethesque (N. C., not Andrew) illustrations in children's books. Details like hats, caps, playing cards, shuttlecocks, quills and ribbons, flat tabletops, and rounded childish hands are seen with easy clarity and exquisite compositional poise. Much of childhood, these images imply, is a still life, a set of objects arranged on a plane. The children gaze into their own worlds, bright cubbyholes within eighteenth-century grandeur. These relatively spacious canvases sunnily partake of the Enlightenment's love of logic, decorum, and play.

In an ajar drawer of *Child with a Top* Chardin has placed a crayon-holder like an artist's signature. He was, in fact, fond of toying with his signature, affixing it to surprising facets of the represented reality. In many of his early canvases, it is inscribed on the edge of a shelf as if carved there—a demure bit of *trompe l'oeil*. His sense of the artist as an undeniable presence and of the painting as not a window into reality but a willful sort of artifact liberated him, in the still lifes to which he returned from genre painting around 1748, to freer brushwork and starker, more frontal arrangements. From 1734 to 1735 date three studies featuring copper kitchen utensils, notably rich in color and impasto; *The Copper Cistern* (c. 1735), housed in the Louvre, rejoices in its range of homely metals and explores their resonances of sheen and reflectiveness with a monumentalizing intentness. So, too, the pots and clay vessels collected around the figure of *The Scullery Maid*.

After 1748 he returned to fruits and bottles, dead birds and rabbits with an assured flamboyance. The small *Grey Partridge, Pear and Snare on a Stone Table* (1748) has the bravura dash of a Sargent. *A Rabbit, Two Thrushes and Some Straw on a Stone Table* (c. 1755) with a kindred swiftness and verve gives us a puddle of brown feathers and fur, death at its meekest. *Bouquet of Carnations, Tuberoses and Sweet Peas in a White Porcelain Vase with Blue Decoration* (c. 1755), Chardin's only surviving painting of flowers, uses reds and blues as suavely as he uses grays and browns; dabs of duller paint, brushstrokes doubling as petals, lend his small bouquet the recession of depth in atmosphere. Among the exhibit's many flurries of bold brushwork, this small canvas is one of the most astonishing and carefreely perfect. A number of small horizontal paintings of edibles, including the well-known *Basket of Wild Strawberries* (1761), rest in their modesty and (but for the triangular mound of strawberries) murkiness like fruit stored in the cool of a cellar.

The larger and more complex still lifes from his last decades, including some carefully worked out commissioned overdoors (*The Attributes of the Arts, The Attributes of Music*, both 1765; *The Attributes of Civilian Music, The Attributes of Military Music*, both 1767), do not make as congenial an effect, to a modern taste, as these fresh and apparently unstudied small canvases. Less has become, for us, more; the virtues prized in academic art—high finish, organization of many elements, a grandiose humanism—are almost valueless now. What we treasure instead is a glimpse, even a fragmented glimpse, rendered so as to reveal a personality in the painter. A plaster cast of Mercury, introduced into *The Attributes of the Arts and Their Rewards* (1766; commissioned by Catherine the Great of Russia), though impeccably enough painted, seems arrived from a dusty attic. Chardin executed several versions of this refined jumble, and the two on view here, from St. Petersburg and Minneapolis, are disconcertingly identical, devoid of creative second thoughts: a machine might have done the work. It suits our modern fancy to think of Chardin as a saint of perception, a kind of monk guilelessly contemplating the glory in a glass of water or an earthenware coffeepot, "giving to each thing its color," Proust wrote, "each form of shining significance for the eye, if obscure significance to the brain." But Chardin was also an unabashed self-copier, once the image was locked in. The "majestic" mallard hanging by one leg becomes a word in a sentence instead of a shout when transposed to a large oval still life, *Duck Hanging by One Leg, Pâté, Bowl and Jar of Olives* (1764). Just as a certain clumsiness reinforces the earnest worth of Chardin's early work, some of his later, more conventionally ambitious pieces are vitiated by his serene professionalism.

And yet less of an artisan might not have resorted to pastels when his eyes, affected by a lifetime of lead-based pigments and binders, contracted, like Degas's a century later, amaurosis—paralysis of the eyes. How much poorer our sense of this painter would be without the self-portraits he executed in pastel, having never attempted one in paints. At last the man himself appears, wearing comical getups of beribboned turbans on his wigless skull, and owlish round spectacles, and, in the self-portrait of 1775, an eyeshade that makes him look like a batty grandmother, yet one full of dignity, with an expression, to quote Proust once more, "daring you to smile, or to make an excuse, or to weep." His last self-portrait was executed in 1779, a few months before his death, and, though signs of age darken and crease his visage, his attitude is alert, the crayon uplifted in his hand. His self-portraits are impish, and cocky in a reserved Gallic manner, "subtly imperious." Some of his late still lifes, too, have an impish touch: the slice of melon in *The Cut Melon* (1760) posed atop the triangular chasm left by its removal, and, in·*The Brioche* (1763)—a painting left in Paris but present in the catalogue—the wonderfully painted double dome of bread topped, as was the custom with a *brioche de mariage,* by a sprig of orange blossoms. The joke, if there is one, is on all those contemporary painters of pomp and sexual power who did not see that the highest subject of painting is the painting itself, and that the ordinary plain things and persons around us offer the painter not just as good an excuse as any, but the best excuse possible, since the everyday world is what is always there.

ROMANTICS AND REALISTS

"Therefore I Print"

WILLIAM BLAKE, at the Metropolitan Museum of Art, New York, March 29–
June 24, 2001.

The Metropolitan's Blake exhibition originated at the greatly enlarged
Tate Gallery, and the London version included over twice as many items
as the current one; such a vast sampling, served up scarcely more than
two decades after another comprehensive show at the Tate in 1978,
reveals an inordinate British affection for Blake. He represents, if we may
presume to extrapolate an English view, an innocent religiosity, both
ardent and nonsensical; a triumph of eccentricity, the Englishman's cherished privilege and informal purchase on freedom; a plea and protest on
behalf of the bejewelled old England buried beneath the grime of indus-
trialism, "the dark Satanic mills" erected on the rational, mechanical,
heartless premises symbolized by Newton and Voltaire; and a thrilling
voice, like that of his contemporary Robert Burns, from the lower classes,
lending proof of the progressive righteousness of Britain's curious
democracy.

Blake, born in 1757, was one of five children of a London hosier; his
artistic leanings were placated by apprenticing him to an engraver, and
Blake for the rest of his three score and ten years was a craftsman, an
engraver, redolent of acids and inks—"still poor, still Dirty," an observer
commented of the artist and his faithful wife, Catherine. Not only did he
engrave his own work and that of others in the painstakingly linear, "dot-
and-lozenge" intaglio style of the time, but he developed his own method
of relief engraving, painting onto the copper with an impervious liquid
and then subjecting the plate to a double acid bath which left his marks
standing. The process involved his laboriously writing his self-published

poems in minute backward lettering, and produced an integrity of text
and illustration not seen since medieval manuscripts, if then. The visions
and rapt enthusiasms to which he was prone at times did distract him—
he wrote, "My Abstract folly hurries me often away while I am at work,
carrying me over Mountains & Valleys, which are not Real, in a land of
Abstraction where Spectres of the Dead wander"—but a great deal of
close, intent work was nevertheless accomplished.

The scaled-down but still-ample American version of *William Blake* is
housed in the lower level of the Robert Lehman Wing, beyond the
medieval hall, beneath a farewell exhibit to Balthus. It is shadowy down
there, and the conscientious viewer emerges with smarting corneas.
Blake's largest surviving works are watercolors, with pen and ink, two feet
wide; his booklets *Songs of Innocence* and *Songs of Experience* (combined in
1794) were printed from plates measuring less than three by five inches,
often in a pale-ochre ink. In the large room containing a spread of these
rare pages the Metropolitan has thoughtfully supplied magnifying
glasses. In the nineteenth century, Blake loosened up: his watercolor
illustrations to Milton's *Paradise Lost* (1808) have a stately, flowing,
flamelike grace; the figures, mostly of Albion, in his *Jerusalem* (1820)
possess a largeness that only with much strenuous foreshortening fits into
the spaces left to them by the crowded text; his illustrations to Dante, a
huge project commissioned by his last supporter, John Linnell, in 1824
and far from completed when Blake died in 1827, show a new sweep and
spaciousness. Certain of them—*Dante Running from the Three Beasts, The
Ascent of the Mountain of Purgatory, The Lawn with the Kings and
Angels*—could claim to be landscapes, airily deepening the shallow space
that customarily backs the weightless acrobatics of Blake's figures.

As befits an engraver, Blake lived in his lines. Energy, energy unbound,
is his gospel, and the line is its vehicle. His colors are generally tints,
varying on each print pulled. In the combative, self-promoting "Descriptive Catalogue" to his ill-fated exhibition of 1809, he proclaimed his loyalty to the "hard and wiry line of rectitude." He wrote, "The Beauty
proper for sublime art is lineaments," and proclaimed, "He who does not
imagine in stronger and better lineaments, and in stronger and better
light than his perishing and mortal eye can see, does not imagine at all."
He denounced "that infernal machine Chiaro Oscuro," claimed that
Rubens loaded his canvases with "hellish brownness," and condemned
the oil technique—"a fetter to genius, and a dungeon to art"—that had
come to dominate painting: "Oil . . . deadens every colour it is mixed
with, and in a little time becomes a yellow mask over all that it touches."
Instead, Blake sought, with sometimes friable and unstable results, to

revive the fresco technique of muralists, using glue-based washes to imitate egg tempera on wet plaster; he never travelled to Europe and never saw at first hand the handiwork of his models Michelangelo and Raphael.

Blake's watercolors and tinted prints come across as drawings first and representations of depth and atmosphere second. In the exceptionally fine and large-scaled illustrations to *Paradise Lost*, the delicate outlines limn both form and the flow of force in a floating world innocent of receding perspective. In *Christ Offers to Redeem Man*, for instance, the double angels on either side of the Christ-God central configuration flow

Blake, Christ Offers to Redeem Man, *1808. Pen and watercolor.*

downward in robes indistinguishable from abstract ripples, and God is surreally reduced to one foot, a head purely of hair, and two massive hands that hold the supple, submissive body of Christ with the hypersensitive apprehension of a lover. In his filmy robe Christ has a shapely calf and more than a hint of buttocks; the sense of erotic currents overwhelms the theological content.

The body in Blake is coterminous with the human spirit: "The notion that man has a body distinct from his soul, is to be expunged." The notion of nudity, in Blake's time as in ours, carried with it the suggestion of a prelapsarian, uncorrupt world: when Blake and his wife were discovered sitting nude in their garden in Lambeth, he purportedly remarked, "It's only Adam and Eve, you know." His nudes are not anatomically correct—the male genitals are fudged and the female is denied her triangle of pubic hair—but they appear naked even when clothed, with the peculiar flayed nakedness of anatomical illustrations. Marilyn Butler points out in her catalogue essay, "Blake in His Time," that "his drawing of the body is visibly indebted throughout to eighteenth-century anatomical drawing." During his brief period of study at the Royal Academy, he attended the classes of the anatomist William Hunter, but it is not clear when, after the Royal Academy, Blake ever looked at a nude body beyond his own and his wife's. His nudes are foreshortened *à la* Michelangelo, but without convincing us, as Michelangelo does, of an internal logic of muscle and bone. Blake's nudes, with their linear indications of vein and sinew, can be expressive, and arouse tenderness in us— consider the two pathetic figures, bowed in parallel as if being whipped, on the title page of *Songs of Innocence and of Experience*, and the long-thighed Oothoon depicted in *Visions of the Daughters of Albion* (1793), tied to her tormented rapist, Bromion, while her love, Theotormon, rejects her in an abject huddle of disembodied arms and legs.

His nudes strike us as above all a set of symbols, pliantly subject to abstract arrangement on the page. In the illustration to page 72 of Edward Young's *Night Thoughts* (c. 1795–97), Hope becomes a six-winged tiny angel, precisely vertical, reaching down to touch the lips of a frowning poet, whose impossibly circular knee floats toward us while his other leg resolves in a spiral of abstract form. Even more amazingly stylized is the tawny watercolor *Christ in the Sepulchre, Guarded by Angels* (c. 1805, and shown at the Royal Academy in 1808), wherein the leaning angels with their uplifted wings, tip feathers touching, form a flamboyant triangle on the base of Christ's supine body. Such maneuvers are more legible but not much less artificial than the neatly packed sardines of *The Rout of the Rebel Angels* (1808) or the rectangular configuration of the color print *The House of Death* (c. 1805) or the march of fists and faces across *The Stygian Lake, with the Ireful Sinners Fighting*, from his unengraved illustrations to Dante. As a drill sergeant for souls, Blake was Dante's soulmate, and his seething *Vision of the Last Judgment* (1808) has a bubbling, plaited, turbulent incorporeality that makes it a more plausible, if less humane, vision than Michelangelo's great wall of struggling nudes. Perhaps Blake saw angels too easily; he skywrites with bodies; they form a species of handwriting, spelling out messages to which we have lost, often, the code.

His humanitarian vision, his cry against repression, springs from the same liberal optimism and sense of infinite human possibility that allow him to manipulate and stretch the human figure, as an emblem of liquid, plastic spirit. His most memorable images depend on contortion: would *Newton* (c. 1805) be iconic—*The Economist* and *Rolling Stone* recently made covers of it—were it not for the magnificent, compressing gesture that lets the unexpectedly curly-haired, Apollonian savant, naked as a syllogism, reach way down with his calipers and forefinger to touch a diagram at the level of his elegant feet? (Blake's feet are invariably elegant.) Would *Nebuchadnezzar* (c. 1805) be nearly as marvellous were the humbled king not on all fours, growing claws on his toes, veined with ribbons of transformation, and registering on his creased face the dismay of metamorphosis? Would *The Ancient of Days* (1824?) be less Godlike if he were not, in his reddish-brown empyrean, composed of two legs, one huge reaching arm, and white hair and beard whipped sideways by a cosmic wind? Gesture, in Blake, links the seen and the unseen; reaching and pointing recur, evangelistically. The catalogue has for its cover *The Angel of the Revelation* (c. 1803–5), who holds in one hand a tiny open book and in the other seems to be hailing or upholding the universe; *Albion Rose* (c. 1796) announces himself with outflung hands in a sunrise of triumphant expectation. Albion becomes Jerusalem; all "Human Forms" become immortal. This color-printed engraving, finished with pen and ink and watercolor, is one of the few Blakes on view that compel awareness of color; a full spectrum encircles the pink youth at the center, as he stands on rocks made unintentionally lichenous by the blotting and blurring of printing inks. *Newton* and *Nebuchadnezzar* also bear this lichenous look, composed of vibrant ochres and blue-greens, but within a cavelike darkness.

I found the exhibit itself a bit cavelike, and confusing. My notes (e.g., *"I labor upwards into futurity" Swimmer*) bear, I discover, little relation to the catalogue, and its index offers an indifferent guide to its contents, involving many bracketed numbers in both boldface and roman type.

The exhibition does not attempt a strictly chronological arrangement; perhaps none was possible. Blake's creative output abounded in delays and abandoned projects—much of what is admired and incorporated into the history of art was intended to be engraved and placed in a book. Books, rather than paintings for sale and display, were his primary creative objective; though he looked backward to Gothic art and mythic imagery, he was thoroughly enlisted in the print revolution. The most lavish of his finished productions, *Jerusalem* (consisting of one hundred plates, all but a few of them illustrated, and printed in six copies, five in black ink and one in orange and hand-painted), opens by stating "To the Public":

> Even from the depths of Hell His voice I hear
> Within the unfathom'd caverns of my Ear.
> Therefore I print: nor vain my types shall be.

The best known of his books, of course, are the *Songs*, of innocence and of experience. It is instructive to see them in the paper, so to speak, tiny and demurely colored—pretty chapbooks meant to be slipped into jacket pockets, in the same decade when Wordsworth, in his and Coleridge's *Lyrical Ballads* (1798), was asking "how far the language of conversation in the middle and lower classes of society is adapted to the purposes of poetic pleasure." Some of the poems seem banal, pseudo-Christian doggerel and others are so laconically profound as to need the twentieth century to appreciate them:

> O Rose, thou art sick.
> The invisible worm
> That flies in the night,
> In the howling storm,
>
> Has found out thy bed
> Of crimson joy,
> And his dark secret love
> Does thy life destroy.

It would take Nietzsche and Freud to explicate those fatal maneuvers on the bed of crimson joy, and Marx to explain how (to quote Blake's "London") "every cry of every Man" testifies to "mind-forg'd manacles," and how (from "The Chimney-Sweeper") "God & his Priest & King . . . make up a heaven of our misery." Blake's anti-repressive wisdom descends to us not in his long, long-lined allegorical epics but in isolated couplets—

> If the Sun and Moon should doubt,
> They'd immediately go out.
>
> A dog starv'd at his master's gate
> Predicts the ruin of the State.
>
> The harlot's cry from street to street
> Shall weave Old England's winding sheet.
>
> The Vision of Christ that thou dost see
> Is my vision's greatest enemy—

and quatrains—

> Abstinence sows sand all over
> The ruddy limbs and flaming hair,
> But Desire gratified
> Plants fruits of life and beauty there.
>
> There is a smile of love,
> And there is a smile of deceit,
> And there is a smile of smiles
> In which these two smiles meet.
>
> What is it men in women do require?
> The lineaments of gratified Desire.
> What is it women do in men require?
> The lineaments of gratified Desire—

and in his marvellous one-liners: Milton "was a true poet and of the Devil's party without knowing it"; "Eternity is in love with the productions of time"; "One Law for the Lion & Ox is Oppression"; "The tygers of wrath are wiser than the horses of instruction"; "To generalize is to be an idiot"; "He who would do good to another must do it in minute particulars"; and, of Sir Joshua Reynolds, "This Man was Hired to Depress Art."

But was Blake sane? His fiery wit, reckless as a prophet's rage, was not for all hands to warm themselves by. Toward the end of his obscure, drudging life he began to attract attention from younger men, who recorded varying impressions of his conversation. Samuel Palmer, the painter, remembered Blake as "anything but sectarian or exclusive, finding sources of delight throughout the whole range of art; while, as a critic, he was judicious and discriminating." Whereas Henry Crabb Robinson in his diary spoke of "the wild & strange, strange rhapsodies uttered by this insane man of genius" and complained that, since there was "really no system or connection in his mind at all, his future conversation will be but varieties of wildness and incongruity." His wife, the docile Catherine, whom he taught to read and write and make prints, famously confided to a friend, "I have very little of Mr Blake's company; he is always in Paradise." When Blake was four, he saw God put his head to the window; six or so years later, walking on Peckham Rye, he saw "a tree filled with angels," and, on another boyhood occasion, saw angels striding amid haymakers.* Crabb Robinson in his 1825 diary recorded that Blake declared the earth is flat and "denied that the natural world is any thing. It is all nothing and Satan's empire is the empire of nothing." He claimed to talk to Milton, Shakespeare, and Voltaire, the last in a language that was "probably French, but to my ear it became English." More pertinently to his visual art, he told another acolyte in his last years, "I can look at a knot in a piece of wood till I am frightened at it." Van Gogh might have recognized the sensation.

The classic doctrine of inspiration made every artist insane, or at least out of his head, at the creative peak. Blake described himself as an "enthusiast," a word that means literally possessed by a god and was applied to all those Protestant sectarians, like the German Anabaptists, who sought religious satisfaction in personal experience, outside the established churches. He confessed, in a letter written at the age of forty-two, "I begin to Emerge from a Deep pit of Melancholy, Melancholy without any real reason for it, a Disease which God keep you from & all good men." On such evidence some modern psychologists venture a diagnosis of bipolar disorder; that is, Blake, like a number of twentieth-century artists, was a manic depressive. The terms feel a touch pat and contemporary; styles change not only in treatments but in maladies. Blake's delusions were by and large fruitful for him. His long life demonstrates plenty of coherence and concentration, as he painstakingly applied learned engraving skills and carried out a succession of extended projects. Yet his artistic achievement does seem to occupy a plane different from that of, say, Dürer or Cézanne or—another worker at grandiose and interrupted projects—Michelangelo. We understand, we feel, what they were getting at. Even Blake's friend Henry Fuseli was fantastic in a more calculated and hence intelligible (and less interesting) way. There is, as we tread through the dim lower galleries of the Lehman Wing, something unsteady underfoot, something slippery, which makes the

*These and other details are from G. E. Bentley, Jr., *The Stranger from Paradise: A Biography of William Blake* (Yale University Press, 2001).

exhibition hard to organize in retrospect, though certain images of uncanny vividness and unabashed loveliness continue to glow in the mind.

Innerlichkeit *and* Eigentümlichkeit

THE ROMANTIC VISION OF CASPAR DAVID FRIEDRICH: *Paintings and Drawings from the U.S.S.R.*, at the Metropolitan Museum of Art, New York, January 23– March 31, 1991.

The melting of the Cold War, whose immediate global result seems to be the release of fresh energies of strife and destruction, has effected some benefits in the world of art, such as the Metropolitan Museum's present show of nine oil paintings and eleven works on paper by the German artist Caspar David Friedrich (1774–1840), on loan from the State Hermitage Museum in Leningrad and the Pushkin State Museum of Fine Arts in Moscow. The pictures were purchased over a period of twenty years beginning when the future Tsar Nicholas I, then the Grand Duke Nikolai Pavlovich, visited Friedrich's studio in Dresden. The visit was made at the urging of the grand duke's wife, Alexandra Fedorovna, daughter of Prussia's King Friedrich Wilhelm III, and his subsequent patronage was carried on through the intermediary offices of the poet Vasily Andreyevich Zhukovsky, Alexandra Fedorovna's tutor in Russian and an enthusiastic admirer of the painter Friedrich. Zhukovsky frequently visited Dresden, and at each visit sent back to the imperial family descriptions and recommendations which resulted in purchases, the last of them from Friedrich's impoverished widow in 1841. The works thus accumulated—an indeterminate number, but considerably more than eventually descended to the care of the Soviet state—constitute the only major collection of Friedrich's work outside Germany. In all of the United States there is but one painting, and that one hides in Fort Worth, Texas, at the Kimbell Art Museum. The art merchants who sold to the great American collectors in the era before World War I focused on the Italians and French, and after 1914 geopolitical factors helped dampen appreciation of German art. Even German appreciation of Friedrich's mystical, parochial, subtle, and stubborn talent—which for a time attracted approval from Goethe and patronage from the Weimar court—waned after 1820. By 1890, he was virtually forgotten. A retrospective exhibition in Berlin in 1906 of a hundred years of German paintings revived interest, and elicited comparisons of his treatment of light to that of the Impressionists. But he was a thoroughly Nordic artist—he attended art school in Copenhagen and never travelled to Italy, and even balked at visiting Switzerland. He was a fierce anti-Napoleon patriot, who dressed his figures in an *altdeutsch* attire symbolic of the heroic medieval era of German unity. This nationalism won Nazi hearts; in 1940, a German critic dated Friedrich's resurgence from 1933 and boasted that "the pinnacle of his influence coincides with the outbreak of World War." Air raids on Berlin destroyed a number of his paintings there in 1945. In the post-war era, Friedrich has arrived as the internationally best-known German painter of the nineteenth century.

The selection on view at the Metropolitan, though it ranges over nearly the full extent of his career and is supplemented by six early (c. 1803) woodcuts from the Met's own collection, cannot approach complete representation; this is a mega-artist but a mini-show. Volumes like Joseph Leo Koerner's *Caspar David Friedrich and the Subject of Landscape* (Yale University Press, 1990) and Helmut Börsch-Supan's *Caspar David Friedrich* (Braziller, 1974; second edition, Prestel, 1990) reproduce masterpieces—*The Large Enclosure Near Dresden* (c. 1832), *Early Snow* (c. 1828), *Evening* (1824), *Arctic Shipwreck* (1824), *Chalk Cliffs on Rügen* (1818–19), *Neubrandenburg* (c. 1817), and the notorious *Tetschen Altarpiece* (1808)—without parallel in the score of works on loan from the Russians. On the other hand, Friedrich was consistent in his themes and style—so consistent that one sepia work at the Metropolitan, *Window with a View of a Park*, is dated "c. 1806–11 or 1835–37"—and among the paintings on display in New York are Friedrich's two largest surviving canvases, the complementary *Moonrise by the Sea* (1821) and *Morning in the Mountains* (1822–23), and two of his most frequently reproduced, *Swans in the Reeds by Dawn's Early Light* (1832) and *On the Sailboat* (1818–19). The show affords only a taste, but a fair taste, of the artist, and a curious penetrating taste it is.

Friedrich's name is reflexively linked to Romanticism; the very title of the show, and of the pleasant and relatively slim catalogue edited by Sabine Rewald, is *The Romantic Vision of Caspar David Friedrich*. Yet Romanticism is so large and moot a topic it threatens to lead us astray, into philosophical and historical considerations far from the question of why the paintings on the wall win and hold our interest a century and a half after their execution. Friedrich spoke little in interpretation of his own paintings, and then in rather strict terms of Christian allegory. Nor was painting Romanticism's chosen arena. The movement, if it is not too large and inevitable a cultural tide to be called that, had different father figures in different countries—Rousseau in France, Kant in Germany, Wordsworth in England—and none of them painters. Goethe and Schlegel first used the term in distinguishing the contemporary writing from "classic" writing, and the term derives from the late-Latin *romanice loqui*—meaning the vulgar Latin vernacular as opposed to book Latin. The expression gradually extended to popular "romances" and to anything with a coloring of the irrational and the passionate. The label scarcely sticks to painting. *The Oxford Companion to Art* states, in its article on the subject:

> Looking back from our vantage point of more than a hundred years we can see that in fact Romanticism never was part of the mainstream of development in the visual arts. Its proper sphere seems to have been a literary one and with perhaps two exceptions it never produced a distinguished artist. One of these . . . is Delacroix, though his distinction lies not so much in his having been a Romantic as in his having managed to surmount this fact. The other is Turner.

And then of course there is Géricault, and Constable in a sense, and Blake and Bewick you could say, and, oh yes, Fuseli perhaps, and—who was that?—Chassériau! For the purposes of reacting to Friedrich's paintings, and for guessing at his intentions, it is perhaps enough to have in mind T. E. Hulme's famous epigram that Romanticism is "spilt religion" and Hegel's epochal announcement, "The world of Inwardness (*Innerlichkeit*) celebrates its triumph over the outer world."

The advance of inwardness in Germany dates back at least to Martin Luther; his anti-institutional bias, once the Lutheran Church became itself an institution, passed to the Moravian Brethren and other pietistic sects that preached a religion of inner spirit and minimal outward trappings. Luther himself had stated, as Joseph Leo Koerner points out, that "it would be better to uproot all the churches and monasteries of the world and burn them to dust." Friedrich was born in what was then the Swedish province of Pomerania, into a soap boiler's household of conventional Protestant piety. Through his first art teacher, his fellow-townsman Johann Gottfried Quistorp, he encountered the pantheist philosopher and historian Thomas Thorild, and the poet, pastor, and theologian Gotthard Ludwig Kosegarten, who, Koerner says, "preached a particular theology of the heart, in which the subjective experience of nature's primal, and therefore divinely created, beauty leads to a direct experience of God." Kosegarten sometimes preached outdoors, by the sea, in *Uferpredigten* ("Shore-sermons"); the Baltic's rocky shores frequently appear in Friedrich's paintings, thrice in this small show, with the

Friedrich, Two Men by the Sea at Moonrise, *c. 1835–37. Pencil and sepia.*

large *Moonrise by the Sea* and the two sepia works *Two Men by the Sea at Moonrise* (c. 1835–37) and *Boat on the Beach by Moonlight* (c. 1837–39). The mood, furthermore, of shoreline silence, of expectancy directed toward a distant horizon, of a barren yet pregnant vastness, pervades his landscapes. Religion has spilt into nature. Philipp Otto Runge, Friedrich's contemporary, a less suggestive but more articulate painter, wrote of art reaching peaks at the junctures where the Greek gods and then the Catholic God were dying, and claimed that

> with us too something again is dying; we stand on the brink of all the religions that originated with Catholicism; the abstractions are fading away; everything becomes more airy and lighter than before; everything draws towards landscape, seeks something definite in this indeterminacy, and does not know where to begin.

For literal-minded Friedrich, Nature is a church not only in its numinous content but in its balanced form. His pictorial approach is strikingly frontal and symmetrical. The moon hangs in his pictures like a perfectly round rose window; in *Two Men by the Sea at Moonrise* it rests precisely on the horizon. The ecclesiastical ruins plentiful in the landscape offered the very image of a burst church from which religion has spilt. The Gothic arches of *The Dreamer* (c. 1835) hold, instead of a stained-glass biblical scene, fir trees and a dying yellowish light. Friedrich's depiction of linear elements—tree branches and trunks, the ropes of ship rigging—

are, at the opposite pole from Impressionism, as rigorously, faithfully articulated as the vertical lines of a cathedral. In *On the Sailboat*, the mast stays and the lines edging the sails turn the boat's movement as much upward, into the sky, as forward toward the misty small city with its steeples. In *Morning in the Mountains*, Robert Rosenblum points out in his catalogue introduction, the "mountain vista with two foreground peaks seems to be bisected exactly by an invisible but abiding vertical presence." One's focus travels backward, in the misty, paling ranges of this painting, from peak to peak along a carefully zigzag path; in the companion piece, *Moonrise by the Sea*, the same sort of path takes us from the foreground anchor to the two women on the rock, back and up to the two men on a farther rock, on to the two sailboats in the empurpled sea, and back at the reversed angle to the moon in its great bowl of tawny sky. The diagonals are regular and do not carry us out of the picture frame; in the depopulated mountainscape *In Memory of the Riesengebirge* (1835) the zigzag is for a while embodied in a receding ridge. Friedrich's method was to assemble pictures in his studio out of careful pencil sketches made on the spot; in even his slightest paintings an exquisite compositional balance reigns, an underlying formality that works tranquillity upon us. This insistent geometry accords with our modern sense of artistic decorum. If Friedrich meant to imply Presence with his controlled, emptied vistas, and we can feel only Absence, well, Absence is an old friend, and we wouldn't know what to do with Presence if It came up and hit us in the face.

The nineteenth century—the Romantic century—sought to save God by empowering inwardness. Figures as disparate as Kierkegaard and Emerson strove to turn the tables on the creeping atheism of empirical science by making the Subjective a player in the game equal to the Objective. Things are composed of our perceptions; reality must include our intuitions. Friedrich's landscapes usually exist in two planes: a dark foreground, the realm of the viewer, and a luminous background, the natural realm that is viewed. The actual substance of what is seen is not at issue. Is the misty city the young couple of *On the Sailboat* gazes toward really there, or is it a hopeful vision? Friedrich's favorite dramatic device, the foreground *Rückenfigur* ("back figure," figure seen from behind), inserts the act of viewing into the picture, and weaves mood and reflection into the natural reality. *In Memory of the Riesengebirge*, based in 1835 upon a sketch the artist made twenty-five years before, moves back, as if in Wordsworthian memory, from a rocky dark-brown foreground to the radiant whiteness of the Schneekoppe, a presiding purity that one can hardly avoid associating with God. A glance around the single room

Friedrich, On the Sailboat, *1818–19. Oil on canvas.*

where most of the Russian pictures are hung reveals that all have a glow; even the nocturnal cityscape, *Sisters on the Harbor-View Terrace* (c. 1820), has a luminous sky, glowing as if with the foggy diffusion of city lights. In the case of the twilit, time-darkened small oil called *The Nets* (c. 1830–35), there is almost nothing to see but the glow. Moravian theology spoke of faith as not in the head "but in the heart, a light illuminated in the heart." Light is the commonest metaphor for divinity, and Friedrich's skies, which often take up more than half of his picture space, show an especial tropism toward the realm of the glowing impalpable. His skies are rarely distinctly blue, as if this color would opacify their luminosity. In a watercolor like *Ruins of Eldena Monastery* (1801) as well as such oils as *Moonrise by the Sea* and *On the Sailboat*, Friedrich gives the sky an anatomy as detailed as the land's; his even focus leaves nothing scrubbed in or casually observed above the horizon. Goethe, noticing this propensity, once suggested that he execute a series of cloud studies based upon the meteorological system recently developed by the British natural historian Luke Howard. Friedrich refused, according to Koerner, "because it would empty nature of any 'higher' meaning, and because the very attempt to classify would violate the essential obscurity of clouds, and with it the radical alterity of nature itself." Yet his paintings do contain identifiable cloud types, so closely did he paint them.

God is in the details as well as the receding prospect. Friedrich's early pen drawings of ruins and plants show a student's careful precision, which he never relaxed. His explorations of branch patterns and rock shapes keep that Renaissance sense, exemplified by Dürer and Leonardo, of microcosmic discovery. He did not draw easily, and his human forms have little anatomy, yet drawing is everywhere in his pictures, pulling them tight—for instance, the beautifully airy sepia *Boat on the Beach by Moonlight*, with its gentle diagonal echoed by the elongated cirrus clouds, and *Coffin on a Grave* (c. 1836), its foreground thistle as momentous as its silhouetted birch bizarrely hung with funeral wreaths. Even his far-off trees, like those seen in the exquisite *Window with a View of a Park*, have the leaf-by-leaf quality of medieval illumination. Precise rendering is the ethical tool that unlocks each thing's *Eigentümlichkeit*—a term favored by Romantic theorists and the theologian Schleiermacher, signifying "peculiarity" in both its English senses, of particularity and strangeness. For Friedrich's owls and crooked, grasping oaks are strange, even sinister. The Gothic was the cradle of the Romantic. Among his eeriest, most original canvases are renderings, with no anecdotal or symbolic indications, of isolated thickets of trees, as if the most random piece of nature, bodied forth with enough attention to each thrusting twig, has a message for us.

Not that his precision is heavy-handed or spectacular; the two big mountainscapes on display, with their rising valley fogs, have a certain recessive fuzziness. Friedrich's color, save for the fruity tints of his sunrises and sunsets, is brownish and rather streaky. The marvel of the small *Swans in the Reeds by Dawn's Early Light* lies not so much in the pink sky and the animated wealth of reed leaves as in the capture, in these leaves' dull green and the white swans' flat gray, of light before the sun has dawned. Generations before Monet, he has succeeded in painting the air that intervenes before the eye. Yet his appeal is not basically sensual, or a matter of paint; his method of repeated thin coats overlaid by a glistening varnish minimizes a sense of brushstrokes. We are conscious of the painter mostly as the viewer of what we now see, a fellow-contemplative, waiting like us for a clearer meaning or mood to emerge from the enigmatic vista with its ghost of a design. Friedrich expressed his theories sparely, but another artist of the time reported him as saying in conversation that "the most important thing about a work of art is that it should have an effect on each person who looks at it."

With the afterimage of these twenty works fresh in my mind's eye, I made my way through the Metropolitan Museum's mazy treasure house to the American landscape painters of the nineteenth century, who share much with Friedrich. These men, too, had a transcendentalist, nationalist bent, and hoped to distill from vastness an inspiring *Eigentümlichkeit*. Thomas Doughty also gives us mountain views and foreground rocks, and Frederic Edwin Church lavishly provides, in his *Heart of the Andes* (1859), a panorama climaxed by a snowy peak. But their canvases, bigger than any of Friedrich's, seem clangorously crowded, bright, and busy; Church's stupendous virtuosity, which throngs the foreground with botanically accurate Andean vegetation and throws a spotlight upon his name carved on a tree trunk, is itself a presence, full of braggadocio. We meekly bend to admire the dashing precision of each detail of the little religious vignette conveniently illuminated; we are in the hands of a showman God. Even where a softer temperament approximates Friedrich's expectant simplicity—as in Sanford Robinson Gifford's golden gorge, for instance, with its almost invisible waterfall, and the luminist Martin Johnson Heade's level quiet marshland—we are in a material world, where the vigorous act of painting suppresses hints of symbolization, of sublimated appearance, of double meaning. John Frederick Kensett renders space and the mood of the sky, but all of a certain moment; he has come to the verge of Impressionism, where the painter, no longer a wistful, yearning *Rückenfigur*, turns to face us with his brushes, his dancing colors. An irresistible materiality infuses the American landscapes, washing away those faint aftertraces of Christian faith, that delicate fog of the spirit, still visible in Friedrich's church of Nature.

Splendid Lies

J. M. W. TURNER, at the Metropolitan Museum of Art, New York, July 1–
September 21, 2008.

The Turner at the Met is a bear of a show—165 items, mostly oils and
watercolors, with a few prints—and the other patrons on the day of my
perambulation staggered from the final chamber into the gift shop's welcoming arms as if after a tussle in a cave. Turner cannot be dismissed, but
he cannot quite be embraced, either. Ian Warrell says, in his catalogue
essay "J. M. W. Turner and the Pursuit of Fame," "Few other British
artists before, or since, have generated such wildly diverse responses to
their work during their lifetimes or have continued to provoke such fervent debate." His contemporaries did agree that he was personally unpre-
possessing; one associate admitted that "at first sight Turner gave one the
notion of a mean-looking little man," and another remarked that "this
man must be loved for his works; for his person is not striking." John
Constable said after encountering the man, a year older than he and
much quicker to achieve success, "I always expected to find him what I
did—he is uncouth but has a wonderfull range of mind." Turner failed to
look like a great painter, but no one, certainly no other British landscape
artist, aspired to greatness more nakedly, with so uninterrupted a productivity and uninhibited an adventurousness.

In the century and a half since Turner's death in 1851, evolving taste
has reversed the debate over his merits: it is the later, nearly abstract
paintings that win our hearts, though contemporary criticism waxed sardonic in their dispraise, and the earlier works that won him wealth and
fame—mythologically tinged landscapes and scenic renderings of ships,
castles, Alps, and English country homes—repel us with their brownish
pomp. They seem so melodramatic, so fusty, so hardworking, so *grande
galerie*, whereas some of the canvases (*Europa and the Bull; Norham Castle, Sunrise*, both c. 1845), to which his brush condescended with a few
cryptic dabbles and golden smears, impress us as thrillingly minimal and
airy. When these unsold, never-exhibited portions of the immense
Turner Bequest left to the Tate were first put on public view in 1906, one
critic exclaimed, "We have never seen Turner before!" Another wrote
analytically, "Turner in his latest development, more than any artist who
had gone before him, painted not so much the objects he saw as the light
which played around them."

Yet the predilections that make Turner special, and even peculiar, were there from the start. He was the artistically precocious son of a Covent Garden barber and a mother who, after leading her husband "a sad life," was committed to Bethlehem Hospital for the Insane, popularly called "Bedlam," in 1800, when she was sixty-one and her only son, known in the household as William, was twenty-five.* Since the age of twelve he had been turning out architectural drawings and hand-coloring prints for a nearby engraver; some of his early drawings were sold in his father's shop, "ticketed at prices varying from one shilling to three." At the age of fourteen, he was admitted to the Royal Academy Schools, which offered free training for artists and was housed five minutes' walk from his home. Although John Ruskin, Turner's great champion, thought that "Turner, having suffered under the instruction of the Royal Academy, had to pass nearly thirty years of his life in recovering from the consequences," the boy's education fixed his attention upon the Royal Academy as the key to respectability as an English artist; he submitted his work to its annual exhibits, and from 1790, when he was fifteen, his watercolors were accepted for display.

His first oil to be exhibited there—in 1796, when he was just twenty-one—was titled *Fishermen at Sea*; it hangs in the show at the Met, and is something of a miracle. A full moon hangs in a gap of fragmenting dark clouds; its light is reflected on the water below, where a masted fishing boat, with its crew, tilts on a wave. White edges of moonlit foam, delicate as lace, define an oval of momentarily concave water rendered with an avid fidelity to its mixture of shadow and translucence; this liquid bowl of moonlight and the heave of wave creating it portend Turner's lifelong obsession, to the point of enraptured obscurity, with light in its ephemeral impressions. Off to the left, dim rocks, and, on the right, a second, shadowy, but solidly anatomized boat and, sunk still more deeply in darkness, a white bird on a bobbing barrel testify to the painter's early fascination with the imperfectly seen.

His boyhood interest was in architecture, and several large watercolors in the exhibition's first room impeccably delineate the ruins of Tintern Abbey and the interior of Salisbury Cathedral. His architectural precision, like a fossil tidily preserved in a tumbled geology, persists even into Turner's most boldly dissolved impressions—for instance, the masts and yards and tipped-up dories of the two *Whalers* oils (RA 1845 and 1846);†

---

*A number of details in this essay are taken from Anthony Bailey, *Standing in the Sun: A Life of J. M. W. Turner* (HarperCollins, 1998).

†Here and elsewhere, I follow the catalogue in dating canvases by the year when they were exhibited at the Royal Academy.

Turner, Fishermen at Sea, *RA 1796. Oil on canvas.*

the little village in the lower left-hand corner of the otherwise hazy watercolor *Lake Lucerne* (1842); the cathedral architecture deftly sketched into the washes of *Eu: The Church of Notre-Dame and St-Laurent, with the Château of Louis-Philippe Beyond* (1845); and, with less haste, the water-carved gneiss in *The Pass of St Gotthard, Near Faido* (1843), commissioned by John Ruskin and polished to perfection for this connoisseur of geology.

The paintings, as the decades and the exhibition rooms unfold, fluctuate; moods of elemental daring alternate with oppressively academic productions. Turner's uncouth ambition included eclectically outdoing other painters at their game. Not only did *Fishermen at Sea* emulate, according to the catalogue, the eighteenth-century styles of Claude-Joseph Vernet, Joseph Wright of Derby, and Philippe-Jacques de Loutherbourg, but it led, in five years, to "an ambitious response to Willem Van de Velde the Younger's *Dutch Shipping Offshore in a Rising Gale* (c. 1672)," called *Dutch Boats in Gale* (1801), which was described by Benjamin West, then president of the Royal Academy, as "what Rembrandt thought of but could not do." The canvas given what must be the longest title on record—*The Decline of the Carthaginian Empire—Rome being determined on the Overthrow of Her Hated Rival, demanded from her such Terms as might either force her into War, or ruin her by Compliance: the Enervated Carthaginians, in their Anxiety for Peace, consented to give up even their Arms and their Children* (RA 1817)—reflects, according to the catalogue, "the unmistakable style of Claude Lorrain," especially "Claude's masterpiece, *Embarkation of the Queen of Sheba*" (1648). Turner's determination to consolidate a distinctive British style left few Continental predecessors unassimilated. Unmarried, reclusive, he travelled widely (standard working procedure for painters of the time), and every new territory brought with it the ghosts of rivals to subdue.

Venice evoked, the catalogue states, "well-known paintings by Titian, Tintoretto and especially Canaletto"; Turner's *Venice: The Dogana and San Giorgio Maggiore* (RA 1834) "was explicitly couched in the style of Canaletto (even introducing an incidental portrait of the artist at work)." It and its companion, *Venice, from the Porch of Madonna della Salute* (RA 1835), display a lighter, sunnier, blue-and-white palette rare for Turner, along with an instinctive clarity in delineating the Grand Canal's palatial shores. By the time of the two Venetian watercolors from 1840 also on view at the Met, his mature touch fudges all but the broadest outlines, and a sunset yellow tinges the smoky atmosphere. Even an early, Poussinesque exercise in the highly valued mode of the historical sublime, *The Tenth Plague of Egypt* (RA 1802), has idiosyncratic atmospherics: the un-Egyptian city in the middle distance is oddly shadowless and two-dimensional, while nearer to hand an inky cloud swallows the un-Egyptian hillside and seizes all the drama from the God-stricken small figures in the foreground.

The human population in Turner's large canvases is rarely more than a footnote, a spatter of colored jellybeans at the base of a mountain or a metropolis. He stood aside from the distinguished British tradition of portrait painting, once he had executed the fine youthful self-portrait of 1798–1800. A certain caricatural verve can be noticed in the visual anecdotes of *The Northampton Election, 6 December 1830* (c. 1830–31), of *Dartmouth Cove, with Sailor's Wedding* (c. 1825), and of *View of London from Greenwich* (c. 1825), but the boneless and vapid central figures of *The Bay of Baiae, with Apollo and the Sibyl* (RA 1823) contribute no focus or weight to the sundry elements of this idealization of an Italian bathing spot. "SPLENDIDE MENDAX"—"a splendid lie"—a friend wrote on the frame, and Turner allowed the verdict to stay. The figures in early picturesque works like *Fall of the Rhine, Schaffhausen* (RA 1806) and *Fishmarket on the Sands—Possibly at Hastings* (c. 1810) were seriously worked at, but if one takes the opportunity, which the museum has provided, to compare Géricault's sensational *The Raft of the Medusa* (1819) with

Turner's boiling, sketchy raftful of victims in *Disaster at Sea* (c. 1833–35), one appreciates the vastly more intelligible human drama that Géricault staged. In Turner's tableau the only actor is the furious ocean.

Not only do his human figures in general lack psychological presence, they lack physical mass, such as another celebrant of impersonal force, Winslow Homer, was able to integrate with ocean and atmosphere—for example, the half-drowned belles of *Undertow* (1886) and the slickered, silhouetted fishermen of *The Herring Net* (1885). The heroes of some large Turner canvases are curiously difficult to locate; the blinded Cyclops in *Ulysses Deriding Polyphemus—Homer's Odyssey* (RA 1829) merges with cliffs and clouds; the dying Nelson in *The Battle of Trafalgar, as Seen from the Mizen Starboard Shrouds of the Victory* (1808) is reduced to an easily overlooked dwarf wearing a comical grimace; and I couldn't find Nelson at all in Turner's largest painting ever, *The Battle of Trafalgar, 21 October 1805* (1823–24), wherein near-naked navvies desperately compete for lifeboat space under a titanic outlay of billowing sails. Turner didn't see human beings as worth much in the balance of things; of his terrifying *The Shipwreck* (1805), the catalogue comments, "The almost absurd futility of the figures' efforts to save themselves in the face of these forces is thus a crucial aspect of the painting's sublimity." The viewer encountering *Fall of the Rhine, Schaffhausen* on its wall at the Met cringes under the torrent of onrushing white water, which seems certain to engulf the colorful little human caravan beneath it.

Slathering on white pigment with a palette knife, working sections of wet canvas with his fingers, Turner early was criticized for (apropos of *Fall of the Rhine*) "negligence and coarseness" and (in relation to 1827's mellow *Mortlake Terrace, the Seat of William Moffatt, Esq.; Summer's Evening*) the "yellow fever" of his coloring, which a critic likened to the cuisine of a cook with a mania for curry powder. This painting contains, as an added ingredient, the pasted-on silhouette of a black dog; it had begun to peel off by Varnishing Day and had to be re-affixed. On this day, or days, the artists represented in the annual Royal Academy show were given the privilege of adding final touches to paintings already hung on the walls; Turner was notorious for creating a work from near scratch, that is, from one of the unfinished paintings that crammed his studio. His headlong virtuoso performances on these last-minute varnishing days became a semipublic spectacle. One witness recalled him "standing all day" wearing "an old, tall beaver hat, worn rather off his forehead, which added much to his look of a North Sea pilot. . . . His colours were mostly in powder, and he mixed them with turpentine, sometimes with size, and water, and perhaps even with stale beer." Another witness, as early as

1803, saw him "*spit* all over his picture, and, then taking out a box of *brown powder* [presumably snuff], rubbed it all over the picture."

When a paint supplier, unhappy at the fugitive colors Turner was buying, sought to advise him otherwise, he was told, "Your business, Winsor, is to make colours for Artists. Mine is to use them." The results of his use, like those of his American admirer Albert Pinkham Ryder, were canvases whose unstable, cracked, and sunken surfaces Ruskin himself, Turner's champion, deplored: "No picture of Turner's is seen in perfection a month after it is painted. . . . The fact of his using means so imperfect, together with that of his utter neglect of the pictures in his own gallery, are a phenomenon in human mind which appears to me utterly inexplicable."

The improvisatory extent of his methods on varnishing days, expanding and deepening paintings with no model or sketches before him, helps explain the apparent wide gap between some of his masterworks and any recognizable visual phenomenon. *Snow Storm: Hannibal and His Army Crossing the Alps* (RA 1812) shows no snow and only the murkiest signs of an army; a tiny silhouette of an elephant pays faint homage to Livy's historical account, while a sort of gray waterspout swallows most indications of the Alps. In *The Field of Waterloo* (RA 1818), a spectral white flare in the sky illuminates what appears to be a colorful harem sleeping intertwined; the sight is clarified by lines of Byron that Turner inserted in his catalogue:

> The earth is covered thick with other clay
> Which her own clay shall cover, heaped and pent,
> Rider and horse,—friend, foe,—in one red burial blent!

But no poetry helps us out with *Snow-Storm, Avalanche and Inundation— a Scene in the Upper Part of the Val d'Aouste, Piedmont* (RA 1837). A giant curve of indeterminate color enclosing some dabbled white diagonals and more luminous smears can be an avalanche or a storm—take your pick— as it crowds some hapless figures into the lower right corner of the picture. (A reviewer for the London *Athenaeum* warned, "To speak of these works as pictures, would be an abuse of language.") Ruskin's *Modern Painters* called it one of Turner's "mightiest works."

The wall commentary at the Metropolitan puts it that Turner went from the picturesque to the sublime—the sublime, here as in the next century's Abstract Expressionism, involved large canvases, abstraction, and a visionary subjectivity. Though he employed his sketchbook tirelessly, and pioneered *plein-air* painting on a series of wooden panels of Thames scenery, he was a studio painter, concocting visions out of remembered weather. The semicircular arcs and arbitrary bursts of tint in Turner's last paintings feel spun almost entirely out of himself. An ultimate of this fearless approach is *Snow Storm—Steam Boat off a Harbour's Mouth Making Signals in Shallow Water, and Going by the Lead. The Author Was in This Storm on the Night the Ariel Left Harwich* (RA 1842). By his own account, the painter had himself lashed to the mast for four hours. He said: "I did not paint it to be understood, but I wished to show what such a scene was like. . . . I did not expect to escape, but I felt bound to record it if I did. But no one had any business to like the picture."

Other startlingly fresh fruits of such defiant willfulness were *Rain, Steam and Speed—the Great Western Railway* (RA 1844), which is not in the show, and *Staffa, Fingal's Cave* (RA 1832) and *Peace—Burial at Sea* (RA 1842), which are. When the sails on the ship central in the latter were criticized as being unrealistically black, he replied, "I only wish I had any colour to make them blacker." Not that his mood always gravitated to darkness. His series of *Deluge* paintings in the 1840s featured incandescent skies; in *Light and Colour (Goethe's Theory)—the Morning after the Deluge—Moses Writing the Book of Genesis* (RA 1843), the sun's glare has become a heavenly circle studded with barely brushed multitudes. Goethe's theory, set out in a new English translation of *Zur Farbenlehre* in 1840, interested Turner with its idea, as Anthony Bailey puts it, "of a circle of colours in which reds, yellows and greens had to do with warmth and happiness, and blues, blue-greens and purples prompted 'restless, susceptible, anxious impressions.'" Immaterial arcs and tinted veils haunt his late impressions.

As the painter aged, and his productions became more eccentric, there was speculation in the press about both his sanity and his eyesight—one critic pronounced his work to be "the fruits of a diseased eye and a reckless hand." A Lady Eastlake reported, "Every object he saw, as he himself told us, was outlined to his vision in prismatic colour." Domes of light dominate his Claudean harbors: the moon casts a glow one commentator called "neither night nor day" in *Keelmen Heaving in Coals by Moonlight* (RA 1835). *Regulus*, exhibited in Rome in 1828 and reworked for a London exhibit in 1837, was based by Turner upon the haunting legend of a Roman general whom his Carthaginian captors tortured by cutting off his eyelids and exposing him to the sun; the painting burns into the viewer's eyes with an empyrean of solid gold and its reflection in rippled water. Turner in fact did not go blind; it was the sardonic critics, instead, who were blind, blind to the obstinately questing quality in Turner that showed other artists a way to the future, where what were scoffingly called "pictures of nothing" were pictures of the truth.

A Lean and Optical Dane

CHRISTEN KØBKE, by Sanford Schwartz. 153 pp. Timken Publishers, 1992.

The economics of global renown oblige small countries to specialize. Holland has its great painters—Rembrandt, Vermeer, Frans Hals—and Denmark its writers: Kierkegaard, Hans Christian Andersen, Isak Dinesen. The notion of a Danish painter worthy of international appreciation taxes our mental budget, and that of a Golden Age of Danish painting seems positively extravagant. Yet there was one, roughly from the 1820s to the 1840s, fitted into the cozy Biedermeier era, when Northern Europe, between the Napoleonic storms and the upheavals of 1848, sought domestic peace. Not that Denmark had done very well out of Napoleon; it had seen its Navy defeated by the English in 1801, large portions of Copenhagen destroyed in a British bombardment of 1807, its grain trade and state bank ruined by seven years of subsequent fighting as Napoleon's ally, and its possession of Norway given over to Sweden by the Peace Treaty of Kiel in 1814. Times were lively but hard in the chastened little kingdom during the Golden Age. One art critic has suggested that the small physical scale of Danish paintings in the 1820s reflects the reduced life-style of the middle classes.

Distinguished by steeples, castles, and coolly classic white houses erected after the Great Fire of 1795, Copenhagen, with a population of about a hundred thousand, was picturesque, and the Royal Academy of Fine Arts, housed in the Charlottenborg Palace, produced, under the aegis of the painter and professor Christoffer Wilhelm Eckersberg, a sudden generation of young painters. Of these, Christen Købke, a short and staid baker's son who began to study at the Academy when he was twelve, did not especially stand out. The portraitists Christian Jensen and Wilhelm Marstrand both had reputations higher than Købke's; the most famous contemporary Danish artist of all was Bertel Thorvaldsen, a sculptor who lived in Rome. Købke, who had ten siblings, was a pious self-doubter and, until his wealthy father died in 1843, under no financial pressure to make a splash. He often gave his canvases away as gifts, sold a mere two to the Royal Collection, and was twice rejected for membership in the Academy. In 1848, at the age of thirty-seven, he died, after a decade of family deaths, straitened circumstances, and artistic wane. Only toward the end of the nineteenth century did his reputation begin to revive. Now he is considered the best painter of his age—"the Golden

Age" has become "the Age of Købke"—if not the greatest Danish painter of all time.

Yet he is still barely known outside Denmark. Sanford Schwartz's *Christen Købke* is the first American book about this painter. The most extensive previous consideration in English was to be found in Kasper Monrad's fine catalogue notes for the Købke items in the 1984 exhibition at the National Gallery in London, *Danish Painting: The Golden Age*. In the fall of 1993, a similar exhibit will be coming to the Los Angeles County Museum and then to New York's Metropolitan Museum of Art. In the meantime, Schwartz's elegant, though annoyingly miniaturized, album will serve as a primer and an appetizer.

Schwartz brings to art criticism a broad knowledge and a hungry but patient sensibility. One assumes, from his reference to sources in Danish, that he knows the language or mastered it for this critical occasion. He is one of a flock of youngish American critics to show the influence of Pauline Kael, echoing the passionate film-reviewer's gangling, slangy, heavily personalized, go-for-all-of-it style. "Købke," Schwartz tells us, "was still on his anti-Eckersberg roll—still trying to shuck his first teacher." Købke's father was "a big-time baker," and the hyphenated adjectives don't stop there. Købke's contemporaries produce "sketch-like, of-the-moment landscapes," Wilhelm Bendz's "dark-yet-streaky pictures seem far afield from the staid Eckersberg," and one of Købke's paintings presents "an extraordinary sense of see-throughness."

Schwartz rather revels in awkward phrasing: "In tone, Købke's work runs the range from being somewhat blank to being youthfully—charmingly—trustful to conveying a jet of pure, frank, penetrating awareness." Conveying his own jet of awareness, Schwartz beclouds simple meanings with an ingenuous wordiness: "His art is one of the products of the social and personal liberties of the era after Napoleon, but it should be said that Købke wasn't in revolt from another way of being an artist." As the critic ponders the canvases, his subtle sensations successfully defy expression:

> The pictures might present the state of someone who is mildly ravaged.

> When he sets a green wagon near a red fence, for instance, the surrounding colors are so balanced that the red and the green spring out on their own.

> There is a melancholy mood to Købke's pictures, but it arrives from between the cracks.

Not the cracks, presumably, of the aging paint. The vivid, chatty viewing persona at times turns petulant: of Købke's later, grander, duller works,

Schwartz complains, "We're not lured into thinking about how he made these pictures," and of Købke's friend and student, Johan Lundbye, we are amused to read, "A viewer quits Lundbye's company with the thought that this man was too talented and too smart to have made his protagonist a distant cow."

Yet, on the not totally satisfactory basis of the color reproductions in this book, one can only agree with Schwartz's basic appreciation of his subject. "Erectness, precision, and gentleness" excellently sums up Købke's virtues. Gentleness isn't commonly listed as a virtue in visual art, but in the surpassingly beautiful canvas *The Landscape Painter F. Sødring* (1832), the quality characterizes both the subject's expression and the way in which Købke's painterly attention envelops and modulates every surface, every texture, from the pencil drawings pinned to the gray-panelled wall to Sødring's pink-tinged right thumb, from the cushion strings and folded camp stool along the lower edge to the tilted oval mirror bisected by the upper edge. The little still life of objects on the table by Sødring's elbow is marked by the tonal hot spot of the quietly colored portrait, a rectangular red case like a distillation of the pink planes that compose the

Købke, The Landscape Painter F. Sødring, *1832. Oil on canvas.*

young painter's faintly quizzical, pale-browed face—a face which is treated, like faces in Vermeer and Manet, dispassionately, as one among a number of objects defined by color and light. An earlier portrait of another colleague, *Marstrand at the Easel in Eckersberg's Studio* (1829), is relatively loaded with chiaroscuro and dramatic atmosphere; it is the quiet, emotionless tone of Købke's mature treatment that enables his somewhat abstract color to strike its balances and to manifest what Schwartz calls "freshly felt formal tension."

As Schwartz says, "Købke's endeavor is remarkably lean and optical, and it's without sentiment." Such an endeavor appeals to the twentieth century, where the Victorians would be bored and possibly alarmed by it; their *horror vacui* has been replaced by our own horror of clutter. Købke worked on the edge of emptiness. His instinct was to work small, beginning with drawings of a meticulous precision, or with oil sketches brushed onto pieces of paper that fit into the lid of his portable paint box. His genius was an intimate one, nurtured by Danish coziness and Nordic reserve. Many of his paintings, including some detailed landscapes, are less than a foot square.

His several paintings of Frederiksborg Castle—one of the biggest things in Denmark—are among his largest, but the most arresting of them are the ones that contain the least amount of castle, the two rooftop views painted in 1834–35. Brick chimneys and ornate copper turrets loom before a far brown landscape and an empty blue-green sky. The canvases, measuring over five by five feet, were painted to share the walls of his parents' large new dining room with two grisaille paintings by Købke of circular plaster reliefs by the sculptor Thorvaldsen, *Night* and *Day*. The rooftops seem raked by a setting or rising sun, and Schwartz, taking as a sign the stork on one chimney, bundles the goddesses and the shifting roof perspectives into a single theme: "Viscerally, at least, the four pictures together become a sort of meditation on the passage of time, on being brought into the world and being taken out of it." What makes the roof views appealing now, and Købke's fuller views of the castle much less so, is their fragmentary and minimal content; as in an unpopulated plaza by de Chirico, an eerie absence shouts out. In the Dane's later paintings of, say, a cliff in Capri (*Marina Grande, Capri,* 1839–40) or *The Forum, Pompeii, with Vesuvius in the Distance* (1841), the absence is, as it were, missing, with nothing to take its place but a conventional grandeur, heavy on antique ochre.

The grandeur in his best landscapes is not imported from ancient Rome but found in the modest country around Copenhagen, where houses and people are never out of sight. In two masterly paintings from

Købke, Ida Thiele, *1832. Oil on canvas.*

1838, both called *View from the Embankment of Lake Sortedam*, human figures are silhouetted on lakeside docks, clustered at the base of a central vertical—a sail-wrapped mast in one, a flagpole in the other. The mood is benevolent, yet tinged by silence, desolation, and poignance. In the smaller, though more stunning, of the views, looking toward Østerbro, an ominous evening shadow darkens the group, in their playful assortment of hats, as they make things tight at their end of their sail.

The melancholy that flits through Andersen's fables and pursues Kierkegaard through his whirlwind of impersonation and polemic haunts the innocent, geometrically taut world of Købke. The absence one feels, perhaps, is that of the Madonnas and crucified Christs, gods and goddesses and nymphs and satyrs and idealized historical figures for whom landscape hitherto has been merely background. Brought to the foreground, will not nature look blank and empty? Købke's paintings are full of light but it is generally a dry, less than refulgent light; thready little white lines—almost his signature—appear on the edges of buildings and collars and wands of grass. His trees, with their blanched leaves and twigs, have a spectral pallor. His exquisite drawing emphasizes line over mass, so that some of his portrait heads quite lack a sense of weight, of existing in the round.

Others of his portraits are superb, with startling psychological presence. His portrait of Christian Petersen (1833) uses the same pink, planar tones as the portrait of Sødring a year earlier, but the face is more troubled and complex, without distracting us entirely from the equable rendering of the flowered brown vest, the lush velvet coat collar, and the splendidly fitted and rendered shirt and collar. The alert, searching, and

Købke, Professor F. C. Sibbern, *1833. Pencil and sepia.*

even agonized face of Lauritz Lyngbye, painted the same year, takes all the focus, however; Schwartz rates it at the Romantic end of Købke's range, heated and pent up where the portrait of Sødring is cool and mellow: "It's hard to recall other paintings of the Romantic period, except Géricault's images of soldiers in moments of doubt and confusion, that convey so freshly the Romantic ache, the mixture of contrary yearnings." Between these extremes lies a remarkable variety of Danish visages—the lumpy, flatly colored *Ida Thiele* (1832), one of the best portraits of an infant ever painted; *An Old Sailor* and *An Old Farmer Woman* (both 1832), full of the pained dignity of age; *Male Model* (1833), an unblinking, antiheroic, yet magnificent male nude; the superbly rounded and realized pencil sketches *Professor F. C. Sibbern* (1833) and *Young Girl* (undated); chalky portraits of his rather crafty-looking parents (1835); the swarthy, hypnotically gazing *Study for the Portrait of Prefect J. A. Graah* (1837–38); and the dashing *Portrait of a Naval Officer* (1834), a companion in picture-making to the portrait of Sødring, with the same dusky-green background and air of urbane good humor.

From portrait to portrait, Købke's intentions seem to fluctuate. Some suggest a less crusty Rembrandt, others a less smoothly modelled Ingres. His mentor Eckersberg's travels had included a year of study in Paris with David, and he had brought back to Denmark a French neoclassicism whose rigor and thinness were, to Købke, both releasing and confining. Eckersberg preached, not quite paradoxically, perspectival construction and life studies. "Draw from nature, no matter what it is," he exhorted. An animated oil sketch of riverside grasses by Købke was included, eleven years ago, in the Museum of Modern Art show *Before Photography*; introducing the catalogue, Peter Galassi pointed out that the fifteenth-century pictorial invention of linear perspective opened the way not only for such marvels of balanced architectural clarity as della Francesca's and Uccello's crystalline panoramas but for the overlappings, fragmentariness, and surprises in apparent size found in Dutch painters like de Witte and Saenredam and, later, in Degas. Købke's rooftops are an impressive instance of what might be called the proto-photographic eye, which includes and excludes not according to an idealistic hierarchy of significance but in mute, enigmatic acceptance of what falls within the viewer's frame.

Eckersberg's proposed turn from the exhausted pomp of historical and mythological tableaux to *plein-air* sketches in the Copenhagen suburbs was undoubtedly healthy, and in the forward direction of Impressionism. But Danish critics had their doubts. One wrote of Købke: "This artist has distinguished himself by conscientious truth and simplicity, but unfortunately also by a conspicuous indifference to his choice of subjects. The latter is highly regrettable, inasmuch as nature possesses much that is trivial and common that cannot serve as a worthy object for art." The issue is metaphysical: If a thing exists in nature, how can it be trivial, and how can it not be, if it is not real? Does art involve the rendering of the actual, or the reordering of it? Is something extra, beyond skillful human imitation, needed to make nature into art? The appreciative Schwartz comes up against these questions in considering two ambitious, hardworked canvases that Købke, seeking a wider public, pitched in a grander mode: *View Outside the North Gate of the Citadel* (1834) and *Østerbro in Morning Light* (1836). The former, Schwartz concludes, "teeters between greatness and emptiness" and ends with "a heart that is too small for the body it's placed in"; the latter, similarly, "seems undernourished. It has more sweat and preparation than innards."

Surviving letters from Købke describe the sweat and preparation, and the obscure depths of struggle from which he prays for God's assistance. His reputation scarcely needs the two big works. Less effortfully, he achieved a dozen or so masterpieces that give him his niche in global renown. Still, one would like to test Schwartz's negative conclusions about the two ambitious pictures. Is there some subtle poetry, some precious grace of rendering, the critic has missed? But he has had the advantage of seeing the paintings themselves, where they hang in Copenhagen, and, infuriatingly, the color reproductions that Timken Publishers have given the pictures in question are too small to judge, as are a number of others. Repeatedly, I had to take a magnifying glass to the color plates. With an opportunity to reproduce many of the smaller paintings near their actual size, the designers have chosen to make them miniatures, with lavish margins. True, a few bled pages do amplify the details so that Købke's stabbingly deft, increasingly "blocky, runny, halting" brushwork can be studied, but such pages are three in number. On the rest, for whatever reasons of cost or style, this volume, meant to enlarge Christen Købke's reputation, presents him as almost too small to see.

Lear Far and Near

EDWARD LEAR AND THE ART OF TRAVEL, at the Yale Center for British Art, New Haven, Connecticut, September 20, 2000–January 14, 2001.

Even during Edward Lear's lifetime, his nonsense verse tended to detract from the seriousness of his landscape painting. In the corner of a letter Lear had written Ruskin in 1883, the great critic non-responsively jotted, "Is this the nonsense man?" A few years later, Ruskin in *Pall Mall Magazine* praised the writer but ignored the artist. Posthumously, appreciation of the art must work its way around (to quote a review from 1930) "the Himalaya of nonsense [whereupon] Edward Lear sits enthroned." The catalogue of one exhibit of his watercolors almost insultingly speaks of "Edward Lear, 'the landscape painter' as he was wont to call himself." The brilliance and even majesty of Lear's best watercolors has been shadowed, too, by the mediocrity of the oil paintings for which they were, often, preliminary studies, complete with written color notations in the spaces of the sketch. Yet, after his early years, when, from the age of sixteen to twenty-five, he labored as a meticulous painter of birds and animals, it was as a landscape painter, or topographical artist, that he supported himself, travelling all over the lands of the Mediterranean and beyond, into India, to turn exotic landscapes into saleable watercolors and oils and books of lithograph illustrations of his own prose.

Words came effortlessly to him, as is evident in the bubbling flow of the letters that survive from the torrent he addressed to friends and patrons (often the same) and his sister Ann, who in effect raised him when the Lear family fortunes, once prosperous, turned sharply downward in the aftermath of the Napoleonic Wars. In his visual art, the pencil was Lear's favorite tool; he wrote, "I am certain, whatever good I may get by 'colour from nature' I get more by pencil." His watercolor method was to produce a pencil sketch on the spot, apply washes usually, but not always, later in the studio, and then trace the pencil lines with sepia ink. From his early ornithological studies he acquired the habit of precision, and though he complained frequently about his failing eyesight—he was, unfortunately for a landscape painter, nearsighted—his work to the last remained markedly linear, with a slightly surreal wiriness. In this he was the opposite of the explosively coloristic J. M. W. Turner, Ruskin's pet contemporary and by general consensus the greatest English landscape painter of the Victorian era.

When Lear, whose impoverished upbringing did not allow him proper training in oil painting, attempted to learn the necessary skill to produce prestigious large canvases in oil, he found a rather grudging instructor in Holman Hunt, one of the three founders of the Pre-Raphaelite Brotherhood, who attempted to overturn the dour, brownish academic style by imitating early Italian paintings, painting on a wet white ground to give their colors brilliance. A jewel-like brilliance was obtained, but the Pre-Raphaelites did not escape a certain sickly literalism, a rather flat, licked, stained-glass look; their work can feel encased and airless. Most of Lear's oils, even of wild terrain, usually stayed canvas-bound, appearing whitish, waxy, and overstudied, though indisputably dramatic and painstaking. His own description of his working at a large oil canvas—"sitting motionless like a petrified gorilla as to my body & limbs hour after hour—my hand meanwhile, peck peck pecking at billions of little dots & lines"—indicates a joyless fussiness of attack. At the same time, his watercolors, rapidly done in transit, became robust and free in feeling; they leap into the third dimension in a way his oils do not. Lear's most dependable living was gleaned from what he called "tyrants"—series of watercolors based on travel sketches, done thirty at a time, applying patches of color assembly-line fashion.

This somewhat pathetic tale of an always struggling artist can be found excellently told in Vivien Noakes's biography, *Edward Lear: The Life of a Wanderer* (1968), and her study *The Painter Edward Lear* (1991). The melancholy facts do not prepare the viewer for the airy happiness of many of the 129 works by Lear on display in New Haven, or for the poet's jubilantly grotesque pen-and-ink illustrations of his own limericks and nonsense verse. In the impudent stretchiness and sketchiness of these comical drawings Lear looks forward to the revolutionary liberties that Picasso took. His rapid tinted sketches of landscape, some of them done five minutes apart as he drifted down the Nile in a small boat, anticipate the capture of shifting light which Monet essayed in his series of haystacks, poplars, and bends in the river.

Lear estimated that he had done as many as thirty thousand watercolors; even at the more likely estimate of ten thousand the number is impressive. Sheafs of them were released onto the market in 1929 with the deaths of Lear's friend and executor, Franklin Lushington, and of his patron Lord Northbrook; in the long lull of Lear's unfashionability many were picked up cheap, for as little as a few shillings apiece, by the American collectors Philip Hofer and W. B. Osgood Field, who gave them to Houghton Library at Harvard in 1942. During the Second World War, Donald C. Gallup, an Army officer and eventually an English professor, began to buy Lear watercolors in a London shop; in 1997, he donated his collection, containing nine oils and twenty-eight prints as well as 356 watercolors and drawings, to Yale. This is the heart of the present exhibition. Scott Wilcox, the exhibition's curator, explains in his introduction to the catalogue that, rather than range—as did, say, the London Royal Academy of Arts exhibit organized by Vivien Noakes in 1985—over the varied Lear production, he has focused on the topographical art, and drawn upon the resources of the Yale Center for British Art to display over seventy examples of British travel art not by Lear, from the late eighteenth century to the 1860s.

An 1842 map of overland routes from England to India shows the romantic world of Britain's imperial adventure: most of Africa's interior is a blank mystery, the Arabian Peninsula likewise, yet the coasts are thickly sewn with ports to feed and fuel the busy maritime traffic. The artists who ventured out into the Mediterranean lands and beyond, braving sunstroke, malaria, bedbugs, banditry, and other indispositions, brought back news to England: pre-photographic pictures of places most Englishmen had never seen but could, increasingly, aspire to see. These images served as reportage and as advertisement, travel posters of a sort, encouraging the elite Grand Tourist of the eighteenth century to become the middle-class Cook's Tourist of the nineteenth. The Napoleonic Wars formed but an interruption in a broadening flow as the English sought to escape their wet, gray climate, their restricting class system, their Victorian inhibitions, their Protestant work ethic with its grim Industrial Revolution. Italy was the principal destination; Iberia (which Lear somehow missed) and Greece, Egypt and the Holy Land, and the Mediterranean islands drew the more devout and determined. The artists, to be interesting, were compelled to venture into ever more exotic locales; Lear's *Views in Rome and Its Environs* (1841) showed more or less standard sights; *Illustrated Excursions in Italy* (1846) presented views less commonly visited. Later books of illustrated travel journals took him to Greece and Albania, southern Calabria, Corsica; he never was able to organize his Egyptian pictures for publication.

Travel, then as now, held the promise of liberation and advancement. Lear had much to escape from: he suffered from asthma in his damp and "smokydark" native environment; he was prone to depression as well as ebullience; his epilepsy, attacks of which occurred as often as twenty times a month, constantly threatened to embarrass and discommode him. How physically realized his homosexual tendencies were remains, as with many other Victorians, hard to determine; Noakes pins the central crush of Lear's life on Franklin Lushington, a slightly younger, "very amiable & talented man" (Lear wrote in a letter to his sister Ann) with whom the artist travelled in Greece for six weeks in 1849, according to Noakes "probably the happiest few weeks of Lear's life." A tender glimpse is given in Lear's diary, where he marvels at the abundance of flowers in the Greek springtime: "As for Lushington & I, equally fond of flowers, we gather them all day like children, & when we have stuck our hats & coats & horses all over with them—it is time to throw them away, & get a new set." Though several times serious in his contemplation of marriage—most often to the Honorable Augusta "Gussie" Bethell—Lear avoided proposing, an avoidance as much, perhaps, temperamental as practical for an unpropertied wandering artist. An incongruous work in the Yale exhibit consists of, in eight manuscript pages, a little nonsense narrative, "St. Kiven and the Gentle Kathleen," scribbled to amuse the children of the Earl of Derby's household while Lear was a young resident artist there. I transcribed one of its stanzas as follows:

> 'Twas from Kathleen's eyes he flew,
>   Eyes of most unholy blue!
> She had loved him all along,
>   Wished him hers, nor thought it wrong.

And another thus:

> Here at last, he calmly said,
>   Woman ne'er shall find my bed.
> Ah! the good saint little knew
>   What that wily sex can do.

Lear himself, with an evasiveness almost saintly, did avoid, to his death in 1888 at the age of seventy-five, that wily sex with its unholy eyes. Nevertheless, the theme of lonely longing and failed courtship recurs in his nonsense verse, perhaps most poignantly in "The Dong with a Luminous Nose":

> For day and night he was always there
> By the side of the Jumbly Girl so fair,

With her sky-blue hands, and her sea-green hair.
Till the morning came of that hateful day
When the Jumblies sailed in their sieve away,
And the Dong was left on the cruel shore
Gazing—gazing for evermore. . . .

At the Yale Center for British Art, the great number of works—more than two hundred in all—threatens to blunt the viewer's keen attention. One gathers a general impression of a tropism, on Lear's part, to dry climates with broad unpopulated views; these scenes breathe with an asthmatic's relieved lungs. He likes the bare, the austere, the cloudless, the wide-open. The many sketches along the Nile, especially, from his tour of 1867, seem more than dutiful in their attention. His diary recorded, of the upper Nile,

> Nubia delighted me; it isn't a bit like Egypt, except that theres a river in both. Sad, stern, uncompromising landscape—dark ashy purple lines of hills—piles of granite rocks—fringes of palm—& ever and anon astonishing ruins of oldest Temples:—above all wonderful—Aboo Simbel which took my breath away.

Yet the majestic cliff statues of Abu Simbel are sketched at a distance, so that they scarcely seem man-made objects within the folds of the bare hills. At Karnak, Lear is more interested in impressionistically recording the surrounding landscape than in depicting the ruined temple, which was carefully and vividly rendered in the watercolors by David Roberts and William James Müller, also displayed at Yale. It is the contours of land and rocks that grab Lear's attention, in a kind of geological rapture. The marble rocks of Nerbudda Jubbolpore (1882), the astonishing crags of Corsica (1870), the riverside formations at Tafa and Gebel Sheikh Abou Fodde (1867), the cliffs of Capo Ducato on the island of Santa Maura, from which Sappho supposedly leapt to her death (1863), the stupendous gorge of Zagóri, Greece (1860), and the dramatically foregrounded rocks and glistening distant peaks in a number of the large oil paintings, including the fine *Forest of Valdoniello, Corsica* (1869)—these mineral conjurations lodge in the mind, as touched by an instinctive search for the sublime within the inhuman. Victorian science and piety meet in this exalted geology. Rocky landscapes even more dramatically embraced are reproduced in Noakes's *The Painter Edward Lear:* a craggy 1858 perspective of Jerusalem; a precipitous 1856 view of the Monastery of St. Paul clinging to the slope of Mount Athos; a stunningly detailed 1838 rendering of Amalfi in pencil, sepia wash, and white body-color; gorges at Syracuse in 1847 and Castelluccio in 1843; Mount Sinai in 1852 and the loftily perched Monastery of Barlaam in Meteora in 1849—in such powerful, cold-eyed watercolors the adamant substance of the planet seethes as if in the moment of volcanic creation. Trees, too, spoke to Lear, a little more sinuously than to other eyes: those in *Corfu from Ascension* (c. 1856–64) seem to writhe in a kind of pain, an agonized chorus waving in lament. The tree in the splendid watercolor *On the Road, Two Hours from Tepelene* (1857) has a mountainous grandeur in its low perspective, rooted on a green ground sprinkled with color notations and animated by a troop of costumed Greeks pausing for rest and water. The work is dated and precisely located, and we indeed are there with Lear that sunny day, that exact distance from the wanderer's next destination. His life flits by in the dates he systematically attached to the visual notations that, in the words of a visitor to his San Remo home late in Lear's life, "he would put on paper . . . with a rapidity and accuracy that inspired me with awestruck admiration."

But even the finest of the watercolors are haunted by a sense of the deferred; these are not ends in themselves but steps on the way to grand oils that will win him the glory and fortune that, in fact, eluded him. The works exhibited at the Yale Center by other travel artists have the unintended effect of reminding us of all that Lear does not customarily deliver. Studious portraits of the Karnak ruins have been already mentioned; equally vivid and circumstantial are John Frederick Lewis's desert encampment, complete with canopy guy wires and recently slain hares

Lear, Garf Hossayn, *February 15, 1867. Watercolor with pen in brown ink over graphite.*

and gazelle, and Thomas Hartley Cromek's cavernous lower Basilica of St. Francis at Assisi, and various Venetian and Portuguese vistas as captured in sparkling, bustling daylight by James Duffield Harding and James Holland. These painters had advantages, a schooled professional briskness compared with which Lear remained a self-taught amateur. How dark, greasy, and uncertain in key many of his oils are compared, say, with the wet, bold, splashy attack of Richard Parkes Bonington, represented among the travel artists by *Corso Sant'Anastasia, Verona, Italy* (1828), or the luminous meltdown of Turner, as seen in his small canvas *Venice, The Mouth of the Grand Canal* (c. 1840).

And yet there is a poetry, a poetry of pleasurable vacancy, that gives Lear his own place in the distinguished annals of English watercolorists. The precision of the young ornithological painter accompanies the vague quest of the aging traveller, as he hobbles from one commission and loan and act of aristocratic patronage to the next. "Alas! I needs must go and call on swells, / That they may say, 'Pray draw me the Estrelles,'" he wrote in the comically complaining "Eclogue, Composed at Cannes, December 9th, 1867," a souvenir of his momentary close friendship with Mr. and Mrs. John Addington Symonds. Lear hungered for friendship, and his irrepressibly frisky letters, increasingly Joycean in their whimsy and wordplay, remain as traces of the personal charm that won him valuable loyalties among the upper classes. After his death, Franklin Lushington said that the love of his friends was "the best and sweetest of garlands

Lear, On the Road, Two Hours from Tepelene, *April 19, 1857. Watercolor with pen in brown ink over graphite.*

that can in spirit be laid on his tomb." Lushington also stated, "He really *lived* upon the letters of his distant friends more than any man I have ever known." Lear did not quite live, and he did not quite paint oils, but he certainly wrote; he let go, as we say now, in the realm of language.

In his letters he eloquently tossed off desolate truths: "I am doing little, but dimly walking on along the dusty twilight lanes of incomprehensible life. . . . I wish I were an egg and was going to be hatched," he wrote Charles Fortescue, who saved all of his letters, giving posterity a major trove. (A regrettable mass of his personal papers were lost in the domestic confusion when Lear died in San Remo, having outlived even his beloved cat Foss.) Bliss and melancholy keep close, manic-depressive company in his letters. From Egypt he wrote, "And to me what wonders of broad beautiful green & lilac vegetation & far hills & mosques—see thro' & beyond gt. palms & acacias! O sugar canes! O camels! O Egypt!" and then, up the Nile among the ruins, "The intense deadness of old Egypt is felt as a weight of knowledge in all that world of utter silence. . . . One peeps into those dark death-silent giant halls of columns—a terror pervades the heart & head." In India he deplored the "frightful fuss-ticket-baggage-bother and tumult" and called the British establishment "Hustlefussabad" yet punned happily of himself in Delhi "making Delhineations of the Delhicate architecture as is all impressed on my mind as inDelhibly as the Delhiterious quality of the water of that city."

His poems exude the same giddy juice. His limericks, not exactly limericks, turn in their repetitive last line on an unexpected adjective; they have the gossamer silliness of days among the children at the Earl of Derby's lavish and carefree mansion, Knowsley. Lear cast himself early as Uncle Arley, the playful big-nosed uncle with his ready pen and nimble hands on the piano, tossing off a verse or song to earn his place at the dining table. If he had his erotic frustrations and his epileptic fits (which, in stout British fashion, he blamed upon a failure of willpower, like masturbation), a fun uncle keeps his pains to himself, or drowns them, as Lear reportedly did, in alcohol.

> O! My agèd Uncle Arley!
> Sitting on a heap of Barley
>   Thro' the silent hours of night,—
> Close beside a leafy thicket:—
> On his nose there was a Cricket,—
> In his hat a Railway-Ticket;—
>   (But his shoes were far too tight).

The tightness eased in the presence of children—the least threatening of human beings—and in that of landscapes, the more barren and lunarly picturesque the better. The Cricket on Uncle Arley's nose might be construed as talent and sensitivity; though not Tennyson or Turner, Lear had his genius, but had to come at it by travelling to the land where the Bong-tree grows.

The Artist as Trailblazer

FREDERIC CHURCH, WINSLOW HOMER, AND THOMAS MORAN: *Tourism and the American Landscape,* at Cooper-Hewitt, National Design Museum, New York, May 19–October 22, 2006.

This engaging, farraginous show at the Cooper-Hewitt Museum, on Fifth Avenue, invites the viewer to think of the nineteenth-century American landscape artist, usually envisioned as the independent producer of a luxury artifact, as, instead, a tool of commerce and real-estate development. Frederic Church, who played the starring role in 2002's travelling megashow *American Sublime* (London, Philadelphia, Minneapolis) and this year's exhibition *Treasures from Olana: Landscapes by Frederic Edwin Church* (National Academy Museum, New York), extends his twenty-first-century revival by dominating the two other named artists in an assemblage subtitled *Tourism and the American Landscape.* Though Winslow Homer is represented by a number of amusing wood engravings and beautiful watercolors, and Thomas Moran adds his otherworldly West to the collective depiction of the relatively unspoiled American wilderness, it is Church whose heirs lodged more than two thousand works in the collection of the Cooper Union Museum (as compared with more than three hundred by Homer and fewer than a hundred by Moran), and it is Church who, in his preternaturally deft and rapid oil sketches, most decisively places before us the thing itself, the New World's nature.

Cooper-Hewitt and its vast collection need some explaining, which Barbara Bloemink's catalogue introduction concisely provides. The Cooper Union for the Advancement of Science and Art was founded by Peter Cooper in 1859 "in order to provide practical courses for the education and self-improvement of the working class, particularly in the trades of engineering, illustration, industrial design, architectural drawing, ornamental drawing, mechanical drawing, and painting." Cooper, born in New York City in 1791, was himself an inventor and a hands-on industrialist, whose fortune got its start in the glue business, greatly expanded in the iron industry, eventually included more than half the telegraph lines in the United States, and was significantly invested in philanthropy and the cause of public education. Cooper Union provided night classes so that working men could attend; an existing art school for women was incorporated into the institution, "in order to provide female students with the practical skills to become self-supporting designers and art teachers."

A committee drawn from the distinguished artists on the faculty acquired contemporary drawings "to be used for teaching purposes," but it wasn't until 1897, fourteen years after Cooper's death, that his three granddaughters—Sarah Cooper Hewitt, Eleanor Garnier Hewitt, and Amelia Hewitt—founded "the first design and decorative-arts museum in the United States." Their models were the Musée des Arts Décoratifs in Paris and the Victoria and Albert in London—stately grab bags whose polymorphous utility was expressed by Eleanor Hewitt at the museum's founding: "For the worker, the source of inspiration is frequently found in the sight of an unexpected object, possibly one of an entirely different trade." The sisters stocked their museum with buying sprees abroad; Dr. Bloemink states, "Many of the objects the sisters acquired were unusual and eclectic, reflecting an enormous range of works, from match-safes and birdcages to wallpaper and fine lace."

It was, then, for the training of artists that works of art were acquired, with a craft emphasis on preliminary drawings and sketches. Toward this pedagogic end the sisters and such advisers as the artist Eliot Clark and the collector Charles W. Gould acquired, in 1912, the gift of hundreds of Winslow Homer's watercolors and drawings from the artist's brother, and, in 1917, eighty-plus works from Thomas Moran himself. The same year saw the massive donation from Church's son Louis, including most of the works remaining in his deceased father's Hudson Valley mansion, Olana. Church's oil sketches, often dashed off on paperboard pinned to the inside of his paint-box lid, are marvels of an artist's habituated eye and hand. Some, such as *Sun Rising Over Bar Harbor* (c. 1860) and *Sunset Across the Hudson Valley* (1870), when reproduced in a catalogue, belie with their grandeur their small size; others, like *Coast at Mount Desert (Sand Beach)* (c. 1850), *Autumn Landscape in New England* (c. 1865), and the seething, spray-filled *Surf Pounding Against the Rocky Maine Coast* (c. 1862), amaze us with the fineness of their quickly captured detail. These *plein-air* notations were meant, of course, to be worked up as stu-

dio canvases of marketable dimension and finish, and were added to the
Cooper-Hewitt collection as a professional master's leftovers; their present aspect as delightfully fresh and free works of art had to wait until
Impressionism loosened our sense of acceptable brushwork. Still, it is
hard to see the two studies by Church of Mount Katahdin's near slopes,
both dated before 1878, one a foot square and the other fourteen by nine
inches, as preliminary works, so poised is their composition and impressive their illusionism.

Church, a decade older than Homer and Moran, had the jump on the
scenic high points of the American Northeast. As a young man he studied
in the Catskills as the only student of Thomas Cole, the founder of
American landscape painting. The Mountain House, Kaaterskill Falls,
the Hudson Valley, the coast of Maine, Niagara Falls—he painted them
all, and produced, in his seven-and-a-half-foot-wide oil *Niagara* (1857),
housed at Washington's Corcoran Gallery of Art, an image that, accord-

After Thomas Moran, Katahdin from the South Shore of the Lake—
from a Study by F. E. Church, *c. 1878. Engraving, by Francis Scott King,
for* Scribner's Monthly Magazine, *May 1878.*

ing to Gail S. Davidson's catalogue essay "Landscape Icons, Tourism, and Land Development in the Northeast," "supplanted Niagara itself as the symbol of America." Images, reproduced in popular magazines by painstaking wood engravings and lavished upon the middle classes in the photographic form of stereoscopic views, were a key to the solidification and spread of American identity from mid-century onward. Semi-tamed landscape had become a middle-class consumable with the development of vacation resorts, a process in which artists served as groundbreakers. The editor of *The Nation*, Edwin Lawrence Godkin, analyzed the process as early as 1883, in a tongue-in-cheek essay titled "The Evolution of the Summer Resort"; the cultural historian Hans Huth, in his serious 1957 work *Nature and the American: Three Centuries of Changing Attitudes*, perceived a

> three-phase development of resorts, which starts with artists and writers exploring a place and locals creating boarding houses to serve them. In the second phase, the boarding house becomes a rustic hotel filled initially by cultured and refined visitors, then by more economically diverse vacationers. In the final phase, the elite clientele, seeking refuge from the larger community of resorters, builds their own cottages with privately owned beaches.

Godkin puts it this way: "The hotel boarders, who have now become second-class citizens, are driven away to seek newer resorts; and the cycle begins again."

Niagara Falls, the first and still-classic vacation site, was swiftly overrun by tourists. Church's magnificent paintings—his second large oil, *Niagara Falls from the American Side* (1867), came ten years after the epic view from the Canadian side—showed nary a soul of the throngs of visitors and vendors (some in Native American costume, the ancestors of the present day's Falls-side casino operators) that are visible in a more naïve canvas like Ferdinand Richardt's *Niagara* (c. 1855). Entrepreneurs on both sides of the river erected industrial mills and ever-larger hotels, crowding views that remained, in Church's representation, pristine. Church also, through the magic of thoughtful observation, triumphantly solved a technical problem which the photography of the time could not yet handle—the representation of running, rippling, falling water.

Though he displayed his most ambitious canvases for an admission fee, Church did not exploit the techniques of mass reproduction, as Homer and Moran did. Homer produced black-and-white images, often reused in his paintings, that could be turned into woodcuts for such journals as *Harper's Weekly*, *Scribner's*, *The Century*, and *Appletons' Journal of Litera-*

ture, Science, and Art. Moran began as a wood engraver; his craggy, rather Gothic views of the arid, mountainous West, based upon his own delicate watercolors, gouaches, and pencil sketches, supplied illustrated magazines and the massive two-volume album *Picturesque America, or The Land We Live In* (1872–74), edited by no less an eminence than William Cullen Bryant. The artist's Western travels to the Yosemite Valley, the Sierras, and the Grand Canyon were underwritten by railroads and hotels hoping to attract tourists. Born in England and raised in Philadelphia, Moran was influenced by Ruskin and the paintings of J. M. W. Turner; his own paintings have a Turneresque, romantic, dematerializing tendency flattering to the stony realms portrayed. From prehistorical cave paintings of hunted bison up to medieval icons and Renaissance panoramas illustrating a cultural mythos, art had served social functions; it still served, as advertisements for travel and land development. Further, in the post–Civil War period, glamorized images of the vast American territory distracted North and South from their wounds.

Winslow Homer differed from Moran and Church in populating his

After Winslow Homer, The Artist in the Country, *c. 1869. Engraving, by John Karst, for* Appletons' *magazine, June 19, 1869.*

vistas with live Americans. The figures in his popular wood engravings from the late 1860s, such as *The Summit of Mt. Washington* and *Summer in the Country*, share an icy lack of facial expression and a lively complexity of costume. The conscious comedy of *The Artist in the Country* (a mustached dauber paints under a tilted umbrella while a comely spectator frowningly eyes his canvas; the original sketch had two painters working in tandem, as on an inspiration built for two) is rivalled by the unconscious comedy of sun hats multiplied like the sharp bills of a flock of birds in *The Fishing Party*, and the heavily garbed women anxiously peering out from *Under the Falls, Catskill Mountains*, and the two uncomfortably stiff gentlemen surrounded by roughing-it equipment in *Camping Out in the Adirondacks*. These representations of the wilderness being breached in clothes designed for the parlor nevertheless spelled out to the middle classes possibilities of activity hitherto restricted to the servant orders. A catalogue essay by Sarah Burns, indeed, accuses Homer of inventing a type of false American pastoral; his sojourns at Houghton Farm, an estate, two hours from New York, run "in accordance with strictly scientific methods" by a well-heeled family, the Valentines, that Homer had known since his boyhood, yielded to the artist's hand images of toothsome, dreaming shepherdesses: *Bo-Peep (Girl with Shepherd's Crook Seated by a Tree)* (1878), *Shepherdess Resting Under a Tree* (1878), *Shepherdess Resting* (c. 1877), and the superb watercolor *Fresh Air* (1878). Such visions of wholesome rural simplicity are, according to Burns, "transparently artificial concoctions that the artist himself had conceived, dressed, and staged" for "urban consumption at a time of vigorous, and problematic, metropolitan expansion." Even Homer's beloved image, painted in two versions, of country schoolboys playing snap-the-whip falls into this category of "concoction," in the form of a study, dated 1872, in black and white chalk.

Homer's drawings, sometimes present as tracings produced in the wood-engraving process, come off as works of art that, however casual, are superior to his rather stiff and surreal magazine illustrations and the colored tiles that, as a member of the Tile Club, a group of New York artists devoted to "ancient methods of hand craftsmanship," he adorned with shepherdesses. His oil paintings on display at Cooper-Hewitt, executed with a broader, slower brush than Church's, provoke some verbal acrobatics in Floramae McCarron-Cates's essay "The Best Possible View: Pictorial Representation in the American West." Having observed the "detached immediacy" and compressed perspective of Homer's wood engravings, she states of two good-sized oils on display, each representing a single erect figure, respectively in fall and in blossom-time (*Gather-*

ing Autumn Leaves, c. 1877; *The Yellow Jacket*, 1879), that "it is almost as if a sheet of glass were held up between the viewer and the figures represented, pulling the background forward, and resulting in an abstracted arrangement of forms." Even those unable quite to grasp this optical stunt can see that Homer of the three artists is the most modern; his early low-keyed Barbizon pastoralism brightened to a homegrown impressionism wherein spatial depth is of small concern. Two watercolors on view, *Landscape with Deer in a Morning Haze* (c. 1892) and *Valley and Hillside* (1889–95), are virtually abstract (but for the tiny, poignantly alert deer), and his late, great oils eliminate humanity and confront, like Church's Niagaras and Moran's buttes and canyons, raw American nature—crashing waves and battered cliffs. The scenic Maine area of Prouts Neck, incidentally, where Homer built his final home and studio, had become, thanks to the shrewd purchases of the painter and his brother, a Homeric real-estate development.

Development and the need to escape the overstuffed Victorian parlor motivated and recompensed American landscape painting, we are told. Karal Ann Marling's concluding catalogue essay, "America Inside Out: The View from the Parlor," wittily speaks of "a dream of some fresh-air utopia visible only from the vantage point of the great indoors." Fresh air, as Eastern American cities, planted in coastal swamps, grew into massive infestations of humanity, was no small blessing in summertime. A wall card at the Cooper-Hewitt exhibition states, "The pictures made by artists . . . brought in ministers, lawyers, doctors, bankers, and teachers for their summer vacations." It wasn't just nostalgia for an imagined Native American freedom that settled the resorts, but concerns of health and comfort, even though the urban parlor accumulated souvenirs like vases depicting an Indian encampment (Edward Timothy Hurley, 1909) and wallpaper of repeating braves in canoes. Longfellow's greatly loved poem *Hiawatha* helped to bring the Midwest's northern lake country into the orbit of vacationers.

Cooper-Hewitt (which has its own pleasant outdoor space, and a panelled staircase evocative of an older, more stately scale of construction) has in its copious collection of designed objects a wealth of tickets, postcards, hotel registers, promotional posters, stereoscopic photographs, woven fishing baskets, and pottery depicting Catskill wonders, a sampling of which is on view to awaken in twenty-first-century breasts nostalgia for nostalgia of a pre-modern, more simply satisfied sort, when Arcadia was just a steamboat ride away and the sublime was a palpable sensation. But perhaps our forebears had a more complex relation to nature than we imagine. Nineteenth-century tourism received its most attentive description in William Dean Howells's first, transparently auto-biographical novel, *Their Wedding Journey*. Its hero, Basil March, enjoying, in 1870, the standard honeymoon swing north, at one point confides to his bride,

> "We come to Niagara in the patronizing spirit in which we approach everything nowadays, and for a few hours we have it our own way, and pay our little tributes of admiration with as much complacency as we feel in acknowledging the existence of the Supreme Being. But after a while we are aware of some potent influence undermining our self-satisfaction; we begin to conjecture that the great cataract does not exist by virtue of our approval, and to feel that it will not cease when we go away. The second day makes us its abject slaves, and on the third we want to fly from it in terror."

VAN GOGH AND SEURAT

Uncertain Skills, Determined Spirit

Vincent van Gogh: *The Drawings,* at the Metropolitan Museum of Art, New York, October 18–December 31, 2005.

For sheer viewer discomfort, the show of van Gogh drawings at the Metropolitan Museum has been topped in my experience only by the once-in-a-millennium assembly of twenty-three Vermeer paintings at Washington's National Gallery in 1995. In both cases, too many people jealously clustered and jostled within inches of hallowed works that demanded close scrutiny. At the Met, the week the exhibition opened, the docile masses straggled in clotted lines, their noses almost grazing the minutely hatched and speckled art, through rooms housing more than one hundred drawings in ink, graphite, charcoal, and watercolor, plus a few oil and watercolor paintings. The first room, in which van Gogh can be seen, in 1881, at the age of twenty-seven, taking up art with the hope of becoming a professional illustrator, is especially hard on the eyes as he scratchily, painstakingly renders grasses, trees, and the undersides of clouds (*A Marsh*) and explores with wash and chalk the stiff poses and creased clothing of Dutch folk engaged in domestic tasks (*Boy with a Sickle, Woman Sewing*). His skills are uncertain but his spirit is determined. Though posterity's image of van Gogh centers upon his mental fragility and lamentable suicide at the age of thirty-seven, this overflowing show, and the wall texts and catalogue that accompany it, remind us of the tremendous industriousness that produced, in the mere ten years between 1881 and 1890, eight hundred paintings and eleven hundred drawings, not to mention the more than eight hundred letters he wrote to his younger brother Theo, composing one of the great literary testaments, eloquent and confessional, left by a supreme painter.*

He signed both his letters and art works "Vincent," explaining to Theo, "I myself am different in character from the other members of the family, and really I am not a 'van Gogh' at all." Given the same name as an older, stillborn brother, he was the eldest of six children of a Calvinist minister, Theodorus van Gogh, from a line of Calvinist ministers. Vincent's last employment before becoming an artist was as a lay preacher in the impoverished Belgian coal-mining district of Borinage; his fervent attempt to live by the ascetic precepts of Saint Francis and Thomas à Kempis did not find favor with the local evangelical committee, which cited excessive zeal as its reason for not renewing his contract. His resort to art in these humiliating straits was a return to a familiar realm: four of his father's brothers were art dealers, including another Vincent, his godfather "Uncle Cent," who from humble beginnings had seen his gallery incorporated into the chain of the Paris art publisher Goupil. At the age of sixteen, Vincent was apprenticed to the Hague branch of Goupil, and four years later, on the enthusiastic recommendation of the manager, he was transferred to London, where he was stationed for a year; he would return to England at least twice, the second time as a teacher in Isleworth. Among the incidental exhibits at the Met are a letter to the Australian painter John Russell written in a quite serviceable English. The young man's initially auspicious employment with Goupil frayed and finally terminated, under the pressure, perhaps, of his religious calling and of temporal-lobe epilepsy, the favored posthumous diagnosis of his mental illness.

His belated turn to art, therefore, had its practical side—he partially knew the ropes, putting himself to school with Charles Bargue's *Cours de dessin* and the wealth of mechanical reproductions published by Goupil—and a religious one; from almost the start, clumsy as he could be, he was able to endow landscapes and still lifes with an extra intensity manifesting his belief, as he expressed it in a layman's sermon, that "God is using the things of everyday life to instruct us in higher things, that our life is a pilgrimage and we are strangers on this earth." In his paintings, the sunflowers, the workers' worn shoes, the famous chair (*Vincent's Chair with His Pipe*, 1888) seem indeed to have arrived from another world, as freshly and startlingly *there* as the annunciatory angel, full of

---

*The estimate of more than eight hundred letters is to be found in *Van Gogh*, by Rainer Metzger and Ingo F. Walther (Taschen, 2005). This review has drawn repeatedly upon its facts.

their news. There is some artistic advantage in feeling like a stranger on earth.

A beautifully lonely feeling wells up from *Country Road* (1882), one of a number of studies in perspective and landscape with which he pursued his self-imposed apprenticeship, having decided, as a letter to Theo puts it, on "active melancholy" in preference to "succumbing to despair." The foreground to the otherwise staid *Nursery on Schenkweg* (1882) shows the weedy, reedy edges of a ditch with the calligraphic energy, the half-suppressed violence, that would become the hallmark of his mature style. His wrestles with the human figure begin to yield anatomically persuasive images, whose peasant lumpiness has an unforced pathos and charm. He thought well enough of *Girl with a Pinafore* (1882–83) to paint a frame of black ink around it, and this study of a silent, muss-haired child (probably the daughter of van Gogh's romantic interest of the time, Sien Hoornik), carried out with pen and brush in lithographic crayon, graphite, ink, and watercolor, does have, for him, an exceptional ease and subtlety. The thicker tools of chalk and crayon free him to create a strong sensation of volume in two studies of figures resting their eyes on clenched fists—*Worn Out* (1882) and *Sorrowing Woman* (1883)—whereas his attempts in pen and watercolor to give life to weavers at work are still painfully awkward. His sympathy with the laboring classes finds its most memorable expression in the often reproduced *Head of a Woman* (1884–85), a profile of brutal ugliness, executed at twice the usual size for the portrait studies he called "heads of the people"; the subject, no doubt younger than her homeliness allows us to realize, turns, like the winsome child in the pinafore, shyly away from the artist.

The somewhat damaged and time-altered *Landscape in Drenthe* (1883), of utterly flat country in the northeastern Netherlands, is strikingly minimalist, piling upon the twilit moors a nearly empty sky lightly laden with reckless scribbles, in early premonition of van Gogh's insistence that the sky is never really empty. His drawings of winter trees (*Pollard Birches, Behind the Hedges, Winter Garden, The Kingfisher*, all from March of 1884) have an agitated angularity—he wrote Theo of a quality "not expressed easily or without effort or by chance"—that remind us of the pre-abstract drawings of another religious Dutchman, Piet Mondrian; the linear, ultimately unsearchable maze of bare branches led the latter to abstraction and the former, in such canvases as *Avenue of Poplars in Autumn* (1884) and *The Parsonage Garden at Nuenen in the Snow* (1885), to the impressionistic resources of oil paints. From 1884 onward, van Gogh, relinquishing hopes of becoming a black-and-white illustrator to compete with Daumier or Doré, diverted most of his energy to painting, and his drawings become somewhat adjunctive—preliminary studies for paintings or, for an inner circle of consultants, copies of paintings already executed. At times, when poverty or seclusion denied him access to painting equipment, drawing again became his principal creative channel.

From the subterranean browns and gnarled peasant faces of *The Potato Eaters* (1885), which is scarcely less monochromatic than a drawing, he moved into color just as, physically, he moved from Holland. His father died in March of 1885, and Vincent's welcome in Nuenen was further cooled when, later that year, the Catholic priest forbade the villagers from sitting for him. Van Gogh went to Antwerp and, briefly, the École des Beaux-Arts there, and then to Paris, and finally the south of France. In Antwerp he discovered Rubens; the former acolyte of Millet's sombre country scenes excitedly wrote Theo, "What color is in a picture, enthusiasm is in life, in other words no mean thing if one is trying to keep a hold on it." In Paris he discovered the Impressionists, the Pointillists, and imported Japanese prints; he met Pissarro, Seurat, Signac, Toulouse-Lautrec, and Gauguin. He coped with what Sjraar van Heugten in his catalogue essay calls "the disconcerting discovery that the style of painting he had practiced for the last three years was hopelessly old-fashioned."

In the course of his self-renovation, his drawings took on more verve and assurance. *The Blute-Fin Mill* (1887) is dashing in its application of soft graphite to the paper; the swift parallel horizontal strokes of the stairs and the kindred vertical strokes of the low building beside them invite the viewer to relish the artist's virtuosity. The Blute-Fin, a windmill-turned-nightclub dating from 1622, is often mistakenly called the Moulin de la Galette, which was the name for a district of Montmartre that held both mills and places of popular entertainment. Vincent and Theo, now an art dealer for Goupil, lived together in Montmartre, at 54 rue Lepic. Vincent's socialist instincts focused in Paris on the working-class recreational sites—dance halls and *guinguettes* (informal outdoor cafés)—and the populace strolling on the still-existent Paris ramparts. Toulouse-Lautrec and Renoir had recorded proletarian pleasures before him, as had the Japanese woodcut depicters of Edo's street life, like Hiroshige, whose influence can be felt especially in van Gogh's brightly tinted *Gate in the Paris Ramparts* (1887). From the same colored series, *Shed with Sunflowers* touches on a subject that van Gogh will make his own, and *View from Montmartre* limns a crisp and cheerful panorama of the city with a detailed finish and formal inked frame indicating unrealized hopes of a sale. The foreground declivity, conjectured to be a quarry, shows in opaque watercolor the staccato broken brushwork, adopted from pointillism, that was to become his signature manner.

Van Gogh, The Blute-Fin Mill, *1887. Pen and ink over graphite.*

When, in February of 1888, after exactly two years of Paris, Vincent left for Arles, in western Provence, Theo, far from relieved, wrote his sister:

> I would never have thought that we could become so close. Now that I am on my own again I feel the emptiness in my home all the more. It is not easy to fill the place of a man like Vincent. His knowledge is vast and he has a very clear view of the world. I am convinced that if he has a few more years he will make a name for himself.

A few years was all he did have (and Theo, too, who outlived him by only six months), but they were full of triumph for his art, if ultimately tragic for him. He hit the southern ground running, with a lovely painting of orchards in bloom. The drawings from Arles, before his self-commitment in May of 1889 to the asylum of Saint-Paul-de-Mausole in Saint-Rémy, twenty kilometers north of Arles, not only accompany the great strides he made in his painting but, with the new energy and scale enabled by his employment of reed pens—reeds peculiar to the Midi region cut and sharpened like goose quills—constitute works of art on their own. *Path Through a Field with Pollard Willows* (1888), one of the first pen-and-ink drawings mailed to Theo from his new location, and copied by an oil painting in the following month, is hesitant but insistent, and uses the reed pen only for dots sprinkled through the grassy ground. *Public Garden in the Place Lamartine*, done the same month of March, of the rather wild-looking gardens opposite the yellow house he occupied in Arles, and *Orchard with Arles in the Background* possess a nearly full set of the calligraphic gestures—quick hatchings and zigzag scribbles, small circles and specks—that are evolving alongside remnants of his Dutch literalist manner, most noticeable in the carefully traced branchings of foreground trees.

Of his reed pens he wrote Theo, "It is a method I already tried in Holland some time ago, but I hadn't such good reeds there as here." The reed pen was more flexible than metal nibs and held relatively little ink, which

Van Gogh, Street in Saintes-Maries-de-la-Mer, *1888. Reed pen, quill, and ink over chalk.*

consorted well enough with van Gogh's emphatic short strokes. The drawings in their range of attack and texture aspire to the condition of paintings. *View of Arles with Irises in the Foreground* (1888) emphasizes the irises in a darker ink brushed over the pen marks, creating an effect of recession more elaborately carried out in *View of Arles from Montmajour* (1888). The first *View* became an oil painting, as did his relatively rough sketches *Three Cottages, Saintes-Maries-de-la-Mer* and *Street in Saintes-Maries-de-la-Mer*, products of a seaside visit in the week of May 30–June 5, 1888. The latter drawing became the basis of a pivotal painting of the same name, his boldest experiment yet in surreal color with its yellow sky and violet thatched roof, and its pink street utterly without shadows; "positively piling it on, exaggerating the color—Africa not so far away," he wrote to Theo. He thought well enough of the breakthrough to send his fellow-artist Émile Bernard a sketch of the painting filled in with the names of the colors, and made similar after-the-fact notations in drawings mailed to Theo, notably one of four beached boats that he made in an hour, without the perspective frame he usually depended on, "just by letting my pen go."

His seaside week was a turning point for van Gogh. He painted a violent oil, as thick and wild in its impasto as a Soutine, *Boats at Sea, Saintes-Maries-de-la-Mer*. His three reed-pen copies of it, executed as the painting dried on the wall, demonstrate, in the sinuous parallel arabesques in the foreground, an almost alarming submission to the watery turmoil. The flamelike dark cypresses, writhing olive trees, blaring oversized suns, convulsed mountains, and vortically churning stars of van Gogh's visionary madness are not far off. But first come the gorgeous landscapes of high summer in Provence: "Everywhere now there is old gold, bronze, copper, and this with the green azure of the sky blanched with heat: a delicious color, exceptionally harmonious, with the blended tones of Delacroix," Vincent wrote Theo in June. At the Metropolitan exhibit, the crowds, their eyes made bleary by dimlit chambers of penwork, stood back with relief from *Harvest in Provence* (1888), a large golden oil canvas preceded by a detailed, lightly tinted drawing and followed by two rather differing pen versions for Émile Bernard and John Russell. The one for Bernard takes more liberties with the painting, and is freer in its use of van Gogh's shorthand of hatching, squiggles, and dots. In the version for Russell, specks appear in the sky where the painting has a blank blue, and these, and concentric lines encircling the sun (*A Summer Evening*, 1888), become an almost compulsive feature of the drawings, as if van Gogh is saying that no space of nature is truly blank, devoid of color and of divine activity. The drawings brim with latent color.

Of this summer's scenic drawings and paintings, he wrote Theo, "Yellow—old gold—done quickly, quickly, quickly and in a hurry, just like the harvester who is silent under the blazing sun, intent only on his reaping." The painting *Arles: View from the Wheat Fields* is as stubby with Pointillist stabs as the drawings derived from it; *Wheat Field with Sheaves* fairly dances in its tousled bundles of pen strokes. He has caught up with an observation made to Theo three years before: "What has impressed me most on seeing paintings by the old Dutch masters again is the fact that they were generally painted quickly. Not only that: if the effect was good, it stood." *Olive Trees, Montmajour; La Crau: The View from Montmajour;* and the surpassingly delicate and swift reprise of *The Langlois Bridge:* these masterly works in reed pen come close to Rembrandt, and have been enriched as much as weakened by the uneven aging and fading of the inks van Gogh zealously experimented with, discussed in chemical detail by Marjorie Shelley at the back of the catalogue.

Two months spent with Gauguin in the yellow house, in vain hopes of inaugurating a Provence commune for artists, disturbed van Gogh's confidence and sent Gauguin fleeing Arles in fear of the other's craziness; the night he left, van Gogh cut off the lobe of one ear and presented it to a young woman residing in the local brothel. One wonders, in reading of these quarrels and strange behaviors of van Gogh, how much should be laid to mental disability and how much to alcohol abuse; even before Gauguin arrived, van Gogh contemplated a clinical report that told him, "Instead of eating sufficiently and regularly I kept myself going (they said) with coffee and alcohol." He added to Theo, "I admit it; but in order to achieve that noble shade of yellow I achieved last summer I simply had to give myself quite a boost."

He drew little in the months on either side of the events in late 1888, and when he took it drawing again, in two farewell sketches of Arles— *The Courtyard of the Hospital in Arles* and *A Garden in the Place Lamartine*, both from early May 1889—the reed pen had thickened, and the effect turned "very dark and rather melancholy," as he confided to Theo. The heavily outlined tree in the garden looks like a shattered lampshade. But in the asylum in Saint-Rémy, the pines and ivy and cypresses, especially the dark, sinuous, aspiring cypresses, acquire a dramatic life of transferred torment (*Pine Trees in the Walled Garden of the Asylum, Tree with Ivy in the Garden of the Asylum, Cypresses,* all from May and June of 1889). The subjective urgency that van Gogh's objective studies often projected, as of annunciatory apparitions, now melts the boundary between seer and seen, sight and psyche. Everything squirms and twists. Clouds and hills, mountains and vegetation appear molded from one wormy, resistant substance (*Wheat Fields with Cypresses*, 1889). *Wild Vegetation*, its paper sheet almost completely covered by restless, hard-to-read wriggles of erratically fading ink, anticipates the "overall" canvases of Abstract Expressionism. In *Walled Wheat Field with Rising Sun*—a drawing that, the catalogue shrugs, might have preceded or followed its partner painting—the field hurtles toward the wall while a swollen sun emits concentric waves like a struck drumhead.

Yet the artist's fortunes were looking up. In Paris, a favorable article on him appeared in *Mercure de France*, and Toulouse-Lautrec challenged to a duel a fellow-painter who spoke slightingly of van Gogh's work. In Brussels, the first sale of a van Gogh painting was recorded—four hundred francs for *The Red Vineyard*. Vincent and Theo agreed that living among the mentally ill was not salubrious, and the painter was moved to a village north of Paris, Auvers-sur-Oise, where a sympathetic doctor, Paul-Ferdinand Gachet, agreed to keep an eye on him. The catalogue tells us, "He worked hard and fast, executing about seventy-five paintings and fifty drawings during the remaining seventy days of his life." But, to judge by three Auvers works on display, van Gogh's hard-won skills and inborn intensity had slackened; *Landscape with a Bridge Over the Oise* (1890) lays on green and white strokes in such cursory fashion that the paper ground shows through, and the brushed lines of blue and black in *Landscape with Houses* and *Old Vineyard with Peasant Woman*, not a straight line among them, seem to me a complete meltdown. But never underestimate van Gogh's posthumous appeal for the art public: a few feet away, a woman said in my hearing, of the two half-blue drawings, "I love those."

The Purest of Styles

Vincent van Gogh—Painted with Words: *The Letters to Émile Bernard*, at the Morgan Library and Museum, New York, September 28, 2007–January 6, 2008.

Renzo Piano's chaste blond addition to the Morgan Library holds for the remainder of the year, in the Morgan Stanley Gallery East, a small but intense exhibition centered on the twenty-two letters written in 1887–89 by Vincent van Gogh to Émile Bernard. Bernard, who was only nineteen at the outset of this epistolary outpouring from the thirty-four-year-old van Gogh, is just a footnote in art history now, but as a painter and critic he enjoyed the acquaintance of a number of important Post-Impressionists. The Morgan displays an elegant, thinly painted portrait of Bernard at a mere seventeen by Toulouse-Lautrec—the boy looks wispy, intelligent, polite—and Bernard claimed to have invented the *"cloisonniste"* style used by Gauguin to good effect; he elicited, in another correspondence, Cézanne's famous wish to render nature "by means of the cylinder, the sphere, and the cone."

The exhibition includes a number of Bernard's paintings and sketches, and the catalogue a good many more, and it is hard to see much talent in them. Of those on view, the portrait of Bernard's grandmother (1887) shows a certain caricatural spark, and *Brothel Scene* (1888) illustrates the lumpy *cloisonniste* style with its heavy outlines and non-receding back-grounds; *Breton Women in the Meadow* (1888), which van Gogh said he liked, isolates various outlined costumed figures on a field of blank green—only two stray dogs and a little girl forlornly sucking her finger seem to have caught the painter's full attention. His paintings at times seem to be etiolated van Goghs. His sketches, even when of nude prosti-tutes, are sketchy to a fault. An attempt at a masterwork, *Madeleine in the Bois d'Amour* (1888), unpersuasively stretches a full-length, fully clothed female daydreamer along the bottom of a large canvas rendering, in edgy parallel brushstrokes resembling Cézanne's, a vacuously tidy woods. Bernard was a Symbolist—that is, a member of the artistic movement that lasted from roughly 1885 to 1910 and favored the symbolic repre-sentation of ideas over the depiction of common reality. Tinged with reli-gious mysticism and a sickly eroticism, Symbolism sanctioned Bernard's fascination with both brothels and religious scenes taken from the New Testament. Van Gogh, himself a Christian believer of a radical sort, deplored modern (as of the 1880s) attempts to revive the manner and subject matter of early-Renaissance masters like Giotto. Almost all of his letters to Émile Bernard express resistance to abstract thought and advo-cate realism, as exemplified by Rembrandt, Hals, and other Dutch mas-ters, including the recently rediscovered Vermeer.

Van Gogh and Bernard met in Paris, and van Gogh wrote the first let-ter, using the intimate *tu*, while both still were there. He paternally advises the young Frenchman, "You'll realize that in the studios not only does one not learn very much as far as painting goes, but not much that's good in terms of *savoir vivre*, either." Don't be a "narrow sectarian," the older painter says—"the equivalent of those who think nothing of others and believe themselves to be the only righteous ones." Bernard evidently showed tendencies that way; fifty years later, in 1937, the art critic Doug-las Cooper, when translating these letters, wrote that Bernard, then all of seventy, was "a very greedy and difficult person who is only interested in capitalizing all he can with regard to his now famous friends."* Yet something about the callow youth engaged van Gogh, and elicited from him, after the expatriate Dutchman moved, in February 1888, to the Provençal town of Arles, letters fuller and franker, in regard to his philosophy and art, than even those he mailed, in his Southern isolation, to his brother Theo.

The letters, a selection of which are displayed at the Morgan in a considerate dim light, have, with their interjected sketches, a holy fragility. The cheap stationery, varying in size and quality, has yellowed, and the once black ink, where based on iron salts rather than carbon, has faded to brown, at places a faint tan. The handwriting varies in size and consistency, often as small and neat as mechanical print, at other places enlarged by haste or for emphasis, but nowhere indicating an unbalanced temperament. Writing came easily to van Gogh; he confided to his correspondent that he found it "restful and diverting" after a long day of struggling with the evasive nuances of portraiture. Writing French as a second language (in addition to his native Dutch, he also commanded a serviceable English), he made some mistakes in grammar and spelling, and was careless with accents, but, the introduction to the catalogue assures us, "he found the words to express the problems and ideals that concerned him as a human being and artist. The style is very direct," and, of his eight hundred surviving letters, those to Bernard are "quite simply the most spontaneous of them all." Charles Bukowski praised "his style, the purest of styles." Bernard carefully saved van Gogh's letters to him, and saw to their publication soon after van Gogh's death in 1890; his own letters have not survived, though their content can often be surmised.

The letters from Arles in 1888, plus the two written, after nearly a year's hiatus, to Bernard by van Gogh from the asylum at Saint-Rémy-de-Provence, form a single outpouring, with faithfully recurrent themes: his concern with Bernard's impending conscription into the Army, which in the end never occurred; his belief that artists should collaborate and communicate, as they did in the Renaissance, without factional war or

---

*The Australian-born Cooper's translation was published in *Letters to Émile Bernard* (Museum of Modern Art, 1938); the complete letters were published in the original by Ambroise Vollard in 1911. The editors of the Morgan Library catalogue—Leo Jansen, Hans Luijten, and Nienke Bakker of the Van Gogh Letters Project, at the Van Gogh Museum, Amsterdam—commissioned a new annotated translation by Imogen Forster. All but three of the letters were acquired by the collector Eugene V. Thaw in 2001 and have been promised as a gift to the Morgan.

Mon cher Bernard, ayant promis de t'écrire, je veux commencer par te dire que le pays me paraît aussi beau que le Japon pour la limpidité de l'atmosphère et les effets de couleur gaie. Les eaux font des tâches d'un bel émeraude et d'un riche bleu dans les paysages ainsi que nous le voyons dans les crepons. Des couchers de soleil orangé pâle faisant paraître bleu les terrains. Des soleils jaunes splendides. Cependant je n'ai encore guère vu le pays dans sa splendeur habituelle d'été. Le costume des femmes est joli et le dimanche surtout on voit sur le boulevard des arrangements de couleur très naïfs et bien trouvés. Et cela aussi sans doute s'égayera encore en été

Van Gogh, from a letter to Émile Bernard, March 18, 1888

jealousy; the inspiring artistic examples set by the Japanese and the Northern Europeans; the incompatibility of pursuing art and having much sex; his own health and the pleasures of the salubrious Southern climate. "For myself," he wrote in June 1888,

> I'm in better health here than in the north—I even work in the wheat fields at midday, in the full heat of the sun, without any shade whatever, and there you are, I revel in it like a cicada. My God, if only I had known this country at twenty-five, instead of coming here at thirty-five—In those days I was enthusiastic about gray, or rather, absence of color.

Moving to Arles plunged him into a world of color—his two years in Paris had already lightened and emboldened his originally sullen palette—and into a furious exploration of color's power on canvas. He became, in the time of writing these letters, the van Gogh treasured by posterity. Again and again, as much for his own appreciation as for his reader's, he paints a new painting in words:

> Large field with clods of plowed earth, mostly downright violet.
> Field of ripe wheat in a yellow ocher tone with a little crimson.
> The chrome yellow 1 sky almost as bright as the sun itself, which is chrome yellow 1 with a little white, while the rest of the sky is chrome yellow 1 and 2 mixed, very yellow, then.
> The sower's smock is blue, and his trousers white. Square no. 25 canvas. There are many repetitions of yellow in the earth, neutral tones, resulting from the mixing of violet with yellow, but I could hardly give a damn about the *veracity* of the color.

The underlined *veracity* (*vérité*, in French) touches on the debate underlying the whole exchange, which led eventually to van Gogh's brusque dismissal of Bernard's Symbolist version of Christianity and to the end of their correspondence, though the two men remained interested in and respectful of each other's work.

The last letter is by far the longest of the series, a summing up of all that van Gogh had learned in the last two years. His objections to Bernard's recent religious pictures, of which he had seen photographs, are preliminary, though sharply put. Of an *Adoration of the Shepherds* (1889), imagined in a rural French setting, van Gogh objects:

> It's too great an impossibility to imagine a birth like that, on the very road, the mother who starts praying instead of giving suck, the fat ecclesiastic bigwigs, kneeling as if in an epileptic fit, God knows how or why they're there, but I myself don't find it healthy.

Another painting, of Christ carrying the cross, is "atrocious . . . commonplace." He accuses Bernard of exchanging the beauty of "those Breton women walking in a meadow . . . the color so naively distinguished" for "something—one must say the word—something artificial—something affected." These dismissals delivered, van Gogh turns to his own struggle for health:

> And if I haven't written for a long time, it's because, having to struggle against my illness and to calm my head, I hardly felt like having discussions, and found danger in these abstractions. And by working very calmly, beautiful subjects will come of their own accord; it's truly first and foremost a question of immersing oneself in reality again, with no plan made in advance, with no Parisian bias.

Parisian bias, abstract thinking—these are irrelevant to his "fighting hand-to-hand with reality." Yet he admits that, in executing his long-harbored intention to paint the starry sky (*The Starry Night*, 1889), he was guilty of "allowing myself to do stars too big, etc., new setback."

Like a former drunk boasting of his present sobriety, he announces, "Here's a description of a canvas that I have in front of me at the moment," and describes, with exhaustive specifics of color and shape, the rather gloomy evening scene before him at the asylum, dominated by a great tree that lost a limb to lightning. In his next paragraph he turns from being all eye, in the Impressionist fashion, to being an Expressionist:

> This dark giant—like a proud man brought low—contrasts, when seen as the character of a living being, with the pale smile of the last rose on the bush, which is fading in front of him. Under the trees, empty stone benches, dark box. The sky is reflected yellow in a puddle after the rain. A ray of sun—the last glimmer—exalts the dark ocher to orange—small dark figures prowl here and there between the trunks. You'll understand that this combination of red ocher, of green saddened with gray, of black lines that define the outlines, this gives rise a little to the feeling of anxiety from which some of my companions in misfortune often suffer, and which is called "seeing red." And what's more, the motif of the great tree struck by lightning, the sickly green and pink smile of the last flower of autumn, confirms this idea.

The phrase *"voir rouge"* ("seeing red"), though clearly enough written, has been always misread as *"noir-rouge,"* and the "black-red" reading made enough sense, given the emotional weight assigned to color itself. The point, as far as the education of Émile Bernard is concerned, is that, in order to give an impression of anxiety, you can try to do it without heading straight for the historical garden of Gethsemane. . . . Ah—it is—no doubt—wise, right, to be moved by the Bible, but modern reality has such a hold over us that even when trying abstractly to reconstruct ancient times in our thoughts . . . our own adventures throw us forcibly into personal sensations.

He goes on to cite failures in contemporary Biblical scenes, excepting only Delacroix, no doubt thinking of his *Christ Asleep During the Tempest* (c. 1853), which he had extolled in an earlier letter.

Van Gogh's achievement was to sublimate his own mysticism in the representation of reality, rather than inventing symbolic images. He made things themselves—worn shoes, a rush-seat chair, sunflowers—symbols, bristling with wordless meaning. Two late paintings bring the Morgan exhibition to a climax: *Enclosed Field with Young Wheat and Rising Sun* and *A Corner of the Asylum and the Garden with a Heavy, Sawn-Off Tree* (both 1889). The latter is the very painting described as a picture of anxiety in his last letter to Bernard—circular swirls and flame-shaped arabesques move like a wind through the branches of the olive trees, against a yellow-and-blue sunset, while small human figures slowly become visible on the asylum grounds. In the former, the undulating field, blue and golden and green, rushes toward the viewer, and the blue mountains beyond seem a roiling river, under a bright-yellow sky where the white sun is pinned like a medal. His impasto has become terrific—ridged ribbons of color as in a heavy brocade. A visionary effect has been achieved through stubborn labor: "What I'm making is harsh, dry, but it's because I'm trying to reinvigorate myself by means of rather arduous work, and would fear that abstractions would make me soft."

The debate between abstraction and representation continues to this day. The international triumph of Abstract Expressionism sixty years ago was great but brief; it left echoes but no heirs as signal as Pollock, Kline, and Rothko; abstraction tapered into minimalism and the pencil lines of Agnes Martin. But its triumph, its bold foray into pure paint and form, left representation, as it crept back by default, with a guilty conscience, which it seeks to dispel with a shambling comedy of irony and unabashed eclecticism. Van Gogh, out in the hot fields, his easel anchored with iron pegs against the winds of the mistral, resolved the debate with acts of submission: "I do what I do with an abandonment to reality, without thinking about this or that." He tried never to work from memory, he told Bernard, but always from the facts before him. After rebuking Bernard's stylized and impossible adoration of the shepherds, he professed, "I adore the true, the possible." But no man's truth is another's, and van Gogh's individuality, extending to his limitations as a draftsman and a painter, provided all the abstraction needed. His furious productivity in the year in Arles, which extended sporadically into his stay at the Saint-Rémy asylum, is that of a man possessed by a fresh sense of his vocation in the world; there is an evangelical urgency in the culminating work of this failed evangelist. Personality and praxis, rather than theory, generate style and veracity. Van Gogh's letters to Bernard form a blazing witness to this process, and a true testament—a testament beautifully presented, it should be said, in the catalogue, a model volume of scholarship and of book design and manufacture.

Pointillism in Black and White

Georges Seurat: *The Drawings*, at the Museum of Modern Art, New York, October 28, 2007–January 7, 2008.

Impressionism, our impression is, proceeded by instinct, its stabs of high color pursuing what the eyes of Monet and Renoir and Pissarro and Sisley found in the open air, as sunlight's spectrum flitted across the sight of haystacks, poppy-dotted fields, and rippled water. Analysis was left to Post-Impressionism, whose varied masters, with a greater or lesser degree of programmatic determination, put forward terms for their own art and the art of the future. Neither Cézanne nor van Gogh was more resolutely theoretical than Georges Seurat. Born in 1859 and dead at the age of thirty-one, in 1891, Seurat was temperamentally taciturn—Pissarro called him "mute"—and confided a statement of his theories to paper only once, in an unsent three-page letter of August 28, 1890, in response to queries from the critic Maurice Beaubourg. In it Seurat wrote, "Art is Harmony," and "Harmony is the analogy of opposites"—that is, of complementary colors, which he lists: "Red–Green, Orange–Blue, Yellow–Violet." But not only opposites (*contraires*) are enlisted in the effects but "similarities" (*semblables*); Jodi Hauptman's introduction to the catalogue of Seurat's drawings translates a section of his difficult text as "The means of expression is the optical mixture of tones, of tints, that is, of the lights and of their reactions (shadows), following the laws of *contrast*, of gradation, of irradiation." From scientific studies of color by Michel-Eugène Chevreul, Ogden Rood, and David

Sutter, Seurat had extracted the concept that, to the human retina, each spot of pure color bears a halo of its complement.

On this abstruse principle he based Pointillism, or divisionism, a painstaking method of painting in discrete dots whose intense colors are mixed in the viewer's eye. Seurat's palette was closely patterned on Chevreul's color disk—four basic colors and their intermediaries were mixed with varying amounts of white and applied in carefully separated dots. So quixotically pedantic a technique achieved vindication in the first two major paintings Seurat produced—*A Bathing Place, Asnières* (1883–84) and *A Sunday Afternoon on the Island of La Grande Jatte* (1884–86)—and several smaller seascapes; they are stately, serene, and soaked in light as few canvases are. *La Grande Jatte*, especially, caused a controversial sensation with its "scientific Impressionism." The influence of Pointillism extended beyond Seurat's few immediate followers, of which Paul Signac was the foremost, to van Gogh, Cubism, Paul Klee, Robert Delaunay, and Wassily Kandinsky, who wrote that Seurat had shown "not a fragment of Nature . . . but Nature complete and entire in all her splendor." The marriage of art to scientific principles remains a chimerical goal appealing to this day; Chuck Close's photorealism by the patient means of a grid of abstract daubs is admired in Richard Shiff's catalogue essay.

The exhibit of Seurat's drawings at the Museum of Modern Art gets some welcome color from a few oil studies for paintings and from small photographic reproductions of paintings for which some drawings were preliminary sketches. But the profound and grainy black of Conté crayon is the dominant shade, and four big rooms of it—130 drawings in all—test the gallerygoer's eyes. The first room's handsome, precocious student drawings of antique casts and nude models (the superb, soulful *Male Nude, Profile* of 1877–78; the gnarly, nearly headless *Aged Hindu* of 1878–79) establish that Seurat began as a disciple of Ingres, with his fine outlines and neoclassic cool. Indeed, Seurat's drawings persistently aspire to the smooth, grave, impersonal essence of Greek sculpture. He said, "The Panathenians of Phidias formed a procession. I want to make modern people, in their essential traits, move about as they do on those friezes."

By 1880, having completed his studies at the École des Beaux-Arts under Henri Lehmann (a pupil of Ingres) and his year of military service in Brest, Seurat began to draw in a new, theory-driven manner. His linear sketches of fellow-soldiers give way, in *Seated Woman* (1880–81), to a figure entirely blocked in with diagonal pencil shading, and in *Woman with*

Basket (1881–82) to a figure sketched from behind in Conté crayon, fundamentally dark against the light paper but with some searching linear swirls reminiscent of Daumier's lithographs. *Nude* and *Nurse and Child* (both 1881–82) banish any hint of an outline; figures are defined as they emerge from a dark ground of Conté crayon—swirls of it like a greasy mist. *Tree by a Road* (1881–82) does away with definition almost entirely—the tree is a blur, the road a double arc of relative pallor—and *Landscape with Houses* (1881–82) poses its geometric forms beyond a foreground, a good half of the image, almost solidly black. Forms feel carved out of an underlying darkness. The elegant profile *Aman-Jean* (1882–83)—Seurat's first publicly displayed drawing, hung at the Salon of 1883—is accomplished in a somewhat conventional range of grays, with a conventional precision, but the contemporaneous heads of his mother, *Embroidery* and *The Artist's Mother*, show how brilliantly for the artist, as the Conté crayon warms in his hand, is willing to go in the direction of minimal linear indication and maximum saturation in black.

From the early 1880s on, Seurat drew almost exclusively on quarter-

Seurat, Aman-Jean, *1882–83. Conté crayon.*

sheets (roughly nine by twelve inches) of a handmade laid (as opposed to machine-made wove) French paper called Michallet. Consisting of pulp dried on a rectangular frame of fine metal rods, Michallet paper retained, as alternately raised and depressed parallels, the impression of the fine rods, and, at right angles, that of the less close "chain" lines impressed by the wires that kept the rods aligned. Conté crayon, a soft mixture of clay and pulverized graphite or carbon or both, brought up the texture of the paper even when very lightly used, and when applied heavily created a dense black. By these means Seurat achieved a sort of black-and-white Pointillism, a style of rendering that employed minute marks as they accumulated in the viewer's eye. A phrase of Seurat's recorded by the Symbolist writer Gustave Kahn can be applied to the drawings as well as the paintings: Seurat spoke to Kahn of *"l'art de creuser une surface"*— translated, rather fancifully by Richard Shiff in the catalogue, as "the art of fathoming a surface." *Creuser* has the basic sense of digging, of excavating. "Hollowing out" a surface is what the drawings do, especially those, like *Woman Reading* (c. 1882) and *Woman with Two Little Girls* (1882–84), where a prevalent darkness yields a few pale areas that read as forms in murky space. In *Night Stroll* (1887–88), which exists in a pen-and-ink version as well as in a stronger Conté-crayon one, a light ground accepts dark blurs that uncannily convey the impression of bodies in a partially occluding and, in the second instance, moonlit atmosphere.

Seurat's secretive, crepuscular temperament was drawn to the tawdry area of Paris just outside the walls, called "the Zone," and to the industrial suburbs—Saint-Denis, Asnières, Courbevoie—"the country of the stinking industries," as Louis Barron wrote, or, in a phrase of Victor Hugo's, "the limbos of Paris." Seurat's first two major canvases, showing suburbanites enjoying sunny leisure, derive from these limbos, but his drawings, often done during walks in the dusk, show a joyless landscape of railway right-of-ways, factories, and lonely laborers. In *Drawbridge* (1882–83), the bridge lifts its iron beams like beseeching arms, right off the Michallet paper's deckled upper edge; in *Steamboat* (1882–83), the dark vessel looks like a squashed bug on the floor of the pale river. In *Wine Tumbril* (1882–83), the great wheels of the vehicle can hardly be disentangled from the writhing scribbles of the surrounding gloom. A ragpicker and a tramp (his hat at a jaunty angle as he slumps under a bridge) loom in stark silhouette; such near-total blackouts as *Cart with Grazing Horse* (c. 1883), *Two Wagons* (c. 1883), and *Rain* (1882–83) lead the dutiful viewer to ask himself, somewhere in his long circumnavigation of the second and third rooms, Who was Seurat doing these for? The drawings were not, except for the showpiece *Aman-Jean* and a few later, picturesque specimens, put on display, or sold. They were done, one must conclude, in a spirit of scientific research—an ongoing experiment in drawing with nothing but masses of shading, thus *creuser* the paper surface. It is paradoxical that this follower of Ingres, concerned with the laws of optics and of orderly artistic procedure, in practice produced drawings so expressionist in their violent scribbles and nocturnal atmospherics. Some figures, such as those in *The Veil* (1882–84) and *The Lamp* (1882–83), approach in their surrealism the charcoals and lithographs of the older French artist Odilon Redon; the landscapes *The Edge of the Forest* (c. 1883), *In a Park* (c. 1883), and *Tree Trunks Reflected in Water* (1883–84) come close to total abstraction. It is a rare scene that, like *Place de la Concorde, Winter* (1882–83), gives us, in its range of white to black and its illusion of recession, the sense of a space in which we might move and breathe.

Things brighten in the fourth and final room of the exhibition, dominated by drawings preparatory to Seurat's precious few paintings. His figures were never more statuesque and classically solid than in his studies of naked boys for *A Bathing Place, Asnières*. Two luminous seascapes—*Grandcamp, Evening* (1885) and *Lighthouse and Mariners' Home, Honfleur* (1886)—illustrate the lessons in tonal contrast that Seurat's drawing exercises had taught him. A piquant model, one of the three depicted in the painting *Poseuses* (1886–88), poses in three media—an oil sketch in rough Pointillism, a relatively tender Conté crayon, and an ink-and-pencil outline, lightly stippled. After his *chef d'oeuvre, La Grande Jatte*, Seurat turned for subject matter to street fairs, music halls, and the circus—a strange turn, since his formalized mature style could hardly have been less suited to animated action. But the democratic instincts that drew him to the Zone and the industrial suburbs relished popular entertainments, and his art included a certain caricatural wit. One wall of the final room holds a series of theatre drawings—*At the Concert Européen, High C, Music Hall Scene, At the Gaîté Rochechouart, Café Singer, Eden Concert* (all from 1886–88)—that show Seurat willing to vary his medium with chalk and gouache and Gillot paper and to subdue his technique to subject matter. We become interested in what the drawings show as well as how they show it. In these gaslit interiors the performers onstage are seen in a pale haze of illumination while the audience—drolly ovoid heads topped with bowler hats and upswept hairdos—and the agitated orchestra populate a dark foreground. The two clowns described as a study for *Parade* (1887–88) are faceless and absent from the painting, but the vivid trombonist in its center is even more of a presence in the Conté-crayon drawing.

Seurat, Seated Woman with a Parasol (*study for* La Grande Jatte), *1884–85. Conté crayon with white chalk.*

It is the figure studies for *La Grande Jatte*, however, that belong, in their delicacy and radical simplicity, among the masterpieces of modern European drawing. *Seated Monkey* (1884), in a pose not used in the finished painting, projects a simian essence, a shadow so faintly swiped onto the paper that its grid of distinct laid and chain lines appears the pattern of a costume, a pattern that, in the very slightly darker head, seems to hold an eye and a hint of a frown. *Seated Woman with a Parasol* (1884–85) is majestic against the paper's white ground, her hat smaller than in the painting, where she seems rather squat, sprouting from the grass like a colored mushroom; in the drawing she has her full height, and a bosom whose softness is suggested by a blur haloing the crayon's darkest, most nearly solid black. *Young Woman* (1884–85), who appears in the painting as a small figure just above the seated woman's parasol, is even more

Brancusi-esque in her streamlined shape, a silhouette so nearly feature-less that we marvel at the artistic conscience that preserved this notation and fitted its tiny piece of humanity into the grand mosaic. And *Child in White* (1884) seems less a representation than an abstraction, with its white rectangle and two trapezoids; but there it is, very near the center of the panorama, those geometric shapes having become the bodice, skirt, and crown of a sun hat worn by a little girl caught up in the enchanted stillness of this Sunday moment—a moment that the young French artist, out to revolutionize the way we paint and draw what we see, froze in time at the threshold of modernism, when the ideals of tranquillity and order could still be thought to rule.

SECESSIONISTS AND SURREALISTS

Can Genitals Be Beautiful?

Egon Schiele: *The Leopold Collection, Vienna*, at the Museum of Modern Art, New York, October 12, 1997–January 4, 1998.

In *Civilization and Its Discontents* (1930) Freud found the civilized love of beauty something of a puzzle: "All that seems certain is its derivation from the field of sexual feeling. The love of beauty seems a perfect example of an impulse inhibited in its aim. 'Beauty' and 'attraction' [the German *Reiz* means "stimulus" as well as "attraction"] are originally attributes of the sexual object." And yet, he goes on, "It is worth remarking that the genitals themselves, the sight of which is always exciting, are nevertheless hardly ever judged to be beautiful; the quality of beauty seems, instead, to attach to certain secondary sexual characteristics."

Breasts, hips, shoulders, and throat, for instance: in females, a rhythmic soft curvaceousness, and in males an angular hardness, signifying strength. The beautiful nudes of Western art aren't close-ups. Only in primitive art, with its urgent need to evoke the sources of fertility, are the phallus and the vulva emphasized, as it were, innocently; by ancient Greek and Roman times there already existed the specialized category of the pornographic—graphic art or writing supposed, like a harlot (*pornæ*), to sexually stimulate. In a compartmentalized society like pre-modern Japan's, *shunga* erotica, with its giant genitals and decorous faces, formed a distinct genre, and a district for prostitution could be set aside as a "floating world." But in a questioning Western world, where the crucifix and the figures of Adam and Eve give the naked body a sacred sanction reinforced, in the Renaissance, by the artistic authority of classical statuary, the genitals awkwardly cling to an artistic humanism whose epitome and measure is the human form. If men and women have sexual parts and a sexual purpose, how can an art of representation suppress them?

Indeed, Leo Steinberg has persuasively proposed, in *The Sexuality of Christ in Renaissance Art and in Modern Oblivion* (1983), that from before 1400 to the mid-sixteenth century, European religious art emphasized the genitals of the Infant Jesus and the dead Christ in an *ostentatio genitalium* that enforced the doctrine of the Divine Incarnation. God became, so to speak, all man. But something, perhaps a sexual puritanism present in both Protestantism and the Counter-Reformation, caused a cloud of fig leaves and gravity-defying loincloths to descend, even upon such splendid works as Michelangelo's boldly frontal *Last Judgment* and his statue of the risen Christ in the Church of Santa Maria Sopra Minerva. Human male genitals are hard to overlook—harder than those of four-legged animals—whereas those of the female, happily, are tucked out of sight. No incarnational theology ever championed pubic hair, and with its conventional omission a Diana or a Venus as smooth and bland as soap could be displayed in parks and on façades and as decoration in bourgeois homes.

The reassimilation of the genitals into art that could be shown in public galleries and museums has been a relatively recent revolution. In 1917, the Paris police closed an exhibit of Modigliani's paintings because he insisted on indicating—with a characteristic painterly tact—the pubic hair on his female nudes; in 1912, an Austrian court found Egon Schiele guilty of "distributing obscene drawings" and sentenced him to three days in jail, on top of twenty-one days of pretrial detention. Certain works are on display in *Egon Schiele: The Leopold Collection, Vienna*, which not many decades ago would have been unthinkable in a public exhibit.

Schiele remains a test case in the moot matter of erotica versus art, the pornographic versus the merely lifelike. He is not the best witness in his own defense: he persuaded adolescent girls, including his younger sister Gerti, to pose for him in positions that thrust their vaginas forward, and he utilized his first long-term lover, Valerie Neuzil (called Wally), and then his petit-bourgeois wife, Edith (née Harms), as models for drawings which were sold to prurient Viennese as hot stuff. His quite explicit *Reclining Woman Exposing Herself* of 1916 is an impressive instance of wifely submission; at this same time in his life Schiele was, according to rumor, having an affair with Edith's sister Adele, and was certainly using her as a naked or half-naked model as well—she was "more audacious in her poses," Magdalena Dabrowski tells us in the exhibition catalogue.

If the litmus test of pornography is that it excite the (typically male) viewer, then Schiele is no pornographer. His nudes, gaunt and splotchy on the whole, make us tense and sad, even though many deserve to be called beautiful. He shares with his fellow-Viennese Freud a dispassionate and rather melancholy sexual realism, with an eye to psychopathology. The genital facts are there, plainly enough, but as checkpoints on a map of anxiety; the figures are feverish not with erotic heat but with the fever of disease. The early nudes, especially, appear emaciated and contorted; there can be felt in Schiele's work, as in Kafka's, a progressive normalization, a good humor, relatively speaking, growing from a stark and dire ground. The impression of unhealth is so strong that we must remind ourselves that, though Schiele died young, at the age of twenty-eight, it was not of a wasting disease like that of Keats but, as with Shelley, of a sudden misfortune—in Schiele's case the great Spanish-flu epidemic, which carried off his wife, who was six months pregnant, three days before his own death on October 31, 1918.

Earlier that year, his mentor and only local equal, Gustav Klimt, had died at age fifty-five, leaving Schiele acknowledged as the premier painter of Austria; his one-man exhibition at the Vienna Secession in March sold out, and, amid the privations of the Great War's final year, mounting commissions and invitations to exhibit encouraged the painter to expand to a larger studio. In that era's millions of casualties, his was one of the burgeoning talents poignantly cut down, though it is hard to imagine him sustaining the pace and surpassing the intensity of his youthful production, achieved in the scant ten years from 1909 to 1918.

The scathing morbidity of his early work owes something, of course, to the ferment of Austrian modernism and the emergence of so-called Secession style, the glittering permutation of Art Nouveau and Symbolism epitomized by Klimt's bejewelled, two-dimensional tableaux. In Schiele and Oskar Kokoschka, a generation younger than Klimt, Secession style became Expressionism, distinguished by violent color and a wiry, bony linearity. But the scabrous violence of Schiele's precocious drawings had personal sources as well; these are described in the fall issue of *Museums New York:*

> The central, traumatizing fact of Egon Schiele's life was his father's syphilis, madness and death. The untreated illness pinballed hellishly throughout the family, infecting (and demoralizing) his mother and killing four of his siblings. Egon, already a brooding adolescent, was psychologically seared by the association of sex, insanity and death—and it shows in his brilliant, disturbing art.

The biography in the MoMA exhibition catalogue disputes some of this melodramatic summary; for syphilis it substitutes "some kind of pro-

312 : SECESSIONISTS AND SURREALISTS

gressive paralysis," and it says that Egon's father was not "actually insane, as scholars would have us believe." But he did die when Egon was four-teen, and Dabrowski in her catalogue essay assumes that venereal disease was the cause, so that Egon "lived in terror of the possibility of his own insanity and death related to his sexuality." She also asserts that the young artist had "a rather complicated relationship with his mother, by whom since the early years he felt victimized and neglected." His oil painting *Dead Mother* (1910) is vivid enough to support a notion that his mother was dead for him; even in the fine portrait profile of Marie Schiele done when Egon was a seventeen-year-old art student, she radiates little warmth.

But psychoanalysis takes us only so far into an artistic accomplishment; suffice it to say that the first works in which Schiele unmistakably strikes his own note show naked males, usually himself, as fearfully thin and iso-lated. In the *Kneeling Male Nude* of 1910, a ruddy stick figure is striking an incongruously jivey attitude. In the *Seated Male Nude* of the same year, the drawing is more polished, even academic in its stylized anatomy; the yellowish body, so distinctly muscled as to look flayed, shows five red spots—two nipples, one eye, a navel, and the genitals—lit as if by a fire within. Emaciation, and a flesh coloring as if of decaying meat, become more pronounced in gouaches later in that same year; *Nude Self-Portrait in Gray with Open Mouth* and *Nude Self-Portrait* could be studies from a Buchenwald where the victims' arms have been lopped off. Concave hairy bellies and tufted armpits have a weedy vitality that succumbs, in oils like *The Poet* (1911) and *Self-Seer II* (1911; also titled *Death and the Man*), to a tilted patchwork of monstrously elongated heads and hands, the fingers spatulate and stiff, like dead men's.

A kind of assault on the painter's own image is in progress; in *Grimac-ing Self-Portrait* (1910) he has knocked out most of his teeth. Gazing even upon relatively undistorted self-portraits like the two showing him in a shirt, and upon the caricatural pair of the nude, dandified mime Erwin Osen, we uneasily feel ourselves in the presence of an ongoing process, a matter not merely of self-examination but of self-flagellation, in cells devoid of any hint of furniture or perspective. A gouache not in the show but reproduced in the catalogue, *Self-Portrait in Black Cloak, Masturbating* (1911), makes explicit a quality latent throughout his stud-ies of males: a joyless, quizzical onanism, a morose fondling of a problem.

The male to Schiele is the self, a realm in essence immaterial. The female is the other, whose material opacity awakens a sense of bulk, of linear grace. Most of us, I suspect, would not really like to live with his lurid male nudes on the wall—their blotchy skins, hectic stares, and dan-

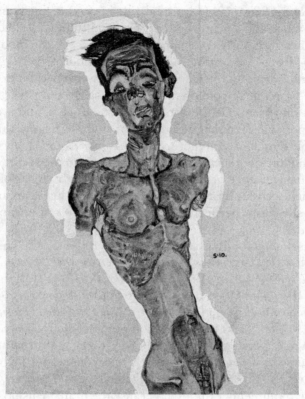

Schiele, Nude Self-Portrait, *1910. Gouache, opaque white, and black crayon.*

gling genitals. His female nudes, however, are among the great drawings of the century, and even those with the vulval cleft foregrounded have the guileless animation that occurs when self-absorption lifts and observation begins. True, *Reclining Nude Girl* and *Three Nude Girls*, both from 1910, have the jittery line and pained elongation of the male figures of the time, but the *Sick Girl, Seated* and the two sketches of pregnant women permitting examination (a friend and collector, Dr. Erwin von Graff, let Schiele draw women and infants at his gynecological clinic) show real presences, whether in the yellow-tinted, hot-eyed face of the first, the dramatic red sprawl of the second, or the intent appraising gaze of the third, who sizes up the viewer while exposing to view a densely curly pudenda and a distended, pale-green abdomen.

Schiele's fascination with female genitals gives many of his pictures a double focus; *Red-Haired Girl with Spread Legs* (1910) and *Black-Haired*

Girl with Raised Skirt (1911) are subdivided into two zones: an upper and a lower, a public and a private, a lightly but skillfully indicated face and a perhaps more studiously dwelt-upon sex. *This is me*, the models seem to be saying—for it is clear that in some of his models, recruited from the more liberated ranks of the fair sex, Schiele provoked a jaunty exhibitionism. Women in the age of voluminous long skirts and petticoats, we are more than once reminded, did not wear underpants, and a casual flash was more possible then than in our age of short skirts revealing only the impregnable crotch of pantyhose. *Seated Woman Clasping Her Feet* (1915) is a beautiful drawing because our eyes are led into the secret cave as if in life, by an inadvertence of natural intimacy, through a maze of lines every one of which reads as limning a woman's figure—her arms and legs laid parallel as she clasps her feet, her sex centered but not pornographically highlighted.

Our sensation is fond rather than lustful, and much the same could be said of such lovely late works as *Reclining Female with Spread Legs* (1913), *Kneeling Girl* (1913), *Girl (Seated with Yellow Cloth)* (1913), the two titled *Crouching Woman* in 1914, and *Nude with Raised Right Leg* (1915). Not all of the sketches disclose genitalia; *Seated Nude with Red Garter, Seen from the Back* (1914) contains the suggestion of masturbation only in a certain tension of the back, and in the more clearly masturbating *Kneeling Woman with Head Bent Forward* (1915), her labia and fingers and the folds of her red slip are indistinguishable. Female privacy, we feel, is observed without being exploited, because the draftsmanship is so evenly intent.

Beauty lies, perhaps, not in the eye of the beholder but in the hand of the creator. Around 1910, Schiele took from Rodin the technique of "continuous drawing"—drawing directly upon the paper without taking one's eyes off the model. The difficulty of so spontaneous a method lies in keeping the segments in proportion and properly integrated; Schiele developed a consummate fluidity, rendering the most complexly fore-shortened poses with an apparently effortless fidelity—e.g., the *Seated Woman* praised above, and the very late *Girl Lying on Her Back with Crossed Arms and Legs* (1918). In the first, the roughness of the underlying drawing board or table was engagingly incorporated into the lines; in his last year he took to using a darker, softer pencil, and to shading with the side of the point. *Nude Girl with Crossed Arms* (1913) and *Standing Nude Girl with Stockings* (1914) could not be more confident; they have the squared-off, slightly metallic elegance of Modigliani's pencil drawings, with not a line wasted or groped for.

In his late paintings, Schiele approaches fussiness, which hitherto was

Schiele, Reclining Female with Spread Legs, *1913. Pencil.*

never a trait. The lightly tinted attack of pencil line gives way to a dabbly oil color and a stolid naturalism. His models become conventionally voluptuous (*Female Nude with Long Hair Propped Up on Her Arm*, 1918) and, in two large unfinished canvases, *Two Crouching Women* and *Three Standing Women*, oddly static—labored studio pieces with which to claim the throne vacated by the death of Klimt.

His drawings and watercolors of females, usually with a peep at their genitals, contain most of this show's electricity. In this narrow but central field Schiele went further than any artist of his calibre had quite gone before, unsentimentally searching out women in their sexual being. Sexuality acquires a nervous system in his best work, though his few renderings of embracing couples—*Lovers* (1914–15) and *Act of Love* (1915)—convey an effect almost comic, of a puzzlement, both wide-eyed and weary, at being caught in such a fix. Schiele's vigorous voyeurism becomes inhibited; the man and woman of both couples are looking away from each other, outward at us, into the unhealthy mirror.

Away from the grip of his own sexual fascinations, Schiele had yet to prove himself an interesting artist. His cityscapes, usually based on sketches of Krumau, his mother's birthplace, suggest a darker, less witty Paul Klee; his topic paintings, such as *Hermits* (1912), a representation of himself and Klimt; *Cardinal and Nun* (1912), a blasphemous parody of Klimt's *The Kiss;* and *Blind Mother* (1914), a variation on the theme of stony maternal inadequacy, all have Klimt's hieratic flatness without the decorative dazzle. His superb drawing skill, when directed, during his military service, to desktops and packing rooms and nondescript architecture, remains in the realm of craft rather than that of art. What he would have done with his talent had he lived—in 1950 he would have been merely sixty years old—cannot be known; he was moving, it would seem, in the direction of a safer, more pompous style. As it is, more than Klimt, more than Kokoschka, he seems a contemporary, a brief jagged flare on the edge of the scandalous, who expressed with a new forthrightness the link between sex and seeing, in the territory that Freud was simultaneously exploring, between sex and "modern nervousness."

New Kind *on the Block*

New Worlds: *German and Austrian Art, 1890–1940,* at Neue Galerie New York, November 16, 2001–February 18, 2002.

Two questions come quickly to mind: (a) Does Fifth Avenue's "Museum Mile"—stretching from the Frick Collection at Seventieth Street to El Museo del Barrio at 104th—need another museum, and (b) What will the new museum, Neue Galerie New York, at Fifth and Eighty-sixth, do for its next show? This inaugural exhibit, like a tell-all first novel, appears to hold little in reserve; the museum, as described in its own press release, "is a museum devoted to German and Austrian art, in particular the art created in . . . the early part of the twentieth century," and the cream of its collections—a generous splash, but on Museum Mile a drop in the bucket—has been put on view. In answer to question (a), business was booming the rainy Monday of my December visit; a Viennese-style café on the ground floor, called Café Sabarsky, had lines waiting to get in, and the two floors of exhibition space above felt congested. The renovated rooms of even an opulent town house make cramped quarters for a rainy-day museum crowd, and no circulatory flow was established; our bodies became bumper cars, propelled toward their targets by the aggressive tendencies New Yorkers share with German tourists. To heighten the congestion, Monday seemed to be Ladies' Day; the fair sex was disproportionately represented, and immovable gabfests developed in the vicinity of, but facing away from, the works of art.

This six-story corner building was completed in 1914 for the industrialist William Starr Miller; later occupants were Mrs. Cornelius Vanderbilt III and the YIVO Institute for Jewish Research. In 1994 it was purchased by Ronald S. Lauder—chairman of Estée Lauder International and Clinique Laboratories Incorporated, chairman of the Ronald S. Lauder Foundation and the Board of the Museum of Modern Art, and a collector of German-Austrian art since the age of thirteen, when he bought an Egon Schiele drawing with money given him for his bar mitzvah—and Serge Sabarsky, a purveyor and promoter of Austrian-German art who operated a Madison Avenue gallery from 1968 on and died in 1996, while he and Lauder were still realizing their dream of a Neue Galerie New York, an institution that would thrust modern art's Germanic stepchildren into the bosom of the Manhattan museum scene, almost directly across from the Metropolitan, two blocks south of the Guggenheim, and a healthy northward walk from the Frick and the Whitney.

Older museums have had to find accessory space for their increasingly important dining and shopping facilities; the Neue Galerie leads off with them, on the ground floor. As stated, the café, with windows on Fifth Avenue, was thriving; in my haste to get to the art I missed the bookstore and "design shop." All these hotbeds of commerce are open six days a week, while the art can be seen during only four, Fridays through Mondays. The second floor, devoted to Austria, is attained by elevator or by climbing the curvaceous grand staircase of white marble and elaborately wrought iron; at the top, the hall landing is paved with black and white marble and the two principal display rooms retain the gilded glamour and fine oak panelling of their heyday as living quarters.

Moving from marble to parquet, one first claps eyes on the large Gustav Klimt *Portrait of Baroness Elisabeth Bachofen-Echt* (c. 1914); she has a floating entourage of small Oriental figures, most conveniently interpreted as a species of wallpaper. The baroness wears an elongated white outfit, with high collar and pantaloons, behind which hangs a triangular train of Chinese symbols signifying, the catalogue tells us in a note, "the typical hopes and dreams of a young woman, which the painter attributes to her." The formally symmetrical face gazes out with a touching, tentative vitality; away from the face, the painting slopes into the bejewelled flatness that was Klimt's way of coping with the modernist question of the representational versus the abstract. No less fashionably elongated than the full-length portraits of Sargent and Whistler, Klimt's cross over into abstraction while keeping intensely studied semblances of the human face, hands, and feet. The other such portrait in the room, *The Dancer* (c. 1916–18), even more boldly turns the space enveloping its subject into decoration; the flowers massed behind the model exist on the same plane as those on a table at her hip, and her robe sustains the pattern with no perspectival concession to the physical body it enwraps. It is customary to speak of Klimt's flattened pictorial surface as jewel-like—as if he were offering up trays of the patterned brooches and tableware of the Wiener Werkstätte, whose artifacts are on view in the adjacent room—but his brushwork upon inspection is surprisingly rough and free, like the mosaic bits in the later Chuck Close.

Klimt's surfaces seem uneasy in these portraits; there is not the seductive, barbaric emanation of design out of misty flesh found in his *Judith I* (1901, in Vienna) or the Byzantine wall of pure gilt and bauble through whose gaps the lovers of *The Kiss* (c. 1907–8, also in Vienna) can be glimpsed. The Klimt landscapes on display, whether the early *Tall Poplar Tree I* (1900) or the Pointillist *Pond of Schloss Kammer on the Attersee*

Klimt, The Dancer, *c. 1916–18. Oil on canvas.*

(before 1910), are untroubled by any homage to the human form; they make the portraits look attenuated and schizophrenic. So, too, from another direction, do his drawings, in the next room, of indecorously relaxed nudes caught in a flowing, confident pencil line. His sketches are less contorted than those of the artist with whom he is forever paired, Egon Schiele, and more amiably erotic. Klimt, the leader of the Vienna Secession and the embodiment of Art Nouveau, searched for styles other than his brittle, theatrical one of despatialized appliqué; the minimalist *Pale Face* (1907–8) shows him open to Munch's undulant forms, and *Forester House in Weissenbach on the Attersee* (1912) suggests, with its decided outlines and flamelike, ominous vegetation, van Gogh.

Schiele was twenty-eight years younger and pushed Klimt's Art Nouveau into Expressionism and an exhibitionism that is not just erotic but psychoanalytical. In Freud's Vienna, everybody was, it seems, neurotic, sex-obsessed, and tense. Schiele's work is uncompromisingly linear; his more complex groups of figures, such as the large, grayish *Man and Woman I* (1914), are hard to read into the third dimension. Strange webs of linear subdivision spread across these ambitious nudes and the furrowed earth of *River Landscape with Two Trees* (1913), cementing their Kafkaesque impression of paralysis, of frustrated effort. But his drawings, and not his drab paintings, are the basis of his fame, both during his tragically short lifetime (he died in 1918 of the Spanish flu, at the age of twenty-eight) and after.

The dozen or so drawings arrayed in the smaller room behind the Klimt salon are as a group one of the museum's central treasures, though less scandalous and on the whole less beautiful than the Schiele drawings gathered at the Museum of Modern Art in 1997. That show included a number of female nudes with vividly depicted genitals; the most provocative example at the Neue Galerie of Schiele's fierce, morose voyeurism is *Seated Nude, Three-Quarter-Length (Moa)* (1911), with her luxuriant spray of black armpit hair echoed by a pubic bush at the other end of a dramatically tapered anatomy. The *Kneeling Seminude* (1917) is shown fingering her own breasts, and two lean women are engaged in a spoon embrace in *Friendship* (1913) ("*Freundschaft*," a female voice behind me said. "And how!"), but the sexual charge is muted, in part by Schiele's later manner of stylized faces, thicker outlines, and dry touches of red and green. The drawings of 1910 are still exploratory, even to their eccentric placement on the paper, and include some hits—a skeletal, angrily glaring *Self-Portrait with Arm Twisting Above Head*, a blearily leaning *Portrait of the Painter Karl Zakovsek*—and some awkward misses, such as a perversely disaffected *Mother and Child*, wherein the mother presents a naked backside with a coy gaze over her shoulder while a large bald infant, with very long brown fingers, adheres in suckling position to her back, unsuckled and ignored. Birth and nurture are misbegotten processes, we are led to feel, and the contorted poses and bizarre emaciation of Schiele's typical male figures imply—and this is 1910, remember, when Vienna was the thriving capital of an intact empire—that all is far from well.

Oskar Kokoschka, whose youthful interim in Vienna, including his art schooling, wins him a place on the Neue Galerie's Austrian floor, also drew gaunt, angular nudes and dreamy Klimtesque designs, but the architect Adolf Loos, Keith Holz tells us in the catalogue, "nudged Kokoschka away from decorative arts and toward painting by arranging numerous portrait sittings." These youthful portraits remain among the peripatetic Kokoschka's best work, and strike here a strong, sensuous note: the portrait of the poet Peter Altenberg (1909) is nervy, crusty painting and captures a moment of agitated gesture with the immediacy of a snapshot. The same year's portrait of Martha Hirsch, her small red mouth pursed as if in the middle of a word, and her hands self-consciously twisted as if she thought them out of sight, has the same nervous presence, though its huge eyes verge on caricature; a drawing identified as *Reclining Seminude Woman* (1908–9) shows that her homely, long-chinned face can coexist with a voluptuous breast. Rudolf Blümner, in the portrait of him (1910), evoked excited painting; Kokoschka digs out white lines with the other end of the brush, applies raw red and sweeps of purple, and works the face with so rich a mix of stabbed-on pigments that he leaves his subject looking cross-eyed.

Another Viennese with a wild brush was Richard Gerstl, who committed suicide over a broken love affair at the age of twenty-five. He was precocious but unruly, and consorted less with painters than with musicians, including the young Arnold Schönberg, who also painted, and is said to have studied with Gerstl. Many of Gerstl's canvases remained rolled up in a warehouse until his family released them in 1931, to acclaim. He is represented here by the dashingly competent but not unconventional *Portrait of a Seated Man in the Studio* (1907) and, from the same year, the dramatically vague *Portrait of a Man on the Lawn*, a man virtually without features, gliding diagonally across a field of violently brushed impasto— a kind of ghost in pure paint, anomalous in German Expressionism before, by a route through Surrealism, it arrived at Abstract Expressionism. Possibly, the painting might be simply unfinished, a hasty laying-out that Gerstl's short and hectic life never went back to; in any case, it is a show-stopper. The Austrian paintings and few sculptures, it should be said, are accompanied, in these sumptuous former living quarters, by furniture and household items—clocks, cutlery, glassware—from the Wiener Werkstätte, variously handsome and innovative and no doubt instructive to a craftsman's eye but affording this viewer the sensation usually engendered by chairs one cannot sit on and eating implements in a sealed case, the sensation of having missed the party.

One ascends to the third floor by means of a back stairs that, though of white marble, is distinctly unornamented. On this floor, where the illusion of a comfortable town house is left behind, the problems of the museum and its mission more plainly emerge. This is not comfortable art; it is fuller of programmatic intentions than of harmonious resolution. The German monarchy Bismarck had hammered together around Prussia had Berlin as a political capital but was still a land of regions, with no cultural equivalent of London, Paris, or Vienna. The floor's four rooms are divided among four labels: Die Brücke, founded in Dresden in 1905; the Blaue Reiter group, formed in Munich in 1911; Dada and Neue

Gerstl, Portrait of a Man on the Lawn, *1907. Oil on canvas.*

Sachlichkeit (New Objectivity), a term coined by Gustav Friedrich Hart-laub, the director of the Kunsthalle in Mannheim, to title a 1925 exhibit of "post-Expressionist" paintings of a relatively naturalistic, conservative style; and the Bauhaus, the art-and-design school founded in 1919 by Walter Gropius in the Thuringian city of Weimar, where Goethe and Schiller lived and died and the pre-Hitlerian republic was founded. The Bauhaus, though ostensibly a school for architecture and the practical arts, with painting and sculpture marginal concerns, yet hired instructors in art theory who included such artists as Paul Klee, Vasily Kandinsky, Oskar Schlemmer, Lyonel Feininger, and László Moholy-Nagy; indeed, American museumgoers will encounter the most names familiar to them in this section, the front room, which also holds steely furniture and household items designed by Marcel Breuer, Ludwig Mies van der Rohe, and Wilhelm Wagenfeld.

The three-dimensional artifacts are models of clean, witty design; the paintings on the third floor sound a chronic note of protest, anguish, scorn, and unhealth. The usual Expressionist nude, as rendered by Ernst Kirchner or Erich Heckel, is yellow and angular; the customary landscape—see August Macke's *Strollers at the Lake II* (1912) or Karl Schmidt-Rottluff's *Landscape with House and Trees* (1910)—presents a strident crush of discordant colors taken less from nature than from the palette of overthrown inhibition. The violent colors of Kandinsky and Franz Marc are yet subdued, or sublimated, by a certain vision of the primitive village, with its gentle, almost speaking animals, but there is, in the work of Kirchner, Heckel, Macke, Schmidt-Rottluff, not to mention Max Beckmann, George Grosz, and Otto Dix, no lack of illustration for the dicta of Oskar Pfister's groundbreaking *Expressionism in Art* of 1922:

> The expressionist artist cannot be merely deduced out of a protest against the artistic or cultural milieu. . . . Expressionism is a "cry of distress," like a stream of lava forcing itself forward prompted by the soul's misery and a ravenous hunger for life. . . . The chaos of the picture betrays the confusion of the expressionist himself, the brutal color and outlines the brutality of his character.

An enigmatic, caustic mood pervades even a Beckmann still life (called, with presumed irony, *Sunrise*, 1929) and Kurt Schwitters's abstract collages; as no less an authority than Joseph Goebbels, who was within the decade to lead the Nazi assault on "degenerate art," wrote in his 1929 novel, *Michael*, "We are all Expressionists today. . . . The Expressionist builds in himself a new world. His secret and his power is this ardor." Within the German-speaking world, the predominantly Protestant north was the province of proper ardor, an emotional fury that considered itself masculine. Reviewing a 1916 Berlin show of Viennese art, the critic Karl Scheffler complained that Viennese painting was "utterly feminine . . . charming but not creative" and claimed it "lacked the spirit of Protestantism. That is to say: the readiness to go into depth." The notion of a barbarian vigor that scorns feminine niceties and seeks a depth beyond the rational can be found in Expressionism and Nazism both. We go, let's admit it, to exhibits of pre-1940 German art in a mood of diagnosis, looking for symptoms of the plague to come. Even in the next century we ask ourselves how a nation of such advanced civilization came to consign itself, with all its military and industrial might, to a government of thugs and criminal cranks and rabid anti-Semites.

A dissatisfaction with the status quo underlies revolutions both political and artistic; Pamela Kort's survey, in the compendious catalogue, of American attitudes toward Expressionism, asserts, "Though not politically radical, pre–World War I Expressionists were united by their disdain for the bourgeois culture and imperial politics of Wilhelminian Germany." After the war, there was the Weimar Republic, ruinous inflation, and the taste of defeat. German art from 1890 to 1940 differs from French art of the same period in its refusal to rest content with visual expression—an exploration of appearances that takes its passion from the process. The subjects of Cézanne's portraits, and Modigliani's, and van Gogh's, have little psychological presence compared with—all in this exhibit—Otto Dix's sly, awry, slump-shouldered Jewish lawyer (*Portrait of the Lawyer Dr. Fritz Glaser*, 1921), or Dix's shopworn, chalky-faced nudes (1926, 1930), or with George Grosz's *Portrait of John Förste, Man with Glass Eye* (1926), glaring into a book with enough force to make the wormy vein at his temple pop, or with Max Beckmann's truculent self-portraits (1923, 1938), or Paul Klee's broken, baleful self-portrait of 1909. These human figures are less objects taking the light than souls in torment; they have the Gothic inwardness of medieval statuary. Northern Europe had its own art tradition, graphic and linear, gaunt and at times gruesome, and visitors to the Neue Galerie expecting the epicurean modernism of the School of Paris will have their sensibilities abraded. The French strategies of refreshed representation take on a new violence from, it seems, the German painters' seething psyches. The Fauves laid on color in boldly vibrant streaks, but there is a world of difference between some gaudy Derain boats moored in the water and the assaultively unnatural colors and brutal brush attack of Heckel's *Bathers in a Pond* (1908). Monet's haystacks evoked, as the day's hours changed, some prickly, counterintuitive patches of paint, but nothing like the gory

Beckmann, Self-Portrait in Front of Red Curtain, *1923. Oil on canvas.*

impasto of Emil Nolde's *Sunset* (1909). Cubism in the hands of Picasso and Braque was a golden-brown walk around a table and a jug; for George Grosz its diagonal chopped perspective became a scaffolding for caricatural images of whores, fat-necked politicians, monocled mustached Junkers, and a welter of other human symptoms of something rotten in Deutschland—*Panorama (Down with Liebknecht)* (1919). The answer to question (a), whether Fifth Avenue needs another museum, may depend on how much willful ugliness the public wants to pay ten dollars for (seniors and students only seven).

The posh bulk of the museum's catalogue offers to cushion the shock; it comes to six hundred pages exactly—fifty-three essays more or less, many translated from the German. Ronald Lauder's preface recounts how, one night in 1968 (a rather expressionist year, come to think of it), he asked Sabarsky if there were any Schiele collectors in America: "He said he knew of two. With that I answered, 'You should also count me and my brother.' He looked at me, smiled, and said, 'I already counted both of you.'" The several collections the museum can draw upon—its own, plus those of Sabarsky and the Lauder family—are choice, but, as the Getty Museum shows, late-starting museums, however well endowed, have a hard game of catch-up to play; celebrity art not already locked into public collections bears prices that bar extensive acquisition. Paul Klee, who was Swiss by birth and in his final residence, and was marginally Expressionist in temperament, is the one painter in this show who ranks with beloved modernist superstars like Matisse, de Chirico, and Picasso; he is effectively but sparsely represented, compared with the Klees one has seen on the walls of MoMA and, indeed, in the German wing of the Fogg Museum at Harvard, a collection begun in 1902 and for decades separately housed in the Busch-Reisinger Museum of Germanic Culture. Klee, who produced over ten thousand of his modest-sized works, is represented at 1048 Fifth Avenue by paintings, two in oil and three in watercolor and gouache, which hint at the tireless wit of his experimentation. Two are still lifes on a black ground, the larger of which (*Gay Repast / Colorful Meal*, 1928) holds objects disparate enough to qualify Klee, in the opinion of the critic and gallery owner Alfred Flechtheim, as "the real creator of Surrealism." But the multiplicity of Klee's visual devices suggests a cerebral source somewhat higher than the fluid subconscious dear to Surrealism: not a flooded basement but a dry playroom whence spill puns, doodles, and philosophical jokes. His inventiveness in making marks on paper spins a giant comic footnote to reality. There almost always is in Klee a certain radiance, and the once-and-done air of musical improvisation. In *Mystical Ceramic (in the Manner of a Still Life)* (1925) he uses a knitwork of dry marks as if with a sponge; in *Yellow House* (1915) envelopelike rectangles of watercolor; in *On the Lawn* (1923) ink lines into wet watercolor furrily limn his frolicking, staring bathing beauties.

More surreal in feeling, though thoroughly representational, like a more explicit Balthus, are Christian Schad's two young masturbating women, with their gleaming eyes lost in a middle distance that includes the uneasy viewer; it is this image, presumably, along with a masturbating nude of Klimt's, that bars children under twelve, as a stern sign downstairs announces, from attending the show at all. The basically representational Neue Sachlichkeit section includes Schad; Dix's two remorseless portraits of puckered, sagging, anxious nudes; George Grosz in a variety of styles, including a dishevelled apartment (*Couple in Interior*, 1915) in feeling like a George Bellows, only more pornographic in its squalor; and three sizable Beckmann oils, of which the two self-portraits linger in the mind's eye longer than most anything else in the exhibit. Among the Neue Galerie's other bright spots should be listed the Kandinskys, though the later abstraction *Black Form* (1923) seems cartoonlike, and Lovis Corinth's windswept still life *Fruit Bowls* (1923) and pencilled self-portrait (1921).

The Beckmanns (*Self-Portrait in Front of Red Curtain*, 1923; *Self-Portrait with Horn*, 1938) are separated by fifteen years. By the time of the latter, Beckmann was already on his way to Amsterdam, where he survived the war before heading to the United States in 1947. From the smooth, blocky style of the earlier work he had evolved the flickering black out-lines and poster-sharp colors of his mature style; but the man is the same, round-headed, unsmiling, and determinedly *there*, a study in *Dasein*, a dis-tinctly German man whose costumes—tuxedo, red scarf, lit cigar, bowler hat tipped back in the one; in the other a V-necked jersey of red and black stripes, clownish to go with the curved horn he is holding—suggest a potential for mischief and battle, a dangerous density of energy. He will not, his posture implies, go away. So much for (a); as to (b), we shall see.

Beyond Real

MAX ERNST: *A Retrospective*, at the Metropolitan Museum of Art, New York, April 7–July 10, 2005.

GHOST SHIPS: *A Surrealist Love Triangle*, by Robert McNab. 266 pp. Yale University Press, 2004.

Not only is Max Ernst the subject of an extensive and eye-challenging retrospective at the Metropolitan Museum of Art, he is winning retro-spective publicity as a romantic principal in a shameless, artistically high-powered *ménage à trois* in the early 1920s, lyrically and speculatively described by the documentary filmmaker Robert McNab in his book *Ghost Ships*. The known facts are not numerous: Ernst, born in the town of Brühl, Germany—near the Rhine, between Bonn and Cologne—into a large middle-class Catholic family, whose father was a teacher of deaf chil-dren and an amateur painter, studied philosophy and abnormal psychol-ogy at the University of Bonn. At the age of twenty he decided to become a painter and joined August Macke's Rhine Expressionist group. In 1919, having served four years in the Kaiser's Army and risen to the rank of lieu-tenant, he helped found, with Johannes Theodor Baargeld, the Cologne

Dada movement. Increasingly well known in art circles, and acquainted with such prominent German-speaking artists as Paul Klee, Hans Arp, George Grosz, John Heartfield, and Otto Dix, he experimented with collage. In 1921 his collages won him a solo show in Paris, but visa trouble in post-war Germany prevented him from attending. The exhibition, organized by André Breton, attracted enthusiasm among the French Surrealists; later that year the Surrealist poet Paul Éluard and his Russian wife, Gala, visited Cologne with the express purpose of meeting Ernst. A photograph was taken during the meeting, showing Max and Luise Ernst with their small son, Jimmy, the two Éluards, and the painter Baargeld. Already a prophetic note of cozy trespass was struck: Gala posed wearing the German Iron Cross, the military decoration which Ernst had won. Éluard, too, four years younger than the thirty-year-old Ernst, had fought (and been severely gassed) in the war. He said, "Max and I were at Verdun together and used to shoot at each other." According to Robert McNab,

> The imaginative and moral sympathy of the two men was immediate. They also felt an instant urge to collaborate, to improvise like jazz musicians, so that Éluard quickly selected eleven collages by Ernst as illustrations for his next book of poems. . . . He also bought a large canvas, the *Elephant of Celebes*, that accompanied him to Paris with Gala. These were the first of many collaborations in book form and the first of hundreds of works Éluard purchased from Ernst.

Éluard, whose poetry has weathered better than all but a few creations by the Paris Surrealist group, was unusual among these bohemians in that he had ample money and a job; he worked for his father, a Parisian property developer. More collaborations with Ernst followed, and more trips to Cologne. When Gala and Ernst began to sleep together was not recorded, but a photograph exists, probably from March of 1922, showing Gala standing between the two men, slightly closer to Ernst than to her husband. All are on skis; the photographer may have been Luise Straus-Ernst, who was later to write of "this slippery, scintillating creature with cascading black hair, luminous and vaguely oriental eyes, delicate bones, who, not having succeeded in drawing her husband into an affair with me in order to appropriate Max for herself, finally decided to keep both men, with the loving consent of Éluard." By the summer of 1922, the affair, and Éluard's complaisance, were public knowledge. Dominique Bona, in her 1995 biography *Gala*, describes Gala (in French) as "the benchmark of their friendship, as their means of communication with each other, as their shared wife. They made love to each other in her."

In August, Ernst left his wife and son in Germany and, travelling illegally on Éluard's passport, moved in with the Éluards in their home in Saint-Brice, a suburb of Paris. He never lived in Germany again. Luise, whom Max had met in art school before the war and married soon after it, was the daughter of a prosperous Jewish milliner who had disapproved of his son-in-law. Finally divorced from Max in 1926, she became a museum curator until ousted by the Nazis; she joined the resistance, was arrested, and died in Auschwitz. Their son, Jimmy, fondly called Minimax to go with his father's nickname, Dadamax, became a Surrealist painter in California.

Ernst's painting thrived in the *ménage*, but the gentle Éluard showed signs of stress, drinking late in bars and nightclubs and, in McNab's telling, "falling asleep at his friends' instead of going home, where Ernst and his wife seemed the resident couple." Eighteen months after Ernst moved in, Éluard one evening "got up from the bistro table to buy some matches, walked out and vanished from Paris." He was on his way to the Far East, and at his urging Gala followed four months later, bringing Ernst with her. She auctioned off a sizable part of her husband's painting collection to buy the steamer tickets.

Only a few photos and brief communications survive from that travelling year of 1924; McNab fills the huge gap by writing, very interestingly, about steamships and their ports of call, about the huge French colony of Indochina, about the call of the Pacific from the eighteenth-century French explorers to the painter Gauguin, the poet Saint-Pol-Roux, and the anti-Eurocentric, culturally relativistic traveller Victor Segalen. Surrealism, McNab argues, began as travel, more or less random, as a trance-inducing escape from the bourgeois Europe that had given the younger generation World War I. In early June 1919, Breton and Philippe Soupault walked all night through Paris, and "at dawn agreed jointly to write something to evoke the peculiar state of mind the experience had induced. . . . At times they wrote for ten hours on end, breaking off for fresh air to roam the streets again in a daze." Other nocturnal rambles, enhanced by cannabis and cocaine, followed; by 1922, Breton was advising his readers, in a short piece titled *"Lâchez tout,"* "Drop everything. . . . Drop your wife, drop your girl-friend. . . . Park your children in the woods. . . . Drop your comfortable life. . . . Take to the road." It was all about *dépaysement*, according to McNab: the word

> translates literally as being outside your own country, but its meaning also encompasses exile and disorientation. . . . *Dépaysement* also defined a favoured Surrealist mood, the feeling we all get when we arrive somewhere new for the first time, our senses sharpened by wonder and tinged with anxiety.

The exhaustion as well as the disorientation of travel was courted as a means to fresh perceptions. Surrealists walked from Blois to Moret and back, having visions and hallucinations in the creepy Solonge, and took steamers to Cuba, the Amazon, the Gulf of St. Lawrence. Freud had discovered a new territory within, the subconscious, and dreams, drugs, word games, séances, automatic writing, virtually random collage, and impulsive exotic travel were ways of exploring it. There was a political dimension to *dépaysement:* direct experience of France's Pacific colonies confirmed the Surrealists' antagonism to the jingoistic, often brutally exploitative colonizers, and to the European establishment.

Of course, breaking through the shell of reason and accepted order to profounder truths beneath is an idea as old as shamanistic trances, Greek oracles, and the mind-emptying exercises of yoga and Zen. Rimbaud, along with Gauguin a stellar example of self-exile, in 1871 had famously asserted that the poet makes himself a seer by a long, immense, and deliberate *"dérèglement de tous les sens."*

Gala, Ernst, and Éluard achieved a *dérèglement* of social custom with their *ménage* and their escape to Saigon, where the three reassembled. Back in Paris, Éluard described it as a *voyage idiot*, a stupid trip, and in fact their triune rapport was never the same. Ernst returned later than the Éluards and took up separate residence in a Montmartre studio; Éluard entered a tuberculosis sanitarium, from which he wrote Gala longing letters, while she had entered into a period of intensified promiscuity and a campaign, successful, to captivate Salvador Dalí. When this was achieved, she made remarks that McNab translates as "Didn't I do well to ditch Max Ernst: he's a loser. But as for Dalí, just look at the success he's become since I took over!" The French for "he's a loser" was *"il n'arrivera à rien"*—"he'll come to nothing" or "he'll arrive nowhere." Life is a journey. One of Éluard's poems to Gala during their separation began, "At the end of a long journey, I can still see that corridor, that gloomy burrow, that warm darkness where a breeze blows in drifting off the surf." What the trio did in French Indochina, besides pose for a Saigon street photographer and make the difficult trip to Angkor Wat, remains mysterious. Éluard burned all of Gala's letters to him, and hers to Ernst are lost; only her actions speak for her. Of the three, Ernst seems the coolest, the blankest. Gala had the satisfaction of being desired by two men at once, and Éluard that of his steadfast forbearance and affection; Ernst's role is purely that of a taker—of the younger man's wife, house, and patronage. Only his artistic diligence can be admired.

* * *

The show at the Metropolitan is itself a long-enough voyage to induce some trancelike feelings, as we wind, "our senses sharpened by wonder and tinged with anxiety," through the Tisch Galleries and the multiple switchbacks of Ernst's techniques and styles. The show quits, in fact, well before Ernst did; only a few displayed works follow the artist back to France after his American sojourn between 1941 and 1953; he lived and produced for more than twenty more years, dying one day short of his eighty-fifth birthday, on April 1, 1976. The 175 items—paintings, collages, sculptures—on view are almost all meticulous and inventive, but Ernst was not a very pleasing painter. A German dryness clings to his brushwork, and his drawing has a stilted quality that makes Dalí and Magritte, say, look like Renaissance masters. His cleverness with picture-generating gadgetry covers up the relative sparseness of his formal artistic education.

The canvases that a viewer can wholeheartedly cherish are relatively few. Beginning, at the age of twenty-two, with a naïve scene of a family embedded in a forest, wryly called *Immortality* (c. 1913), and moving, after the war, to gaudily colored animals and villages in the manner of Chagall or Franz Marc (*Town with Animals*, 1919), Ernst arrived, in 1921—having momentarily put aside Dadaesque collage and fantastic mechanical drawings in the style of Kurt Schwitters—at the painting that Paul Éluard purchased: *Celebes*, in which the form of a Sudanese corn bin is transformed into a blue-green elephant, its thick ringed hose of a trunk terminating in a white cuff shaped like a crown. A chalky headless nude in the lower right corner and several fish swimming in the sky in the upper left submit the requisite Surrealist credentials; but this canvas in its firmly rounded central enigma manifests a presence achieved through painterly rather than quasi-literary means. Surrealism was a thinking man's movement. The poet Robert Desnos wrote, "*Pour toujours la peinture est grosse de parole, la parole grosse de peinture*"—"For always painting is pregnant with words, and words with painting"—and to an unparalleled degree artists in the two media collaborated and crossbred under Surrealism's banner. For the viewer it too often means an uneasy wait in front of a rebuslike canvas in hopes that its verbal meaning will dawn. *Celebes* needs no help from words, and is beyond them. The influence of de Chirico, whom Ernst discovered in 1919, is happily at work here, subduing the German's magpie mind to a single dominant image, sturdily shadowed and outlined in black.

Saint Cecilia (1923), playing an invisible organ and half enclosed in rough tan masonry, is one of a series of encased women. This one seems less a victim than most; her delicate hands hover in midair at the same

Ernst, Celebes, *1921. Oil on canvas.*

level as the nearby bird thrillingly standing on its tail. *Woman, Old Man, and Flower* (1924), a bit of a jumble as its title suggests, with its peg-legged lion-man and fan-shaped great headdress, is structured by a sequence of verticals and swept together into a kind of beckoning by the calligraphically outlined arms of the transparent central figure: some invisible force is being welcomed. *The Forest* (c. 1924) presents one of his recurrent themes—Ernst was born among the Rhine forests—with the jagged boldness of Max Beckmann. *Le Déjeuner sur l'herbe* (1936), a borrowed title he was to use more than once, takes a leaf less from Manet's than from Picasso's book in its elastic distortions and neoclassic air; it has among its pale gargoyles the round-eyed cartoon bird that, under the name Loplop, was to inspire a Dadaesque series early in the decade.

Birds, rendered in contours that from across the room suggest the deformed and foreshortened nudes of Francis Bacon, take an especially alien form in his two paintings of identical style and title, *Monument to the Birds* (both 1927); suspended rather than flying, the birds seem wooden forms torn from a baroque organ. *Blind Swimmer: Effect of Touch* (1934) is one of Ernst's rare abstractions, and a brilliant one, of a striped curtain agreeably rough to the eye yet flowing like water around the two interruptions, a white lens and a peacock-feather eye. Nearly as abstract, *A Night of Love* (1927), painted the year he married his second wife, née Marie-Berthe Aurenche, took its main lines from paint-soaked strings tossed onto the canvas, but seems unusually personal and vital nevertheless, with stylized breasts and grasping hands scattered on a brown blanket while one lover's teeth, two glowing arcs in an emptied head, join the nocturnal background of stars. *The Bride of the Wind*, from the same year, seems also exuberant and ethereal, a horse galloping itself to pieces. His bride was the product of a convent education and ultra-respectable parents; they at first tried to get Ernst arrested for interfering with a minor.

The original exhibition including Ernst's assaultive painting *The Blessed Virgin Chastises the Infant Jesus Before Three Witnesses: A.B., P.E., and the Artist* (1926) was closed by church pressure because of it; at the Met, alone on a large wall and protected by glass against possible Christian vandals, it exerts a sensuous spell. Perhaps Ernst was spurred by memories of his Catholic boyhood to revel in the intensely local colors, the delicately painted halos (the Virgin's casts a dotted shadow on her hair; that of the Infant Jesus is jarred loose onto the floor), and such tender details as the blush on the Christ Child's spanked buttocks, the Pieroesque tinted planes of the outdoor environment, and Mary's impossibly widespread bare feet, blurred as if by the vigor of her discipline, which is administered with a gesture reminiscent of Michelangelo's Sistine Chapel Christ imposing the Last Judgment. Though this scene cannot be enrolled in Christian iconography—it has no Gospel authority, for one thing—Ernst has created something iconic, which all who take seriously the doctrine of the Incarnation, and all it entails, cannot lightly dismiss.*

Ernst was a zealous technician, who after mastering collage went on to *frottage*, the producing of an image by rubbing a relief, and *grattage*, the

---

*See the article by Leo Steinberg ("This Is a Test," *New York Review of Books*, May 13, 1993) concerning this painting; Steinberg makes the surprising point that the "three witnesses" (André Breton, Paul Éluard, and the artist) are none of them witnessing the shocking scene. The two French poets are pointedly looking elsewhere, and the artist, from his background vantage, is watching us, the viewers. Steinberg wrote, "The painting is engineered to embarrass: so long as I look, I am exposed to the artist's accusing gaze as he watches the churl in me trapped in the act of ogling a sacrilege—a provocation which my betters scorn to acknowledge."

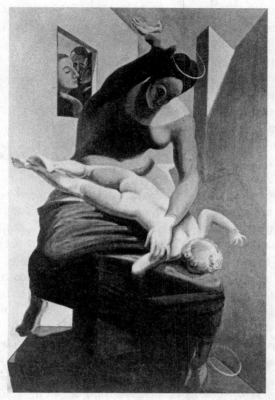

Ernst, The Blessed Virgin Chastises the Infant Jesus Before Three Witnesses: A.B., P.E., and the Artist, *1926. Oil on canvas.*

same process applied to scraped paint. Both these methods of making marks tend, in my view, to produce stiff and standoffish results, though in *The Petrified City* (1935) and its superior successor *The Entire City* (1935–36) the buildings, formed by the *grattage* of Rajput wood blocks used for printing muslin, do loom under their huge full moons as ominous memories, perhaps, of Angkor Wat's immense ruins, or as contemporary foreboding at the rise of fascism, with its merciless architecture.

The technique oddly named decalcomania, however, was very fruitful for Ernst, figuring in several masterpieces around the time of his narrow escape from Europe. The process, related to the monoprint, was invented by his fellow-Surrealist Oscar Dominguez and involved putting paints on canvas, pressing a sheet of paper or glass upon them, and then lifting. The effect, as described by Pepe Karmel in a catalogue essay, "pushes and pulls the colors into strange, visceral ridges, like those on the surface of a sponge." As manipulated by Ernst in *Totem and Taboo* (1941), *Napoleon in the Wilderness* (1941), and, with supreme effect, *Europe After the Rain* (1940–42), the effect is of coral or rotted rock spun out into structures populated, with the artist's fine and patient brush, by growths and creatures and human survivors in the sinister wreckage. *Europe After the Rain*, we are told, was begun by Ernst in a European prison camp and finished in the United States—a precarious transit, in that dire time, for a crusty canvas two feet by five.

The year 1940 saw the production of the one canvas that must have a place of honor in any history of Surrealism, the magnificent *Robing of the Bride*. Decalcomania contributes to the uncanny texture of the bride's feathery orange robe and of the female attendant's trapezoidal headdress. Both women are naked, with long ivory-white legs that augur well for the unseen groom's happiness, but something has gone fearfully wrong with the bride's head: it is much too small, and sits atop her petite, appetizing breasts like a shrunken head worn as a neck amulet. But perhaps it is not *her* head; a single eye peeks through a bulky hood of feathers capped by an owl's cruel beak and staring eyes. In the bridal chamber, with its checkerboard floor as in a late-medieval palace, hangs a miniature version of the same scene, without the attendants, and the long white leg and torso emerging from not a robe of feathers but a heap of corroded minerals. The tableau is erotic and menacing, and pierces close to the heart of Ernst's only partially friendly feelings concerning the fair sex, with which he was so successful. The work hangs in the Peggy Guggenheim museum in Venice; after a brief farmhouse idyll with the English artist and writer Leonora Carrington ended in Ernst's being interned by the French as an enemy alien, it was Guggenheim who managed to get him out of Europe and who became, in New York, the third Mrs. Ernst.

Decalcomania figures, too, among the teeming array of techniques employed in *The Temptation of Saint Anthony* (1945), in which Ernst declares his German heritage by managing to out-Grünewald Grünewald and out-Bosch Bosch. As Robert Storr points out in his catalogue essay, whereas Grünewald gave his saint a fighting chance against these diabolical apparitions from the animal world, Ernst's Anthony is being helplessly consumed by what seems a swarm of magnified lice—the artist was, as we know from his earliest collages, a connoisseur of magnification as illustrated in biological texts. His compulsively horrific painting won a competition, sponsored by a moviemaker, over entries by Dalí, Ivan Albright, and Dorothea Tanning, who became Ernst's fourth wife in 1946. Among the other canvases produced in America, *Surrealism and Painting* (1942) struck me as oddly consummate; Ernst's rather arid and logolike simplified birds have become flamingos of a sort, iridescent and obscenely flexible, snuggling into one another while a long-necked hand works away at a canvas displaying the artist's newest resort to technical sorcery: the mathematically pure ellipses formed by a swinging paint can.

In addition to paintings there are Ernst's celebrated collages, at which museumgoers dutifully squinted, bemused by a parade of ungettable jokes. Ernst fashioned them with remarkable care, rendering the seams all but invisible, and with an excellent, unwrinkling glue. A furiously energetic melodrama surges through these nineteenth-century woodcuts—wood engravings, more exactly, mass-produced for popular magazines and novels before the advent of photoengraving. A fanatic precision guided Ernst's hand as he grafted birds' and lions' heads onto these agitated scenes, wreaking mutilation and metamorphosis upon the frock-coated, mustached men and the *déshabillées* maidens caught in some Gothic tale's toils. But how much of the hybrids' aesthetic interest—their perverse beauty—should be credited to the original illustrators and painstaking engravers? A fair amount, I decided after leafing through my own copy of *Une Semaine de bonté*. Onto these mass-produced popular materials Ernst soldered an inscrutable message, dredged, he confessed, from dreams and childhood memories. The effect is a childish, sadistic one, of an insatiable, ingenious taunting.

And there are sculptures, some of which—the horned chess player titled *The King Playing with the Queen* (1944)—are familiar and others of which—*Bird Head* (1934–35), *Moonmad* (1944)—go somewhat beyond what he learned from the young Giacometti. The stone sculptures with which he decorated the desert home he shared with Tanning were present only in photographs in the last room of the retrospective. His life's journey arrived, for a time, at the red rocks of Sedona, Arizona—*dépaysement* with a vengeance. But enlarged photos of Ernst in ripe middle age show that though he sported an American tan he carried himself with a Puckish poise that only a European man could project. He and Tanning returned to France in 1953, where he became a legal French citizen and, heavy with years and honors, eventually died in Paris.

The Enduring Magritte

A TRIBUTE written for *Los Angeles* magazine, occasioned by the exhibition *René Magritte: The Poetry of Silence*, at UCLA's Armand Hammer Museum of Art and Cultural Center, September 17, 1996–January 5, 1997.

The Surrealists have not aged well. Dalí seems in retrospect to have gone from sick to slick, from sensational to sentimental, his intensity too much a matter of bejewelled surface detail. The celebrated collages of Max Ernst savor of yellow paper and dried glue; the whole principle of incongruous juxtaposition has been turned into an MTV cliché. And Miró seems too much the cartoonist, his linear fancies centerless and spindly. Shock value fades; enduring resonance is an elusive quality not always spotted immediately. René Magritte, initially regarded as a staid Belgian outrider to Surrealism's Paris-based movement, did not command much attention until after World War II, but now, nearly thirty years after his death in 1967, enjoys a high esteem in the art world. A few years after a large retrospective show that travelled from London to New York and thence on to Houston and Chicago, Magritte is now on display in Los Angeles through early 1997.

Magritte is not just a curator's artist; he exerts an incalculably large influence in the imagery of advertisements, of posters and, one can say, of thought. Before deconstruction existed as a concept, when the philosophy of signs was a matter of obscure technical interest, he promulgated an impeccably straightforward painting of a burnished curved-stem pipe captioned *"Ceci n'est pas une pipe"* ("This is not a pipe") and titled *La Trahison des images* (1929). The treachery of images is his constant, fertile theme. We stand before the painting with our minds in a buzz of alternating contradiction: it is a pipe, that is to say, an image of a pipe, which is not, come to think of it, a pipe. The fine seam between the real and its image is tirelessly traced in paintings which are, after all, only paintings. A window frames a scene which turns out to be painted on the window glass (*La Lunette d'approche*, or *The Field-Glass*, 1963; *Le Soir qui tombe*, or *Evening Falls*, 1964) or, in *La Condition humaine* (1933), a painting on its easel blends, but for the visible edges of the canvas, with the landscape being painted. Magritte, a willing explicator—unlike many painters—of his art, said of this last work:

> The tree represented in the painting hid from view the real tree situated behind it, outside the room. It existed for the spectator, as it were, simultaneously in the mind, as both inside the room in the painting, and outside in the real landscape. Which is how we see the world: We see it as being out-

Magritte, La Trahison des images, *1929. Oil on canvas.*

side ourselves even though it is only a mental representation of it that we experience inside ourselves.

The tricks of *trompe l'oeil* bring us up against this inner nature of a reality; the world is what we perceive of the world, and if, as in *Les Promenades d'Euclide* (*Where Euclid Walked*, 1955), a receding road bewilderingly resembles a conical tower, so be it. Reality is a thin skin of perception; the panorama of sea and clouds in *Les Mémoires d'un saint* (1960) is a papery arc which surrounds an invisible viewer. It opens, like the illusion of the stage, with curtains drawn apart. The world is a theatre of appearance that, as Shakespeare's Prospero said, "shall dissolve, / And, like this insubstantial pageant faded, / Leave not a rack behind. We are such stuff / As dreams are made on. . . ."

Dreams, given new significance and importance by Freud's theories, were a cornerstone of the Surrealist aesthetic. "Pure automatism," in which the subconscious was encouraged to take over the pen, would, according to André Breton, generate a fresh literature. Miró's wandering line was the painterly equivalent. Free association, part of Freudian therapy, became, in Dalí's medleys of limp watches, dismembered anatomies, and Spanish deserts, a doorway to a deeper reality, the world of our private psychologies. Few artistic movements have been as self-consciously promulgated as Surrealism, with as coherent and plausible a program, and yet the ground of automatism proved to be shallow soil, producing some luxuriant growths but much weedy ephemera.

Magritte, like Giorgio de Chirico, the painter of the first great canvases that can be called Surrealist, was a technically conservative painter, whose literalist brushwork lends a certain weighty calm to his bizarre juxtapositions and daring visual deceptions. Using the freedom of dreams, he çomposed meditative puzzles upon meaning and signification. Written language, as much as the representations of graphic arts, presumes to substitute for reality, and frequently in the late 1920s Magritte contented himself with simply spelling out on a canvas, in a lucid and pretty script, words such as *"horizon," "cris d'oiseaux," "salon," "fores," "femme triste."* The viewer feels cheated, but should he? Are not painted images themselves a vocabulary? And what is more surreal, more enigmatic in its juxtapositions, than a list, an inventory, such as we find in paintings like *Le Dormeur téméraire* (*The Daring Sleeper,* 1928), which embeds representations of a bird, a candle, an apple, a bowler hat, a hand mirror, and a tied ribbon in a tablet of lead, or *Les Six Éléments* (1929), which in six irregular panes presents such images as a nude woman, clouds, house fronts, trees, hells and flames? In *L'Évidence éternelle* (*The Eternally Obvious,* 1930), five parts of a nude woman are framed discretely—a piquant catalogue of what most attracted the painter's attention, ending with the humble bare feet. Magritte's habit of notation translates, in his manner of painting, to a conscientious clarity that never requires any flourishes of brushwork or color; he coolly stands at the opposite temperamental pole from the feverish virtuosity with which Dalí insisted on his visual non sequiturs.

He painted in a corner of his comfortable home south of Brussels, and worked intermittently as a commercial artist, even in a wallpaper factory for a time. His first paintings are done in a neo-Cubist style that became Art Deco; his early Surrealist works, dating from the mid-Twenties, are greasy in texture and dull in color and show barely enough skill to create *trompe-l'oeil* effects. He improved as a painter through much of his life; his paintings from the Fifties and Sixties show a delicate touch and brightness of tone absent from his work before the war; the late canvases that recast familiar objects in stone, such as *Souvenir de voyage* (*Memory of a Journey,* 1951) and *Le Manteau de Pascal* (*Pascal's Coat,* 1954), depend upon a confident technique. His levitating loaves and apples and little bowler-hatted men would have no power to charm and startle us if they were not persuasively solid. The disturbing power of *Le Survivant* (which roiled a 1950 exhibition of paintings by members of the Belgian Communist Party, to which Magritte faithfully paid dues) lies not just in the blood but in the impassive correctness of the gun's detail and the obsessively rendered middle-class wallpaper, wainscoting, and wood-grained floorboards. The same deadpan fidelity to bourgeois décor creates the neoclassic dignity in *La Durée poignardée* (*Time Transfixed*, 1938), whose marmoreal fireplace is so memorably pierced by the emergence of a smoking locomotive instead of a stovepipe. The monstrous joke of the notorious *Le Viol* (*The Rape*, 1934)—another of his most famous images—enfolds into its *double entendre* a skillfully, even reverently rendered female nude.

In *Le Viol*, the doubling of the female pudenda as a furry mouth is certainly assaultive and prickly, a kind of fur teacup. The fur teacup remains the ultimate Surrealist object, the paradigm of Surrealism's procedures of aggravation and abrasive resistance to conventional expectation. *Les Amants* (*The Lovers*, 1928), in wrapping the kissing heads of lovers in white cloth, rubs disagreeably against the imagined sensation of a kiss— as well as awakening, in this era, sinister thoughts of hooded terrorists. Surrealist shock tactics remain effective and commercially viable; there is a contemporary television commercial, for a make of golf club, which shows flinty-looking rocks being addressed as if prior to being struck. Any golfer, to whom hitting rocks is the worst of sensations, finds his attention concentrated.

Yet such perversities lose their interest; having delivered its shock, the image has nothing left to tell us. Surrealism suffers the danger of any art of ideas: the delivery of the idea exhausts the content. The overturning of conventionality becomes as boring as conventionality. We give highest honors, in art, to the artists who widen our discourse with reality and who in their work give the impression of holding themselves open to the last minute to further impulses from nature. Cézanne and Vermeer, for instance, keep receiving messages—glints, tints—that modify and even override whatever intention they began with. Their canvases brim with being. The allegorical and sentimental content of Vermeer's canvases becomes the least of it, though it remains there; the formal intent gathers a halo of reality, of unsayable thingness. The artist as showman and preacher moves to the side of the stage, and his self-effacement leaves us with a work of art that is more than an argument, a defiance, or a more or less political proclamation. Even in abstract art we can feel this evolution; Pollock, for instance, is a more replete artist than Newman, and Mondrian than Malevich.

Les Jours gigantesques (*The Titanic Days*, 1928) is about rape, or attempted rape, and vividly illustrates the victim's struggle and fear. Yet Magritte's Surrealist trick, learned from his experiments in collage, of giving the rapist substance only within the victim's outline, creates an image of heated intimacy, in which the relations of victim and assailant are transformed into a metaphor for struggle within the self. It is inter-

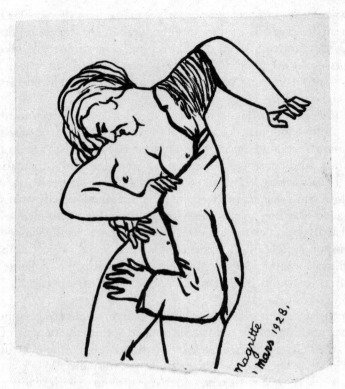

Magritte, L'Aube désarmée (*after* Les Jours gigantesques), *1928. Pen and brush.*

esting how his later revision of this powerful image, adding to the woman full-length, heavily Légeresque legs and to the surrounding space a rudimentary geometric logic, fatally weakens its suggestive power. The artist must tread delicately through our psyches to make a mark. The wonderfully comic and mysteriously consoling painting of the great green apple in a windowed room just big enough to hold it (*La Chambre d'écoute*, or *The Listening-Room*, 1958) fails, when the oversize object is a red rose (*Le Tombeau des lutteurs*, or *The Tomb of the Wrestlers*, 1960), to evoke much more than a corsage in its box. A number of Magritte's enigmatic signifiers—the slotted bells and the humanoid forms suggesting balustrade supports of turned wood—signify little to this viewer, and remain private clutter.

A striving toward an elemental idealism ran through Magritte's work, and strengthened toward the end. Late paintings like *Les Mémoires d'un saint* and *La Clef de verre* (*The Glass Key*), both from 1960, have the blue largeness of Romanticism, at the moment it discovered that mountains and ocean were sublime. That other traditional epitome of beauty, the female body, figures in Magritte's work from the start and achieves apotheosis in *La Folie des grandeurs* (*Megalomania*, 1967), the bronze-sculpture version of a telescopic conceit present in an oil of 1927, *L'Importance des merveilles* (*The Importance of Marvels*). Another large bronze of 1967, "*Madame Récamier*" *de David*, refers back to a painting of 1949; the homage to the most sternly neoclassic of French artists is both droll and sincere. The bent coffin is one of Magritte's simplest and most resonant images. Another, the floating loaf of bread, seen in *La Force des choses* (*Inevitably*, 1958), suggests a miracle of the Middle Ages; levitation has been ever a symbol of spiritual grace. Magritte has survived the stale furors of Surrealism by virtue of a humanism that transcends shock and scorn; there is a benign grandeur in his best work, and its surprises have the surprising effect of making the viewer feel good.

Jean Ipoustéguy, 1920–2006

A TRIBUTE published in *Le Transréaliste*, the bilingual newsletter of the Friends of Ipoustéguy, March 2007.

The work of Jean Ipoustéguy first struck me in the Sculpture Garden of the Hirshhorn Museum, in Washington, D.C. There, within sight of the great obelisk erected to the honor of George Washington and amid a host of modern outdoor sculptures from Rodin to David Smith, Ipoustéguy's vigorous male nude *Homme poussant la porte* (*Man Pushing the Door*, 1966), wearing the expressionless face of a doll or a robot, pushes two hands and part of a leg through a louvered door while on the other side of the door a dog's head nuzzles the hip of the man's partially flayed body. *What can this mean?* I asked myself—this solemnly comic "double take," this mixture of well-muscled human anatomy and straight-edged forms: the louvers, the doorposts, the blank disk in one of the man's hands. "*J'ai cassé l'oeuf de Brancusi,*" Ipoustéguy once said—"I broke Brancusi's egg." It is in one of the many witty self-explanations with which he has offered to clarify sculpture that remains resolutely and aloofly yet energetically enigmatic.

In a single work, passages of an Ipoustéguy hark back to the physical realism exultantly explored by Renaissance and neoclassical masters, while other, closely juxtaposed passages look ahead to the simplifications

Jean Ipoustéguy, 1999

of modernism and, even, minimalism. A brilliant, provocative restlessness keeps us off balance as it flays, corrodes, and layers consummately representational figures. *La Femme au bain* (*Bathing Woman*, 1966), her long-legged body brought to a high burnish and nicely detailed from teeth and toes, comes with a hinged carapace that reveals, when lifted, nipples and navel and a beautiful belly. The copulating woman in *La Maison* (1976) wears a formalized, impassive mask hiding a head thrown back in orgasmic ecstasy.

"*Toute oeuvre vient du corps et y revient,*" he said—"All work comes from the body and returns there." Yet the organic is subject to the inorganic: he once described an aspect of his work as "*l'anatomie des hommes mêlée à une sorte d'environnement*" ("human anatomy mixed up with some kind of environment"). His mature sculpture is not Cubist, but it insists on what he called "*plusieurs points de l'espace à la fois*" ("many points in space simultaneously"). He works in the traditional materials of permanence—bronze, marble—but playfully imitates the textures of paper and the shape of fractures, seeking "*vivantes contradictions*" ("living contradictions"), improvising at the intersections of the inner and the outer, the architectural and the human, the fluid and the frozen, the multiple and the single. Further subverting the illusion of stable volume, his later work became more and more linear—drawing in the air with lines of inflexible metal.

Though he was awarded a major prize at the 1964 Venice Biennale and a number of prominent public commissions within France, Ipoustéguy is but lightly noted in surveys of modern art, and has received few exhibitions in the United States. His sculpture confounds, perhaps, with its restless complexity and its considerable, if obscure, narrative content. It seems "literary" when this is not a compliment. An Ipoustéguy sculpture would not self-effacingly adorn a luxurious modern apartment or serve, like a riveted and painted Calder stabile or a patiently rounded Henry Moore monolith, to ornament a peaceful outdoor space. An Ipoustéguy agitates; it demands second looks; it defies expectations. The art which found iconic favor in the second half of the twentieth century did not ask for a complex interaction; Brancusi's eggs, Pollock's evenly spattered canvases, the large abstract forms of Newman and Rothko, the machined boxes of minimalism all stun us into the silent suspension of thought with which we stand before colossal works of nature or human engineering. This art asserts rather than invites discourse. Ipoustéguy, a connoisseur of integuments, seeks to get under the viewer's skin, and to itch there. Alluding to a host of earlier sculptural styles—battered barbaric, Roman monumental, medieval devotional, medical-school *écorché*—he exploits a full range of techniques and methods, but all under the aspect of permanence. No fragile rope sculptures or temporary assemblages of bricks or plastic dolls for him. He belongs, if with conscious irony, to the grand tradition of sculpture, and sounds in that company a French note of hearty wit, of strenuous introspection.

I was enough struck by the two works at the Hirshhorn (the other is *David et Goliath*, of 1959) to do some research in Harvard's Fogg Museum Library and to compose an article on Ipoustéguy for my book of art essays *Just Looking* (1989). On the strength of that modest work of appreciation, I was invited to meet Ipoustéguy when he visited the United States some years later. The photographs of him that I had seen often showed him working bare-chested, like a Gallic Vulcan at his forge; he startled me by being short, though his frame was knotted with muscle. His English was as fragmentary as my French, and in any case I could only attempt to repeat phrases of admiration I had already expressed in print. But it was an encounter still impressed in my memory, and precious to my sense of art and who forms it. The origin of so much epic creative force was revealed as merely human in size. I am pleased to learn that, a year after his death at the age of eighty-six, a society of his admirers, Les Amis d'Ipoustéguy, has been founded to keep alive and to refine awareness of his intricate, spacious, and unique achievement.

PHOTOGRAPHERS

Visual Trophies

THE ART OF THE AMERICAN SNAPSHOT, 1888–1978: *From the Collection of Robert E. Jackson*, by Sarah Greenough and Diane Waggoner with Sarah Kennel and Matthew S. Witkovsky. 294 pp. National Gallery of Art / Princeton University Press, 2007.

Among the homely staples of twentieth-century life that have been unceremoniously retired by the microchip revolution—the typewriter, the pressed-wax record, the card catalogue—the camera loaded with film has met a swift and stealthy end. Digital cameras look much like their analogue predecessors, but the viewfinder is different—a tiny TV screen, held at arm's length—and we don't have to wait for the mistakes to come back from the drugstore before discarding them. We didn't, in fact, often discard silver-based snapshots, but kept them, with their negatives, in boxes and drawers to await a definitive culling that rarely came. They began to slide into obsolescence before the turn of this century, and had already become "collectibles," with a fellowship of collectors and dealers feeding on the shoals of these silverfish as they raggedly rose from the depths of the private realm to surface in the marketplace. One prominent collector, Robert E. Jackson, of Seattle, struck up a relationship with the National Gallery of Art, in Washington, D.C., that has resulted in his donation of 138 snapshots to the institution and an exhibition, titled *The Art of the American Snapshot, 1888–1978*. The exhibition, which runs through the end of the year, includes 254 items, all from Jackson's gift or his collection, and is commemorated with a 294-page catalogue of the same name.

The volume defies easy handling—it is heavier than one expects, and wordier—and an easy aesthetic response. The brief foreword, by the

National Gallery's director, Earl A. Powell III, poses the critical problem nicely:

> In the years since 1888, when George Eastman and others made it possible for anyone to make a photograph, billions of snapshots have been made in this country alone. Most of them poignantly remind their makers of a person, place, or event with special meaning or importance to their lives.

My own shoeboxes of curling, yellowing snapshots derive their fascination almost entirely from my personal connections with the depicted matter—grandparents and parents, cousins and schoolmates, houses I once lived in, vistas and furniture lifted from my private *temps perdu*. The fascination extends to snapshots of my father in his First World War soldier's uniform and my mother in her college hockey outfit, youthful and hopeful in the void before I was born, but thins with snapshots *they* saved of people I never knew, and reaches the vanishing point in stiff studio portraits, not snapshots at all, of ancestors to whom no narrative has been attached. A little halo of photographic illumination, in other words, accompanies us in our traversal of the decades, and any aesthetic or sociological values that the photographs possess are incidental. With a poignance peculiar to photographic images, the past is captured while its obliteration is strongly implied. Susan Sontag wrote in the first of the brilliant essays collected in her book *On Photography* (1977):

> All photographs are *memento mori*. To take a photograph is to participate in another person's (or thing's) mortality, vulnerability, mutability. Precisely by slicing out this moment and freezing it, all photographs testify to time's relentless melt. . . . A photograph is both a pseudo-presence and a token of absence.

Without a felt connection to one's own mortal course through a lifetime of circumstance, snapshots become baffling and boring, their "qualities and intentions," as Sontag says, "swallowed up in the generalized pathos of time past." The generalized pathos, however, needs less than a multitude of illustrations. Most amateur snapshots fall short of being either art or news. An album by a professional art photographer, such as Richard Kalvar's recent *Earthlings*, has us studying each page for the joke or trick or shock—the news—in each elegantly composed example, selected from sheaves of less happy exposures and reproduced large enough for every detail to tell. The prints in *The Art of the American Snapshot* are reproduced at their actual modest size, with lots of blazingly white space, and have taken their riddles into oblivion with their anonymous creators. Is the baby, for instance, lying on an open packed suitcase,

apparently asleep, alive or dead? What impulse led someone, probably not the photographer, to scribble a ballpoint dress over a man in bathing trunks and pen the words "Hey Big Boy, come up & see me some time!"? What is the woman standing in a field and covering her face with her shapely hands while being photographed trying to tell us? Is she peeking at the photographer (and at us) through her fingers? Is she being coy or grief-stricken? The image is arresting enough to use on the book's dust jacket, but its peculiar agonized playfulness hangs enigmatically in the general pathos of lost time.

Such images may baffle interpretation, but they do not repel commentary. Four National Gallery curators write at some length on four periods of snapshot-taking: "Photographic Amusements, 1888–1919," "Quick, Casual, Modern, 1920–1939," "Fun Under the Shade of the Mushroom Cloud, 1940–1959," and "When the Earth Was Square, 1960–1978." Diane Waggoner tackles the thirty-year era after George Eastman's promulgation of the first Kodak cameras: "They had a string mechanism to cock the shutter and a button to release it, and they made exposures at a shutter speed of 1/25 second." The significant novelty wasn't in the construction of the camera but in that of the film. Eastman had founded a company in Rochester to mass-produce gelatin dry-plate glass negatives, and after a few years he did away with the glass, inventing paper negatives that spooled onto a roll holder that fit into a standard plate camera. After a few more years, he launched a hand camera preloaded with paper negatives; he named the camera Kodak, "coining the name because it was unique and could not be mispronounced." These early Kodaks produced

round images, two and a half inches in diameter, which were developed and printed in the Rochester factory; the customer sent in the entire camera, which was returned to him, loaded with new film, along with the prints from the old, all for the not inconsiderable fee of ten dollars. "You press the button, we do the rest," was the captivating slogan.

The Eastman Kodak Company proved as prolific of slogans as of technical innovations. Within a year, the complicated transfer of emulsion to a glass plate and then to a thin, flexible gelatin support had been simplified to a one-step negative on transparent film of cellulose nitrate. Within two years, a folding camera had been introduced, with a viewfinder, characterized in its early state as a "dimly lit one-inch square." Refinement followed refinement, and slogan followed slogan: "Kodak as you go"; "A vacation without a Kodak is a vacation wasted." By 1900, when the first Brownie was marketed for one dollar, with rolls of film at fifteen cents apiece, America was hooked. More than 150,000 Brownies were sold in the first year.

The early users were a methodical, tricksome lot; they compiled careful albums and took elaborately posed pictures, with mirrors, intentional double exposures, and *trompe-l'oeil* feats of perspectival foolery. The spiritualism and stage theatricality of the time were echoed in tableaux vivants, eerie masks, ghostly illusions, and fancy costumes, including some jaunty cross-dressing. Summer vacations and snowstorms were snapped up as especially worth preserving. A steadying tripod and judicious use of magnesium-based flash powder enabled indoor shots. The shutter speed was still slow enough to blur action, though by 1909 Kodak

had introduced Speed Kodak film, with exposure times as fast as a thousandth of a second. America was speeding up; Waggoner writes, "When middle-class America increasingly enjoyed time at play and time on the go, the camera went along for the ride—quite literally, as cameras designed to hang on the bicycle were sold for convenience of travel." The camera and the bicycle both generated, in this clubbable era, organizations for their group enjoyment, as did the automobile in the early decades of the twentieth century. When soldiers went off to the First World War, Eastman ads offered this advice to loved ones: "The parting gift, a Kodak. Wherever he goes the world over, he will find Kodak film to fit his Kodak." Even in the trenches, over there.

In 1922, Sarah Kennel tells us in treating the years 1920–39, the poet Vachel Lindsay wrote that "the acres of photographs in the Sunday newspapers make us into a hieroglyphic civilization far nearer to Egypt than to England." Though increasingly commonplace and versatile—"quick, casual, modern"—the camera still found employment as a faddish toy; the booklet *Picture Taking at Night* instructed readers how to create silhouettes with backlit models. Trickery with shadows and with perspective figures in a number of the shots that have made their way into *The Art of the American Snapshot*. Stop-action dives and acrobatics take us back to a more muscular, outdoorsy America; there are two discreetly non-frontal views of skinny-dippers. A number of racy exposures hint at the camera's significant role as a de-inhibitor, an enabler of what Kennel calls "home-grown pornography." Nudes in provocative poses were among the earliest fruits of big-box, slow-tech photography in the mid-nineteenth century; something about the camera's impassive appropriation of what-

ever is set before it invites, like a psychoanalyst's silence, self-exposure. Another new work on photographic folk art, Näkki Goranin's *American Photobooth*, relates how, beginning in the 1950s:

> Complaints started coming in, from Woolworth's and other stores, that people, particularly women, were stripping off their clothes for the private photobooth camera. Couples started being a little more adventurous in the privacy of the curtained booth. As a result, many of the Woolworth's stores had to remove their curtains to discourage naughty encounters.

It is good times, happy times, that we wish to preserve. In its ads of the Twenties and Thirties, Kodak insistently pushed its product as the recorder of family life. "I'll show 'em a *real* family!" one jubilant snap-shooter brags ("He's something to brag about, that new baby of yours"); another spread shows two commuters on a railroad platform, one of them enviously studying the other's snapshots and thinking, "I felt ashamed. *He* was so proud of *his* children; why hadn't I taken snapshots of *mine*?" A third ad simply advises, while a proficient mother photographs her two children in their lunch booth, "Let Kodak keep the story." The camera both exalted and invaded domestic privacy—"Candid photography is making us human goldfish," one pundit wrote in the journal *Photography* in 1938. Letting Kodak keep the story constituted one more formerly human operation delegated to machines; our anniversaries and children's birthdays were remembered for us, in caches of snapshots. A vacation became a string of photo ops, a mechanical escape from what one writer, in 1928, called "the circumscribed routine of factory, store, or office." At many a wedding, the hired photographer replaced the minister as the central officiator.

Sarah Greenough deals with the years 1940–59, under the rather frantic head "Fun Under the Shade of the Mushroom Cloud." By 1940, flashbulbs, the color film Kodachrome and Agfacolor-Neu, and the superb Leica camera, using 35-millimeter film, had been invented. Increasingly cheap and handy color film followed. In 1948, the Polaroid Corporation offered the Land Camera, which made black-and-white prints in sixty seconds, thus cutting out the local developer and making snapshot-taking more private than ever. But perhaps these innovations, and ever more automatic features relieving the photographer of control over focus and exposure time, made amateur photography too easy, for there is a discernible falling-off of artistic energy in the post-war snapshots exhibited. Except for a joyous nude of a fat girl with her eyes shut in an ecstasy of embarrassment, and a stunning pair of tan legs that are, Greenough tells us, a man's, and a scrawny Arbusian Christmas tree in a corner, and some few others, the photos tend to look like television—fuzzy slices of life, cut with a dull knife. This section is the only one that presents a named photographer, a young Midwestern woman identified as Flo; she lived at a Milwaukee YWCA and snapped shots of the other young women living there, none of whom, from the evidence, wanted to be photographed. Greenough tells us, as we can see, "They covered their faces with their hands or magazines; they turned and walked away or closed their doors in her face; they stuck their tongues out at her unwelcome intrusions." Flo's photographs, of which thirty-two, usually flash-lit, examples are included in the catalogue, rarely peek outdoors; their invariably female subjects, caught doing dishes or washing their hair, seem to nervously inhabit a flimsy bomb shelter. Greenough gamely theorizes:

> From our own experiences, we instinctively know when viewing snapshots like these that they, unlike many carefully crafted works of art or fully articulated documents, possess a kind of truth that is both profound and unassailable. But what that truth is precisely remains forever unknown.

Fifties existentialism, which also gave us the deadpan facticity of the *nouveau roman* and, in cinema, the *nouvelle vague*, gives us the dogged dreariness of Flo's unknown, though profound and unassailable, truth. The camera has acquired a will of its own, blindly recording unwilling subjects like a robotized vacuum cleaner nosing into every corner of the room.

Matthew S. Witkovsky, taking up the years 1960–78, heaves the most ornate critical language into the bottomless pit of the ordinary. He claims that the square shape favored by Brownies and Polaroids "supplants narrative flow with iconic stasis, and it tends to draw attention away from the picture toward the object as such." He mischievously proposes that "making one's own pictures in these years might be said for the first time to match in its breadth and banality the daily experience of seeing pictures by others." Public and private achieve a null parity. Photographs of children, common in every era, "reveal a perhaps unaccustomed level of nonchalance that separates them from earlier family snapshots and potentially from those made more recently as well"; several show children in perilous situations and suggest "a remarkable, even disconcerting privileging of humor over safety." The week's funniest, most brutal videos are around the corner. Over all, Witkovsky decrees, "many of these pictures seem insistently mundane and emotionally awkward"; the vulgar or obscene gestures in a number of them "might be interpreted as a sign of increasing social recklessness, part of 'sixties culture,' its echoes and aftermath." American mores and manners, in short, are going to pot, and Kodak is there to keep the story. Art photography, once distinctly aloof, with its sharp-focus nudes, mountains, and still lifes, from amateur snapshooting, now "takes a turn toward unremediated—and therefore highly provocative—banality" in the work of "avant-garde artists such as Acconci, John Baldessari, and Dan Graham, all of whom use photography (or so they claim) as a mute and inexpressive tool." Garry Winogrand photographed with a random lavishness that left thousands of undeveloped rolls at his death, "a snapshooter run amok." The determination "to drain formal interest, to de-skill the creative process, generates an aesthetic that many at the time called 'neutral' or 'affectless' but which seems more accurately described as somewhere between kitsch and tedium." Where Kodak set up shop to glorify the American family, a modern master like Diane Arbus makes it appear appalling.

The photographic impulse, as I experienced it in my days as a Nikon-toting daddy, wore two aspects, the creative and the commemorative. The first sought to catch, in the plump snap of the shutter, something vivid and even beautiful in its color and contour; the second aim, more realistic though in a sense grander, was to halt the flow of time. The camera, that highly evolved mechanism, put into Everyman's untrained hands the chance to become, if half by accident, a death-defying artist.

The collector Robert Jackson deserves the last shot; his afterword to the catalogue manages to cast a pall of reasonableness over his curious passion. He coins the phrase "a visual trophy" for a medium that "seeks to preserve an idealized and individualized moment in time." Attempting to explain the collector's motives, he claims, "It is the anonymous snapshot's immediacy, inherent honesty, and unstudied freedom from external influence that are the draw. . . . The personal can therefore become impersonal." Ah, but, then again, "a collector can have a subjective interest in a snapshot's narrative content as a surrogate for life experiences. Thus the personal remains personal, if you will." Like novels and scandal sheets, snapshots are windows, however smeary, into other lives. Jackson goes on to name, in four broad columns of print, 107 dealers, fellow-collectors, and flea-market merchandisers who assisted his macabre traffic in silver-based shadows. For those who care, he confides that a leading bazaar for these souvenirs of the pre-digital age is eBay.

Aftermaths

NEW ORLEANS AFTER THE FLOOD: *Photographs by Robert Polidori*, at the Metropolitan Museum of Art, New York, September 19–December 10, 2006.

AFTER THE FLOOD, by Robert Polidori, with an introduction by Jeff L. Rosenheim. 333 pp. Steidl, 2006.

AFTERMATH, by Joel Meyerowitz. 349 pp. Phaidon, 2006.

Twenty-four chromogenic prints each measuring three by five feet: the exhibition begins with six of them in the Metropolitan's Tisch Galleries, the long upstairs corridor customarily devoted to etchings, drawings, and photographs, and continues, after two left turns, in the modest spaces of the Howard Gilman Gallery. The show concerns the aftermath of Hurricane Katrina's ruinous pass over New Orleans on August 29, 2005, as recorded by the distinguished architectural photographer Robert Polidori in four visits between September 2005 and April 2006; it is being attended, to judge from the day this viewer was present, by more youthful African-Americans than usually make their way into the Met. Katrina, as the disaster is called for short, was a black disaster, exposing the black poverty that, dwelling in the low-lying areas of the metropolis, stayed out of the view of the tourists who flocked to Bourbon Street for a taste of Cajun cuisine and old-fashioned jazz, or who admired the fluted columns and iron lace of the gently moldering Garden District, or who were unthriftily prepared to *laisser le bon temps rouler* at Mardi Gras or the Super Bowl. Good times were what the city had to sell, trading on its racy past as a Francophone southern port. Founded in 1718, it flirted from the start with sea level, as the surging Mississippi and Lake Pontchartrain hung over its shoulder; like Los Angeles on its fault line, and New York City in its congestion, it borrowed glamour from a hypothetical precariousness. Not merely hypothetical, Katrina proved: 160,000 homes were swamped, and, to quote Jeff L. Rosenheim's succinct introduction to Polidori's massive album *After the Flood*, "street after street, block after block, from Chalmette and New Orleans East to the Lower Ninth Ward, Lakeview, Metairie, and Gentilly (where Polidori lived as a teenager)," added up to "widespread urban ruin" and "community disintegration." Many thousands of the displaced have still not returned; an estimated two hundred thousand never will. A major American city was depopulated with a suddenness and thoroughness war itself could not top.

The event was mostly just news, like tornadoes in Kansas and mudslides near Malibu, to the rest of us; Polidori's big prints take us there with a lofty dispassion and even focus. Eerily, no human beings are present in the photographs, so they have the uncanny stillness of Piranesi *carceri*, of Richard Estes's glittering cityscapes, of Egyptian tombs unsealed after millennia.* The circumstances in which these impassive exposures were made were not studio-ideal; there was no electricity in most of the interiors, and, to quote Rosenheim again:

> When Polidori arrived in New Orleans on September 20 . . . 80% of the city was still under water. The temperature was close to 90° F and the smell of rotting flesh and food was putrid. Downed electric cables draped the streets and sidewalks. Toppled live oaks lay like fallen colossi, except there was no grandeur to the scene, just despair. Most traffic lights and streetlamps had long stopped working, and exhausted relief crews were still discovering and collecting the dead.

But Polidori, with the same devotion that led him to explore the abandoned and radioactive apartments, schoolrooms, hospitals, machinery, and nuclear-power facilities around Chernobyl (*Zones of Exclusion: Pripyat and Chernobyl*, published by Steidl in 2003), persisted, employing in some electricity-less interiors film exposures that ran into the minutes. In the haunting Chernobyl book, he wrote in a terse afterword, "I felt personally compelled to confront and witness this ongoing tragedy that no ritual can heal." In New Orleans, he dealt not with invisible radioac-

---

*Two exceptions: one photograph, *Deslondes Street, September*, contains a pink coathanger that slipped slightly during the exposure, leaving a small blur, and another, *2606 St. Peter Street*, shows, if I read it right, the top of the white-haired head of a blanket-swaddled corpse.

Polidori, 5417 Marigny Street, 2006. Chromogenic print.

tivity but with a city like, he has said in an interview, "a decomposing body"; photographs taken six months after the hurricane still show scant signs of cleanup, reclamation, and recovery.

The first photograph in the show, *Industrial Canal Breach, Reynes Street*, presents, under a powder-blue September sky, water flowing between banks of washed-up lumber, insulation, and overturned automobiles. Automobiles, those stolid American necessities, turn out to be susceptible and rather comically buoyant in a flood; the second photo, *2600 Block of Munster Boulevard*, captures two of them with their rear ends elevated, like a pair of saucy chorus girls, in a row of brick bungalows. In the full tide of Polidori's 333-page album *After the Flood*, ruined automobiles—upended, overturned, mud-filled, pinched beneath buildings, caught up on fences, buried beneath lumber and sea straw, mashed in mock copulation one against another—are as prominent as fallen trees and skewed ranch houses separated from their cement-block foundations. *2732 Orleans Avenue*, the jacket photo of the album, shows an intact white coupe parked at an angle before an exiguous but apparently unharmed two-family house; the subtle message of the picture, clearer in the blowup at the Met, lies in the horizontal lines of dirt on the car's chassis, marking the gradual recession of the waters.

Arresting though the outdoor photos are, with their silent testimony to

Polidori, 6328 North Miro Street, *2006. Chromogenic print.*

a catastrophe that swept through humble neighborhoods accustomed to being ignored, it is the wrecked, mildewed interiors that take our eye and quicken our anxiety. Would our own dwelling quarters look so pathetic, so obscenely reflective of intimate needs inadequately met, if they were similarly violated and exposed? The third photograph in the Tisch Galleries, *6328 North Miro Street,* brings the viewer shockingly close to a four-poster bed sagging beneath a dark weight of dried and crackled mud; carved pineapples blandly stand watch at the head of the posts, a chunky cabinet of some sort has been tossed by the evaporated flood into a corner, and lace curtains admit daylight between yellow curtains that have bent their valence under a weight of water. *5417 Marigny Street* displays a gruesomely stained and still-soggy-looking orange sofa holding a lamp, TV table, and gaudy throw pillows amid a surrounding clutter that includes a vacuum cleaner, a broom, a baseball cap, a TV set. On the mold-spotted wall a small sign distinctly promotes SOUTHERN COMFORT. Another enlarged interior, more *moderne* in its furnishings, *1401 Pressburg Street,* suffers terminal dishevelment for all the aspiration of its crisp blue walls and blue Barcalounger, its boxy sofa and arctic landscape painting, its brass floor-to-ceiling lamp whose three cylindrical shades are wrapped in primary colors, and its little framed text headed DON'T QUIT. Another interior on display, *5000 Cartier Avenue,* might have been a rumpus room or studio, with tangerine walls, a tiled floor, an electric organ, a piano on its back, an exercise bike, a utilitarian oak table, a framed motto of which the word BLESS is legible; on view are formal photos of three black children, and, most conspicuously, as if propped up by a returning inhabitant, of a young black woman wearing a military uniform, with service ribbons.

For many of us gallerygoers, this is as close as we will ever get to the insides of ordinary African-American homes—their touches of sometimes garish comfort gone, as Mark Twain wrote of the wreck of a raft, "all to smash and scatteration." First the muddy waters let loose by broken levees invaded these rooms, then the police and military units searching for dead bodies and marooned pets, then Robert Polidori and his voracious camera, and now our fascinated, sociologically prurient gaze. The exhibition and the far greater selection bound into *After the Flood* call to mind two of the tenets of Susan Sontag's book of essays *On Photography:* "There is an aggression implicit in every use of the camera," and "the camera makes everyone a tourist in other people's reality, and eventually in one's own." From this second observation she argued that photography as an art is intrinsically surreal, presenting us with reality not as filtered through the humanity of a painter or wordsmith but as captured by an emotionless, thoughtless mechanism, in a moment of time that instantly begins to recede. "What renders a photograph surreal is its irrefutable pathos as a message from time past, and the concreteness of its intimations about social class." The class intimations of these images are plain enough, though Polidori in his exhaustive effort of preservation did not scruple to include upper-end or highland stretches—Canal Street, say, with its two-storied, sometimes stuccoed domiciles set back on lawns, including a pert example of old-fashioned flat-roofed, parallelepiped-pure modernism, with Art Deco stripes and a little penthouse. The occupants of such homes, surely, if they came to New York might not be beyond a visit to the Metropolitan Museum of Art, where they would find themselves surreally represented. Even the bleakest of the shelters that caught the photographer's attention—the single-story shack on Tupelo Street, for instance, a missing wall baring a bright closetful of abandoned clothes; or the wrecked salmon-colored cabin at Law and Tupelo streets; or the grimly simple bedroom on presciently named Flood Street, with its careening mattress and ceiling fan wilted like a Dalí timepiece—hold bits of decorative art and vibrations of life, cut off as suddenly as occupancies at Pompeii.

There are signs that residents of the flood zone sought to defend themselves from oppressive attention. Visible in *1728 Deslondes Street*, a neatly lettered sign in the fender of an upside-down sedan proclaims "Tourism HERE is Profane!" At 1498 Filmore Avenue, a game local contractor made a rhyming joke, advertising his willingness to undertake "Tree Cutting and House Gutting." Polidori's book has a rough order to it: it progresses from shots of still-present floodwater to the extensive, picturesque property damage inside and out, and then to indications of cleanup climaxed by several shots (*6409 Louis XIV Street, 6525 Wuerpel Street, 539 Rocheblave Street*) of interiors stripped of plaster and ruined furniture, getting ready to be rebuilt and inhabited, while pristine temporary trailers at last appear, courtesy of a sluggish government. The photographs of the cleanup stage, however, are among the most dismaying. Heaped onto the street and sidewalk are tons of the flimsy stuff of American housing—fiberglass insulation like poisonous cotton candy; sheets of warped plywood; mock-pine pressed sheathing; pulverized plasterboard; aluminum siding splayed like palm fronds as houses floated and twisted; strips of metal and molding; plastic-covered shelves and countertops; shower curtains and mattresses, downspouts and lawnmowers, air conditioners and refrigerators mired in a state of eternal paralysis. Catastrophe feeds the dump. Short-cut American construction, from wigwams to balloon frames, welcomes the easy transition to trash. The very idea of shelter, *our* shelter, feels threatened and mocked as we contemplate Polidori's tireless panorama of automobiles dropped here and there like the playthings of a tired child at the end of the day and of wooden houses that, resting without basements on already saturated soil, took off at the first tug of floodwater.

Polidori, his work makes clear, loves the grave, delicate, and poignant beauty of architecture when the distracting presence of human inhabitants is eliminated from photographs. The bleak utilitarian works of Chernobyl and its associated workers' town of Pripyat, vacated by an explosion of radioactivity, formed an ideally drastic subject, its commemoration self-evidently justified by the admonition the images project, not just to shoddy Soviet management but to all guardians of the nuclear genie. His *Moods of La Habana*, published in Hamburg in 2003 to accompany four CDs of Cuban music, shows a pastel Havana emptied of the capitalist wealth that would sustain its elegant buildings. The Cubans, generally smiling and clothed in light tropical style, who are visible amid the moldering, flaking old architecture, seem amiable ghosts, as politically innocent as the bulbous, expansively oversized Fifties models of American cars that are patched up and kept running for lack of alternatives. The message, if any, is muted; the iron grates and graceful archways and fading façades and crumbling Beaux Arts cornices exist in a gentle limbo, an economic miasma suggested by the misty look of photographic reproduction on relatively inexpensive, non-glossy paper.

But *After the Flood* is an opulent volume, brilliantly sharp in its large, ten-by-fourteen-inch reproductions, bound in lavender cloth, and difficult to manipulate anywhere but on a coffee table. It weighs nearly ten pounds and costs ninety dollars; a consumeristic paradox hovers over the existence of so costly a volume portraying the reduction of a mostly poor urban area—"the funky urban environment that gave birth to jazz," a wall legend has it—to a state of desertion and deeper destitution. Who is this book for? Not the flood's victims, who could not afford it. Nor, one suspects, very many well-heeled connoisseurs of fine photography, though there is an abstract beauty in Polidori's close-focus studies of patterns of mold and paint distress, and an occasional Pop humor in the tinselly shoes and glitzy wall decorations the victims left behind them as the floodwaters rose, and a macabre Art Brut in shadowy rooms crowded with cheap furniture as tightly as passengers in a sinking ship.

As it happens, another enigmatically magnificent album of photographs is also on the market these days—*Aftermath*, by Joel Meyerowitz, an extensive, big-format pictorial record of the cleanup of the World Trade Center site. On September 23, 2001, Meyerowitz, wearing his worker's badge, began to photograph the gigantic tangle left behind by the attack on September 11 and the myriad workers who carried out the daunting and dangerous task of clearing the site. Adrian Benepe, the Manhattan Borough commissioner for parks and recreation and the son of a friend of Meyerowitz's, cleared the bureaucratic hurdles balking the photographer's desire to document progress with a large-format wooden view camera. The engineers, policemen, civil servants, and construction men on the site were already, in an age when photographs verify reality, taking surreptitious snapshots. When Meyerowitz, his status still uncertain despite his badge, explained his presence to a group of NYPD Arson and Explosion Squad detectives, one immediately said, "Yeah, we need this history, for our children and our grandchildren."

The formulation is about as a good as any we will get. It is for our children and our grandchildren—for the historical record—that Meyerowitz and Polidori zealously labored over many months to capture on film (a phrase the digital camera may soon render archaic) the aftermaths of the two most spectacular disasters on American soil in this young century. This is what it looked like; this is what we don't want to happen again. Since the Brady studio photographed the aftermath of Civil War battles, war has worn a new, less acceptable face. Photography, Sontag pointed out, is naturally drawn to misfortune and the unfortunate; in some cases, such as Jacob Riis's photos of New York slums and Lewis Hine's of child laborers, a public reaction effected some reform. The bourgeoisie must be continually discomfited. If the discomfort that *After the Flood* and *Aftermath* arouse contains an increment of discomfort at the poshness of the volumes and the aura of glamorous selflessness bestowed upon the photographers and their photographic appropriations, the record is indeed enhanced, for posterity to consult, and to use in ways we cannot imagine.

Pet Topics

THE UNIVERSE

The Valiant Swabian

WHEN YOUTHFUL AND FRISKY, Albert Einstein would refer to himself as "the valiant Swabian," quoting the poem by Ludwig Uhland: "But the valiant Swabian is not afraid." Albert—the name "Abraham" had been considered by his unreligious parents but was rejected as "too Jewish"— was born in Ulm, in March 1879, not long after Swabia joined the new German Reich; he was the first child and only son of a mathematics-minded but financially inept father and a strong-willed, musically gifted woman of some inherited means. A daughter, Maria, was born to the couple two and a half years later; when shown his infant sister, Albert took a look and said, "Yes, but where are the wheels?" Though this showed an investigative turn of mind, the boy was slow to talk, and the family maid dubbed him *der Depperte*—"the dopey one."

As the boy progressed through the schools of Munich, where his father had found employment in his brother Jakob's gas-and-electrical-supply company, Albert's teachers, though giving him generally high marks, noted his resistance to authority and Germanic discipline, even in its milder Bavarian form. As early as the age of four or five, while sick in bed, he had had a revelatory encounter with the invisible forces of nature: his father brought him a compass, and, as he later remembered it, he was so excited as he examined it that he trembled and grew cold. The child drew the momentous conclusion that "something deeply hidden had to be behind things." That intimation was to carry him to some of the greatest scientific discoveries of the twentieth century, and to a subsequent persistent but unsuccessful search for a theory that would unite all the known laws of nature, and to a global fame impossible to imagine befalling any mere intellectual now.

Walter Isaacson's thorough, comprehensive, affectionate biography of

Einstein* relates how, in 1931, during the fifty-one-year-old scientist's second visit to America, he and his second wife, Elsa, attended, in California, a séance at the home of Mr. and Mrs. Upton Sinclair. He must have allowed a little skepticism to creep into his polite conversation, for "Mrs. Sinclair challenged his views on science and spirituality." His own wife overheard and indignantly intervened, telling their hostess, "You know, my husband has the greatest mind in the world." Mrs. Sinclair didn't dispute the assertion, replying, "Yes, I know, but surely he doesn't know everything." On the same excursion, Einstein, at his own request, met Charlie Chaplin, who, as they arrived at the première of *City Lights*, said, of the applauding public, "They cheer me because they all understand me, and they cheer you because no one understands you."

In 1905, Einstein, a twenty-six-year-old patent clerk in Bern, Switzerland, had produced in rapid succession five scientific papers that (a) proposed that light came not just in waves but in indivisible, discrete packets of energy or particles called, after Max Planck's discovery, quanta; (b) calculated how many water molecules existed in 22.4 liters (a number so vast that, Isaacson tells us, "that many unpopped popcorn kernels when spread across the United States would cover the country nine miles deep"); (c) explained Brownian motion as the jostling of motes of matter by invisible molecules; (d) expounded the special theory of relativity, holding that all measurable motion is relative to some other object and that no universal coördinates, and no hypothetical ubiquitous ether, exist; and (e) asserted that mass and energy were different manifestations of the same thing and that their relation could be tidily expressed in the equation $E = mc^2$, where c is the speed of light, a constant. Only a few friends and theoretical physicists took notice.

In 1903, Einstein had married a woman three years older than he, Mileva Marić, a lame, homely Serbian he had met when both were students at the Zurich Polytechnic. It emerged only in 1986 that before their marriage the couple became parents of a girl, Lieserl, whom Einstein probably never saw and whose fate is unknown. A legitimate son, Hans Albert, was born in 1904. Einstein had not been able to secure any teaching job; his cavalier and even defiant attitude toward academic authority worked against his early signs of promise. He had left Germany and renounced his citizenship at the age of sixteen, and for four years was too poor to buy Swiss citizenship, depending for sustenance on a monthly stipend from his mother's family and some fees from private tutorials. In the pinch,

---

Einstein: His Life and Universe (Simon & Schuster, 2007).

Marcel Grossmann, a brilliant math student whose meticulous lecture notes helped Einstein get high grades at the Zurich Polytechnic, managed to secure him a job at the Swiss Patent Office, in Bern. His long stint there figures, in the conventional Einstein mythology, as the absurd ordeal of a neglected genius, but Isaacson thinks it might have been a good thing:

> So it was that Albert Einstein would end up spending the most creative seven years of his life—even after he had written the papers that reoriented physics—arriving at work at 8 a.m., six days a week, and examining patent applications. . . . Yet it would be wrong to think that poring over applications for patents was drudgery. . . . Every day, he would do thought experiments based on theoretical premises, sniffing out the underlying realities. Focusing on real-life questions, he later said, "stimulated me to see the physical ramifications of theoretical concepts."

"Had he been consigned instead to the job of an assistant to a professor," Isaacson points out, "he might have felt compelled to churn out safe publications and be overly cautious in challenging accepted notions." Special relativity has a flavor of the patent office; one of the theory's charms for the fascinated public was the practical apparatus of its exposition, involving down-to-earth images like passing trains equipped with reflecting mirrors on their ceilings, and measuring rods that magically shrink with speed from the standpoint of a stationary observer, and clocks that slow as they accelerate—counterintuitive effects graspable with little more math than plane geometry.

The general theory of relativity took longer, from 1907 to 1915, and came harder. Generalizing from the special theory's assumption of uniform velocity to cases of accelerated motion, and incorporating Newton's laws of gravity into a field theory that corrected his assumption of instant gravitational effect across any distance, led Einstein into advanced areas of mathematics where he felt at sea. He turned to his invaluable friend Marcel Grossmann, now chairman of the math department at the Zurich Polytechnic; Isaacson quotes him as saying, "Grossmann, you've got to help me or I will go crazy." After consulting the literature, Grossmann "recommended the non-Euclidean geometry that had been devised by Bernhard Riemann." Einstein, beginning with the insight that acceleration and gravity exert an equivalent force, worked for years to find the equations that would describe

1.) How a gravitational field acts on matter, telling it how to move;
2.) And in turn, how matter generates gravitational fields in spacetime, telling it how to curve.

"I have gained enormous respect for mathematics," he wrote a friend, "whose more subtle parts I considered until now, in my ignorance, as pure luxury!" For a time, he discarded Riemannian tensors, but eventually returned to them, and, to quote Isaacson, "in the throes of one of the most concentrated frenzies of scientific creativity in history," he felt close enough to the solution to schedule four Thursday lectures at the Prussian Academy, in Berlin, which would unveil his "triumphant revision of Newton's universe." Then, heightening the suspense, another player entered the game. Einstein, still a little short of the full solution and beset with nervous stomach pains, showed one of his lectures to David Hilbert, "who was not only a better pure mathematician than Einstein, he also had the advantage of not being as good a physicist." Hilbert told Einstein that he was ready to lay out his own "axiomatic solution to your great problem," and the physicist battled to establish the priority of his theory even as he was putting the last, perfecting touches into his fourth and final lecture. It all came down to:

$$R_{\mu\nu} - \tfrac{1}{2}g_{\mu\nu}R = 8\pi T_{\mu\nu}$$

The other giants of physics in the first half of the twentieth century applauded. Paul Dirac called general relativity "probably the greatest scientific discovery ever made," and Max Born termed it "the greatest feat of human thinking about nature, the most amazing combination of philosophical penetration, physical intuition and mathematical skill." In 1919, the discovery was given empirical proof when Arthur Eddington, the director of the Cambridge Observatory, led an expedition to equatorial realms to observe a solar eclipse and see if, as Einstein's field equations predicted, stars near the sun's rim would be apparently displaced 1.7 arc seconds. With a little massaging from Eddington, they were. Einstein, asked what his reaction would have been if the experiment had shown his theory to be wrong, serenely replied, "Then I would have been sorry for the dear Lord; the theory is correct."

Though Einstein was to reap many honors (including the 1921 Nobel, belatedly, for his early work on the photoelectrical effect) and was to serve humanity as a genial icon and fount of humanist wisdom for three more decades, he never again made a significant contribution to the ongoing life of the physical sciences. Beginning around 1918, he devoted himself to a quest even more solitary and visionary than his relativity triumphs. "We seek," he said in his Nobel Prize lecture, "a mathematically unified field theory in which the gravitational field and the electromagnetic field are interpreted only as different components or manifestations of the same uniform field." Quantum theory, with its built-in uncertainties and paradoxes, struck him as a spooky violation of physical realism. "The more successes the quantum theory enjoys," he lamented to a friend in 1912, "the sillier it looks." In an autobiographical sketch published in 1949,* he described his frustrated attempts "to adapt the theoretical foundation of physics" to quantum science: "It was as if the ground had been pulled out from under us, with no firm foundation to be seen anywhere," leaving "an intermediate state of physics without a uniform basis for the whole, a state that—although unsatisfactory—is far from having been overcome."

His faith that a unified theory of all the fields exists went back to his childhood sense that "something deeply hidden had to be behind things," a something that would evince itself in an encompassing theory of elegant simplicity. Isaacson tells us: "On one of the many occasions when Einstein declared that God would not play dice, it was Bohr"—the physicist Niels Bohr—"who countered with the famous rejoinder: Einstein, stop telling God what to do!" God, sometimes identified as "the Almighty" or "the Old One" (*der Alte*), frequently cropped up in Einstein's utterances, although, after a brief period of "deep religiousness" at the age of twelve, he firmly distanced himself from organized religion. In a collection of statements published in English as *The World As I See It,*† he wrote:

> The scientist is possessed by the sense of universal causation. . . . His religious feeling takes the form of a rapturous amazement at the harmony of natural law, which reveals an intelligence of such superiority that, compared with it, all the systematic thinking and acting of human beings is an utterly insignificant reflection. This feeling is the guiding principle of his life and work, in so far as he succeeds in keeping himself from the shackles of selfish desire.

The apparition of a superior intelligence behind the impassive arrangements of nature was more than a playful metaphor for Einstein, and the escape from selfishness through scientific thought was a principle he lived. In composing, at the request of an editor, his "Autobiographical Notes," he concentrated almost exclusively on his thought processes, complete with equations.

* * *

---

*"Autobiographical Notes," in *Albert Einstein: Philosopher-Scientist*, edited and translated by Paul Arthur Schilpp (Library of Living Philosophers, 1949).
†"The Religiousness of Science," in *The World As I See It*, by Albert Einstein, edited and translated by Alan Harris (Bodley Head, 1935).

Yet things happened to him; he had a life. In 1909, the University of Zurich upped an initial offer, and Einstein, "four years after he had revolutionized physics," resigned from the patent office and accepted his first professorship. "So, now I too am an official member of the guild of whores," he told a colleague. In 1910, Mileva gave birth to a second son, Eduard, who as he grew older developed mental illness and was to end up in a Swiss asylum. In 1911, the Einsteins moved to Prague, where Einstein accepted a full professorship at the German part of the University of Prague. Offers kept coming; in 1912, he returned to the Zurich Polytechnic, which had become a full university, the Eidgenössische Technische Hochschule. Mileva should have been happy back in Zurich, among old friends, but her health was uncertain, carrying with it depression, and continued to decline. In 1913, an invitation was personally delivered by two pillars of Berlin's academic establishment, Max Planck and Walther Hermann Nernst, to come to Berlin as a university professor and the director of a new physics institute, and to become, at the age of thirty-four, the youngest member of the Prussian Academy. Einstein stayed in Berlin until 1932, when the combination of rising Nazism and tempting offers from America impelled him to leave Germany, never to return.

In America, Robert A. Millikan, a physicist whose experiments had verified Einstein's photoelectrical equation, was now the president of Caltech, and he aggressively courted Einstein to come to Pasadena. However, the educator Abraham Flexner, a former officer of the Rockefeller Foundation, was in the process of establishing, with funds from the Bamberger department-store fortune, a haven for scholars named the Institute for Advanced Study, to be situated in New Jersey, next to but not affiliated with Princeton University. Einstein, intending to split his time between Europe and America, accepted the Princeton proposal. He and Elsa moved there, and in 1935, after renting for a few years, they bought a modest frame house at 112 Mercer Street, where Einstein lived until his death, in 1955.

He and Mileva had divorced, after many difficulties, in March 1919. One of the attractions of Berlin in 1913 had been the presence of his divorced cousin Elsa Einstein. During the First World War, while Mileva stayed in Zurich with the two boys, Elsa and Einstein shared a life in Berlin—in his divorce deposition he gave the period of "intimate relations" as "about four and a half years." After some friction (Einstein wasn't sure that he wanted to be married at all, after the mental exertions of general relativity, but Elsa's respectable family wanted her reputation salvaged), he and Elsa married, in June 1919. In their "spacious and somberly furnished apartment near the center of Berlin," with her two daughters, he seemed, a colleague remarked, "a Bohemian as a guest in a bourgeois home." Elsa was shrewd but, unlike Mileva Marić, not scientific, which at his stage of life and eminence may have been a blessing. Einstein and women are a complicated story, and Isaacson doesn't attempt to tell it all. There were a number of extramarital relationships; how many of them tipped from companionship into sex is, like the electron, difficult to measure. (One startling fact, according to Isaacson: beginning in 1941, Einstein was sleeping with an alleged Soviet spy, the multilingual Margarita Konenkova, though the FBI, which was keeping close tabs on him, never twigged.)

Isaacson, a former managing editor of *Time*, whose previous biographies dealt with Benjamin Franklin and Henry Kissinger, writes in short paragraphs; taking up in rotation science and politics and personal developments, he has much material to compress. He notes that, at Elsa's untimely death, in 1936, "Einstein was hit harder than he might have expected," and pronounces on their marriage:

> Beneath the surface of many romances that evolve into partnerships, there is a depth not visible to outside observers. Elsa and Albert Einstein liked each other, understood each other, and perhaps most important (for she, too, was actually quite clever in her own way) were amused by each other. So even if it was not the stuff of poetry, the bond between them was a solid one.

Yet when Michele Besso, an old friend from his youth in Zurich, died, not long before Einstein's own death, he wrote to Besso's family that the deceased's most admirable trait had been to live harmoniously with a woman, "an undertaking in which I twice failed rather miserably." He was married to the universe, and gave back to people less love than he attracted. Max Born said, "For all his kindness, sociability and love of humanity, he was nevertheless totally detached from his environment and the human beings in it."

But he loved America, and America reciprocated. Its informality, optimism, and emphasis on free speech delighted him: "From what I have seen of Americans, I think that life would not be worth living to them without this freedom of self-expression." Except for a brief trip to Bermuda as part of his application for citizenship, he never left; he never returned to Europe, let alone to Germany, whose crimes, he wrote the chemist Otto Hahn, "are really the most abominable ever to be recorded in the history of the so-called civilized nations." To America, Isaacson says, he projected a "rumpled-genius image as famous as Chaplin['s] little tramp." As famous as Chaplin, he appeared, to Americans of my age, as saintly as Gandhi. Einstein's public political life—his initially reluctant but eventually committed Zionism, his initially militant but eventually modified pacifism, his wartime patriotism (including a sponsoring role in the creation of the atomic bomb), his scorn of McCarthyism, and his good humor and amiable wit in shouldering all the causes and interviews he was asked to shoulder—contributed to American morale in the challenging years between 1933 and 1955. Having the greatest mind in the world on the premises lifted American spirits. In his own freedom of thought, the valiant Swabian demonstrated how to be free.

Visions of Mars

MARS has long exerted a pull on the human imagination. The erratically moving red star in the sky was seen as sinister or violent by the ancients: the Greeks identified it with Ares, the god of war; the Babylonians named it after Nergal, god of the underworld. To the ancient Chinese, it was Ying-huo, the fire planet. Even after Copernicus proposed, in 1543, that the sun and not the earth was the center of the local cosmos, the eccentricity of Mars's celestial motions continued as a puzzle until, in 1609, Johannes Kepler analyzed all the planetary orbits as ellipses, with the sun at one focus.

In that same year, Galileo first observed Mars through a telescope. By the mid-seventeenth century, telescopes had improved enough to make visible the seasonally growing and shrinking polar ice caps on Mars, and features such as Syrtis Major, a dark patch thought to be a shallow sea. The Italian astronomer Giovanni Cassini was able to observe certain features accurately enough to calculate the planet's rotation. The Martian day, he concluded, was forty minutes longer than our twenty-four hours; he was only three minutes off. While Venus, a closer and larger planetary neighbor, presented an impenetrable cloud cover, Mars showed a surface enough like Earth's to invite speculation about its habitation by life forms.

Increasingly refined telescopes, challenged by the blurring effect of our own planet's thick and dynamic atmosphere, made possible ever more detailed maps of Mars, specifying seas and even marshes where seasonal variations in presumed vegetation came and went with the fluctuating ice caps. One of the keenest-eyed cartographers of the planet was Giovanni

---

Written for *National Geographic*, December 2008.

Schiaparelli, who employed the Italian word *canali* for perceived linear connections between presumed bodies of water. The word could have been translated as "channels," but "canals" caught the imagination of the public and in particular that of Percival Lowell, a rich Boston Brahmin who in 1893 took up the cause of the canals as artifacts of a Martian civilization. As an astronomer, Lowell was an amateur and an enthusiast but not a crank. He built his own observatory on a mesa near Flagstaff, Arizona, more than seven thousand feet high and, in his own words, "far from the smoke of men"; his drawings of Mars were regarded as superior to Schiaparelli's even by astronomers hostile to the Bostonian's theories. Lowell proposed that Mars was a dying planet whose highly intelligent inhabitants were combating the increasing desiccation of their globe with a system of irrigation canals that distributed and conserved the dwindling water stored in the polar caps.

This vision, along with Lowell's stern Darwinism, was dramatized by H. G. Wells in one of science fiction's classics, *The War of the Worlds* (1898). The Earth-invading Martians, though hideous to behold and merciless in action, are allowed a dollop of dispassionate human sympathy. Employing advanced instruments and intelligences honed by "the immediate pressure of necessity," they enviously gaze across space at "our own warmer planet, green with vegetation and grey with water, with a cloudy atmosphere eloquent of fertility, with glimpses through its drifting cloud wisps of broad stretches of populous country and narrow, navy-crowded seas."

In the coming half-century of Martian fancy, our neighboring planet served as a shadowy twin onto which earthly concerns, anxieties, and debates were projected. Such burning contemporary issues as colonialism, collectivism, and industrial depletion of natural resources found ample room for exposition in various Martian utopias. A minor vein of science fiction showed Mars as the site, more or less, of a Christian afterlife; C. S. Lewis's *Out of the Silent Planet* (1938) invented an unfallen world, Malacandra. Edgar Rice Burroughs's wildly popular series of Martian romances presented the dying planet as a rugged, racially diverse frontier where, in the words of its Earthling superhero John Carter, life is "a hard and pitiless struggle for existence." Following Burroughs, pulp science fiction, brushing aside possible anatomical differences, frequently mated Earthlings and Martians, the Martian usually the maiden in the match, and the male a virile Aryan aggressor from our own tough planet. The etiolated, brown-skinned, yellow-eyed Martians of Ray Bradbury's poetic and despairing *The Martian Chronicles* (1950) vanish under the coarse despoilment that human invasion has brought.

But all the fanciful Martian megafauna—Wells's leathery amalgams of tentacles and hugely evolved heads; American journalist Garrett P. Serviss's fifteen-foot-tall quasi–red men; Burroughs's ten-foot, four-armed, olive-skinned Tharks; Lewis's beaverlike hrossa and technically skilled pfiffltriggi; and the "polar bear–sized creatures" that Carl Sagan imagined to be possibly roaming the brutally cold Martian surface—were swept into oblivion by the flyby photographs taken by Mariner 4 on July 14, 1965, from six thousand miles away. The portion of Mars caught on an early digital camera showed no canals, no cities, no water, and no erosion or weathering. Mars more resembled the moon than the earth. The pristine craters suggested that surface conditions had not changed in more than three billion years. The dying planet had been long dead.

Two more Mariner flybys, both launched in 1969, sent back fifty-seven images that, in the words of the NASA release, "revealed Mars to be heavily cratered, bleak, cold, dry, nearly airless and generally hostile to any Earth-style life-forms." But Mariner 9, an orbiter launched in 1971, dispatched, over 146 days, seven thousand photographs of surprisingly varied and violent topography: volcanoes, of which the greatest, Olympus Mons, is thirteen miles high, and a system of canyons, Valles Marineris, that on Earth would stretch from New York City to Los Angeles. Great arroyos and tear-shaped islands testified to massive floods in the Martian past, presumably of water, the *sine qua non* of life as Earth knows it. In 1976, the two Viking landers safely arrived on the Martian surface; the ingenious chemical experiments aboard yielded, on the question of life on Mars, ambiguous results whose conclusions are still being debated into the twenty-first century.

In the meantime, our geographical and geological intimacy with Mars grows. The triumphant deployment of the little Sojourner rover in 1997 was followed in 2004 by the even more spectacular success of two more durable rovers, Spirit and Opportunity. In four years of solar-powered travels on the red planet, the twin robots have relayed unprecedentedly detailed images, including many clearly of sedimentary rocks, suggesting the existence of ancient seas. The stark, russet-tinged photographs plant the viewer right on the surface; the ladderlike tracks of Spirit and Opportunity snake and gouge their way across rocks and dust that for eons have rested scarcely disturbed under salmon-pink skies and a pearlescent sun. In this tranquil desolation, the irruption of our live curiosity and systematic purpose feels heroic.

Now the Phoenix Mission, with its surpassingly intricate arm, scoop, imagers, and analyzers, takes us inches below the surface of dust, sand, and ice in Mars's north polar region. Spoonfuls of another planet's substance, their chemical ingredients volatilized, sorted, and identified, become indexes to cosmic history. Meanwhile, the Mars Reconnaissance Orbiter, the newest of three operational spacecraft circling the planet, feeds computers at the University of Arizona with astoundingly vivid and precise photographs of surface features. Some of these false-color images appear totally abstract, yet they yield to knowledgeable eyes riches of scientific information.

The dead planet is not so dead after all: avalanches and dust storms are caught on camera, and at the poles a seasonal sublimation of dry ice produces erosion and movement. Dunes shift; dust devils trace dark scribbles on the delicate surface. Whether or not evidence of microbial or lichenous life emerges amid this far-off flux, Mars has become an ever-nearer neighbor, a province of human knowledge. Dim and fanciful visions of the twinkling fire planet have led to panoramic close-ups beautiful beyond imagining.

Extreme Dinosaurs

BEFORE THE NINETEENTH CENTURY, when dinosaur bones turned up they were taken as evidence of dragons, ogres, or giant victims of Noah's Flood. After two centuries of paleontological harvest, the evidence seems stranger than any fable, and continues to get stranger. Dozens of new species emerge each year; China and Argentina are hot spots lately for startling new finds. Contemplating the bizarre specimens recently come to light, one cannot but wonder what on earth Nature was thinking of. What advantage was conferred, say, by the ungainly eight-foot-long arms and huge triple claws of *Deinocheirus*? Or, speaking of arms, by *Mononykus*'s smug dependence on a single, stoutly clawed digit at the end of each minimal forearm? Guesses can be hazarded: the latter found a single stubby claw just the thing for probing after insects; the former stripped the leaves and bark from trees in awesome bulk. A carnivorous cousin, *Deinonychus*, about the size of a man, leapt on its prey, wrapped its long arms and three-fingered hands around it, and kicked it to death with sickle-shaped toenails.

Tiny *Epidendrosaurus* boasted a hugely elongated third finger that served, presumably, a clinging, arboreal lifestyle, like that of today's aye-

Written for *National Geographic*, December 2007. Adam Gopnik chose this for *Best American Essays 2008*.

aye, a lemur that possesses the same curious trait. With the membrane they support, the elongated digits of bats and pterosaurs enable flight, and perhaps *Epidendrosaurus* was taking a skittery first step in that direction. But what do we make of such apparently inutile extremes of morphology as the elaborate skull frills of ceratopsians like *Styracosaurus* or the horizontally protruding front teeth of *Masiakasaurus knopfleri*, a Late Cretaceous oddity recently uncovered in Madagascar by excavators who named the beast after Mark Knopfler, the guitarist and singer of the group Dire Straits, their favorite music to dig by?

Masiakasaurus is an oddity, all right, its mouth bristling with those slightly hooked, forward-poking teeth; but, then, odd too are an elephant's trunk and tusks, and an elk's antler rack, and a peacock's tail. A difficulty with dinosaurs is that we can't see them in action and tame them, as it were, with visual (and auditory and olfactory) witness. How weird might a human body look to them? That thin and featherless skin, that dish-flat face, that flaccid erectitude, those feeble, clawless five digits at the end of each limb, that ghastly utter lack of a tail—*ugh*. Whatever did this creature *do* to earn its place in the sun, a well-armored, nicely specialized dino might ask.

Dinosaurs dominated the planet's land surface from some two hundred million years ago until their abrupt disappearance, 135 million years later. The vast span of time boggles the human mind, which took its present, *Homo sapiens* form less than two hundred thousand years ago and began to leave written records and organize cities less than ten thousand years in the past. When the first dinosaurs—small, lightweight, bipedal, and carnivorous—appeared in the Triassic, the first of three periods in the Mesozoic geologic era, the earth held one giant continent, Pangaea; during their Jurassic heyday, Pangaea split into two parts, Laurasia and Gondwana; and by the Late Cretaceous the continents had something like their present shapes, though all were reduced in size by the higher seas, and India was still an island heading for a Himalaya-producing crash with Asia. The world was becoming the one we know: the Andes and the Rockies were rising; flowering plants had appeared, and with them, bees. The Mesozoic climate, generally, was warmer than today's, and wetter, generating lush growths of ferns and cycads and forests of evergreens, ginkgoes, and tree ferns close to the poles; plant-eating dinosaurs grew huge, and carnivorous predators kept pace. It was a planetary summertime, and the living was easy.

Not *that* easy: throughout their long day on earth, there was an intensification of boniness and spikiness, as if the struggle for survival became grimmer. And yet the defensive or attacking advantage of skull frills and back plates is not self-evident. The solid domed skull of *Pachy-cephalosaurus*, the largest of the bone-headed dinosaurs, seems made for butting, but for butting what? The skull would do little good against a big predator like *Tyrannosaurus rex*, which had the whole rest of *Pachy-cephalosaurus's* unprotected body to bite down on. Butting matches amid males of the same species were unlikely, since the bone, though ten inches thick, was not shock-absorbent. The skulls of some pachy-cephalosaurs, moreover, were flat and thin, and some tall and ridged—bad designs for contact sport. Maybe they were just used for discreet pushing. Or to make a daunting impression.

An even more impractical design shaped the skull of the pachy-cephalosaurid *Dracorex hogwartsia*—an intricate sunburst of spiky horns and knobs, without a dome. Only one such skull has been unearthed; it is on display, with the playful name derived from Harry Potter's school of witchcraft and wizardry, in the Children's Museum of Indianapolis. Duck-billed *Parasaurolophus walkeri*, another Late Cretaceous plant-eater, sported a spectacular pipelike structure, sweeping back from its skull, that was once theorized to act as a snorkel in swimming; but the tubular crest had no hole for gathering air. It may have served as a trum-peting noisemaker, for herd communication, or supported a bright flap of skin beguiling to a parasaurolophus of the opposite gender. Sexual suc-cess and herd acceptance perpetuate genes as much as combative prowess and food-gathering ability.

Dinosaurs have always presented adaptive puzzles. How did huge her-bivores like *Brachiosaurus*, *Apatosaurus*, and *Diplodocus* get enough daily food into their tiny mouths to fill their cavernous guts? Of the two famil-iar dinosaurs whose life-and-death struggle was memorably animated in Walt Disney's *Fantasia* (though in fact they never met in the corridors of time, failing to overlap by fully seventy-five million years), *T. rex* had puzzlingly tiny arms and *Stegosaurus* carried on its back a double row of huge bony plates negligible as defensive armor and problematic as heat controls. Not that biological features need to be efficient to be carried along. Some Darwinian purists don't even like the word "adaptive," as carrying a taint of implied teleology, of purposeful self-improvement; all that is certain is that dinosaur skeletons demonstrate the viability, for a time, of certain dimensions and conformations. Yet even Darwin, on the last page of *The Origin of Species*, in summing up his theory as "Natural Selection, entailing Divergence of Character and the Extinction of less-improved forms," lets fall a shadow of value judgment with the "less-improved."

In what sense are living forms improvements over the dinosaurs? All life forms, even such long-lasting ones as blue-green algae and horseshoe crabs and crocodiles, will eventually flunk some test posed by environmental conditions and meet extinction. One can safely say that no dinosaur was as intelligent as *Homo sapiens*, or even as chimpanzees. And none that is known, not even a heavyweight champion like *Argentinosaurus*, was as big as a blue whale. One can believe that none was as beautiful in swift motion as a cheetah or an antelope, or as impressive to our mammalian aesthetic sense as a tiger. But beyond this it is hard to talk of improvement, especially since for all its fine qualities *Homo sapiens* is befouling the environment like no fauna before it.

The dinosaurs in their long reign filled every niche several times over, and the smallest of them—the little light-boned theropods scuttling for their lives underfoot—grew feathers and became birds, still singing and dipping all around us. It is an amazing end to an amazing evolutionary story—*Deinonychus* into dove. Other surprises certainly lurk within the still-unfolding saga of the dinosaurs. In Inner Mongolia, so recently that the bones were revealed to the world just this past spring, a giant birdlike dinosaur, *Gigantoraptor*, has been discovered. It clearly belongs among the oviraptorosaurs of the Late Cretaceous—ninety-pound weaklings with toothless beaks—but weighed in at one and a half tons and could have peered into a second-story window. While many of its fellow-theropods—for example, six-foot, large-eyed, big-brained *Troödon*—were evolving toward nimbleness and intelligence, *Gigantoraptor* opted for brute size. But what did it eat, with its enormous toothless beak? Did its claw-tipped arms bear feathers, as did those of smaller oviraptorosaurs?

The new specimens that emerge as tangles of bones embedded in sedimentary rock are island peaks of a submerged continent where evolutionary currents surged back and forth. Our telescoped perspective gives an impression of a violent struggle as anatomical ploys, some of them seemingly grotesque, were desperately tried and eventually discarded. The dinosaurs as a group saw myriad extinctions, and the final extinction, at the end of the Mesozoic, looks to have been the work of an asteroid. They continue to live in the awareness of their human successors on the throne of earthly dominance. They fascinate children as well as paleontologists. My second son, I well remember, collected the plastic dinosaur miniatures that came in cereal boxes, and communed with them in his room. He loved them—their amiable grotesquerie, their guileless enormity, their unassuming small brains. They were eventual losers, in a game of survival our own species is still playing, but new varieties keep emerging from the rocks underfoot to amuse and amaze us.

THE COMMONWEALTH

Harvard Square in the Fifties

IN 1950, Harvard Square and the nearby business blocks were, to this homesick freshman, a sore—in the dictionary sense of "extreme, very great"—relief from the pressures within the Yard of learning and social adaptation. I would gaze from the windows of the Union toward the gas station pinched in the acute corner of Mass. Avenue and Harvard Street as if at a vanished paradise, where my vanished small-town self would pump free air into his bicycle tires and watch the rickety family car being greasily repaired. On Sunday mornings I would give myself the treat of sleeping through the bells from Memorial Chapel and then walking in the opposite direction from the Union to the drugstore next to the UT; there I would dip into my modest allowance to the extent of a cup of coffee and a cinnamon doughnut at the counter, whose marble top seemed continuous with the marble countertops at home. The helpful maps in Mo Lotman's priceless assemblage of photographs tell me that this haven from Latin and calculus was called Daley's Pharmacy. There was an even more intimate escape hatch where Mass. Avenue curved into Boylston Street, just up from the Wursthaus, whose exiguous triangular interior shape accommodated only a few hot-dog addicts at a time; this was, I am reminded, the Tasty Sandwich Shop. Furtively I sought out places that seemed to me anonymous and exempt from Harvard charm. Later, as I matured enough to join the *Lampoon* and acquire a Radcliffe girlfriend— feats achieved, I now realize, against considerable odds—she and I nur-

---

Written for *Harvard Square*, an illustrated history by Mo Lotman (2009). The UT was the University Theatre (1926–61), a nineteen-hundred-seat movie house that, as late as the middle Fifties, had velvet drapes, a gilded proscenium, usherettes, and a double bill of first-run films every night.

tured our romance at tables in Albiani's, the Hayes-Bickford's, and Cronin's, with always the guilty thrill that I wasn't back in my monk's cell studying the humanities. We huddled in the darkness of the single-screen UT, and descended into the damp chill of the Red Line, whose shrieking cars would take us to Boston. The commercial surround of Harvard Square—the ugliest spot, William Dean Howells called it, on the planet—saved me from the academic vapors, as it saves the university from preciosity. For all my four years there, I remained grateful that this colonial and neo-colonial palace of higher learning had pitched itself in a down-to-earth, if not downright grubby, American city.

Ipswich in the Seventies

WHEN I FIRST SAW IPSWICH, I had been married about three hours, was twenty-one years old, and didn't much care where I was. One of my newly acquired father-in-law's parishioners had lent us a little house behind an apple orchard. My bride and I bicycled to the beach, shopped in the A & P, played croquet on a tiny lawn, bit the apple from the Tree of Knowledge, and left. A few years later, seeking escape from Manhattan, I remembered not so much the Ipswich beach, which is splendid and famous, as the something comfortingly raggle-taggle about Market Street, where the grocery store had offered oranges beneath an awning and the five-and-ten had possessed the deep-aisled navelike cool of a Woolworth's from my boyhood. It felt like a town with space, where you could make your own space. We moved, impulsively, tentatively, and fifteen years later still live here, still on honeymoon.

Happily, the town is rather hard to get to. U.S. 1, in its haste to reach New Hampshire, barrels through the shaggy outskirts, and Route 1A from the south, coming through North Beverly, Wenham, and Hamilton, acts as a natural barrier, choked as it is with addled-access shopping malls and some of the pokiest blue-haired drivers in the East. On its northern flank, Ipswich is guarded by Rowley, a hamlet with an oddly Midwestern air of desolation, and by Linebrook Road, a tortuous lane that some dastardly planners project as a superhighway. Ipswich was first approached from the sea, by a distinguished party of settlers led by John

---

Published, as "The Dilemma of Ipswich," in the Ford Motor Company's *Ford Times* (September 1972), and reprinted, as a pretty little pea-green pamphlet sewn with yellow thread, by Aloe Editions under the happier title *A Good Place* (1973).

Winthrop, Jr., in 1633, and the site thrived for a while as a port; but, as no less an authority than Captain John Smith had predicted, the Ipswich River sleepily silted it over. The clipper ships of the China trade went elsewhere. Population ebbed in the nineteenth century, and a unique number of pre-1725 houses escaped the destruction that goes with thriving in America.

"Yet," as a local friend recently insisted to me, "this was *never* a hick town." The first generation of citizens, including not only young Winthrop but future Governors Dudley and Bradstreet and the misogynistic legalist Nathaniel Ward and the colony's first poet, Bradstreet's wife, Anne, gave Ipswich a good self-image from which it never recovered. It bills itself, on Chamber of Commerce billboards (on the basis of a not very glorious scuffle between some selectmen and Governor Andros in 1687), as "The Birthplace of American Independence" and notes with pride that, alone of the major towns of Essex County, it never hanged a witch. Never a hick town, always with just enough industry—lace, farming, hosiery, clamming, electronics—to sustain an independent population, Ipswich at present stands to be eaten by the megalopolitan monster of expanding Boston. Its surviving farms and empty spaces, its casual heritage of historicity and charm, its mini-city perkiness, are all delicious, and what developers from outside are not allowed to do, local developers will. Our town is no longer hard enough to get to.

The Boston doctors who came around the turn of the century and summered on the land along the beach road were perhaps the first, after the Indians, to seize this place as a place of visible glory. The marsh, though men and wide-shoed horses no longer harvest its salt hay, is not an idle piece of scenery. It rarely rests, changing its tint every month, playing host to a plague of greenhead flies in August, becoming a Carthage of ice rubble in February. Subtle and abiding, the marriage of earth and ocean that the marsh represents pacifies all the elements, absorbs the tide and releases it, warms the wind, prepares the eyes and spirit for the implacable otherness of the Atlantic—which breaks on Ipswich sands so tamed by the arms of the bay that an infant can dabble in it safely. Nor does Ipswich lack beauty inland; its westernmost point cuts into a freshwater pond as cherished by its pines and cottages as any in New Hampshire, and the Ipswich River before it turns salt flows through miles of state forest. The town has no country club. The one golf course is delightfully public, a cozy 66-par where the young learn the game and the old retire with it. Though sea-bathing north of Cape Cod is a stoic sport even in July, there are few swimming pools. The Ipswich style makes do with what God provides—swim when the tide is high, clam when it is low. Conservationist attitudes run deep and strong. It was an Ipswich summer resident, Dr. William Shurcliff, who led the successful lobbying fight against the SST.

Yet, in the same style, Ipswich is traditionally careless of itself. Sidewalks exist or do not exist by whim of the individual householder. When we moved here in 1957, an open sewer with the lyrical name of Farley Brook ran through the middle of town; the remarkably belated program of town sewers is still far from complete. After ten years of stalemate, a new high school was voted in by rigging the bylaws, and now a newer one, badly needed, has several times been defeated at the polls. The attempt to create a legal historic district, in the manner of Concord, has been rebuffed by homeowners fearful of having their right to choose a speckled siding or to build a sun porch infringed. Even the dogs in Ipswich enjoy an exceptional freedom; they sleep in the middle of North Main Street and wander through the fenceless back yards like a pack of sacred cows. A leash law was defeated at the last town meeting by a margin of one.

Market Street is still comfortingly raggle-taggle, but increasingly hard to park on. We moved to a town of not seven thousand; the population is now twelve thousand and growing irresistibly. Not that resistance is absent. Plans to construct an atomic-energy plant on the marsh are nipped each time they try to bud; an entrepreneur anxious to build us a Robert Trent Jones golf course, with a few high-rise apartments posed between the sand traps, has been successfully enmeshed in town bickering. But such triumphs of forestallment do not slow the bulldozers clearing half-acre lots for ranch houses, or put money into the hands of a Conservation Commission eager to buy up a green belt.

Two splendid prominences overlook Ipswich Bay and Plum Island. One, consisting of Castle Hill and Steep Hill, contains only the mansion and accessory buildings built by Richard T. Crane, a Chicago tycoon who early in the century bought up a baronial amount of coastal Ipswich, most of which, including a beach, has passed to the town as a public reservation, a park that becomes more precious (and more vandalized) every year. The other prominence, across the Ipswich River, is Jeffreys Neck, named after Ipswich's first known white resident, a squatter farmer. The Neck has been freely given over to the perpetrators of summer cottages, so that its silhouette bristles like a cogwheel with rooftops, and even more are being crowded in, with much scraping of land and much importation of plywood and tarpaper. Yet though the view *of* the Neck is dispiriting, the view *from* it is still grand, and in the sum of human happiness which accounts for more, the lonely Castle or the crowded Neck? One's instinct, having arrived at a good place, is to bar the gates, but there are no gates on this permissive and accidental paradise, this is America, and we are all *arrivistes*, from John Winthrop, Jr., on—all exploiters and developers and spoilers.

A town begins by being anyplace and ends as the Only Place. Ipswich has long been alive for us with people we know, people who, my impression is, distinctly lack the personal smallness associated with small towns. Perhaps the great Puritan beginning, or the proximity to that master ironist the sea keeps them alert and open and kind. Big enough to be yourself in, yet so small political enemies must link hands in a Greek dance line, Ipswich has subdued its once bitter ethnic rivalries to a town identity all feel is threatened. The dilemma is typical, widespread, perhaps perennial; everything flows. Population crushes what it would love. Yet for a time longer the marshes will serenely mirror the seasons; the old houses, having survived centuries of being taken for granted, will ride easy in the harbor of antiquarianism; and the newcomers to the town will be grateful for the space, never dreaming how much it has shrunk.

Three Texts from Early Ipswich

STAGE: *The rocks of Meetinghouse Green. Stockade fencing, lecterns, pulpits, microphones. Chairs for congregation.*

This pageant was commissioned by the town of Ipswich, Massachusetts, for performance on Seventeenth Century Day, August 3, 1968. It is composed of texts taken from *Ipswich in the Massachusetts Bay Colony*, Volume I, by Thomas Franklin Waters (Ipswich Historical Society, 1905); *History of Ipswich, Essex, and Hamilton*, by Joseph B. Felt (Charles Folson, 1834); *The Simple Cobler of Aggawamm, in America*, by Nathaniel Ward, edited by T. F. Waters (Ipswich Historical Society, 1906); and Anne Bradstreet's poems as printed in *The American Puritans: Their Prose and Poetry*, by Perry Miller (Doubleday, 1956). "Only the connecting thread of narration, the modernization of spelling, and the utterances of Masconnomet are mine," Updike wrote in a note to the performance text, which was designed and printed, as a saddle-stitched booklet, by Lovell Thompson for the Seventeenth Century Day Committee in the summer of 1968. The present, slightly revised version appeared in *Audience* magazine, in 1972.

The performance, directed by Bradford Lucas, was staged at South Parish Church (Congregational), on the Ipswich Meetinghouse Green. The Reverend Edward French read the part of the Narrator; Ben Collins played Masconnomet; John Pechilis, John Winthrop, Jr.; and Homer White, the Reverend Nathaniel Ward. Meredith (Mrs. Roger) Burke read the poems of Anne Bradstreet. Other actors were Hollie Bucklin, Jean Bucklin, Robert McGarty, Hiram Sibley, and Robert Weatherall.

NARRATOR: The Puritans. We have all heard of them; but who were they? They are around us in the shape of half our houses; the marks of their axes can still be touched on the great summer beams they hewed from the forests of oak and pine. On our older streets, our automobiles obey the curves their footsteps determined. We honor by use the names they bestowed: Jeffreys Neck, Turkey Shore, Labor-in-Vain, Castle Hill, so called three centuries before there was a castle to adorn it.

Their voices, their faces, have vanished; but they left us, on scattered and fragile bits of paper, records, texts in which, if we listen closely, we may hear the breath of their lives, lives far removed from our own, but perhaps not as different as we have supposed.

(WINTHROP, MASCONNOMET, WARD, SALTONSTALL, SMITH, *other Indians, and other Puritans enter. These last will also serve as the congregation for Ward's sermon and as dancers to Bradstreet's poem.*)

NARRATOR: Our first text is a legal document, a deed. Its date is the 28th of June, 1638; its author, or principal indictor, John Winthrop, Jr., Governor Winthrop's eldest son. (WINTHROP *steps forward.*) Five years earlier he had led a band of twelve men, in March of 1633, by boat from Boston to this region, then called Agawam, to make a settlement. Big-nosed in his portrait, and rather sad-eyed, he was a student at Trinity College, Dublin, and a barrister at law, and a soldier serving with the British fleet under the Duke of Buckingham. His special passion was scientific experimentation. Winthrop's personal competence and magnetism soon established Ipswich as a center of enlightenment, and the town of the colony second in importance to Boston. When, a year before our deed is signed, the governor was reported to be recalling his son to Boston, three Ipswich citizens drew up a petition of remonstrance to the governor:

SALTONSTALL: It was for his sake that many of us came to this place, and without him we should not have come. His abode with us hath made our abode here much more comfortable than otherwise it would have been. Mr. Dudley's leaving us hath made us much more desolate and weak than we were, and if we should lose another magistrate it would be too great a grief to us and breach upon us, and not a magistrate only but our Lieutenant Colonel so beloved of our Soldiers and military men that this remote corner would be left destitute and desolate. We find his affections great and constant to our town, and we hope ours shall never fail towards him and his. We therefore humbly beseech you that we may still enjoy him. The distance we are set in hath made us earnest for the company of able men, and as loath to lose them when we have obtained them.

NARRATOR: The signer of this document, this deed, was an Indian, Masconnomet, the Sagamore of Agawam.

MASCONNOMET (*steps forward, reads*): I, Masconnomet, Sagamore of Agawam, do by these presents acknowledge to have received of Mr. John Winthrop the sum of twenty pounds, in full satisfaction of all the right, property, and claim I have, or ought to have, unto all the land, lying and being in the Bay of Agawam, alias Ipswich, being so called now by the English. . . .

NARRATOR: In 1614, Captain John Smith landed in Agawam, and wrote:

SMITH (*a bearded voyager, gaudy in his armor*): This place might content a right curious judgment; but there are many sands at the entrance of the Harbor, and the worst is, it is embayed too far from the deep sea. Here are many rising hills, and on their tops and descends are many corn fields, and delightful groves.

MASCONNOMET: My people burned the underbrush each November, allowing the hunter to pass through easily, and the great trees to grow; we cleared the hilltops and planted them with corn: that is what brought the English to us. To steal our fields.

SMITH (*continuing*): On the East is an Isle of two or three leagues in length; the one half plain marsh ground, fit for pasture or salt ponds, with many fair high groves of mulberry trees and gardens. There is also Oaks, Pines, Walnuts, and other wood to make this place excellent habitation, being a good and sage harbor.

MASCONNOMET: We called it Agawam, which means: Place Where the Fish Run.

NARRATOR: As early as 1620, the Pilgrims at Plymouth had heard of Agawam—"a place," it was written, "which they heard to be an excellent harbor for ships, better ground and better fishing." Traders and fishermen came first, and squatter farmers like William Jeffreys; Great Neck was called Jeffreys Neck years before Winthrop's party landed.

MASCONNOMET: A terrible plague carried off nine out of ten of my people; the Tarratine tribe from the North made war upon the few that remained. That is why we had to bargain with the English.

WINTHROP (*comes up and prompts, reading*): I hereby relinquish . . .

MASCONNOMET: I hereby relinquish . . .

WINTHROP: . . . all the right and interest I have . . .

MASCONNOMET: . . . all the right and interest I have . . .

WINTHROP (*his voice clear, cold*): . . . unto all the havens, rivers, creeks, islands, huntings, and fishings, with all the woods, swamps, timber, and whatever else is, or may be, in or upon the said ground to me belonging . . .

MASCONNOMET: . . . to me belonging . . .

WINTHROP: . . . and I do hereby acknowledge to have received full satisfaction from the said John Winthrop for all former agreements, touching the premises and parts of them; and I do hereby bind myself to make good the aforesaid bargain and sale unto the said John Winthrop, his heirs and assigns, forever . . .

MASCONNOMET: . . . forever . . .

WINTHROP: . . . and to secure him against the title and claim of all other Indians and natives whatsoever. Witness my hand. (*Passes over twenty pounds.*)

(*Four men step forward, saying:*)

FIRST: Thomas Coytmore, Witness.
SECOND: James Downing, Witness.
THIRD: Robert Harding, Witness.
FOURTH: John Jollife, Witness.
WINTHROP (*indicating*): Masconnomet, his mark.

MASCONNOMET *makes with difficulty his squiggle and hangs his head.*

NARRATOR: In 1644, Masconnomet agreed to place himself and the remnants of his tribe under the protection of the government of Massachusetts, and to be instructed in the Christian religion. Some of their catechism survives:

WARD: Will you worship only true God, who made heaven and earth, and not blaspheme?

MASCONNOMET: We do desire to reverence the God of the English and to speak well of Him, because we see He doth better to the English than other gods do to others.

WARD: Will you cease from swearing falsely?

MASCONNOMET: We know not what swearing is.

WARD: Will you refrain from working on the Sabbath, especially within the bounds of Christian towns?

MASCONNOMET: It is easy to us—we have not much to do any day, and we can rest on that day.

NARRATOR (as MASCONNOMET, SMITH, *and* WINTHROP *slowly leave*): Masconnomet, the last of the chiefs of the Agawam, lived to see his people almost extinct. In 1658, the records tell us, his widow was granted a parcel of land, and that "idle curiosity, wanton sacrilegious sport, prompted an individual to dig up the remains of this chief and carry his skull on a pole through Ipswich streets." John Winthrop the Younger, after service in many towns of New England, and repeated terms as governor of Connecticut, died in Boston in 1676, and was laid beside his father in King's Chapel graveyard. Historians, though praising his virtue and intelligence, deny him the heroic stature of his father; his heart belonged to science, and throughout his career he corresponded voluminously with the Royal Society for Improving Natural Knowledge about such matters as tides, waterspouts, caterpillars, comets, minerals, sea-dredging, corn blight, the effects of lightning, and the fifth satellite of Jupiter, whose existence was not confirmed until this century.

(Bells toll.)

Church. At first, a meetinghouse of logs and thatch, surrounded by a stone fort. Men attended carrying muskets. (*As Puritans file in.*) As early as 1640, there was a bell to summon the farmers of Ipswich to worship. They came afoot; by law no house could be built more than a half-mile from the meetinghouse, which, "commanding a good prospect to a great part of the Town," probably from the first was located on this site. The interior was bare, furnished only with the Bible and the Psalm Book and the hourglass, to render visible the length of the sermon. The order of seating was rigid; on one side of the aisle sat the magistrates of Ipswich, Winthrop and Richard Saltonstall and sometimes Governor Thomas Dudley, and the Bradstreets and the Appletons. Behind them sat the lesser gentry and substantial yeomen, and behind them the servants and the poor. Across the aisle sat the wives, arranged also by order of station. Before them, in the pulpit, clad in black Geneva gown and skullcap, stood the pastor, on this Sabbath the great Nathaniel Ward. In England a lawyer by profession, Ward at the age of forty entered the ministry; his Puritanism was uncompromising. Asked to conform to the canon of the Church instituted by Archbishop Laud, Ward commented:

WARD: The Church of England was ready to ring changes in religion, and the Gospel stood a tip-toe, ready to be gone to America.

NARRATOR: Ward was excommunicated in 1633. The same year, his wife died. Sixty-four years of age, he came to the New World, and with his motherless children he spent the winter of 1634 in Ipswich, in Winthrop's own house, and took charge of the newly founded church. Life in the wilderness was not easy for an old man; in his letters to Winthrop he wrote:

WARD: I entreat you to reserve some meal and malt, till our river be open. I am very destitute; I have not above six bushels of corn left. I acknowledge I am tender and more unfit for solitariness and hardship than some other, especially at this time, through many colds and seeds of the bay sickness I brought from thence.

NARRATOR: In a few years, his health compelled him to resign the active ministry. But his great accomplishments, the two foundations of his fame, lay ahead of him. In 1638, he was invited, as the most legally learned man in the colony, to draw up a code of laws; after three years of labor, he produced a code of one hundred laws, the so-called Body of Liberties, of which the scholar F. W. Poole has written — Mr. Poole.

POOLE (*a man in modern clothes, fussily adjusting his glasses*): The sublime declaration standing at the head of the first Code of Laws in New England was the production of no common intellect. It has the movement and the dignity of a mind like John Milton's or Algernon Sidney's, and its theory of government was far in advance of the age. A bold avowal of the rights of man, and a plea for popular freedom, it contains the germs of the memorable declaration of (*consults notes*) July 4th, 1776. Ah, furthermore —

NARRATOR: Thank you, sir. The congregation has prayed and is anxious for the sermon to begin. No Ipswich sermons from the seventeenth century have survived, but Ward's second claim to fame is a book, *The Simple Cobbler of Agawam*, composed around 1645, and published in London the following year, when Ward had returned to England. *The Simple Cobbler* is a strange and somewhat repellent work, extravagant in its language and ferocious in its political views. Its latter half is addressed chiefly to the problems of the Cromwellian revolution, then in progress. His proposed treatment of the Irish does not strike modern ears as Christian:

WARD (*thumping pulpit*): Cursed be he that maketh not his sword stark drunk with Irish blood, that doth not recompense them double for their hellish treachery to the English, that maketh them not heaps upon heaps, and their country a dwelling place for Dragons, an astonishment to Nations. Let not that eye look for pity, nor that hand to be spared, that pities or spares them, and let him be accursed that curseth not them bitterly.

NARRATOR: Nor are his views of women very charitable. One famous couplet runs:

WARD:

The world is full of care, much like unto a bubble;
Women and care, and care and women, and women and care and
    trouble.

NARRATOR: The opening pages of *The Simple Cobbler*, however, set forth the cosmic and general framework of his discourse. They are sufficiently theological to suggest what a sermon of that time must have been like. So let us imagine ourselves in church, near this very spot, in Ipswich in the first decade of its settlement, listening, while the hourglass runs, to Nathaniel Ward preach on the subject of religious toleration:

WARD*: Either I am in an apoplexy, or that man is in a lethargy who does not now sensibly feel God shaking the heavens over his head, and the earth under his feet. The heavens so, as the sun begins to turn into darkness, the moon into blood, the stars to fall down to the ground, so that little light of comfort or counsel is left to the sons of men; the earth so, as the foundations are failing, the righteous scarce know where to find rest, the inhabitants stagger like drunken men. And no marvel, for they have defiled it by transgressing the laws, changing the ordinances, and breaking the everlasting Covenant.

The truths of God are the pillars of the world, whereon states and churches may stand quiet if they will; if they will not, He can easily shake them off into delusions and distractions enough.

Satan is now in his passions; he feels his passion approaching; he loves to fish in roiled waters. Though that dragon cannot sting the vitals of the Elect mortally, yet that Beelzebub can fly-blow their intellectuals miserably. The finer religion grows, the finer he spins his cobwebs; he will hold pace with Christ so long as his wits will serve him. He sees himself beaten out of gross idolatries, heresies, ceremonies, where the Light breaks forth with power; he will, therefore, bestir him to prevaricate Evangelical truths and ordinances, that if they will needs be walking, appointing for his engineers men well complexioned for honesty, for such are fittest to mountebank his chemistry into sick churches and weak judgments.

Nor shall he need to stretch his strength overmuch in this work. Too many men, having not laid their foundation sure, nor ballasted their

---

*During this sermon there can be some by-play in the congregation: sleepers woken by ushers with sticks, etc.

spirits deep with humility and fear, are pressed enough of themselves to evaporate their own apprehensions. Those that are acquainted with Story know it has ever been so in new editions of churches: such as are least able, are most busy to pudder in the rubbish, and to raise dust in the eyes of more steady repairers. Change of air discovers corrupt bodies; reformation of religion, unsound minds. The devil desires no better sport than to see light heads handle their heels, and fetch their careers in a time, when the roof of Liberty stands open.

The next perplexed question, with pious and ponderous men, will be: What should be done for the healing of these comfortless exulcerations? I am the unablest adviser of a thousand, the unworthiest of ten thousand; yet I hope I may presume to assert what follows without just offense.

First, such as have given or taken any unfriendly reports of us New English, should do well to recollect themselves. We have been reputed a colluvies of wild opinionists, swarmed into a remote wilderness to find elbow-room for our fanatic doctrines and practices. I trust our diligence past, and constant sedulity against such persons and courses, will plead better things for us. I dare take upon me, to be the herald of New England so far, as to proclaim to the world, in the name of our colony, that all Familists, Antinomians, Anabaptists, and other enthusiasts shall have free liberty to keep away from us, and such as will come to be gone as fast as they can, the sooner the better.

(*Noises of approval from congregation.*)

Second, I dare aver, that God does nowhere in His Word tolerate Christian states, to give tolerations to such adversaries of His truth, if they have power in their hands to suppress them.

My heart has naturally detested four things (*ticks them off*):

the standing of the Apocrypha in the Bible;

foreigners dwelling in my country, to crowd our native subjects into the corners of the earth;

alchemized coins;

tolerations of diverse religions, or of one religion in segregant shapes. He that willingly assents to the last, if he examines his heart by daylight, his conscience will tell him he is either an atheist, or a heretic, or a hypocrite, or at best a captive to some lust. Poly-piety is the greatest impiety in the world.

The power of all religion and ordinances lies in their purity; their purity in their simplicity. Then are mixtures pernicious. I lived in a city where a Papist preached in one church, a Lutheran in another, a Calvinist in a third; the religion of that place was but motley and meagre; their affections, leopard-like.

He that is willing to tolerate any religion, or discrepant way of religion, besides his own, unless it be in matters merely indifferent, either doubts of his own or is not sincere in it.

He that is willing to tolerate any unsound opinion, that his own may also be tolerated, though never so sound, will for a need hang God's Bible at the devil's girdle.

(More indignation, approval from congregation.)

That state that will give liberty of conscience in matters of religion must give liberty of conscience and conversation in their moral laws, or else the fiddle will be out of tune, and some of the strings crack.

I take liberty of conscience to be nothing but a freedom from sin and error, and liberty of error nothing but a prison for conscience. Then small will be the kindness of a state to build such prisons for their subjects.

The Scripture saith, there is nothing makes free but truth. And Truth saith, there is no truth but one. If the states of the world would make it their summoperous care to preserve this one truth in its purity and authority, it would ease them of all other political cares.

I am sure Satan makes it his grand if not only task to adulterate truth; falsehood is his sole sceptre, whereby he first ruffled, and ever since ruined, the world. Amen.

NARRATOR (*as* WARD *and congregation file out*): Thus ends our second text. Its sternness and harsh piety must be understood against the background of the wilderness, where unity could mean survival, and of the century, when, in the words of Ipswich's foremost historian, Thomas Franklin Waters:

WATERS: It was a matter of common belief in England, as well as in the Colonies on this side of the Atlantic, that Satan and his angels were actively engaged in assaulting the kingdom of the Lord Jesus Christ, and disturbing the peace of mankind.

NARRATOR: The peace of mankind—what was the ordinary life of the Puritans; what was inside the stockade of religious prohibition? Some glimpses of the intimate life of the first settlers are afforded by the records of the courts, whose duty it was to administer the code of regulations ranging from the sale of "strong water" to the wages of crafts-men, from the amount of lace or silk that might be worn by a com-moner to the delicate issues of domestic peace. The Reverend Waters tells us:

WATERS: Mark Quilter was put under ten dollar bonds in 1664 to be "of good behavior toward all persons, but especially his wife." Daniel Black and his wife were both condemned to be set in stocks, with instructions not to "miscall each other" while in limbo. Mary Bidgood was ordered to England to live with her husband. John Tellison was duly punished for tying his wife to the bedpost with a plow chain to keep her at home. Humphrey Griffin's difficulty with his mother-in-law led to two prosecutions: she was fined for cursing and reviling her son-in-law, and he for reviling her.

NARRATOR: The numerous inventories of domestic possessions describe the Puritan home, by our standards a strange mixture of austerity and luxury. Instead of candles, strips of pine, moist with turpentine and pitch, were burned; hence the name, sacred to local golfers, of Candle-wood. There were no forks, and plates were often square pieces of wood slightly hollowed. Weapons, however, were in abundance: Matthew Whipple's hall contained three muskets, three pairs of ban-doleers, three swords, a fowling piece, some breast armor, a pike and sword, a halberd, and a rapier. His best feather bed, bolster and *nine* pillows, weighed one hundred and six pounds. The early Puritans lived in a world of wood and cloth: John Winthrop's inventory of 1636 included:

WATERS (*reads*):
One mantle of silk with gold lace
One holland tablecloth some three yards long
Five child's blankets whereof one is bare million
Four aprons of which one is laced
One dozen holland napkins
One gown sea green
Two old petticoats one red one sand collar serge
One pair leather stockings one muff
One tapestry coverlet
One red bays cloak for a woman.
(*Looks up.*) Many fair English costumes found place in their chests and strong boxes that came over the seas, and the plain houses and plainer meetinghouse were radiant, on Sabbath days, and high days, with bright colors and fine fabrics.

NARRATOR: A tender glimpse of the Puritan family is afforded by the valedictory of Sarah Goodhue, who foresaw her own death in the birth of her twins, and wrote to the eight other of her surviving children:

SARAH GOODHUE: Your father hath been loving, kind, tenderhearted towards you all: and laborious for you all, both for your temporal and spiritual good. You that are grown up, cannot but see how careful your father is when he cometh home from his work, to take the young ones up into his wearied arms; by his loving carriage and care towards those, you may behold, as in a glass, his tender care and love to you every one as you grew up.

NARRATOR: But the supreme poet of Puritan domesticity, and the first considerable poet of America, was of course Anne Bradstreet. Born the daughter of Thomas Dudley in 1612, and raised in the mansion of the Earl of Lincolnshire, she was married at the age of sixteen to Simon Bradstreet, and came with the Great Migration of 1630 to New England.

ANNE BRADSTREET: I found a new world and new manners, at which my heart rose. But, after I was convinced it was the way of God, I submitted to it and joined the church at Boston.

NARRATOR: With her husband and father she moved to the new settlement of Ipswich; here, in the intellectual company of Ward and Nathaniel Rogers, the Denisons and the Saltonstalls, her muse quickened to an astounding productivity. In the eight or nine years of her residency in Ipswich, Ipswich was the most aristocratic and cultured of the Massachusetts communities. When the Bradstreets moved to a North Andover farmstead, her muse languished, though she was only thirty.

ANNE BRADSTREET:
The world no longer let me love.
My hope and treasure lie above.

NARRATOR: Her long poems, pious and scholarly, in the manner of Du Bartas and Spenser, won her the proud title of The Tenth Muse, Lately Sprung Up in America. But it is her occasional lyrics, based upon her domestic life, that still live. She addresses her poems as if they were her children:

ANNE BRADSTREET:
My rambling brat (in print) should mother call;
I cast thee by as one unfit for light,
Thy visage was so irksome in my sight;
Yet being mine own, at length affection would

Thy blemishes amend, if so I could.
I washed thy face, but more defects I saw,
And rubbing off a spot, still made a flaw.
I stretched thy joints to make thee even feet,
Yet still thou run'st more hobbling than is meet;
In better dress to trim thee was my mind,
But nought save homespun cloth in th' house I find.

NARRATOR: And she speaks of her children as if they are her poems. To her husband, in case she dies in childbirth:

ANNE BRADSTREET:
If any worth or virtue were in me,
Let that live freshly in thy memory;
And when thou feel'st no grief, as I no harms,
Yet love thy dead, who long lay in thine arms.
And when thy loss shall be repaid with gains,
Look to my little babes, my dear remains.
And if thou love thyself, or loved'st me,
These O protect from stepdame's injury.
And if chance to thine eyes shall bring this verse,
With some sad sighs honor my absent hearse;
And kiss this paper for thy love's dear sake,
Who with salt tears this last farewell did take.

NARRATOR: It is in the poems to her husband that Anne Bradstreet most closely approaches greatness, as, surprisingly, a passionate celebrant of love, of married love. "A Letter to Her Husband, Absent upon Public Employment," was considered too personal to be made public during her lifetime; it appeared six years after her death in 1672, in a collection entitled *Several Poems Compiled by a Gentlewoman in New-England*. It is the third of our texts. Listen to the ardor that breathes through these sturdy couplets; feel how the wife and mother lifts these conventional celestial conceits into the grandeur of honest emotion— and believe that the Puritans were alive, as we are alive.

ANNE BRADSTREET:
My head, my heart, mine eyes, my life—nay more,
My joy, my magazine of earthly store,
If two be one, as surely thou and I,
How stayest thou there, whilst I at Ipswich lie?
So many steps head from the heart to sever,
If but a neck, soon should we be together.
I, like the Earth this season, mourn in black,

My Sun is gone so far in's zodiac,
Whom whilst I 'joyed, nor storms nor frost I felt,
His warmth such fridged colds did cause to melt.
My chilled limbs now numbed lie forlorn;
Return; return, sweet Sol, from Capricorn;
In this dead time, alas, what can I more
Than view those fruits which through thy heart I bore?
Which sweet contentment yield me for a space,
True living pictures of their father's face.
O strange effect! now thou art southward gone,
I weary grow the tedious day so long;
But when thou northward to me shalt return,
I wish my Sun may never set, but burn
Within the Cancer of my glowing breast,
The welcome house of him, my dearest guest.
Where ever, ever stay, and go not thence,
Till nature's sad decree shall call thee hence;
Flesh of thy flesh, bone of thy bone,
I here, thou there, yet both but on

NARRATOR: Winthrop, Nathaniel Ward, and Anne Bradstreet had all left Ipswich by 1645. But the life of intellectual distinction and adventure to which they contributed here established a tone that lingered for generations. In 1687 the town meeting of Ipswich, led by Samuel Appleton and the Reverend John Wise, refused to comply with a tax that—quote—"doth infringe their Liberty as Free born English subjects of his Majesty." Though the town leaders were jailed, and compliance was enforced, the principles of self-government had been proudly asserted. Five years later, in 1692, Ipswich alone among the important towns of Essex County resisted the witchcraft delirium that swept outwards from Salem.

Winthrop legally purchased this land, though for a modest sum, and wisely administered the settlement. Ward's legal code, based upon the more liberal aspects of English common law, held the seeds of a toleration and pluralism he would have detested. Anne Bradstreet, though condemned to the hard life of a pioneer woman, yet found space here in which her female spirit could flower and bear poetic fruit special to America. Our texts illustrate the nobler elements of the Puritan heritage—a faith in the law, a passion for the things of the mind, a habit of independence. Without exaggeration, it might be said that the Puritan flame, taking hold in the New World, burned brightest at Ipswich.

Lovell Thompson, 1902–1986

I CANNOT IMAGINE anyone meeting Lovell Thompson and not feeling
that this was an extraordinary man. He was extraordinary-looking, for
one thing, with his intensely blue eyes, his baroque eyebrows, and his
noble sea captain's head. Extraordinary, too, in his soft-spoken courtesy,
and his quickness to understand and to be amused, hesitating now and
then to wrap his mouth a bit more securely around his pipe stem, and his
words around his thought. He brought to everything, it seemed to me, a
truly fresh attention, relying not on rote usages and conventional reactions but on a scrupulous thinking-through, like a perfect student of
some foreign language for the first time confronted with native speakers,
in a native situation. He descended to earthly intercourse from some residence within an ideal state, and those aspects of his life to which I was a
witness were characterized by a rigorous caring about quality and a stubborn fidelity to his vision of the best.

I think, for example, of the beautiful folded guide-maps that Lovell
used to produce for the biannual (more or less) recurrences of Ipswich's
Seventeenth Century Day, of which he and his wife, Kay, were founders.
Though the event was thoroughly local, the maps in their beauty and
professional polish would have graced a metropolitan event a hundred
times the scale, and gave everyone connected with the day a sense of
being connected with something substantial, something done in fine and
affectionate style. On a more personal level, I recall how, when he and I
were both householders in Ipswich, and both needing new roofs on our
houses, we discussed the choice between asphalt and cedar shingles. As if
to convert me to the more historically correct and aesthetically pleasing
choice of cedar, he told me that he had looked into the price of both and
been assured that the cedar shingles cost only three times as much. That
he had, for his own life, fine houses in Louisburg Square and in the rural
reaches of Argilla Road did not prevent him from investing not only time
and energy but, most impressively, money in the fight to preserve the
architectural heritage lodged in Ipswich's unruly and not always grateful
downtown. I had the pleasure of serving with him on the Historical
Commission, and the bracing experience, once, of being in the opposition in regard to the construction of a new church building he deemed
unworthy. He was, in his obstructionist cause, implacable and resource-

---

Read at the memorial service in King's Chapel, Boston, on January 2, 1987.

ful, but I can say that not only I, who had many reasons for affection, but the church people as a group recognized that Lovell was a stubborn foe for selfless reasons—he simply wanted the best for Ipswich. His philosophy comes out in these sentences he once wrote: "In the grand rush down the main road we have lost sight of alternatives—pastoral detours, pleasant rest areas and country towns. The economics of mass production have overwhelmed the variety and frugality that arise from individual local solutions. It is important, then, to preserve the best models from the past."

One wonders if such powers of civic caring and discrimination are not dying with such men as this. His civic sense was just one facet of a general aspiration toward the good life, which also showed in his hospitality, in the home environments that he helped to construct, in the books that Gambit Inc. published under his direction, in the genial and undiscouragable spirit that controlled his demeanor. Having worked for forty-two years for Houghton Mifflin, in offices only a few blocks from where we are gathered, he did not retire but instead embarked, at age sixty-seven, on an entrepreneurial gambit. When, in 1977, the exquisite Beacon Street quarters for his publishing house were gutted by fire, he did not, as he might gracefully and understandably have done, give publishing up; he instead relocated at an Ipswich location as choice, in its way, as the uphill part of Beacon Street, and adorned Meetinghouse Green with his special branch of this most civilized of industries. Of all the letters I have received from people in publishing, his were the most witty and thoughtful, and always held at least a phrase of that Thompsonian twinkle, that almost eighteenth-century twist of lucid awareness, of harmless irony. Even his handwriting—I recently found an old letter of his in a book I was consulting—bespoke, in its snub-nibbed, fluent, steady, and legible elegance, the man.

The book I was consulting was called *Fifty Best American Short Stories*, in which Lovell has a story, written in 1937. An artistic sensibility surely informed his concerns and the conduct of his life. I am a late witness to that life, to its afternoon and evening, and not a very close witness; but yet close enough to be warmed by a passion and originality that were artistic. Just dinner at Lovell's Argilla Road house—the friendly way one sneaked along a brick walk, and entered a porch, and then immediately, at a right angle on the left, negotiated another door, and upon being admitted, or admitting oneself, found, again on the left, the party spread out in merry progress, on sofas and chairs in perilous proximity to a roaring fire in a big fireplace, while directly ahead lay the dining table already set and glimmering, and beyond it the porch where memories of summer drinks still lingered—all this felt unique, and kind, and expressive of a man who had made the world within his reach as good as it could be, as graceful and gracious as the world itself permits. His life was long, and he paid the price of a long life in pain and infirmity during his last years, and a price in grief, too, as he thrice became a widower. The three children of his first marriage are here, and their children, and many others who knew Lovell better and longer than I. I am honored to be considered by his family a good enough friend to say these words. Truly, he raised my consciousness, and set a standard for us all, and lived a life whose example of discrimination and caring and intelligent joy we can carry with us.

Open Spaces

THOSE OF US who have lived in Ipswich know the moment when Argilla Road, heading toward Crane Beach, slips its sheath of roadside houses and trees and the view on the right becomes an immense one of salt marshes and, beyond their grassy extent, sand dunes and the horizon of the ocean. This is open space, the kind that the Trustees of Reservations has been preserving in Massachusetts since 1891. The Trustees' holdings in Ipswich are especially vast and varied—nearly three thousand acres, including miles of spectacular white sand beach, a number of hills, several sizable islands, and a fifty-nine-room mansion with outbuildings, not to mention, on the other side of town, a nearly one-thousand-acre working farm. The more than eighty properties under the protection of the Trustees of Reservations in the Commonwealth of Massachusetts stretch from the Coskata-Coatue Wildlife Refuge on Nantucket to Field Farm in the Berkshires. The view from my present house in Beverly includes Great and Little Misery islands, whose pleasantly unpopulated condition was recently assured by the Trustees of Reservations' acquisition of the last three acres still in private hands.

If Massachusetts, one of the longest-settled and most populous of the states, remains one of the most livable, one reason is the formation, over a century ago, of a group of citizens whose public spirit dedicated itself to the acquisition of "bits of scenery" as "public parks" for the growing and crowded masses of greater Boston. The quoted phrases are from the flu-

---

Foreword to *Land of the Commonwealth: A Portrait of the Conserved Landscapes of Massachusetts*, an album of photographs by Richard Cheek commissioned and published by the Trustees of Reservations (2000).

ent pen of Charles Eliot, the son of Harvard professor (and later president) Charles William Eliot. Young Eliot apprenticed for two years in the Brookline office of Frederick Law Olmsted and then travelled through parts of Europe studying public parks, gardens, and great private estates. At the age of twenty-seven he opened an office in Boston, at the corner of Beacon and Park streets, as a landscape architect. Writing to the periodical *Garden and Forest* in 1890, he observed that close to the metropolis remained "several bits of scenery which possess uncommon beauty and more than usual refreshing power." He cited the narrows of the Charles River in Sherborn, which became in 1897 one of the first acquisitions of the Trustees of Reservations, an organization "empowered by the State," as Eliot proposed, "to hold small and well-distributed parcels of land free of taxes, just as the Public Library holds books and the Art Museum pictures—for the use and enjoyment of the public." Eliot died at the young age of thirty-seven, but his noble idea flourished, along with his brainchild, the first private statewide organization devoted to the preservation of open spaces—"surviving fragments," as he wrote, "of the primitive wilderness of New England."

Not many of the reserved properties are "primitive wilderness"; they include the Great House at Castle Hill, the Old Manse, Long Hill, as well as a number of other domiciles, gardens, and working farms. But each holding, it could be said, rescues a certain moment of landscape from the predations of unbridled development. Since we are all part of the press of population that would replace wilderness with human habitations, industry, and commerce—the Native Americans cleared fields and erected dwellings, and even the seemingly virgin salt marshes have been trenched and drained—it would seem paradoxical to resist, by means of advanced organization and substantial funds, the triumph of our own species over the surface of the earth. An asphalt parking lot is, in a sense, as natural as a lava spill, and a factory as a honeycomb. The nineteenth-century mills of Lowell have become themselves the objects of preservation efforts, their beauty and splendor revealed as their utility subsides. The first McDonald's, in Des Plaines, Illinois, is now a piously visited museum. Still, nature without man, or with selective human refinements modestly added to a natural effect, possesses, in Eliot's phrase, "refreshing power."

Nature has its balances, and the human race is not so omnipotent as to avoid the penalties of a persisting imbalance. Deforestation brings floods, overgrazing produces deserts. The Trustees of Reservations was founded in an era that lacked the word "ecology" and that knew far less than our own about the environmental value of lands too wet for houses or crops, or the role that plants' emission of oxygen plays in our atmosphere. What at first seems waste in nature turns out, often, to be essential. An efficient inefficiency presides above the workings of the planet in its full range of flora and fauna, of water and air and permeable soil. We belong to this lavish dispensation, an animal evolved on the East African grassland, a hunter and harvester among many, accustomed to wide spaces and small tribes. "I love a broad margin to my life," Henry David Thoreau wrote in *Walden*, and, in his journals, "The savage in man is never quite eradicated."

The New England conscience, brought by the Puritans to a rocky, resistant terrain, is prone to a certain parsimony with regard to its natural inheritance. Thoreau's essay "Walking" begins, "I wish to speak a word for Nature, for absolute freedom and wildness, as contrasted with a freedom and culture merely civil,—to regard man as an inhabitant, or a part and parcel of Nature, rather than a member of society." Thoreau's New England had still enough untrammelled spaces in it—Cape Cod, in his day, provided a walk on the wild side and not a mile-long traffic jam on Route 6—for him to feel an opposition between nature and society. One could escape from one into the other. His little Walden wilderness, never as isolated as his great book suggests, is now a heavily used suburban preserve.

Having endured utopian visions of Bauhausian "machines for living" and towering apartment blocks where greenery is kept like a lapdog and all neighborhood scale is lost, we can see that some protected aboriginal nature is essential for social health. The town of Ipswich, for instance, benefits as a whole—acquires a communal panache—for the presence within it of upland, beaches, dunes, and marshes kept relatively pristine. Charles Eliot's perception that spaces uncluttered by human enterprise feed our spiritual and physical well-being was not unique; such a perception lay at the heart of Romantic poetry and was extended by ecstatics like John Muir, who chose for the motto of the Wilderness Society Thoreau's remark "In wildness is the preservation of the world." Muir provided the theological paraphrase "In God's wildness lies the hope of the world—the great fresh, unblighted, unredeemed wilderness."

The Trustees of Reservations, without much rhetoric but with much patient study and quiet generosity, has acquired and maintains for our commonwealth more than eighty tracts of land, large and small, beautifully portrayed herein by the photographs of Richard Cheek. Nature's gifts have been seconded by the gifts of human benefactors and workers committed to the vision of a planet shared among all its life forms, an Eden under human stewardship.

Memoirs of a Massachusetts Golfer

I THINK OF MYSELF as a Pennsylvania native and a New York writer, but 100 percent a Massachusetts golfer, never touching a club until, at the age of twenty-five, I became resident in the Bay State. An aunt of my wife's put a driver into my hands on her side lawn in Wellesley, and complimented me on my swing at a phantom ball, and thus sent me haring, for over forty years now, after my unfulfilled golf potential.

It was in Wellesley, the bards of golf history tell us, that golf took root in the commonwealth. A Miss Florence Boit (who can be seen in the Museum of Fine Arts, in the celebrated John Singer Sargent portrait of the four Boit sisters) had played the game in Pau, France, and in 1892 she brought some clubs and balls back to the home of her uncle, Arthur B. Hunnewell. To demonstrate the purpose of these curious implements the athletic lass proceeded to lay out a seven-hole course on her uncle's land and that of some neighbors. Among the astonished audience of her exhibition play was one Laurence Curtis, of Boston, who, ere the year was out, persuaded The Country Club in Brookline to devote some of its turf to golf. So, without young Florence Boit and her *bons temps* at Pau, there might have been no course at The Country Club, and hence no venue wherein Francis Ouimet would beat Harry Vardon and Ted Ray at the U.S. Open in 1913, and Julius Boros would vanquish Arnold Palmer and Jacky Cupit at the U.S. Open in 1963, and Curtis Strange would hold off Nick Faldo at yet another U.S. Open, in 1988—and thus Massachusetts golf would have missed out on three of its great moments. Likewise, if that aunt-in-law hadn't played golf, I would have spent a lot more summer afternoons working in the yard or answering my mail.

I had moved, as it happened, to the North Shore, where the virus imported by Miss Boit was festering within a year or two, causing primitive layouts to spring up on the land of the Essex County Club, in Manchester; the Appleton Farm, in Ipswich; the Moraine Farm, on Wenham Lake; and Prides Crossing, in Beverly. The Myopia Hunt Club, in Hamilton, against the better judgment of the red-coated fox chasers, had nine holes by 1894; the club hosted the first of its four U.S. Opens in 1898 and the last in 1908.

My own obscure golfing career, however, developed, in the 1950s and

Written, at the invitation of editor Laurence Sheehan, for *A Commonwealth of Golfers, 1903–2003*, the sumptuous centennial publication of the Massachusetts Golf Association (2002).

1960s, far from these storied private venues, on a number of public courses in the area. Each had its distinctions. Candlewood Golf Course, on Essex Road in Ipswich, was a converted farm, and the farmer's widow, kindly Mrs. Whipple, took your fees (less than a dollar, can it be?) in a roadside cottage, distinguished, if my faltering memory serves, by a soft-drink cooler as murmurous as a mountain stream and a large photograph of Dr. Cary Middlecoff's swing as captured by stroboscopic camera. The Candlewood layout was on the flattish, shortish side, but a sufficient challenge to my novice skills; my majestic beginner's slice posed a considerable threat to the motorists on the roads passing to the right of the first and ninth fairways. There were two long holes, then two short ones, and a fifth which asked that you walk back to a tee framed by apple trees and hit a blind drive which, if errant, could threaten players on the sixth tee and fairway. At the center of the course a number of fairways came together on a knoll of desolate bareness, all its grass and mayflowers worn to dust by the intersection of many wheels and dragging cleats. From this lunar knoll, the highest point on the course, there was a 360-degree battle panorama of loping pre-adolescents, white-haired retirees, and off-duty clammers as they struggled to move the ball along circuits of the hard-used little layout. My older son, at the age of ten, would play Candlewood all of a summer day, working in as many as fifty-four holes.

A mile farther down Essex Road, in the hamlet of Essex, where clipper-ship building had, within a century, given way to the fried-seafood business, the Cape Ann links offered nine holes of greater length and less harrowing contiguity than Candlewood, with some exhilarating views of marsh and sea. The seventh hole, a longish par-3, asked that you hit across a stretch of mudflat; more than once, at icy high tide, we took off our shoes and socks to reach the hole and, on a parallel causeway to the eighth fairway, to wade back. Beside the green of the ninth hole one was rewarded with a handshake from the owner, who proprietorially basked in one of the few golf carts available. It was a Depression-era course of minimal amenity and maximum intimacy; the owner's son drove the gang mowers, the daughter-in-law sold the Cokes and second-hand balls, and the aging holder of the course record (Frank Brady, 62) often acted as starter. Weekends saw long waits on the first tee. Greenheads, an insatiable fly bred in marshes, were a seasonal torment. You teed off on broken tees pried into the interstices of rubber mats. There were soggy patches and parched stretches on the fairways at the same time of the year. But the sea air and short-sleeved bonhomie were hard to beat. It was on this modest par-70 that I had my best round ever: a 38 on the first nine was topped by a par-35 on the second (the same nine), making a marvellous 73. My opponents refused to pay their debts, I had played so far above my head.

And other courses beckoned, a bit inland: Ould Newbury, with its aggravatingly elevated greens and pleasantly elevated screened clubhouse veranda; the Rowley Country Club, constructed as a lark by a retired Peabody contractor, its fairways newly seeded and its third hole an imposing watery dogleg; New Meadows, where the buzz of traffic along Route 1 mixed with that of the Topsfield mosquitoes. Some public courses boasted eighteen holes: Wenham, whose linkslike back nine throbbed to the passage of B & M commuter trains; Lynnfield's Colonial, where Canada geese and their spoor were superabundant and Red Sox players could occasionally be spotted, treading lightly; Boxford's Far Corner, its precipitous fairways on one witnessed occasion the scene of a spectacular roller-coaster ride, the rubber-tired golf cart doing slow wheelies on the wet grass all the way down to the eleventh green, while its duo of passengers, my playing partners, yelped.

It was a happy and varied world, public golf, but an increasingly crowded one, as televised tournaments gave the sport glamour, and the population of eastern Massachusetts grew, and a prospering economy freed ever more wage slaves to the joys of recreation. My old companions in driving miles to make a hard-won Publinx tee time slowly faded away, and my dying battery was recharged by membership in a private club. I came to know the privileged, curried terrains of Myopia and Essex, of Peabody's Salem and Salem's Kernwood, of Brookline's Country Club and Newton's Brae Burn and Wellesley's Wellesley. Gradually I acquired a country-club manner, an ease with chits and caddie tips, and an expectation of lush green spaces populated by discreetly scattered golfers, of three- or even four-level tees and carts equipped with grass-seed ladles that make replacing divots a *faux pas*, of clubhouses whose walls shone like those of Byzantine churches with gold-lettered walnut plaques proclaiming tournament results from bygone ages and with silvered clubs and balls of intense historic interest, and of pro shops stocked as densely as a flower shop with fanned bouquets of high-tech multi-metal clubs, of locker rooms scaled like the Baths of Caracalla, and of dining facilities that made upstairs at the Ritz look like a pizza parlor. However hard I endeavor to blend in, in costume and manner, my golf, I fear, has betrayed me, remaining ragged and unmannerly—public-course golf, formed in the school of hard knocks. Never mind; onward I go, spring, summer, and fall, in pursuit of that vision glimpsed in Wellesley nearly half a century ago.

* * *

Now, what, in all this rich experience, is distinctly of a Massachusetts character? The Puritan founders of this commonwealth have contributed, it may be, a certain Spartan tang to the sport, a tang less to be tasted in the plush precincts of Connecticut, so much of it suburban to New York City and its grotesque fortunes, or even to the precious courses carved from Rhode Island's meagre, inlet-nibbled acreage. Massachusetts clubhouses, by and large, rarely are cast in the mock-Tudor, half-timbered style favored in Greenwich, Stamford, and the Hudson Valley, nor are the waiting lists for memberships as elaborately staged or as cruelly prolonged as there; it is easier and quicker to help crew a spaceship to Uranus and back than run the hurdles at, say, Darien's Wee Burn. On the other hand, Massachusetts golf is not as rugged, or as truncated in the length of its season, as that in the three states of northern New England. Cape Cod can entertain play at any month of the year, and even north of Boston a good season stretches from a muddy start in April to an Indian-summer round in late November. As opposed to Florida golf, that of Massachusetts offers an entertainingly unflat terrain, rich in sidehill lies and blind spots over this or that immediate horizon. Hilly, but, unlike that of Vermont, not showily dependent on mountain views and prodigious feats of bulldozing to achieve a teeing area.

And, in distinction from Florida or Arizona or Alabama golfers, those of Massachusetts can venture out under the noon sun of most any summer day without suffering heat prostration. The summer is slow to come, with many a Maytime feint, but when it does it is a temperate sweetheart that rarely lacks a cooling breeze and a bearable humidity. No dawn risings to avoid the cruel scorch of midday; no late-afternoon rounds dragging past dinnertime. In Massachusetts one strides or rides cheerfully into the heart of the day, as through the warm months the scenery rings its changes from blossom time to leaf season, each with its own glories, its height and texture and tint of rough, its qualities of turf underfoot and of cloud overhead. Golf becomes an exhilarating reason to get outdoors and take a long soak in Nature. Insects, except for spring blackflies and August greenheads in some coastal locales, are no problem; nor does an alligator threaten to slither ravenously up from a water hazard, or a rattlesnake to uncoil from behind a red rock, or a scorpion to skitter hissing out of a burrow in a sand trap. Nature has been tamed, but for the wilderness wind that produces wild and wooly golf shots.

The character of one's companion Massachusetts golfers deserves to be particularized. They are not the high rollers of Palm Springs or Winged Foot; a dollar a side, or a quarter a skin, is enough to whet a thrifty Yankee's competitive edge and to bring the excitement of financial concern to a four-foot putt. In keeping with the commonwealth's Puritan heritage, we (if I may) know that life is a vale of tears, all is vanity, and earthly comfort is not the main issue. Cold days, damp days, nasty days are nevertheless days for golf.

Having been weaned on the essays of Ralph Waldo Emerson, Massachusetts golfers know that "a foolish consistency is the hobgoblin of little minds"; the inconsistencies of their game do not trouble them so much as philosophically amuse them. Aware, too, that "if the single man plant himself indomitably on his instincts, and there abide, the huge world will come round to him," they are loyal to their instinctive, untutored swings, and do not hurry off to seek instant relief in the faddish lessons of the golf pro, who comes from California and winters in Sarasota. The Massachusetts golfer wears his golf as he wears his turtleneck and uncreased corduroys and ten-year-old golf shoes; they may sag and hurt a bit, but they are his own, and "in self-trust, all the virtues are comprehended." Yet the self-trust is tempered by, as Emerson's disciple Thoreau put it, knowledge that "the mass of men lead lives of quiet desperation" and each man is "a parcel of vain strivings." Vainly striving together on the golf course, Massachusetts golfers evince a puckish stoicism and, usually, an unforced good humor. "Manners," to quote Emerson once more, "are the happy ways of doing things," and amid the laconic courtesies of an afternoon foursome one is not permitted to forget that golf is, as well as a competitive ordeal, a form of socialization.

One might wonder if the common philosophical wealth that Massachusetts inherits hasn't sapped our lust for victory. A relative few native golfers have excelled at the national level. There was Ouimet and his epic feat in 1913, but in modern annals the non-sportswriter is hard pressed to come up with names beyond those of Paul Harney, Bob Toski, and Pat Bradley. Toski rapidly won six tournaments in 1953–54, and then slumped into a distinguished career as a golf instructor. Little Rhode Island and Connecticut have done slightly better, producing Julius Boros, Brad Faxon, and Ken Green. The climate can be blamed, but is it much worse than that of western Pennsylvania, which produced Arnold Palmer, or of Rochester, New York, whence came Walter Hagen? It is certainly better for golf than Sweden, but look at Jesper Parnevik and Annika Sörenstam. Compared with, say, bleak and windy Texas, with its parade of greats from Byron Nelson to Ben Hogan to Lee Trevino and Ben Crenshaw and beyond, Massachusetts has kept its golf to itself, a green secret tucked here and there among its spired towns and bravely surviving farms. I like it that way. I never feel closer to my adopted state than when I am perambulating those green spaces, searching for the philosopher's stone behind a sweet, repeatable swing while casting a sideways glance at the early-budding willows and late-budding oaks, the swampy groves with their mossy stumps and springtime skunk cabbage, the wooden-bridged rivulets, the shimmering high rough of summer, and autumn's blazing fringe of hickories and maples all along the fairway.

THE GAME

In Love with a Wanton

I FELL IN LOVE with golf when I was twenty-five. It would have been a healthier relationship had it been an adolescent romance or, better yet, a childhood crush. Though I'd like to think we've had a lot of laughs together, and even some lyrical moments, I have never felt quite adequate to her demands, and the bitch has *secrets* she keeps from me. More secrets than I can keep track of; when I've found out one, another one comes out, and then three more, and by this time I've forgotten what the first one was. They are sexy little secrets that flitter around my body—a twitch of the left hip, a pronation of the right wrist, a cock of the head one way, a turn of the shoulders to the other—and they torment me like fire ants in my togs; I can't get them out of my mind, or quite wrap my mind around them. Sometimes I wish she and I had never met. She leads me on, but deep down I suspect—this is *my* secret—that I'm just not her type.

Who is her type? Well, go figure. Fat guys like Craig Stadler and Tim Herron, and skinny wispy guys like Corey Pavin, and lanky skinny guys like Tiger Woods, and grim intense guys like Jack Nicklaus and Ben Hogan, and laid-back jokers like Fuzzy Zoeller and Walter Hagen and Lee Trevino. Golf isn't exactly choosy, you'd have to say, but she can turn a cold shoulder to anybody on a given date. If there's one kind of suitor she consistently rejects it's the jittery, overanxious kind, worryworts who for all their lessons and driving-range prowess whiff on the first tee and stub a crucial three-foot putt on the eighteenth green. Golf likes a bit of sangfroid, the "What, me worry?" slouch, and spurns those who care too much and try too hard. I've tried not caring, but maybe I've tried too

Written for The Talk of the Town, July 31, 2000.

hard. She's an intuitive old girl; she sniffs you out. Those extra ten yards you think you can squeeze out of your swing—she's on to you while the club is still approaching horizontal. She likes guys (gals, too—she's through with gender hang-ups) who keep things simple and don't mind repeating themselves. And that, it breaks my heart to have at last perceived, lets me out.

So: why do I still love her? Why do I continue to pour hours and treasure into a futile and unreciprocated courtship? Well, she's awfully pretty. All those green curves, and dewy swales, and snug little sand traps; and the way she grassily stretches here and there and then some. She makes you think big, and lifts your head up to face the sky. When you connect, it's the whistle of a quail, it's the soar of a hawk, it's the sighting of a planet hitherto unseen; it's mathematical perfection wrested from a half-buried lie; it's absolute. And golf never lets you go a whole round without your connecting once or twice. You think she's turned her back on you forever, but with a little smile over her nicely mowed shoulder she lets a long putt rattle in, or a chip settle up close, or a 7-iron take a lucky kick off a greenside mound. Another foot to the right, and . . . Oh, she is quite the tease.

And quite the accountant, too. How can you not love a game where a three-hundred-yard drive and a two-inch putt each count the same? I mean, that's a sport with a sense of proportion. And the shapely rhythmic way a round dwindles down, hole after hole, far and then closer, and closer yet, and in. It's a journey ending in a burial and—*whoa!*—up out of the grave again, eighteen times in all, twice a cat's number of lives. In other games, somebody else is always getting in your way, all elbows and trash talk, brushing you back from the plate, serving to your backhand, giving you aggravation. Golf lets you do the aggravation all by yourself: there is nothing between you and the hole but what you've managed to put there. She's no flatterer, but she can give a sucker an occasional break: a scuffed drive, a skulled approach, and a putt that would have rolled ten feet past still make a par-3 on the scorecard.

The tools—is it too intimate to talk about the tools, the tender way the leather grips invite the fingers to curl around them and adhere, the grainy grooved faces of the irons, the slither of a club being withdrawn from the bag, the flexing elegance of the tapered shafts, even the merry dimples on the ball and the tiny sensation of "give" when the wooden tee penetrates the turf? Golf has the equipment to please a man, and she's not ashamed to use it. She's been around since the Scots monarchs were stymieing the English and Old Tom Morris would spend a drizzly afternoon stuffing a single feathery with duck down; but you're as young as you feel, and my sweetheart still runs me ragged. And ragged, she keeps letting me know, isn't good enough. We'd break up in a flash, except we never really got together.

Playing with Better Players

UNHAPPY GOLFERS are each unhappy in their own way, but it is not true, as Tolstoy's well-known formulation would have it, that all happy golfers are alike. Some, as we see on television, have flowing, picture-book swings, and others, especially among the seniors, swat at the ball, after short and choppy backswings. Arnold Palmer leaves his club out in front of him like a rifle, Lee Trevino seems to be trying to slap his drive through the right side of the infield, and Jim Furyk resembles, a commentator has said, an octopus falling out of a tree. But all seem to get the job done, or did get it done in their prime, and the mystery of how lingers somewhere out of the range of TV cameras. A viewer basically sees the ball vanish off the right of the screen like a banana slice and hears the commentator excitedly bleat that the shot is bending in, on top of the flagstick.

No, being there in three dimensions is the only way to see for yourself, and for that reason a mediocre golfer needs now and then to play with better golfers. They show up in club tournaments or as the brother-in-law of a weekly partner; they can be college students or company salesmen or vagabond scions of a snake-oil fortune. Their togs are color-coördinated, the pockets of their bags bulge with towels, rainsuits, and spare gloves. As they take practice swings on the first tee, the *swish* of their clubs has a higher pitch than you hear in your usual, companionably inept foursome. Without seeming to strain, they generate clubhead speed where it counts, at the bottom of the swing, where the ball is. Doesn't everybody? No: the virtually universal tendency of duffers is to hit from the top, expending wrist-cock in the first ninety degrees of the arc and thus arriving at the ball late and weak, giving it an armsy, decelerating hit that makes the fingers tingle and digs a deadening divot on the wrong side of the ball. With that little white orb sitting up on tee or turf begging to be spanked, our lunging into the downswing as swiftly and passionately as possible makes good sense to the warrior within us—*Look out! The other fellow has a broadsword, too!!*—but couldn't be more coun-

---

Contribution to *The Ultimate Golf Book*, edited by Charles McGrath and David McCormick (2002).

terproductive. The good player waits that heartbeat for the club to swing itself. His grip shows no white knuckles; the club adheres to him of its own sweet will. *Swish, swish:* a new beast has been released, there on the first tee.

Watching your accustomed friends set up, waggle, and attack the ball, you are conscious of their bodies as a collection of separate units struggling to get together. The arms go back as far as they conveniently can, and then fear of failure, of generating insufficient distance, pushes them up some more inches, tipping the shoulders into a reverse pivot and making the feet fight like Tinker Bell's to keep contact with the earth. The knees gyrate in agitation and the head bobs as if signalling assent to the hopelessness of it all. First the right leg locks straight as a stick, and then the left. It is all too much activity to squeeze into two seconds. The ordinary swing encompasses a roughly circular area full of muscular yearnings; propelled by such a rich mix of motions, the clubhead is lucky to graze the top of the ball or to get an open toe on a couple of dimples.

The better golfer, contrariwise, seems to have only a waist, which twists slightly one way, to square his shoulders at a right angle to the flight line, and then the other way, to send the club into the ball and way beyond, so that the shaft winds up behind his back. That is what you miss on television, the quick way the center of the body—the waist and hips— *slings* the arms, as passive spokes, through the swing's wide arc. The happy player gives the impression of big muscles used sparingly; the unhappy use all their little muscles, including those for pursing the lips and grinding the teeth, in order to propel a ball impossibly small and obdurate along a line as narrow and scary as a tightrope. The integrated, waisty (not wristy) swing makes the ball harder to miss; a simple coiling and uncoiling sweep it away, to distances we have trouble believing. Once I marvelled at where a diminutive veteran had put his 4-iron, way past my drive, and he bristled as if I were accusing him of cheating. As indeed, in a way, I was: it's cheating to make golf look that easy.

There is also a look the good players have of *rolling the shoulders*—for us lesser players the shoulders are a kind of seesaw, clenched and angular, whereas for our betters the suggestion is more of a tilted roundabout softly surging through a half-circle. Sam Snead exemplified this look, a kind of pantherish padded motion around his Panama-hat brim, as casually smooth as stepping onto an escalator. A fellow-student of the game once came back from watching a professional tournament with the wide-eyed revelation that the pros, seen up close, aren't really swinging easy; their hands are a blur. A blur, I think, the way the end of a whip is a blur; the big body parts move the unresisting arms and loose, light hands through the hitting area before we know it. There is an enviable way in which a well-struck ball, in the moment of impact, seems already to be *halfway there*.

Good players chase after the ball with the clubhead. The rest of us tend to hit and quit. The difference may not be apparent, but the ball feels the difference, and quits on us in turn. Also, good players on the green express, with their springy steps and earnest squats and squints, a certain expectancy of making the putt, though it be a downhill fifty-footer. Their faith is sometimes rewarded, certainly more often than our lack of faith, with its woefully short, absentminded lags and, in compensation, nervously jabbed six-footers, which rim the cup and end up a bit more than a gimme away. Good players expect, too, to get up and down, from a sand trap and elsewhere close, while we mentally chalk up three shots—the short approach and two putts.

Finally, good players are pleasant to play with as well as instructive. Snug within their low-handicap comfort zone, they maintain a cheerful temper, never condescend to a sputtering duffer, demonstrate a scrupulous but unlawyerly regard for the rules, and rarely lose a golf ball. Only when one of them pounds a 3-wood right through the first part of a dogleg do they oblige their companions to visit with them the woods, brambles, swamp, or gorse.

Good golfers show what golf can and should be. Nevertheless, they lack one lovely quality that your wristy, reverse-pivoting, heads-up, where-did-it-go buddies in the regular Wednesday foursome ever so delightfully possess: you can beat them.

Walking Insomnia

TIGER WOODS, after his narrow victory in the 1999 PGA, slumped and sighed as if he'd been carrying rocks uphill all afternoon. His suddenly weary demeanor reminded me of a curious physiological phenomenon: one is rarely tired while playing golf. Afterward, yes, and beforehand, very possibly, but while the score is mounting and the tees and fairways and greens are passing underfoot, fatigue is magically held at bay. I have flown overnight to London, taken the morning commuter plane from Heathrow up to Edinburgh, and driven several hours through a winding

---

Written for *Golf Digest*, March 2001.

chain of Scots villages to a golf course, delirious with jet lag. But once I stepped with my group of groggy Yanks onto the springy turf of the first tee, a rejuvenating exhilaration set in, dissipating fatigue as does the sun the mists of morning. We frisked around like a pack of schoolboys, and only after the eighteenth hole, in the creaking leather armchairs of the clubhouse bar, partaking of lulling liquors, did we feel our years again.

And in this country, too, the aftereffects of a short night's sleep and a premature arising are suspended during play. How can this be? The answer can only be that golf is so entertaining and various in its challenges that the mortal frame is wholly engaged; weariness finds no cranny whereby to enter. Think of an average par-4 as a duffer plays it. First, the perilous, all-important drive, which can evade any fairway no matter how wide and can be sliced, hooked, or topped into any patch of rough no matter how out of the way. Then, once the wee orb has been maneuvered with one blow or many to within, say, 150 yards of the green, there is the iron shot, demanding not the drive's sweeping motion but a sharper, more simultaneously upright and downward swing, ideally culminating in a smart divot and a soaring straight shot. If ideality does not become reality, a chip of some length is left, requiring crisp contact and a judiciously partial swing. Then, if the chip is not skulled across the green, or chunked into more short rough, or shanked sideways into a sand trap, there remain, most likely, two putts—the long putt, requiring a slippery mental image of lagged distance and estimated break on the swales and humps of the green, and the short putt, a testing little snake with its own fangs of dire possibility.

At every point on this progression the mind is challenged by fresh problems; it is as if a sculptor were to move around his studio carving first in granite, then in soapstone, then in tight-grained wood, in friable plaster, and finally in butter. Each substance demands its own technique, its own backlog of previous experience and helpful admonitions to oneself. *Don't overswing. Don't hurry from the top. Turn your back. Keep the triangle of the arms and chest. Don't grip too tight. Don't baby it. Pick your spot, and trust it. Get it up to the hole. Don't overread the break, or underread it.* Each touch of the club on the ball is a test, and a chance for redemption. A good iron can redeem a mediocre drive. A good chip can redeem a poor iron. A good putt can redeem a bad chip. There is hope at every juncture, until the ball rattles into the cup and sends us on to the next tee, where fresh hope springs up as readily as dandelions in April.

Oh, to be sure, other sports have their variety, too. In tennis, there is the forehand, the backhand, the overhead smash, and the drop volley, each with a different grip. Baseball skills schizophrenically encompass a batter's and a fielder's. Still, only golf sets up its challenges in such a tidy row, a telescoping succession like that of Russian dolls nested one inside another. There is space between each shot, providing time in which to contemplate and conceptualize. The classic and best way to play is to walk, coming up on the ball from behind with a firm and thoughtful tread, rather than zigzagging at it with a cart partner's chatter in your ears and his ball cluttering your view. Connecting the dots is the method of golf's puzzle, the prize going to the fewest connections. The course is a diagram in your head, and you are the dot, moving along in as straight a line as you can manage.

If the course is one you play often, you have hit most of the possible shots well enough at some time or other, and one of the stimuli keeping you awake is this rivalry with your best self. Golf at its measured pace permits an electric excess of mental activity. Your brain pours a rain of advice down upon your body, like a seasoned old coach who is at first patient and fatherly with a dull-witted athlete, then louder and blunter in his sideline advice, and finally livid with frustration. Who could sleep in such a racket of inward stricture?

And always the next shot lures us on, making the heart race with hope, even though the ball be found in the rough beneath a tangle of running raspberries, or in the woods behind an arched beech root, or in the sand nested within its own concussion crater. But recovery is not utterly impossible; the green is but 120 yards away; a deliberate slice might well curve into the hand's-breadth of space between two stout trunks. So: keep the head down and the hands ahead of the clubhead. *Pow!* The ball vanishes—no, there it is, skipping along on the cart path, taking a fortunate kick right off the trap rake, dribbling onto the green, settling close to the hole, from here it looks like a gimme. Your buddies cheer. Another addition is made to the sparse annals of your wonderful shots.

Even in the depths of a dismal round the possibility of a miracle lingers. Despair relaxes the swing, and things look paradoxically up. Many a long putt wanders in for a nice quadruple bogey. Many a soaring wedge caps a succession of tense foozles. The possibilities are always there, and keep our energy high. There is never a juncture where the adrenaline can stop flowing. And who could be bored or long disconsolate amid the spreading scenery that unfolds around us, the heedless wildlife that twitches at the edges of our journey, the silvery clouds that cap it? Who could be tired with so much to think about, so much to hope for, so much to laugh about, so much to redeem? Space brims all around us, and vaster yet is our room for improvement. I have, I confess, sometimes wondered how some of my more retired friends can play golf every day without any sign of surfeit. Well, the man is the same, and the course is the same, but the golf is never the same, and those wide-awake synapses just keep firing.

Lost Balls

And the wind shall say: "Here were decent godless people:
Their only monument the asphalt road
And a thousand lost golf balls."
　　　　　　　　　　　—T. S. Eliot, chorus from *The Rock*

I HAVE SEEN news videos of outfielders rummaging for a baseball lost in the ivy on the quaintly leafy wall at Wrigley Field, and I have experienced mis-hit tennis balls flying over the court fence deep into an impenetrable grove beyond, but no sport offers the sensation of lostness as often and enragingly as does golf. The damn thing *has* to be here, we think as we thrash at a clump of blueberry bushes or buffalo grass with the 7-iron we hopefully brought with us into the wilderness. Our obliging partners tramp in circles with us for a few minutes, peeking into drainage ditches and under fallen palm fronds, but their hearts aren't in it the way ours are; this lost ball represents two strokes, and two extra strokes could mean the hole and even, it could be, the match, the entire outing, the day itself. *Why me?* one wonders. It was just a little slice, a tiny tail exaggerated by a gust of wind. It carried only a tad, a mere yard or two, into the woods, or the marsh, or the tall grass. Why couldn't it have been the other fellow, the loudmouth buddy smugly announcing, "O.K., we've given it five minutes, let's get a move on. It's getting dark, guys"? Not as dark, actually, as the inner weather as one trudges along, dragging like the foursome's crippled foot, "out of the hole," as they say, headed for an ignominious triple bogey, a condescending, token "paper seven."

The whereabouts of the ball are in a sense the key to every ball game, but the whereabouts are most picturesque in golf. Tangles of running raspberry, the shadowy depths of a deep sand bunker, the sandy beds of shallow little watercress-choked creeks, the weedy lees of lichen-laden stone walls, the snake-infested moonscapes of Precambrian basalt just off the plush watered fairways of a desert course, the pulpy flesh of a venerable saguaro cactus, the leaf-mulched floor of a hushed beech forest, the

---

Foreword to a book of golf photographs by Charles Lindsay (2005).

squishy tummocks of a reedy marsh, the hot and sere macadam of the club parking lot, the concrete curb next to the snack shop, the bed of petunias and pansies lifted up on creosoted railroad ties beside the eleventh tee—all these nasty patches of environment can play host to a misplayed golf ball. We have been there.

And others have been there before us. All but buried in the sun-dried mud of a bygone spring day, an ancient cut-up Acushnet glimmers to catch the golfer's restless eye. Or perhaps, in a patch of low-lying, seldom-visited bog, a waffle-patterned gutta-percha antique comes to light, browned on its underside by its ages-long bath in the slow-acting acids of Mother Earth. For every lost ball, there was once a forlorn search, perfunctory or thorough; these questing ghosts haunt the course, hovering at the juncture of their interrupted game. "Found it!" one wants to cry out in triumph, though the loser has been decades in his grave. Golf thus leaves a residue, thin but detectable, on the hundreds of acres set aside for play. Not only lost golf balls but broken tees, detached cleats, withered gloves, and the occasional broken shaft, petulantly snapped in two, mingle their mournful testimony with the silent turf.

A player interacts with the landscape at a visceral level, his natural difficulties translating into rage and even tears. At times, analyzing the niceties of a "close lie," he takes a worm's-eye view of the ball as it nestles amid pebbles and tufts; at others, his eye soars like that of a lordly hawk, seeking the telltale glint of his ball in a wide, wind-whitened world of rough. Goose feathers and dandelion polls and balled-up Kleenexes cruelly tease him with optical illusions. Nature is his companion, but, like a nagging wife, she persistently points out his inadequacies and cloaks her scenic beauties in the ongoing quarrel of the game itself. We struggle to experience the course as something other than an enemy challenging and taunting us at every swing—to experience it instead as a site of seduction, of artful landscaping, of birdsong and wild berry and pale blossom and scarlet autumnal leaf, all tamed to our use in an enchanted blend of natural creation and human recreation. But a greenside bunker leaps up and pounces on a singing 9-iron and shatters our mood, narrowing our perspective to a square foot of damp sand.

The camera of Charles Lindsay knows how to see the game. It not only sees the variety of turf and the luxuriant obduracy of rough but it hears the *plip* of the sadly underclubbed approach as it sends out the ripples from its irrevocable submersion, and it smells the tonic freshness of morning dew and rising mist, and it feels the effort of a sand wedge digging deep to lift the ball over the trap's hairy lip. From Ireland to Arizona and back his camera has journeyed to record golf's sensations—the weave of interlocking incident that makes up a round. Some golf balls are lost, and with the things now retailing for twelve dollars a sleeve of three Pro V1s, this borders on tragedy. But some are found, right where we thought we had looked a half-dozen times before. Not only is it ours (a theatrical examination, *sans touche*, confirms it) but it is sitting up on a bed of pine needles. There is an opening back to the fairway. There is even a shot—a chancy shot, with a deliberate slice, cunningly controlled—at the green. So keep your head down and swing easy. Golf may not be a lost cause after all.

Being Senior

I SEEM TO REMEMBER, from my hundreds of hours spent watching televised golf, a bulky senior pro (Gay Brewer? Charles Coody?) leaping up into the startled but smiling embrace of Sam Snead, who had just carried the two of them, with his ageless swing and sidewinder putting style, to a match-play victory. It was the kind of jocular moment we used to expect of the Seniors Tour, when the stakes were low enough and the I've-been-there factor was high enough to permit some foolery to squeak through. In the first decade, the 1980s, Chi Chi Rodríguez and then Lee Trevino brought their Latin levity into the winner's circle, and nobody made a million dollars in a season. Trevino was the first, in 1990. Now two million is par, and the big money winners the last three years, Hale Irwin, Larry Nelson, and Bruce Fleisher, are amiable sportsmen but too intent to be comedians. The stakes have gone up, the field is keen, and you better make your killing before your fiftieth birthday has settled too deep into your bones.

The Senior PGA Tour, as it evolved, turned out *not* to be the regular tour transcribed up a decade or two in the age scale. It was dominated, in its early decades, by unspectacular regular-tour players like Don January and Miller Barber who proved insouciant and durable enough to thrive in the senior altitudes. On the other hand, Jack Nicklaus and Arnold Palmer failed to have Senior careers commensurate with their regular-tour achievements. Hale Irwin, who recently became the all-time Senior winner, now dominates, but at his heels there is a hungry pack of names we've never heard before—club pros and British/Aussie also-rans who

---

Written for the official program for the 2001 U.S. Senior Open Championship, held in June at the Salem Country Club in Peabody, Massachusetts.

find after half a century of ill-rewarded labor the opportunity to cash in. Success at the highest levels of golf is much a matter of intensity, and perhaps only so many decades of intensity are given to an athlete: burnout is a natural consequence of competitive fire. The man at last released from the thralldom of a pro shop, where his time is consumed with giving lessons and selling equipment to the relatively inept, may well come forth at fifty, his children's educations secured and his mortgage at last paid off, ablaze with a pent-up will to dominate. Certainly the Senior Tour offers us a revised star system, featuring such unfamiliar names as Tom Wargo and Bruce Summerhays and Don Bies and John Bland and cigar-chomping Larry Laoretti and, indeed, top-ranking Bruce Fleisher, who won a single tournament on the regular PGA tour and whose best finish on the money list, in 1992, placed him sixty-eighth. A delayed dose of prowess seemed to kick in for these middle-aged men.

To those of us who never won more than a low flight in the club four-ball, senior status also holds out a chance of rewards. Retirement brings with it more time on the course and the practice range. Senior sagacity, honed in forty years of carving a living from a cruel world, can surely tame at last that youthful slice. The old body doesn't seem so bad, if we tighten the belt a notch and remember to do those stretching exercises on the tee; its very stiffness may be the enforced path to a slowed tempo and a shorter backswing. Golf is 90 percent in the head, and a man is more and more head as he ages. Mind over matter at last. If all it takes for a solid hit is a fuller shoulder-turn and a lighter grip, why, here they are, delivered by the mature brain to the muscular system as faithfully as a Social Security check plopping through the letter slot. It's a simple game, after all. And, with this new equipment, it virtually plays itself. Why, I can remember (you tell yourself) when a 3-wood was literally that, a little persimmon knob with a face no bigger than a quail egg, and the shaft was raw steel, with as little flex as a car jack. These new MegaMagnum Quadra Metals, and their matching scoopback krypton irons with annealed plastic insets, zing the ball virtually while they're still in the bag; the laws of physics allow you no way to miss.

Yet somehow the old landmarks on the course seem to be receding like the top of the down escalator. The drive that used to reach the swale now hangs back on the flat: the bunker an 8-iron used to clear in a breeze has been expanded (drat those cocky young upstarts on the greens committee!) to swallow a 6. And yet you never struck a 6-iron more cleanly, with more seasoned know-how. Clearly there has been lots of fiddling with the course, under cover of night. The greens have been shaved to a glassy smoothness, so that an ideally hit chip nevertheless has no bite and slides off into the nasturtium bed at the base of the next tee. Whose fancy idea was it, anyway, to plant nasturtiums there?

The course seems a little stranger each day, though you bring to it ever more senior wisdom. At times, on the greens, while your senescent opponent hangs for three minutes over his sidehill two-footer, you forget where you are, let alone what the score is. A sliver of cloudiness, like a plastic insert, slides between your intention and the execution. On the fairway, as you step up to your shot, the key swing-tip slips from your consciousness and you hit with a blank pleading mind, like a hurt boxer waiting for the bell to ring. At times, even, the senior golfer is prey to wondering, while he sweats over a six-foot putt to salvage a double bogey, if it's worth it, all this anxiety, suppressed rage, expense, and waste of hours to determine whether or not a little ball will slip into a hole. Such thoughts are heresy—look at how Tiger Woods winces, crumpling as if stabbed, when a putt slides by. But such irreverent doubts do enter the senior head, and make the old quest for perfection, like other instances of youthful ardor, seem a touch silly.

And yet the beauty of a well-struck shot and the happiness of being in nature continue to lure us outdoors. The great gap between a duffer's skills and those of the senior professionals who are strutting their stuff at the Salem Country Club this week invites us to believe we might still, in spite of our deteriorating bodies and emptying heads, improve. The room for improvement is exhilaratingly large; we might, by the mellow light of the sunset years, whittle away at it, reducing the number of three-putts, fluffed chips, thinned approaches, pushed irons, and topped drives that have kept our handicap, these many years, so far above our true potential.

Handicap: how apt that word is! Every golfer is handicapped, and increasingly so, by aching joints, fuzzy vision, and diminished muscle tone. But diminishing expectations can bring with them a relaxing modesty. It is too late—too late!—for us to qualify for the Senior circuit, but in the tiny circuit of our equally aging golfing acquaintance, we can, with a little refreshed focus, still cut a swath, wreaking vengeance for past defeats and reaping a harvest of quarters and dollar bills in Skins or low-stakes Nassau. So on we seniors soldier, a vincible doughty army, ever hopeful, ever grateful for those moments of the game when a good or lucky shot allows us to forget our age.

Table Talk

THE END OF AUTHORSHIP: *Words addressed to booksellers attending Book-Expo America, in Washington, D.C., in May 2006.*

Booksellers, you are the salt of the book world. You are on the front line where, while the author cowers in his opium den, you encounter—or "interface with," as we say now—the rare and mysterious Americans who are willing to plunk down twenty-five dollars for a book. Bookstores are lonely forts, spilling light onto the sidewalk. They civilize their neighborhoods. At my mother's side I used to visit the two stores in downtown Reading, Pennsylvania, a city then of a hundred thousand, and I still recall their names and locations—the Book Mart, at Sixth Street and Court, and the Berkshire News, on Fifth Street, in front of the trolley stop that would take us home to Shillington.

When I went away to college, I marvelled at the wealth of bookstores around Harvard Square. In addition to the Coop and various outlets where impecunious students like myself could buy tattered volumes polluted by someone else's underlinings and marginalia, there were bookstores that catered to the Cambridge bourgeoisie, the professoriate, and those elite students with money and reading time to spare. The Grolier, specializing in modern poetry, occupied a choice niche on Plympton Street, and over on Boylston there was the Mandrake, a more spacious sanctum for books of rare, pellucid, and modernist water. In the Mandrake—presided over by Irwin Rosen, a soft-voiced short man, with brushed-back graying hair—there were English books, Faber & Faber and Victor Gollancz, books with purely typographical jackets and cloth-covered boards warping from the damp of their transatlantic passage, and art books, too glossy and expensive even to glance into, and of course New Directions books, modest in format and delicious in their unread content.

After Harvard, I went to Oxford for a year, and browsed for dazed hours in the rambling treasury, on the street called the Broad, of Blackwell's—shelves of Everyman's and Oxford Classics, and the complete works, jacketed in baby-blue paper, of Thomas Aquinas, in Latin and English. Then I came to New York, when Fifth Avenue still seemed lined with bookstores—the baronial Scribner's, with the central staircase and the scrolled ironwork of its balconies, and the Doubleday's a few blocks on, with an ascending spiral staircase visible through plate glass.

Now I live in a villagelike corner of a small New England city that holds, *mirabile dictu*, an independent bookstore, one of the few surviving in the long coastal stretch between Marblehead and Newburyport. But I live, it seems, in a fool's paradise. Last month, the *New York Times Magazine* published a lengthy article that gleefully envisioned the end of the bookseller, and indeed of the writer. Written by Kevin Kelly, identified as the "senior maverick" at *Wired* magazine, the article describes a glorious digitalizing of all written knowledge. Google's plan, announced in December 2004, to scan the contents of five major research libraries and make them searchable, according to Kelly, has resurrected the dream of the universal library. "The explosive rise of the Web, going from nothing to everything in one decade," he writes, "has encouraged us to believe in the impossible again. Might the long-heralded great library of all knowledge really be within our grasp?"

Unlike the libraries of old, Kelly continues, "this library would be truly democratic, offering every book to every person." The anarchic nature of the true democracy emerges bit by bit. "Once digitized, books can be unraveled into single pages or be reduced further, into snippets of a page," Kelly writes. "These snippets will be remixed into reordered books and virtual bookshelves. Just as the music audience now juggles and reorders songs into new albums (or 'playlists,' as they are called in iTunes), the universal library will encourage the creation of virtual 'bookshelves'—a collection of texts, some as short as a paragraph, others as long as entire books, that form a library shelf's worth of specialized information. And as with music playlists, once created, these 'bookshelves' will be published and swapped in the public commons. Indeed, some authors will begin to write books to be read as snippets or to be remixed as pages."

The economic repercussions of this paradise of freely flowing snippets are touched on with a beguiling offhandedness, as a matter of course, a matter of an inexorable Marxist unfolding. As the current economic model disappears, Kelly writes, the "basis of wealth" shifts to "relationships, links, connection and sharing." Instead of selling copies of their work, writers and artists can make a living selling "performances, access to the creator, personalization, add-on information, the scarcity of attention (via ads), sponsorship, periodic subscriptions—in short, all the many values that cannot be copied. The cheap copy becomes the 'discovery tool' that markets these other intangible valuables."

This is, as I read it, a pretty grisly scenario. "Performances, access to the creator, personalization," whatever that is—does this not throw us back to the pre-literate societies, where only the present, live person can make an impression and offer, as it were, value? Have not writers, since the onset of the Gutenberg revolution, imagined that they already were, in their written and printed texts, giving an "access to the creator" more pointed, more shapely, more loaded with aesthetic and informational value than an unmediated, unpolished personal conversation? Has the electronic revolution pushed us so far down the path of celebrity as a *summum bonum* that an author's works, be they one volume or fifty, serve primarily as his or her ticket to the lecture platform, or, since even that is somewhat hierarchical and aloof, a series of one-on-one orgies of personal access?

In my first fifteen or twenty years of authorship, I was almost never asked to give a speech or an interview. The written work was supposed to speak for itself, and to sell itself, sometimes even without the author's photograph on the back flap. As the author is gradually retired from his old responsibilities of vicarious confrontation and provocation, he has grown in importance as a kind of walking, talking advertisement for the book—a much more pleasant and flattering duty, it may be, than composing the book in solitude. Authors, if I understand present trends, will soon be like surrogate birth mothers, rented wombs in which a seed implanted by high-powered consultants is allowed to ripen and, after nine months, be dropped squalling into the marketplace.

In imagining a huge, virtually infinite wordstream accessed by search engines and populated by teeming, promiscuous word snippets stripped of credited authorship, are we not depriving the written word of its old-fashioned function of, through such inventions as the written alphabet and the printing press, communication from one person to another—of, in short, accountability and intimacy? Yes, there is a ton of information on the Web, but much of it is egregiously inaccurate, unedited, unattributed, and juvenile. The electronic marvels that abound around us serve, surprisingly, to inflame what is most informally and noncritically human about us—our computer screens stare back at us with a kind of giant, instant "Aw, shucks," disarming in its modesty, disquieting in its diffidence.

The printed, bound, and paid-for book was—still is, for the moment—more exacting, more demanding, of its producer and consumer both. It is the site of an encounter, in silence, of two minds, one following in the other's steps but invited to imagine, to argue, to concur on a level of reflection beyond that of personal encounter, with all its merely social conventions, its merciful padding of blather and mutual forgiveness. Book readers and writers are approaching the condition of holdouts, surly hermits who refuse to come out and play in the electronic sunshine of the post-Gutenberg village. "When books are digitized," Kelly ominously promises, "reading becomes a community activity. . . . The universal library becomes one very, very, very large single text: the world's only book."

Books traditionally have edges: some are rough-cut, some are smooth-cut, and a few, at least at my extravagant publishing house, are even top-stained. In the electronic anthill, where are the edges? The book revolution, which, from the Renaissance on, taught men and women to cherish and cultivate their individuality, threatens to end in a sparkling cloud of snippets.

So, booksellers, defend your lonely forts. Keep your edges dry. Your edges are our edges. For some of us, books are intrinsic to our sense of personal identity.

IN DEFENSE OF THE AMATEUR READER: *Remarks upon accepting the National Book Critics Circle Award in Criticism, for* Hugging the Shore, *in January 1984.*

Winning a prize for criticism from a circle of critics is a wonderful thing, and I thank you. I do not presume to call myself a critic, while paradoxically harboring the hope that some of what I write might be dignified with the name of criticism. I am a free-lance writer who writes on occasion about books, bringing to the task a rusty liberal-arts education, an average citizen's spotty knowledge of contemporary issues, and a fiction writer's childish willingness to immerse himself in make-believe. My embarkation, twenty-five years ago, on my first book reviews was prompted, perhaps, by a dim sense that the humanities and arts need repeated injections of amateurism.

In this country now, public considerations of literary effort fall into two camps: there are those who, in newspapers and magazines, review the new books that are simultaneously appearing in the bookstores, and there are those who, in universities and colleges, present to students works of established merit. The former, in that even an adverse review constitutes publicity, function as arms of the publishing industry, as the latter function as employees of the educational industry. A task of the educational professionals is to advance literary theories, preferably with some shine of the newly invented or imported, whereby the students can process in their required papers works already exhaustively discussed by prior generations. A task of the journalistic professional is to suggest that, regardless of the ups and downs of individual cases, the world of books—the world of *new* books—is an exciting one, and bookstores are places, like Greece and the savings bank, that one really should visit. The two camps are not exclusive—professors review books all the time—and between them do mighty work in keeping the book industry humming. But one's elusive fear, amid so much industry, is that an aura of duty will oust all joy from the situation.

Whatever art offered the men and women of previous eras, what it offers our own, it seems to me, is space—a certain breathing room for the spirit. The town I grew up in had many vacant lots; when I go back now, the vacant lots are gone. They were a luxury, just as tigers and rhinoceri, in the crowded world that is making, are luxuries. Museums and bookstores should feel, I think, like vacant lots—places where the demands on us are our own demands, where the spirit can find exercise in unsupervised play. Our artistic heroes tend to be those self-exercisers, like Picasso, and Nabokov, and Wallace Stevens, who rather defiantly kept playing past dark. There should always be something gratuitous about art, just as there seems to be, according to the new-wave cosmologists, something gratuitous about the universe. Art, out of its own freedom, should excite and flatter our sense of our own. Professionalism in art has this difficulty: to be professional is to be dependable, to be dependable is to be predictable, and predictability is aesthetically boring—an anti-virtue in a field where we hope to be astonished and startled and at some deep level refreshed.

A man who reads a book for no particular profit becomes, while he reads, a gentleman, a man of leisure, a dandy of a sort; one would hate to see this dandyism entirely squelched, whether by the analytic mills of the universities or by the scarcely less grim purveying of animated information and automated thrills reflected by the best-seller lists. An occasional sport, a *White Hotel* or *Name of the Rose*, does show up in these lists to remind us that a certain whimsy, an ineluctable hankering for the elegant and unclassifiable, does persist in the soul of that rough beast, the book-buying public; but in general the list is all too predictable, and the industry as a whole is all too dependent upon the list. This potentially mirthless situation we self-appointed critics—and who will appoint us if not ourselves?—can ameliorate by being, within measure, self-amusing, by indulging our own tastes and pursuing our own educations, by seeking out the underpublished wallflower on the edge of the dance floor and giving her a twirl, by reminding ourselves that literary delights are rarefied delights, that today's blockbuster is tomorrow's insulation, that books are at best a beacon in the darkness but at second best a holiday that lasts and lasts.

A POETICS OF BOOK REVIEWING, *codified for the foreword to* Picked-Up Pieces *(1976).*

My rules, drawn up inwardly when I embarked on this craft, and shaped intaglio-fashion by youthful traumas at the receiving end of critical opinion, were and are:

1.) Try to understand what the author wished to do, and do not blame him for not achieving what he did not attempt.

2.) Give enough direct quotation—at least one extended passage—of the book's prose so the review's reader can form his own impression, can get his own taste.

3.) Confirm your description of the book with quotation from the book, if only phrase-long, rather than proceeding by fuzzy *précis.*

4.) Go easy on plot summary, and do not give away the ending. (How astounded and indignant was I, when innocent, to find reviewers blabbing, and with the sublime inaccuracy of drunken lords reporting on a peasants' revolt, all the turns of my suspenseful and surpriseful narrative! Most ironically, the only readers who approach a book as the author intends, unpolluted by pre-knowledge of the plot, are the detested reviewers themselves. And then, years later, the blessed fool who picks the volume at random from a library shelf.)

5.) If the book is judged deficient, cite a successful example along the same lines, from the author's *oeuvre* or elsewhere. Try to understand the failure. Sure it's his and not yours?

To these concrete five might be added a vaguer sixth, having to do with maintaining a chemical purity in the reaction between product and appraiser. Do not accept for review a book you are predisposed to dislike, or committed by friendship to like. Do not imagine yourself a caretaker of any tradition, an enforcer of any party standards, a warrior in any ideological battle, a corrections officer of any kind. Never, never try to put the author "in his place," making of him a pawn in a contest with other reviewers. Review the book, not the reputation. Submit to whatever spell, weak or strong, is being cast. Better to praise and share than blame and ban. The communion between reviewer and public is based upon the presumption of certain possible joys of reading, and all our discriminations should curve toward that end.

AN AMERICAN VIEW OF ENGLISH FICTION: *Comment solicited by the* Times Literary Supplement *(London) in the spring of 1964, when Murdoch and Spark and the world were young.*

It is difficult for me to conceive of English fiction as something susceptible to telescopic examination of the sort we give a star: in most ways I feel closer to Muriel Spark than to Norman Mailer, though I may not be typical in this. At any rate my sense of instantaneous participation, as a reader, in English writing makes it absurd for me to say what is so obvious: that I enjoy, admire, and hope to have learned something from, say, E. M. Forster and Evelyn Waugh. It is perhaps less obvious, and more useful to say, that in my early reading the very beautiful and surprising novels of Henry Green were a revelation to me comparable only to my first readings of Proust and Kafka—and that if I were able to rub a lamp and have a new book by any living Englishman, it would be a book by him. To this I could add that, for a superbly cadenced examination of emotional states, I have read nothing recently to compare with Iris Murdoch's *A Severed Head.* And, while we are at it, let me express my enduring affection and admiration for a generation of English writers—that of Chesterton, Belloc, Shaw, and Conrad—who, while no longer held in the esteem their living presences could command, have remained readable in a way true of no American writer between Henry James and Hemingway.

In general, it seems to me possible that Americans trying to write can learn from their English cousins the valuable lesson of modesty. I do not mean to suggest that the English have "much to be modest about"—I mean that a certain vague assurance that society has a place (however modest) for him enables the English writer to utilize his gifts with a directness and ease denied the American. For the American writer, feeling the lack of such assurance (in fairness, it is not part of the American style to hand out assurances to anyone), must rather desperately try to rise above society, as a priest or Messiah, or stand outside it, as an expatriate or crank, or crouch beneath it, as a mock-criminal or pseudo-Negro. Or try all three poses in rapid alternation. In America, the strenuous task of *being* a writer always threatens the task of writing: the books of some of our fiction writers are indeed not so much a series of tales as a succession of self-aggrandizing protests, a row of hastily hewn props to keep an ever-tottering reputation from sinking out of view. In England I suspect it is easier to get an honest day's work done.

Adversely, let me say that no literature is as non-existential as the English. That is, the Englishman does not really seem to be aware of any *intrinsic* problem in human existence. It can all be patched up and muddled through. Hence the survival of satire—an instrument for piecemeal correction. Hence the extraordinary fluency with which novels of social circumstance are still produced—as if society were the universe. Hence the virtual absence of radically formal experimentation—although Nathalie Sarraute has clasped hands across the Channel with Ivy Compton-Burnett. Hence, finally, the uniquely sweet and seductive voice, which would call us back from the edge of the abyss in whose depths answers might lie—would call us back, from our shadowed armchairs, to green meadows where the May Queen still reigns.

COMMENT, *solicited by the editors of* Poetry *in 2006, on the effects of* "*poetry's failure in the marketplace*" *on the Updike* oeuvre.

Had poetry paid as well as fiction, I would have written more of it. In the first decade of my free-lancing, the checks from *The New Yorker* for my (mostly light) verse were not, in my budget, insignificant. Back then, Robert Frost and Ogden Nash were living examples of the professional poet. I wouldn't call poetry's present marketplace position a "failure," since no contemporary poet expects to make a living by it. He or she teaches, rather, or has an independent income. While making my living elsewhere, I have never stopped writing and reading poetry, as the exercise of language at its highest pitch. But let me add that I am dismayed by the recent rise of the term "literary fiction," denoting a genre almost as rarefied and special and "curious" in its appeal, to contemporary Americans, as poetry.

FOREWORD *to the 1982 edition of* The Carpentered Hen and Other Tame Creatures.

This my first book yet had a long foreground of verse written since my early teens in imitation of Ogden Nash, Phyllis McGinley, Arthur Guiterman, Richard Armour, Robert Service, E. B. White, and others; the magical progression from *frisson* to words and thence from words to print first seemed feasible, to me, as a matter of stanzas and rhyme, and more poems than the number collected here were published in such available display cases as the Shillington High School *Chatterbox*, *The Harvard Lampoon*, and Jerry Kobrin's hospitable column in the Reading (Pennsylvania) *Eagle*. So when, in the June of my graduation from college, *The New Yorker* accepted "Duet, with Muffled Brake Drums," a long campaign bore fruit and an old dream came true. This was in 1954. In the following three years—spent in Moretown, Vermont; Plowville, Pennsylvania; Oxford, England; New York City; and finally Ipswich, Massachusetts—I ruthlessly exploited with my offerings the editorial breach I had made, and *The New Yorker*, perhaps bemused by the apparition of so eager a young practitioner of the dying art of light verse, accepted enough to make me feel that I had become a professional writer.

The oldest poem in *The Carpentered Hen* is, if memory serves, "Why the Telephone Wires Dip and the Poles Are Cracked and Crooked," written in high school, under the influence of science fiction. "The Population of Argentina" is one of many composed at Harvard, though not one of the three included in Max Shulman's *Guided Tour of Campus Humor* (Hanover House, 1955). The translation of a Horatian ode was done in my senior year for a competition, which it did not win; but years later, Garry Wills, then a classics scholar, chose it for his anthology *Roman Culture* (Braziller, 1966). The latest poems here are "Planting a Mailbox," penned in observation of a rural rite soon after my hopeful move to a small New England town, and "A Cheerful Alphabet of Pleasant Objects," written one letter per day while I lay on the sands of Crane Beach in the summer of 1957. The infant son the alphabet was dedicated to now is twenty-five; twenty-four years have passed since Harper & Row, then Harper & Brothers, brought out *The Carpentered Hen* in a pretty mint-green jacket, and twenty-three years since my first novel was published by Alfred A. Knopf, who now, as a present to me on my fiftieth birthday, issues this new edition of my slim and no doubt expendable fledgling volume. Thank you, Alfred. Thank you, all, from the *Chatterbox* on.

Light verse did not need to exist as long as its qualities of playfulness and formality and mundane perception were present in the high verse of Donne and Marvell, Dryden and Pope. Even Blake, in such quatrains as those of "Infant Sorrow" and "Mock On, Mock On, Voltaire, Rousseau," had the trick of it. But with the onset of Romanticism an alternative convention emerged in the society verses of W. M. Praed (*Don Juan's* tune minus Byron's bass) and became mixed, in Carroll and Lear and Calverley, with parody of Victorian solemnities. Calverley, the most exquisite of these, had a pedantic, Horatian streak also present, some generations and an ocean removed, in that American promulgator of the deft art Franklin P. Adams. Light verse as practiced by F.P.A. and Guiterman, and then by White and McGinley and Morris Bishop, can now be seen as a form of Georgian poetry; the modernism of Eliot and Auden and Marianne Moore and Wallace Stevens leaves no space where wit can strike its own separate music.

Polishing my post-adolescent jingles, I took small notice of these historical trends. But I did notice, around the time of John Kennedy's assassination, that the market for comic, topical rhymes was slowly drying up, and my inspiration docilely dried up with it. Light verse makes up the bulk of this collection and exactly half of my next, *Telephone Poles* (1963); the fraction in *Midpoint* (1969) and *Tossing and Turning* (1977) is progressively smaller. I write no light verse now. Yet the aesthetic bliss of generating such lines as "My stick fingers click with a snicker" or "Superphosphate-fed foods feed me" or "thusiastically, and thus," is as keen as any I have experienced, and this week of preparing *The Carpentered Hen* for its new venture forth—changing a few words, readjusting the order slightly—has been one of peaceful communion with an estimable former self. Of course, in my early twenties I attempted not only light verse. The second poem here, and the second accepted by *The New Yorker*, is "serious" and has enjoyed a healthy anthology life, though its second stanza now reads strangely to students.* The lines welcoming my first child to the month of March (in fact she arrived late, on April Fools' Day, the joke being on me) and those describing the inside of an English train compartment and Room 28 of the National Portrait Gallery seek to express what perhaps flickers at the edge of the light verse as well—the forebodings of a shy soul freshly embarked upon the uncharted ocean of adult life. "The blue above is mostly blue. / The blue below and I are, too."

---

*That is, young readers of "Ex–Basketball Player" have never seen glass-headed pumps, or gas stations selling a medley of brands of gasoline, or the word ESSO. Other irredeemably obsolete references include the first-wave trade names invoked in "A Rack of Paperbacks," the forty-eight states and innocent patriotism of "Quilt," and, in "Popular Revivals, 1956," the motion picture *The Last Hunt*, which starred Robert Taylor and Stewart Granger.

Those lines were written in anticipation of the sea voyage that would take me and my pregnant young wife to England. Many of these poems were written there, of the oddities around me in a land whose details seemed lifted, page after page, from the illustrations to books of my childhood, and of an America that when glimpsed through the telescope of an overseas edition of *Life* also seemed quaint. England, where Belloc and Stevenson wrote their *Cautionary Tales* and *Child's Garden of Verses*— models of the light mode—and where the present poet laureate is the supreme neo-Georgian Sir John Betjeman, indulges sheer versifying more freely than our no-nonsense republic, and this collection (titled in its British edition *Hoping for a Hoopoe*) is colored for me by a green English something that tinged as well my few years in gray Manhattan.

Like any art, light verse aspires to maximum density and an appearance of inevitability. On the other hand, any ordering of language by means of meter and rhyme and their ghosts partakes of that "encrustation of the mechanical upon the organic" which Bergson defined as the essence of the comic. There is a lightness to all poetry, it being so drastic a distillation, and an echo of the primitive chant raised against the darkness. Light verse's hyper-ordering of language through alliteration, rhyme, and pun is a way of dealing with the universe, an exercise of the Word not entirely lacking in Promethean resonance. High spirits are what Nature endows us with, that we may survive her crushing flux long enough to propagate. It will brighten my second half-century to have these old evidences of my own high spirits still in print.

INTRODUCTION *to the 1977 edition of* The Poorhouse Fair.

The present is the future of the past. Driving back into Boston the other night, I looked across the river at the not especially spectacular skyline of East Cambridge and saw it as a nineteenth-century man might have seen it: as parabolic and luminous splendor continuously and coolly on fire, as pyramids piled of cubes of light, each high-rise apartment building a gigantic perforated lantern twinned in the black river and crowding the sky with golden outpourings of energy. Even the glowing advertising signs—FOOD FAIR, ELECTRONICS CORPORATION OF AMERICA— appeared magnificent, unaccountable, authoritative in their strangeness. Who had set such a marvel there? Only a race of gods, it seemed, could inhabit and power this ribbon of the future unrolling on the far shore of the Charles. I was amazed, an alien.

Twenty years before, I had stood by a low wall in Shillington, my birth-place in Pennsylvania, and looked down at the razed acres where for all my boyhood the poorhouse had been. I have described it elsewhere:

> At the end of our street there was the County Home—an immense yellow poorhouse, set among . . . orchards and lawns, surrounded by a sandstone wall that was low enough on one side for a child to climb easily, but on the other side offered a drop of twenty or thirty feet, enough to kill you if you fell. Why this should have been, why the poorhouse grounds should have been so deeply recessed on the Philadelphia Avenue side, puzzles me now. . . . But at the time it seemed perfectly natural, a dreadful pit of space congruent with the pit of time into which the old people (who could be seen circling silently in the shade of the trees whose very tops were below my feet) had been plunged by some mystery that would never touch me. That I too would come to their condition was as unbelievable as that I would really fall and break my neck.*

Now the poorhouse was gone. Out of the hole where it had been, there came to me the desire to write a futuristic novel in commemoration of the fairs that I had attended here as a child.

Backward time, forward time carve the same abyss. The novel of the future seeks to give us in concentrated form the taste of time that flavors all novels, that makes their events more portentous than the events of our lives, where time passes unnoticed, but for the rare shudder, and the mechanical schedule. With superb and dreadful poetry H. G. Wells's *Time Machine* moved its hero through time so fast that he "saw the sun hopping swiftly across the sky, leaping it every minute, and every minute marking a day"; upon acceleration "the palpitation of night and day merged into one continuous greyness" and "the jerking sun became a streak of fire, a brilliant arch, in space." The sun, simultaneous symbol of life and of its transience, is visited by the Time Traveller on the verge of its own extinction, when it hangs in the sky "red and very large, halted motionless upon the horizon, a vast dome glowing with a dull heat." He pushes thirty million years further on, to when "the huge red-hot dome of the sun had come to obscure nearly a tenth part of the darkling heav-ens." It is bitterly cold. The sea is blood red and tideless. The sole signs of life are green slime and a vague creature out on a sandbank—"it was a round thing, the size of a football perhaps, or, it may be, bigger, and ten-tacles trailed down from it; it seemed black against the weltering blood-red water, and it was hopping fitfully about." How horrifyingly real, to

---

*"The Dogwood Tree: A Boyhood," *Assorted Prose* (Knopf, 1965), p. 156.

my thirteen-year-old imagination, was that animated-cartoonish survivor (oblong in my mind like an American football, instead of round like an English one) at the end of the world. The vision could not be dismissed; it was a nightmare that, as would my own death, *would come to pass*.

The totalitarian nightmare of *Nineteen Eighty-four*, like the Eloi/Morlocks class war of Wells's fable, would *not* come to pass, at least in the United States: so it seemed to this patriotic adolescent. Reading Orwell's novel in my late teens, I was titillated by its anti-Soviet allegory; but the book developed a claw of iron when O'Brien, Big Brother's spokesman (and a cousin perhaps of my Conner), told the captive hero:

> "You must stop imagining that posterity will vindicate you, Winston. Posterity will never hear of you. You will be lifted clean out from the stream of history. We shall turn you into gas and pour you into the stratosphere. Nothing will remain of you: not a name in a register, not a memory in a living brain. You will be annihilated in the past as well as in the future. You will never have existed."

Orwell knew he was dying as he wrote that terrible imprecation; personal dread drove him to touch futurism's black center: the death of everything. The ultimate fruit of the future is nonexistence. Not only our egos but all their memorials and progeny are swallowed by the sun's bloating, by the stars' slowing, by entropy. Congealed of gas, we return to gas. In Huxley's *Brave New World*, which I read at a still later, admittedly less impressionable age, deaths occur, but without immensity. The Savage's suicide at the end is mockingly objectified, trivialized even: the corpse's dangling feet, slowly twirling, give the directions of the compass. As in our mundane reality it is others that die, while an attenuated silly sort of life bubbles decadently on. This is, one could say, the vision of the future offered in *The Poorhouse Fair*.

The novel was written in 1957, as a deliberate anti–*Nineteen Eighty-four*. Its events, I asserted in the solicitous flap copy that was then left off the first printing, occurred "about twenty years from now"—that is, now, twenty years later. The pre-dating was done with some accidental imprecision. John Hook, the hero, is ninety-four; in the first pages he remembers himself freshly graduated from normal school in "the fat Taft's administration." Taft was President from 1909 to 1913; assuming that normal school in Hook's day meant a two-year post-high-school curriculum, he would be twenty years old upon graduation, which would put his birth between 1889 and 1893, and the time of my novel right around 1984. But I wanted it to fall short of that year, as its political ambience fell short of *Nineteen Eighty-four*'s dire absolutism; in the Modern Library edition (now out of print) I amended the administration to "the first Roosevelt's," Taft's predecessor. TR's ample reign (1901–9) places my future's near rim in the late months of 1975 (McKinley was assassinated in September of 1901) and is amply congruent with the novel's other muddled checkpoint, the anniversary of the St. Lawrence Seaway, whose opening in 1959 was itself in the haze of the future when I pinned my novel to it. At first I had the anniversary "silver," the twenty-fifth, which again nudges 1984; for the Modern Library I altered this to "crystal," which, as the fifteenth, places it *too* near; "china," the twentieth, is about right, though it sounds brittle. But the entire editorial, as a piece of prediction, lives up to its quaint style.

How do they match up, the world of *The Poorhouse Fair* and the world that surrounds us now? As long ago as 1964 it seemed necessary to say, in a brief foreword to the Modern Library edition, that

> I meant the future it portrays to be less a predictive blueprint than a caricature of contemporary decadence. Though I expected that some details would be rendered obsolete, I did not imagine that Hook's rhetorical question . . . "Isn't it significant, now, that of the three presidents assassinated, all were Re-publican?" might abruptly become impossible. I have let it stand, as a vivid anachronism. I thought, in 1957, fondly composing this latter version of the stoning of St. Stephen, that the future did not radically differ from the past; and this notion now seems itself a product of the entropic years of the Eisenhower lull.

Not only was John Kennedy assassinated in the twenty years prior to 1977, but another President resigned, and the Vietnam Involvement escalated and collapsed, and with it a wave of civil dissent such as has not been seen in this country since the Civil War. It is hard to know what Hook refers to when he says, "This last decade has witnessed the end of the world, if the people would but wake to it." He cannot be referring to the Arab oil boycott and the rising squeeze on raw materials, for the automobiles that come to the poorhouse seem to be still of Fifties dimensions, and the poorhouse furniture has a reassuring ring of solid stuff, of brass and rubber and frosted glass; the tags on the porch chairs are sturdy metal, and simple "soybean plastics" represent our throwaway multitude of synthetic polymers. Nor can Hook be thinking of the global realignments that place the Soviet bloc with the "have" nations and turn Russia and China to enemies and encourage our own surprising rapprochement with the red dragon, for Truman is still remembered as the President who "gave away China to the Russians." Something called the "London Pacts with the Eurasian Soviet"—a bow, it may be, to *Nineteen Eighty-*

four's division of the planet into Eurasia, Eastasia, and Oceania—dominates the peace wherein American population soars "like diffident India's." Our population no longer soars, as it turns out. *The Poorhouse Fair* foresees widespread voyeurism but not the pornography boom; its popular culture has a wrong Hispanic accent, but the brown tint seems right. The romantic vanities of Ted the truck driver and Conner the youthful poorhouse prefect savor more of a Forties boyhood than of our guarded, unenthusiastic Seventies. The characters reflect back through the riots and revolts of the Sixties as if they had never occurred—and so, to an extent, do we. There is a present truth in the sentence "The nation became one of pleasure-seekers; the people continued to live as cells of a body do in the coffin, for the conception 'America' had died in their skulls." There are striking technological omissions: where are the computers, and the Xerox machines? Buddy should be using an electric typewriter, and can his typing table really be porcelain? Drugs, so much in our news and so prominent in *Brave New World*, figure only as a dose of flavored penicillin exclaimed over as a novelty by an anonymous fairgoer. An even stranger absence is that of television, crucial in Orwell's scheme of tyranny and the present-day mainstay, the continuous electronic *soma*, of nursing homes and retirement villages. Nothing is quainter about my old people than their never seeming to watch television, and their having to fall back for entertainment upon reminiscence and mischief. But, if the next seven years bear me out, I was right where Orwell was wrong: no atom bombs have fallen, and the governmental forms of the major Western democracies have not succumbed to Big Brother. In 1977, Hook continues his inward walk down a "long smooth gallery hung with the portraits of presidents of the United States," though a President Lowenstein has not been one of them.

The main flaw of my "predictive blueprint" inheres in any attempt to predict the course of multiple and intercausative phenomena such as make up the life of a nation or a planet. We can extend the graph curve of present trends and be certain that existent vitalities will decline, but we cannot conceive of the new, of the entities born by intricate synthesis from collisions of the broadly known. Models of the future tend therefore to be streamlined models of the present, the present with its corners cut off. But it is these very corners that move into the center and become the future. They move unexpectedly and perhaps unpredictably, even to the supreme intelligence hypothesized by Laplace, who said, "Nothing would be uncertain for such an intelligence, and the future like the past would be present to its eyes." Determinist faith in essential predictability has been challenged, recently, by David Layzer, who, deploying the laws of thermodynamics and the concept of phase space, concludes that "not even the ultimate computer—the universe itself—ever contains enough information to completely specify its own future states. The present moment always contains an element of genuine novelty and the future is never wholly predictable."* It is such a future, an unpredictable one wreathed in mists as of nostalgia, a fuzzy old-fashioned non-future of a future, that I tried to render in this novel, imitating not the science-fiction classics mentioned above but the obscure poetic *Concluding*, by Henry Green. *The Poorhouse Fair* shares with *Concluding* an embarrassing number of particulars: an old estate housing a vague state-run institution (a girls' school, in Green's case), a not-too-distant time-to-come (fifty-five years hence, *Concluding*'s jacket flap stated in 1948), an elderly mono-syllabic hero (Mr. Rock), a multilevelled action drifting through one day's time, a holiday (Green's fête, Founder's Day, even falls, like the poor-house fair, on a Wednesday), heraldic animals, much meteorological detail, and a willful impressionist style.

> —Old and deaf, half blind, Mr Rock said about himself, the air raw in his throat. Nevertheless he saw plain how Ted was not ringed in by fog. For the goose posed staring, head to one side, with a single eye, straight past the house, up into the fog bank which had made all daylight deaf beneath, and beyond which, at some clear height, Mr Rock knew now there must be a flight of birds fast winging,—Ted knows where, he thought.

That is from Green's first page; this is from mine:

> In the cool wash of early sun the individual strands of osier compounding the chairs stood out sharply; arched like separate serpents springing up and turning again into the knit of the wickerwork. An unusual glint of metal pierced the lenient wall of Hook's eyes and struck into his brain, which urged his body closer, to inspect.

The innocently bold eclecticism of my youth rouses my envy now. A million or more published words later, my sentences are less purely mine than these stolen from Green, with their winsome inversions confident as a child's speech ("With the eye it was not difficult to follow the shining squares all the way down the line") and their soft straining to combine sensual "touch" and subjective mythifying ("Despite the low orange sun, still wet from its dawning, crescents of mist like the webs of tent caterpillars adhered in the crotches of the hills").

The novel, reread, seems best when it deals with John Hook and at its

---

*"The Arrow of Time," *Scientific American*, December 1975, pp. 56–69.

THE POORHOUSE FAIR : 435

weakest with Conner; the antagonists rotate the novel in and out of credibility. Conner, in his thirties, was too young for me to understand; what
goes on in his cupola I guessed at as I guessed at what went on in the principal's office of my high school. ("A principle is a ru*le*," the teachers used
to tell us, "but the principal is your *pal*.") A nervous self-conscious shyness, and maneuvering around that shyness, dominate Conner and Buddy
as if they were adolescents. Conner is a high-school goody-goody, trying
to make his way among sardonic rowdies, tied by pious ambition to invisible grown-ups—invisible like the grown-ups in *Peanuts*, like the human
beings in Kafka's "Investigations of a Dog." He should have been more.
Whereas Hook's antiquity shrinks him to the scope of my still basically
childish imagination. His physical and visual impairments impose the
same magical discontinuities that a child's handicaps of perspective and
ability do. Like a child he is in love with the world and hopes that the
world loves him. He is alert for clues, though blind to patterns. His per-
ceptual style controls the book; the parakeet, the rabbit on the lawn, the
"silver zeppelins" of Lucas's pigs (there are swine in Green, too) are
seized upon with relief, as something alive but intelligible, by the presiding, animistic imagination. The flap copy went:

> Animals haunt the landscape, and inanimate objects—a sandstone wall, a
> row of horsechestnut trees, a pile of pebbles—strain wordlessly toward the
> humans, who act out their quarrels of tradition versus progress, benevo-
> lence versus pride, on a ground riddled with omens and overborne by a
> massive, variable sky. The author seems to separate sense and existence; the
> chatter of the mob that comes to the fair in its sense illustrates the national
> decay that obsesses the pensioners, yet in its existence, isolated by bits in the
> air, shares with grass and stones a positive, even cheering, *anima*.

There is, then, a philosophical ambition here: an attempt, no less, to
present the meaning of being alive, as conveyed by its sensations. Our
eager innate life, rebounding from the exterior world, affirms itself, and
the quality of affirmation is taken to be extrinsic, immanent, divine. I
needed God to exist. My claim that the banal American chatter that dis-
solves the novel at the end manifests "a positive, even cheering, *anima*" is
a leap of aesthetic faith sheerly—a child's delight in being up late, eating
licorice while grown-up conversations make a sky of safety above his
head, recalled fifteen years later and forcibly assigned a clinching position
in an argument sketched, I see now, along Thomist lines. Like a Thomist
proof the novel moves from proposition to objections to counter-
objections. The distinction between essence and being (*essentia* and *ens*) I
took from Saint Thomas; with his help I sought to consecrate, to baptize

into American religiosity, those three very atheistical Englishmen, Wells, Orwell, and Henry Green. The original manuscript ended a page sooner, upon the Chestertonian lament "to guard the gates of the deserted kingdom." Small wonder the ending baffled what were to have been the book's publishers; good luck or Providence led me to an editor, Stewart Richardson, and a publisher, Alfred A. Knopf, who to my lasting gratitude printed this book in a format as exquisite as my intentions, my text unaltered.

That was twenty years ago. Now I notice, in this text, amid the religious schemata, a less conscious pattern, announced by the sentence already quoted, about the strands of osier arching like separate serpents springing up and turning again into the knit of the wickerwork. The image forced itself upon me at the outset of the action; it returns on page 27, as Hook remembers himself as a child examining his bedcovers, "searching for the deeper-dyed thread that occasionally, in the old woven cloth, would arch above the others." This microcosmic event is dramatically enlarged when, amid the schoolyard rumpus of the stoning, Hook, studying the interwoven clouds of the sky, has "his narrow field of vision crossed by a flow of arrowing stones, speeding through the air in swift flocks, and before he considered, he had the thought that here was something glorious. Battles of old had swayed beneath such a canopy of missiles." The hurled stones arch; and so the entire incident itself arches up out of the fabric of the day, and then is turned again into the knit of the gossip that ends the day. Buddy carries the scandal into the crowd and composes a comic headline in the air; by page 180, amid the threads of several other rumored scandals, the event is anonymously made to yield a moral ("you sometimes need a man with a look of authority") and allowed to fade from the common discourse.

> The people who had come to the fair talked more slowly, tending toward affectionate gossip about the past they had in common as citizens of the town, and about roads and schools and old houses sold. Coarsened hands of still handsome women nervously tucked back stray strands of hair; young mothers pouted under the weight of sleeping babies.

Ipswich has displaced Shillington behind this evocation. The Massachusetts town where I wrote this novel, in the three summer months of our first year there, has begun to intrude upon the remembered town; young mothers and sleeping babies join my cast of characters.

Life goes on; stray strands are tucked back; the stoning has sprung up and been turned again into the knit. All is flux; nothing lastingly matters. Such pessimism came more naturally to the author of *The Poorhouse Fair* than his hopeful detection of a world-soul. For me, the most surprising—the most abruptly *given*—image occurs on the penultimate page; the stars are perceived as "not specks but needles of light suspended point downward in a black depth of stiff jelly." Earlier, Hook, praying, had felt his mind as "a point within an infinitely thick blanket." We are *within*, the young author feels, honestly claustrophobic—within a universe where the sun daily grows "orange, oblate, and distended"* and then plunges to its death like some Titanic deity. For a while the furrow plowed by its plunge glows "the color of an unnatural element, transuranic, created atom by atom in the scientist's laboratory, at inestimable expense," but, as the sick-ward patients watch, clouds propelled by evening winds obscure the golden chasm. The poorhouse is fair, I wanted to say, against my suspicions that it is, our universe, a poor house for us.

The book was published early in 1959. Wright Morris and Mary McCarthy found kind words to say of it, and Mary Ellen Chase published in the *Herald Tribune* a review of extraordinary enthusiasm and warmth. Others found it precious, for all the "phenomenal composure" of the prose. *Time*, after what I took to be a panning, cited it among "The Year's Best," and I had the pleasure of seeing myself anointed, in their regal way, "Gifted Writer Updike." *The Poorhouse Fair* arched back smoothly into the vast knit of past seasons' books. It sold about eight thousand copies, and has been kept in print by the publisher's generous policy in this regard. This is its sixth printing; the fifth was in 1966. A few lingering typographical mistakes have been cleared up, the historical clues have been adjusted as mentioned above, Gregg's expression "a.h." has been liberalized to "a.hole" (though I am pleased with my solution, for those days, to the problem of printed obscenities; better my abbreviations than non-words like "fug" or eye-catching dashes), and what appears to be the same boy at the fair has been given the same name throughout, Mark. Otherwise the text is unchanged; I could not write this novel now, and will respect the man who could. He wanted to lay down in these theorems and raptures the foundation for a tower of volumes, its title a slogan to prosper by. A few days ago I submitted the manuscript for my twentieth book. The future is now; it is as if, standing by that poorhouse wall, I threw myself down, into the pit of time, and, my neck unbroken, find myself here.

---

*Cf., of course, the sun at the end of *The Time Machine*. And, of the stars, this sentence by Wells may have been in my memory: "The circling of the stars, growing slower and slower, had given place to creeping points of light."

APOLOGIA PRO OPERE SUO, *from the Afterword to* Buchanan Dying *(1974).*

> I wanted to write a novel in which the chief character was to have been a
> man who had a pair of spectacles with one lens that reduced as powerfully as
> oxy-gas-microscope and the other that magnified equally powerfully; in his
> interpretation, everything was very relative.

This entry in Kierkegaard's *Journals* (December 10, 1837) excited me
nearly twenty years ago; I, too, "wanted to write a novel in which the
chief character" etc. To this fallow inspiration (I did try a few dozen
pages, the journal of a wicked man, a high-school principal) time added
the idea of a novel with a stationary hero, a man in bed dying. Learning
that Samuel Beckett, Hermann Broch, and Carlos Fuentes had already
written such books dampened but not quite extinguished this ambition,
which was vaguely intermixed with a youthful vision of a tetralogy, of
which the first novel would be set in the future, the second in the present,
the third in the remembered past, and the fourth in the historical past.
The first three materialized obediently enough (*The Poorhouse Fair*, *Rabbit, Run*, and *The Centaur*), but the fourth hung unachieved, attracting to
itself, over the years, the lint and interstellar matter of fragmentary inspi-
rations. The discovery that Buchanan had mismatched eyes fitted the
Kierkegaard, and the fact that he was Dying worked in with an overall
alphabetical scheme of writing in my lifetime twenty-six novels, each to
be dominated by one letter of the alphabet—the "B" in *Rabbit, Run* and
the "C" in *The Centaur* need scarcely be emphasized. But, while I waited
for the "D" to pull together (the first sentence would go, *During the
night, the old man had a strange dream*), many other books presented
themselves to be mustered through the presses, and the tetralogy
remained open on one side to the wind and bad weather.

James Buchanan had to be the historical figure. Who was he? In my
Pennsylvania childhood, I knew him to be the only President our great
and ancient state had produced; but where were the monuments, the
Buchanan Avenues, the extollatory juvenile volumes with titles like *Jim-
mie Buchanan, Keystone Son in the White House*, or *"Old Buck," the Hair-
Splitter Who Preceded the Rail-Splitter*? Lincoln and Washington were
drummed into us but Buchanan went unmentioned. When, in 1968, as an
act of penance for a commercially successful novel set in New England, I
began my research, I discovered, of course, that Buchanan's Administration had ended under a cloud of disgrace that after a century still glow-
ered. The Covode Investigation, the Floyd scandals, General Scott's
published charges, a campaign of press vilification led by Forney, Gree-

ley, and Bennett, the Lincoln Administration's self-serving innuendoes,* a congressional vendetta that stooped to abolishment of the franking privilege of ex-Presidents and to Thaddeus Stevens's claim that Buchanan had defrauded the government of eight thousand dollars for White House furnishings—all did their work. Not Buchanan's tediously dispassionate self-defense, nor the grand and tragic fatalism which informs Lincoln's second inaugural—giving the war the cast of divine foreordination, of an inexorable justice whereby "every drop of blood drawn with the lash, shall be paid by another drawn with the sword"—could dissipate the impression of bad performance and worse faith on Buchanan's part. Even modern historians, a century remote from the wounds of the Civil War, sometimes jeer vindictively at "Poor, foolish Buchanan!" who "prayed and twittered and did nothing."[†]

And yet my grandfather John Hoyer, born in Berks County in 1863, spoke of Lincoln as of someone who had personally swindled him, and to his death at the age of ninety voted the straight Democratic ticket. I felt a mystery here. My father, born Republican, became a Roosevelt Democrat in the Depression; this was understandable, the Depression was in my marrow. (And the opprobrium that attached to Hoover in the 1930s, if heightened by imputations of treason and the fact of a million dead in civil war, approximates Buchanan's disgrace.) John Hoyer, for whom I was named, retired from farming before I was born, and appeared to me as a sedentary talker, with an ash-colored mustache, high-top buttoned shoes, and a beautiful stately way of delivering his pronouncements to deaf ears. He should have been a politician, my father always said of "Pop" Hoyer. This was not entirely a compliment; my father's generation had a Menckenesque contempt for politicians. My grandfather, on the other hand, owned a keen country sense of the courthouse as a holy center, pronounced the words "burgess" and "alderman" and "judge" in a reverential manner, and took that genially reductive view of human motives that is, after all, the basis of the American political system. In men like him, ornate arguers and ironical listeners, the citizens of the

---

*Lincoln, in his war message of July 4, 1861, found that "A disproportionate share of the federal muskets and rifles had somehow found their way into these [seceding] states, and had been seized," that "The Navy was scattered in distant seas," and that his efforts to reinforce Fort Pickens were frustrated by "some *quasi* armistice of the late administration." In the next paragraph, however, he cashes in resoundingly the net result of the unmartial Buchanan policy: "It is thus seen that the assault upon, and reduction of, Fort Sumter, was in no sense a matter of self-defence on the part of the assailants."

[†]Samuel Eliot Morison, *The Oxford History of the American People* (1965), pp. 593, 608.

rural republic sought their spokesmen and discovered their provincial interests. Through his Democratic prejudices I looked back, unknowingly, into the Jacksonian democracy—anti-tariff, anti-Bank—whereby America's yeomen, North and South, took power from the seaboard aristocrats and bankers. Four decades later, under the stalking horse of abolitionism,* these same urban forces, swollen black and mighty, took power back. Like Buchanan, my grandfather depended upon and distrusted women; smoked cigars; obeyed the law; was a Mason; loved cronyship.† And as with Buchanan, though he read his Bible to tatters, he lived, I fear, in a world purely human. Will people ever talk about each other so avidly again, or fashion of the lives of those they know such a treasure of polished nuggets and gimcracks of gossip? How telegraphic, how unloving, by comparison, our own gossip is!

Even older than my grandfather was Uncle John Spotts, his sister Hannah's husband. Uncle John, shorter than five feet, with a hook nose and large-lidded eyes in deep sockets, spoke with an antique voice, an old-fashioned superpalatal wheeze that merged with the dark, somehow tropical greenery outside his house and the smells of fresh-baked pie dough and unused plush parlor chairs inside. Though his hand bunched into blue knobs as it gripped the curve of his cane, he was dapper, in starched pinstripe shirt and broad suspenders, and his inner knit, I felt as a child, was as clean and tight as the wickerwork of his porch chairs. Nearly a hundred Pennsylvania summers lived in him, hazy farm summers where only the springhouse was cool. His kindly, eerie wheeze of a voice, sighing "Johnny," with a caressing tone of lament, arose from a green world where men would not breathe again, a Pennsylvania dying about us, though its buildings like bones remained. I wanted to dive into that lost green, and set a novel there.

At some moments of research I touched something live. In the great

---

*The only political story of my grandfather's that I remember concerned the hypocrisy of abolitionist Quakers. Here is the story as told by John Hook, in *The Poorhouse Fair* (Knopf, 1959), pp. 92–93: "The Quakers among the city dwellers had a great reputation for good works, and in Buchanan's day were much for passing the runaway slaves on up to Canada. Ah. But the truth of it was, this old fella who was the patriarch of the sect would harbor the negroes in the summer, when they would work his fields for nothing, and then when the cold weather came, and the crops were in, he would turn them out, when they had never known a winter before. One black man balked, you know, and the old fella standing on the doorstep said so sharp: 'Dost thou not hear thy Master calleth thee?'"

†"He . . . delighted more than any public man I have known in what is sometimes called 'cronyship.'" (Henry S. Foote, *Casket of Reminiscences* [Chronicle Publishing Co., 1874], p. 113).

round reading room of the British Museum, with its aquarium whisper-
ing, they brought me a book about Henry Clay published in 1864; its
pages had never been cut, I had to slice them with the edge of a credit
card. Startled British faces looked around at the tearing sound. I wanted
to explain, I was innocent, more than innocent; I was the prince whose
kiss this book had been awaiting, asleep, for over a century. Then, at the
Historical Society of Pennsylvania, a few floors above the muggy hulla-
balloo of Philadelphia, I held in my hands the very sheets of paper—
eight of them, legal-length—upon which Jeremiah Black, his gorgeous
flowing hand intact after a sleepless night and a hectic month, had written out his objections and emendations to Buchanan's proposed reply to
the South Carolina "Commissioners." For a moment—December 30,
1860—American history had flowed through these sheets, these
arabesques and furious hatchings of ink. A tide had turned that morning.
The South's long hold on Washington had been broken; the possibility of
a negotiated, peaceful secession had passed. The Union's course had been
set, here, in my hands. And again, one winter, unable to make the novel
move, unable to strike the music—the chords of detail given momentum
by significance—that, as Henry James had warned, can only be elicited
from "the palpable present *intimate* that throbs responsive,"* I impul-

---

*On October 5, 1901, James wrote to Sarah Orne Jewett apropos of her novel *The Tory
Lover:* "The 'historic' novel is, for me, condemned, even in cases of labour as delicate as
yours, to a fatal *cheapness,* for the simple reason that the difficulty of the job is inordinate
and that a mere *escamotage,* in the interest of ease, and of the abysmal public *naïveté*
becomes inevitable. You may multiply the little facts that can be got from pictures and
documents, relics and prints, as much as you like—*the* real thing is almost impossible to do
and in its essence the whole effect is as nought: I mean the invention, the representation of
the old CONSCIOUSNESS, the soul, the sense, the horizon, the vision of individuals in
whose minds half the things that make ours, that make the modem world, were nonexistent. You have to *think* with your modern apparatus a man, a woman—or rather
fifty—whose own thinking was intensely otherwise conditioned, you have to simplify back
by an amazing *tour de force*—and even then it's all humbug." (*Selected Letters of Henry
James,* edited by Leon Edel [Farrar, Straus & Cudahy, 1955], pp. 202–3.)
  In his introduction to *The Aspern Papers* in the New York edition (1909), however,
James concedes "a palpable imaginable *visitable* past—in the nearer distances and the
clearer mysteries, the marks and signs of a world we may reach over to as by making a long
arm we grasp an object at the other end of our own table. The table is the one, the common expanse, and where we lean, so stretching, we find it firm and continuous. That, to
my imagination, is the past fragrant of all, or of almost all, the poetry of the thing outlived
and lost and gone, and yet in which the precious element of closeness, telling so of con-
nexions but tasting so of differences, remains appreciable. With more moves back the element of the appreciable shrinks—just as the charm of looking over a garden-wall into
another garden breaks down when successions of walls appear."

442 : TABLE TALK

sively, desperately flew south from Boston, hoping that the sight of Wheatland, in Lancaster, might break the block. The flight to Newark was delayed; I missed the connecting flight and had to drive a rented car through New Jersey, to the Pennsylvania Turnpike. Winter held the woods and wide fields in suspense. I passed the Morgantown exit that so many times had taken me home and drove into Lancaster as dusk was falling. Buchanan's dusty road to Marietta is now a residential street. It rises out of the old downtown, where the courtly street names and colonial brick houses persist amid a modern clutter of commerce and reconstruction; and then Marietta Avenue slightly falls, and on the left, back safe on its great lawn, stands Wheatland. Of orangish brick, the mansion, with its narrow windowless sides and rather sprightly, Frenchified façade, feels intimate—or felt so that day, when snow hushed its grounds, and I was the only visitor. The driveway had been plowed, but the paths were unshovelled. No caretaker moved to intercept me. Solitary as a burglar, as a lover, I waded to the windows and looked in. Through wavery panes rapidly darkening, I glimpsed planes of wallpaper, an oval mirror topped by an eagle, balusters of the stairway in whose newel post is sealed the rolled-up mortgage papers and at whose head rests (I knew) the porcelain bowl given Buchanan by the Mikado of Japan, the largest piece of porcelain in the world, mistakenly sold out of the White House by Mary Lincoln and many years later recovered for Buchanan's estate. Creeping along the wall, I peered, as into Henry James's "garden," into the windows of the library where the old Functionary had spun his web of letters and received job-seekers, power-brokers, cronies, and neighbors. The leather settee, the glass-fronted bookcases, the framed posters and flags, even the basket of pretzels the Lancaster Historical Society has set up on the center table—I could make out all these, but coming closer had put me further away. The furniture of his life remained sealed upon its mystery. The house was closed for the season. I could not get in.

Nor could I get into his life and make my novel there. The plan was to have him dying and in delirium or dream reliving. His days, the correct dates running along in the margin like the ticking of a clock, would flow unchronologically one out of another, revealing the "veins" of his psychology, of his fate. There were even four chapter titles, alliterative as I like them: "Love," "Law," "Duty," "Death." But researched details failed to act like remembered ones, they had no palpable medium of the half-remembered in which to swim; my imagination was frozen by the theoretical discoverability of *everything*. An actual man, Buchanan, had done this and this, exactly so, once; and no other way. There was no air. Atoms of the known lit up an abyss of the unknowable. In the end, a play seemed possible. Let the designers of sets and costumes solve the surfaces. Let theatrical unreality equal historical unreality. Let the actors themselves be the "veins." Let speech, which is all impalpable that remains to us of the dead, be all. Some scenes, like that of the Colemans' party, I took from the aborted novel; other scenes, like Buchanan's walk with Jackson and the Cabinet struggles, had only to be synthesized from existing accounts. The pages did at last accumulate. In the course of their accumulation, I broke my leg, turned forty, buried my father. So be it. *Sufficient to the day is the evil thereof.* Here is Buchanan, I am rid of him, and this book, a mosaic with more tesserae than matrix, constitutes, I trust, my final volume of homage to my native state, whose mild misty doughy middleness, between immoderate norths and souths, remains for me, being my first taste of life, the authentic taste.

REPLY *to an essay by the historian Paul Boyer, in a collection of twenty such essays-and-replies called* Novel History: Historians and Novelists Confront the American Past—and Each Other *(2001).*

Paul Boyer's lively, friendly appraisal of my novel *Memories of the Ford Administration* (1992) does not mention what I considered the pivotal intersection of Alf Clayton's Buchanan saga with his real, as remembered, life: his swooning into the arms of a student's mother, Mrs. Arthrop, upon hearing that her name, like that of Buchanan's lifelong love object, was Ann. "Oh. Ah. 'Ann,' I repeated. That tore it." This particular, history-inspired infidelity, discovered by Alf's own love object, Genevieve Mueller, tears their romance and sets Alf's life back, with a jolt, on track.

Nor does Professor Boyer identify by name my previous work on Buchanan, the long play *Buchanan Dying*, published in 1974 and performed in cut versions in 1976, twice—in Lancaster, Pennsylvania, and in San Diego, California. Though my publishing firm of Alfred A. Knopf, Inc., made a handsome volume of it—perhaps the handsomest, in design and typesetting, of any of my books—I remained unsatisfied with this packaging of the Buchanan matter, and tried again nearly twenty years later. The reasons for my dissatisfaction were, basically, the unwieldiness of an actual life, especially a long political one lived in the public eye from 1814 to 1868, and the embarrassments, forcefully described by Henry James in a memorable letter to Sarah Orne Jewett, of writing what he called " 'historic' fiction"—"*The* real thing," he warned, "is almost impossible to do and in its essence the whole effect is as nought." The novel, I think, delivers better than the play what I have to say about Buchanan, because it wears its aesthetic discomfort, as it were, on its sleeve, in the person of the discomfited, all-confessing narrator, a teacher of history.

I do not want to repeat here what is spelled out in the long afterword to *Buchanan Dying*, and in a number of paragraphs on Buchanan to be found in my two most recent non-fiction collections, *Odd Jobs* (1991) and *More Matter* (1999). Buchanan was a Pennsylvanian, and one of the history books' losers: these were my incentives to love him enough to risk research. It was pleasant and, the mind ever accumulating rust, salutary for me to delve into the history of antebellum America, and to feel how one's ignorance widens along with one's researches, wherein book would lead to book *ad infinitum*. When I thought I knew enough, I began; of course more could be known, but the kind of fact which a fiction writer depends upon, the witnessed and experienced particular, does not come swimming out of memory where memory, however saturated with texts, has never been. The fearful effort of constructing a simulacrum of, say, Ann Coleman's suicide—itself far from historically certain—produces a glaze, a sweat on the surface of it quite absent, one hopes, from my narrator's freely recalled details of the Eastern United States in the mid-Seventies. And yet, just as I am chastised by Professor Boyer for not knowing enough of the "social history" (whatever that is—isn't all history social?) of Buchanan's lifetime, a young reviewer called David Lipsky chastised me for getting wrong many details of the Ford Administration years (1974–77). Apple computers did not exist, he wrote me, and futons were not yet fashionable; video games were not evolved beyond the rudimentary, nonchirping Pong; boom boxes had yet to appear; and Pachelbel's Canon in C, the theme song of Genevieve and Alf's romance, did not become popular until 1980, when it made the soundtrack of the film *Ordinary People*.

I could swear that my informant is wrong on some of these details, but where he is not, he bears out Alf's assertion that he remembers nothing. We remember, certainly, less than we think, and the engines of distortion begin to work long before events pass into the distances of history. Journalists simplify what they learned an hour ago, eyewitnesses hallucinate, stenographers misspell, and each consciousness plays Hamlet in its own botched, truncated version of the drama. And there are nuances and elusive flavors in the living present, even the somewhat abstracted present of political events, that, like jellyfish, are too delicate to be lifted from the support of their vast momentary context; what will historians make of the Clinton/Monica/Starr/Hillary constellation, and contrive to know how the second presidential inauguration was both very serious and, in its workings and significance to the public, not serious at all—a watery farce of personality tics transposed to the national stage? The worst-case scenario, history may forget, would have given us President Al Gore, a less-than-earthshaking eventuality.*

My own life story has the quirk that, for almost the entire period of the Ford Administration, my concerns were so exclusively personal that I subscribed to no newspaper and learned of national events (which luckily were in a minor key) quite by the way. A quirk of Buchanan's Administration is that, between Lincoln's election in early November 1860 and the incumbent's surrender of the presidency in March 1861, an almost unprecedentedly hectic atmosphere generated conferences of which a remarkably full record, in the form of memoirs and documents and letters, exists. The Cabinet meetings in my novel are taken from the record. The drama of a legalistic, compromise-minded President elected by Southern interests being brought, crisis by crisis, to a minimum sticking point in defense of the Union, and the drama, furthermore, of a man early traumatized in life being led, through a long lifetime of cautious and evasive dealing, into the center of the supreme national trauma— such drama is there, in Buchanan's story, whether or not I had the wit to bring it out.

Some fakery is present in any fiction; among my own novels I count one set in the African Sahel, where I have never been, and one set in a Brazil I never experienced, and most recently an excursion into medieval Denmark. These are all as real as I could make them, while aware, on the reader's behalf, that their reality is in a large proportion fantastic. The act of writing and the format of fiction in themselves aërate the most mundane reconstruction with the fizz of the unreal. We shorten, we skirt, we skim, all to deliver back to the reader his own reality. Of the two worlds of *Memories of the Ford Administration*, my own pleasure and recognition attach more readily to the contemporary one, as, for example, in the scenes concerning Alf's involvement with Ann Arthrop. I am charmed by the little illuminations they generate as they unfold: "Ann answered my knock instantly, as if poised by the door; she was already in a bathrobe, in a room where but one dim bedside lamp, its parchment shade decorated with a pointing Labrador, added its beige glow to the moonlighted pressing on the drawn curtains." A glimmer ricocheting off the surface of known things is where the fiction writer finds his poetry and his *raison d'être*. He rotates the contemporary details his mind has unwittingly

*And a possible crimp in the political fortunes of George W. Bush.

stored. Yet I could not have written the episodes of the Ford era without the frame of the NNEAAH,* of *Retrospect*, of my impudent assumption of the historian's robes.

I do not, may I add, consider Allan Nevins's prose purple,† or anything but a regal shade of that color; I emerged from my own labors in mauve ink awed by the ability of narrative historians like Nevins and Roy Nichols and Philip Klein to take all their vast musty reading and give it the momentum and particularity of fiction. Insofar as history lives in the telling, and persuades us we are there, it is a species of fiction.

LETTER *to Rosemary Herbert, Book Review Editor of the* Boston Herald, *anent* Gertrude and Claudius *(2000).*

Thanks for your interest, and for your questions. In my limited experience of interviews, spoken ones never take less than an hour and leave you limp. There is always the anxiety that what you say is not being heard or understood, even with a tape recorder going. In any case it becomes a social experience rather than a literary experience. So let me respond in this way to your questions, more or less in order.

In fact it was pleasant, for a writer accustomed to isolation, to be in Shakespeare's company, and to have him as a collaborator, much as he collaborated with the authors of old and foreign plots to make the bulk of his plays. The larkiness of the project became quickly absorbed in the hard work it entailed—reading the pre-Shakespearean sources of *Hamlet*, working up the Middle Ages (castles, costumes), and trying to make sense of the play itself, which is not easy. It is full of inconsistencies, blithe elisions, and loose ends. I wanted my little novel to dovetail smoothly into the beginning of Shakespeare's action, and to contain nothing in utter contradiction to the text, though I invented a complicity between Gertrude, Claudius, and Polonius that underlies the play rather than lies on its surface.

Yes, writing is risk-taking, and you are never quite certain how well it will work out. But in that it resembles every earthly enterprise.

Just as Shakespeare had to give Elsinore a more or less Elizabethan cast, so I had to animate the plot with emotions that might be called suburban and modern. (I was reminded lately, by the way, that the word

---

*The fictional Northern New England Association of American Historians (Putney, Vermont), publishers of *Retrospect*, a tri-quarterly journal.
†As did Professor Boyer.

"suburbs" occurs in Shakespeare: Portia asks, "Dwell I but in the suburbs / Of your good pleasure?") But the characters' feelings became real to me in the context I created. The status of women in the Middle Ages possibly made Claudius's possession of his dead brother's queen as brutally matter-of-fact as his seizure of his brother's crown; but Shakespeare didn't see it that way, and neither did I.

I love Gertrude, and always have. Everything she says is to the point, and much of it is witty. Her description of death, to her disturbed son— "Thou know'st 'tis common; all that live must die, / Passing through nature to eternity"—is so beautiful I used it as an epigraph for my novel *Brazil*, another attempt of mine to retell an old story. It wasn't Shakespeare who saw her as "stewed in corruption," it was her fastidious son.

As to the voices, I couldn't have them speak blank verse—it would become parody—but I did try to give their utterances something of the formal dignity and speedy concision of Shakespeare's stage language. I curbed modern expressions, most regretfully when I struck out the elder Hamlet's saying it was time his son came back from Wittenberg and "got real."

After a while, these imaginary houses and castles you construct for your characters become real to you, so that you move around in them with a friendly familiarity; but I wouldn't call in an architect to examine the blueprints, or an inspector to check the wiring. *Life in a Medieval Castle*, by Joseph and Frances Gies, was a help, but in the end you must be your own designer. I liked the secret passageway, the way back, and the way her father's oriel room became Gertrude's private room—or "closet," as Shakespeare says.

Again, there are a number of guides to costume through the ages, and old Hollywood movies, whatever their defects in other regards, were often beautifully researched in details of dress. "Wadmal" is in the dictionary; and the arrival of silk in Northern Europe is an incident in my drama. Authentic ancient food is less frequently documented than clothes (and is hard to imagine, pre-refrigeration), but I came across a French book, *A History of Food*, by Maguelonne Toussaint-Samat, that was helpful. As with other details of bygone living, you do enough research to feel the ground solid under you, and then take your leap of imagination. Henry James thought the whole process was bogus, and he was no doubt right: the authenticity that the present has is sacrificed. But, then, even the present—which the writer must fashion, in the end, out of his own subjective experience—can include factual mistakes. I suspect some of my costumes in *Gertrude and Claudius* are too late for my time-frame, around A.D. 1250.

Though *Hamlet* begins as if there is going to be a lot of political action, Shakespeare in the end made Elsinore the site of a domestic drama: an intensely verbal son "working through" his relation to his dead father and live mother and, through her, with the female sex. Hamlet's treatment of Ophelia is more shocking, to me, than Claudius's usurpation. Claudius's hopes of making it all good, and his love of Gertrude, and hers of him— in some productions she protects Claudius from Laertes and his mob with her body—are all there, in the play, asking for acknowledgment. My novel is an attempt to make the acknowledgment. Several Shakespeare commentaries, especially one by the Spanish thinker Salvador de Madariaga, helped me see that Hamlet is in fact the callous, egocentric villain of *Hamlet*.

INTRODUCTION *to* Rabbit Angstrom: The Four Novels *(1995)*.

The United States, democratic and various though it is, is not an easy country for a fiction writer to enter: the slot between the fantastic and the drab seems too narrow. An outsiderish literary stance is traditional; such masterpieces as *Moby-Dick* and *Huckleberry Finn* deal with marginal situations and eccentric, rootless characters; many American writers have gone into exile to find subjects of a congenial color and dignity. The Puritanism and practicality of the early settlers imposed a certain enigmatic dullness, it may be, upon the nation's affective life and social texture. The minimization of class distinctions suppressed óne of the articulating elements of European fiction, and a close, delighted grasp of the psychology of sexual relations—so important in French and English novels—came slowly amid the New World's austerities. Insofar as a writer can take an external view of his own work, my impression is that the character of Harry "Rabbit" Angstrom was for me a way in—a ticket to the America all around me. What I saw through Rabbit's eyes was more worth telling than what I saw through my own, though the difference was often slight; his life, less defended and logocentric than my own, went places mine could not. As a phantom of my imagination, he was always, as the contemporary expression has it, *there* for me, willing to generate imagery and motion. He kept alive my native sense of wonder and hazard.

A writer's task is not to describe his work but to call it into being. Of these four related novels, I know principally—and that by the fallible light of recollection—what went into them, what stimuli and ambitions and months of labor. Each was composed at the end of a decade and published at the beginning of the next one; they became a kind of running report on the state of my hero and his nation, and their ideal reader became a fellow-American who had read and remembered the previous novels about Rabbit Angstrom. At some point between the second and third of the series, I began to visualize four completed novels that might together make a single coherent volume, a mega-novel. Now, thanks to Everyman's Library, this volume exists, titled, as I had long hoped, with the name of the protagonist, an everyman who, like all men, was unique and mortal.

Rabbit, Run was begun, early in 1959, with no thought of a sequel. Indeed, it was not yet clear to me, though I had one short novel to my credit, that I was a novelist at all. At the age of twenty-seven I was a short-story writer by trade, a poet and light-versifier on the side, and an ex-reporter for *The New Yorker*. I had come, two years before, to New England to try my luck at free-lancing. *Rabbit, Run* at first was modestly conceived as a novella, to form with another, *The Centaur*, a biune study of complementary moral types: the rabbit and the horse, the zigzagging creature of impulse and the plodding beast of stoic duty. *Rabbit* took off; as I sat at a little upright desk in a small corner room of the first house I owned, in Ipswich, Massachusetts, writing in soft pencil, the present-tense sentences accumulated and acquired momentum. It was a seventeenth-century house with a soft pine floor, and my kicking feet, during those excited months of composition, wore two bare spots in the varnish. The handwritten draft was completed, I noted at the end, on September 11, 1959. I typed it up briskly and sent it off to my publisher just as the decade ended and headed, with my family, to the then remote Caribbean island of Anguilla.

There, after some weeks of tropical isolation, I received a basically heartening letter from my publisher, Alfred A. Knopf himself, indicating acceptance with reservations.* The reservations turned out to be (he could tell me this only face to face, so legally touchy was the matter) sexually explicit passages that might land us—this was suggested with only a glint of irony—in jail. Books were still banned in Boston in those days; no less distinguished an author than Edmund Wilson had been successfully prosecuted, in New York State in 1946, for *Memoirs of Hecate County*. My models in sexual realism had been Wilson and D. H. Lawrence and Erskine Caldwell and James M. Cain and of course James Joyce, whose influence resounds, perhaps all too audibly, in the book's

---

*See *Odd Jobs* (Knopf, 1991), p. 845, for the text of this letter.

several female soliloquies. Not wishing, upon reflection, to lose the publisher who made the handsomest books in America, and doubting that I could get a more liberal deal elsewhere, I did, while sitting at the elbow of a young lawyer evidently expert in this delicate area, consent to a number of excisions—not always the ones I would have expected. It was, I thought, a tactful and non-fatal operation. The American edition appeared toward the end of 1960 without legal incident; in England, Victor Gollancz asked for still more cuts and declined to publish the Knopf text as it was, but the youthful firm of André Deutsch did. The dirty-word situation was changing rapidly, with the legally vindicated publication of Lawrence's *Lady Chaterley's Lover* and Henry Milller's *Tropic of Cancer.* Censorship went from retreat to rout, and when I asked Penguin Books, late in 1962, if I could make some emendations and restorations for their edition, they permissively consented. For ten pages a day that winter, sitting in a rented house in Antibes, France, I went through *Rabbit, Run*, restoring the cuts and trying to improve the prose throughout. This text was the one that appeared in the Modern Library (and eventually in Knopf hardcover); I have made a few further corrections and improvements for this printing. *Rabbit, Run*, in keeping with its jittery, indecisive protagonist, exists in more forms than any other novel of mine.

Yet my intent was simple enough: to show a high-school athletic hero in the wake of his glory days. My father had been a high-school teacher, and one of his extracurricular duties was to oversee the ticket receipts for our basketball games. Accompanying him, then, at home and away, I saw a great deal of high-school basketball, and ten years later was still well imbued with its heroics, as they are thumpingly, sweatily enacted in the hotly lit intimacy of jam-packed high-school gymnasiums. Our Pennsylvania town of Shillington was littered, furthermore, with the wrecks of former basketball stars, and a thematically kindred short story, "Ace in the Hole," and poem, "Ex–Basketball Player," had preceded Rabbit into print:

> Once Flick played for the high-school team, the Wizards.
> He was good: in fact, the best. In '46
> He bucketed three hundred ninety points,
> A county record still. The ball loved Flick.
> I saw him rack up thirty-eight or forty
> In one home game. His hands were like wild birds.

To this adolescent impression of splendor my adult years had added sensations of domestic interdependence and claustrophobia. Jack Kerouac's *On the Road* came out in 1957 and, without reading it, I resented its apparent instruction to cut loose; *Rabbit, Run* was meant to be a realistic demonstration of what happens when a young American family man goes on the road—the people left behind get hurt. There was no painless dropping out of the Fifties' fraying but still-tight social weave. Arriving at so prim a moral was surely not my only intention: the book ends on an ecstatic, open note that was meant to stay open, as testimony to our heart's stubborn amoral quest for something once called grace. The title can be read as a piece of advice. (My echo of a British show tune from 1939, by Noel Gay and Ralph Butler, was unintentional; just recently I was given the sheet music of "Run, Rabbit,—Run!" and read the lyrics' injunction "Don't give the farmer his fun, fun, fun. / He'll get by without his rabbit pie.")

The present tense was a happy discovery for me. It has fitfully appeared in English-language fiction—Damon Runyon used it in his tough tall tales, and Dawn Powell in the mid-Thirties has a character observe, "It was an age of the present tense, the stevedore style." But I had encountered it only in Joyce Cary's remarkable *Mister Johnson*, fifteen or so years after its publication in 1939. In a later edition of that groundbreaking portrait of a West African entrapped by colonialism, Cary wrote of the present tense that it "can give to a reader that sudden feeling of insecurity (as if the very ground were made only of a deeper kind of darkness) which comes to a traveller who is bushed in unmapped country, when he feels all at once that not only has he utterly lost his way, but also his own identity." At one point Rabbit is literally lost, and tears up a map he cannot read; but the present tense, to me as I began to write in it, felt not so much ominous as exhilaratingly speedy and free—free of the grammatical bonds of the traditional past tense and of the subtly dead, muffling hand it lays upon every action. To write "he says" instead of "he said" was rebellious and liberating in 1959. In the present tense, thought and act exist on one shimmering plane; the writer and reader move in a purged space, on the travelling edge of the future, without vantage for reflection or regret or a seeking of proportion. It is the way motion pictures occur before us, immersingly; my novella was originally to bear the subtitle "A Movie," and I envisioned the credits unrolling over the shuffling legs of the boys in the opening scuffle around the backboard, as the reader hurried down the darkened aisle with his box of popcorn.

A non-judgmental immersion was my aesthetic and moral aim, when I was fresh enough in the artistic enterprise to believe that I could, in the Poundian imperative, "make it new." *The Centaur*'s fifteen-year-old narrator, Peter Caldwell, awakes with a fever after three trying days with his plodding, prancing father, and looks out the window. He is a would-be painter:

> The stone bare wall was a scumble of umber; my father's footsteps thumbs of white in white. I knew what this scene was—a patch of Pennsylvania in 1947—and yet I did not know, was in my softly fevered state mindlessly soaked in a rectangle of colored light. I burned to paint it, just like that, in its puzzle of glory; it came upon me that I must go to Nature disarmed of perspective and stretch myself like a large transparent canvas upon her in the hope that, my submission being perfect, the imprint of a beautiful and useful truth would be taken.

The religious faith that a useful truth will be imprinted by a perfect artistic submission underlies these Rabbit novels. The first one, especially, strives to convey the quality of existence itself that hovers beneath the quotidian details, what the scholastic philosophers called the *ens*. Rather than arrive at a verdict and a directive, I sought to present sides of an unresolvable tension intrinsic to being human. Readers who expect novelists to reward and punish and satirize their characters from a superior standpoint will be disappointed.

Unlike such estimable elders as Vonnegut, Vidal, and Mailer, I have little reformist tendency and instinct for social criticism. Perhaps the Lutheran creed of my boyhood imbued me with some of Luther's conservatism; perhaps growing up Democrat under Franklin Roosevelt inclined me to be unduly patriotic. In any case the rhetoric of social protest and revolt which roiled the Sixties alarmed and, even, disoriented me. The calls for civil rights, racial equality, sexual equality, freer sex, and peace in Vietnam were in themselves commendable and non-threatening; it was the savagery, between 1965 and 1973, of the domestic attack upon the good faith and common sense of our government, especially of that would-be Roosevelt Lyndon B. Johnson, that astonished me. The attack came, much of it, from the intellectual elite and their draft-vulnerable children. Civil disobedience was antithetical to my Fifties education, which had inculcated, on the professional level, an impassioned but cool aestheticism and implied, on the private, salvation through sensibility, which included an ironical detachment from the social issues fashionable in the Thirties. But the radicalizing Thirties had come round again, in psychedelic colors.

I coped by moving, with my family, to England for a year, and reading in the British Museum about James Buchanan. Buchanan (1791–1868) was the only Pennsylvanian ever elected to the White House; the main triumph of his turbulent term (1857–61) was that, though elderly, he survived it, and left it to his successor, Abraham Lincoln, to start the Civil War. A pro-Southern Democrat who yet denied any constitutional state's right to secede, he embodied for me the drowned-out voice of careful, fussy reasonableness. For over a year, I read American history and tried unsuccessfully to shape this historical figure's dilemmas into a work of fiction. But my attempted pages showed me too earthbound a realist or too tame a visionary for the vigorous fakery of a historical novel.

By the first month of 1970, back in the United States, I gave up the attempt. But then what to do? I owed my publisher a novel, and had not come up with one. From the start of our relationship, I had thought it a right and mutually profitable rhythm to offer Knopf a novel every other book. In the ten years since *Rabbit, Run* had ended on its ambiguous note, a number of people had asked me what happened to Harry. It came to me that he would have run around the block, returned to Mt. Judge and Janice, faced what music there was, and be now an all-too-settled working man—a Linotyper. For three summers I had worked as a copy boy in a small-city newspaper and had admired the men in green eyeshades as they perched at their square-keyed keyboards and called down a rain of brass matrices to become hot lead slugs, to become columns of type. It was the blue-collar equivalent of my sedentary, word-productive profession. He would be, my thirty-six-year-old Rabbit, one of those Middle Americans feeling overwhelmed and put upon by all the revolutions in the air; he would serve as a receptacle for my disquiet and resentments, which would sit more becomingly on him than on me. Rabbit to the rescue, and as before his creator was in a hurry. An examination of the manuscript reveals what I had forgotten, that I typed the first draft—the only novel of the four of which this is true. I began on February 7, 1970, finished that first draft on December 11, and had it typed up by Palm Sunday 1971—which means that my publisher worked fast to get it out before the end of that year. If the novel achieved nothing else, it revived the word *redux*, which I had encountered in titles by Dryden and Trollope. From the Latin *reducere*, "to bring back," it is defined by *Webster's* as "led back; specif., *Med.*, indicating return to health after disease." People wanted to pronounce it "raydoo," as if it were French, but now I often see it in print, as a staple of journalese.

Rabbit became too much a receptacle, perhaps, for every item in the headlines. A number of reviewers invited me to think so. But though I have had several occasions to reread the novel, few excisions suggested themselves to me. As a reader I am carried along the curve that I described in my flap copy: "Rabbit is abandoned and mocked, his home is invaded, the world of his childhood decays into a mere sublunar void; still he clings to semblances of patriotism and paternity." The novel is itself a moon shot: Janice's affair launches her husband, as he and his father witness the takeoff of Apollo 11 in the Phoenix Bar, into the extraterrestrial world of Jill and Skeeter. The eventual reunion of the married couple in the Safe Haven Motel is managed with the care and gingerly vocabulary of a spacecraft docking. It is the most violent and bizarre of these four novels, but, then, the Sixties were the most violent and bizarre of these decades. The possibly inordinate emphasis on sexual congress—an enthusiastic mixture of instruction manual and de Sadeian ballet—also partakes of the times.

In *Rabbit, Run*, there is very little direct cultural and political reference, apart from the burst of news items that comes over Harry's car radio during his night of fleeing home. Of these, only the disappearance of the Dalai Lama from Tibet engages the fictional themes. In *Rabbit Redux*, the trip to the moon is the central metaphor. "Trip" in Sixties parlance meant an inner journey of some strangeness; the little apple-green house in Penn Villas plays host to space invaders—a middle-class runaway and a black rhetorician. The long third chapter—longer still in the first draft—is a Sixties invention, a "teach-in." Rabbit tries to learn. Reading aloud the words of Frederick Douglass, he becomes black, and in a fashion seeks solidarity with Skeeter. African-Americans, Old World readers should be reminded, have an immigrant pedigree almost as long as that of Anglo-Americans; "the Negro problem" is old in the New World. The United States is more than a tenth black; black music, black sorrow, black jubilation, black English, black style permeate the culture and have contributed much of what makes American music, especially, so globally potent. Yet the society continues racially divided, in the main, and Rabbit's reluctant crossing of the color line represents a tortured form of progress.

The novel was meant to be symmetric with *Rabbit, Run:* this time, Janice leaves home and a young female dies on Harry's watch. Expatiation of the baby's death is the couple's joint quest throughout the series; Harry keeps looking for a daughter, and Janice strives for competence, for a redeemed opinion of herself. Nelson remains the wounded, helplessly indignant witness. He is ever shocked by "the hardness of heart" that enables his father to live so egocentrically, as if enjoying divine favor. *Rabbit, Run*'s epigraph is an uncompleted thought by Pascal: "The motions of Grace, the hardness of the heart; external circumstances." In *Rabbit Redux*, external circumstances bear nightmarishly upon my skittish pilgrim; he achieves a measure of recognition that the rage and destructiveness boiling out of the television set belong to him. Many of the lessons of the Sixties became part of the status quo. Veterans became doves; bankers put on love beads. Among Harry's virtues, self-centered though he is, are the national curiosity, tolerance, and adaptability. America survives its chronic apocalypses. I did not know, though, when I abandoned to motel sleep the couple with a burnt-out house and a traumatized child, that they would wake to such prosperity.

Rabbit is rich, of course, in 1979, only by the standards of his modest working-class background. It was a lucky casual stroke of mine to give the used-car dealer Fred Springer a Toyota franchise in *Rabbit Redux*, for in ten years' time the Japanese-auto invasion had become one of the earmarks of an inflated and teetering American economy, and the Chief Sales Representative of a Toyota agency was well situated to reap advantage from American decline. As these novels had developed, each needed a clear background of news, a "hook" uniting the personal and national realms. In late June, visiting in Pennsylvania for a few days, I found the hook in the OPEC-induced gasoline shortage and the panicky lines that cars were forming at the local pumps; our host in the Philadelphia suburbs rose early and got our car tank filled so we could get back to New England. A nuclear near disaster had occurred at Three Mile Island in Harrisburg that spring; Carter's approval rating was down to 30 percent; our man in Nicaragua was being ousted by rebels; our man in Iran was deposed and dying; John Wayne was dead; Skylab was falling; and Rabbit, at forty-six, with a wife who drinks too much and a son dropping out of college, could well believe that he and the U.S. were both running out of gas. Except that he doesn't really believe it; *Rabbit Is Rich*, for all its shadows, is the happiest novel of the four, the most buoyant, with happy endings for everybody in it, even the hapless Buddy Inglefinger. The novel contains a number of scenes distinctly broad in their comedy: amid the inflationary abundance of money, Harry and Janice copulate on a blanket of gold coins and stagger beneath the weight of 888 silver dollars as they lug their speculative loot up the eerily deserted main drag of Brewer. A Shakespearean swap and shuffle of couples takes place in the glimmering Arcadia of a Caribbean island, and a wedding rings out at the novel's midpoint. "Life is sweet, that's what they say," Rabbit reflects in the last pages. Details poured fast and furious out of my by now thoroughly mapped and populated Diamond County. The novel is fat, in keeping with its theme of inflation, and Pru is fat with her impending child, whose growth is the book's secret action, its innermost happiness.

My own circumstances had changed since the writing of *Rabbit Redux*.

I was married to another wife, which may help account for Janice's lusty rejuvenation, and living in another town, called Georgetown, twenty minutes inland from Ipswich. Each of the Rabbit novels was written in a different setting—*Redux* belonged to my second house in Ipswich, on the winding, winsomely named Labor-in-Vain Road, and to my rented office downtown, above a restaurant whose noontime aromas of lunch rose through the floor each day to urge my writing to its daily conclusion. Whereas Ipswich had a distinguished Puritan history and some grand seaside scenery, Georgetown was an unassuming population knot on the way to other places. It reminded me of Shillington, and the wooden house that we occupied for six years was, like the brick house I had spent my first thirteen years in, long and narrow, with a big back yard and a front view of a well-trafficked street. The town was littered with details I only needed to stoop over and pick up and drop into Mt. Judge's scenery; my evening jogs through Georgetown could slip almost unaltered into Rabbit's panting peregrinations three hundred miles away. In two respects his fortunes had advantage over mine: I was not a member of any country club, nor yet a grandfather. Within five years, I would achieve both privileged states, but for the time being they had to be, like the procedures of a Toyota agency, dreamed up. A dreamy mood pervades the book; Rabbit almost has to keep pinching himself to make sure that his bourgeois bliss is real—that he is, if not as utterly a master of householdry and husbandry as the ineffable Webb Murkett, in the same exalted league.

Once, in an interview, I had rashly predicted the title of this third installment to be *Rural Rabbit*; some of the words Harry and Janice exchange in the Safe Haven Motel leave the plot open for a country move. But in the event he remained a small-city boy, a creature of sidewalks, gritty alleys, roaring highways, and fast-food franchises. One of *Rabbit, Run*'s adventures for my imagination had been its location in Brewer, whose model, the city of Reading, had loomed for a Shillington child as an immense, remote, menacing, and glamorous metropolis. Rabbit, like every stimulating alter ego, was many things the author was not: a natural athlete, a blue-eyed Swede, sexually magnetic, taller than six feet, impulsive, and urban. The rural Rabbit turns out to be Ruth, from the first novel, whom he flushes from her cover in his continued search for a daughter. Farms I knew firsthand, at least in their sensory details, from the years of rural residence my mother had imposed on her family after 1945. Rabbit spying on Ruth from behind the scratchy hedgerow is both Peter Rabbit peeking from behind the cabbages at the menacing

Mr. McGregor and I, the self-exiled son, guiltily spying on my mother as, in plucky and self-reliant widowhood, she continued to occupy her sandstone farmhouse and eighty acres all by herself. She did not, in fairness, keep the shell of a school bus in her yard; rather, the town fleet of yellow school buses was visible from the window of my drafty study in Georgetown.

Though 1979 was running out, I seem to have worked at a leisurely speed: the end of the first draft is dated April 19, 1980, and seven more months went by before my typing of the manuscript was completed on November 23. Happily, and quite to my surprise, *Rabbit Is Rich* won all three of 1981's major American literary prizes for fiction (as well as a place in critic Jonathan Yardley's list of the Ten Worst Books of the Year). An invigorating change of mates, a move to a town that made negligible communal demands, a sense of confronting the world in a fresh relation cleared my head, it may be. The Rabbit novels, coming every ten years, were far from all that I wrote; the novel that precedes *Rabbit Is Rich*, *The Coup*, and the semi-novel that followed it, *Bech Is Back*, in retrospect also seem the replete but airy products of a phase when such powers as I can claim were exuberantly ripe.

Ripeness was the inevitable theme of my fourth and concluding entry in this saga. By 1989, my wife and I had moved to Beverly Farms, a bucolic enclave of old summer homes. Most of our neighbors and new acquaintances were elderly; many spent part of their year in Florida. My children were all adult, and three stepsons nearly so; as it happened, my wife and I each had a widowed mother living in solitude. My mother, well into her eighties, was my principal living link with Rabbit's terrain; countless visits over the years had refreshed my boyhood impressions and reassured me that southeastern Pennsylvania was changing in tune with the rest of the nation. Thirty years before, a reader had asked me if Harry didn't die at the end of *Rabbit, Run*, and it did seem possible that death might come early to him, as it often does to ex-athletes, especially those who are overweight and not usefully employed. All men are mortal; my character was a man. But I, too, was a man, and by no means sure how much of me would be functioning in 1999. The more research I did to flesh out my hero's cardiovascular problems, the more ominous the pains that afflicted my own chest. As a child, just beginning to relate my birth year to the actuarial realities, I had wondered if I would live to the year 2000. I still wondered. I wanted Harry to go out with all the style a healthy author could give him, and had a vision of a four-book set, a squared-off tetralogy, a boxed life. I began *Rabbit at Rest* early in 1989, on

January 12, as if anxious to get started, and finished the first draft on the last day of September, and the typed draft on January 20, 1990. Like *Rabbit, Run*, it was published in a zero year.

And, like *Rabbit, Run*, it is in three parts. The hero of both novels flees south from domestic predicaments. In March of 1959 "his goal is the white sun of the south like a great big pillow in the sky." He fails to get there and, lost and exasperated on the dark roads of West Virginia, turns back; but his fifty-six-year-old self knows the way. Harry has acquired the expertise and the money and he gets there, and lays his tired head upon that great big pillow. No distinctly American development, no moon shot or gas crunch, offered itself as a dominant metaphor, at this end of Reagan's decade; instead, the midair explosion of Pan Am Flight 103 over Lockerbie, which occurred before Christmas of 1988, haunts Rabbit acrophobically. And he senses the coming collapse of the Soviet Union and its empire, whose opposition to the free world has shadowed and shaped his entire adult life. Freedom has had its hazards for him, and capitalist enterprise its surfeit, but he was ever the loyal citizen. God he can doubt, but not America. He is the New World's new man, armored against eventualities in little but his selfhood.

The novel's two locales have an exceptional geographical density. For the Florida city of Deleon, I did several days of legwork in the vicinity of Fort Myers. To give substance to Harry's final, solitary drive south, I drove the route myself, beginning at my mother's farm and scribbling sights, rivers, and radio emissions in a notebook on the seat beside me, just as, more than three decades previous, I turned on my New England radio on the very night, the last night of winter 1959, and made note of what came. Accident rules these novels more than most, in their attempt to take a useful imprint of the world that secretes in newspapers clues to its puzzle of glory. The fictional name "Deleon," along with the murals Rabbit notices in the hospital lobby, constitutes homage to my mother, whose cherished project it had long been to write and publish a novel about the Spanish governor of Puerto Rico and discoverer of Florida, Juan Ponce de León. She enriched, too, the city of Brewer, for a grim interplay developed between my novel, in the year of its writing, and her physical decline. Her several hospitalizations generated medical details that I shamelessly fed into Rabbit's ordeal; my frequent filial visits exposed me more intensely to Reading and its environs than at any time since the Fifties, and so Rabbit's home turf, especially as evoked at the beginning of Chapter II, acquired substance and the poignance of something slipping away. I became, as I have written elsewhere, "conscious of how powerfully, inexhaustibly rich real places are, compared with the paper cities we make of them in fiction. Even after a tetralogy, almost everything is still left to say. As I walked and drove the familiar roads and streets, I saw them as if for the first time with more than a child's eyes and felt myself beginning, at last, to understand the place. But by then it was time to say good-bye."*

My mother died two weeks after I had completed the first draft of *Rabbit at Rest*. If she pervades its landscape and overall mortal mood, my father, who died in 1972, figures strongly also. Rabbit, in his near-elderly, grandpaternal condition, more and more talked, I could not but notice, like George Caldwell in *The Centaur*. My two projected novellas had merged: the dodgy rabbit had become the suffering horse; the man of impulse and appetite had aged into humorous stoicism. In trying to picture a grandfather (my own enactment of that role had just barely begun) I fell back upon memories of my father, whose patient bemusement and air of infinite toleration had enchanted my own children. A number of readers told me how much more lovable Harry had become. My intention was never to make him—or any character—lovable. He was conceived, at a time when I was much taken with Kierkegaard, as a creature of fear and trembling; but perhaps my college exposure to Dostoevsky was more central. Rabbit is, like the Underground Man, *incorrigible*; from first to last he bridles at good advice, taking direction only from his personal, also incorrigible, God.

His adventure on the Sunfish with Judy rehearses once more the primal trauma of *Rabbit, Run*, this time successfully, with the baby saved by a self-sacrificing parent. Ripeness brings to fruition many of the tendencies of Rabbit's earthly transit. His relations with the opposite sex appear to have two main aspects, the paternal and erotic; they come to a momentarily triumphant climax in his contact with his daughter-in-law. His lifelong involvement with Ronnie Harrison—that repugnant locker-room exhibitionist whose very name seems a broken mirroring of Rabbit's—reaches its terminus in a tied golf match. Harry's shy but determined advance into the bodies of women slowly brings him to a kind of forgiveness of the flesh. Whatever his parental sins, their wages are generously paid him by his son in an act of corporate destruction. Harry's wary fascination with his black fellow-Americans leads him to explore the black section of Deleon, in its stagnation comfortingly similar to the Depression world of his childhood. So many themes convene in *Rabbit at Rest* that the hero could be said to sink under the burden of the accumulated

*See *Odd Jobs* (Knopf, 1991), p. 872.

past, and to find relief in that "wide tan emptiness under the sun," the recreation fields next to the abandoned Florida high school.

A problem for the author of sequels is how much of the previous books to carry along. The nuclear family—Harry, Janice, Nelson—and Ronnie Harrison figure in all four installments of *Rabbit Angstrom*. The older generation, potently present in the first two novels, has dwindled to the spunky figure of Bessie Springer in *Rabbit Is Rich;* I was charmed to find her so spirited and voluble as she manipulated the purse strings of her little dynasty. Characters dominant in one novel fall away in the next. Ruth vanishes from *Rabbit Redux* but returns in the next decade. I have restored to *Redux* an omitted brief reappearance by Jack Eccles, who almost became the co-protagonist of Rabbit's first outing, and whose own "outing" seemed to deserve a place in the full report. Skeeter, who takes over *Redux*, dwindles to a news item and a troubling memory; what later novel could hold him? Perhaps he returns in the form of Tiger. That the neo-Babbitt of the third volume contains the witness to the apocalyptic events of the second would strain plausibility did not so many peaceable citizens contain lethal soldiers, so many criminals contain choirboys, so many monogamous women contain promiscuous young things. An adult human being consists of sedimentary layers. We shed more skins than we can count, and are born each day to a merciful forgetfulness. We forget most of our past but embody all of it.

For this fresh printing, apt to be the last I shall oversee, I have tried to smooth away such inconsistencies as have come to my attention. Various automotive glitches—a front engine assigned to a rear-engine make of car, a convertible model that never existed in all of Detroit's manufacture—have been repaired. The flora and fauna of commercial products and popular culture posed many small spelling problems that should be now resolved. Birthdays: real people have them, but fictional characters usually do without, unless an extended chronicle insists. To my best knowledge Harold C. (a mystery initial) Angstrom was born in February 1933, and Janice Springer sometime in 1936. They were married in March of 1956, and their son, Nelson, was born the following October, seven months later—on the 22nd, by my calculations. Nelson's daughter, Judith, was born in January of 1980 and his son, Roy, in November of 1984. *Rabbit, Run* takes place from March 20, 1959, to June 24 of that year; *Rabbit Redux* from July 16, 1969, to late October; *Rabbit Is Rich* from June 23, 1979, to January 20, 1980; and *Rabbit at Rest* from December 28, 1988, to September 22, 1989. Spring, fall, summer, winter: a life as well as a year has its seasons.

FOREWORD *to* The Early Stories: 1953–1975 *(2003)*.

This is a collection. A selection, surely, is best left to others, when the writer is no longer alive to obstruct the process. Any story that makes it from the initial hurried scribbles into the haven of print possesses, in this writer's eyes, a certain valor, and my instinct, even forty years later, is not to ditch it but to polish and mount it anew. However, I did omit two stories, "Intercession" and "The Pro," which were already safely reprinted in *Golf Dreams* (1996), and two more, "One of My Generation" and "God Speaks," which, both of them first-person reminiscences based on college memories, trembled insecurely on the edge of topical humor, and felt dated.

These grudging omissions left 103 stories, composed between 1953 and 1975. The oldest is "Ace in the Hole," submitted toward the end of 1953 by a married Harvard senior to Albert Guerard's creative-writing course. Guerard, the very model of a cigarette-addicted Gallic intellectual, who nonetheless faithfully attended the Crimson's home basketball games, liked the story—he said it frightened him, an existential compliment—and suggested I send it to *The New Yorker*, which turned it down. The next year, though, after "Friends from Philadelphia" and some poems had been accepted by the magazine in my first post-collegiate summer, I resubmitted the story and it was accepted. With modifications to the coarse exchange with which it begins, it was run in April of 1955, toward the back of the magazine; such was the reading public's appetite for fiction then that "casuals" (a curious in-house term lumping fiction and humor) appeared in "the back of the book" as well as up front. The story is entangled, in my memory of those heady days of the dawning literary life, with the sudden looming, in the lobby of the Algonquin, of J. D. Salinger, a glowingly handsome tall presence not yet notoriously reclusive; he shook my hand before we were taken in to lunch with our respective editors, William Shawn and Katharine White. He said, or somebody later said he said, that he had noticed and liked "Ace in the Hole." His own stories, encountered in another writing course (taught by Kenneth Kempton), had been revelations to me of how the form, terse and tough in the Thirties and Forties, could accommodate a more expansive post-war sense of American reality; the bottle of wine that ends "Friends from Philadelphia" owes something to the Easter chick found in the bottom of the wastebasket at the end of "Just Before the War with the Eskimos." But my main debt, which may not be evident, was to Hemingway; it was he who showed us all how much tension and complexity unalloyed dialogue can convey, and how much poetry lurks in the simplest nouns and predicates. Other eye-openers for me were Franz Kafka and John O'Hara, Mary McCarthy and John Cheever, Donald Barthelme and Vladimir Nabokov, James Joyce and James Thurber and Anton Chekhov.

The year 1975 seemed an apt cut-off; it was the one and only full year of my life when I lived alone. My marriage, of twenty-two years, to a barefoot, Unitarian, brunette Radcliffe graduate was ending, but all of these stories carry its provenance. Perhaps I could have made a go of the literary business without my first wife's faith, forbearance, sensitivity, and good sense, but I cannot imagine how. We had lived, from 1957 on, in Ipswich, a large, heterogeneous, and rather out-of-the-way town north of Boston, and my principal means of support, for a family that by 1960 included four children under six, was selling short stories to *The New Yorker.* I had in those years the happy sensation that I was mailing dispatches from a territory that would be terra incognita without me. The old Puritan town was rich in characters and oral history. Though my creativity and spiritual state underwent some doldrums, the local life and the stimulation of living with growing children, with their bright-eyed grasp of the new, never left me quite empty of things to say. A small-town boy, I had craved small-town space. New York, in my twenty months of residence, had felt full of other writers and of cultural hassle, and the word game overrun with agents and wisenheimers. The real America seemed to me "out there," too homogeneous and electrified by now to pose much threat of the provinciality that people used to come to New York to escape. Out there was where I belonged, immersed in the ordinary, which careful explication would reveal to be extraordinary. These notions propelled the crucial flight of my life, the flight from the Manhattan—the Silver Town, as one of my young heroes pictures it—that I had always hoped to live in. There also were practical attractions: free parking for my car, public education for my children, a beach to tan my skin on, a church to attend without seeming too strange.

I arrived in New England with a Pennsylvania upbringing to write out of my system. The first section of these early stories, "Olinger Stories," appeared as a Vintage paperback in 1964. It has been long out of print, though a few professors who used to assign it have complained. Its eleven stories constitute, it may be, a green and slender whole—the not unfriendly critic Richard Locke once wrote of their "hothouse atmosphere"—but the idea of assembling my early stories (half of them out of print) presented, to me, no temptation stronger than the one of seeing *Olinger Stories* back together. Their arrangement, which is in order of the heroes' ages, has been slightly changed: "Flight" and "A Sense of Shelter" both feature a high-school senior, but the one of "Flight" seemed on reconsideration older, further along in his development. All the stories draw from the same autobiographical well—the only child, the small town, the grandparental home, the move in adolescence to a farm—but no attempt is made at an overall consistency. As I wrote in the original introduction,

> I have let the inconsistencies stand in these stories. Each started from scratch. Grand Avenue here is the Alton Pike there. In "Pigeon Feathers" the grandfather is dead, in "Flight" the grandmother. In fact, both of my mother's parents lived until I was an adult. In fact, my family moved eleven miles away from the town when I was thirteen; in "Friends from Philadelphia" the distance is one mile, in "The Happiest I've Been" it has grown to four. This strange distance, this less than total remove from my milieu, is for all I know the crucial detachment of my life. . . . The hero is always returning, from hundreds of miles finally.

And, intoxicated by the wine of self-exegesis, I went on:

> It surprised me, in making this arrangement, to realize that the boy who wrestles with H. G. Wells and murders pigeons is younger than the one who tells Thelma Lutz she shouldn't pluck her eyebrows. But we age unevenly, more slowly in society than in our own skulls. Among these eleven brothers, some are twins. John Nordholm and David Kern, having taken their turn as actors, reappear as narrators. And optically bothered Clyde Behn seems to me a late refraction of that child Ben who flees the carnival with "tinted globes confusing his eyelashes."

Of the sections that follow, two, "Out in the World" and "Tarbox Tales," take their titles from a Penguin collection, *Forty Stories*, selected by me and published in London in 1987. Their contents, however, have shifted and expanded, and the remaining five sections are newly invented, to give some friendly order—as in my five non-fiction collections—to so large a number of items. As the writer-editor shuffles his stories back and forth, he begins to see all sorts of graceful and meaningful transitions and sub-surface currents: each set seems to have a purling flow that amounts to a story of its own, a story in turn part of a larger tale, the lived life evoked by these fragments chipped from experience and rounded by imagination into impersonal artifacts. The reader, however, does not have access to the writer's core of personal memory, and is furthermore free to read the stories in any order he chooses. Each is designed to stand on its own, though perhaps the stories concerning Joan and Richard Maple, scattered herein though collected in a Fawcett paperback called (after a television script) *Too Far to Go* (1979) and in a Penguin edition titled (by me) *Your Lover Just Called*, do gain from being grouped. My other sequential protagonist, the writer Henry Bech, is represented only by his first manifestation, when I didn't know he was to star in an ongoing saga, now bound in *The Complete Henry Bech* (2001).

The index dates the titles by the time of composition rather than of publication. Introducing *Forty Stories*, I wrote, "Social contexts change; it is perhaps useful to know that 'The Hillies' was written in 1969, and 'A Gift from the City' in 1957." And that "Ethiopia" was written when Haile Selassie was still in power and "Transaction" when "transactional analysis" was the hottest psychological fad. Rereading everything in 2002, I was startled by the peaceful hopes attached to Iraq in "His Finest Hour," amazed by the absurdly low prices of things in Fifties and Sixties dollars, and annoyed by the recurrence of the now suspect word "Negro." But I did not change it to "black"; fiction is entitled to the language of its time. And verbal correctness in this arena is so particularly volatile that "black," which is inaccurate, may some day be suspect in turn. "Negro" at least is an anthropological term, unlike the phrase "of color," which reminds me that in my childhood the word "darky" was, in the mouths of middle-aged ladies, the ultimate in polite verbal discrimination. As to the word "fairies," used twice in "The Stare" to refer to gay men, I doubt that it was ever not offensive to those designated, but it was much used, with its tinge of contempt, by heterosexuals of both genders, and after pondering, pencil in hand, for some pained minutes, I let it remain, as natural to the consciousness of the straight, distraught male who is my protagonist. After all, *The New Yorker*'s fastidious editors let it slip by, into the issue of April 3, 1965. In general, I reread these stories without looking for trouble, but where an opportunity to help my younger self leapt out at me, I took it, deleting an adjective here, adding a clarifying phrase there. To have done less would have been a forced abdication of artistic conscience and habit. In prose there is always room for improvement, well short of a Jamesian overhaul into an overweening later manner.

My first editor at *The New Yorker* was Katharine White, who had done so much to shape the infant magazine only three decades before. After accepting four stories of mine and sending back a greater number, she, with her husband, came to visit the young Updikes and their baby girl in Oxford, and offered me a job at the magazine. Of the year or two when we shared the premises—before she followed E. B. White to Maine, giving up the high position of fiction editor—I remember her technique of going over proofs with me side by side at her desk, which made me fuzzy-headed and pliant, and how she once wrinkled her nose when asking me if I knew why my writing, in the instance before us, wasn't very good. She had made her way in Harold Ross's otherwise all-boy staff and could be brusque, though there was no mistaking her warm heart and high hopes for the magazine. My next editor, until 1976, was never brusque; William Maxwell brought to his editorial functions a patient tact and gentle veracity that offered a life lesson as much as a lesson in writing. My fiction editor since has been Katharine White's son, Roger Angell, whose continued vitality and sharpness into his eighties gives me, at the outset of my seventies, hope for the future. All three, not to mention the unsung copyeditors and fact checkers, contributed many improving touches to these stories and on occasion inspired large revisions, though my theory in general is that if a story doesn't pour smooth from the start, it never will. Though it was more than once alleged, in the years 1953–75, that *The New Yorker* promoted a gray sameness in its fiction, it permitted me much experimentation, from the long essayistic conglomerations capping the Olinger stories to the risky and risqué monologues of "Wife-Wooing" and "Lifeguard." The editors published so much fiction they could run the impulsive brief opus as well as the major effort, and as William Shawn settled into his long reign he revealed a swashbuckling streak of avant-gardism, a taste for Barthelme and Borges that woke up even the staidest in his stable to new possibilities.

Some of the more far-out stories are unduly precious to me, but readers of *Museums and Women* will not find here the illustrations of pond life, Jurassic life, horse-harness technology, or the baluchitherium that adorned the relevant pages; after a long, would-be cartoonist's flirtation with graphic elements, I have decided that pictures don't mix with text. Text, left to its own devices, enjoys a life that floats free of any specific setting or format or pictographic attachments. Only a few Greek letters and a lone bar of music (in "Son") have posed a challenge to the hard-working keyboarders of the volume at hand.

The technology reflected in these stories harks back to a time when automatic shifts were an automotive novelty and outdoor privies were still features of the rural landscape, and it stops well short of the advent of personal computers and ubiquitous cell phones. My generation, once called Silent, was, in a considerable fraction of its white majority, a fortunate one—"too young to be warriors, too old to be rebels," as it is put in the story "I Will Not Let Thee Go, Except Thou Bless Me." Born in the early Depression, at a nadir of the national birthrate, we included many only children given, by penny-pinching parents, piano lessons and a confining sense of shelter. We acquired in hard times a habit of work and came to adulthood in times when work paid off; we experienced when young the patriotic cohesion of World War II without having to fight the war. We were repressed enough to be pleased by the relaxation of the old sexual morality, without suffering much of the surfeit, anomie, and venereal disease of younger generations. We were simple and hopeful enough to launch into idealistic careers and early marriages, and pragmatic enough to adjust, with an American shrug, to the ebb of old certainties. Yet, though spared many of the material deprivations and religious terrors that had dogged our parents, and awash in a disproportionate share of the world's resources, we continued prey to what Freud called "normal human unhappiness."

But when has happiness ever been the subject of fiction? The pursuit of it is just that—a pursuit. Death and its adjutants tax each transaction. What is possessed is devalued by what is coveted. Discontent, conflict, waste, sorrow, fear—these are the worthy, inevitable subjects. Yet our hearts expect happiness, as an underlying norm—"the fountain-light of all our day," in Wordsworth's words. Rereading, I found no lack of joy in these stories, though it arrives by the moment and not by the month, and no lack of affection and good will among characters caught in the human plight, the plight of limitation and mortality. Art hopes to sidestep mortality with feats of attention, of harmony, of illuminating connection, while enjoying, it might be said, at best a slower kind of mortality: paper yellows, language becomes old-fashioned, revelatory human news passes into general social wisdom. I could not but think, during this retrospective labor, of all those *New Yorker*s, a heedless broad Mississippi of print, in which my contributions among so many others appeared; they serviced a readership, a certain demographic episode, now passed into history— all those birch-shaded Connecticut mailboxes receiving, week after week, William Shawn's notion of entertainment and instruction. What would have happened to me if William Shawn had not liked my work? Those first checks, in modest hundreds, added up and paid for my first automobile. Without *The New Yorker*, I would have had to walk. I would have existed, no doubt, in some sort, but not the bulk of these stories.

They were written on a manual typewriter and, beginning in the early Sixties, in a one-room office I rented in Ipswich, between a lawyer and a beautician, above a cozy corner restaurant. Around noon the smell of food would start to rise through the floor, but I tried to hold out another hour before I tumbled downstairs, dizzy with cigarettes, to order a sandwich. After I gave up cigarettes, I smoked nickel cigarillos to allay my nervousness at the majesty of my calling and the intricacy of my craft; the empty boxes, with their comforting image of another writer, Robert

Burns, piled up. Not only were the boxes useful for storing little things like foreign coins and cufflinks, but the caustic aura of cigars discouraged visitors. I felt that I was packaging something as delicately pervasive as smoke, one box after another, in that room, where my only duty was to describe reality as it had come to me—to give the mundane its beautiful due.

FOREWORD *to* Too Far to Go: The Maples Stories *(1979)*.

The Maples presented themselves to the writer in New York City in 1956, dropped from his sight for seven years, and reappeared in the suburbs of Boston in 1963, giving blood. They figured in a dozen stories since, until the couple's divorce in 1976. Their name, bestowed by a young man who had grown up in a small town shaded by Norway maples, and who then moved to the New England of sugar maples and flame-bright swamp maples, retained for him an arboreal innocence, a straightforward and cooling leafiness. Though the Maples stories trace the decline and fall of a marriage, they also illumine a history in many ways happy, of growing children and a million mundane moments shared. That a marriage ends is less than ideal; but all things end under heaven, and if temporality is held to be invalidating, then nothing real succeeds. The moral of these stories is that all blessings are mixed. Also, that people are incorrigibly themselves. The musical pattern, the advance and retreat, of the Maples' duet is repeated over and over, ever more harshly transposed. They are shy, cheerful, and dissatisfied. They like one another, and are mysteries to one another. One of them is usually feeling slightly unwell, and the seesaw of their erotic interest rarely balances. Yet they talk, more easily than any other characters the author has acted as agent for. A tribe segregated in a valley develops an accent, then a dialect, and then a language all its own; so does a couple. Let this collection preserve one particular dead tongue, no easier to parse than Latin.

NOTE *on "The Indian," a short story published in* The New Yorker *in August 1963 and reprinted, with this commentary, eight years later as a special number of* The Blue Cloud Review, *a publication of the Benedictine Missionaries of Blue Cloud Abbey, Marvin, South Dakota.*

"The Indian" was written early in the 1960s around the germ of a gentleman, himself not an Indian, who hangs around Market Street in

Ipswich with a proprietary and watchful air. In this short story I coined the name "Tarbox"—an authentic if rarely encountered Yankee name—for the small New England town that for all its charm seems to me to be the arena of the Decline of the West. Indeed, readers of my novel *Couples* would do well to have this little preliminary evocation of Tarbox in mind. The idea of the Indian, as Leslie Fiedler keeps telling us, is central to the American mythology, and we are all haunted by these dispossessed—and were long before the New Left seized upon the Indian Wars as a (not especially apt) metaphor for our Asian adventures. The key word in the first paragraph is the "unpossessed" of "unpossessed abundance."* The North American abundance was of course already, in a shadowy way, possessed, and it does not seem unlikely to me that Chief Musquenomenee, that "shadowy chief" who is buried "presumably upright," in fact haunts our shabby and garish downtowns, waiting for the astonishing ramshackle construction Caucasian Man has imposed upon the world to collapse, and to restore to him—primitive man—his primal inheritance.

NOTE *on* Bech: His Oeuvre, *privately printed by William B. Ewert in 2000.*

I had thought that the publication of *Bech at Bay* in 1998 would close the book, as it were, on the character of the Jewish-American writer Henry Bech, born as a fictive person in 1923 and as a literary creation in 1964, in the short story "The Bulgarian Poetess." He survived that brush with a Communist beauty to figure into eighteen more stories, collected in three small but tasty volumes: *Bech: A Book* (1970), *Bech Is Back* (1982), and the above-mentioned *Bech at Bay*, which contains the two longest Bech stories ever and ends with a highly fantastic apotheosis in Sweden. Yet within the year the scheme of one more Bech story abruptly came to me and, amid the press of much other business, I executed it, scribbling

---

*"The town, in New England, of Tarbox, restrained from embracing the sea by a margin of tawny salt marshes, locates its downtown four miles inland up the Musquenomenee River, which ceases to be tidal at the waterfall of an old hosiery mill, now given over to the manufacture of plastic toys. It was to the mouth of this river, in May of 1634, that the small party of seventeen men, led by the younger son of the governor of the Massachusetts Bay Colony—Jeremiah Tarbox being only his second in command—came in three rough skiffs with the purpose of establishing amid such an unpossessed abundance of salt hay a pastoral plantation. This, with God's forbearance, they did. . . ."

the first draft on airplanes taking me to Kansas City and back, and sending the typescript off to *The New Yorker* on the day before Christmas. They published it with equal dispatch, in the issue of January 25, 1999. I am delighted that to my friend Bill Ewert it appeared worthy of becoming a little book in itself. To me it seems one of the purer Bechian flights, holding at its center the humbling but shining truth that artistic creation is at best a sublimation of the sexual instinct, and subsidiary to it. Bech almost never appears in my fiction without an erotically charged companion; he is first seen with his mother and last with his infant daughter, and is more or less in love steadily meanwhile. In this he is not only a representative writer but, I think, a representative human being. Art is his pastime, but love is his work.

REPLIES *to three questions posed by* Le Nouvel Observateur *upon the publication, in September 2005, of the French translation of* Licks of Love *(2000), a collection of twelve short stories and a novella, "Rabbit Remembered."*

Q. *The stories in* Licks of Love *are nostalgic in tone, and their characters' best days are mostly over. What do you feel nostalgic about?*

A. They are the work of an elderly man; what else can you expect? The past, Proust pointed out, is Paradise. We cannot help revisiting Paradise, and the writer has his own magic carpet woven of words to take him there. I feel nostalgic about almost everything I have experienced—people I knew, brand-name products I consumed, movies I saw, books I once read, certain tints of weather that return to me unexpectedly. It is marvellous, to have lived, and the longer one lives the more marvellous it seems. As a child I used to hear a horse-drawn wagon come down the street, and coal noisily pour down a chute; I watched a man haul a block of ice into our kitchen and put it in a wooden "icebox"; I listened every day to the gracious, unhurried voice of my grandfather, a man born in the middle of the American Civil War. Is this not marvellous? Not to mention the presence of my young mother and father in the background. In *Licks of Love* the details are lit by love, love for what we can no longer have. Two examples: the title story, "Licks of Love in the Heart of the Cold War," about a kind of cultural-exchange mission that once felt dangerous and useful, and "How Was It, Really?," about the difficulty of remembering the daily details of a bygone marriage.

Q. *You have written more reviews for* The New Yorker *than any other writer. How, as a reviewer, would you approach* Licks of Love? *Which details would you linger over?*

A. Oh, my. I never set out to be a reviewer, and certainly try to hush up my reviewer's voice when I am writing creatively. But I did feel, as best I remember, happy, writing "Rabbit Remembered," to be back in Rabbit's territory, even with my hero only haunting it. There is a kind of human event I find only in that territory—a warm confusion, perhaps, deriving from the somewhat desperate comedy of my first, childish impressions of family life—and I loved watching Annabelle and Nelson get together (the very consonants of their names hinting at a genetic connection) and riding with them into the new millennium, to the tune of a traffic jam and a Christian-rock concert in the shell of a once thriving small-city downtown. As to the other, mostly suburban stories, they embody for me tender encounters of the kind that keep the world turning. Besides the stories singled out above, I would bestow special praise upon the first paragraph of "The Women Who Got Away" and the poignant coda of "Metamorphosis."

Q. *What is your America? Is the America that you love gone forever?*

A. It is true, I have trouble, writing about America, in reminding myself that everybody now has cell phones, that sex without condoms is flirting with death by AIDS, that everybody under forty has grown up with computers and computer games, that people get cash day and night by feeding a plastic card into a machine, and so on. The America that automatically presents itself to my imagination is a semi-rural one where the telephone and the movies are the latest thing, and Jack Benny and Benny Goodman dominate the airwaves, and the spectres of Protestant morality still exercise a powerful pull. In a way, my imagination has not "kept up," however zealously I read contemporary fiction and gossip magazines. But history proceeds, I console myself, less like a parade than like an onion or a cabbage, wrapping its older layers in thin newer ones. But the older ones gave it its essential shape, and the America I love, the land that trusts its citizens to know what is best for them and to pursue happiness without undue impediments, is still there for me. And it is there for whole classes of people—notably people of color and women—who were, not many decades ago, matter-of-factly disenfranchised. With all its faults— vulgarity, self-indulgence, youth-worship, romanticism in thought and ruthlessness in practice—it is still a template for the world, as the races and nations inevitably mix.

THE "ORIGINAL ENDING" *of* Self-Consciousness, *rescued from the files for a 1990 collection of "literary outtakes" compiled by Larry Dark.*

. . . Even toward myself, as my own life's careful manager and promoter, I feel a touch of disdain. Precociously conscious of the precious, inexplicable burden of selfhood, I have steered my unique little craft carefully, at the same time doubting that carefulness is the most sublime virtue.

OPPOSITIONAL OTHER: *Pfauggggh!* Fearfulness and selfishness, that's all I've been hearing. What a little Fafner you are—"I have and I hold!" Clinging to a creed demolished everywhere you look, to a patriotism as obsolete as blood sacrifice, to a storybook small town that never existed, least of all in the dingy Thirties; toadying to any establishment that comes your way, from a high-school faculty to a Communist Writers' Union; so anxious to please and afraid of a little normal opposition your tongue and lungs can't get the words out; so afraid of losing a flake of your precious dragon's hoard of you-ness you resist every change from the condominium next door to the junking of the Electoral College and even think ending the Cold War may be a bad idea; in love with the status quo under the delusion that you've done well by it; obsessed with a painless harmless skin disease as if without it you'd be a raving male beauty; and now in this present chapter of egocentric rambling even slyly confessing to wanting, on the basis of medieval or at best eighteenth-century metaphysics, to preserve your miserable, spotty identity forever! What about the *big* picture! Where in all these millions of words you boast about is there any serious consideration of the large issues that concern humanity in the mass? Nuclear war! Holocaust! The industrial-military complex! Birth control! The rust belt! The national deficit! AIDS!

SELF: Well, I *have* written a play about a President and a novel about a coup. But morality and politics in general, it seems to me, were definitively handled in the works of George Bernard Shaw. All that a lively intelligence, generous spirit, and tireless style could do along these lines, he did. In any case the large ground is heavily trod. My own concern gravitates to the intimate, where the human intersects with something inhuman, something dark and involuntary and unsubmissive to man-created order. After all that Kierkegaard and Barth that I once consumed, it is hard for me to be reverential about the purely human. Nevertheless, I unfailingly vote; I contribute to charities, and even sometimes respond to especially shaming solicitations by mail; I recognize that the good and legal thing, in a well-policed society, is generally also the convenient thing—

o. o.: Scandalous! To put down—in limp parody of Fifties mandarinism—the core concerns of human society and enterprise as issues of convenience, and to find reality only in your chaos of intimate particulars, this babble of random and cagey candor sliding in slippery, unconscionable fashion from point to misremembered point—*aaargggh!* The title of this opus should be *Self-Serving. Self-Promotion.* One more slyly aggressive tome that the poor dear librarians think they have to buy. One more egotistical tax upon the stifling bookstores and groaning forests. You have your nerve, whining about the whale and the buffalo and how you and your alphabet blocks rose above dog eat dog.

No argument. I am weary of *Self-Consciousness.* What I have written here discomfits me: it is indiscreet and yet inaccurate, a greedy squandering of a life's minute-by-minute savings, a careless provisional raid upon the abyss of being. Fiction, which does not pretend to be true, is much truer. This stuff is embarrassing. The reviewers will jump all over it. I think I'll save myself a peck of trouble and not publish.

SELF: Oh, go ahead. It was written, after all, only by Updike; it has nothing to do with *me.*

ON ONE'S OWN STYLE: *Statement contributed to* The Sound on the Page: Style and Voice in Writing, *by Ben Yagoda (2004).*

Style as I understand it is nothing less than a writer's habits of mind—it is not a kind of paint applied afterward, but the very germ of the thing. One has certain models of excellence, certain standards of prose evolved with the help sometimes of teachers and editors, and certain readerly expectations that one hopes, as a writer, to satisfy. Just as one's handwriting tends to come out the same way every time, with certain quirks of emphasis and flow, so does one's writing, with its recurrent pet vocabulary and concerns.

I usually begin a new project excited by the idea of *not* sounding like Updike. *Rabbit, Run,* for instance, was an attempt to provide a prose more freewheeling and uninhibited than that in my *New Yorker* stories, which in general have an *en brosse* quality, sticking up in little points. When I began to write *Rabbit, Run* in the present tense, it was a conscious effort to escape the me who writes in the past tense and tends to get mired in elaborate backward-looking syntax. With *Rabbit* and his subsequent brothers, there was little looking back, just an impressionistic momentum and a fresh grasp of the language; lots of sentences that would be ordinary in the past tense take on a hasty poetry in the present; even the "he says" expresses something different.

And so forth, story to story, book to book. The mandarin explosions of *A Month of Sundays* and *The Coup* sought relief from the drab Rabbit terrain. In *Seek My Face*, I tried to write the way Jackson Pollock painted, in long stringy loops. Nevertheless, there will be a sameness due to the limits of a single personality. One's effort as an artist is to extend those limits as much as possible. When I read my old prose, usually aloud before audiences, I am aware of phrases I would not use now, things I have forgotten I ever knew, imitations of Proust and Henry Green that would not be so naked now, but in general I am comfortable. As in a real voice and body, changes occur—but organically, within one identity.

LETTER *included as an afterword to the introduction of* Updike in Cincinnati: A Literary Performance, *edited by James Schiff (2007).*

Dear Jim:

I am happy to repose in your too-generous account of my public readings and appearances; would that it were exactly so. Since you ask in the course of your description, "Why does he do so much of it?," permit me a response, though you answer the question well enough on your own. For one thing, I don't think I do a lot of it—almost none in recent years, and, overall, less, surely, than Vonnegut, Mailer, Oates, Wolfe, and a dozen poets. My reasons, as best as I can understand them myself, are

1.) I may not need the money, but I *feel* I need it. For two days or, in the Cincinnati case, three of travel and amiable socializing I receive twice or more the payment than for a short story that took many days of intense and chancy mental effort to compose. "Chancy"—a story can always be rejected, and come to nothing. As long as posing as a writer pays better than *being* a writer, a child of the Depression, as was I, will be tempted.

2.) I get to see, in the margins of my appearance, a bit of the country, this wonderful federal republic that it is my job to know and love. And I meet a lot of bright professorial people and hopeful young students that I would not otherwise; just the deportment and dress of a student audience tells you something about where you are. And how would I otherwise get to hang out with great guys like Jim Schiff, Bill Pritchard, and Don Greiner?

3.) I began late—until 1965 or so I read in public only in a few New England venues—and was pleasantly surprised to discover that I could do it, without much stuttering. The microphone and the attentive audience allay a stutterer's basic fear, the root of his vocal impediment—*the fear of not being heard.* The speaker tries, at a cocktail party or in a telephone conversation, too hard to be heard, to be understood, and anxiety jams his throat and blocks speech. Instead, a soothing honey of attention and responsive laughter eases the platform performer's voice box, and he luxuriates in a degree of attention not experienced since his parents stopped hearkening to his first babbling.

4.) Reading something aloud is a good way to test it, to see if the words do flow as when heard in one's head. My effort while reading is to pronounce the words slowly and distinctly, letting them speak for themselves. You have to have faith, in the surrounding silence as you drone on, that the listener—*any* listener—is with you.

5.) I have been known to write out speeches and give them, *à la* Tom Wolfe, but really that seems too much effort for fifty minutes or an hour in the limelight, between the dinner with the English faculty beforehand and the book-signing afterward. Also, it bends my mind in a crippling way; there is something fishy and forced about opinions manufactured on mighty topics (e.g., "Are public libraries good things?" and "Is the planet going to the dogs?"). My fiction and poetry are my fullest and most honest attempt to describe my realities and contribute to society's net wisdom. If reading a selected sample, with what comments occur to me, is not enough for the audience, let it go down to the cineplex instead.

I had a great time in Cincinnati, but why is there no shrine to Doris Day?

All best,
John Updike

THE COURAGE OF BALLPLAYERS: *A comment solicited, in 2002, by Curt Smith and the Baseball Hall of Fame and Museum for a coffee-table book celebrating the national pastime.*

What baseball means to me is standing as a child on third base of our local softball field and praying that no ball would be hit my way. Even a softball seemed hard to me, and what came up to the plate in a hardball game looked like a bullet. An imperfectly aimed bullet. My admiration for the men who play this game has been intensified by this early revelation of the courage it takes. The courage, too, to stand alone, surrounded by green space, and have your mistakes show in full view of the stadium.

POST-HUBBLE ASTRONOMY: *A gloss on "The Accelerating Expansion of the Universe," a short story published in* Harper's *in 2004 and reprinted, with this commentary, in* Physics Today, *April 2005.*

It is not true that developments in physics go ignored by professional humanists or by the common man. The basic facts get to us all and frame the way we think and even, in this instance of the fictional Martin Fairweather, feel. The picture physics paints of the material universe is arresting enough to make the newspapers but far from flattering to our individual identities. Astronomy is what we have now instead of theology. The terrors are less, but the comforts are nil.

ON "THE AMERICAN IDEA": *Written, in 2007, for the sesquicentennial issue of* The Atlantic Monthly, *which featured a symposium on this theme.*

The American idea, as I understand it, is to trust people to know their own minds and to act in their own enlightened self-interest, with a necessary respect for others. Totalitarian governments promise relief for deprived and desperate people, but in the end are maintained in power by terrorism from above rather than the consent of the governed. Empowerment of the individual was the idea in 1857, the year of *The Atlantic's* founding, and after a century and a half of travail and misadventure among human societies, there is no better idea left standing. The idea of individual freedom, undermined by a collectivist tide in the first half of the last century and disregarded by radical Islam today, now spreads through an electronic culture of music, television, and the Internet, even under governments fearful of losing control.

Not only are ordinary citizens to be trusted, in the American idea, but leaders of government, too. Those who have lost the people's trust can be voted out. To be sure, there is a lag in the process, but a process more immediately responsive to the people's will might have ousted Lincoln and Washington in their unpopular moments. A certain trust in a nation's overall soundness and stability is implied in the contract between the governed and the governors. American democracy speaks not just in votes and policies, but in the buoyancy, good nature, and mutual tolerance of its people. These qualities persist even in difficult times—and what times are devoid of difficulties, of contention and conflict and challenge? The American idea builds them in, creating not a static paradise but a productively competitive section of the earth's humanity.

The challenges ahead? A fury against liberal civilization by the world's poor, who have nothing to lose; a ruinous further depletion of the world's natural assets; a global warming that will change world climate and with it world geopolitics. The American idea, promulgated in a land of plenty, must prepare to sustain itself in a world of scarcity.

COMMENCEMENT ADDRESS *delivered at the University of Massachusetts, Amherst, on May 23, 1993.*

Mr. Chairman, Mr. President, Mr. Chancellor, fellow-honorees, members of the platform, members of the faculty, gratified parents, and grateful graduating students: you are about to see a vow being broken. Decades ago, in the innocent purity of my avant-garde beginnings, I vowed never to give a commencement speech. I had heard a number in my progress through the American educational system, and as an occasional honoree at college ceremonies since I have heard a number more, always with the nagging thought, *Is this necessary?* The commencement speech, like the weather forecast on television, is a ceremonial space in American life, a spirited spouting of words whose value is not factual content but homage to the empyrean, to the heavens that send us rain and sunshine, good fortune and bad, out of those invisible tiers where atmosphere becomes stratosphere, and stratosphere becomes virtual vacuum.

At this moment, you graduating seniors are brim-full of yourselves— your twenty-plus years of life have reached a culmination that gives your brief personal history a certain drama and shape, arrowing as it has toward this very point in time. You are surrounded by buildings and scenes you will rarely if ever see again, and by friends most of whom, incredible as it seems, will fade forever from your lives. You are each pregnant with the person you will become, and this pregnancy is preoccupying and disquieting, dreadful and wonderful. At this sensitive moment of morning sickness, then, appears a more or less elderly, in some remote sense eminent, person, who will talk to you about himself, or herself, or his or her favorite cause. In my idealistic youth I vowed never to be that person.

But here am I, and my topic, predictably, is myself. In trying to imagine my audience today, I reflected back upon my own few graduations—

from a small-town high school in Pennsylvania in 1950, from Harvard College in 1954. The world of the early Fifties was, compared with the world you know, in some ways touchingly innocent and underequipped. Our electronic expertise extended little beyond knowing how to turn on a radio. Television existed, but as a black-and-white novelty; the screen was small and round, and we had not grown up with it. Popular music came out of jukeboxes, and its stars—Bing Crosby, Frank Sinatra, the Andrews Sisters, Nat "King" Cole—were admired by our parents as well as ourselves; it was not until Elvis Presley's emergence in 1956 that the generational divide in musical taste established itself as a canyon in our cultural landscape. The movies, too, catered to all ages, and their repertoire of sanitized, romantic imagery had been brought, in the Thirties and Forties, to a high pitch of expressiveness and penetration; my generation's aspirations, ethical values, and notions of social etiquette were in large part shaped by the movies. The bias of the men in Hollywood who made the movies was intensely patriotic and populist-conservative; that is, the American people, we learned, had a heart of gold. We had witnessed, as children, the United States send its men and women across the world's two great oceans to defeat two cruel fascist empires; we had little reason to question that heart of gold. By "we" I suppose I have come to mean young white males; in 1954 women were expected to marry, and African-Americans to know their place. Further, homosexuals were expected to stay in the closet, Latin Americans to stay south of the border, sin to stay in the red-light district, and abortions to stay in the back alley. Keeping the Communists at bay was the main political agenda, and the principal domestic question was "Why is the Man in the Gray Flannel Suit so unhappy?"

Mine was, I can see now, a rather fortunate generation. We were born into the heart of the Depression, yet our childishness sheltered us from any radical doubt of capitalism's essential benevolence. Too young to be out of work, we were then too young to fight the Second World War but old enough to participate vicariously in its excitement and triumph. There were not many of us, thanks to the pinched domestic budgets of the Thirties, and we graduated, in the early Fifties, into a nation where prices were still low but opportunities were multiplying. It was not difficult, as we slipped into our first jobs, to buy our first automobiles for a few thousand dollars or our first house for—as mine was in 1958—$18,500. We married young and thought nothing of having four or five children. Suddenly, we were too old for Vietnam, and for the next wave of radical doubt and potential revolution. Our goals were personal and particular and we never elected a President from our number; national leadership has recently at last passed from the generation that fought the Second World War to the generation that fought or protested the war in Vietnam. What did we do? A minority of us fought in Korea, and most of us, by paying our taxes and believing our leaders, saw the Cold War through. They called us, long ago, the Silent Generation. Now we are old enough to take early retirement and paint watercolors in Arizona, but many of us still cling to positions of power, and in our silence have carried forward the work of industry and the arts, agriculture and business, advertising and bureaucracy. Of course, I love my generation; I have spent my professional life mostly writing about myself and my peers, our gradual loss of sexual and political innocence, our experience of the last four decades of history and of the timeless human experience of growth, work, change, and decay.

My thought for you this morning is that you may not be much different. The generational rhythm dictates that grandparents and grandchildren resemble one another; you, too, are graduating into times when history is more like a short-story collection than a novel. You are concerned about finding your niche in the economy, as were we; you are looking to family life as the vehicle of happiness, as did we. And perhaps you distrust generalizations as did we. I distrust even the ones I am now making. All generations, when the dust has finally settled, are mostly silent. The world is always with us, and is never without danger and woe. History tints us, like fish that swim through colored water; but our bones are all fish bones. The human species, with its internal drives and conflicts, is a constant. A Cro-Magnon man of thirty-five thousand years ago, were he dressed in academic garb and placed on this platform, would not look out of place. We are born into history, and graduate into it, but our animal optimism and our cerebral capacity to plan our own personal futures exist independently of history. The individual is the unit of measure and of national movement; nowhere is this more true than in the United States.

I have said that I was conditioned to believe that America has a heart of gold; mine may be the last generation that could believe this easily. But international events in the four years since you entered this university make it easier, it seems to me, and newly exciting to be American. We are no longer obliged to pour our strength into a cold war of reaction and counterblow; we have moved from a dualistic to a pluralistic world, a world in which our national gifts are by no means obsolete. What are those national gifts? At a stab, they are good humor, optimism, the ability to improvise, the willingness to learn, and respect for the individual. You graduating seniors are the latest embodiments of these qualities, the newest edition. Thanks to television and computers, and to an openness that came with the Sixties, you are savvy in ways my generation was not. What you know about the facts of life, and what you understand of tolerance and acceptance and multiform ways of being human, puts 1954 to shame. But your generational savviness, it could be, in our age of imagery and sound bites is a matter more of imagery than of the heft of real things, of earth and the tools that bit by bit move it. You cannot but learn more of the world's heft, as you take it now into your hands. Take it up reverently, for it is an old piece of clay, with millions of thumbprints on it.

REPLY *to a commendation by Stephen H. Webb, presenter of the Lifetime Achievement Award of the Conference on Christianity and Literature, delivered at the meeting of the Modern Language Association, in Philadelphia, on December 29, 2006.*

Let me extend my thanks to you, Professor Webb, for your most generous words, and to all of you of the Conference instrumental in giving me this award. Any literary award prompts some guilt in me, for to have lived since the age of twenty-two as a published writer, with the lenient hours and craftsmanly pleasures the vocation bestows, is surely reward enough. The productivity that Mr. Webb mentions, although somewhat intimidating, not to say suffocating, in its accumulated fruits over these five decades, was for me a less than onerous daily duty to earn my privileges as a self-employed, and virtually unsupervised, worker in one of the last cottage industries, one wherein impulsive marks on blank paper are gradually turned into print and snugly bound pages.

My connection with Christianity is unremarkable. Raised in the pious precincts of Berks County, fifty miles northwest of here, in a small town where the season of our Saviour's birth was openly celebrated with civic lights and town-hall ceremonies, in a school system where Bible passages and the Lord's Prayer began each day, and the son, furthermore, of a Presbyterian minister's son who obligingly, with marriage to my mother, became a Lutheran deacon and Sunday-school teacher, I accepted churchgoing as part of a respectable and orderly life, and even in college and youthful periods of city residence never quite forsook the habit. I felt lost and lonely without it. As I aged, much of my life took on the aspect of answered prayers, and not to acknowledge, to the object of these prayers, my gratitude would have struck, to my sense of things, a wicked imbalance. In my twenties and early thirties, especially, I sought to firm up my supernatural inklings by reading theology and professedly Christian authors, of which there were a significant number in the 1950s.

I never, however, presumed to think of myself as a Christian apologist—the difficulties and embarrassments of faith in a disbelieving age are all there, in my fiction and poetry, as part of reality. I believed that realism even in its darkest aspect formed a homage to the God of creation, and a gesture of trust in Him. My work, as I fallibly understand it, concerns itself with issues of religion and belief from the first novel, *The Poorhouse Fair*, which houses an extended religious debate and a latter-day version of the stoning of Saint Stephen, to the most recent, *Terrorist*, which underlines the lethal dangers of any absolute supernatural faith— it makes us ruthless and disregardful of *this* life and *this* world. This world is the one we see and experience, the one we should treasure and praise. I do not think of myself as a witness to faith but as a witness to life. Even in those many works of mine in which religion plays no overt role, mundane events are considered, I like to think, religiously, as worthy of reverence and detailed evocation. Much in our lifetimes dazzles and puzzles; much invites us to doubt and despair; yet a world in which no better is imagined, and the motions of our spirits are not at all valorized, would be one not only without religion but also without art.

My kind commender mentions "The Deacon," a short and perhaps small story about the humble, marginal position of churches in our contemporary landscape. That dogged deacon was, in a way, my father; and also the many, including clergy, who, against the modern grain, borrow light and lightness from ancient lamps, suffer from a Sabbath compulsion, and take comfort in the periodic company of like-minded others who—to quote from "The Deacon"—"share the pride of this ancient thing that will not quite die."

Index

Note: Italicized numerals indicate pages with
illustrations. Boldface numerals indicate pages where
the author and/or work is specifically the subject
of a review or prose piece.

Illustration Credits

The photographs and images reproduced in this book were provided with the permission and courtesy of the following:

pages 276, 277: Lear, *Garf Hossayn* and *On the Road, Two Hours from Tepelene*. The Yale Center of British Art, New Haven, gift of Donald C. Gallup, B.A. 1934, Ph.D. 1939. Images courtesy of the Yale Center for British Art.

page 281: After Moran, *Katahdin from the South Shore of the Lake*. Image courtesy of Olana State Historic Site, New York State Office of Parks, Recreation, and Historic Preservation.

page 283: After Homer, *The Artist in the Country*. Image courtesy of the University of Michigan and the Making of America collection (http://moa.umdl.umich.edu).

page 291: Van Gogh, *The Blute-Fin Mill*. The Phillips Collection, Washington D.C. Image courtesy of the Phillips Collection. All rights reserved.

page 292: Van Gogh, *Street in Saintes-Maries-de-la-Mer*. The Metropolitan Museum of Art, New York, bequest of Abby Aldrich Rockefeller, 1948 (48.190.1). Image copyright © The Metropolitan Museum of Art/Art Resource, N.Y.

page 298: Van Gogh, from a letter to Émile Bernard, March 18, 1888, illustrated with a sketch, *Drawbridge with Walking Couple*. Autograph letter, signed. The Pierpont Morgan Library, New York, gift of Eugene V. Thaw in honor of Charles E. Pierce Jr., 2007 (MA 6441.2). Image courtesy of the Pierpont Morgan Library/Art Resource, N.Y.

page 304: Seurat, *Aman-Jean*. The Metropolitan Museum of Art, New York, bequest of Stephen C. Clark, 1960 (61.101.16). Image copyright © The Metropolitan Museum of Art/Art Resource, N.Y.

page 307: Seurat, *Seated Woman with a Parasol*. The Art Institute of Chicago, bequest of Abby Aldrich Rockefeller, 1999 (1999.7). Image copyright © The Art Institute of Chicago.

pages 313, 315: Schiele, *Nude Self-Portrait* and *Reclining Female with Spread Legs*. The Leopold Collection, Vienna. Images courtesy of the Leopold Collection.

page 318: Klimt, *The Dancer*. Private collection. Image courtesy of Neue Galerie New York.

page 321: Gerstl, *Portrait of a Man on the Lawn*. Private collection. Image courtesy of Neue Galerie New York.

page 324: Beckmann, *Self-Portrait in Front of Red Curtain*. Private collection. Copyright © 2011 by Artists Rights Society (ARS), New York / VG BildKunst, Bonn. Photograph by Hermann Buresch, courtesy bpk, Berlin / Hermann Buresch /Art Resource, N.Y.

page 331: Ernst, *Celebes*. Tate Modern, London. Copyright © 2011 by Artists Rights Society (ARS), New York/ADAGP, Paris. Image courtesy of Tate/Art Resource, N.Y.

page 333: Ernst, *The Blessed Virgin Chastises the Infant Jesus Before Three Witnesses*. Wallraf-Richartz-Museum & Fondation Corboud, Cologne. Copyright © 2011 by Artists Rights Society (ARS), New York/ADAGP, Paris. Image courtesy of Snark/Art Resource, N.Y.

page 337: Magritte, *La Trahison des images*. Los Angeles County Museum of Art, purchased with funds provided by the Mr. and Mrs. William Preston Harrison Collection (78.7). Copyright © C. Herscovici, London/Artists Rights Society (ARS), New York. Image copyright © 2009 by Museum Associates / LACMA/Art Resource, N.Y.

page 340: Magritte, *L'Aube désarmée* (after *Les Jours gigantesques*). The Royal Museums of Fine Arts of Belgium, Brussels. Copyright © C. Herscovici, London/Artists Rights

JOHN UPDIKE was born in Shillington, Pennsylvania, in 1932. He graduated from Harvard College in 1954 and spent a year in Oxford, England, at the Ruskin School of Drawing and Fine Art. From 1955 to 1957 he was a member of the staff of *The New Yorker*. His novels have won the Pulitzer Prize, the National Book Award, the National Book Critics Circle Award, the Rosenthal Foundation Award, and the William Dean Howells Medal. In 2007 he received the Gold Medal for Fiction from the American Academy of Arts and Letters. John Updike died in January 2009.

CHRISTOPHER CARDUFF was born in Kansas City, Missouri, in 1956. Since graduating from Macalester College in 1979 he has worked in publishing in New York and Boston, and is currently an editor at The Library of America. He lives in Melrose, Massachusetts.